# The Journals of David E. Lilienthal

## VOLUME II

## THE ATOMIC ENERGY YEARS

*Books by David E. Lilienthal*

BIG BUSINESS: A NEW ERA

CHANGE, HOPE, AND THE BOMB

THIS I DO BELIEVE

TVA — DEMOCRACY ON THE MARCH

# The Journals of David E. Lilienthal

VOLUME II

# THE ATOMIC ENERGY YEARS 1945-1950

HARPER & ROW, PUBLISHERS

NEW YORK, EVANSTON, AND LONDON

FIRST EDITION

LIBRARY OF CONGRESS CATALOG CARD NUMBER: 64:18056

H-O

DEDICATED TO
HARRY S. TRUMAN

# CONTENTS

*A section of illustrations follows page 276.*

# PUBLISHER'S NOTE

This is the second volume in Harper & Row's publication of the private journals of David E. Lilienthal. It is a large and in every sense major venture in publishing, which will ultimately record a period of some forty-six years in Mr. Lilienthal's career in public and private life.

Volume I, *THE TVA YEARS,* is the private and personal record of Mr. Lilienthal's leadership of the Tennessee Valley Authority in its pioneering period of the late 1930s and early 1940s, when it was achieving recognition as one of the enduring accomplishments of the New Deal.

Volume II, *THE ATOMIC ENERGY YEARS,* opens with the entry of August 7, 1945—the day after the first atomic bomb was dropped on Hiroshima. At this time, Mr. Lilienthal had more than a year remaining as TVA Chairman, but he was soon drawn into the national and world-wide issues of atomic energy. In January, 1946, he was made chairman of the special State Department Board of Consultants which developed the basic American plan for international atomic control, and in October of that year, President Truman appointed him as the first chairman of the new U.S. Atomic Energy Commission. This was the stormy period of America's atomic weapons monopoly, of spy scares and Congressional investigations, of a secret struggle between civilian and military leadership within the government, and, finally, of the gravest of issues—the decision to make the H-bomb.

The Lilienthal Journals form a frank and lively account of these crucial years, written from the inside of events by one of the major participants—an account written *at the time* and published now without essential change. The Journals are therefore not a history, but part of the contemporary record which is the raw material of history. Here is the story of an intense and active experience, set down as the experience itself was being lived, in the center of the tumult and controversy of public life.

Men engaged in the world of action rarely provide more than a glimpse of that world, except in the mellow afterthoughts of a memoir. The Lilienthal Journals are not a memoir. They are instead an immediate and living record. They have the vital spirit of human reality which we believe has created a unique and valuable American narrative.

# The Journals of David E. Lilienthal

VOLUME II

THE ATOMIC ENERGY YEARS

# I

# THE ATOMIC ENERGY YEARS

# AUGUST-DECEMBER, 1945

AUGUST 7, 1945
HOME [NORRIS, TENNESSEE]

The story of the "Mystery Plant" near Clinton is out.

Whether or not the atomic bomb proves to be so devastating as to mean the end of the Japanese War in a few weeks, it is perfectly clear that here is one of the greatest events in American history. And it took place largely in the Tennessee Valley not ten miles away from where I am ticking off this journal.

We have had notice, from the first, that this was something of great portent. The first visit of Dr. Arthur Compton and his physicist associates, way back there, when they asked for a certain kind of site, with unlimited power and a certain quality of water, showed that they had backing that must come from the President directly. We didn't want them to take over such vast areas of land of such fertility, and tried to get them to consider western Kentucky. But they knew what they wanted: the "climate" here suited them better, they said, for the kind of workers, who would be the cream of America's scientific crop. And that was that. My sessions with the Under Secretary of War, Judge Patterson, and General Farrell* were always marked by tenseness on their part; it must have been a terrible responsibility—and it still is. For if it is not as the country is led to believe—a full-blown discovery, ready to annihilate the Japs—then they are in trouble. If it is as terribly effective as represented, their responsibility is even greater.

* Deputy commander of the atomic bomb project.

[ 1 ]

The effect of this research, as it moves into non-military fields, upon our governmental and economic life may be very great. Industry will try to get control, and at first will be successful. But as it goes on, it will be clear that no such control over the destinies of us all can be left in the hands of private corporations. The profound effect of Muscle Shoals upon public thinking may be as nothing compared to the debate and decision affecting this undertaking.

SEPTEMBER 18, 1945

WASHINGTON

I came into the President's office at 3:15. He was standing, looking at some correspondence piled up on his desk for signature.

After the usual greetings he said he wanted to talk to me about TVA and how "I can get another one in the Columbia Valley, and what are we going to do about the Missouri Valley." He has a very jaunty look, but he is worn. "There just isn't time to do everything around here." He had the labor situation on his mind, with the Detroit strikes threatening and his announcement concerning the reorganization of the Labor Department to be made in a few minutes at his press conference. "I am going to upset a lot of apple carts around here with what I am doing about the Labor Department. I'm transferring a lot of things to that department and holding the Secretary responsible. I can't get into all these things. I want more of these things put under Cabinet officers, and if one doesn't deliver the goods, then I'll get another who will."

Thinking of TVA, I didn't like the sound of this a bit.

I had thought about my "story" a good deal, but decided not to fix on a definite "outline." But I had decided I would somehow make one point and proceeded to do so: that TVA was different, a new way of doing things, and he should deal with it as such. When people said, "Why should TVA be exempted?" (I referred to the Whittington Bill†); "why should it be different from all the rest of the bureaus?"—the answer should be: "Of course it's different; it was supposed to be different." We were happy that TVA had been so generally accepted, in spite of bitter opposition ("Yeah—they're singing a different tune now, aren't they?" he stuck in, grinning), and I thought it was important to point out to him *what* it was about TVA that made people think it was good, especially the people of the Valley.

The reason it had achieved a measure of success was because it went at resource development in a unified way. I tried to show how soil

† A House bill providing for stricter Congressional fiscal control over Federal agencies—but exempting TVA.

conservation, forestry, river development are carried on elsewhere and, by contrast, in the Valley—and that was an essential part of the "different-ness." I don't think I got over this "unified idea" too well, but the companion idea of decentralization was clear. "Surely the country can afford one experiment in a way that is different"—indicating again what the existing way was—and I hoped he would see that it wasn't messed up from within the Government, as almost everyone was constantly suggesting—Civil Service, Ickes, etc.

He was quite emphatic: "It has gone over well," he said, "and as long as I have anything to do with it, and I guess that will be quite a while" (smiling) "it won't be changed." As much to say: That is that—anything else on your chest?

Well, that was fine, and assuming (1) he understands what is involved and (2) that we follow up on it, that was very good indeed.

He was quite evidently anxious to get on with the talk so he could discuss the other authorities; TVA was something that was in good shape and didn't need more attention. Just as he started on this line the telephone rang, and after a delay, during which the President kept saying, "Hello, Lew, Hello, Lew," the Secretary of Labor finally got on. (No irritation from the President—he sat patiently waiting till the connection was completed.) Schwellenbach was upset about something, and gently had to be reassured about the pending executive order enlarging the powers of the Secretary of Labor; he was apparently quite disappointed that the National Labor Relations Board wasn't included. His order, the President said, was under the war powers and NLRB didn't have anything to do with war, so it probably would have to wait until the reorganization bill was passed. He wheedled a bit: "I'm playing a little politics there; want the support of the Wagner people on my reorganization bill."

Then: "Where were we—oh, yes, the Columbia Valley."

A regional authority in the Columbia Valley he thought could be had; the people were for it. Could be just like TVA. There were only two states affected, and only power and irrigation. But in the Missouri Valley—he took off his glasses and rubbed his eyes—that's the hard one.

Then he explained the conflicts between the downstream people and those upriver, how dams below Sioux City wouldn't do, would fill up with silt in a year; there wasn't any power in that part of the river. Flood control dams would have to be built on the little streams and kept empty—and so on, with a loquacity and excited interest that reminded me of his predecessor on such a subject. He went down the list of Senators in each of the nine states—all against MVA except two. The people up there sending in resolutions dead against. "We'll have to figure out something." I didn't want to go into detail at that late hour, but I said, "It may take some time for people to realize it, but it is perfectly clear that all those conflicts can't be resolved unless there is one agency responsible for resolving them—that's the lesson of the TVA experience." It seemed to ring a bell, but a small one, and he looked at me sternly and said, "Maybe so; we have got to figure out something that they will accept."

The high point of the meeting came with these words: "Oh, that's Ickes' idea; I'm against it. If these things are going to be just part of the bureaus here in Washington we might as well leave them in the hands of Congress. What people like about TVA is that it is regionalized, and that's what they want. I can't see what there was in the Message that you say some people interpreted as being for the Ickes idea, and I ought to know; I wrote that part of the Message myself."

All of this, of course, was occasioned by my comment that it is wrong to ask for regional agencies to blanket the whole country, and then couple that with an insistence that they must be "coordinated" in Washington, which simply means run from Washington. I referred specifically to the fact that one of the bills for the Columbia Basin (the President had just mentioned the Columbia as the next place where a regional authority could be "had") provided for that kind of "coordination" by the Secretary of Interior. (This is Ickes' National River Basin Board.) It was at this point that he rared back and said, "Oh, that's Ickes, etc."

That was a mighty comforting discussion.

I asked him what he wanted me to do about invitations I received in numbers to speak about TVA in other parts of the country; that I had been declining them until I had a chance to ask him.

"It is perfectly all right to accept them. Of course, you should use good judgment about it, but that's the only way the people will get to know the facts—they sure won't know them through the newspapers." (The first touch of that kind about the press I had ever heard from Truman or attributed to him.) "Go to it," he said.

I explained that I had been reluctant because there were people in Washington who were very super-sensitive about things like that, always worrying about their "jurisdiction." He picked it up: "Isn't it the Goddamnedest thing—what happens to people when they come to Washington? Why even some of these new Cabinet members of mine start right out being that way." Then he repeated the remark of Wilson as to what happens to people who come to Washington: "Some grow, some swell up." (He put in the "up.")

I said that was one of the fine things about working in a decentralized agency, where the people are; they can get at you and you feel you are part of their life.

"Well, sir, do you know why I go back home every once in a while? So people can kick me around."

He is a tired man, but a square-shouldered, plucky one. You can't help admiring him; and being struck with the extraordinary contrast with Roosevelt.

He seemed to be completely satisfied with the way things were going in TVA and after saying so, added, "That's why I reappointed you." I said that took some guts, since it meant a fight. "I never run away from a fight—don't invite 'em, but don't run away from them," he said.

Standing in the doorway of his office: "Tell Charley O.K." (Charles Ross, the press secretary.) "Enjoyed talking to you. Come back again when you haven't anything better to do." (This remark epitomizes the humor of the Middle West, its barbershops and filling stations where men pass the time of day, but can you imagine a Groton President saying that? F.D.R.'s humor had a different kind of expression. Also, F.D.R. laughed; Truman grins broadly and he does laugh, but it is so fleeting that it is hardly a laugh at all—a chuckle, or more the sound effect of a grin.)

Then he went out the next door, and there were the correspondents, hundreds it seemed, lined up, ready for the race to his office for an important four o'clock press conference. (He announced Stimson's resignation as Secretary of War, Patterson's appointment to succeed him; also the nomination of Justice Burton, the new Labor Department reorganization, etc.)

P.S. (Note of September 26, 1945)

Confirmation of the President's rejection of the Ickes position came today. Congressman Henry Jackson of the State of Washington saw the President yesterday, and Senator Mitchell, he told me by phone. The President will support a bill for a CVA, but it must exclude the pet Ickes provisions for "supervision" by the Secretary of the Interior. We are to help in drafting the bill.

OCTOBER 14, 1945
SUNDAY

Things have been happening fast of late. Too bad I haven't been able, somehow, to keep a journal record of them.

This last week, for example:

1. David was sworn in as an apprentice seaman in the United States Naval Reserve. I had signed a parent's waiver a couple of weeks ago, and then enlistments were cut off, to his utter dismay. While he was in Washington visiting Nancy (where we joined him a week ago for a

memorable visit), word came that they would take him, and last Wednesday he was in Nashville and took the oath. A two-year hitch. It hurts to see him spend that time away from his education, but we are so much luckier than most people; besides, the time won't be entirely wasted, of course. It may prove to be a very useful experience.

2. On the same day President Truman dedicated Kentucky Dam and made a speech endorsing the TVA idea completely and with great emphasis. The speech was substantially what I dictated as a draft in an hour, before a board meeting on October 2, based on an idea of presentation that I got up in the middle of the night to note. But he knew what he was saying, and believes in it, for it follows the line of thought we discussed in our conference of a few days before.

The dedication was very impressive. The President's car, preceded by Secret Service, etc., drove up the long earth fill; I greeted him as he got out, introduced him to a number of TVA staff, and then conducted him around the top of the dam, and then down a long flight of stairs to the platform before which 10,000 people had been gathered for several hours. Here he delivered his speech. I had a good chance to show him how a dam can be both for power and flood control, by pointing out the floodgates and the present level of the water—many feet below the height of the floodgates. But the most important part of the dedication shindig is that he spent more time thinking about TVA and its application elsewhere than would have been possible in almost any other way— for he edited the draft of speech, then read it over several times before delivery, then read it aloud (plus emphatic interpolations!) so it is now (we can assume) pretty firmly fixed in his mind.

I feel that we can assume that this "buttons up" my long controversy with Ickes about putting TVA into Interior, and the ensuing issue of the character of the new regional agency, if any. The Interior boys will keep on trying to have their way, but they certainly have a large-size and explicit tank-trap in their way now, something that never happened under F.D.R.

After the ceremonies I had a long visit with Cap Krug, on the way to Fontana, which he, John Lord O'Brian, and some others visited that same evening. He has been offered any number of important jobs, outside the Government, and is considering them with the vast care he exercises about his career.

He says he must make some money to recoup, but that he wants to make it in a way that will not prevent his returning to public life later on. This return to an important administrative position in the Government seems to weigh most heavily with him—and this surprised me, for I rather assumed that now he would be out to make money and plenty of it, and that was that. He liked the kudos and fascination of large affairs, naturally enough, and wants some more. He has great ambitions, and the ability to justify them. Clearly one of the most capable men I have ever known—in some ways the ablest. The most interesting prospects relate to trade with China (a scheme of Floyd Odlum, the investment banker, and Harry Hopkins) and an important post in the motion picture industry with Eric Johnston, the new czar.

OCTOBER 16, 1945
WASHINGTON

Harold Smith, Director of the Budget (with whom Clapp and I had luncheon today), said he had just reached this conclusion about Truman: that he is less orderly than Roosevelt. The conclusion seemed to surprise him, for F.D.R. was not orderly (in an administrative sense, of course), and Smith had the distinct impression, at first, that Truman's natural inclinations for order would make him superior in this respect. But he has fallen into the error of inadequate staff preparation, and as a result has committed a number of messes. He "fesses" up to them as mistakes and asks to be pulled out of them. Smith was quite impressive in his description of Truman: a fine, keen intelligence, the highest of motives and sincerity, high purposes. He sees him a great deal, of course, as he did Roosevelt, which is what makes these observations interesting.

The use of staff is a kind of art, one of the finest of the arts of administration. This is not generally understood, and particularly by men who have had legislative experience only, and have only seen administration from the outside.

OCTOBER 18, 1945
HOME

The Army's bill to "control" atomic energy and research was almost railroaded through the House Military Affairs Committee last week, after five hours of hearings. One of the most far-reaching pieces of legislation in the history of the country!

Patterson, Groves, took most of the time; a halfhearted appearance by Vannevar Bush and Pres. Conant. No scientists at all, all of them being under the gag. Don't want to hear from anyone else, says Chairman May.‡

‡ Several atomic energy control bills were drafted in the early fall of 1945. The first to be seriously considered was the one pushed by Representative May, with strong War Department backing. It was, of course, finally sidetracked in favor of the all-civilian Atomic Energy Commission proposal sponsored by Senator McMahon and enacted in the summer of 1946. Bush, Conant, and General Groves were the three leading figures in the wartime bomb project, called the "Manhattan District."

Then the very issue I underlined at Chicago§ began to get attention—why don't we hear from the scientists? what are the consequences of trying to "control" science? And in what John Sparkman (a member of the committee) described to me as a memorable session, May was overruled and the committee reopened the sessions to hear from a few scientists who are on the project. My hunch was right that time.

NOVEMBER 7, 1945
ON THE TRAIN FOR NEW YORK

Nancy and I had a big time at the Russian Embassy, celebrating the October Revolution, eating the famous Communist sturgeon and seeing the most amazing variety of international faces I have ever seen. Dazzling: the uniforms of every country, and the international sex set (I can still feel the effects of *my* several vodkas and Nancy's, too, she having taken one sip and left me to finish it).

It was a great event for the kid, to see such celebrities as General Jimmy Doolittle; the former Ambassador to Russia, Joe Davies; meeting Secretary of Agriculture Anderson, the Mexican Ambassador (who was embarrassingly agog at meeting the "world-famous Lilienthal," as he said), and so on. The quaintest was what looked like a Greek Orthodox priest, with jeweled crown, a roving eye, and a wild-looking blonde. I always said the clergy is *the* profession.

Nancy and I had dinner together last night, at Hogate's, out of which came a story that pleases my vanity as well as both our senses of humor. She had to get home early to write a report, so having snared a cab on the waterfront I got out at F Street, telling the driver, "Take my daughter home, to Monroe NE." He was a young fellow, and grinned at me as I left. Nancy said, after they were on their way the driver said, "Is that your father, on the level?" Nancy opined as how it was. "Well, I thought he was the boy friend; looks too young to be your father."

DECEMBER 27, 1945
TAXCO, MEXICO

The first impression our trip to Mexico has made upon me has been change, a complete, utter change. Some of it has been fantastic—this town of Taxco, for example. Some has seemed so unreal that I wondered if we really were there, or whether it had not been dreamed up—our being guests at the elaborate rancho of the famous Mexican "bull-fighter"

§ This refers to a conference on atomic energy control which I attended in September at the University of Chicago. My notes on this conference are contained in Appendix A to this volume.

and motion picture comedian Mario Moreno—the Cantinflas of the posters all over Mexico. The casualness and lack of any sense of time, schedule, or need for them, of the assorted group that picked us off the train at Monterrey. ("Assorted" meaning a Nicaraguan, a Frenchman born in Poland, a Chinese young woman, born and brought up in Trinidad and married to an American by the name of Von Hohenlerten!)

The impressions are almost countless:

The market at Taxco the Sunday before Christmas, crowded into narrow, almost subterranean windings.

The Indian beside his five-gallon tin of huge meatless bones, for sale.

Charcoal, in jute sacks, coming through the streets on the backs of burros.

A sackful of eggs, suspended from the metal gutter on a tile-covered house.

The square-headed Indian, in his tight white pants, sombrero and serape, shuffling into the great church beside us, kneeling, then squatting almost like an animal through the mass.

The houses, of all kinds, perched on the mountainside—the view that is before me as I write these hand notes.

The Cathedral always dominating everything, with the dark green of the plaza trees before it.

The startling beauty of so many of the women and girls, some of them really breath-taking, with their regular features, high cheekbones and incredible eyes. If I don't get shot or stilettoed for staring before I leave Mexico, it will be surprising.

The curious and pleasing effect of hearing people speak without understanding their words, so that you hear the sound of voices (such as those of the men working in the garden just below me) but not the distraction of words. And a mixture of languages—French particularly, among the visitors, as well as good old Michigan.

The incredible climate—sunshine, not rationed but unlimited, brilliant, warm (and dry), and when it is gone, quite cool. Indeed, it is cool in the shade even when it is hot in the sun.

And, of course, poverty, poverty so general and common that it only occasionally curls your hair, as when I saw the derelict asleep on a stone bench in a little plaza, a complete and abject collapse of human dignity. I climbed the mountain one evening and saw some farm living, outside the town (which I suppose is relatively well-off). Lord—beyond belief. And yet the children look well nourished and the men not too bad. The women are either young and handsome—mostly—or old, which probably means they do much of the work, and age in their thirties.

# II

# THE ATOMIC ENERGY YEARS

# 1946

JANUARY 16, 1946
WEDNESDAY

Saw Acheson◖ at 9:15 until 10:00.

He talked frankly and in detail: Those charged with foreign policy —the Secretary of State (Byrnes) and the President—did not have either the facts nor an understanding of what was involved in the atomic energy issue, the most serious cloud hanging over the world. Commitments, on paper and in communiqués, have been made and are being made (Byrnes is now in London before the United Nations General Assembly) without a knowledge of what the hell it is all about—literally! The War Department, and really one man in the War Department, General Groves, has, by the power of veto on the ground of "military security," really been determining and almost running foreign policy. He has entered into contracts involving other countries (Belgium and their Congo deposits of uranium, for example) without even the knowledge of the Department of State.

Finally realizing that this could not go on, Acheson was able to persuade the President and Secretary to do something about it. A committee was appointed by the Secretary of State for the purpose of advising what position the United States member of the UNO should take respecting control of the atomic weapon, safeguarding the "secret" and working out the terrible position we are all in because of this discovery.

◖ Then Under Secretary of State. (The discussion with Acheson is more fully recounted in the following entry.)

The committee consists of Acheson as chairman, President Conant of Harvard, Vannevar Bush, Gen. Groves, Jack McCloy, former Asst. Secy. of War.

JANUARY 20, 1946
HOME, SUNDAY

(It is a rainy, overcast day. Helen and I are conscious of every minute, for David will be back from boot camp at San Diego sometime today. Every telephone call we are sure is IT; every sound out front is that long-legged kid coming down the walk. It's now 2:30 P.M.; for all we know it may not be till midnight.)

Last Monday Acting Secretary of State Acheson phoned me, asking that I come to talk with him about an important assignment having to do with atomic energy and our international relations. I saw him Wednesday morning for an hour (Jan. 16). One of the most flattering proposals ever made to me, and yet one of the most humbling possible.

Boiled down, it is this: that I become responsible, as the directing head of an Advisory Panel of three or four men, for a knowledge of *all* the facts concerning the atomic bomb project in all of its ramifications, and for an interpretation of those facts. This interpretation, with its recommendations, would be for the purpose of advising the President and Secretary of State, and more particularly so they could instruct the American member of the United Nations Security Council as to what should be the position of that member (and the U.S.A.) on the problem of the atomic bomb.

The initial assignment would have particular reference to two issues: (a) methods of control, safeguarding, inspection, etc., involved in any proposals for international action on the bomb, and the enforcement of such international action; and (b) a judgment (on the basis of all the facts, including top secrets secured by our military intelligence) of the industrial and scientific potential of other nations (really meaning Russia) for the development of atomic bombs; in other words, the relative hazards to us.

Inevitably (as I see it), the assignment would force an examination of the crucial question: *What* is there that is secret? Are those facts really "secret" in the sense that is assumed by our international policy, and by the communiqués and commitments of our Govt., the British, etc.?

If my hunch, expressed in the opening hours of the Chicago University conference, that in the real sense there are no secrets (that is, nothing that is not known or knowable), would be supportable by the facts, then real progress would be made. For then it would be clear that the basis of present policy-making is without foundation. For present policy and commitments are made on the Army-sponsored thesis that there are secrets. And since it is in the Army's hands (or, literally, Gen. Groves') to deny access to the facts that would prove or disprove this vital thesis, there has been no way to examine the very foundation of our policies in the international field.

An amazing situation. For Gen. Groves determines whether a fact can be divulged, to anyone, by anyone, on the basis that such facts involve our military security. And that power over the facts has prevented anyone knowing whether we are on the right track or not. Example: the Atomic Energy Committee of the Senate has been refused access to the facts they thought they needed. Example: dealings with other nations involving uranium materials are not known to the State Department.

Clapp and Dr. H. A. were very seriously opposed to my undertaking this assignment; Pope thought I should, because of its importance. I am trying to cut down the requirements of the job, so I can be of some help without injury to TVA. I expect to meet with Acheson, Conant (pres. of Harvard), Vannevar Bush, Gen. Groves and the advisory group in Wash. next Wed.

. . . the phone; David is in town and we're off to get him.


JANUARY 22, 1946
WASHINGTON

Saw Herb Marks (Acheson's assistant) at the Hay-Adams. I had read the Joint Declaration of Truman-Attlee-King. The importance of trying to develop a policy or plan on the basis of a study of the facts seemed terribly clear. For example, the Joint Declaration and Byrnes' interpretation of the UN resolution for an international UN Atomic Energy Commission "to inquire into all phases of the problem" both implied that we would not supply facts until safeguards had been established.* And yet without supplying facts to other countries how could they know enough to discuss safeguards? The facts are the beginning place for the development of any intelligent public policy. I told Herb that the proposition about safeguards, as stated by the Joint Declaration and the Byrnes statement, reminded me of the Nebraska statute Dean Pound was fond of quoting: "When two trains approach each other at gradings, neither shall pass till the other has gone."

He retorted by telling me what Acheson had said to the President,

---

* The Truman-Attlee-King declaration of November 15, 1945, proposed the establishment of a United Nations Atomic Energy Commission to develop a proposal for international atomic control. In London, where the UN was about to approve a resolution to set up this commission, Secretary Byrnes had declared that no international body could compel the U.S. to release A-bomb information.

apropos the necessity of having men schooled in government or state-craft take a concentrated look at the facts, so the facts about atomic energy could be translated into terms of public policy. Without such men, Acheson had said, it would be "as if one called in a very intelligent and well-intentioned South Sea Islander and said, 'There are too many cows being killed on railroad tracks and I want you to do something about it.' But the South Sea Islander, although smart and meaning well and want-ing to be helpful, has never seen a cow or a railroad."

Herb seemed overjoyed that I got the point about the necessity for an analysis of the facts before any sense could be made in terms of a method of international control, to which we had committed ourselves as a nation. He said he had been batting around the Department of State for months, trying to find someone who could see how important this was, and they all thought he was crazy. Even Acheson, he said, had difficulty with the idea (and took it, I rather guess, largely because Herb pressed for it so hard).

Late in the evening we went out to the Shoreham and saw Oppen-heimer, who had just come in by plane from California. First time I had seen him. The setting was curious, too: a newly decorated room, very fancy, with a bed in the room, eight feet wide, and the atmosphere hardly that of a physics laboratory or an atom bomb assembly plant. We had a couple of drinks. He walked back and forth, making funny "hugh" sounds between sentences or phrases as he paced the room, looking at the floor—a mannerism quite strange. Very articulate. He did not have any idea what Herb's point was, really: "What you mean is there should be a kind of Atomic Primer?" Well, this certainly wasn't it, except that such a primer would be one way of laying the foundation for the search for a policy. I left liking him, greatly impressed with his flash of a mind, but rather disturbed by the flow of words.

JANUARY 24, 1946
ON THE TRAIN, HEADING
FOR HOME, THURSDAY AFTERNOON

I am going through one of the most memorable intellectual and emotional experiences of my life. And I have one of the most remarkable opportunities to accomplish something toward the peace of the world that could come to anyone. It is a very sobering and yet highly stimulat-ing experience.

Yesterday I sat at a table in the somber office of the Secretary of State. History crowds around one in that room, and a sense of continuity with the past is in the air. At the head of the small table sat the Acting Secretary of State, one of America's ablest lawyers, a former law secretary of Brandeis, Dean Acheson. At his right was the president of Harvard, and next to him Major General Groves; at his left was Dr. Vannevar Bush, perhaps the leading administrator of science in the country. Those latter three men supervised and directed the atomic bomb from its very inception; they were there on that dawn when the bomb proved its terrific powers, on the desolate desert.

At the end of the table was J. R. Oppenheimer, the scientist who more than anyone else was able, at Los Alamos, to find a way to turn the knowledge of nuclear forces into a weapon that shattered the whole world, as we knew it, at Hiroshima; an extraordinary personage (and as I learned today, a really *great* teacher). I sat on Bush's left. At my left was Harry A. Winne, vice president of General Electric in charge of engineering, whose organization contributed a great deal to solving the fantastic industrial production problems of the atomic bomb; next to him Chester Barnard, president of the New Jersey Bell Telephone Company (my nominee for the panel of consultants), and across from him, Dr. C. A. Thomas, vice president and director of research of the Monsanto Chemical Company, who had a major part in research and production problems worked out at Clinton and Los Alamos—he was one of those who saw the results of their work at Alamogordo on July 16, 1945, one of the vital dates of history.

I won't go into the details of the discussion; the records will show the results, including an indication of what was expected of the group of consultants, my designation as chairman and director of the work of the panel, the fact that, upon my questioning, it was understood by General Groves and the entire group that we five would have unrestricted access to any and all facts and facilities, including the very "top secrets," all of which, taken together, are now known to only a handful of men on this earth, and the possession of which may change my prospects for peace of mind for a long time to come.

It was made evident that the committee of Acheson, Conant, Bush, and Groves (McCloy was unable to be present because of illness) expected our committee to draft recommendations and reports on the very heart of the question: Can a way be found, a feasible, workable way, to safeguard the world against the atomic bomb?

Today it was announced from London that the General Assembly of the United Nations Organization approved the creation of an International Commission, responsible directly to the Security Council, to report on methods, by international action, of preventing the use of atomic energy as a weapon of war. Our work, the work of this group for which I have been made chairman, is to develop a position, based on facts not now known by our political officers, that will "work," and have a good chance of being accepted, especially by Russia.

After 1½ hours of discussion, the Advisory Group went to luncheon for further discussion, and then met in the offices provided for us. President Conant spent an hour setting forth some ideas he had, then we discussed procedure. This morning Oppenheimer talked to us, without limitation (i.e., including some of the top secrets, chiefly scientific discoveries not "released" about fundamentals).

It was tough going for me; but there was some comfort to find that it was also tough going for Barnard, Winne (though an engineer), and Marks. But I think I got the "feel" of it, and understood more than I would have supposed two days ago.

This afternoon we discussed problems of the scope of our inquiry, driven by my constant insistence that we keep that scope manageable, that we do not fall into the illusion that there is "*a*" solution, one answer that we must seek for and that will answer everything, but rather perhaps a number of partial answers, and that we not be distracted by side issues or abstract propositions. As one man put it: Let us first see, in the light of the facts that are known, what is possible in the way of safeguards and control, before discussing what is desirable. What I am trying to do is to emphasize the fundamental importance of the *facts*. It is an absence of knowledge of the facts that has led to some of the unfortunate occurrences in the field of policy thus far, and they must be corrected as well as they can be.

This is a supreme test—and by all odds the most intricate and subtle—of my faith that it is not in the discussion of dogma or abstract propositions that social progress lies, but in ascertaining the facts and evolving policies and action from them. Already we have made headway on that proposition, even in two days' discussion.

Dr. Morgan and Clapp are quite upset and disturbed that I am undertaking this assignment, even though it is clear that we can be prepared to report in a few weeks. This worries me, I confess, and there is something to their concern about what my absence from TVA will do in slowing down decisions, losing momentum, etc. But I am deeply persuaded that this is one of the great chances of a lifetime to do some bit of good in a supremely grave and portentous situation, a chance that I cannot ignore and live with myself.

Furthermore, I am convinced that it is a natural and proper part of my work as chairman of the TVA, for the knowledge I will acquire, and the experience in this matter, is part of my education as a leader in seeking to bridge the desperate and continuing crisis of modern science and the human spirit. This is a major issue of statecraft; it is what TVA is concerned with, at bottom (as I said in a commencement address at Radcliffe last June); and it is part of my life's work, if TVA may be said to be that.

Furthermore, it seems to me clear that TVA will gain in prestige by the very fact that I am called upon to head so important a piece of work, considering from whom the invitation comes and who my associates on the committee and the Advisory Group are. Finally, I am convinced that this experience can help me to help TVA avoid one of its continuous dangers, that of mental isolation. We are so sure of ourselves in TVA, and must so constantly fight outside forces that the chance of cross-fertilization is not as great as it should be; this experience already proves that it can be helpful in that direction. As for the fear that this will be the means of weaning me away from TVA (which is really what was beneath Dr. Morgan's angry and hurt protests), there is nothing in it; I should know if anyone does.

Sunday I go to New York, where for several days we continue, listening to a group of experts from nine different parts of the Manhattan Project, then to Washington to hear all about such matters as ores, the potential of other nations, and more of Oppenheimer's explanations, and to block out the various roads that may lead to specific recommendations.

JANUARY 28, 1946
NEW YORK, MONDAY

No fairy tale that I read in utter rapture and enchantment as a child, no spy mystery, no "horror" story, can remotely compare with the scientific recital I listened to for six or seven hours today. Seated in a prosaic office high above Lexington Avenue, I heard more of the complete story of the atomic bomb, past, present, and immediate future, than any but a few men have yet heard. It was told well, technically, dispassionately, but interspersed with stories of the decisions that had to be made, the utter simplicity and yet fantastic complexity of the peering into the laws of nature that is the essence of this utterly bizarre and, literally, incredible business. There were things that have never been even hinted at that are accomplished, or virtually accomplished, facts, that change the whole thesis of our inquiry, and of the course of the world in this generation.

None of this can be written down. These are the very top of the top secrets of our country; some of them are likely to remain secrets for some time to come.

The subject matter is very complex and highly technical, even for a scientifically trained man. For me it is doubly difficult. And yet under the necessity of learning about them, of getting the "feel" of the subject, I find, to my great relief, that by a process of deposit I am getting "on" to what this is about.

We are going to know the facts about this whole business as no one else, having similar purpose, has ever known those facts. When that happens, we may get some insight into the very grave difficulty involved in building some kind of hope for the future out of what, on the face of things as they now stand, gives little basis for hope for the world within the next decade. This is a fearful responsibility. I am quite sure I was right, whatever may come, in making the effort to inch us along somewhat toward ground that is more solid beneath our feet.

This is a soul-stirring experience. One must be far more insensitive than I—the same thing is plainly written on the utterly solemn and grim faces of my associates—not to feel deeply moved by having the terrible facts of nature's ultimate forces coolly laid before him as on an operating table, almost feeling them warm and stirring under one's probing fingers. Mixed with that the constant element of international rivalry and intrigues, and I feel that I have been admitted, through the strangest accident of fate, behind the scenes in the most awful and inspiring drama since some primitive man looked for the very first time upon fire.

FEBRUARY 15, 1946
FRIDAY, FLYING ACROSS OKLAHOMA
(IN A LUXURIOUS ARMY
TRANSPORT PLANE,
HEADING FOR LOS ALAMOS, N.M.)

Last Wednesday, at noon, Ickes announced his resignation as Secretary of the Interior, in a violent and nasty attack on the President, dealt in tones of unctuous self-righteousness that Arthur Morgan couldn't have beaten.

Our atomic bomb consulting board was to have left, by Army plane, for Knoxville at noon on Wednesday; about eleven o'clock word came from the pilot that the weather was getting too bad at Knoxville and the flight was off. So we got train reservations and came down Wednesday night on the train that leaves Washington at 4:30 P.M.

At about 6:30 that evening the White House called Miss Owen saying, "The President wants to talk to Mr. Lilienthal as soon as possible." She said she didn't know where I was, but suggested that I might be at home. Later in the evening Connelly, the President's secretary, called her again: "Had she any idea where I could be found? The President wanted to see me."

That same afternoon John Sorrells (I think it was he) of the Scripps-Howard management (executive head, I believe) came into Ed Smith's office at the News-Sentinel in Knoxville. He had just come down from New York, and had stopped in Washington. He was quite excited. Had he heard that Lilienthal was to succeed Ickes as Secretary of the Interior? No, Ed hadn't heard. He called Helen; of course, she said I was on the train and couldn't be reached.

Last evening we had the members of the consulting board as dinner guests (and a very nice party it was, too, by the way, topped off by our all going over to the Norris Dam overlook and seeing the dam by (1) moonlight, (2) by a slight touch of my last remaining Kentucky Tavern, and (3) through snow flurries).

It was during this evening that Clapp, who was there, hinted that the President had tried to get to see me, as he was given to understand, about the Interior, and that I probably ought to call Miss Owen. So after the party left, about 10:30, I called her.

In addition to the word about the telephone call, as recorded above, she said that Connelly had given her the impression that he would call again in the morning, i.e., Thursday morning, but that he hadn't done so. She construed this as meaning that between the time he first called for me and Thursday morning he had been prevailed upon to change his mind, or had himself thought better of the idea (if offering me the post *was* the idea behind the call, as Owen thinks was the case).

Prior to the telephone calls from the White House (that is, during the afternoon of Wednesday), she had a visitor, Kirby Billingsley, a newspaper editor from Wenatchee, Washington. Billingsley and his boss, Rufus Woods, are Republicans, and long-time progressives; Woods being known as the father of Grand Coulee Dam. Woods, a figure in the state, has visited us, and is very enthusiastic about TVA, a convert to a TVA kind of Columbia Valley Authority, and a strong believer in me.

Billingsley told Owen that he had been talking to a number of progressives of both parties, from the Western part of the country, and they expressed a favorable opinion about urging the President to name me as Secretary of the Interior. He said that he had talked with Henry Wallace that morning (this was before Ickes' announcement was made official), and he had urged the idea as a sound one. Billingsley's question was: "If the post is offered to Lilienthal would he accept it?" Naturally, Owen declined to speculate on such a question; only I could answer that one. But she was troubled that some of our friends might start such a movement and then it could become a problem.

I told her that the chance that such an offer ever would be made seemed to me almost fantastic, for many reasons. I didn't want to be in the position of commenting on an offer that had never been made and wouldn't be made; that looks silly. And I certainly wouldn't want to let our friends make me appear to be a candidate and then have that work against TVA later on. If the situation would provide an opportunity to see the President so I could talk to him about TVA, and the effect of his appointment of an Interior Secretary upon TVA and other regional developments, that would be grand.

As for the post itself, I said that I had no interest in becoming a member of this Cabinet. I meant just that. I don't have that kind of ambition.

After talking to Owen, and feeling quite relaxed about the whole thing, Helen (obviously proud and pleased that such a thing was being considered) gave me a very sweet pep talk. Of course, it hadn't been offered to me, and perhaps it wouldn't be, as I said. But, she said, I should think ahead, of what I would say if the opportunity *were* made, and not just turn it down without giving it some thought. Now was the time to think about it, however remote I thought the possibility. (It was quite evident that *she* didn't think the idea absurd! Neither did Owen, by the way: a good way to slap Ickes hard, at the same time shutting the mouths of his friends, who could hardly attack me for not being a liberal, etc.).

The decision was for me to make, Helen continued, and like all the other decisions of that kind, whatever I decided would be fine with her, and she would adjust to them. If it was the high cost of being in the Cabinet on $15,000, I wasn't to worry about that—we could manage that as we managed the $5,000 a year as a commissioner at Madison, years ago. I should take my standing in the public confidence more seriously, and not let personal modesty obscure my judgment. And especially, I shouldn't just dismiss the whole thing, and then, if the offer did come along, handle it as I did over the phone with Owen, with an instant decision.

It seems to me highly unlikely that anything more will come of this. I shall certainly not start a campaign to promote the idea. I think a lot better of the idea this morning, however, if it should come that the offer is made without any effort whatever on my part. For it might give me (if the President backed me up) a chance to present and promote the TVA idea in a way that I couldn't hope for otherwise.

These things have a way of developing naturally: if nothing further happens, that means that it wasn't in the cards, and my purpose in life is to be fulfilled by carrying on in my present work, which I love and can do effectively. If it develops further, then it is time enough to see whether my appointment under the circumstances of the time would be something seriously to consider.

Yesterday we spent a whirlwind day going through the mammoth works at Oak Ridge. I saw the "end products" (something very few people have seen, including men who have done much of the top echelon work), saw a pile operate, heard discussion of new developments. Intensely interesting. And I think our ideas are becoming clearer as we move along. Now to Los Alamos.

A postscript (Feb. 21): That my name was being considered last week was again confirmed this morning when I met David Niles, administrative assistant to the President (and Harry Hopkins' close friend for so many years). But I don't believe the idea got too far. The President has almost certainly offered the post to Bill Douglas, who hasn't yet decided what to do about it. Kirby Billingsley continues his campaign, reports to Owen that he has talked to a lot of people, still thinks the post may be offered to me. I have plunked for Oscar Chapman, who would be less vigorous than one might wish, but who has the right point of view. Patton of the Farmers Union now sees him as the best bet available. This would be as good a solution as we can hope for.

P.S. Later: Jerry Kluttz's column in the Wash. *Post* confirms the story, as recited; the source: "a White House intimate."

FEBRUARY 16, 1946
SANTA FE, NEW MEXICO, SUNDAY

It is snowing: a heavy, lovely snow. All day.

Yesterday I had one of the most dramatic and deeply moving experiences of my life, an inspection of Los Alamos, where the atom bombs that shattered the world were made. I can't write these things down, safely at least, until I return home so I won't be carrying the notes around with me without the precautions that top secret limitations require. But I shall certainly never, never forget them. There on that mesa, with the high mountains forming a majestic backdrop, we went into casual little buildings, saw things only few men have seen, talked with soft-spoken, gentle, intelligent men about the things they had done—all most disinterested. Now I have a sense that this thing of atomic bombs is *real,* and to do something about it is a matter of immediacy, of urgency.

FEBRUARY 21, 1946
WASHINGTON

Called on Justice Frankfurter this afternoon. He had sent out what he called an "urgent SOS" for me to see him at the time I was in doubt about accepting the atomic energy panel chairmanship. He was with

Justice Murphy, and called me in to meet him; we chatted awhile, the three of us. Murphy said some pleasant things about having watched my work for years. I said I remembered him very well indeed, for I sat at Clarence Darrow's side (as junior counsel) during the Sweet murder case in Detroit, a race riot case in which Murphy sat as the trial judge. He was surprised to hear this, of course, as was Felix, for that matter. I told him how deeply impressed I had been by his calm, fair way of handling a terribly explosive situation—it was that and more. He said Darrow wasn't a good lawyer (true enough), but he was a remarkable human being. He told a story about Darrow that is new to me; here it is:

"Darrow said to me, 'Judge, I think I have got a good jury.' I asked him why. 'Well, six of them are Irish Catholics.' I asked him if he meant by that that Irish Catholics wouldn't find a hanging verdict. 'No, it isn't that. It's just that I never met an Irish Catholic yet who didn't think that someday he might be in trouble himself.' " Nice story, I thought.

F.F. said he had wanted to tell me (explaining the occasion for his urgent message about seeing him—I had been too busy at the time to respond) that by all means I should understand how terribly important it was for me to accept the assignment about the bomb; that it was nothing short of a miracle that David Lilienthal should get the chance, and it took a good deal of courage to make the tender. He said some rather extravagant things about the turn of events that put just the right person in a position where he again had hope that a catastrophe might be avoided in world affairs; that one as self-effacing and as free of shibboleths as I am, with such proved ability to get things done, and with my unique background of changing the course of social history would do this job if it could possibly be done, etc., etc.

Well, it was very impressive to me, really, for it was lighted with his eloquence and a kind of intensity I had never seen in him before. F.D.R. had discussed this business (the bomb project) with him over a period of years: "I think it was one of the things that gnawed most at his vitals, and concern about the outcome and the consequences had a good deal to do with his death." His death, he said as an aside, was providential—not that I don't see how much we miss him now—for they would have torn him limb from limb like a pack of wolves.

As I came walking across Capitol Park after leaving the Supreme Court, a bright-eyed, red-cheeked man gave me a big hello, and we immediately launched into a lively conversation about the Tennessee Valley. It was one of the Pullman conductors on the Southern. He explained to the man who was with him ("He's a conductor on the Seaboard") as follows: "Well, I saw my friend, Lilienthal, coming along and I just thought I would stop him and pass the time of day." It was pleasant; just right. We had a big laugh about my never having seen him in a regular hat before, always a Pullman cap.

It was a good idea to forget the atomic bomb and all its works for a couple of days. This I was most successful in doing in Santa Fe, for a number of reasons, perhaps better than any other place. Among other reasons was Taos, where I spent an interesting day on Tuesday. To reach this Indian pueblo village we drove through a magnificent valley in sight of the Sangre de Cristo range, beautiful almost beyond belief in their coating of new snow and under the amazing light. I forgot atomic bombs, and assorted anxieties of that order. And someday I shall try to write a novel; I reached that conclusion somewhere on the highway to Ranchos de Taos.

At 7:30 I careened up a long gangplank with my luggage and took my place in the barn-like interior of a C-54 of the Air Transport Command. Heading back through the high mountain pass. I wonder when I shall ever be back there again, and under what circumstances.

FEBRUARY 22, 1946
WASHINGTON

I am bothered a good deal by the displeasure I have incurred for accepting the responsibility involved in the State Department assignment. Dr. Morgan and Clapp felt strongly that I should not undertake the assignment. How deep their feeling in the matter may go it is hard to say. It may, conceivably, become a serious situation, though I shall do everything I can, once I am back again, to alleviate the wounds. But it bothers me more than I should allow it, for I now know what I only suspected before, namely, that *no one* could possibly decline to try to do something helpful in this terrible situation, whatever its effect on his ordinary work or however important that work might be.

I am also considerably concerned that the strength of feeling exhibited may be a symptom that TVA has become too dependent upon me—not that it won't go along smoothly, in an administrative sense, but that no one will be willing or perhaps able to stir things up. This might not be true if I were definitely and permanently out and someone else in. This might mean that I can't plan to do much collateral work— or even plan the trip to Sweden and France for this fall. If this is true, the attractiveness of the TVA job becomes less at once.

At breakfast this morning my friend, Morris Llewellyn Cooke, told me a story that illustrates a current form of madness.

It arose apropos our discussion of two international meetings a number of people are interested in having me attend, the International

Engineering Conference at Paris and the American Management Association meeting at Stockholm, both in September.

The story, however, happens to be concerned with Czechoslovakia. An official of the Masaryk Institute of Prague explained to Mr. Cooke that the Nazis had taken all their books, including everything of a scientific and engineering character. They were eager to have these replaced as rapidly as possible; would American technical organizations be interested in helping?

Cooke thought it was a wonderful opportunity, of course, so he talked to the president of the American Society of Mechanical Engineers, his own profession (and with which he has been feuding, successfully, for a generation over its incredible stupidity). No, said the president, he didn't see how the American Society, representing as it does free enterprise, could supply any books that would be of interest or of usefulness to a country that had just expropriated and nationalized 144 private industries! And this, says Mrs. Cooke (the memory of her summer in Prague lighting up her eyes), about "the sweetest, most solid people in the whole world"!

The fact that engineering is engineering, and not free enterprise or any other kind of engineering (it is like talking about *American* nuclear physics, or American blood corpuscles), and that the reason these businesses were seized was because they had been taken by Nazi henchmen from the owners, and that the only way to retain them in "private" ownership was to let these Nazi robbers keep them—little things like this didn't seem to bother this gent. It is an illness.

There is quite a bit of furor about my going to the Stockholm meeting. I have decided that I can't afford to pay my own way, and that I should not charge it to TVA, though it would be in line of duty. Even if some other way is found to pay for the trip, there would be a problem about leaving my work, considering how much difficulty it has produced for a much more important thing, namely, the State Department task. If I go, though, perhaps I could combine with it a trip to Vienna (where Llewellyn Evans is at work on a Danubian problem for General Clark, and could use me) and to Prague, where I would very much like to go. Perhaps Mr. Cooke could get me also made a member of the Masaryk Institute.

FEBRUARY 25, 1946
WASHINGTON, MONDAY

I am very happy tonight. We have developed a really original, distinctive, and I think completely sound idea as the theme of our recommendation on the atomic bomb. After weeks of sweating blood, of weary hours when we went every which way, we now have arrived, together—a beautiful demonstration of what well-directed discussion can do. When everyone instantly accepted as his own a completely new set of words to describe what we were after—security through cooperative development—as a substitute for the term "control," which has been habitual in every preceding discussion not only of our group but in all the official dissertations on the subject—I knew we had made great headway, and that the worst, for this job, was over.

There is still a very considerable job of drafting, of rewriting, and, of course, of persuading others of the wisdom of the idea. But to come up with something distinctive and appealing to all of us—who appeared so barren, and who were so apparently far apart—this gives me enormous satisfaction.

FEBRUARY 28, 1946
WASHINGTON

Cap Krug† called for me and drove me out to his house for a talk. He will be before the Public Lands Committee next Tuesday. What should he say, especially if questioned (as he probably will be) about valley authorities?

I reminded him that when he went to the WPB way back in 1940, and asked my advice, I suggested one simple rule to apply in the inevitable series of pressures as between private and public power advocates, etc.: Will this help win the war? That formula worked. I now suggested a similarly simple one, but one that would seem startling to people accustomed to the grabbing, power-hungry official. It is this: "I am only interested in measures that will advance the interests of the people, and the fact that such measures may cut down the jurisdiction, prestige, or authority of the Interior Department is something I am not concerned about." I elaborated on this, as a device for answering questions, and indeed as a rule of conduct. This fits into his record in WPB, where he liquidated the agency rather than tried to prolong it (I told him I thought he had overdone it, as a matter of fact, but that isn't the point). And for that attitude he received considerable acclaim.

We talked about valley authorities, and many other things.

I talked history to him—his background isn't too extensive—of how for 75 years the country was influenced by the development of

† Krug had been appointed to succeed Ickes as Secretary of the Interior. Oscar Chapman, mentioned earlier as a possible appointee, was made Under Secretary.

the West, from the Mississippi, and that in the past 40 years that same region (much of it) has been slipping, with profound effects upon the whole country. He has a great chance to reverse the process, through this new post.

He is a very able fellow. What he will be able to do with this job is hard to say, but he seems entirely devoted to the idea of disinterested public service. I believe he will make a good Secretary.

Working hard as the very devil on the atomic bomb report— have written one section, and gone through the agony of rewriting and rethinking the damn thing. In a week we must face the test of our ideas in their first go-round. In the meantime, the situation in respect to a rational dealing with the problem has been deteriorating, though it is by no means hopeless. I refer to the announcement of Russian spies and what not issuing from Canada,‡ and the Army's renewed efforts to take over permanent control of the atom in this country.

That my long controversy with old Ickes should have this curious turn, namely, that one of "our" boys, as close to me as Cap, should succeed the old devil is a curious bit of irony!

MARCH 6, 1946
WASHINGTON

I have just come back across Lafayette Park from an hour and a half's talk with Acheson.

About three weeks ago General Groves came in to see him, "a very scared man." "This is the mess we are in," Groves said, quite upset; "you have got to get us out of it." This was the story (as fantastic in its way as anything in the whole atom story) that Groves told:

At the time of the Attlee, King, Truman meetings here (November, I believe) an agreement was drawn up in the form of a memorandum, by Vannevar Bush, which the three "great men" initialed, providing for future cooperation between the three nations, in development, etc. It was quite broad and general. Then Truman told Groves to go off with one of the British and make this more specific. They produced a memo providing for assistance to the British, including aid of a

---

‡ This was the case of Alan Nunn May, a British physicist assigned to the Canadian atomic energy project who transmitted some information about the American effort to Soviet agents. It came at a time when the Army was still pressing for an atomic energy law that would give it strong representation.

technical and other kind for the actual construction of a plant in England. This was done without the knowledge of Acheson (who told me these things because of their bearing on the report we present tomorrow at Dumbarton Oaks) and without the knowledge of his immediate superior, Byrnes.

Groves' agitation came from the fact that now the British wanted action on the promise of cooperation. Acheson said he would try to work it out.

Yesterday, nothing having happened and the British becoming increasingly pressing and rather indignant, they met with Acheson. He said it was quite impossible to fulfill the obligation of the arrangement. If a secret arrangement were carried out, it would blow the Administration out of the water. If it were carried out by some shenanigan of an exchange of notes, to evade the plain provision of the UNO Charter requiring summaries of all agreements between nations to be submitted to that body, that evasion would be fatal and wouldn't work. They must just resign themselves to the fact that, although we made the agreement, we simply could not carry it out; that things like that happen in the Government of the U.S. due to the loose way things are handled, and they would have to face the problem of their own country's feeling of being let down, just as we would have to face our problems.

This comes on the very eve of our presentation of a plan for joint international development. Nothing could be more timely, in the sense that our report may become the basis for international discussion and therefore help stave off just such things as this U.S.A.-U.K. joint enterprise which might permanently forestall international action.

I was permitted to read a very long and well-written dispatch from Moscow from Kennan of our Embassy staff there. It spelled out his interpretation of Russian policy for the future, in terms of their relations to the West and to non-Communist countries. When he says that the position of the U.S.S.R. as he believes it to be presents the greatest test of diplomacy and statecraft in our history, he certainly does not overstate the matter. And the atom bomb will, as I said to Acheson, be one of the very first real tests of our ability to understand the Russian problem (essentially that of an effort to break down all other systems than theirs throughout the world, as this man believes) and also of our own willingness, here in the U.S., to face the implications of international organization, whether UNO or some other development.

I didn't sleep well last night, and little wonder. I find myself in the midst of wholly strange and fearsome things. And as a result of the past six weeks, these seem quite close and real.

MARCH 9, 1946
WASHINGTON

I put down the copy of our report on international control of atomic energy, the concluding paragraphs of which I had just read aloud and said: "This, gentlemen, is our recommendation of a plan for security in a world of atomic energy."§

I sat at the end of a long table in the great hall of Dumbarton Oaks. At the other end was Dean Acheson. He put down his copy (we had read the entire report together, one of us reading aloud the while), removed his glasses, and in a warm, low tone said, "This is a brilliant and a profound document."

This was on Thursday, the 7th. All that day, and beginning again yesterday and continuing until about four we talked over the plan. All kinds of difficulties were raised; some of them were answered; some did not seem adequately met. General Groves made some shallow comments about how he could circumvent the plan, but he didn't get very far—my fellow-members had at him with the facts in a vigorous way. President Conant and Bush had formulated the policies of the President and Secretary Byrnes (Conant went to Potsdam and Bush practically ran the Attlee-King-Truman session here, including drafting the "Agreed Declaration"). Our report presented quite a different scheme, and I had entertained scant hope of getting their approval— if they didn't disapprove, I thought that would be good.

But after the long discussion Bush expressed himself enthusiastically—this was by all odds "the best proposal that has ever been put forward." They wanted more light (and here John McCloy joined them, though heartily and extravagantly praising the job) on what would happen in the "eventuality" that the plan broke down after it was launched, or while it was being launched. This led to a long and to me rather discouraging discussion. For they were committed to a "step-by-step" program, in their earlier statements; our plan is integral. They both agreed that it had to be integral, and yet they still wanted us to develop an additional chapter on what "safeguards" there were in the event of failure. We agreed to try, and until late last night, and again all morning, meeting separately, we have been struggling with this.

§ In brief, the report proposed the establishment of an international Atomic Development Authority (ADA) which would have exclusive control of all "dangerous" aspects of atomic energy. National activity in these "dangerous" areas would be outlawed. At the same time, the ADA would promote the cooperative development of the atom's peaceful potentialities. We concluded that an inspection system alone would be ineffective as a protection against nations attempting to build up a secret atomic arsenal.

About 11:30 Oppenheimer hit upon a way of stating the fallacy in the Bush-Conant point; it was pounced upon by Thomas and Winne, and in no time we "had it," and adjourned to get a draft written that would make perfectly plain what risks the plan entails (in relation to America's present situation) at various stages, from its initiation to its full operation, say seven to ten years hence.

Something Bush said to his former assistant, Carroll Wilson, pleased me more than anything else. He remarked on the way we all pitched in, as a unit, when questions were put or points needed discussion: "I couldn't have told which were scientists, which were industrial men, which the administrator of a public enterprise." And they were impressed, all of them, not only by our unanimity at this stage, but our obvious liking for each other. Considering the long strain, the forbearance that working together so long on so difficult a subject requires, the fact that we are speaking to each other, much less enjoying each other's company, means a good deal. I am given the credit, as chairman, for this sort of thing. I have worked hard to accomplish it, it is true, for I know how important it is in its effect on the substantive job of the board. But actually it was possible because these are really remarkable men, as fine a group as I have ever seen.

One further note: It is sobering to realize how seriously this report is taken. It is the only thing that has been done that bears the mark of careful thought and originality. This means that it may have considerable influence. We meet again with the Acheson group on March 16. The next step would be the submission of the report to the Secretary of State and the President. What will happen then no one can tell, of course.

It would be quite wrong if I did not record how weary I have been (tomorrow will be the third Sunday in a row that I have worked) and how often there have been periods of almost unimaginable gloom. The gloom has come not only when we hit a serious snag, or can't seem to keep on the beam, but from the terrible realities of the bomb, so close to us in our work, and the constant fear of a long, bitter period of antagonism and strain and perhaps war with the Russians. I can't make clear how this hangs over everything. We try to be objective about it, but it is part of the calculations, part of the planning, part of the weighing of alternatives. And if that doesn't represent an amazing collection of raw materials for five men to be struggling with, I never heard of one.

The setting in which all this went on for two days is a part of the story. On the walls some of the most magnificent tapestries men have ever devised; in a glass case, a priceless ebony cat, Byzantine. The ceiling, three stories high, decorated with the beams of some castle, carved and painted. And dominating the whole thing in a strange and lovely way, a painting by El Greco, "The Visitation." This painting had a fascination for us. It was hung, not flat against a wall, but in a bracket at an angle from one of the great French doors that led to the garden, so that it caught the light in a beautiful way. And moving by, from time to time, outside the windows on the garden terrace were workmen, the people who had most at stake, and too little to say as to whether someday the order is given and an atomic bomb, perhaps a thousand times greater than Nagasaki, starts on its way against other workmen.

MARCH 17, 1946
WASHINGTON, SUNDAY

God, what an experience!

Yesterday we had a long session with the Acheson Committee at Dumbarton Oaks all afternoon. It did not go so well, and I became belligerent, and we all were on edge. But we genuinely felt we were nearing the point where our report would at least be received, not rejected, despite the animadversions of Conant, Bush, Groves. Then we went to dinner and had a number of drinks and became quite gay— we might be near the end. About 9:30 Herb Marks, who had been sitting with the Acheson Committee while they deliberated in our absence, came in. He looked as if the end of the world had come. They had hopped all over us, and things looked very bad indeed.

I talked over this sad turn of events with some of the men until midnight. I don't know when I felt more miserable; all our work might be wasted, and some cheap alternatives offered, for reasons that would be cowardly and could only lead to the certainty of atomic warfare.

I was determined to maintain some perspective; we might have to hang on, working with these men until they saw that their objections were simply a refusal to face the inescapable price of international action, or an attempt in that direction. I appeared at Dumbarton Oaks this morning, early (I didn't sleep much, I can tell you), determined to set that kind of tone to the meeting today.

And at four o'clock this afternoon the entire Acheson Committee (not excluding General Groves) had signed a fine letter of transmittal of the report to Secretary Byrnes. What happened in between now seems nothing less than a miracle. Such praise of the report and of those who developed the plan! Bush even said it was, so far as he was concerned, "the" plan. The difficulties that were so acute and apparently fatal yesterday yielded to a persistent pounding away of the facts, and a narrowing down of the objections, whittled steadily to smaller and smaller dimensions by some interesting work on our part.

By Tuesday it will be in the hands of the Secretary of State. Then what? In the middle of the discussion this noon, when General Groves and Conant were insisting that we provide definitely that we should continue to make bombs and to make that a part of their approving our plan, Acheson told us something of the Russian situation and how it may disintegrate in the Middle East in the near future. This gave a note of grim reality to the whole business. It made me feel (that and the quite warm praise of the committee) that whatever happens, the misery and exhausting work of the past two months could be counted as my contribution toward something better in the world than perhaps we must look forward to. It wasn't all misery, though; much of it was genuinely exciting and pleasurable.

MARCH 19, 1946
FLYING HOME—AT 210 MILES AN HOUR! (EARLY MORN)

While I am sitting in the radioman's jump seat of a B-25, roaring like all hell due westward and home, our report is being handed to Secretary Byrnes.

This is a crazy kind of finale—or is it the curtain-raiser?

(On all sides of me are gadgets, wires, valves, for this is a working Army plane, cold—I have flier's lined boots on—uncomfortable— but fast as hell. There won't be enough ceiling at Knoxville to handle a really tall giraffe, but this young pilot—a great guy, Pete Young by name—will ease her in.)

But the crazy part is that last Sunday, while we at Dumbarton Oaks were hammering out a complete agreement on the report and plan I have been nursing along all these weeks (two months almost to the day), Byrnes was asking Bernard Baruch to be United States member on the UNO Atomic Energy Commission. When I read this news last night, I was quite sick. We need a man who is young, vigorous, not vain, and whom the Russians would feel isn't out simply to put them in a hole, not really caring about international cooperation. Baruch has none of these qualifications. And this morning comes the list of men who will, as he says, really do the work—which is substantially true. It is the old crowd: Hancock, Eberstadt, Swope (Herbert Bayard), and that familiar bull in the china closet, Searls. God! Isn't *this* something!

This is the hottest seat B.B. has occupied since War I. He has responsibility this time, and not just a chance to kibitz.

I can imagine how heavy Acheson's heart must have been Sunday, knowing that this was going to happen. B. is, of course, Byrnes' idea.

Yesterday morning I walked into the Interior Building for the first time since my talk with Ickes when he tried to keep me from fighting the idea of bringing TVA into that department. This time I was greeted by those who have been writing nasty letters about me for Ickes' signature, but butter wouldn't melt in their mouths. For I was there for Cap Krug's induction as Secretary. While it was unusual to have a swearing in made into a public meeting (this was in the auditorium) and accompanied by a "speech of acceptance," it was all right, I thought. Miss Owen was appalled at the whole thing (except the graceful way Cap conducted himself, and the wonderful poise of his family whom he introduced to the crowd), and Herb Marks said these "Presidential boom launchings" turned his stomach. I thought it was all right; that the people in the department felt they were participating in something very important to them, and that asking all Cap's friends, instead of a few, was all right. His speech, of course, was pure corn.

I couldn't sleep last night—finally had to take a sleeping pill— because next door some men were talking and quietly drinking. They talked earnestly, solemnly, unceasingly, about—canned goods. This was business talk, of course. There was one man who spoke with vast profundity, and then a kind of boy-like earnestness about jellied consommé! The possibilities hadn't been realized. Nothing to add, no heating up; you put it in the refrigerator for two days, open the can, and there are two servings (he amended this, clearing his throat: "two *generous* servings") of jellied consommé. "This salad dressing entered our home for the first time twenty-five years—wait a minute—twenty years ago." "To my mind, it is like this. . . ." And then a dissertation about salad dressing—it is so good that they eat what's left under the salad with a spoon—go after it with a spoon—do you get that?

There is a terrible point about these hours of talk about groceries, by grown men to whom this is the center of life. And it should make me stop fretting so damn much about what I am doing with my life.

MARCH 24, 1946
HOME, SUNDAY

Bernard Baruch just phoned me. He had read our report "two or three times." As he understood it, said he, the report had been approved by the Acheson Committee. If it was also approved by the Secy. of State and the President, then the policy of the country was fixed, for this "is more than a report—you recommend a definite policy." The Pres.

and Secy. of State must either adopt the policy, modify it, or reject it. If they adopt it, then there isn't anything for him to do, he said; just be a messenger boy, and lay it before the other nations.

What about it? he asked.

I told him I didn't know whether the Secy. of State and the President had adopted the plan proposed; it was my understanding that they were considering this merely as a place to begin negotiations, and a wholesome discussion to clarify the whole atom bomb business. But even if they did adopt it as their own, there was still a whale of a job, the job of getting 11 other nations on the United Nations Atomic Energy Commission to agree to the plan in general, and then to work out by negotiation the important details we didn't fill in.

Well, he said, we who worked out the plan were the ones who knew how to fill it in, and we ought to be the ones to do that. Then he went on to explain that he could do it himself, and he would have good technical advisers. He had explained all that when he accepted the post a week ago (though the only "technical adviser" by any remote interpretation would be Fred Searls, a mining engineer. I told him the only dependable technical advisers I knew of were the members of our own board of consultants—stressing Oppenheimer, but also Thomas. Yes, Conant and Bush had said the same thing, he said, and he would get in touch with them.

I was appalled by the fact that he thought that somehow this terrific responsibility could be carried through having people around him, so I told him he would have to have good technical men, but he would have to go through the painful process of absorbing the technical stuff himself, just as we did on our Board of Consultants. He said, well, he wasn't much on technical scientific stuff, but he could smell his way through it—and that's the way he did things, smell his way.

"Don't think, young man, you won't be pulled back into this. When are you coming to Wash. to go over this with me?" I dodged, feeling it important that the report be presented to the McMahon Committee◖ (scheduled for Tuesday) and if possible be published before I get involved again, if I do. Here I am torn between a desire that this terribly important matter not be left to the judgment of an old man and my intense desire to stay on the TVA job.

He gave me a big talk about how much he thought of me, that he had recommended me for Secretary of the Interior, along with Krug, O'Mahoney and Douglas (all of which I must admit I don't quite believe).

◖ The special Senate committee established the previous October to work out U.S. atomic energy legislation.

I immediately called Herb Marks, and fortunately got him just before he took off to see Acheson. They are to see Baruch tomorrow, and present the report to the McMahon Committee in executive session on Tuesday.

MARCH 30, 1946
HOME

Great excitement these days.

Although Baruch protested against it to the President, the green light to publish our report came through about Wednesday, a "background" press conference was held by Acheson on Thurs. and the report was released Thurs. night.

I read the AP account at Gatlinburg (Tennessee) Friday morning: columns and columns. I really was sick. The story (Knoxville *Journal*) described the plan as "drafted" by an official committee of which Acheson was head: not one single word about our Board of Consultants in the whole four or five columns. I thought it was a deliberate effort in Washington to take the report over, since it was evident that the preliminary leaks had demonstrated that it was going to go over quite well. I even phoned Sturdevant to see what he could do to save something from the wreckage.

The worst thing about the next two or three hours was realizing how unhappy I could be made by such a failure to get credit for what is a very important thing. I thought I had enough objectivity to take it in stride, happy in the thought that we were getting the two things we wanted: publication so the public would have a chance to judge the plan, and sponsorship by the State Depart.

I stayed somewhat mad most of the day (I spoke to a big teachers' meeting, state-wide, at Asheville), but I had myself in hand by nightfall. Today I saw that it wasn't a deliberate effort to deny credit to us, just a mistake by the AP man, or an effort by him to blow it up, since it was released by the State Dept. and the form of the report was ambiguous on quick reading. I hear that our board and myself as its chairman did get noticed in some of the publicity; and anyway, today it doesn't seem to matter so much whether we did or not. Apparently our long work has met with a grand response all over.

APRIL 4, 1946
HOME

Monday last we were before the Special Senate Committee on Atomic Energy, the McMahon Committee. Oppenheimer did a brilliant job of explaining denaturants, and fitting it into the whole plan. They were disappointed, in a kind of kid way, that some simple, easy way out of the whole thing had not been developed. Must say I was impressed with Vandenberg and Connally, certainly by comparison. It is quite evident that they have "put their money" on the UNO idea, and this fits into it. Curious how it calms down the skeptics when you ask or present the alternatives!

Have just heard that Baruch has decided to accept his appointment.

APRIL 5, 1946
HOME

I have learned somewhat more about myself out of this atomic bomb experience. Thrown into a new problem, with new kinds of people to work with, without the support of staff—it was quite a revealing thing.

On the debit side I found that while I don't give up, actually, when things don't "go"—and they didn't many times—I get much too low about it, draw too long a face, take it much, much too hard. What is equally clear is that I seem to try to get others to feel the hurt of the bad way of things, by exaggerating my own sense of impending defeat. I found myself, on one or two crucial occasions, one when we were together at Dumbarton Oaks, talking in the language of defeat, not because I actually would have given up for worlds (I am really tough and stubborn in the pinch), but seemingly (not a deliberate process) to make others feel as badly as I—a kind of play-acting that would induce certain feelings and perhaps get people to urge me not to take it so hard.

At one stage it worked, actually. We were asked to cover certain contingencies of our plan (this from the Acheson group) that we thought should be excluded; we didn't see the answers, and said they were for others to work out, at a later stage, etc. I put on a show (I see it was that now; then it seemed more or less the McCoy) that we were through—that I wanted to go back to Tennessee; that if this didn't do the job they had in mind, then someone else would have to do it. This didn't make a good impression at all, but it did have the effect of making them see that many of the issues they wanted answers on couldn't be answered at this point. My own motive, I can see, was that, being awfully tired and wanting to get through, I used the device of appearing ready to quit to force the issue. Not good, Dave. Arguing it out is much better.

On the credit side there are things to be said. I showed far more patience than anyone would have guessed; indeed, at the beginning and for three weeks it was my patience and more patience that kept us from falling apart. I showed human resourcefulness in judging the people I was trying to keep together, giving them the right kind of assignments, being candid at the right times and soothing at about the right times. I showed more resourcefulness about the subject matter, and about unsnarling differences that developed, than I thought I would be able to. While I didn't follow the scientific detail as well as the others, I think, I did get the essentials more quickly than I thought I could. I kept my "chairman" function out of the picture almost throughout, so that for the first time in our experience—all of them said the same thing, Barnard being especially vehement on the matter —all five men participated actively all the way through, rather than one or two doing the work and the others either coasting or criticizing from the back seat.

APRIL 13, 1946
NEW YORK (12:30 A.M.)

Have just come from the dinner in memory of F.D.R. Saw more New Deal people than I have seen in years and years.

Wallace mentioned the "Acheson-Lilienthal Report" in his speech, with warm approval ("F.D.R. would have been for it"). Got a round of applause at the reference. Said to me that he believed I was chiefly responsible for it—which I denied, but those things always sound coy.

Frances Perkins: When she was in Europe, all over the one thing people would speak about, hopefully, was TVA. This seemed to astound her; she doesn't know much about it, really. But you could see she had taken a new interest in TVA and me. She was quite moved as she spoke —talked about the Rhone; Lyons, where the only sewage system they have is the one the Romans left.

Jerome Frank; Rex Tugwell, looking a bit fat, as cynical and superior as ever. Helen Gahagan looking very thin—she doesn't look anything like the buxom gal I drove to Washington with just barely over a year ago; but quite striking and lovely in an evening gown. I never saw such a change in anyone. Wearing herself out, I would say. Leon Henderson, looking wonderful. My egg man story (really Helen's, of course) he heard me put over at the Washington Press Club he was still chuckling over; said he stole it and used it in a speech the next day, and it is all over the place.*

* During the war, when Oak Ridge was still the "mystery plant," the farmer who sold us fresh eggs got a job there as a laborer. After a while, he quit, and one day reappeared at our door with his basket of eggs. When my wife asked him why he hadn't stayed on his new job, he disapprovingly described the extravagant activities he'd seen there—all the plants and houses and streets being so hastily

Much praise, quite extravagant, about the job we did on the atom: from Senator Pepper, Max Lerner, Gardner Jackson, Robert Nathan, Jim Patton, John Carmody, Paul Appleby—extravagant, Lee Pressman; Sidney Hillman said it was "must" reading, though as Jim Warburg said yesterday, "I doubt if Sidney has read 80 pages himself in the past 10 years."

Orson Welles gave a dramatic and stylized speech—I don't care for anything so studied, though of course it made a big hit.

They introduced everyone in the dais places—must have been 40 people, including some dopes. I got a real walloping applause— the bomb report is still news.

Good deal of talk about organizing support for the report on a "mass organization" basis. Well, we'll see.

Talked to the church leader group yesterday afternoon—Bishop Oxnam, Bishop Tucker of the Episcopal Church, and perhaps 25 or 30 others. It was quite apparent that they were surprised that it was so simple and clear. I think that will do a lot of good. Yesterday Herb Marks, who was with me, said, "No wonder you are the darling of the church people. There was no unction in that, and yet you let in the outside world as if you assumed they knew something about it." I do have a remarkable standing with church leaders—have two important invitations for large church gatherings in the Midwest just this week.

APRIL 14, 1946
WASHINGTON, SUNDAY EVENING

Clare Luce gave me a long, appraising look and said, "You are the only living New Dealer—I underline *living*—who is still popular. It is a considerable distinction and it must give you a very good feeling. I say living because death casts a mantle of popularity that did not exist in life." I said something vague and mumbled that I hadn't thought of myself that way.

This is the way our luncheon conversation began at Mark Childs' house today. She is quite a puzzling person. At times that gift for the cutting and clever phrase, at other times extraordinarily obtuse, in getting the point of a quite simple statement—Mark had to shout at her finally when she stubbornly persisted in saying she didn't understand and, innocently or otherwise, got things all mixed up. She has a weird kind of mysticism. This is very bad in men; in women who have

---

built in that little valley. "I don't know what it is the Government's makin' there," he concluded, with a shake of his head, "but it'd be a darn sight cheaper if they went out and bought it!"

power—of money, beauty, wit and political talent (she has all of them) —it can become even worse.

She can be very amusing and clever—as when imitating people, like one of the other guests, Señor Martíns, Ambassador of Brazil, or silly Lady Astor. And the coolness that seems such a pain in the neck can change to a warmth of look and color that is quite surprising and really attractive, though she is certainly not my type even at the top of that particular form. But there is an underlying strangeness and bitter touch that made me quite uneasy.

I thought at a certain juncture that she was just a plain phony and that was that. But she isn't a phony. The reason I had thought so was this sort of thing: "Yes, I would run again" (to young Senator Fulbright and Mark, who were with us at this point) "if there were a party I believed in to run for. What kind? Socialist, a Republican Socialist party. Socialist, of course; the country inevitably will be socialist. What do I mean by socialist? Public ownership and control of all utilities, for one thing." (When I said that didn't seem very startling; I believed in a good deal of that myself; indeed, had done something about it, and I hardly regarded that as socialism, she said, well, she would put me in her Cabinet if she were President. This latter part of the conversation got around and before the afternoon was over, people were remarking that I was to be in Clare's Cabinet.)

That was one example; followed by this: Mark asked if she would support Bricker if he were the candidate. She certainly would. "He is at least an honorable man, and that is no inconsiderable virtue as things now are." Bricker, the Republican Socialist.

I mean: This was childish stuff said with great cleverness, dolled out in what I suppose were very expensive clothes and a little round straw hat that probably cost as much as Helen's last five hats.

She gave me a lot of the full-look-in-the-eyes stuff of a woman who can turn it on and off, and since she is a member of the House Military Affairs Committee and the wife of the editor of Life-Time, etc., I more or less did what was expected of me in that kind of exchange. But it wasn't fun, and it makes me uneasy yet—if she were just a handsome fool, but she is certainly no fool, it wouldn't matter. She does not believe in the material interpretation of history—and then was off on a spiel about spiritualism that one couldn't object to, literally, but you just somehow knew wasn't genuinely part of her.

The Ambassador of Brazil was all upset. At the Gridiron Dinner last night he was put fourth from the President instead of next to him (he is the Dean of the Diplomatic Corps), and he did not touch a bit of food or drink the whole evening! Was still boiling about it: now that the war is over and we do not need them any longer, the United States is showing its contempt for the Latin Americans.

The Gridiron Dinner was a big, garish display of celebrities in a huge room, filled with the din of the Marine Band, loud "acts," and well-fed, successful men, with the lighthearted aspects of politics, as just a lot of fun among friends, as the theme. I was glad of an opportunity to go, and I enjoyed it. But I certainly don't crave much of that.

Met many people, and was showered with extravagant comments upon our report and just praise in general. I have become something of a phenomenon—a minor one perhaps—but something rather extra; somewhere between a prize fighter who reads the classics, say, and a man who can wiggle his ears.

Eric Johnston (who really *is* a glamour boy—he was tossing his genuinely handsome profile about like an actor) was very hearty and cordial. Cap Krug looked like a monolith, up on the dais. Halleck of Indiana and I had a lot of vigorous chatter, and he seemed overcome: "So this is Lilienthal—what do you know?" That sort of thing. Tom Stokes, Mark Ethridge, Don Richberg, Lowell Mellett, Kaltenborn, H. L. Mencken (looking like a boozy old man, the kind who goes to Senate committee hearings day after day just to stay in out of the cold); Mark Sullivan, General Eisenhower, Governor Dewey—well, the works. Stassen delivered the traditional speech of "advice" to the President, and for the first time I have heard him was light, witty, and his delivery speeded up, excellent. It was a good, courageous speech, in which he not only pitched in his hat, but thumbed his nose and made other even more unmistakable gestures at the Old Guard. "We Republicans have a Solid South." I was delighted with him in every way, and wish I had a chance to vote for him.

Walked home—at 1:30, when the parties were still going strong— with Joseph Pulitzer. What about Baruch, he asked, was he still miffed? I said I didn't know about that; that Baruch had stopped me at the Gridiron to tell me that he had asked that we continue in existence— our board. I said I wanted to talk to him about that request, for I had to go back to my work; from here on it was his ball. "Well, I am 75 years old; you young fellows have to keep right on with me." I tried to make it plain that this was out for me.

Pulitzer made a curious statement, but considering how close he is to Baruch, one that I have pondered. "What is he up to? He is a shrewd old man. Is he trying to give you enough rope to hang yourself?"

Mark pointed out that if I persist in dissenting, and choose not to hang myself by continuing to act as an adviser to the "Great Adviser," then Arthur Krock's column will begin to contain stories that Lilienthal is sulking, etc., etc.

I would like to have a showdown on this soon.

APRIL 15, 1946
WASHINGTON

Byrnes wrote all of us, including members of the Acheson Committee, that Baruch was "quite earnest" in his desire to have us continue to serve in an advisory capacity to the President and Secretary of State. This I don't want to do at all, but it is a most difficult thing to get out of completely. Baruch does not realize, I fear, what he has let himself in for in this assignment, or how much staff work and close and exacting work lies ahead for him. This afternoon he phoned me, saying he wanted to see me for a talk, and warning me that we could not fail to help. He wanted me to come early in the morning "while I am still fresh"—what a practice for a man who faces such terrific responsibilities! I shall see him at eleven; before that I hope to see Acheson.

Spent the day on TVA materials, preparing for the appropriation hearings.

APRIL 20, 1946
HOME

Stripped to the waist, and sweating like a stevedore—just in from the garden for a moment because I really must record something of my talk with Baruch—from 11 to 12:30 of the 16th.

I had grimly determined that I would remember that he was the vehicle of our hopes, and that the choice seemed to me fantastic— his age, his unwillingness to work, his terrifying vanity—nevertheless he was the representative of this country. But I was not prepared, even so, for the flow of words about things quite irrelevant. Fully a fourth of the time (he talked almost continuously) he spent saying that it was a shame that the President had insisted on choosing him, that he had tried to get out of it, had held up his confirmation, that it should be a younger man, that he had urged that someone else do it, etc.— this was the opening and the closing note.

Of course, he didn't believe a word of it, and it went on so long because I didn't take my cue and assure him that he was the wisest man in the world, that he wasn't really old, and that he must by no means withdraw. I just couldn't say those things, even to be polite to an old man. So he had to keep repeating the cue. When it was evident I wouldn't come through with the goose grease, he went on for another fourth of the time telling me how smart he is, how he doesn't need to study the facts, and how he will be in this thing to the end, that he isn't senile (he said it just that way a half-dozen times), and that he would outfox everybody.

After about an hour of his telling me these things, and urging me (with much palaver and praise put on with a trowel), I spoke up, but I had to fight to keep the floor. I wanted to resist the idea of being drawn in with no clear definition of what we were to do, and wanted to make clear what I thought was the nature of his own responsibility, that it required well-organized staff work. I told him he was famous as Dr. Facts, and that without the facts carefully developed, these advisory groups were a menace.

When I got through indicating how exacting a job I thought he had before him, how badly it needed extensive staff preparation, how important it was for him to establish clear lines of responsibility unconfused by vague committees wandering around being consulted, several things happened: (1) he didn't like his job as well as he did before; (2) he didn't like me too well (my guess is that I'm not too likely to be called upon again, by him); and (3) he admitted that he was groping, and that his impulse had simply been to "reach out" (this accompanied by gestures) and take in these men who had given so much thought to the subject. It is significant that at no time did he say that he approved our report, thought it a sound policy, etc. The most he said was that it was "thoughtful."

He made one good line of argument, to wit, the domestic legislation providing a U.S. Atomic Energy Comm. is part of the international matter, and the members and their staff—when that time comes— should be chosen and work with the internatl. situation in mind. He said I ought to become head of the U.S. Commission. I had been told by Acheson (who saw him from 9 to 10:30 the same morning) that this was the line, and I refrained from any comment at all.

Jim Pope told me that Pres. Conant fought vigorously for "the panel's" report in a meeting of the Carnegie Endowment in N.Y. against the roarings of Manley Hudson,† who said what do these amateurs mean invading our field, and Gano Dunn, who thought it was a public power scheme. Such old dodos.

† Harvard law professor and specialist in international law. A Carnegie Endowment committee was preparing a report proposing a draft treaty for UN atomic control, with emphasis on inspection and punishment for violations. (This is referred to in the entry of May 4, 1946.)

MAY 2, 1946
HOME

Just talked to Herb Marks. Very low. He and Acheson talked to Hancock, Baruch's right-hand man, and they were deeply depressed. Apparently Baruch hasn't yet the slightest conception of what he is into, and neither have his "aides." They want Oppenheimer to join them, on the scientific side, but he has no intention of doing so. Terrible stalemate. If the President were to adopt the report as policy, that might start things again. In the meantime Russia has named Gromyko to the UN Atomic Energy Comm., and when Mexico names their member, that Commission could hold its first meeting.

MAY 4, 1946
HOME

Must be pretty tired, with all the overexcitement and hard work: slept till ten almost. Downpour last night, so no gardening today, so may stay in bed and read and drowse. Reading Milton's *Samson Agonistes*—such power. Frustration—what a theme for tragedy. Blindness could not be half so bad as that. And alongside Samson I've dug up *Now We Are Six*—the Milne book we read and reread to the kids at Palos,‡ till it's practically fallen apart. Also reading Stanley Walker's *City Editor* and William Allen White's autobiography, just out. He isn't nearly as appealing, so far, in his own words about himself as my picture of him in less personal writings; my hunch that autobiography, just that, is something I should avoid would be supported by this taste of his.

Doubleday Doran's issue of The Report came yesterday, a 35¢ booklet with wild type on the cover—à la Willkie's *One World*. And yesterday I finished revising a piece for the Sunday supplement magazine, *This Week*—one of these breezy and breathlessly informal things that I have successfully avoided thus far. But it will get into 8 million homes, some of which can read beyond the comics, and it does make the point well, that this concerns everyone, so it seems worth doing, at the risk of seeming pretty undignified. (Maybe I've carried that too far; after all, I am a darn informal guy, so it isn't quite Cal Coolidge pitching hay with stiff cuffs.)

Shotwell of Carnegie Endowment for Peace phoned last night; to see him in Wash. at his request, to review a report a big name committee has prepared; wants it to jibe with our plan, he says.

‡ Palos Park, a Chicago suburb where we lived, 1927–30.

Nancy still without a job; poor kid. David will be out of the Navy by midsummer. Agreed to speak at Utah Ag. College June 8—first time I've been in that part of the country.

## MAY 6, 1946
### HOME

All day with presidents of the Land Grant colleges—all there but Mitchell of Miss. and Caldwell of Georgia. Went over the issue of our keystone policy of carrying out TVA agric. program through the colleges and extension services, heart of which is that we reimburse the colleges for assist. agents, etc., instead of TVA's employing them directly. They are going to the Secy. of Agriculture, Anderson, with the issue raised by his refusal to follow along on this policy, esp. respecting the Soil Conservation Service.§ May be a very important and broad issue; I may use it as theme of my commencement speech at Utah Ag. College June 8.

Oppenheimer called from Ithaca. He spent hours with Baruch *et al.*; declined to join them as technical delegate, and for good reason. B. is off of me, as I knew he would be, because I refused just to yes-yes him and feed his vanity. Opp. will be in the same boat, I guess. Why do we need a staff? these fellows say; and they are planning to appeal for general disarmament and a lot of other things that will nicely mix things up and get nowhere. What can we do? If we nurse them along to try to affect their decisions, we get nowhere and are blanketed; if we don't, we'll have to try to make a public ruckus, which isn't good either.

## MAY 7, 1946
### WAITING AT KNOXVILLE AIRPORT

Talked at length yesterday by phone to Oppenheimer, who is at Cornell lecturing. He had spent a long time with Baruch, Hancock, Searls. Baruch urged him to become his technical adviser. He declined, and was worried badly by the way these men are going at it. They have a fancy set of ideas and think, or say at least, that they are in pursuance of our Report. Examples: (1) A call for total disarmament; this would hopelessly confuse and mix issues, and obscure the hope of working out something on the atom bomb, and then move on to other things. (2) UN should maintain a large stockpile of *bombs,* on the theory that retaliation is a great deterrent—but this would be fatal and we rejected the notion. (3) Uranium mines should not be

§ The Agriculture Department had for several years refused to take part in the TVA-college program. The college presidents visited Secretary Anderson in June, but the department's policy remained unchanged.

worked by the Atomic Development Authority, but it should only own the concentrates. Hancock explained—in one of the most significant statements of the conference—that this was because the Government couldn't operate anything successfully. (4) Much to-do about the veto power.

Oppenheimer was right in declining to serve, for despite his hours and hours of talking to them they still come up with such notions as these. He says they are enthusiastic about proceeding right away with negotiations and proposals, but have no hope of an agreement. They talk about preparing the American people for a refusal by Russia.

As the others left, Baruch took Oppenheimer to the elevator and said, "Don't let these associates of mine worry you. Hancock is pretty 'Right,' but" (with a wink) "I'll watch him. Searls is smart as a whip, but he sees Reds under every bed."

I hope to see Acheson this afternoon. The gravest danger is that they will put forward proposals in a spirit that will insure their refusal, and the pattern of the UN Security Council now will be repeated. This might happen in any case, since virtually all the members of the UN Atomic Energy Commission are also the Security Council members—except Baruch.

(LATER, IN WASHINGTON)

Just spent an hour with Acheson, Acting Secretary in Byrnes' absence at the Paris Conference. He gave me a careful blow-by-blow report of the atomic bomb situation—which is mostly about Baruch.

He talked to the President yesterday. The Baruch idea of calling for a general disarmament conference the President said he wanted none of, and would tell Baruch so. No one can be sure of this, but that is what he said, and emphatically. Baruch's idea of having Secretary General Lie call an initial meeting of the UN Commission for May 20 he said he would not have either. He said he supported Acheson's alternative, i.e., a meeting just before the UN delegations take off for the Bikini tests in the Pacific in early June, at which time our Report would be distributed to the other members as a "working paper" and they would be asked to supply such studies as they might have made. It is likely that the Report will be supported by at least one other nation to start with, Canada. Then take a six-week recess to study and prepare further, more detailed proposals. The President thought this was a good idea and says he will tell Baruch so Thursday, when Acheson and Baruch will meet and will also meet with the President.

Baruch says I am "sour" and won't cooperate; that Oppenheimer is the same. That he can't understand what is the matter—most of this reached Acheson via a newspaperman, Alsop, who is doing a *Saturday Evening Post* piece on the Report.

I suggested that while I doubted if it would do any good in any way, except to show that we "tried," perhaps we should have a meeting of the Acheson Committee and our Consulting Group with Baruch and his advisers. I hate to have to undertake this, but perhaps we must.

Had a nice visit with Nancy; she has a possible job with a union in Philadelphia. Sweet kid. She waited in Acheson's outer office—it was exciting for her to hear calls coming in from Lord Halifax, etc.

MAY 11, 1946
HOME

Baruch saw Acheson Wednesday. Marks reported on it to me. Three hours of talk.

Acheson said he thought the Report should be put forward by Baruch to the UN Atomic Energy Commission as the United States' "working paper." Baruch said that if he insisted on that he, Baruch, would resign. Why? Well, there were some things in it that he couldn't agree with. What, for example? Well, the ownership of uranium mines by the ADA. They wouldn't object to complete control; but ownership, no. What silly men. So "dominion" was substituted for ownership. What else does ownership mean, except for formal title? Childish.

What else is wrong? The Report doesn't go far enough. By that, he was asked, do you mean that some broad proposal for world disarmament should be put forward—this was what Baruch was talking about before and that produced a row. No, just that the people of the world be given hope. Do you mean that you want to make an eloquent speech? Yes, that's it. Hancock put in: "What the Chief means is, he wants people to see the light at the end of the tunnel." Well, of course, that's fine; that is what the Report implies in many places and if you spell it out that's fine.

What else?

There were one or two other things of this absurdly limited character.

Acheson said that he wanted the UN Commission to meet just as the foreign representatives left for the Bikini tests—all countries represented on the Commission are invited. So about June 10 there should be an initial meeting of that international Commission. Before then Baruch should meet with the Acheson and the Lilienthal groups. Baruch objected to that, the reason for this not being quite clear in Marks' report, since Baruch has been complaining to everybody that we won't help him, etc., etc. In any case we have been notified to try to be on hand next Friday, Saturday, and Sunday. I will be there.

Talked to Cap Krug Wednesday afternoon—that would be May 8; chiefly about his position on valley authorities and particularly the Columbia Valley Authority.

Hearings on a CVA—the bill by Senator Mitchell—have been set for June 24 before Overton and his Army Engineer wrecking crew sub-committee of the Commerce Committee. I explained my interest in his (Krug's) position and that of Interior; when the MVA Murray Bill was on for hearings a year ago, Ickes and the Interior witnesses smeared TVA and cut the throat of the MVA by being "for" it if it were rewritten so as to be wholly unacceptable to everybody.

Cap was cagey at first. What possible chance has the bill before Overton? So I told him what the public support picture was—in contrast to the MVA. The farm organizations of both Washington and Oregon, labor, Governor of Washington, all the Democratic members from both states, etc. The opposition is the usual: reactionary interests, friends of the Army Engineers, utilities, railroads, etc. But, he said, the reason the TVA bill passed was because the people were almost solidly for it. No, I pointed out that this wasn't true—it is true now but wasn't when the bill was considered. That is what Norris continually complained about. The basis of the opposition from the Valley varied, but it was there and strong. Indeed, I said I could not think of any compar-able piece of legislation that had as much support as CVA has in that region.

He said he had asked Steve Raushenbush and a fellow by the name of Dixon to prepare a report and get ready for the hearings. In con-fidence, he thought he would come out for the CVA, and if he did, it wouldn't be a "Yes, but" sort of approval—here he looked belligerent, and I was quite pleased.

As I left, I reminded him of two things: first, that his reputation in WPB was due (as I had told him in my talk with him just before his confirmation hearing) to his refreshing attitude of not caring about perpetuating his jurisdiction—that was definitely involved here; and second, that business people were for him—they had worked with him in WPB. But the progressives still weren't sure about him, and were reserving judgment. This CVA issue was a grand opportunity to show them on that score, and they would watch for it for that reason. He looked at me in a rueful way as I said this—which was pretty straight talk, really—but I don't think it was wasted.

It was a friendly but a very forthright conference.

Judging from an interview he gave the St. Louis *Post-Dispatch* the other day, and from a story about him in *Look* the other day, he is not going to hide his TVA background or its decentralization ideas under a bushel. He stated flatly that valley authorities should be autonomous; and that if they required coordination in some particulars later on if and when there might be several of them, it should not be in the Department of Interior. These talks with him are definitely useful. It may be that getting the regional authority idea really rolling in the United States may be well served by having Cap in that spot. It looks better right now than ever before.

The preceding day the Interior budget had been reported to the House cut in two, and the transmission line requests butchered. While much of this will doubtless be restored, Cap didn't lose the significance of it. He said that "none of those guys" could be elected if they are against public power, but they figure they can cut out lines that make public power from the dams possible and call it economy. "We have got to have some way of dividing the sheep and the goats. It is the whole Muscle Shoals issue all over again." This kind of fight talk I haven't heard out of Cap in a long time.

Staying in bed; it is raining like mad, a wonderful rain that makes the green even deeper. The sound is a happy one; even the occasional thunder under the steady drum of rain seems friendly. That's because I'm home and feel secure in this little house that has Helen in every room and corner of it.

Came home by plane last night after two full days of an annual ordeal, the appropriation hearings. For this I have been preparing and worrying since last November, for ordinarily it comes in late December, and this year was postponed. The subcommittee—on "Government Corporations"—is a new one. So I had the task—and this made it tough—of presenting a complicated and varied budget, providing a lot of money (we spent about 70 million in the year) to a committee that had not been hearing the story year after year.

The first morning I didn't do well on the questions. The critical members asked: Why can't this and that (farm demonstration, farm machinery research, etc.) be done by the Department of Agriculture? I wasn't sufficiently clear and firm on the distinctive way we do these things, being more concerned to establish that such functions were not unprecedented by the Federal Government.

Clapp and Owen talked to me at noon, and when we returned at 2:30 I did a much better job; in fact, it was quite good, much more specific, aggressive, certain. Then Friday (yesterday) morning I was "rolling," and bore down on the distinctive character of TVA, making a virtue of it rather than "appeasing." I did rather poorly on some critical and badgering questions (chiefly from Ploeser of Missouri) on finance questions. But in the afternoon session under the friendly questioning by Gore, we got the record in good shape and Ploeser seemed a quite different man. It is often difficult to answer a man's question satisfactorily because you imply into those questions things that may not actually be in the man's mind.

Jensen of Iowa, who had before him a typed list of the conventional utility questions, said he thought what we had done had been a good job, but said that the power of spending our revenues without Congressional approval each year leads him to say that "You are the most powerful man in the United States Government" because no one else has such complete authority over what is done with public property and money. That gave me a chance to explain the necessities for the revenue authorization and how it is limited, etc.

MAY 16, 1946
WASHINGTON

Arrived in Washington about five; found a message from Acheson at the airport, and the State Department car, so I went at once to his office. We went over his conversation with Baruch of a week ago. I'm too tired tonight to repeat it all here. To Acheson's proposal that our Report be made American policy, Baruch said that if that were done he would resign. The meeting begun today was arranged, Baruch protesting against it at first, but agreeing at last.

Acheson summed up his conversation with Baruch by saying in his dry, even voice, "Mr. Baruch is in the grip of two metaphors." This delicious phrase referred to Baruch's and Hancock's constant reference to Baruch's desire to start the UN Commission sessions off by "showing the broad highway" and "the light at the end of the tunnel." Closer inquiry as to what this meant did not help very much.

At six or so I went to the Wardman to meet Herbert Morrison here from England. He was still at the State Department on the famine business, so I had an interesting talk with Marriner Eccles, Leon Henderson, Harry White of the Treasury, Harold Smith, Louis Bean of Agriculture, John Coil of the National Planning Association, Bill Batt, etc.

Morrison, introduced to me, said, "I remember talking with you

That is, to help work out an Anglo-American plan to distribute emergency food supplies in Europe and Asia.

in my office at the London County Council years ago." Quite a memory: that was 1934, and while I remember it in detail, this surprised me. Impressive man—short, has the vernacular of a well-adjusted man of experience and savvy. The questions put to him were of two kinds: What is England prepared to do, with her continued controls, if a slump should begin? What about nationalization—what are the problems, etc.?

What he said about the coal industry is something that should be preserved, for its great understanding and relaxed simplicity. (I wish I had Helen's positive genius for remembering colloquy down to the last inflection.) The point was, however, that they must improve management, which meant a public corporation, autonomous (he and I had a colloquy about this, in terms of political and financial interference with management), with well-paid management ($100,000 a year if necessary), but it was about the men that he spoke most feelingly. The trouble with the mines is something in the minds of the coal miners; and the outcome depended on whether the miners' minds could be changed.

Under private ownership the miners' minds had been poisoned; could they feel there was a change? The whole question was: What can we do to get miners to dig coal? (Which, of course, confirms my feeling that nationalization, per se, is not of too great significance; in the end the question remains: Can you get miners to dig coal, do it continuously, do it at decreasing cost and under increasing conditions of well-being?)

He showed his broad politician's touch when he said that whether they would dig coal (i.e., greatly increase output) depended upon such things as whether there were things they could buy in the stores. Come Friday and a miner has his 30 bob and he says, "I'll knock off; what good is another few bob?" But if the stores have attractive things to buy (which they haven't now and in the miserable coal villages never did have), then he will go down in the mines for another day. "If there is a frock the old woman wants, he won't dare stay above ground."

This gives an inadequate picture of his talk, and of his relaxed simplicity. He spoke of my book, and said TVA was the only experience in the world where "new techniques" were being developed. I retaliated by saying that many of the things in his book *Socialisation and Transport* had been of great help and guidance to me, especially the principle that labor must not be represented in public corporations *as* labor. He was pleased at this: "We had a nasty fight over that in the party, and I took a bit of kicking around over it, but it stuck."

His assistant is Max Nicholson, a harassed, hollow-eyed fellow of about 40, former chairman of PEP (Political and Economic Planning). He told me with his eyes aglow of how you would see workmen "in the trams" solemnly reading my book in "the Penguin," as he put it.

MAY 17, 1946
WASHINGTON

We met with Baruch and his advisers at Blair Lee House all afternoon. There were Hancock, Eberstadt, Swope, Searls; Acheson, McCloy, Bush, and "the Lilienthal Committee."

Hancock ran the show for Baruch and did a good job of it—affable, followed a list of questions. Baruch's manner had *none* of the complaining and hurt business that I had heard reports about from all over.

What made me feel very good was that our five stood right up to all the questions, and resisted any of the efforts to develop differences among us. From my viewpoint this was very gratifying. One fellow would answer and all of us would reaffirm. This is both because we understand the problem in the same terms and also because we have developed a philosophy that we share in common. This rather amazed these gentlemen, accustomed to quite different committee operations.

Some of their discussion was pure "moonshine," to use Acheson's pointed expression. At 4:30 or so we paused for refreshment. Swope, who had said nothing thus far, began a stuffy, pompous lecture about "sanctions," how violations would be "punished," etc. It was unrealistic, silly, but time-consuming. Some of it was mischievous in the extreme.

They began with a Searls proposal, harbored by the group for several weeks and put forward to us by Hancock, as follows: At the first meeting of the UN Commission, Baruch would sponsor a resolution that, prior to any agreement on a plan, the UN would organize a world survey of raw materials, and send "fifty two-man teams" all over the world. Searls said that in this way we would find out what is going on in Russia. And if the Russians refused to accept this proposal, then we would know that they would not go along on any international scheme, and  . . . he didn't finish the statement, but his eyes indicated what he thought should then be recommended, and it was anything but pleasant.

When I was asked to comment—this was at the very beginning of the afternoon—I said I thought we ought to think it over and respond later; others, however, pushed right into it, Winne doing a wonderful job. (My admiration for him grows constantly.) But this is a very bad idea for it can be made quite plausible to people on the Hill, and yet it would explode the international conference, if so much as proposed.

Whether they will proceed on the basis of our Report, or on some other, is still not clear, though they said the usual general approving things about the Report.

Baruch had me sit next to him at the long table. He is really quite an old man, and it is painful to contemplate—he fidgets with his hearing aid and sagged badly as the afternoon proceeded—in fact, he wanted to quit at 4:30 and would have if Hancock could have stopped the talk —but our boys were going good.

Tolman appeared, as Baruch's technical adviser. A great comedown from Oppenheimer and Thomas. Oppenheimer is suffering terribly because he turned down the opportunity to serve Baruch *et al.*, and yet I am sure he realizes that he did the only thing he could.

Acheson did a magnificent job, as always. His summaries are simply beautiful to see. Bush was blunt and good. I did one good job. They kept talking about "going beyond your Report" and "setting our sights higher" and so forth until I got worried about it, and took that apart, saying that this was of a piece with the World-Government dogma.

But where will it all come out? They have been at this now for two months—the period it took us to write our Report. I insisted, at the outset in my first telephone conversation with Baruch, that this was a task that called for hard, close preparation. No, they thought they could get it by "talking" with people of "different viewpoints." They are hardly further along in understanding now than they were at the beginning, and in the end they will have to come to grips with the problem anyway. As the final evidence of how little they understand the purpose or spirit of our Report, hence the character of the problem, here is one of Searls' gems: a proposal that each nation be permitted a stockpile of bombs, as a deterrent against atomic warfare; and that the UN also have a stockpile of bombs for retaliation.


MAY 19, 1946
IN THE TVA PLANE OVER VIRGINIA,
SUNDAY AFTERNOON

Pretty tuckered. We were at it until 12:30 last night (began working at 9 A.M.) and had another session this morning from 10:45 till 12:30.

The session yesterday morning at Blair Lee House seemed to me a little better than that of Friday. I thought this was really the first time they were exposed to the ideas in our Report long enough so that they began to see that there might be something to them. When it was all over, about 12:30, Van Bush, seeing I didn't look too happy (for it is necessary to look for reasons for encouragement in this picture, as things stand), expressed his firm belief that the "Old Man" is too smart politically to do otherwise than adopt our Report as the basis of his proposals to the UN Commission, and that all this bucking and argument, that seemed so antagonistic, was just part of the window-dressing.

This may prove to be correct; and a report Charlie Thomas gave us at noon today of his breakfast meeting with Hancock, taken at face value, would support the hope that the violent antagonism to the basic proposition of our Report is being modified in the direction of its acceptance, in essentials.

The procedure yesterday morning (like that on Friday afternoon) was for Hancock (who ran the meeting) to ask questions or ask our views; they "put out" nothing. This caginess wasn't very pretty nor flattering to us, but none of us said anything about it. It was part of the atmosphere of suspicion of us; and perhaps of our lack of confidence in their capacity to do this job, especially in the continued absence of staff work which we have recommended all along (since my first telephone talk with Baruch before the Report was made public) and which we included in a joint telegram to Byrnes a few weeks ago.

The present attack on the Report in both sessions was directed against our recommendation of complete ownership or control of mines and mining. Searls, a mining engineer and entrepreneur (he has spent many years in the gold and diamond regions of South Africa), was the chief protagonist. (At the opening session Baruch referred to "my one infirmity," his very bad hearing, turned the meeting over to Hancock, and thereafter said almost nothing, except at the end of today's session, of which more later.)

Searls also pressed his proposal for national and international stockpiles of bombs, "as a deterrent by way of retaliation," a crazy notion indeed.

I told them how deeply we opposed the preliminary survey idea, but whether what we said made any impression I don't know. It would, we thought, endanger the whole negotiation. Extraordinary how united we continue to be—on this proposition we again spoke with one voice and one tone.

One of the most revealing remarks came from Hancock, who continued to handle himself in a really fine, dignified way, despite his unwillingness to be more explicit about their own thinking, an arrangement apparently agreed upon in advance. I asked, and pressed the question: What is the basis for their objection to international ownership or management of uranium and thorium mines? Hancock said, "We feel it would be too great an interference with private enterprise." Two things about this: (1) It shows quite a lack of apprehension of how grave an issue we are dealing with. As Winne said, that is one of the very least interferences with our accustomed ways of doing things that the bomb will necessitate. (2) They had not looked into the facts carefully to learn how much uranium mining there is to be "interfered" with, even including possible by-product activities such as vanadium. In other words, their failure to realize the importance of first getting the facts —a point we emphasized in our Report and that we urged them to remedy—was tending to lead them into a broad and fatal error, i.e., leaving raw materials in the hands of nations.

They finally said they had no more questions. We started to break up. Acheson asked us to wait a moment. In the calmest way imaginable he said, "Where do we go from here?" The Senate Atomic Energy Committee had been put off, in their desire for hearings on the international aspects, by the promise that after the meetings just concluded he, Byrnes, and Baruch would meet with them. That was fixed for Monday. What would we say to them about the American position? Baruch said, "I'm not ready to say. This hasn't jelled in my mind yet." But we can't put it off much longer, Acheson said. The first meeting of the UN Commission has been put off until June 14 at our request, and that is less than a month off. Between now and then we must explain what our position will be to the Senate committee and get the President's and Byrnes' approval.

"Well, I am not ready to make a recommendation to the President, and I am not ready to talk to the McMahon Committee. I will take responsibility for not appearing. I am not going to say anything until I understand all this. The gentleman here at my left" (putting his hand on my knee) "told me quite frankly over the telephone back in March that it would take me eight weeks of study to understand this subject, and it is going to take even longer." (He apparently continues to hold that remark against me, the implication being that I thought he wasn't any smarter than we were.)

Acheson was plainly baffled. His mouth dropped open. The Old Man was getting quite excited—unusual for him. Hancock stepped into the breach (it looked pretty explosive for a while): Can't we say that in two weeks—no promises, mind you—in two weeks we may have something that we are ready to go ahead on? Not a commitment, but a hope.

Acheson took a long look, and then said, "All right, Mr. Baruch"; and we broke up. He and Baruch had been to the airport to greet Byrnes on his return from the Paris (and fruitless) "peace" conference; Acheson probably thought: Well, now Jimmy is back *he* will have to handle this. Byrnes and Baruch are conferring today.

Then Baruch said, speaking directly across the table toward Winne, but meaning the five of us, "I want you to put down on paper what *you* would say. Write down the charter that you think should be drawn. What would you say if you were in my place when the UN Commission first meets?" This rather baffled everyone. We had been explaining for hours and hours that writing a charter required a good deal of staff study. I had, at the opening session (in response to question), stated a dozen or more categories of studies that needed to be made, ranging from personnel administration to location of raw materials. So we just gaped. Then he said, "Write down what your Report means to you. It has been studied by every chancellory in the world, it has been commented on by the press all over the country. Now tell me what it means to you." We were flabbergasted.

So afterward Winne, Barnard, and I talked to him further, and decided that he wanted, really, a summary of the plan so he could be sure that he had the highlights as we saw them.

This turned out to be quite a chore, more than you would suppose. It wasn't over until after midnight.

They have named Richard Tolman, of Cal Tech, I believe, as technical adviser, in view of Oppenheimer's refusal to serve (which still harasses his conscience). Thomas and Oppenheimer declined Tolman's request that they serve on a panel of advisory scientists. When Oppenheimer, Thomas, and I got back to their room, after a walk, we found a message: Oppenheimer was to phone Baruch. Baruch said: How is Tolman, how is he feeling? He looked so tired.

None of us could figure this out. And Baruch had phoned to the State Department to ask the secretary, Miss Wilson, the same question. What curious business.

Hancock told Thomas at breakfast this morning that they began to see the point of factual investigations about raw materials. Also this extraordinary information, that Baruch had talked to Gromyko, the Russian member and Security Council member. He had assured him of his desire to be generous and to avoid suspicions and caginess in the efforts to "save the world." Baruch expressed a desire to talk to Stalin about the whole thing, and Gromyko had said he was sure Stalin would want to talk to him. I don't know, but I doubt whether this was with the knowledge of the State Department. Another Colonel House. This kind of informality can become very confusing indeed.

In our letter summarizing the Report we volunteered to be as helpful as we could in the future. Of course, we have no alternative than to try to be helpful. Fortunately, the Report is published and many people look to it.

There below us is Cherokee Lake. Home now before long, thank God.

I have been so absorbed in telling this rather bizarre tale that the fact that we came within moments of a nationwide railroad stoppage, or that the coal strike still hangs over the country, hasn't appeared in these notes. People are worried, but feel that "they" will take care of it.

MAY 21, 1946
KNOXVILLE

Oppenheimer spent two hours with Baruch Sunday, just as I was leaving for home.

The "Old Man" said that many of the proposals put forward for discussion by his advisers were "nonsense," and were put forward because it was necessary to have the answers. He assured Oppenheimer that he was prepared to follow the principles of our Report and "had no thought of deviating" from it. But to me this is just part of an effort to dissever Oppenheimer from our board and begin the process of breaking it up.

Oppenheimer said that he was not optimistic in any particular about the outcome, because the negotiations require insight, judgment, knowledge, and luck of a high order. But he was sure that the strong points in the situation are (1) the presence of our board as an entity, a unit, as we so clearly demonstrated at the two-day session; and (2) the possibility that the scientists from many countries could be welded together.

MAY 25, 1946
HOME, SATURDAY

Came in a bit ago, dripping, an oats sack over my shoulders. Was transplanting some wonderful zinnia seedlings in my garden near the barn when a dark, beautiful storm came up, sudden and fierce. For some perverse reason I went on with my planting, while the rain whipped me.

Maybe I was trying to wash out of my mind the misery I felt when, a half-hour before, the President of the United States angrily asked the Congress for authority to try slave labor methods on striking workmen. I thought his appeal last night was excellent, though the ultimatum was neither necessary nor more than a gesture. But painting the consequences—utter disaster—was well done. But this today! Byrd has taken him over, or rather, Whitney and Johnston* have put him right into the hands of the most horrible forces. The cheers that went up when he proposed drafting men into the Army who didn't work in an emergency.

I did a radio broadcast about labor today. But it was a different kind of story, thank God. A CBS nationwide program, sponsored by CBS itself, part of a series on labor, from "sites," this time the power-

* Heads of the trainmen and engineer railroad brotherhoods. The national rail strike lasted for a few days, being called off in the face of the threat that Congress would rush passage of punitive legislation.

house of Norris Dam. As we sat down with the script this morning—we talked from a rehearsed outline—I was pretty sick—saying anything pleasant about labor with the rails and mines closed down wasn't too good. But here was a story of a public necessity, too, like transport, in which there had never been a major stoppage and no strikes. I emphasized "the public interest in TVA being paramount"—a phrase I got written into the very preamble of the TVA labor contract, and Googe, Southern rep. of the AFL, was ready to take it straight, and said he agreed with my interpretation of what that meant in the contract— that the 5 million who depend on TVA must come first, and where a contract represents the spirit of fair dealing . . . etc. I won't ever be ashamed of that broadcast, but Truman will of his, I fear.

MAY 31, 1946
HOME

Talked by phone with Acheson this afternoon; called to read him parts of my letter from Baruch. He said he and Byrnes had spent all day and evening yesterday with the Old Man; that he was pretty badly mixed up still. Acheson seemed no happier about him than when we had our meeting two weeks ago—perhaps less so. Said they tried to talk him out of the business of widening his efforts to take in all instruments of war and that the President would probably instruct him to eliminate that. He is also mixed up on raw materials. He starts out by saying that he accepts the Report in its entirety, and then begins these vague excursions.

I am deeply concerned about this, because for better or worse B.B. is the vessel, and we must try to help as much as we can. But how? I wrote another little personal note today, since that seems to make him feel better and perhaps more receptive to our ideas.

Finished the Utah Agriculture College speech today, after a terrible grind on it. It takes the farthest position yet on our ideas of decentralization, and "takes on" the Dept. of Agriculture. Coming a mere ten days before the seven college presidents see Secretary Anderson it may create quite some excitement; as we revised it today it is pretty pointed, and it should be.

JUNE 1, 1946
HOME

Saw a new kind of "line" yesterday in Knoxville. Unemployed men, veterans. The line began at the Veterans Service Center next door to the New Sprankle Building, stretched past the entrance of the TVA office, past the telephone office, turned the corner and stretched down the hill half a block. It was that long when I went to lunch; it was even longer when I returned. Men getting their $20-a-week unemployment benefits. There is quite a good deal of unemployment in this section. This is something new.

I confess to a cold, queasy feeling when I saw them and later when I thought about it. And now. These "declines" have a way of building up. But surely there is no reason to worry about them now, for a while at least. The coal strike is settled—(Cap Krug did a good job on it, it seemed to me, as he would in that kind of situation, for he can grasp facts with amazing rapidity, and is tireless; besides, he had Lewis under pressure)—production will get going again.

But I keep thinking of those men in that line. We must never let that snowball begin again.

JUNE 9, 1946
FLYING ACROSS NEBRASKA, HEADING HOME,
SUNDAY AFTERNOON

The Utah-Colorado trip was well worth doing; and, on the whole, it was fun. A bit too worn-down from the last five months of work and excitement to be up to standard performance here and there; but I wouldn't brood about that, and really enjoyed everything to the full.

The mountain country and Salt Lake City were revelations. The high mountains, with their snow, and great crenelated gorges, seen from the air or from a car, the fantastic afterglow on the brooding crags for a few moments after the sun had set (one evening the glow was vermilion; another night the sky was positively green, no less; a dark, lovely green). These really were experiences.

I had a room at the Hotel Utah with an enormous window facing west, looking out over the Mormon Temple, the garden around it, and the tar-colored, ugly Tabernacle. Some gilt angel tooting his trumpet practically looked into my window from his perch on top the Temple. The Temple itself is almost beyond belief, with its stiff, proper lines, squinched narrow and upright, which make me think of Vermont under the influence of the Western mountains, which is probably what it is; or Grant Wood's "Gothic" portrait of the Iowa couple.

But at night the Temple is lighted up—the exterior, I mean—and then it is quite something else. Then it looks gay enough, and a little naughty. Perhaps chuckling over the fact that the Temple owns the fancy Utah Hotel right across the street (which it does) where setups (but no liquor—that is brought in by hand!) can be purchased for a price, including a reasonable profit for the Church.

The Mormon Church ought to chuckle, discreetly, for it really is an institution that combines the love of organized do-gooding with the love of making a nice juicy profit and seeing the "business" expand year by year. Even to the "traveling salesmen." For most young Mormons must go on a Mission. (The plane is tossing around again, so that it is hard to write these shorthand curlicues.) The purpose of the Mission is to get new converts. (Marriner Eccles, chairman of the Federal Reserve, went on a Mission to Scotland.)

The Church, I was told, owns not only the biggest hotel, a radio station, a newspaper, large department and other stores (called ZCMI—Zion's Cooperative Mercantile Institute, although it is no longer a co-operative, though it was originally—the Church owns it and runs it and keeps the considerable profits for Church work). The Church even runs a bank cater-corner from the Temple. Which led to the following comment by a somewhat cynical young man (not a Mormon) with whom I had dinner on the hotel roof garden overlooking the square: "See that status of Joseph Smith down there in the square in front of the Temple? They say around here, and you will see that it is true, that he has his rear" (not quite his word) "to the Church and his outstretched hand to the Bank. That's the Mormon for you."

The commencement exercises yesterday appealed to me strongly. And I was taken with the contrast with the commencement of just a year ago at Radcliffe, when I addressed Nancy's graduating class, in the "cultural" and intellectually "accepted" atmosphere of Cambridge.

(Standing, mind you, in a corner of the madhouse of the Chicago Airport on a Sunday evening—waiting to see how I get home. It is now 9 P.M.

(Hardly the place to write; looking at this crowd is a little disturbing, frankly: these somewhat too prosperous people, and the aggressive, cigar-smoking, loudly dressed men of a typical Chicago crowd, with their too many, rather repugnant children chewing gum with their mouths open—a kind of crowd that makes me less friendly toward people in general. This antagonism to that type is a curious quirk in me, but I think I would be prepared to defend it.

(God, what an insane place—there isn't room to operate a peanut stand in this whole terminal.)

But, as I was trying to say, about the Logan commencement. The 200 men and women were the sons and daughters, almost entirely, of Mormon farmers, largely poorer farmers from the rim of Utah and south Idaho. The "dean" of "Forestry, Grazing and Wild Life Management" would arise, in his academic robes complete with hood, etc., and ask the graduates in that branch to rise, etc.; and so with Home Economics,

"Bachelors of Science in Agriculture," etc. My speech dealt with this "unique American institution," the Land Grant college, and its extraordinary history, reflecting the firm intention of the Westerners as far back as the '60s and before to have their children get an education, too, and one that would equip them in the mechanical and agricultural skills—not just Latin and law. And yet here are the paraphernalia of the "classical" education—the diploma, the formula pronounced, the mortar board and gown—to adorn the graduate who knows more about cows than anyone else in his class, and whose education, historically, was a kind of revolt against the traditionalism of which the robes, etc., are the outward marks.

A far cry from Cambridge, Massachusetts, to Logan, Utah.

(Still waiting—"Don't go away," says the plump gal at the Delta counter.)

JUNE 13, 1946
HOME

Tomorrow morning at eleven at Hunter College Baruch will read his statement of the American position to the UN Commission on Atomic Energy. This is a critical time, and the past few days have been trying.

Monday night (the 10th) Marks called to say that Eberstadt, one of Baruch's banker-promoter advisers, wanted me to come to Wash. at once to go over the speech B. was to make on the 14th. Acheson, Marks, Eberstadt, and I spent the whole of Tuesday evening, till midnight, in Acheson's office. It appeared that on the previous Friday, the 7th, the President approved (by initialing paragraph by parag.) a ten-page or so statement of directions to Baruch on the policy and proposals to be followed. I read this with care; it was our Report to the "T," even to the terminology, the name "Atomic Development Authority," etc. B. and his advisers had tried to get it changed, especially in respect to raw materials; they retained their old objection to ownership and management of mines and mining by the ADA, and wanted mere licensing and inspection—this is disclosed by the drafts they submitted and which were not accepted. But they managed to get ambiguous language adopted —"dominion," a word Acheson suggested to try to smooth things over some weeks ago, and which they grabbed and gave a quite different content.

When we went over B.'s draft of the speech (B. wasn't there), it consisted of much mediocre oratory, an adoption of our plan in a rather confused and badly organized form of statement, some absurd stuff about sanctions and penalties. On raw materials they said "tight control" was the key to the plan, and then gibbered about "dominion," and would not consider ownership of mines; even balked at ownership of primary plants!

We had it hot and heavy, Eberstadt trying to be suave and we pitching in. Acheson was wonderful. He got mad and let them have it. Said that the plan meant nothing unless uranium mines were owned or subject to managerial control that would place the ADA in position of supreme authority as to source materials. I told E. I would blow my top if they went ahead on the indicated basis, and of course I shall have to. I doubt if it made any impression. E. said they were worried about the effect on such enterprises as the Rand gold mines of South Africa.

A typical piece: the speech said that if a plant in a country were seized by a nation intent on war, it would take "three months to nine months" before they could make a bomb. Of course, if this were true, there would be nothing to our plan and we would be fools. But how did they get that figure? E. had "recalled" that Oppenheimer had said that at Blair Lee—just that. We phoned O. at Berkeley; if he had the job, he would say it couldn't be done in less than two years; a year is an absolute minimum. Just a sample. And E. didn't seem bothered by the terrible almost-error.

B. sent an invitation for me to attend the opening tomorrow; I declined. I don't want to be roped into that.

I spent a lot of time phoning: to Thomas, Oppenheimer, Winne, Barnard and Carroll Wilson, Bush's assistant, asking him to call Conant and Bush. They all agreed that the raw materials thing would be terrible, and that we will have to say something vigorous if it is still in.

After days of arguing with the Old Man, Byrnes told A., "This is the worst mistake I have ever made. But we can't fire him now, not with all the other trouble."

They will wish they had now, before it gets them into even worse troubles, which are ahead.

JUNE 15, 1946
HOME

I was in my vegetable garden at the barn yesterday, thinning my carrots and enjoying myself thoroughly. It was about 10:15; I had risen late, to recover from the Washington strenuosity. A TVA police car hove in sight; I knew somehow that I was being "summoned." A call from Helen: there is something on the radio—better come right away. When I got here, Baruch was in the middle of his rhetorical flourishes in the fore-part of his speech to the UN Commission on Atomic Energy. With my hands still covered with mud from the garden, and in my blue jeans and quite excited, I sat me before the radio with a pad of paper, a pencil, and my trusty shorthand. This was the verdict. Would what he said make it necessary for me to do as I told Eberstadt I would, to wit, "blow my top"? Helen, I may say, was as excited as I, especially since she had a time getting hold of me.†

Baruch's speech had been considerably improved, compared with the Tuesday night version. It was ambiguous on raw materials, but subject to the right interpretation as well as to the interpretation that its authors had in mind—I'm sure we didn't persuade them, but only made them cautious and hence vague.

I rushed into the office; talked with Raymond Swing, who had been calling all morning. Pointed out the raw material ambiguity and its importance; said as to "sanctions" that this talk of "condign punishment" set another and a discredited tone—the outlaw of the weapon business—and was contradictory to the spirit of our Report, but perhaps wasn't fatal; that would depend upon the course of the negotiations—in any case it didn't affect operability of the plan itself. As to the veto, that was a step forward‡ as was the talk about "stop making bombs." I listened to the latter part of Swing's broadcast at six; he seemed to have taken my points.

I was in a considerable dither during the afternoon. Drafted a brief statement saying, isn't this fine that our Report has been so helpful? Then as call after call came for off-the-record comments from St. Louis, Wash., etc., I decided, at least till I had talked to others of our board and thought about it I'd better sit tight and take the chance of being accused of being ungracious. This latter would be a minor transgression compared to the fact that the Baruch speech made no acknowledgment of the fact that the whole ADA setup comes from our Report.

Talked at great length with Oppenheimer and Thomas last night; they called me from N.Y., where they attended the affair. Said they had made a statement approving the "14 points" in B.'s speech and were troubled that I might not agree. They admitted there was still ambiguity, but I agreed the thing to do was to assume that it was to be resolved by reference to the Report. O. was deeply troubled by the sanctions talk, and by the implications of it; he has no faith that B. can negotiate an agreement since he doesn't understand our position, and this he confirms by the sanctions stuff, which is a far cry from "international cooperative

† I must have forgotten the time difference between Tennessee and New York, which was on daylight saving time.

‡ Baruch's insistence that the veto right of the chief UN powers be waived in atomic energy matters was the major difference between the American plan he presented and the Board of Consultants' program on which it was based. My colleagues and I agreed completely with the "no-veto" principle, but we felt that the injection of this issue prematurely would endanger consideration of the affirmative basis of the plan itself.

development." In the present state of suspicion vis-à-vis the Russians, if the proposal doesn't emphasize this constructive side, it may well be less than worthless. This we recognized early in the game. I'm glad my *Atlantic Monthly* piece (for the July issue) bears down on that.

Had a wonderful time in my garden again this morning; cleaned the weeds out of the millions of onions. The heavy rain made everything prosper, not excluding the weeds. I like to see that kind of progress. In the meantime, I'm sitting tight. . . . Tonight I am to be host to a dinner for the Prime Minister of Hungary, at Norris Lodge. I am something of a case study in the fluidity and opportunity of American life, considering that my parents were poor Hungarian youngsters and Jews to boot—just one generation. And the P.M. thinks he is being honored by me; and that's right, too.

Acted as host at dinner tonight at Norris Lodge to a party of Hungarian officials, the Prime Minister, Deputy Prime Minister, Foreign Minister, etc. (Names—P.M., Ferenc Nagy; D.P.M., Rakosi; F.M., John Gyongyosi; Minister of Justice, Stephen Riesz; and so on—12 in all.)

They arrived last week to work out the issue of return of Hungarian property, including their gold reserve, now in the zone of American occupation in Germany and Austria. They were largely successful and were quite happy. They have to return to London on Tuesday. When they were asked what they wanted to see in America, they said (so the State Dept. man along said), "Why, TVA." It was explained they would only have time for one trip, outside Wash.—didn't they want to see something else? Nope; TVA. "We couldn't understand it," said the S. Dept. guy, but that was the way it was. When I learned this, I commented on it; the Prime Minister told me via an interpreter of his legation here, "In Europe the thing everybody knows about in America is TVA. Oh, sure."

Their Government is a coalition; the Deputy is a Communist, with his little star in his buttonhole, a very bald, very round, firm little man, very interesting, for he was enormously well informed about the U.S., spoke excellent English, and had stock phrases. "Power politics," "Imperialism of the U.S. and Great Britain." But very mild, very restrained. Once in a while he couldn't take it (obviously he had been told not to talk his line—this is America where Communists aren't highly regarded and it might cost Hungary), so he would get up and walk away and look out over Norris Lake till he had himself in hand.

I asked the P.M. why the small nations of S.E. Europe couldn't somehow get going together on some project: electrification, the river Danube, coal mining or something, to take their minds off their hatreds for each other.

The P.M.'s answer was that till they got a fair peace treaty (meaning, getting Transylvania back, etc.) the people were in no mood for projects—hardly a response. The Buddha-like Deputy Prime Minister couldn't contain himself longer: "Your question, Mr. President Lilienthal, interests me greatly as a Communist. All of these hatreds get better; then imperialistic greeds stir them again. . . ."

As we said good-bye (the P.M.'s formal invitation to me to visit him in Budapest being repeated three times), the economist and interpreter hung back and said, "I should explain"—this sotto voice—"that Hungary has a coalition government including the Communists, but you should not take anything said amiss." No need for it; I thought the little man (Rakosi) interesting, though full of familiar capsules.

I asked them did they know the little village of Neutra (now Nitra) —my mother (or my dad, I'd just forgotten) was brought up near there. They all leaped as if shot; I had uttered a familiar word. Not really; not my own very own mother. Then, sadly, Neutra is no longer in Hungary; since World War I it is part of Czechoslovakia. But it made me seem nearer. They talked of orchards and vineyards and the breaking up of the large estates; and this reminded me of Mother's stories about her girlhood.

There is something dramatic and American about this: it was more than evident that they looked on me as a world figure and said so in many ways, and that this was doing them honor. But my father and mother were born in their country, children of poor and humble people. Just one generation, and I am listened to as an interpreter of the life of this country. Fantastic.

JUNE 19, 1946
WASHINGTON

Talked to Walter Lippmann by phone, to tell him how good I thought his article day before yesterday was. He sees that the "veto" stuff is a bad thing to infuse into the picture, and seemed to understand what I said about the unfortunate "sanctions" bombast, and said that he was having a piece about it tomorrow. Wanted to see me; too bad I am tied up.

"You are doing a wonderful job," he said as we rang off.

JUNE 21, 1946
BUFFALO, N.Y.

I had quite an experience tonight. Spoke to the annual conference of the American Library Association (title of my talk, "Science and the

Human Spirit") in a large hall—with people standing because all the seats were filled—from all over the country. In spite of a terrible public address system and bad acoustics, they were intent to an extraordinary degree; I took 50 minutes, ordinarily too long, and at the end the applause continued so long that I rose, and then they just went on, and even after I finally got up and grinned a second time it kept up.

I really have something to say—that speech and those ideas are right and timely. I used a good deal on atomic energy, and I could tell that very few of them really knew much if anything about it; that will change in libraries all over the country—as the presiding officer predicted when I was through. The great interest in TVA and the deep respect for it, and the encomiums on my book are really something. This sort of thing makes up for the troubles of travel, the wear and tear, even the being away from home. This is being useful in the world.

JUNE 26, 1946
HOME

McKellar's campaign has opened.§ He asked me a series of skillful questions at the appropriations hearings—loaded they were. I resisted the temptation to reply cagily, thinking that I must keep my eye on the ball: get the appropriation through and avoid any hint that I had his election in mind. The papers have used it to the hilt as a "whitewash" of the old boy's long violence against TVA. I think most people will take a different slant: that he has to try to climb on the bandwagon just before election.

Jennings Perry of the Nashville *Tennessean* phoned me late today, insisting I should answer some questions about our position: Have we changed our mind about the hamstringing effect of McKellar's bill to change our fiscal policy, etc.? He was vigorous, and it seemed harmless enough; but it would be construed as an entry into the campaign. Worried me a lot, to have a good friend feel I was letting him down— their campaign for Carmack has been badly handled. Perry put on the pressure, implying that people would say I had made a "deal" with Mc-Kellar unless I spoke out; that when he was elected he would say it was a mandate to continue his fights against us and that then the people couldn't be expected to rise up against him if I had failed to speak out when he was up, etc., etc., for 30 minutes. But I should keep my mouth shut, however much it hurts.

Tomorrow is my last day at the office for a while; Helen and I leave for a holiday at Pawleys Island. I am very, very tired, though I am

§ For re-election. (McKellar defeated E. W. Carmack in the Democratic primary in August, and won in the November general election. It proved to be his last Senate term.)

in good spirits and not ill. But I will be if I keep up this mad pace; canceled the Iowa Centennial speech—just too much travel. Spoke in Utah, Buffalo, Grinnell, Ia., Denver, Chattanooga, and made three trips to Wash. all in a single month. I have a tough constitution and am stubborn as hell. *N.Y. Times* gave me double-column head on my crack at Gromyko's proposal—also the Carnegie Foundation's to same effect: queer bedfellows, also editorial quote.◖

JULY 8, 1946
PAWLEYS ISLAND, S.C.

Another birthday. Now I manage to take them as they come. I've stopped brooding on the subject quite a long time ago—1940 to be exact.

Greatly refreshed—it has been only about a week since we got away. Still don't let go entirely, and perhaps that is a good sign; I don't feel weary of *spirit,* no need to have to escape entirely.

I have been thinking a good deal, as I walk the beach or read, about a long-time project of thinking and writing, the sort of thing that could 20 years in developing and writing. Perhaps the way to begin would be an article or two in a serious magazine or professional journal, outlining the idea, and illustrating briefly, and then to continue to preach it and gather material.

The theme is: The Manageable Job. I described it, in one context, in *Democracy on the March.* There it was the idea that the United States as a whole is not a manageable unit for natural resource development. In the Atomic Energy Report I hinted or suggested the idea (and used the term "manageable" so often that it became a subject of gentle banter by my colleagues, like Oppenheimer's "valid" and Marks' "knowledgeable"). I have since elaborated on the idea a bit, in the context of international affairs, as in the *Atlantic Monthly* piece that has just appeared (July issue, 1946).

The notion there is that you don't build "peace" all at once; you look for units, for jobs, in other words, that are manageable for human beings at the time and under the circumstances; you seize those manageable jobs as opportunities. Instead of despairing because they don't solve everything—witness Lewis Mumford's letter along these lines to me of a few weeks ago, and many others these days—you embrace such limited opportunities because they can be handled with a fair degree of success; whereas the all-embracing undertaking, so entrancing in logic and in rhetoric, is simply not manageable by human beings.

◖ The Russian atomic control plan, presented by Gromyko on June 19, called for outlawing the bomb, destroying existing bombs, and establishing penalties for nations violating an international atomic agreement. The Carnegie proposal also placed heavy stress on a system of prohibitions, laws, and punishments.

This could become a penetrating technique, as well as a philosophy. It is adapted to our modern problems—labor, Negro problem, anti-Semitism, etc. Those are not manageable problems. But segments can come along that are. And those one must seize upon.

There is another tangent of the theme of the "manageable job." It inheres in the implications of the word "manageable." The word does not imply "solution," the handling of a problem so that it is "solved," put away, never more to bother us. It does not imply perfection, a task completed. It sounds of the attainable but less than perfect, "the problem under a degree of control"—that sort of thing. This is not defeatism—it is the way the world is put together, and instead of being the occasion for a sense of defeat or despair, should be quite the reverse, for it implies constant struggle but one that is rewarding because not beyond human possibility.

The theme of the "manageable job" has still another interesting and useful facet. It will be challenged on the ground that what the complicated modern world needs is not separate tasks of small caliber but vast coordination. Coordination is something done at the center; that coordination is the important thing, because the world is so interdependent, it is "One World," etc. The replication will bring out the fact that "coordinating" pieces that are themselves badly done is no coordination at all; and to be preoccupied with coordination, to the neglect of the units being harmonized, is not to coordinate at all.

The theme has a further advantage. It can deal with the issues of "bigness"—the Brandeis-Ernst thesis—but in quite different and less dogmatic terms. There is beneath it a similar philosophy: that man's capacity is finite and relatively limited, though growing; that remote control is injurious to the spirit and development of men. But it does not fall into the fault of a concept of "bigness" that is inevitably dogmatic and yet vague, i.e., subjective (everyone having a different idea of what is "big," and everyone knowing that some little things are not good and some big ones are good). The manageable job is a better idea.

JULY 11, 1946
PAWLEYS ISLAND

I haven't managed to sever myself from "thinking" this vacation. That isn't because we are not isolated here—though I have had a good many telegrams (including a hot "Have you quit beating your wife?" one from McKellar, no less) and have been concerned about our appropriation bill, still not approved. Nor is it because this isn't a wonderful place to rest. My walks up the strand go far into an absolutely uninhabited stretch of dunes. I was on the beach for three hours continuously this morning, and another couple of hours this afternoon; four swims a day is my quota, and I am burned as dark as a ripe zucchini squash.

Whatever the reason, it is a rather pleasant place to try to think about things. What about the future of TVA—and of DEL? One can't "plan" these things too particularly, and the most important things apparently one can neither plan nor vaguely anticipate—witness the atomic energy task for the State Department. (And, incidentally, it discloses the questionable value of "advice" from trusted friends; if I had taken their advice—Helen excepted—I would have turned it down cold, as of no importance and something for which I wasn't qualified, indeed something that would or might throw discredit on me and TVA—this is a composite summary of that advice.)

But there may be a decision soon, and I can't help giving it a going over. Suppose the McMahon Bill, or something substantially like it is enacted in the next fortnight or so—it is on the House calendar after the British loan, now pending, I believe. Suppose (as many people are suggesting these days) that the President should offer me the chairmanship of the Atomic Energy Commission? (A position on the five-man Commission would be an easy decision—definitely no.) But suppose it were the chairmanship, with assurance that I would be chiefly responsible for results and with some voice perhaps in the selection of associate members and a large voice in the selection of major staff? Then what?

To many people it would seem strange that I should hesitate to take such a post. "TVA is a going concern; its chief problems are over, and the major fights. Atomic energy is the most important of all new problems. It involves the new and modern problems of the relation of science and politics, which you have been preparing yourself to meet all these years. The scientists would be with you because of your Report, and many others who look to it and to you. You would have a responsibility in the international field, inevitably. The salary is 50 percent and more greater, which must mean something, the way things are these days. Why should there be any question?"

But there is: a big question. TVA is, or could be, more important than ever. It can be made—it already is, in many places—a sample and proof that non-coercive methods can be developed and used that will put technology to work for the people generally—a trump card, plain and simple to read, in the great contest of our time (not decided by the victory over Hitler) between the coercive and the cooperative society. And there is much more to say—but not today.

The *New York Times Magazine* wants to know if I will contribute an article on how we can be safe from the atom bomb, and especially to discuss "the veto." I said, no—not now at least.

But a really interesting article could be written on this topic:

How are we to attain "World Government"? And use our Report as the framework of the answer, with Lewis Mumford and the Cord Meyer line on the one hand, and the nationalist proposals, à la Gromyko and Carnegie Foundation, on the other.

## JULY 14, 1946
### CATALOOCHEE RANCH, N.C.

Have been reading some from William Allen White's autobiography.

Isn't the whole notion of "reform" as a fight by one class or economic group against another pretty well a museum piece, without much present relevance? Much of our contemporary "issues" still use the language and the strategy, but isn't that just a hangover, a legacy of a period when that meant something?

My feeling is made somewhat closer to the top of my mind by reading White's recollections of the early years of the twentieth century, with its insurgents, progressives, trust-busters, etc., and the outpouring of feeling against the greedy trusts, J. P. Morgan, etc. But this only confirms the growing sense that I have that the equivalent of that, going on today, is almost irrelevant and outmoded; that perhaps the issues we think of in connection with radicalism, Russia, the struggle of the dispossessed to wrest more of a share from the owners, etc., is just going through the motions of an earlier and now quite unimportant struggle.

The issue now is the use of science, which can produce enough to shift the whole center of the struggle from its historic locale. And perhaps even the question of who shall "control" science and technology is no longer greatly relevant as the center of a struggle, for the "control" of land or scarce commodities—coal, copper—was a matter of possession. But technology can only be controlled (in any perspective of time) by those who *know*, rather than those who merely own.

It is very difficult to see these things clearly while they are going on—these vast changes in basic and transcendent issues. We must ordinarily wait until the change is nearly complete, before we recognize that we are fighting over something that no longer means much. I don't want to be caught in that kind of shortsighted business. It is a temptation to be slovenly and accept the terminology of the struggle between the fat-cats and the underdog on the theory that this is essentially a moral issue of the rich and powerful against the poor and humble. We could continue our struggles on that basis tangled in those concepts and especially the words and slogans that go with them, to the place where we actually don't see that they are as pointless and *unreal* today as— well, the analogy escapes me.

We reached this ranch at dinnertime last night, after a beautiful drive through the mountains. The ranch is atop a 5,500-foot mountain, and 3,500 feet of that you climb in the last three miles, on a rocky, narrow stretch of straight up-and-down road. We hit it at an exciting time—it had just rained a gully-washer, and the stream beside the road was a torrent, the road slick in spots, and the sides soft. At the last spurt a car appeared around a corner; I was on the inside, and worrying about forcing anyone coming down into the soft side which goes off hundreds of feet, without protection, so I turned out too sharply and two wheels went into the ditch. I thought we were sunk. But by backing perilously close to the other edge, and with some luck, I got out, and then, miracle of miracles, was able to make a cold start on a mean grade. Rather fun, in a way.

JULY 23, 1946
WASHINGTON

Long talk with Nancy last evening. She is fed up with her job: too much routine. "It is making me bats." Quite on her own, she got an interview with Jim Patton of the Farmers Union, who encouraged her in the idea of a job with the organizing forces in the field. "I'm ready for some adventure," says our 21-year-old daughter. I warned her about getting bored too easily, etc. But no one should make any mistake about it: the kid has a kind of shrewdness and she definitely has a quality of judgment—not only "for her years," but without respect to age. With real grace, humor, but firmness she changed my opinion on two things last night: one about David, the other about my trip to France.* She is really quite a person.

Dr. Ecker examined me today; I am in perfect condition, physically—blood, heart, liver, and lights. My only troubles are with nervous fatigue, and that is just a matter of getting exercise and relaxation. He was quite lyric about my heart; that is his specialty.

Talked with Bob Nathan (the economist) about the France trip. He thinks Monnet is one of the ablest men in the world. He is going to Paris in a few days and will report then on what he thinks about the proposed trip.

The March of Time is doing a shot of Acheson and myself this afternoon. Lunching with Marriner Eccles.

* This trip never took place. I do not recall the purpose, but apparently it was to have included a visit with Jean Monnet, then head of the French Planning Commission.

JULY 24, 1946
WASHINGTON AIRPORT

Met J.R.O.† last night, just in from New York; talked until 1:30 this morning. He is really a tragic figure; with all his great attractiveness, brilliance of mind. As I left him he looked so sad: "I am ready to go anywhere and do anything, but I am bankrupt of further ideas. And I find that physics and the teaching of physics, which is my life, now seems irrelevant." It was this last that really wrung my heart. Here is the making of great drama; indeed, this *is* great drama.

(As I am writing this the control tower man's voice comes booming into this small room. He is talking to pilots: "There, there, that is it, now make a precision turn," etc., etc. "Why don't you come down to 500 feet?" Fascinating.)

O. is in deep despair about the way things are going in the negotiations in New York. He sees no hope of agreement; he doesn't feel that our plan is understood by the American delegation, that Baruch's preoccupation with "punishment" and "veto" has done great harm so that there is little or no discussion of the essentials of the plan. The whole business is quite undirected; he makes suggestions and quite uncritically they are accepted. There is no real discussion. The subcommittees are going through motions that induce what he feels is a wholly false sense of encouragement.

It is difficult to record how profoundly hopeless he thinks it is; indeed, when I said that there are some situations in which one cannot acknowledge despair, he took me to task for this, in a gentle but firm way, saying that it was this sense of a "reservoir of hope" that was quite wrong, for it does not exist.

I told him the "joke" about the Old Man's (Baruch's) glowing report of progress made to the President yesterday: "We have made great progress; the Commission is with us by a majority of 10 to 2"—the "joke," of course, being that since it is Russia's agreement that everyone knows must be secured, this baseball score way of judging progress is rather funny if it were not actually pretty tragic.

O. took this quite sadly, too, and held out no hope for a change of position by the Russians. Gromyko does not have any authority, and the men who do have are unknown, no one can talk to them, no one can have any assurance that they know, firsthand, what this is all about. But he did have a talk, in San Francisco, with the technical adviser, a

† Robert Oppenheimer, who was with the American UN delegation which had begun after Baruch's speech in June the process of trying to negotiate an atomic control plan.

prim little physicist who went to Bikini for the Russians. The Russian stressed the point that the American proposal was designed to permit the United States to maintain its own bombs and plants almost indefinitely—30 years, 50 years, as long as we thought necessary—whereas it wants Russia's uranium, and therefore her chance of producing materials would be taken over and controlled by the ADA at once. This is what they mean by their talk about the proposal insuring an American monopoly. Gromyko is to expand their position in a speech today; it will make interesting reading.

What happens if no agreement is reached; if, in the end, the negotiations fail? This is what O. said: The American disposition will be to take plenty of time and not force the issue in a hurry; that then a 10–2 report will go to the Security Council and Russia will exercise her veto and decline to go along. This will be construed by us as a demonstration of Russia's warlike intentions. And this will fit perfectly into the plans of that growing number who want to put the country on a war footing, first psychologically, then actually. The Army directing the country's research; Red-baiting; treating all labor organizations, CIO first, as Communist and therefore traitorous, etc. He paced up and down in the frenetic way he has as he spoke in a really heart-breaking tone.

Well, this is nerves. But it is a fair sample of the kind of emotional state (and with cause) many will be in when, perhaps, they have reached the state of *realization* that O. now has, because of his superior knowledge and his special sensitiveness.

B.B., as I had sensed, continued to be irritated and even angry at me, O. reports. I felt this, but this was direct and recent confirmation.

B. said to O. about me, "It is too bad about that young man. Such great promise. But he won't cooperate, ought to be up here working with us, but he won't cooperate. He will regret his attitude."

To this tale should be added a single fragment of comment: "They are very open-minded up there; just so long as you don't criticize; no one can criticize."

It is contrary to my nature to fall down and worship and say "aye" (which is what is required); I couldn't even do it for F.D.R., who I thought was the greatest man alive, a really great human being. How could I do it for these men? But it throws light on why I persist in holding back, and why they sense an antagonism. Some of it may be superficial: their lack of graciousness, for example, in acknowledging their debt to our Report, etc. I say superficial, for of course the important thing is that the plan of the Report was adopted, despite all their squirming.

"So, Dave, we have failed," said O. (No use my adding much to that, except I'd put it this way: "So, to date, it certainly appears that our efforts have resulted in nothing that can save the world.")

O. reported some scuttlebutt: that B. had submitted a list of names to the President for members of the Atomic Energy Commission. Conant as Chairman, Hartley Rowe,‡ and, save the mark, General Groves. I have no doubt that it was their intention that O. get this word and that he pass it on to me, to show how B. was "punishing" and "finishing" me for my intransigence.

There may be nothing in it, of course. But just hearing him pass the rumor on gave me a great sense of relief inside—the way one feels, after a hard day, when the first big swallow of an Old-Fashioned meets the stomach—an inhalation and the slow exhalation of relief. However much of a problem continuing in TVA may present—that is, a problem of keeping active and busy with things that seem important—the prospect of undertaking that other job has really had me sick, the thought of giving up the thing I am doing well for a madhouse of frustration, confusion, back-biting, under a law that is an administrative cretin.

An addendum or two:

1. After Evatt (the Australian who was chairman of the UN Commission for a time, and quite a lawyer) had delivered himself of a statement, he was questioned by O. because one of his points we had covered in our Report. "Frankly," he said, "I haven't read the Report; haven't had time." Isn't that something?

2. The British are against our plan, though very cagey. They see atomic energy as a source of power, a way of pulling themselves out of their economic troubles. So they want to be running their own power plants. Cadogan's statement was cautious and did not commit them to our ADA.

JULY 26, 1946
KNOXVILLE

Have just talked to four journalists from Czechoslovakia who have been here for four days.

TVA appeals to them because it is "planning," as they say. They think it represents a complete break from American free enterprise, and they have certain curious notions derived from reading, I suppose, that this country has completely abandoned everything Roosevelt estab-

‡ A top executive of United Fruit Company who had been a consultant in the Manhattan District; he was later a member of the AEC's General Advisory Committee.

lished and has gone back to the days of Hoover. The fact that TVA isn't that way is a mystery to them and they want to know why.

The worst thing that foreign visitors do is to speculate, on very limited information, usually, on the state of political and public opinion in America. It is a natural enough thing to do, but it so often leads them into failing to look sharply and clearly at the things that are going on rather than being preoccupied with an interpretation of them in terms of certain fixed standards of political and economic conduct.

As to Czechoslovakia, they seem to be quite hopeful. Of course, they are moving in the direction of more and more "state enterprise," as they call it. I said that I had the impression that the Czechs were, unlike the Latins, people who were hard-headed enough to go ahead and see what the problems were and get done the things they wanted done and leave the question of labeling it, whether socialistic, etc., etc., to the professors. I used the Atomic Energy Report as an example. This seemed to make sense, and they responded more to this point about going ahead and doing what needed to be done and not quarreling over abstract slogans than anything else we said.

Cap Krug has just phoned me to say that Baruch lunched with him Thursday of last week and that, at the risk of offending me, he wanted to discuss the bad situation that has developed between Baruch and myself.

The Old Man says that here he is badly in need of help and the two men in the whole country who could really help him—namely, Lilienthal and Van Bush—refuse to do so. He professes to be deeply hurt and quite unable to understand why I refuse to help him, except on the basis that I didn't think he should take the job in the first place. Proceeding on this assumption, he said he didn't want to take the job and that now that he is in it and so much is at stake he must see it through.

Cap says Baruch realizes things are not going so well, but apparently has no real understanding of why not. He told Cap that here he had accepted the Lilienthal Report from A to Z, with the sole exception that he added we would destroy our bomb supply, and yet I won't help; and the Old Man is brooding about it.

Cap said that he hoped I wouldn't feel offended by his calling me to urge that I go to see the Old Man if he asks me to come to see him. I told Cap, of course, that he could tell Baruch that I would be glad to go anywhere to see him and he could be completely reassured on that score.

But I did explain what the difficulties were and something of the background. Particularly, I emphasized the fact that the Old Man is so touchy and has been so accustomed to adulation and obeisance that when you express your honest opinion to him, it being asked (as in the case of my first visit with him at the Shoreham several months ago), this gives him offense. Well, it's pretty hard for me to change my whole nature and way of dealing, but I could even try that if he thought it would help the dismal and ghastly state of affairs approaching a debacle.

I told Cap about the Blair Lee House meeting at which Acheson, Van Bush, and all five of the Board of Consultants urged Hancock, Eberstadt, and Swope, and Baruch, of course, for God's sake not to inject the veto and sanction issue at the outset, but to discuss the substance of the plan at length and patiently before going into such questions as enforcement; and that Acheson, Marks, and I had sweat one whole evening with Eberstadt a day or two before Baruch's speech on June 14, urging that that stuff be left out of the speech. We were completely unsuccessful and therefore had some basis for treating that as a vote of no confidence.

Cap was wonderful. He understands the core of Baruch's difficulty: to wit, his terrible pride. But he said that under the circumstances it was up to me to try to do something in spite of that. He recognized, however, that since it was the veto and sanctions issue that was causing the trouble and since Baruch was so flatly on record about it, it may be there was no way of working it out without forcing the Old Man to change a position now publicly taken—something his pride would make most difficult for him to do.

God knows I squirm at the thought of having to go through that confusion and vagueness once more; but I guess I can stand that if others can. I have no hope it will do any good.

Krug said that he had strongly urged the President (even without clearing the State Department, whose recommendations he is not familiar with) to make me Chairman of the Atomic Energy Commission under the legislation for an American Commission. I asked Cap if he thought that was something I should even consider, and he said he thought it was the most important job in the world today and that I certainly should and must consider it. He said that he had urged that our State Department Board of Consultants be appointed as a group for the board. I told him that if anything so happy as that should happen that I would be inclined to accept because I know I can work with these men in harmony and effectiveness and that one of the terrible things about the task is trying to administer something with a five-man group.

A half-hour or so after I talked to Krug, Marks called me to say that legislation had now been enacted, the House having voted to accept the report of the conference between the House and Senate, such report being a purely civilian administration and actually not much worse, if at all, than the McMahon Bill as it passed the Senate. While that bill has a lot that needs improvement from an administrative point of view (such as Civil Service, relations to the General Accounting Office, et cetera), one has to admit that it is not a wholly unworkable bill, as the bill passed by the House definitely was.

So now what?


JULY 27, 1946
HOME, SATURDAY

About noon a telegram from Baruch: "Would be delighted to see you some time soon and talk over atom control for which you have done so much. You can contribute more. We need your experience and help. I am [at] Camp Uncas, Raquette Lake, New York, for about ten days. I should be pleased to have you visit me here. If you would like to come, take New York Central [to] Utica where my car can meet you or I shall be in New York in about ten days. Warmest personal regards."

This, of course, was the result of the Krug conversation.

I wired at once that I would be happy to do anything I could to help and would leave tomorrow if that would be convenient; he has replied that it would and I take off in the TVA plane tomorrow morning.

This comes at an important time, for the decision about the chairmanship of the Atomic Energy Commission will probably be made in the next few days; Congress expects to adjourn next Friday.

My mind is now made up: if I am offered the chairmanship, and have some reasonable assurance about TVA and the other members of the Commission, I will accept; indeed, now I want the appointment. I have done nothing to further it, though, except to talk to Marsh McNeil of Scripps-Howard in Wash., an old friend, and to Coghlan of the St. Louis *Post-Dispatch*. Krug is moving down the line (I reported the Baruch development to him by phone today, and he will press it with the President again tomorrow), and I think I can assume that Acheson will do what he can. The Wash. *Post* this morning urged it editorially, and I can count on quite a little support, as well, of course, as much determined opposition.

So the next few days will be quite lively.


JULY 28, 1946
CAMP UNCAS
IN THE ADIRONDACKS, SUNDAY NIGHT

I am writing this in a quite beautiful lodge, on the shores of a tranquil Adirondack lake, after a long evening of talk with Mr. Baruch.

Of all the settings in which somehow things happen to me, this is one of the strangest. This lodge—it consists of the quite spacious lodge and, some distance away, another group of buildings, including kitchen, dining room, etc.—was built originally by J. P. Morgan, Sr.; as Mr. Baruch said, "If it is good enough for Old Man Morgan, it is good enough for us, I guess."

He is here quite alone—that is, except for his valet; his nurse, a personable young woman indeed; his cook; and chauffeur.

The talk ranged all over everywhere. Part of it concerned the situation with the Russians. He quite evidently is prepared not to push things too fast. He says that Gromyko understands about the veto, etc., but that his real objection isn't the veto but rather the whole idea of permitting their country to be subjected to inspection from without. He says it is clear that Gromyko has no independent discretion in negotiation but is just playing the record over and over again. He harps on the fact that ten or eleven of the countries are with the American proposal; I didn't think there was any point in asking why that was helpful if Russia remains adamant.

He brought up the question of the commission to be appointed under the McMahon Bill. I was discussed, he said, as a possible chairman, in a meeting between the President, Byrnes and himself ten days ago. He urged that I be "saved" so I could be proposed as head of the international ADA: "I look farther ahead than they do. The head of the international will have to be an American, and it can't be the head of the American commission." (Why, he didn't explain and I don't understand.)

I gather this was to be notice to me that he did not recommend me for the American chairmanship, and whether this was the basis given or not, the fact is that he either opposed the idea or wouldn't favor it. I told him that Krug had urged me and had recommended my appointment to the President; whether he told Krug of the position he took with the President he didn't say; Krug didn't mention it at all.

He was exceedingly interesting this evening: telling me about F.D.R. upon his return from Yalta—how worn he was, his memory failing so that he couldn't remember what had been agreed upon there, and repeating himself. He had told Baruch that he wanted him to go to Yalta with him—"But he didn't take me and there was no one there who knew anything about the Balkans, about Germany, about any of the things I knew about because of my Versailles experience." He talked about many things—he delights in Oppenheimer, discussed all his advisers, etc.

He wants me to go to New York and sit down with the others and get the feel of things, especially in the Control Committee, which is devising the setting up of the ADA (on paper!), "because you are the only one who has any experience with that sort of thing."

It is a beautiful starlit night.

JULY 29, 1946
CAMP UNCAS

Spent most of the day talking with Mr. Baruch. With all the luxury around this "camp," we sat on the hard ground, looking out at the lake, most of the time, he resting on his elbow, I with my back up against a rough bench.

He has no illusions, I find, about how little progress there has been made, nor any notion that the 10-to-2 vote means anything. And he knows how terrible the alternative of no agreement will be. I had today by far the most satisfactory talks I have ever had with him—more relaxed, more interesting. It is clear that he recommended against my appointment as Chairman of the Atomic Energy Commission; the grounds he assigned, that I would be the only American who (because of my liberal reputation) would have a chance of being accepted as head of the ADA, don't change the result. He asked me not to mention this to Krug because "It might be construed as indicating I opposed your being named." Which, of course, it does. But this may prove to be the greatest favor he could have done me, for the job is a terrible one.

JULY 30, 1946
EN ROUTE BY PLANE TO NEW YORK

We are flying in a DC-3 Mr. Baruch chartered to bring the safari back to his New York summer home: five servants, a nurse, and God knows how many boxes (including kitchenware), suitcases, seven cases of liquor, frozen steaks, etc.

This morning he finally told me what I sensed—that he was returning to New York because of the discussions going on about the Atomic Energy Commission posts. I now know, too, that he has not favored my nomination; and he may be right, too. The business about holding me back for the international organization is, of course, just so much malarky. There are very good reasons why someone else—or more accurately, a few other men—would do a better job or be publicly more acceptable, so the result is probably O.K. He says he will get the whole background tomorrow and then we will talk it all over. I don't like the idea of being in the middle of such maneuvers, but what the hell can I do?

I think I have made one point at least, as the result of these many hours of talk and listening: that an agreement with the Russians may not result, and that if it does not, his mission is a failure. I thought that was obvious, but apparently not. I hope it sticks.

He has been a most gracious host, and very entertaining, and I have really enjoyed the experience. One of the best things about it is that it has made me realize how empty great wealth can be. Not that great wealth ever had any attractions for me, really.

Tomorrow I go to a meeting, which I understand Gromyko is attending, of one of the Control Committees that are working hereabouts. They don't sound as if they were getting anywhere; in fact, it sounds as if they were farther apart than when they started. But negotiations sometimes go that way.

JULY 31, 1946
KNOXVILLE, TENNESSEE

This seems to me rather interesting.

Following are lists as of the first of this year of:

1. Invitations to write or speak which I have declined:

*Speeches*

National Education Association
Municipal Forum (New York)
Friends of the Land (Athens, Tenn.)
Ossoli (Knoxville)
Agriculture Club (Knoxville)
National Farmers Union (Kansas)
Vocations Day (Athens, Tenn.)
Oak Ridge Parents & Teachers Association
Ohio University
Tennessee Eastman Corporation (Oak Ridge)
Mississippi AAA Committee
Yale Divinity School
North Wilkesboro (N.C.) Kiwanis Club
Hiwassee College Seminar
American Seminar
Harvard Law School Association
Temple Brotherhood (Chattanooga)
Chemical Institute of Canada
Oberlin College
Knoxville Furniture Association
Overseas News Agency

Oak Ridge Association of Scientists
Des Moines Public Forum
Georgia Conference of Social Welfare
American Institute of Architects
Mouse River Cattlemen's Assn. (Minot, N.D.)
University of Chattanooga
Vanderbilt University
Power Managers, Eastern Division, Tennessee
Iowa State Centennial
Huntsville (Ala.) Rotary Club
New School for Social Research
Institute of Pacific Relations (San Francisco)
American Fund for Palestinian Institutions
Berea College
Georgia League of Women Voters
Boston Arena
Civitan Club of Asheville (N.C.)
Independent Citizens' Committee (Philadelphia)
Electric League of Cleveland, Tenn.
Division of Surveys & Field Services (Peabody)
Oregon State Grange
National Convocation on Church in Town & Country
American Public Power Association
National Committee on Atomic Information
Tennessee Press Association
Joint Superintendents' & Managers' Meeting at Pickwick Dam
Conference of Public School Educators
Briarcliff Junior College
Association of American Law Schools
Columbia Broadcasting System—Bikini Tests
Akron (Ohio) Civic Forum
United Steelworkers of America
Iowa State College
Spring City Kiwanis Club
American University Institute
Hollins College
Estes Park Convention
Denby Lecture Series (Detroit)
World Brotherhood Convocation
Middle Tennessee Managers' Association
National Council of American-Soviet Friendship
Rutgers Labor Institute (New Brunswick, N.J.)
Citizenship Institute (Atlanta, Ga.)

Clinton (Tenn.) Youth Council
American Whig-Cliosophic Society (Princeton U.)
Class Day, DePauw University
Memphis Public Affairs Forum
Sevier County Unit Demonstrators
Baltimore Chapter, Union of Democratic Action
Cullman (Ala.) Rotary Club
Southern Animal Nutrition Conference
Potomac Cooperative Federation
Nebraska (Lowell News Service)
Congregation Emanu-El
Clinton (Tenn.) Civitan Club
Third Conference Childhood & Youth
Concord Community Forum
Baltimore Rotary Club
University of Chicago
Lyceum Association & Tulane U. lecture series
Institute of Industrial Administration (London)

### Articles

*The People's Lobby* (Washington)
*The New Leader*
*International Management Congress* (Stockholm)
*Yale Law Journal*
*The Nation's Schools*
*International Engineering Congress* (Paris)
*Conference on Science, Philosophy and Religion*
*Harvard Law Review*
*Southern Packet*
*State Government*
*Educational Leadership*
*Journal of Air Affairs*
*The New Republic*
*Journal of Higher Education*
*The Nation*
*This Week*
*New York Times*

2. A list of things I have written or speeches made since then:

### Speeches

Outdoor Writers Association
The City Club (Cleveland, Ohio)

United Nations Educational, Scientific & Cultural Organization
North Carolina Education Association
New York Herald-Tribune Forum
Americans United for World Government
Church Leaders of Methodist Church (New York)
National Press Club
General Council Meeting, Congregational Christian Churches (Grinnell, Iowa)
American Federation of Labor (CBS)
American Library Association
Volunteer Electric Cooperative
Utah State Agricultural College
Iowa State College
Norris (Tenn.) Forum
TVA Engineers Association

*Articles*

*The Eagle Magazine*
*New Republic Roosevelt Memorial Supplement*
*News Bulletin,* National Committee on Atomic Information
*Press Book,* National Committee on Atomic Information
*Post-War World*
*Southern Packet*
*Atlantic Monthly* (2)
*This Week*
*The New Republic*
*Farmers Educational Fund*
*The Nation*
*Social Science Foundation*
*The Progressive Farmer*

AUGUST 1, 1946
IN THE OFFICES OF THE AMERICAN
DELEGATION, ATOMIC ENERGY
COMMISSION, EMPIRE STATE BUILDING, NEW YORK

Yesterday afternoon I attended a session of what is called the "Working Committee" of the UN Atomic Energy Commission, but what is for all practical purposes the Commission itself, with different hats.

The whole thing didn't seem real. It seemed definitely *unreal.* Around three sides of a rectangle were the representatives of twelve countries, and behind them their technical and other colleagues. The chairman, a Brazilian, was full of charm and smiles—the way to agreement lay in being very pleasant—and he certainly was that. Gromyko and the Polish representative sat together; back of Gromyko was Dr. Skobeltzyn, the physicist, a round-faced, gray-haired man with the soft, unlined, amorphous face of a banker or the possessor of inherited wealth. With him was a constantly half-smiling young fellow—a translator, perhaps. Gromyko was the very picture of composure and self-control.

Hancock, heavy-footed and with great earnestness, started off by urging Gromyko to expand on his ideas about an international convention against atomic weapons, a discussion which Gromyko had begun at an early session. It would be helpful if he would throw more light on the Russians' ideas in this matter. General McNaughton, for Canada, followed, pressing the request further. An extremely handsome man, very strong face, shrewd, firm but quite friendly. The Australian, a young man (in Evatt's place) followed, with a rather lengthy statement also urging a further statement of how Russia proposed to make such a convention enforceable and effective. All this time Gromyko sat impassive; everyone wondered whether he would "open up," and apparently few believed that he would. This might carry us somewhere if he would—one way or the other. He made marks on a pad of paper; I could see the marks over his shoulder and thought for a while he was doing some Russian "doodling." Actually, they were notes for his response—just a few lines of them.

Finally he raised his finger to the chairman and began: in Russian, which of course no one there among the other nations understood. But how intently everyone watched his face: McNaughton under his bushy brows; the Australian with great intentness, as if they understood every word. And Gromyko (talking entirely extemporaneously from these few notes) gestured and ran his eyebrows up and down and looked from one of his auditors to another just as if they understood every inflection. Then the French translation—which relieved the suspense for most people; and then the English translation, which finally told me what he was saying—which was very skillful, extraordinarily skillful from his point of view, and very good propaganda stuff. But of course quite without meaning in terms of the problem that should be met.

At this juncture Mr. Baruch came into the office that had been assigned to me here. He said that he had talked to the President by phone yesterday about the Atomic Energy Commission membership: that one man had already been told he would be appointed, for reasons of friendship and politics—Pike, Baruch thought was his name. That Conant had been offered the chairmanship and had not accepted, and was apparently reluctant to do so. That two or three others were actively under consideration for membership, among them Gustavson of the University of Chicago, Barnard, Admiral Strauss.§ That he had told the President that he withdrew his "idea" about my being held in reserve on the chance that I could be made head of the international agency if and when created—I never took any stock in this idea—that is, I think it was simply a "tactful" way of saying that he objected to my appointment or perhaps, less actively, preferred Conant. Conant is being pushed by the Army, particularly Groves, as he is very close to Groves, who is determined to continue to run things.

I said nothing to the Old Man except that it was a terrible setup— five men trying to administer something, and that the least the President could do would be to name a chairman who had an opportunity to help select his colleagues—but this wasn't to be the case, which made the whole thing highly questionable. I made it plain that I am not actively seeking the job.

Almost immediately after we finished our talk, my call to Cap Krug came through. I told Cap my understanding about Conant, and he said that checked with his information. He said the obstacle in the way of his "campaign" had been the President's fear that if I left TVA it would go to pot, fall into the hands of the politicos, and lose its character. (This conversation took place on the Potomac last Sunday.) Truman told Cap the story, "in considerable detail," of how McKellar and Stewart had come to him in 1945 demanding that I not be reappointed to TVA; how and why Truman reappointed me nevertheless. Cap said Truman considers the TVA a "concrete demonstration" of what he, Truman, stands for in public affairs and he doesn't want anything to happen to it. I told Cap this was comforting, for before I would consider the AEC business at all I would insist on a successor who would carry on.

Did I have any names of Southerners in mind for TVA, in my place? I suggested Frank Graham and Clapp. Graham was new to him, but Cap had suggested Clapp, and the objection had been made that he wasn't well enough known, but more particularly he doubted if he had the strength to beat off political attacks. I said Clapp was known, and favorably, in the Valley, and that he could stand up against anything, but I don't think I impressed Cap. What did I think of Joe Starnes? This shook me; if such a notion was worth repeating, it showed how dangerous the situation might be. Of course, I said he was a politico, and a beaten one, and that his labor record was particularly bad. What about Dykstra?◖ This seemed to me a good idea, an excellent one,

§ Lewis L. Strauss and Sumner Pike had actually accepted Commission appointments offered by Truman a few days earlier; no announcement was made until October 28, when the entire Commission was introduced at a White House press conference.

◖ Clarence A. Dykstra, provost of the University of California.

though I doubt if he would consider it. What pleased me so much was that the President should consider TVA as his responsibility—and whether all this was simply to divert Cap from pressing my name for the other thing or not is not too important on that point. The thing that would kill me would be to be under a "draft" and no satisfactory understanding about TVA succession.

(Well, I have broken into the story of the UN committee meeting.)

Oppenheimer and I took a walk, after the shindig, and then had drinks and dinner at the Plaza with Sir George Thomson, the British physicist; van Kleffens, head of the Dutch Foreign Office, and Security Council member for the Netherlands, Dr. H. A. Kramers, Dutchman and chairman of the Technical Committee. As we came into the dining room there was Skobeltzyn, the Russian scientist, dining alone. There was a painful moment as he pretended not to see us. There was a suggestion of inviting him to join us, but Oppenheimer said there were things to discuss alone, so he wasn't invited, though everyone felt rather badly about it.

I found it difficult to keep my face straight as these men discussed what "the Lilienthal Report" said on this page and that. And they got me into talking about TVA, which seemed to interest them enormously —like some vast and fabulous tale from another world.

This morning I attended a meeting of the Technical Committee—a committee to whom was assigned a very difficult and important job at yesterday's meeting. This was in a small room—the private office of Lie, Secretary General of UN. The same curious feeling of seeing men of so many different kinds, even colors (the dark Egyptian, and a delightful Chinese), and again the funny feeling about the "Lilienthal Report" being discussed, chapter and verse, as clergymen might cite the scriptures as a base of reference. The Russian position had changed; Skobeltzyn told Oppenheimer, "My orders have been changed," and their position was quite reasonable and workable. Whether this will help or not no one can say. It encouraged J.R.O., and that is quite a feat in itself. He wants the Russians to feel that the "facts will suggest a way out," and that the scientists (all of them) will work toward unity and against the forces that divide mankind.

Now for the plane and home tonight.

AUGUST 5, 1946
HOME

David has just phoned from Memphis. I don't know who is more excited, the returned "vet" or his poppa and momma. Peace, it's wonderful. Can hardly wait till he is "processed" and back with us—probably Wednesday, he thinks.

Last Sunday morning we had a wire from San F. saying he'd arrived there by plane from Hawaii; now he's this much nearer, and soon he'll be here. And then the problem: What next for him? He has some rather definite, albeit they may not be feasible, ideas.

AUGUST 10, 1946
HOME, SATURDAY

Mr. Baruch phoned at about 7:30, to tell me what a fine speech I had made (this was the CBS broadcast of Thursday night). Said it would have a very good effect, that he hoped I would do some more, and that if I would talk to the scientific members of the UN Commission it would be very helpful—had Eberstadt or Hancock called me about that? Told him E. had phoned yesterday, expressing warm approval of the speech and asking me if I would come up for that purpose, that I had said I would.

"Has the President called you about that other matter?" he asked. No, not a word. Well, Baruch said, he had talked to him about "my friend" (telephone code for me) and urged him to make the appointment, but he asked, "Could he be confirmed?" Told the President he would go to bat and help, and thought it would be O.K. Also Acheson had asked the same question about confirmation. Pres. said he thought he would let it "rock along" for a while. B. thought it would be very useful if there was close understanding and unison between the new Commission and the work he was doing. We wound up with mutual expressions of friendliness—how much he'd enjoyed having the visit with me at Uncas, etc.—and then his nurse Miss Novarro asked to come on; she asked for a copy of the script of the radio talk, and said Mr. Baruch had listened to it with great satisfaction, and then called a half-dozen people about it.

Score: naught to naught.

AUGUST 26, 1946
KNOXVILLE

Congressman Rankin was in this morning to talk about TVA. As he left, he repeated his speech: "You have done a great job and TVA is the greatest work of man of modern or ancient times." All of this is somewhat on the ironic side.

But I had a little fun out of it at that. This morning the Knoxville *Journal* quoted Rankin as saying that my friend Bishop Oxnam is a pink and has been discovered among the Communist-favoring organizations, etc., his usual line about practically everybody. So when he started talking about the enemies of TVA and how he would throw his figures about power bill overcharges at them (that is, comparing rates in, say, Pennsylvania with TVA rates, the difference being robbery), I said, "Well, those arguments don't work any more; none of the arguments work based on the facts. People have found out that all they need to do is say that TVA is Communistic and then that settles it for most people. The other day at Cincinnati before a service group a TVA-baiting speaker put up a big map showing how the United States would look under the Rankin Bill providing for seven TVAs, describing this as Communism and the directors of these as Commissars." I explained that no amount of argument on the merits would shake people and that the opposition had learned that it was only necessary to yell Communist to put TVA in a bad light.

This didn't do much good with Rankin, but it was fun.

SEPTEMBER 15, 1946
HOME

Still not a word about the Atomic Energy Comm. Have been a number of editorials urging my appoint't. as Chairman, including the Denver *Post*—shades of Bonfils and Tammen. But no hints or feelers or anything. I think I would be relieved if I didn't have to face it.

David wants to enter Harvard; he won't return to U.N.C., and I'm so hopeful he gets what he wants. Think he is right about it. We have a great time playing badminton, and sober talks. Now we've been analyzing and drafting a letter to the Committee on Admissions—fun to work with him.

The speech to the Methodist bishops, etc., at Grand Rapids last week was a great success; they got what I was driving at, the delivery went well, and all the trouble and time I put in on it now seems worth it—though I had my low moments during the two weeks that it bothered my sleeping and waking moments.

Next week to New Orleans to receive the award of the Catholic Committee of the South. The Moslems next!

SEPTEMBER 19, 1946
FLYING TO WASHINGTON FROM
NEW ORLEANS

I repeat myself, but "the darnedest things happen to me." For example:

There I was in a procession, just a few steps behind a "Prince" of the Catholic Church, in his Cardinal's red flowing cape and cap, filing down the center aisle of the Municipal Auditorium in New Orleans, under a canopy of crossed swords of the Knights of Columbus. Then we were on the brilliantly lighted stage. Cardinal Stritch on his throne, flanking him Archbishop Rummel of the New Orleans Diocese and Archbishop Lucey of the San Antonio Diocese, the latter a youngish, bland, genial man—a modern type, I note, compared to some of the roly-poly bishops (thus Bishop O'Brien of Chicago), right out of Chaucer, or the spare ones like Bishop Gerow of Natchez, with the light of Jesuits in their eyes, or the dreamy, soft Bishop Adrian of Nashville, drifting among us as if he were hardly there, and soon to be back in his cell with his dreams and his prayers—the only "spiritual" face in the whole company.

There they were, in a great semicircle, facing a large audience in the front ranks of which were the Brothers, the young men in their blackbird dress, and back of them row on row of just an ordinary audience of Americans, half of them women. Outlining the edges of the center aisle, like a "facing," the Knights—in their white uniforms. The very young and strikingly handsome new Mayor of the City, DeLesseps Morrison, in a stylish white dinner jacket, the Cajun Lieutenant Governor, and I (in my no longer fitting black dinner jacket) were the only "civilian" touches on the platform. The Most Right Reverends—"Their Excellencies"—wore their three-cornered hats, with the puff on top, and their "purple" (actually rose) robes.

The Holy Heart band played—terribly. School hasn't opened yet, I would judge—or they hadn't had a chance to "practice"—but they played a lot (including "On Notre Dame" or whatever it is) because we were ahead of the radio time. Then the Archbishop of New Orleans, the host, spoke. A square-built man, with such perfect iron-gray hair, parted so exactly and brushed back so carefully that you would swear that he was the special pride of a make-up man—except that I stood near him at dinnertime and he is authentic.

There was an ominous note in what he said—to me. Has the war, and all our sacrifices, been in vain before the new and yet ever old enemy—must we soon fight again, to insure the victory? He didn't say Russia, not quite, but this was what he was talking about. Would the peacemakers in Paris not listen to the voice of Christ's vicar on earth, who from the Vatican had . . . etc. Pictures of Spain came drifting across my mind, for his voice was the heavy, booming voice of a political leader, and his frame, his great square jaw was not that of a philosopher or an ascetic—by a long shot. Then he read a message to the Conference from His Holiness, and the circle of little three-cornered hats were briefly removed—just a motion but quite impressive, so solemn it was.

He preceded the Cardinal, who floated down from his throne in the middle of our "circle," his crimson robes sailing off rather like two long wings. He is a smiling, kindly, soft-spoken man, bears the mark of a hard worker, something shrewd and "politic," but not political, in him— without the robes and the great ring he might be the president of a big state university, meeting the legislature in an informal way—the scholar who knows how to talk to the "practical" men, and yet preserve his poise.

What he said was a good prelude (as he himself told me later when I spoke to him about his speech) to my own line of remarks—the prime importance of human personality. Indeed, some of it sounded much like one of the earlier drafts of the opening of my Grand Rapids speech to the Methodist bishops of a week ago! But the Marxists came in for a going over, in this genteel and soft-voiced way. Actually, a very good speech—though I couldn't hear quite everything because I sat behind him, and he didn't speak too loudly.

Then Father O'Connell of Richmond, head of the Catholic Committee of the South (the whole gathering of prelates was to attend their sessions), made a witty and quite eloquent epigrammatic talk about me and my work. As he went on he told about the work of the TVA—things I had in my MS on my knees—and I began thumbing it and deciding hastily to leave out this and that as already pretty well said. Then the final blow: he said that in my book I quoted from Pope Pius XI's encyclical—and read the quotation. I had planned to conclude with that. Helen says that at this point I riffled the pages of my now pretty well dwindled speech and took a page out and stuck it under me. This turns out to be correct, though I don't quite remember being so obvious about it. This laudatory stuff—being compared to "David of old," called "Young Man River," etc.—went on and on, and finally the square-built Archbishop Rummel and I were before the microphone, then flash bulbs going, and he reading (not too smoothly, for the copy he had before him was darned near too faint to see) the citation—and then handing me the plaque—a beautifully done thing in illuminated lettering.

When I finished my "response"—ten minutes perhaps—knowing that it had hit the spot, for the audience and the prelates (to whom I turned occasionally for emphasis or for some special reference to "you who are churchmen, etc."), I gathered my papers and started to return to my seat, and there was the Cardinal floating with hand outstretched to congratulate me. This was really quite a moving business, at that, and of course the audience loved it.

We met at Antoine's for dinner—and what a dinner. Starting with Old-Fashioneds, which I noticed that everyone but the Cardinal drank—oysters Rockefeller, terrapin soup, Pompano en Papillote, crêpe suzette with the most delicious burned brandy. Quite a contrast with the Methodist bishops—where I got pretty thirsty.

As I say, the darnedest things happen to me. A week before we were at Grand Rapids speaking to more than thirty bishops and almost all the 900 district superintendents of Methodist Church. The response was one of the most satisfying in my whole speaking career. By the time I had gone a few minutes you could see that they were getting "the point," and from then on it was wonderful—to see growing understanding. I left my MS to interpolate some fun to ease the tension of their desperately close attention, and when I reached the last five minutes it was like a small group. The applause was of that kind which comes with such a rush that you are sure it is "spontaneous" and then continues, while the chairman asks you to rise, then goes on and the whole audience rose. Bishop Oxnam, sitting next to me, said as if to himself, "A modern Old Testament prophet."

Well, considering everything, to have this Catholic group reacting the way they did—this was quite a week.

SEPTEMBER 21, 1946
HOME, SATURDAY

(I started to write this yesterday afternoon, on our plane in which Helen and I were returning from Washington; but we were over 10,000 feet and going through squalls—a great spectacle it was, with vast blazing rainbows and such—so I gave it up.)

I entered the President's office from the Cabinet Room, for I had been told this was to be "off the record" and so was brought up from the east entrance. The room seemed very large, and the President, standing beside his desk, seemed small. It is difficult to forget how that room seemed when Roosevelt sat behind the desk.

We shook hands; I noticed he looked worn, as if he hadn't been sleeping well. In fact, they were up most of the night (so his aide, Clifford, told me) preparing the affirmation of foreign policy and the decision to fire Wallace.* Only a half-hour before he had made the announcement.

He turned to me and began at once in a very direct fashion—no "How have you been?" etc.

* The former Vice President, then Secretary of Commerce, had attacked the Administration's policy toward Russia, and particularly the atomic control plan. Both Byrnes and Baruch had threatened to resign unless Truman repudiated Wallace's views.

"I want you to go on the Atomic Energy Board, as Chairman. Will you do it?"

Of course, I wasn't unprepared for this question, nor for my answer, though the bluntness of the question wasn't quite what I expected.

I told him that I couldn't answer the question directly with a yes or no. "Well, talk to me about it," he broke in, with a wave of the hand.

I did have a chance to "talk" about it, but not very consecutively nor in too orderly a fashion. He has something of the F.D.R. habit of talking, more than listening, frequently about things that seem extraneous to the business at hand.

The "he said" and "I said" of the conversation—which went on for perhaps 20 or 25 minutes—isn't particularly important. But the points are:

1. That I said I would accept the chairmanship of the Atomic Energy Commission provided a successor were found and appointed whom I believed could carry the TVA work forward. I made it clear that this was an express condition of my taking the job. This he not only accepted, but said that it was because of his concern for TVA and his desire not to interrupt the fine course of its success that he had "put off" talking to me about the AEC. He spoke of TVA as a great asset, and one that he wouldn't consider impairing, etc.

2. Because the kind of successor he should appoint could only be judged in the light of TVA's current problems and opportunities, I wanted a chance to talk to him about TVA. This he agreed to, and asked that I send him a memorandum of the points I wanted to make so the conference could be more useful.

3. As to the Commission, I told him that he must recognize that although the law was as good as could be expected, everything considered, it was a difficult thing to administer, partly because a five-man board is a "monstrosity," and would require that the men selected could work together. He agreed, and said that only two men had been appointed and accepted; that the other two (other than myself) would not be selected until I had a chance to consult about them.

He seemed to recognize that it wasn't right to pick men, as he had, before the Chairman had been appointed, but he didn't tell me the names of the men. "I can assure you they are neither of them crooks or fools" —which isn't too helpful. One was a man "with fifty million dollars who sold all his holdings and put them in Government Bonds." This is quite evidently Strauss, the Navy ordnance chief for whom Joe Swidler worked, formerly a banker with Kuhn, Loeb & Co. The other, it is reported, is Sumner Pike, formerly of the SEC, though I wasn't told this. I didn't particularly relish this unwillingness to tell me the names of the men already appointed, and tried to show it.

I let him know that I knew he had asked Conant and Karl Compton, who had refused to accept, and said something, with a laugh, about being a third or fourth choice. He said, "Well, these schoolteachers, they are worried about security—they have long-term contracts." He implied strongly that anyone who wanted security probably should not be in public service. Whether he thought so or not, it is perfectly true that this is a job for one who is a gambler, or in any event, it *is* a gamble—perhaps a big one. And for me a real gamble because I am pretty secure in what I am doing and get a big kick out of it.

I am to come back as soon as I can with the memorandum and a list. If the story "leaks"—and it usually does—then we may be up against doing something under pressure. If we can't find an answer to the TVA problem that is reasonably good, then I stand by my refusal to accept the other. That won't be easy, but it is what I shall do.

After I left the White House I felt perfectly sure that my inner doubts were resolved. I shall have my ups and downs, of regrets and doubts, and plenty, plenty headaches. But this is a job that needs doing even more than the TVA job does—in this stage—and it must be done by somebody. How well it can be done, with things as they are, and with that law, I am not sure; but I can do it as well or better than anyone else. I won't be happy, I am sure, in the way I have been so much of the time in TVA, nor so free. And change from so pleasant and free an existence isn't something one contemplates with joy. But after I have said that, all the rest of the reasons are on the other side.

SEPTEMBER 22, 1946
HOME, SUNDAY

Gordon Clapp and I spent several hours yesterday forenoon. The upshot of our talking is that I realize rather more clearly how difficult it will be to find a man to do my job on the TVA board, and, secondly, that it can be done. The latter is not due to the fact that we have two or three names of the right kind of men whom we know are eligible—the fact is that after all these years of thinking of a successor (because of Doc's age) we are really no farther along, if as far, as to a particular man. I say the replacement can be made because it is now clearer to Clapp we must not look for another Dave, or even for someone who can do the particular things I do, but rather for a man whom TVA can shape and develop as it has all of us, and who will fight for the things TVA stands for. We will make a search in as nearly a systematic way as we can. I did make it plain that if we can't get the right kind of man for TVA, I am not committed to take the new post.

Of course, I am sad at the thought of leaving. Norris seems more peaceful than ever. The independence and flexibility of my life seem especially desirable, knowing I won't have it on the AEC. The pleasure I get out of knowing people—the trips to the small towns and the barbecues. The absence of the kind of pressures I don't find worth what they cost—especially, daily seeing a long line of people, as I must in AEC. The fact that we have a superb staff, so I have to think of administrative knots only rarely.

But what makes me saddest—and a twinge of "Did I do the right thing?"—comes when I see how hard Doc Morgan and Clapp take it. Or rather, how disappointed they were with me for accepting the State Dept. assignment, and then continuing to interest myself in atomic energy since then. This rankles with them, as they didn't disguise. But yesterday I learned for the first time, explicitly and candidly, why this was so. And this made me sad—sad that TVA has become such an obsession. But this "devotion" accounts, I suppose, for the high quality of the work, the enthusiasm and sense of dedication. But at a price, for some at least: lack of perspective about the rest of the world.

When I said that we must remember that atomic energy and the great peril it is for the world affects TVA, too, no matter how good a job we do in the Valley, Clapp's agreement was more verbal than real. And then he went on to explain (in words I had myself used, and then had scolded myself for—indeed, the very figurative language). "The fact is," he said, "that we felt as we did about your taking the State Dept. assignment, and then establishing a position of public confidence on this issue because we think TVA is the most important thing in the world, and we were jealous of this other thing, that it could attract and interest you. I suppose that's just it."

Later, in speaking of the feeling of disappointment with me in preferring this new issue to the extent that I gave it attention after my return from the State Dept. assignment, he said, "Leaving the TVA for anything else is a painful thought, for some of us feel married to TVA, and leaving is like being divorced."

When I found that the conversation was sufficiently personal to permit it (he is always so restrained and ritualistic about staff-chairman relations that this is the first frank discussion we've ever had—he usually freezes it completely), I said, "Not that it matters any more perhaps, but I could never understand why neither you nor Owen ever spoke to me of the Report. You knew it was a good job, and important, and yet you carefully refrained from saying so. Why?"

"It may be cheap," he said, looking a bit sheepish, "but I was so

upset by the whole thing and especially the way you handled the acceptance of the assignment that I didn't want to have to think about the
Report or anything about it." I told him this I could understand; and
dropped it.


SEPTEMBER 23, 1946
HOME

Have just been reading Dos Passos' account of the Wright Brothers,
the Dayton bicycle mechanics and how 43 years ago they licked the
problem of flying.

Nothing worthwhile is done without these terrible frustrations, the
time-consuming and wasteful wearing down of obstacles, most of them
so unnecessary, so heart-breaking. You had them in the TVA. You will
have them, aplenty, in the pioneer work that Fate seems to have in store
for you, in putting the energy of the nucleus to work for men.

Remember this, when the frustrations come: the stupidities of the
"Civil Service," the General Accounting Office, the dopey Army officers,
the hours and hours and hours with the Congressional Joint Committee,
the State Department, and perhaps some of your colleagues. Remember
that nothing useful and new can be done without enduring these frustrations. They are part of the process of doing something new and
useful.


SEPTEMBER 27, 1946
WASHINGTON, FRIDAY

Another talk with the President this morning, and a very satisfactory and reassuring one. He made a strong impression on me this time,
quite in contrast to the other day. Perhaps because then he had his mind
on that damned Wallace mess; I saw him ten minutes after his press
conference when he announced that he had asked for Wallace's resignation, and the wear of being up much of the night and his feeling bad
about it showed on him.

But this morning was quite different.

On last Monday I talked to the other TVA board members about
the President's proposal and my conditional answer, i.e., conditioned
upon finding a successor who would be satisfactory and keep the TVA
on its present plane. Dr. H.A. (actually the sweetest and best-balanced
man in the world) was wonderful. He had heard of it from Clapp the
preceding Friday—the day I saw the President and had phoned Clapp.
He was disappointed but thought it was inevitable. He felt I might find

the new post wouldn't work out (which it may not) and I would be "wasting" myself. But he put up the kind of front that was grand—vigorous, undaunted, and accepting a result that he had brooded about for a long time. Pope was very gloomy. Full of distrust of Truman. "I know Harry Truman as well as anyone in this room. He has good intentions, but he is weak in carrying them out." He was full of anger about the way Wallace was treated, and took this as proof that the President couldn't be trusted to carry out what he said he might; more specifically, that he would agree to replace me with a progressive, and then put in someone who was a half-progressive. And so forth.

On Wednesday morning Clapp and I came to Washington. At 2 P.M. we sat down at the office, with Owen, to work out the memorandum about the TVA that the President had requested, preliminary to my seeing him—the meeting that I had this morning.

Owen had been working several days on such a memo. It was very long and quite preachy, and full of a tone of preoccupation with ourselves that doesn't seem to me very persuasive. But it had the essential points. I suggested a different approach: one that I thought built upon the President's own experience and interests. This was to assert that TVA was still in danger from its enemies, but that this time the danger came from efforts to break down the autonomy and freedom from red tape that provides our chief armor against attacks; namely, our ability to do a good job and one that evokes the approval and support of the people. So I drafted a rough statement along that line. By the time Owen and Clapp rewrote it, it was again obscure and much too long, I thought. By this time it was 10:30 P.M. This went on and on. At 12:40 A.M. we had another draft, briefer, but still not too good. I was so whipped down that I would have accepted it, but Owen saw its weaknesses and insisted on doing something with it. At two o'clock we quit, *still* without a memorandum. I didn't get to bed until 3 A.M.

I got off by myself at 9:15 and wrote the introductory part on a new basis, in longhand, and revised the balance; Clapp made some suggestions, and at 2:45 I was with the President's special counsel, Captain Clifford, with a copy of a 5½ page, double-spaced draft.

This tale of a memo is almost incredible—that's why I have taken the trouble to tell its story in such fullness. No one seeing the memo would believe that it represented so much work.

But it appears that the care was worth it. For the President did read it, and he began our meeting this morning by pointing to it on his desk and saying, "I've read your statement and I agree completely. But where are we going to get someone to take your place so TVA can go on that way, the way I want it?"

Clifford (with whom I spent 45 minutes before seeing the President) had "warned" me that the President might want to discuss names of a possible successor, and that I should be prepared for his rather urging Bob La Follette. I didn't want to discuss names at this juncture, and was prepared to resist doing so, so I quickly put in, "Even if we don't find anyone, and I must therefore stay on, there are some things that ought to be done about this situation described in that paper; and if we do find a successor, he will need your help just as much, probably more. What I hope you will do is tell the Director of the Budget that you want TVA to be different—it is supposed to be different, and that proposed legislation or executive orders that might fit centralized agencies won't fit and TVA should not be expected to conform to regulations suited for centralized agencies."

Yes, he said, that will be done. (I have just sent a proposed draft of that kind over for the President's signature.)

He didn't mention "names" of successors, though I had the chance to say that the man should not be a politician. And I told Clifford that if La Follette were the choice, we could find it would be better for me to stay where I am, and that I would probably insist on that; but that I felt sure we could do better. Which I suppose will stop the La Follette talk.

I talked about the great importance of TVA as a demonstration that big government, highly centralized, is *not* inevitable. The President took that up and said some genuinely understanding things that greatly increased my sense of assurance and my respect for his intelligence and "management" sense.

"The way the TVA is set up is the way the Columbia Valley Authority ought to be set up—make it an essentially local affair. Of course, there is a national interest, and that's why Congress must enact the legislation and the President pick the men. But after that they must be the kind of men who will run that development. That's the way it has been in TVA and that's the only way to do it."

I said that whether there ever were another TVA or not it was important to make this one demonstration work, for the influence it could have on decentralization. He broke in: "The same principle ought to be applied all through the Government, and I intend to apply it if I can. I don't want to try to run the country from this desk. A lot of these bright fellows around the Government keep trying to get me to put my oar in here and put my oar in there—the strike in Pittsburgh, and so on. They want me to get in it so they can run it for me from Washington. I won't do that. Let the communities and the states do their job. Roosevelt never understood that. I used to tell him he would kill himself letting the people in the Government pull him into everything. I proposed to get Cabinet officers I can depend on and have them run their affairs, and when I can't depend on them I'll keep on firing Cabinet members until I can get that kind.

"And that's the kind of man we must get for TVA. That's the secret of your success with TVA and why the people like it so—it is run right down there by a man who can take responsibility and not keep running up here all the time. That's the way it has to continue to be, and if we can't find that kind of man, we'll just have to find another man for the chairmanship of the Atomic Commission."

"Government in the legislative sense ought to be inefficient," he said, "but administration must be efficient." I liked this simple way of drawing the line I have drawn more ostentatiously in the distinction between centralized authority and decentralized administration of that authority.

He said he thought I had what it took to make a success of the Atomic Energy Commission, and hoped I would be back soon with names for my successor.

Previously I had talked with Clifford about the new post. He told me the names of the men who had already been offered and had accepted appointments. This was done before he came to the White House, he said. He took the position that no appointments should be made except upon the recommendation of the Chairman of the Commission, and only after he had been selected. He assured me that the other two places were ones that I could select. I urged Winne and Thomas, on the ground that I am sure we can work together, and that is the important thing. I pointed out that action would be expected, and because these men had the necessary background and we knew how to work together and all understood organization, we could produce action. I hope these seeds mature.

The rumors about me in this connection popped up again today. I must continue to deny "all" and stick to "no comment." But apparently the leaks are getting bigger—don't know how long this can go on.

SEPTEMBER 29, 1946
HOME, SUNDAY

Been having a bad time.

But a *bad* time. Tormented about what I am about to get into, and afraid of it. Worried that it will wear me out, crack me up. TVA seems so peaceful and secure and good—the other filled with frustrations, neurotic scientists, insensitive Trumanites. The troubles of finding a place to live where I can refresh myself from fatigue and have a bit of fun—these in contrast to the almost idyllic conditions here—which seem all the more wonderful in this beautiful fall weather.

So I toss and agonize and wish I had not done this and that, wish there were a way out, etc.

Most of this is due, as I know, to the fact that I am very tired, going on my reserves of late. But much of it is the kind of buck fever or panic that one has, faced with a test that you aren't sure you can come through with credit, the buck fever of leaving the security of where you are for the insecurity of someplace else.

My great joy in Helen is something that goes on steadily, day in and day out. But there are "special" times when I realize, more than others, my wonderful luck in living with her. A tough period like this one is such a "special." Her good sense, her compassion for me in my inner struggles, and her utter poise when such troubles rise—God. We've been through so much, some I knew I couldn't make—but did, and her eyes steady me now as nothing else. Great woman, really.

OCTOBER 6, 1946
HOME, SUNDAY

Bad news. Dr. Frank Graham (so Gordon has just phoned me) wires he finds TVA chairmanship out of the question; a following phone call by G.R.C. [Clapp] confirms it as not worth pursuing further. This is too bad. He would have given TVA a real lift, I believe, moved it on a few notches.

On Thursday at his press conference the President answered a question about the Atom Commission by saying he was considering me for the chairmanship. McKellar popped off and made it news; would fight me to the last ditch for reasons too numerous to mention—not worth a tinker's, etc. Which again confirms how lucky I am—nothing would be better than that, for then no one would believe there was any "deal" and appeasement with the politicos, and to be confirmed over his opposition, which I would be, would start things off right.

Met Dr. Hugh Dalton, Chancellor of His Majesty's Exchequer, last night at the airport; Helen and I had dinner with him. Talk about British "reserve": he is breezier and more personal in his breeziness than any Kiwanis-ite I've met lately. Don't think he knows much about TVA, but is a keen, intelligent man. Have a feeling the trip is partly recreation, but if he stays till Tues., it will give him a good picture. He was overwhelmed to learn how many foreign visitors we have: "When do you have time to do any work?" Spoke of the Penguin edition and how very widely circulated my book is in England. I said this was surprising—even here we had a pocket edition, usually reserved for mystery stories.

His lively secretary, Young, said, "Well, your book IS a whodunit."
Not bad.

Climbed Mount Le Conte with John Ferris Wed. and Thurs. A
wonderful experience; the sunset from the summit was something never
to be forgotten. It was so peaceful and beautiful.

Am quite over the jitters about the new work—know I must do it
and can do it.

OCTOBER 14, 1946
WASHINGTON

More than ever convinced that I must take on the atomic task—
but the solution of the TVA successor problem is still not apparent.
We got a cable from Jack Blandford—saying sorry, he wants to stay
in international work. Graham had declined ten days earlier; Lloyd
Garrison last Saturday. Not too encouraging. I am going to see Mark
Ethridge in Louisville Wednesday, then perhaps on to Hannah, president of Michigan State. If those fail, as the chances are they will, then
what?

But after my talk with Acheson Saturday evening (I had dinner
and a long talk with him) and with Van Bush today, it is perfectly
clear that I must find a way and soon. It is hard going, this part of the
course, but I feel pretty sure that once the field is cleared for action, I
can do a rather good job of it, and get a good Commission. Lunched
with George Taylor today—fine record in labor arbitration—and asked
him to consider himself "available" for the A. Commission. Rejected
it at first, then became somewhat more interested. Charles Merriam of
Chicago is troubled about his age and whether he would be attacked
for that and his National Resources Board connection. Must just keep
plugging away at the problem.

OCTOBER 17, 1946
FLYING (AT 10,000 FEET), SOUTH OF CINCINNATI, THURSDAY

Still on the search. And the urgency of getting an answer grows
every day.

Ethridge in Louisville said he was sure he couldn't be confirmed.
That he had attacked too many of the Southern Senators, notably Byrd
and George. I was forced to agree with him, though he would have
been a great man for TVA.

Spent four or five hours with President Hannah of Michigan
State. He impressed me very greatly. He has prescience, force, apparently feels things deeply, stable. How he would be on particular

TVA issues (except for decentralization, keeping it out of politics, where he is clearly just right) I couldn't determine, though I brought the matters up. He showed considerable interest, and I should think we would have some chance that he would permit us to submit his name.

My trip to Des Moines to see Waymack† turned sour; a low has moved in. Rather than chance being held up in Chicago or some other spot, I decided suddenly that we had better go back home and make a new start from there after the weather has improved.

Have been thinking hard about the Atomic Board. Why wouldn't Bill Batt be just right for one of the two other memberships? And he might well be available. Going to do some checking as soon as I get in. Merriam hasn't been heard from, nor Taylor. I am somewhat concerned, as he (Merriam) is himself, about his age—72. I am also troubled a bit about his contribution, should his energies be rather low. But we must have someone with some ability to look far ahead, and great perspective.

OCTOBER 18, 1946
FLYING OVER IOWA (WITH A FANTASTIC VISIBILITY), HEADING FOR HOME

The tide has turned. (I hope.)

Waymack was interested at once—I made about the best presentation of this sort of thing I have ever managed—and he wasn't coy. Yes, I could put his name on a list of five. If the President asked him, he would talk to him, and with a sense of favoring the idea. This is all I asked for, but it is clear that if asked he would accept.

My talk with him was very satisfactory and confirmed the things I think he has that this board needs. He is not an "intellectual"—will give us the flavor of a man who is close to people, public opinion, etc. And yet he has had a really very wide experience in a great variety of public activities, national and international. He isn't a profound man, nor probably especially ingenious or original. But he is not afraid of new ideas, is genuinely progressive, has courage and a kind of quiet distinction. He is modest and yet the magnitude of the problem doesn't and wouldn't overwhelm him.

After threshing about, the first good news. And Clifford called from Washington that G.R.C. [Clapp] was satisfactory with the President for the TVA chairmanship. I asked him to wait until we heard, Monday, from Hannah, which he will do. I shall see Batt, who appeals to me as a good idea on a number of grounds, and then, if he will come along, it may be that the torment of in-between will be over—perhaps even by the end of next week.

† William W. Waymack, then editor of the Des Moines *Register and Tribune*.

One thing amused me. Waymack was afraid that I intended to ask him to consider TVA. He said that kind of administrative responsibility he felt he shouldn't take. Actually, his concern that this was what I came for made the actual proposition seem easier.

I left home this morning after breakfast, flew to Des Moines, spent a couple hours, and will be back home tonight by nine or ten. That is really thumbing one's nose at space.

OCTOBER 23, 1946
FLYING HOME

It would be quite impossible to describe the dizzy pace and the happenings of the last few days.

Went to Philadelphia Monday; Bill Batt said "No"—his personal obligations to his company. This was a blow—I think he would have been a great help. I was sorely disappointed because I had hoped that the torment of the search might be over.

Spent the night at the Union League Club, which is the original, I would guess. A bit of crepe would have cheered the place up! Jack Wright, our personable pilot, stayed there, too; he couldn't make it all out. I suggested we ought to give the rebel yell as we left.

Tuesday we flew to Washington, and I went immediately to the White House and a long session with Clark Clifford. (I have come to have a very high opinion of him—clear-headed, decisive, and with none of the maneuver complex, none discernible at least, that so marred some of his predecessors.) I made a quick decision to recommend Bacher‡ for the AEC, rather than Winne or Thomas, and he agreed to this, and thought the idea of a scientist rather important. I told him about Hannah, but said there was still no word from him.

We went in to see the President, who approved the idea of Waymack, Bacher, and Hannah for TVA chairman.§ After some uncertainty about sending for Waymack, I said I thought he would accept by telephone, though there was a risk that it might rock the boat not to have him come on to see the President. We tried it; Waymack said O.K.

I called Bacher, put up to him what I had in mind (which floored him, naturally), and asked him if he would come down to see us at once. Ten minutes later Jack Wright left the airport for La Guardia, and three hours later Clifford and I, complete with White House car, picked up Bacher at the Washington airport. (The way the tall Clifford and

‡ Robert F. Bacher, one of the top physicists on the bomb project at Los Alamos, was professor of physics at Cornell and also was assisting the American delegation to the UN Atomic Energy Commission.

§ Hannah made it plain he was not available. Clapp, though most reluctant to leave the general managership, agreed to accept and was appointed TVA chairman.

my robust figure surrounded Bacher and "spirited" him off to the big black car reminded me of the Gary Cooper picture I had seen the evening before in Philadelphia, *Cloak and Dagger*—the kidnaping and counterkidnaping of the atomic scientists. S-s-st.) We had dinner together, and then went to Clifford's office. We really worked, and the longer we talked, the more convinced I was that Bacher was the right man.

We stayed at Clifford's house—the hotel strike is still on, and I didn't want to cross the picket line. By this time I was pretty worn down and it was quite a while before I could sleep—so much hung in the balance at this stage. In the morning Bacher and I resumed our talks. He has just what we need—a feeling for the subject, an understanding of how important the Atomic Energy Commission's work is and can be, and a clear recognition of the central importance of an adjustment of the international impasse.

Sent him off by plane to Ithaca, to talk things over with his wife. She will be badly disappointed, he feels sure, as he is personally upset by the idea that he wouldn't be able to resume his work in the laboratory. But he is a man of real sense of duty and great purity, and this will make it somewhat more difficult for him to say "No." Also his close friend Oppenheimer (with whom I talked by phone twice) will strenuously urge him to accept. Should this happen, we will be ready to begin. The first weeks will be rather confusing and irksome. But on the whole I am more than ever sure that this is what I should do and must do; and that somehow, with my luck, a rather creditable performance can be turned in.

Now to wait word from Bacher. Should this fail, the torment will go on for I do not know how much longer, searching for someone else.

OCTOBER 25, 1946
HOME

Yesterday for five minutes or so I thought the agony of suspense was over and I was about to "take off." But it is otherwise, and I'm still on the anxious seat.

Bacher called about noon. "The answer is in the affirmative." I was so relieved I think I said, "Thank God." I put in a call to Clifford, who was delighted, of course, and then said Sam Rosenman had called him to say he'd dined with Lewis Strauss and that the latter was doubtful about going ahead with the Commission—the delay had been so long, he was worried about who his associates might be, etc. Clifford was annoyed.

Later he called me after a half-hour talk with Strauss by phone; he said that S. expressed worry that if the Republicans took the Senate the nominations might be kept dangling; also that the men named, "except for you," are not well known and this would be bad. C. asked him to come to see him today. He will go over it with him and if he is still reluctant will say that's that, and we'll try to get Charlie Thomas, who would certainly be a much stronger man. If S. decides to go along (I doubt it myself), then we are ready for an announcement Monday.❡

OCTOBER 28, 1946
COSMOS CLUB, WASHINGTON
(WRITTEN ON A TELEGRAPH BLANK)

Quite a day!

Everything worked out on schedule: our first meeting of the "5 Atoms" at 220, State Department Building; Clapp and I saw the President at 11:15. We saw Byrnes and Acheson at 2:45; the President's press conference at 4—this was quite an experience, facing the special conference crowd and watching the President operate and read these statements; then an incredible 30 minutes with the President in the rose garden outside his office, with "pitcher"-taking and grinning and movie cameras *ad nauseam*. How patient he was. Then a quite important conference with Secretary of War Patterson, General Groves, and that remarkable character General Eisenhower* until after six.

Quite a day indeed.

I phoned Nancy. Asked her how she was, etc. Said she had secured a promotion—had a new job. So have I, said I—and then told her she need not pretend any longer that she didn't know. She was so happy— this was quite a lot of compensation for me.

Tomorrow to Philadelphia and a speech at the Academy of Music.

OCTOBER 30, 1946
EN ROUTE TO WASHINGTON FROM NEW YORK

I got into this atomic brawl at quite a time. Trust me to pick something nice and peaceful.

This morning's paper had Molotov's attack on our atomic proposals and a rather senseless strike—a personal thing—at Baruch. (I got off the train and found myself paged in Penn Station—one's name sounds

❡ Strauss did accept, of course.
* Then Army Chief of Staff.

mighty large in that space. A porter recognized me and asked, wasn't I, etc.? He wanted to thank me for my work in TVA—imagine! The paging was due to a newsreel shot for Universal—they missed out, of the four companies that made one in Wash. yesterday.)

Went directly to see Baruch. He looked older, rather bad color, but cordial and not disturbed, visibly, by the general tumult, which I imagine he must enjoy. A conference was staged into which I was plunged immediately, on some specific questions of "security." The Old Man took me into his office to "talk." What he actually wanted to say, I think, was that he had suspected Herb Marks of "chipping" at his policy, and hence we should not have him around; but he stopped short of saying that and remarked generally about how important it was to have people in "your organization," i.e., AEC, who were 100 percent for the American Plan, meaning the Baruch Plan of course.

Swope (Herbert) later blurted something about people saying that with my appointment to AEC and all the publicity concerning it, did that mean that "B.M." was out?—that's the sort of thing that bothers him. Hancock is quite a different sort—steady, dignified, highly responsible, and candid. We talked at some length about the importance of conferring with the church groups, so they wouldn't get confused about the talk about stopping the making of atomic materials, which Henry Wallace and Ickes are furthering. Saw Bacher in action, and again thanked God for *that* selection. He will make all the difference in the world.

After luncheon—at about three, called on Merz of the *Times*, at his invitation. Told him (and Bob Duffus) how grand it would be if they would do an editorial about Clapp, and I think they will. Told him the greatest danger to success of the AEC were the antiquated provisions respecting the General Accounting Office and the potential difficulties re Civil Service. They will be glad to call attention to this. This is terribly serious and must be faced as such. Markel wants an article, but I begged off—this is for the Sunday *Magazine*—but said their suggestion of a piece by Duffus about me and my ideas would be all right—discussed those ideas at some length.

Newspaper reaction to the appointments continues unbelievably good. N.Y. *Daily News*, a strong editorial about me (also same in Wash. *Times-Herald*); superlative ones in N.Y. *Times*, Phila. *Record*, Phila. *Inquirer*, Wash. *News*, etc. Baruch said he sat next to Senator Vandenberg Monday, and V. said he didn't anticipate any problem for confirmation.

I am having a hell of a good time, and that's a fact. The panic and doubts, so acute a couple weeks ago—where are they now?

NOVEMBER 1, 1946
HOME (8:30 P.M.)

And so the TVA chapter closes.

At quarter after five I took the oath as Chairman of the Atomic Energy Commission, in Federal Judge Taylor's chambers in Knoxville, with Helen, David, Doctor H.A., Pope, Gordon Clapp, and George Gant† there, and, at my special invitation and their delight, Bishop and Mrs. Oxnam.

This morning my last board meeting—a brief and unimportant session. At the end of which I talked for a few moments—not personal things, but about TVA, and how fortunate it was that it was a "vital institution," not one built upon the tenuous foundation of personal loyalty to any individual; that the difficult part, the subtle part, and the most satisfying part was right ahead—that's why I envied them and knew they would deliver. It was only five minutes, but it meant a lot to me and to them.

I said I wasn't having any "leave-taking" but that from two to five my office door would be open and anyone who felt like it should come over and visit. And I was at that all afternoon—streams of people, many of them stenographers, file clerks, people who said they'd been with TVA for 10, 12, or 13 years and hadn't met me. It was difficult; they all spoke with such feeling, and yet most of them seemed proud and gratified because what I am taking on is so important to everyone.

Quite a day.

NOVEMBER 8, 1946
HOME, FRIDAY AFTERNOON

I am trying to rest, somewhat; reading, loafing, in bed a good deal, getting ready for the rigors ahead. Have had a very painful back, but I suspect it is partly twisted sacroiliac and mostly the fatigue of the last two or three months of transition and excitement.

Great flood of letters and wires of good wishes—hundreds of them from all over. So many of them speak of their children, these well-wishers, or that they will sleep better at night knowing I am on this job. This is a disturbing note to recur, for it measures somewhat how much, how very much, is expected of me.

I don't yet quite know how great a responsibility this is; a sense of it is coming over me, as much as I can take, or should. I need wisdom and judgment very much indeed. I am not mystical about it all, I think,

† Gant succeeded Clapp as TVA general manager.

but I feel so clearly the need for a source of strength outside and beyond myself, and that is what I call, to myself, a sense of God. The other
night I went to bed full of this feeling of inadequacy with my own
powers, and quite spontaneously prayed to God with a depth of feeling
I haven't known about anything for a long, long time.

The sense of God has become rather clearer to me. I have no
awareness of it, as a source of strength, when I am concerned much
about myself; I feel it most when I am least aware of concern about
my "career," my "reputation," having my own way, getting personal
credit. I feel it most when I think (and this is quite honest with me
much of the time) of my real faith in people and my love for people.
This will be sorely tried many times, I know, but there is in this love a
kind of purpose and focus.

Spent last Monday and Tuesday at Oak Ridge, in the role of "the
new boss"; Monday I'll be in Wash., discussing "intelligence," FBI, etc.;
Tues. my swan song at Phila.;‡ Wed. we begin on a trip to the various
plants, Oak Ridge, Los Alamos, Hanford, etc.


NOVEMBER 11, 1946
EN ROUTE TO PHILADELPHIA

This day was a pretty good illustration of the variety of this new
undertaking.

Item: A discussion of "foreign intelligence" by a slim young fellow
—Gary Cooperish—turned out to be General Hoyt Vandenberg, head of
all "clandestine" intelligence—his word. The talk cannot be committed
to paper—not now—but it sounded like a Hitchcock movie and the
quite tall young man like a character just off the set.

Item: General Groves, for two hours. A chapter all by himself.
It is not going to be easy to find out what has been going on, that is
evident.

Item: A luncheon given by Senator McMahon, attended by the big
names of the press, columnists and radio: Walter Lippmann, Eric
Sevareid ("Laski asked me, 'Do you know David Lilienthal? You should;
he is the greatest man in the United States.'"). Martin Agronsky,
Raymond Swing, Blair Moody, Philip Graham, Al Friendly, Herbert
Elliston, and Eugene Meyer of the *Post;* Drew Pearson, Ernest Lindley,
Arthur Krock ("That is a fine speech you are making at Philadelphia
tomorrow; I have sent it on to the *Times* recommending that they use
a good deal of it"), David Lawrence, Marquis Childs, Tom Stokes,
Joseph Alsop, etc. The members of the Commission were presented,

‡ My last speech written as TVA chairman was made to the National Municipal League at Philadelphia on November 12.

and I made a ten-minute talk, quite impromptu, and rather well received, considering that there was little we could say. I used two of my total stock of four stories!

This for a sample of public relations.

Item: A confab with the Attorney General and the FBI.

Item: Long sessions with the Commission on organization, and with the staff.

Item: A session with Senator McMahon.

Item: A session with Volpe and Marks about our relations with England preparatory to my seeing Sir John Anderson tomorrow.§

Item: Catching a train heading for a speech.

There will surely never be a dull moment—not for quite a while. And the throat-slitters will soon be at us in volume.

NOVEMBER 14, 1946
FLYING WEST TO LOS ALAMOS

My four associates and I have just broken up a huddle in the compartment of this plane—a Douglas fitted out for the Secretary of War. Bob Bacher has just given us a vivid picture of the making of the bomb, and some things ahead. We were so enthralled that for an hour or so we were hardly conscious of being anywhere at all.

This is the second such trip. Last February we, the State Department Board, made our now celebrated trip. "Little did I think," etc., that I would be making the same journey—but this time what a difference. Now I have a kind of responsibility that becomes more gripping and more overwhelming and more intensely interesting almost by the hour.

Yesterday morning we met—the five of us—in a conference room in the "temporary" building that houses the administrative offices of the "District" at Oak Ridge. With us were Herb Marks, Carroll Wilson, and Joe Volpe. I asked each man if he had taken the oath of office and filed his papers with the Secretary of State. Being assured that this was true, I said, "I call to order this, the first meeting of the Atomic Energy Commission of the United States. The last words of the oath of office which each of us has taken are these: 'So help me God.' Those words were never more appropriately used. So help us God. We will need that help."

And then we set out upon an agenda prepared jointly by Carroll

§ Sir John Anderson was the British counterpart of Vannevar Bush in the wartime development of the bomb, and took a leading part in Allied policy discussions. Joseph Volpe, Jr., was a member of Groves' legal staff during the war. He, Herbert Marks, and Carroll Wilson were the Commission's chief staff in the early days of its establishment.

and me a few days ago. The meeting went beautifully, with a fine spirit, clear discussion, decision quickly where things were in shape for decision, new ideas received, added to and adopted with clarity and without chatter or steam-roller methods. Where we did not have sufficient facts—as in the case of a matter involving international relations—we did not refuse to act, as we had been urged to do by General Groves, but rather decided to wait upon further information and to confer with the Secretary of State and others first. A remarkable meeting, and one that encouraged me enormously.

The evening was even more encouraging. We set out about six o'clock for Norris, the eight of us. There was no tension, no awkwardness, much laughing and joking and genuine, not synthetic, good feeling. Sumner [Pike] turns out to be a most delightful talker, out of a rich and bouncy experience all over the world and in all kinds of work. Lewis [Strauss] has a wit that is light and warm. We enjoyed each other—that is the point. And that, if carefully nourished and worked at—this I know how to do, it is one thing I have some skill at—this can carry us over many of the difficulties inherent in a five-man board.

These are men of very considerable ability as well as resilience. It will be quite feasible, if this first day of working together continues and is carefully encouraged, for us to do many more things *as a commission* than is ordinarily thought possible.

NOVEMBER 16, 1946
ALBUQUERQUE, NEW MEXICO

This has been a day that has made the words about "great responsibility" seem very real, immediate, and sobering. We visited the DP vault, then a second vault, both on the Hill; and this afternoon the Sandia base near here. The rather somber but highly intelligent scientists at Los Alamos, with their pleasure in tough problems and their names—"alarm clock," "little boy," "fat man," "Archie"◄—for rather terrible things; and at Sandia the alert and handsome young West Pointers, eager to learn the art of putting things together—a rather "getting in on the ground floor" sort of thing. Well, it is quite a lot to absorb. I asked some questions that disturbed some of them, and learned quite a lot, particularly about what has *not* been done in the way of planning, coordination, and the like.

Was in considerable pain all morning. Blasted sacroiliac, that had just about cleared up, got too much of a pounding yesterday, when we

◄ Code-words for various weapons. "Little Boy" was the uranium bomb dropped on Hiroshima, and "Fat Man" the Nagasaki plutonium bomb, for example. Sandia was where the bombs were assembled, and the DP vault was where our existing bombs were stored.

spent the day wandering all over Los Alamos. Doctor taped me up, but I was in quite a lot of discomfort, to say the least. Felt better tonight— was more careful and have taken some pain dope. Hope I can get this cleared up before it really lays me out. But I have luck about such things, and somehow I manage.

These mountains are so beautiful—the ride from Santa Fe to Albuquerque was simply wonderful. There is something ironic about the contrast between these magnificent vistas of nature and the things I saw during the day.

Tomorrow we take off for San Francisco, Berkeley, E. O. Lawrence and the giant cyclotron, and Robert Oppenheimer.

NOVEMBER 18, 1946
BERKELEY, CALIFORNIA

It is early—about 7:30—and before breakfast. I am writing this, on 3x5 cards—all the paper I can lay my hands on at the moment— in a room overlooking fog-filled San Francisco Bay and a sad croaking of a foghorn far, far off. I am dressed.

We arrived in The Unwary Turtle or The Flying Neutron, our Army plane, at three o'clock yesterday. The flight from Albuquerque was a beautiful one. We flew over the Grand Canyon, circled Boulder Dam. But what we saw below, majestic and inspiring as some of it was, was not nearly so heart-warming for me as what was going on in the plane, in the process of annealing five men, strikingly different men, into the unity that will make our very considerable task a possible one. Being together continuously that way could work very badly or, as it is this time and as it was on the State Department Board, could work beautifully. Little informal knots of four or five will gather around some fellow's seat to thrash out a point, to listen to Bob Bacher talk about cosmic rays, say, or to laugh together over some of our already "standing" jokes. It is the laughing *at* ourselves, which is the theme I set in my little impromptu remarks to the radio and column people the other day, that gives me most hope for a successful journey. We are really having a good time together.

And yet it is by no means a junket—I mean we are working hard at our job, including reading long and difficult contracts (as the one with General Electric) or difficult texts on technical matters.

Last evening the annealing process went on. Dr. Ernest Lawrence, head of the Radiation Laboratory, and a rather fabulous figure in the nuclear field—indeed, in research generally—came up to Robert Oppenheimer's home with the members of the Commission about 7:00. (Bob Bacher and I are staying here on this lovely hilltop home of the

Oppenheimers.) Lawrence is a very youthful-looking man—big, red-faced, full of vitality and enthusiasm. Looks nothing at all like the picture of a great scientist—not at all. You get a sense of drive in talking with him, and that impression is in accordance with the facts. Afterward we went to Trader Vic's for a wonderful dinner—a kind of smoked sparerib, eaten "by hand" and a coffee plus brandy—these were special items. In the course of the dinner the Atomic Commission and two of the world's greatest scientists rose to sing "Happy birthday, dear Anne" at the request of a very nice-looking man who was giving his wife a birthday party at the next table—of course, the man didn't know who we were, but we did, and this all seemed a very natural thing to do at the time.

Lawrence's theme was: Electric power for ordinary uses can be made from atomic energy, and can be made in a very short time—say a year or even less. He described what was a quickest, surest way— via the Hanford pile, etc. He was fearful that longer delay in order "to hit the jack pot," by the longer-range plans of General Electric and others, was a terrible mistake, and might result in a reaction and skepticism against the whole built-up beneficial-uses story. He hammered this hard, and this gave the five men a chance to work together in a wonderful fashion, which I utilized to its fullest. Today we visit the new super-cyclotron.

LATER, AT ALAMEDA NAVAL AIR STATION
WAITING TO GET ON OUR WAY TO CHICAGO (WE HOPE)

This morning we gathered with a whole passel of brains to hear about the new 184-inch cyclotron, etc. We have been laughing like mad ever since—and this shows the kind of humor of this crowd. The laugh comes from the fact that this galaxy could split and photograph something that isn't there, but they can't operate the simplest thing. The "magic lantern" was snapped on and a picture came on the screen, intended to illustrate something about the use of isotopes for medical treatment. But the picture was way out of focus and meant nothing. Just a big blur. Everybody in the audience protested just the way they do in a movie if the talkie part isn't working. So the operator-genius fiddled and fiddled and then said plaintively, "It won't focus any better than that." So the lecturer said, "Well, anyway, this is a picture of a mouse—that blur there to the left, that's a mouse." And all through the performance a public address loudspeaker would interrupt these precious words of wisdom: "Telephone for Mr. Gurk, telephone for Mr. Gurk."

It reminds me: When we were going through Los Alamos, getting to be more and more wound up in complicated gadgets, fractions of microseconds, etc., etc., we grew more and more solemn. At which juncture I cleared my throat, and in a loud voice said, "Now, gentlemen, if you will step this way there is a device *I* would like to demonstrate to you. This" (pointing to a post in the middle of the room) "this is called a pencil-sharpener. It operates in the following manner—I will demonstrate." It helped.

NOVEMBER 19, 1946
CHEYENNE

My fault as much as anyone's; I'm the shepherd of this little atomic flock, if there is one; but we delayed our departure from San F. so that weather conditions over the mountains worsened. The young Army pilots said we'd make a try. What a try it turned out to be.

Icing. Icing of the wings that we could *see* out the windows. Lewis sat up forward, in the special plane, looking mighty worried; said he was making notes for a talk he was to give to his partners at a farewell dinner (partners of Kuhn, Loeb). But he was mighty pale. And no wonder; we were losing altitude, it was by now dark. Col. Nichols* came from the cockpit with a rather wolfish grin (any grin, though, was a victory) to say that we had to go over 14,000-foot mountains but we couldn't get above 9,000 with the load of ice we'd picked up.

So there we sat, the five men (and my secretary, Miss Reames, as imperturbable as ever), the five men who were touted to have more power than, etc., etc. And our plane gathering ice and losing altitude over the high Rockies. I was worried about Bill Waymack—I'd had notice that he'd had some kind of cardiac problem—and was considering asking for some oxygen for him, he was sleeping so profoundly, I thought. (Damned imagination, as it turns out.) To keep my mind off the troubles and Nichols' bulletins (he said the pilot was sweating like a farm hand up there, and when we landed he came through looking like he'd been in a Turkish bath, though it was cold as hell), I opened a copy of some magazine and contemplated Betty Grable's legs. Sumner looked over his silver specs, reading something, and in his Down East grump said, "Someone better tell Harry to warm up the second team." I kissed the ground when we landed at Cheyenne.

(LATER: FLYING OVER NEBRASKA)

Last night's flight from San Francisco to Cheyenne was rather something. I needn't have recorded it to remember it, believe me. We

* Kenneth D. Nichols, General Groves' liaison officer to the new Commission.

are going to set up some more conservative flying standards—on this we were unanimous when we began joking again.

Reached Cheyenne about midnight and needed no lullaby to get to sleep. A hard, trying day. Picked up Harry Winne at Denver and have just had two hours' session on the Hanford operation and troubles, the research program at Schenectady, etc. This is hard going.

The elaborate procedure for the guarding of what I have dubbed our "hope chest" is interesting. Said hope chest is a wooden box about five feet long containing a whole file of everything under the sun, much of it top secret, all of it "highly classified." Lt. Col. Noble, a young and handsome West Pointer, is along primarily to watch over it and disburse and account for its contents; we are studying these files and discussing them en route. When we stop, the chest is locked, and carried out, Noble with a revolver on his hip watching over it as a couple of armed M.P.s cart it off to stand guard over it until we have it carried back again and start off on the next leg of our journey. Some of the documents are such that Noble never lets them out of his sight, off the plane, and he goes around carrying them on him, also with a revolver. I think if we did crash, what the Army would be really worried about wouldn't be recovering us but the contents of our hope chest.

NOVEMBER 23, 1946
WASHINGTON, SATURDAY NIGHT

This morning Helen and I rented a new home! This is very reassuring. Somehow it makes the adventure we are setting out upon seem honest-to-goodness and real. It is a rather small house in a lovely setting, out in the country beyond Bethesda. We are very, very lucky to get it. It is within our means, and it means I will not be cooped up in an apartment. And it is available immediately, which is very important.

Yesterday noon our Commission had the Military Liaison Committee, provided for in the McMahon Act, for lunch at the Metropolitan Club. We sat at a rather large round table in a private dining room and had a delicious luncheon—through the arrangements of Lewis Strauss. The meeting was my idea, as a way of getting acquainted before we had any particular things to discuss. The Army men are quite outshone by the Navy members—Admirals Ofstie, Solberg, and Parsons, quite able technical men. The chairman is the famous airborne commander, General Brereton. His two associates are not particularly well-equipped men: an old Corps of Engineers division engineer, who was in command of an armored division in Germany, Major General Oliver, and a young artillery colonel, Colonel Hinds. This is apparently their only assignment, and they don't quite know what to do with themselves. Have quite lush offices—much fancier than ours, of course.

Brereton, in response to my little speech after the lunch, predicting cooperation, etc., said he thought of their committee as serving not only "with" but "under" and as a part of the Commission. This I don't care for. They have agreed on Colonel Nichols as our Director of Military Application, and he is putting on a campaign for the appointment. They even suggested they would like to be housed with us when we get permanent quarters, and made a considerable point of our using a B-17 luxuriously furnished, for Commission air travel, a craft Brereton got Spaatz to set aside for that purpose.

Our efforts to find a general manager haven't progressed too well. We have decided to set up a panel of three or four men to help recommend such a man. But the tough job will be to persuade a genuinely qualified man to undertake so tough a job. Also, it will be difficult to get a man with industrial experience who won't be *too* business-minded, or to put it another way, who will have some sense of public policy and its primacy.

Helen was guest today at Mrs. Helm's, the White House social secretary, and was surprised to find Mrs. Truman was one of the seven guests.

The coal strike is under way, and serious trouble looms. I feel very bad about the way John L. Lewis is feeding the anti-labor forces.

The Army people—especially Groves and Nichols—are getting pretty restive. They don't like one bit the fact that we don't assume that everything in the Manhattan District is all right, personnel, policies, contracts, and our examining them independently with our own temporary personnel—Marks, Volpe, Paul Ager of TVA, etc. This may blow up. Might as well be faced.

My Philadelphia speech ("Big Government Is Not Inevitable"), according to Zimmerman, White House personnel adviser, and others, "has set the town by its ears." There have been quite a lot of editorial comments—Washington *Post*, *Courier-Journal*, etc. *Reader's Digest* and *American Mercury* have indicated an interest in making a magazine article of it. Since I have been preaching this very same doctrine for years, this burst of interest is rather curious. Some things are news as often as they are repeated. The timing of this was good, and the tone of the first part of the speech—which I used almost as I had dictated it in a single sitting—was rather well put for such things.

Some of my friends are boiling over a column of my dear old pal, Harold Ickes. It was one of these adolescent boy pieces—really quite childish. I thought it was just plain funny, and so did my colleagues to whom it was shown on the plane returning from Chicago. But others thought it ought to be "answered." Saw Lowell Mellett last night—he thought it would have been a good thing if my friends had written letters about it. Doesn't seem that important to me somehow. (Among people I have seen, briefly, in the past few days: Rex Tugwell, now quite plump, gray, and no longer the dashing knight of 1933; David Cushman Coyle, Larry Duggan, Louis Brownlow, Morris Cooke.)

NOVEMBER 24, 1946
WASHINGTON, SUNDAY

Have just read Raymond Fosdick's article in the *New York Times Magazine*, which, like many others of its kind, compares the great advances in the physical sciences with those in the social sciences and humanities, and directly and by inference bemoans the great "unbalance" between them.

There is something quite wrong in all this doleful talk about great advances in science, in physical science. We should be joyous about the discovery of new knowledge. That is item one. We should stop being apologetic for learning the truth.

Item two: We should stop talking about Nature ("the control of nature") *and* Man. Man and Nature—these are one.

Item three: The talk about unbalance between advance in physical science and in man's social institutions is somehow out of perspective, too. Isn't the fact something like this: that our social and political institutions are not changed by a process of pure reasoning, objective reasoning, as are our physical scientific theories or conclusions; that we change our social institutions because of and after we are more or less compelled to do so by the force of physical facts, or because of an attractive alternative that our greater knowledge of the control of Nature provides?

This does not mean, of course, that we do not need more and more knowledge in that field known as social science—knowledge of social institutions, human relations, etc., etc. But we must understand that the application of that greater knowledge about institutional adaptations will remain unused except as physical science presses ahead more and more rapidly to compel institutional changes, or, in the alternative, to make those changes seem attractive. Much of the TVA story is just this latter.

Hence, we should stop talking about slowing up our knowledge (learn less that is true, actually). We should press ahead harder and harder. For the more control we have over Nature, the more we know about the world (including man, of course), the more rapid will we change our institutions. This is revolution, genuine revolution.

The idea that the way to make social adaptation is to narrow the gap between physical knowledge and human institutions which are to catch up with that knowledge seems wrong; wrong, that is, as a way to effect changes in institutions. For to slow up so institutions can catch up is to neglect the fact that institutions do not catch up that way.

NOVEMBER 26, 1946
WASHINGTON

I have been going through a rather grim hell. The back injury I got three weeks ago is still with me. I forced myself through the long trip with this business hanging on. But today it really has given me 13 kinds of hell. A tough break!

In commenting on today's Commission meeting, I said, "This convinces me once more that on matters of considerable difficulty and complexity, the decision of a group of men who are each qualified is better than the decision of one man."

We spent most time on a contract with General Electric for the operation of Hanford *and* the operation of an expensive laboratory at Schenectady which the contract provides that the Government will pay for. When I first heard of this, I didn't like it; didn't like it at all. It would never have come before us if the definitive contract, through delay, had been executed before August 1, when the McMahon Act was passed. Groves urged us to approve it as it stood. But there were a number of things about it that we wanted to look at. And the more we looked at it, the less we liked the deal.

For example, the Schenectady laboratory was provided as a means of inducing General Electric to operate Hanford, though the two are not otherwise related. And the company could stop the operation of Hanford almost whenever it chose, and still have the laboratory. Such things, and others.

But I felt that the good faith of the Government had been pledged and that therefore we had no alternative but to go ahead, simply stating that we would not have done it that way, and that we would try to work out changes later. Two others rather agreed with me. Strauss felt that we ought to take more time, get a 60-day extension to think about it more. Said: "In a business deal the rule is if you are in doubt, don't." That is pretty good counsel here. Bacher felt that the commitment for a research program at the laboratory was too vague, and too definite, too, because a $20-million figure was set. I said that as long as anyone had any doubts about what to do, we would defer action—that it wasn't a matter of counting votes, but of getting a Commission consensus.

On another matter—the condemnation of a site for the Argonne Laboratory near Chicago—an hour's look at the file disclosed that the Army had not examined carefully into a site of land already owned by the Government. So we delayed that, too. We aren't going to be pushed headlong, apparently.

NOVEMBER 29, 1946
NORRIS

Called on Gordon at "his" office today. Somehow it wasn't quite as difficult and puzzling as I might have thought: seeing him behind a desk in the office I had known as home for so very, very long. Partly because he and I have talked together in that same office so many times —and happy times they were. Partly because I have really gotten myself separated better than I realized.

Everyone made a fuss over me—and especially the dusky elevator girls, the guard downstairs (Mr. Stookesberry) and the stenogs that I met in the halls and on the streets. They really seemed right glad to see me, and they all looked wonderful to me. I shall miss all this genuine friendliness.

Dr. Leach had good news for me. 47½ years old and still a long way from bifocals. He was quite impressed: I can read the finest type and the last row on his little illuminated blackboard without help. He did change my glasses to give me, he said, a bit more reading help, but said I could go without glasses as much as I pleased, and commented that I would probably live forever—the ability to focus plus the condition of the arteries in the eyes (which are related) is a point insurance companies rely on a good deal, and speaks of longevity. Though I must admit that the *quality* as well the the length of life is a matter of larger concern, and a measure of a successful life.

Tuesday or Wednesday we move—the "we" is by courtesy, as Helen will be in full charge. I hope to take some plants from the garden along.

DECEMBER 1, 1946
NORRIS, SUNDAY

This is the last of these journal notes I shall write in this little study in the house at Norris. In a couple of hours I'll be off for Washington, and this will no longer be home. This is a sad feeling indeed.

I've just come from saying good-bye to the Jandrey children, Fritz and Judy, and they have quizzed me about "what will you do with Mac"; that horse of mine deeply concerns them at this juncture. Earlier I dug plants out of my garden, putting them into flats and baskets for carrying to our new home in Maryland. The holes look as if a vandal had been through the place, but it is just too much not to have some of these beloved plants to recognize among the alien ones up there—and how happy I am that I have a place to put them. But we left most of the garden, and I only hope our successor here will do right by the rock garden, the rock wall, and the lovely wildflower spring garden down below.

We have had a happy time here. In this little porch-room I wrote my book, wrote many letters that meant much to me, held the first board meeting after the worst of my undulant fever was over, the meeting approving the deal with Willkie (and on the telephone in the bedroom I talked with and got F.D.R.'s approval of that deal, and finished the details over the phone in the kitchen, talking with Willkie as I leaned against the Frigidaire). And in this room I wrote my resignation and the President's statement about Gordon.

Yesterday the house was filled with *House Beautiful*: a trio of photographer, interior decorator, and writer, doing a "How they live" piece. It was fantastic: they were like people from another world in their preoccupations, and very nice and friendly.

DECEMBER 4, 1946
WASHINGTON

This has been about the toughest day so far, and I am pretty tuckered. But, as I put it to my fellow Commissioners, we do have "interesting troubles."

Met this morning in the office of the Secretary of State with the Commission and Acheson, Patterson, and Groves. Subject: well, let's say "raw materials." As Bill Waymack says, "We pull at a worm, like a robin, and the whole earth explodes and out comes a two-headed elephant." As we left the meeting, the boys got a look-see at what we have undertaken, and one or two were pretty worried, if not rattled. Bill said, "This gives a fellow a case of cerebral hernia," and that let down the tension.

Then we went to meet with Karl Compton, Georges Doriot, John Lord O'Brian, and Herbert Emmerich, who are helping us to find a general manager. I expanded further on my ideas of organization, which I have been developing bit by bit in the Commission's meetings. At this point I added another note: that the Chairman was not to be a kind of super-general manager. I think this point, without their knowing it, has rather worried some of the boys, and I was glad to have a natural occasion on which to say it.

Last evening I had dinner at the Achesons. Phyllis [Mrs. James] Warburg and one "Eddie" Miller were the only other guests. Miller,† an engaging fellow, said to Dean, "You and Lilienthal are the most famous team since Weber and Fields."

Yesterday we met all afternoon with General Groves, a hard session, and reached a kind of tacit understanding that we would try to transfer the responsibilities on December 31. I have concluded that the only way we will get to swimming will be to jump in the water, and that *thinking* about swimming won't help much.

## DECEMBER 5, 1946
### WASHINGTON

Was talking with Clark Clifford in the Cabinet Room, where he was "hiding out," working on the President's speech of Sunday night on the coal strike. This was about 5:10 this afternoon. It was dusk, almost completely dark outside. He turned his head and looked out of the windows that open on the outside passageway, then motioned toward me. It was the President, standing at the glass door, smiling and waving to me. I stood and bowed rather awkwardly and grinned. And then on he went, the Secret Service man half a step behind. Clifford looks very tired; he read me, from a paper pad, the opening lines of the speech: "I bring you tonight a report of a major American disaster."‡

Arranged with Clifford for the President to see the Commission (not just its Chairman—this I am insisting upon as a regular practice) next Wednesday, to report. We have something to report—not much, but a good beginning.

Saw Bandi Marton's film *Gallant Bess* tonight. Beautiful color photography of the genuine old Wyoming country, and perfectly magnificent horses. The theme of emoting quite so much about a horse gets rather tiresome, though.

We continue to maintain the note of enjoying ourselves. Even have a joke about what we call "the hearing aid"—the dictaphones we half-pretend we are convinced are recording our deliberations. So far the relations between the members, and the consequent growth of confidence, is most heartening.

† Edward G. Miller, Jr., then Acheson's special assistant, and later Assistant Secretary of State.
‡ The speech was canceled, because John L. Lewis called off the coal strike the day before its scheduled delivery.

DECEMBER 8, 1946
SUNDAY

We are making headway. I can feel it. There is a sense of traction, of taking hold. And though I look rather on the worn side—dark around the eyes as I've never been before and heavy lines from the cheekbones to the mouth—I'm standing it very well indeed. I don't really worry much; now and then a bit of a spell, but not bad. (For example, I got troubled last week about "security," for we are definitely responsible for frightfully important secrets, and yet we are letting people sit in our discussions that I really don't know well—a board secretary, for example.)

I worried the other day about how Congressman Taber, now chairman of the House Appropriation Committee, would treat me, for he is not only a general ogre for agency heads, but he naturally was opposed to TVA. I thought I had better face it rather than just worry. So I asked to see him. The meeting yesterday was a great surprise; he was actually gracious and considerate and respectful. He even apologized for being late for the appointment and keeping me waiting. And he showed real interest in the purpose of my visit, which was to urge that a special subcommittee of his committee visit Oak Ridge before the appropriation hearings.

Carroll§ is proving the wisdom of our choice more every day, by his sweetness of character, his firmness, his skill with other people. That was the most important decision since the Commission membership itself was selected. And he will probably find division heads who will follow what we call our "personnel policy," namely: "Carroll, are there any more at home like you?"

So, tired as I am, it is a "good" tired, not too much unlike the pleasant weariness you get from a hard day's physical work out of doors. And quite happy. It was so right, my leaving TVA and this gamble. There is one more pioneering job in the old boy!

DECEMBER 11, 1946
AT THE NEW HOME ON THE ROCKVILLE PIKE,
IN MARYLAND

The President greeted me heartily today, leading my little flock. I sat in a chair at his right, and my chums in a straight row of chairs in front of his desk—I used to wonder, in the F.D.R. days, who in the hell's idea it was, setting chairs in a straight row, like in front of teacher.

He didn't start talking (the way F.D.R. did, so you had to count

§ Carroll Wilson, who had been appointed Acting Administrative Officer on November 12.

out the first ten minutes of your time with pleasant talk about nothing in particular, usually; frequently about what the fellow just ahead of you on the appointment list had gotten around to talking about). So I started off—we thought we ought to tell him what we had been doing in the month since we had our first meeting—the trip around to see the "show," the gradual familiarizing ourselves with the enterprise, and the decision, subject to his views in the matter, of taking over the properties and the operation of the Manhattan District on midnight of December 31.

That was fine, he said, the sooner the better. It was very important to get the whole atomic energy business in civilian hands completely. This would do more than anything else to make people in this country and all over the world get over this great fear about it. The other day he had read the "first sensible article by a scientist." (He grinned at Bacher and said, "If you'll excuse my saying so," and then interpolated the story he had told me before about the scientist who sat there and wrung his hands—he motioned—and who had said, "I have blood on my hands" because he helped make the bomb. "I told him the blood was on my hands—to let me worry about that.") This article said that we must understand that atomic energy wasn't just a weapon of destruction—it could be a boon to mankind. Then he went on to say that we will come to see that its beneficial uses are the really important ones— that this was really what was behind what we were doing. "And what you men have to do is the most important thing in the whole world today—no question about that."

Well, of course, we were "charmed" by this clear-headed and simple talk. I went on to explain how we planned the transfer, that he would be asked to sign certain orders. "Send them along; I'll sign whatever you recommend." I said that we might as well mention the fact that, though we hoped for agreement with the War Department, there might be some differences we couldn't adjust that would have to come to him. "I expect that. The Army will never give up without a fight, and they will fight you on this from here on out, and be working at it in all sorts of places. But you can count on it, I am your advocate."

"No, you're not an advocate, Mr. President," I said, "you are the judge—and it's a lot better to have the judge on your side than the most persuasive advocate." This seemed to amuse him a lot, and he said, "Well, I know how they are, they are trained never to give up. I know because I am one of them." "Well," I said, "if you are, you are a lay brother." This was all lighthearted, but very, very important. It meant that in our negotiations with the Army about transferring Sandia and so on we could draw the line where we thought it wise, rather than where we thought we must as a compromise.

I told him how we were going about trying to find a general manager. "I'll appoint anyone you recommend to me, so you better pick a good man because he will be on your hands, whoever you recommend." He said that was a mighty good list of men we recommended for the General Advisory Committee. I said we had received acceptances from every one of them. He grinned at me and said, "You had better luck than I have had." I said that he had broken a precedent lately—he had done with John Lewis what no one else had ever done.

We rose to leave; the whole talk didn't take more than ten minutes and we had really covered a lot of important ground. "Come in whenever you want to; I don't mind trouble. I get plenty of it." As we left, shaking hands, Strauss said to him, "Good luck, Mr. President." "I need some luck. But my luck has been better lately." There was a kind of grim gaiety in his tone and manner at this.

## DECEMBER 14, 1946
### AT "HOME," SATURDAY

This has been a week in which things have begun to happen. The cohesion and understanding among the Commission has increased markedly. We decided to take over the Manhattan District at midnight December 31. The issue between what the military retains and what we take over has been sharpened. We visited the President, and announcement was made of our Advisory Committee. I am quite happy and enjoying life, though it is very strenuous. The damn back is getting better. Helen and I are quite at home in the new place. Tonight I go to the Gridiron dinner.

It is a quite new life. Life begins at 47—that silly kind of expression has occurred to me a number of times this week, for somehow it is actually difficult to believe that it was only six weeks ago that TVA was my whole life, and my channels of thinking were shaped by it. Now that seems a long way away—and when, as this morning, I read a letter from Germany about my TVA book, it seems to be to another guy.

## DECEMBER 17, 1946

Dramatic and important meeting late today. First formal session with the Military Liaison Committee. I sat at one end of a long table and down the line were lots of braid and stars, and my associates. After a preliminary discussion, I said we now needed certain "numbers," that we had intentionally not requested these "numbers" earlier because we recognized they are among the most critical in the world, and must be most closely held; that we are informed that only two or three persons had been given this information; that now it was needed in order that we could work out the problem of custody.

Everyone except the members of the Commission and the committee was invited to leave, Colonel Nichols was sent for, the doors were locked, and the "numbers" explained. Rather clumsily explained, I may add. My guess turned out to be almost exactly correct, and what is more interesting, even the proportion or ratio that I had been using as between these and total fish❡ was almost exactly correct. This afforded the source of amusement from my colleagues, one of whom said I was clairvoyant and another that "you must have been peeking."

At the White House, attending the state dinner for the Cabinet tonight.

### DECEMBER 20, 1946

The development of five men into a unit goes on, and it is a source of great joy to see this growth. There is such great respect, affection, a freedom to laugh at the other fellow (perhaps the surest sign of friendship), and a real common purpose. Some of the discussions go on hour after hour, and if one were not so sure that this is the right process and that out of it great good comes, it might be very trying. But it isn't trying, really, and after each discussion the problem has taken on a new color or shape.

We have spent many, many hours talking about a matter regarded as one of the top secrets of the country, one that involves directly this nation's position among the nations, and our relation to the Congress and the Constitution. This is a high order of discussion we are carrying on, and much hangs on the decision. I am determined not to put the matter to a vote, although at one time there were enough of us satisfied with one course that a motion would have carried. And in the end the result will be a better one, I am quite sure, and the unity of the group will be saved from a severe strain.

Have just come back from a meeting on this matter with the Acting Secretary of State, Dean Acheson (at whose home Helen and I had a delicious dinner and evening last night), and in a few minutes I start out to see the Secretary of War on matters of high policy concerning the military aspects of our work.

David got a letter that Harvard has admitted him beginning in February. He is in Florida visiting his grandfather and grandmother and working on a "project" of the story of their youth in the "old country"— his idea, largely. This news delighted us more than almost anything, for he had his heart so set on it.

❡ That is, fissionable materials.

DECEMBER 21, 1946
AT HOME

Drove through a cold rain to see Secretary of War Patterson at his office late yesterday afternoon. He is a rigid, intense man, but I have always found him fair, from the time way back before the war when he called me by phone to do something about the Aluminum Company's shortage of power. He sits very erect, and as I sat down, he eyed me sternly and with some curiosity, rather expecting, I think, that there was some dispute about the terms of transfer to the Commission.

So I reassured him on that score, saying that we are apparently in agreement on present plans and that I did not anticipate any real difficulty. (This appears to be the case, though, because of Nichols' rather denseness, or some orders from someone else, we spent quite a lot of time arguing about nothing really at all.)

Then I told him that what I really had in mind concerned the Division of Military Applications provided for by law. At the time he had phoned me to say that the Army, with Navy concurrence, thought Nichols was the man we should name to that post, the directorship of the division was thought of as a line or operating position, the man to run Los Alamos, in short. But the Commission had now concluded that our division heads should be essentially staff officers, planning, developing, and integrating program, evaluating it, rather than operating people. This changed the whole conception of the Director of Military Applications. (Later yesterday I sent him a copy of a memorandum indicating how we now thought of the division—as a kind of bridge between military planning for war centering around atomic weapons, and the responsibility of the Commission for the design, development, and production of these weapons.) Nichols was an able supervisor of contracts for construction and production, but had no experience in the development of weapons (he had not been at Los Alamos until after the bomb drop) nor in military planning. Would the War Department give us the names of other officers from whom we might make the selection?

He tilted back in his chair, looked worried, and said he couldn't think of a better man than Nichols. Then he sent for the Deputy Chief of Staff, General Handy, a four-star general, in charge of operations during the war, and a very easygoing and unmilitary sort of man. I repeated my story to General Handy, to whom all this seemed something quite new and interesting. He didn't seem to have the high regard for Nichols that the Secretary had, admitted there might be something to what I said.

Then Patterson said, "Dave, there's no magic about war planning; it's not a technical matter, and there isn't much that combat experience can teach an officer about it. Nichols hasn't had any such experience, it is true, but he is able and intelligent and he could learn whatever there is to learn." I said I felt that the Commission shouldn't be asked to "break a man in." Then he expanded on the idea that there really isn't any special skill in war planning. He mentioned a number of officers—among them General Lauris Norstad—but said they wouldn't know anything about the Manhattan Project and their combat experience wouldn't help them in the kind of function I had been describing.

We went at this for almost an hour. I asked him to think about it further, but he said he didn't think he could possibly think of anyone better than Nichols. I was rather discouraged by this session, but more than ever impressed with the importance of the subject.

I hadn't planned to go to the office today (Saturday), but about ten o'clock Carroll Wilson called to say that if I were to see Forrestal on the same subject, as planned, it would have to be today, as he was leaving. So at twelve I spent 30 minutes or so with the Secretary of the Navy. He seemed to approve and understand my position; said that Admiral Parsons was the best man he could think of in the Navy; that Patterson had called him on the matter and said that he couldn't think of anyone better than Nichols and that he, Patterson, felt that I had put too much importance on the idea of war planning and execution. Forrestal said that the Navy gave more attention to the technical side because so much of their plans depended upon such matters as steam pressures, etc. He asked me to see Fleet Admiral Nimitz and Admiral Ramsey, Nimitz being Chief of Naval Operations and the Navy Chief of Staff. He was very friendly, took me to Nimitz' office.

Nimitz listened very intently, seemed impressed with my analysis of the primary importance of the Commission's responsibility respecting the "common defense" (a statement which I had also made to Patterson while the news was coming in that the UN Commission had voted "favorably" on the American proposal for atomic control). He asked me to have lunch with him, which we had in the Chief of Naval Operations' mess. A very fine luncheon indeed, with filet mignon, which he felt required explaining. Admiral King sat on Nimitz' right, I on his left. King is a quiet, poised man, impressive-looking. After lunch we finished our conversation. Nimitz suggested Parsons' name, subject only to a check to see if Parsons would permit it to be submitted, since it would change his entire Navy career.

Then Wilson and I went to see Van Bush at his house, and told him the same story. He began to think of people at once, in both services, who might fill the bill.

This has provided an important way of discussing such issues with the heads of the military establishments. Where it will come out, however, isn't clear at the moment.

Morris L. Cooke phoned to say that he had heard that McKellar and Taft had agreed on a program of opposing my confirmation. This could be, of course, though it may be only one of the many rumors in which Washington abounds. Strauss saw Taft the other day, and certainly did not tell me, as I am sure he would have, that Taft had any such definite plan in mind. Taft had said that Jenkins of Ohio was raising Ned about me, charging that I was a dictator, etc. Lewis told Taft that if I were, he, Strauss, wouldn't have to work so hard. It is quite conceivable that a formidable opposition will develop. But that will be as it will be.

DECEMBER 22, 1946
AT HOME, SUNDAY EVENING

Baruch has just called. A long talk about the doings in New York. After some preliminaries he asked me if I had seen what Pearson had said; then he read something that said that Acheson and I had told Byrnes that Baruch's insistence on the veto was endangering the peace of the world. I broke in to say that this was a lie, as he probably realized, that I had not seen Byrnes for six weeks. He spent a good deal of time answering my questions about the procedure up there, etc., because I didn't want him to be developing some kind of record about my own views. I did say that I thought it unfortunate that he had retreated from the position of international ownership of the mines to a position of control of ore after it is severed from the ground. He said this had been forced by Mexico, Brazil, Australia, and Canada.

"You'll have to clamp down on these foreigners, don't give them a thing," he said. I don't know exactly what he was referring to, but he was evidently in a jumpy state. He said he wanted the treaty itself to state just what constituted a violation and how that violation was to be punished, whether by an international army or by "concerted action."

I was rather taken aback with Baruch's strong, almost bitter remarks about the British. "The British are in a bad situation, that Government is in a bad shape," he said, and somehow his voice seemed grimly pleased about it. "They are losing India, their home situation is bad."

He concluded by saying that he was going to insist on the American position. "America can get what she wants if she insists on it. After all, we've got it and they haven't and won't have for a long time to come; I don't know how long, but it will be some time."

It may be a most unhappy circumstance that America's fate in this matter is in the hands of a man to whom a period of ten years in the future is longer than in the natural course of events he has much personal interest.

## DECEMBER 23, 1946
### AT HOME ( 10:00 P.M.)

A great day—and I'm very happy tonight. We decided on Carroll Wilson as general manager and he accepted. This is a grand foundation. He has the talents and the character. And the momentum we have developed in the past six or seven weeks will continue. It is fortunate that we moved toward this decision *together* so it leaves only good feeling among us. That part is as important, almost, as the appointment itself. (It is, of course, the President's appointment, but he has told us that he will name whomever we want.)

## CHRISTMAS DAY, 1946

Christmas. Both the children home. In a new home, off on a new adventure. We had a Christmas tree, the smallest one I think since Nancy's "first" one, the little one on the bookshelf in the little apartment on 67th Street in Chicago, a couple of weeks before she was born. But I strung the lights, we all marveled when they worked, David's height now made him the fellow who put the bird at the top, the same bird we've had for years and years. In the morning, instead of the kids getting us up at dawn, and our groaning about it, we all slept late, and then we waited and waited downstairs before David finished his leisurely shaving, etc., and finally came to join us—a handsome rascal and somewhat above such things. I handed out the presents, read the little verses (Nancy's doggerel now added to Helen's). Now I can hear them downstairs talking and laughing together, David's voice quite deep and resonant. They do enjoy each other, those kids, and each of them, separately, commented on it to their Mother. David's conclusion was that this was a rather good family to grow up in.

I like this little room, the "study." Sunny, great trees outside, books around. Will we ever have a home of our own?

## DECEMBER 29, 1946
### AT HOME, SUNDAY

Sent a letter to Baruch yesterday, saying that, "hinting" in the public prints and otherwise to the contrary notwithstanding, I was supporting the "American proposals." He is running into a surprising amount of critical opinion for his insistence on nailing down the veto-on-punishment issue. This is the thing we urged him against at the Blair Lee House meeting. He told the President that if that didn't stay in he would resign, so it stayed in. But there is no point whatever in my involving myself in this dispute at this juncture. This is just a phase of what will be a long discussion. There will be some more meaningful issues when they actually begin to do what they should have tried to start long ago, i.e., write a treaty.

Yesterday afternoon we went to a party at Wilson Wyatt's. It is a pity he is leaving public service, and he said he looked forward to private practice with a feeling that it would seem very tame and irrelevant.* Many people there: among them the Richbergs; Tom Stokes; Nelson Poynter of the St. Petersburg *Times,* whom I met for the first time; Leon Henderson, who can be quite a bore with his super-self-assurance and his interminable stories about what he did when he was Price Administrator; Sonia Chase, Stuart's daughter, fine-looking youngster.

Friday afternoon I had a talk with Clark Clifford. Told him of the recommendation of Carroll Wilson, which presumably will be announced Monday. He looked very tired but seemed to want to talk. Asked me to look at his draft of the labor portion of the State of the Union speech. Its tone seems quite good, and I shall urge some stronger statement about the President's stand on catastrophic strikes, and ask him to reconsider the Joint Council idea.† But it is about all that can be said now.

My high opinion of Clifford—formed almost from the first when no one had heard of him—this was only September—continues. I hope this terrible deluge of publicity won't hurt him. It has so often been the kiss of death.

We are approaching the end—"we hope"—on the transfer to the Commission, and I am naturally concerned about it, as I always am about "deadlines." We are pushing toward signing of the executive order for tomorrow or Tuesday! The problems involving international relations can't be completely worked out by then, but they may be far enough along to permit us to go ahead. We are all now clear that there simply must be no further delay in informing the Senate of the background of certain war transactions.‡

* Wyatt had resigned early in December as National Housing Expediter.

† This idea was that industry-wide labor-management councils should be established to make continuous review of problems, instead of waiting for issues to come to a boil at contract negotiation times. This technique had worked well in TVA.

‡ Secret wartime agreements between Roosevelt and Churchill provided that A-bomb work would be carried on in the U.S. under American direction, and that the U.S. would not use the bomb without British consent. The U.S. also agreed to

I am rather tired, and my back still gives me some trouble, enough so that I can't do anything by way of exercise. But I am going through hard and long days, one after another, that would have laid me out in TVA. I mustn't keep this up too long, but I see no let-up for at least two months more. By that time the Senate confirmation problem will be behind us, and organization work will be well along. Until then I must somehow make it, tired or no, back or no back.

TVA seems very far away, but what I learned at its expense is never far from the way I do things. And I feel greatly reassured by my performance in two particulars especially: I find I can do a job of organization, and think in organization terms (this I didn't have to do in TVA for years and years, because it was in such good managerial hands, some of the best), and second, I seem to be able to "take it." The real test of this lies ahead, but I have acquired quite a lot of confidence, based on the last two months.

There is also reassurance in the feeling that I am not empty of ideas, that is, that I had only a set TVA tune and couldn't develop new ideas. I am beginning the business again of writing notes about all sorts of new things to get started. One that interests me the most is the problem of informing the American people of what lies ahead for them as a result of the entry of this new source of energy and means of learning about the world. I think a great deal can be made of the part-time "thinking squadron"—a variation of the advisory committee. In this way we can draw upon the cream of the crop in America. If we prepare for it, this can have a profound effect on what is superficially called "public relations."

NEW YEAR'S EVE, 1946
AT HOME

What a year *this* has been!

And it came to a close with a flourish this afternoon, so far as I am concerned, in the President's office, where I sat beside him while he signed the transfer order, to the clicking of news and movie cameras.

We set the target for a January 1 transfer about a month ago. At that time it just didn't seem possible to make it, but going on my old theory that getting way out on a limb is the best way to get things done, we announced that as our purpose. Then all kinds of difficulties intervened: the raw materials complications with the State Department,

cooperate fully with the British and Canadians in post-war atomic energy development. (The "problems involving international relations" referred to in the text included the transfer to the AEC from the Army of U.S. membership on the Allied board for joint procurement of uranium ore supplies.)

inhibitions within the board about this and that, what appeared to be very deep troubles with the War Department about who got what. And yet, one by one the troubles were ironed out, one draft followed another, one conference another.

I got the notion some days ago that the way to bring these to a head would be to persuade the President to make something of a ceremonial of the transfer—which would give a deadline. This was fixed, between Press Secretary Charley Ross and me this morning about 11:30. The hour for the public signing was set for 2:45. I scurried around getting people invited—General Groves, Nichols, Patterson. At 2:10 Ed Huddleson, one of our wonderful young lawyers, phoned from the Department of Justice that the best he could do on a snarl-up there was thus-and-so. I told him to take it, and get a document for signing to the White House or our name would be mud. At 2:46 Judge Patterson arrived at the White House, at 2:47 the President was settled at his desk, and we were arranged in our places, and at 2:48 Judge Latta, White House clerk, walked in with the order—the "papers" of the old melodrama—which I looked at in a hurry, and at 2:50 the doors of the President's office admitted the photographers and we were off.

What a year it has been, I say. Helen and I got back from our wonderful Mexican trip about January 11. On the 14th, as I recall, Dean Acheson called me to Washington, and in a week I was launched on what has quite changed the course of my life, if not some things much more important still. Today the substance of our "plan," which we thought would never see the light of day, much less be adopted as American policy, is probably the principal item of importance in international discussions, in the New York negotiations.

While I was in Mexico a request came from James Newman, counsel to the McMahon Committee, inviting me to testify before the committee on my return from Mexico. I sent word that I would not do so as I knew nothing about atomic energy—which was certainly an understatement. This was in January. In March our report was top news in atomic energy. And tonight I am the head of a vast enterprise in that field. It is a strange and interesting world, at that.

God grant that in the coming year I may by a bit lessen the cloud of dread and fear that hangs over the world since Hiroshima. For I am sure that if we have some wisdom and patience, and divine guidance, we will find, we mortals, that the cloud has indeed a lining of silver. And my other wish is that I may be humble in the doing of the heavy but exhilarating tasks I have to do.

# III

# THE ATOMIC ENERGY YEARS

# 1947

JANUARY 3, 1947
HOME

Handed President Conant a "diploma" this morning—his Presidential commission as a member of the AEC's General Advisory Committee —saying that I gave it to him "with all the privileges and headaches appurtenant thereto." I told him I hoped he would, in two years, be doing as much for our son.

Lunched in a terrible little cafeteria in the War Department building with Enrico Fermi and I. I. Rabi, two Nobel Prize winners in physics. To have spent the day with Fermi is like saying that one spent the day with Copernicus or Galileo or the primitive who discovered fire.

JANUARY 5, 1947
SUNDAY NIGHT

David is restless. He can hardly wait until the end of the month, when he takes off for Harvard. He will be setting out on a jaunt in a few days; where he is going he hasn't told us and I haven't inquired. I know how much of a kick he gets out of his independence, and to have to tell where he is going might make it seem less like an adventure.

He has told me, in one way or another, several times lately: "I am 19. You can't possibly know what that is." But tonight he relented, because I haven't argued but rather agreed—how can your generation possibly understand another, quite? So he said, just a few minutes ago, rather fondly, I thought, "Do you remember how you were when you were 19?" Yes, I thought I could pretty clearly: I worked on the Gary *Tribune*, doing the rewrite on wire reports on the last drive of the Allies across France; I lived in a barracks at DePauw; I remember the Armistice; I didn't find enough to do in classes, so I did a lot of other things—campus politics, a big play, and so on. I must have been pretty sure of myself, I said. "I'm sure of myself," said David. "That's fine," I said, "you have every reason to be." The reason part didn't seem important. He wants me to know he feels sure of himself, and, in the way of someone about to run a race, is rather relaxed about it all, he is quite sure. That's good news.

This is Nancy's twenty-second birthday. How well I remember this day—the business at the Chicago Osteopathic Hospital, how worried I was, how I didn't have the slightest interest in the baby at all, hardly listened to Dr. Peckham when he said something, with a sidelong smile in the way he had, about a fine girl—I was really frantic about Helen. Well, she was a fine baby and I became so proud of her as I paraded her around the park that it was worth a man's life if he didn't grin approvingly as I pushed her by in her huge battleship of a brown buggy.

Tonight we are going to dinner at Joe Alsop's; expect the Herbert Agars to be there. I am reading Marquand's latest, *B. F.'s Daughter*, and enjoying it; the fire, the quiet, and a general sense of good feeling inside.


JANUARY 6, 1947
HOME (EVENING)

Ups and downs: That's the way it goes. I felt pretty whipped down tonight, for no very good reason; which is often the case. There are certain kinds of things, though. For example: Elizabeth Dilling, the Red Network lady, gave me some idea of the kind of dirt that will be thrown, by issuing a mimeographed leaflet about the "four Jews" that make up the Atomic Board. An ugly thing. But this sort of thing will happen. And a careless piece of criticism of the Commission from Acheson via Oppenheimer troubled me, though I know Acheson is rather weary and discouraged, and quite doubtful of anything being any good at this stage; nevertheless it bothered me, I must confess. I record these things only because for so much of the time I am exhilarated by this whole experience—the good, the bad, and the difficult—but it is not all that way by a long way.

The party last night was rather fun, though the conversation was by no means remarkable, or witty or special, particularly. It was at Joe Alsop's Georgetown house; very attractive place. Herbert Agar, back from England.§ Poor man has had a time: five years of the war in London, the loss of his only son in the war, his new wife lost all four of her sons, and then, on top of it all, a thrombosis that has robbed him of the sight of his left eye. Even Job might have groaned over such an assortment of ills. He was so cordial, and so hearty about TVA as a symbol of hope for people everywhere—"You have shown that there is a way," he kept saying, and this made me feel as if I were somehow getting credit not perhaps under false pretenses, but certainly beyond, way beyond, my deserts.

There was the British Ambassador, Lord Inverchapel, a quite thoughtful-looking Scotsman; Francis Biddle and his lovely poet wife; a Mrs. Eustis; and Justice and Mrs. Frankfurter. Later, Ben Cohen and a young newspaperman, Richard Kerr.

The President read his message to Congress today, and tomorrow our nominations go to the Senate.

JANUARY 11, 1947
HOME, SATURDAY MORNING

Last evening Mr. Baruch called me; he was on his way through from his holiday in South Carolina; would I come in to see him in the morning? I have just returned from 40 minutes or so; he left to pay a visit to General Pershing. He looked fine and was in fine spirits.

He made some statements that were new to me.

1. Byrnes and the President strongly urged him to begin the negotiations at the UN Commission simply by presenting the Acheson-Lilienthal Report as a basis for discussion. This he refused to do, he said: "We needed a program." No comment from me.

2. He said he made up his mind to resign [as U.S. delegate to the UN Atomic Energy Commission] rather suddenly, on a "hunch." It was about Wednesday of last week. His associates asked why he shouldn't let it go until Monday. "No," he said, "when I make up my mind to something I want to do it right away. Good thing I did," he said. "I called up Jimmy Byrnes on Friday." (This would be the 3rd of January.) "He said, 'Well, if that's what you think you ought to do, send it along.' He didn't plead with me to stay on. I thought that was strange and that something was wrong. Good thing I hurried with it, because if I had waited until after he resigned it would have looked bad."❡

§ Agar had been with the U.S. Embassy and was director of the British division of the Office of War Information.

❡ Baruch's resignation was announced on January 4, only three days before Byrnes'. (General George C. Marshall succeeded Byrnes as Secretary of State, and Baruch's responsibilities fell to Warren Austin, the U.S. representative on the Security Council. Later, Austin's deputy, Frederick Osborn, took the American seat on the UN Atomic Energy Commission.)

3. He commented about Byrnes. "I have known him all his life, but he never would talk things out with me. Never told me what was in his mind." Sounded rather sorry for himself.

4. He talked rather warily about Acheson, but said several things to make me understand that he knew that Acheson had a "private opinion" that Baruch's pressing the veto and punishment matters was a mistake. "No one should have private opinions," he said. He referred to the Blair Lee meetings "that Saturday" (the Old Boy has a terrific memory), which was when Acheson and several others expressed themselves against the idea of injecting the broad veto and sanctions question into the negotiations. "I didn't have my mind made up at that time," he said. He explained his reasons better than I have heard them. Article X of the League of Nations, Wilson said, was the "heart of the League." If that had been in effect, Mussolini couldn't have invaded Abyssinia, and Hitler wouldn't have gotten started. That was the great mistake we made, and we should not make it again. "And I didn't want anyone to fail to understand the importance of punishment as a part of this program—no use waiting until later, and then spring it on them. That's why I insisted on it. And if we remain firm, they will come through."

5. Whenever the British or the other countries on the UN Commission would appear to waver or to be critical of his pushing for a decision now, or pressing the punishment issue, he would say, "Do you want me to give the bomb to Russia?" and that would stop them. They are scared to death of Russia, especially in Europe. And the one thing they know keeps Russia from overrunning Europe is our possession of the atomic bomb.

Continuing about Acheson: Baruch said that at one time, a year or so ago, when he knew that Byrnes was considering retiring, he recommended Acheson as Secretary. He also recommended him for a place on the Supreme Court. He gave me to understand that if Acheson had not appeared to differ with him on the atomic program, he might be Secretary today. No comment, by word or, I hope, by facial expression, on this one.

6. Two Senators had told him they were going to vote against my confirmation. (I broke in to say that was fine, as that was the only way I could honorably get out of a terrible and onerous job—though, of course, I don't believe this and naturally neither did he.) But he said to them, "Lilienthal is all right; you can count on that." So they said, "Well, if you say so, then we will vote for him."

7. He tried to explain his reasons for resigning, but they were not too clear. As I got it, it was like this: "I had reached the end of the furrow" (this was the same expression he used in telling me over the phone some weeks ago that the reports that he planned to resign were

wrong, that "I have put my hands to the plow and I will keep them there until the end of the furrow"). The next stage would be in the Security Council. "*There* would be Austin" (he demonstrated with his hand) "and here I would be" (gesturing at a lower level) "and we would get badly mixed up, back and forth." Just why wasn't made particularly clear.

At this point Karsh, the famous portrait photographer, arrived, and Helen and I spent hours and hours before his camera here in the house —upsetting the whole place. But a very interesting time really.

## JANUARY 17, 1947

"Senator Austin terrifies me. 'I can handle the Russians.' God! Famous last words."

This was Dean Acheson in his office yesterday afternoon, where I went on a number of matters of top secret business, recorded afterward in a memorandum to the Commission. Dean was as tense as I have ever seen him, and so worried-looking that his usual dry humor, even the sour variety, wasn't forthcoming. With pressure being brought that General Marshall should not continue him as Under Secretary, with the atomic bomb business so badly fouled up, it's no wonder.

He wants to "liquidate" the Baruch chapter, he said, but how to do it? Someone must be found so that Hancock can be replaced, and he hasn't been able to think of anyone (except Oppenheimer) who knows the subject and has "a feeling for international relations." We must talk about it later, he said.

## JANUARY 26, 1947
### HOME, SUNDAY

What a time we are having!

Tomorrow morning I appear before the Senate part of the Joint Committee on Atomic Energy, to establish that I am that paragon of all the virtues and wisdoms: a "qualified" Chairman of the AEC. If they ask me if I consider myself "qualified," I am tempted to say, "Hell, no. And any man who thinks he is really qualified for such a fantastic responsibility proves by that admission that he isn't qualified."

Meanwhile McKellar has been warming up in preparation for me by keeping on the front page and filling hour after hour before the Public Works Committee on Gordon's nomination as TVA chairman. "Communism," that's the theme, as one might guess, and he has been having a field day reading eight- and nine-year-old Dies Committee investigator reports, etc. These are intended to show: (a) that TVA was a hotbed of Communism; (b) that Clapp did nothing about them; (c) that I recommended Clapp. Ergo: one so friendly with Communists cannot be trusted with the great "secrets."

I have just talked to a Catholic friend of mine in Richmond who says he will see that the Catholic Committee of the South award to me is called to the attention of the committee. That's the simplest answer. But there are others. Joe Starnes is coming up to testify next week that as a member of the Dies Committee in charge of the investigation of TVA he found things in good shape and that Clapp handled the situation admirably.

Friday morning I had a conference that put us over a hurdle I have been fearing for months. It was with Comptroller General Warren. I never had more admiration for the breadth of judgment that a man can get by being a legislator and a good human being, as compared with the narrowness and arbitrariness that some people get from being "experts"—in this case accountants. The report being prepared in the General Accounting Office that was going to be so critical, and under present circumstances, so dangerous to the TVA's good name, will be so modified that it will do us no harm, and may even do a good deal of good, for it will contain statements of praise in respect to management.

I can't deny I have been worrying some about the coming confirmation ordeal, and fuming a bit under the kind of stuff that the papers carry on the McKellar business. And it is undeniable that I am tired, added to which my damned back is kicking up again. But I will get through this, and creditably, I am sure.


JANUARY 27, 1947
OFFICE

The hearings opened this morning. Much flashing of bulbs and crowding around. It is now by no means clear whether before the hearings are over we shall find it necessary to ask that our names be withdrawn. For Senator Vandenberg insists that it was the intention of Congress that the Military Liaison Committee sit with the Commission in its meetings, and the position of Senator Hickenlooper is that members of the Joint Congressional Committee's staff also sit with the Commission in its meetings. We can hardly see how this is workable, and yet we would be held responsible for the results.

This is no time to get downhearted—too early—but one wonders what it is in a man that makes him willing to risk his name, his health, and his chance of a decent way of living to get into such an impossible setup.

JANUARY 28, 1947
HOME

What a world of difference in twenty-four hours!

This afternoon I took the stand, and by the time I left it an hour later the tide had turned completely. It was done largely by the device I believe in so completely—taking the offensive, and believing deeply in something and showing it.

But all morning I worried and worried with my brethren about whether, if pushed right up against it, I should admit that we would somehow try to work under the proposal put forward yesterday so vigorously by Vandenberg, Millikin, and Knowland. And by the time things had gone very far it was clear that they were ready to back away from their proposal in its raw form, and I had switched the issue by an attack on existing security control.* I had the chance I wanted to discuss "management" and how our organization depends upon the development of a "fraternal spirit."

McKellar is yet to come. But my guess is I am as good as confirmed tonight.


JANUARY 29, 1947
HOME

My testimony of yesterday was, of course, quite a splash on the front pages this morning. And, of course, the point I was trying to make wasn't clear in all the reports. But the essential point was made, and we are no longer holding quite as big a bag as we were. There will be a reaction—and a rather unhappy one—from the scientists, partly because of the way the story was headlined. I stepped on some toes— Groves, probably President Conant—but I'm not going to explain things or backtrack. Bacher says he wouldn't have been quite so emphatic, but he doesn't disagree with the point. Volpe apparently was rather jolted, but seemed all right this morning. Herb [Marks] was greatly pleased; thought it was right, and that evidence would prove that there is a philosophy beneath the remarks made. Of course, it was the denunciation of the Smyth Report that was singled out—which is a distortion of my point, but helped make it. Tomorrow McKellar.

* The three Republican Senators had insisted that the Military Liaison Committee attend all AEC meetings. This in part reflected a belief that civilians would not be as tough on security matters as the military. I countered by declaring that the security system we had inherited from the Army was not good enough. What the press headlined was my remark that the Smyth Report—the official Army report on the bomb, released under Groves' authorization—was "the principal breach of security since the beginning of the atomic energy project."

JANUARY 29, 1947

There has been quite a tempest over my testimony of yesterday, chiefly over the reference to the Smyth Report. Of course, it wasn't understood entirely. But I am not worried. We had to crack the situation, and it certainly worked to stop the hysteria that was being developed that the civilian Commission can't be trusted with the "secret." President Conant, I hear, is quite angry, which is too bad; the Smyth Report is a sacred cow with him. But the point I am trying to make will get over in time if we keep hammering at it.

There is great laughter in the hearing room every time McKellar's future appearances with me are referred to by the chairman, and much amusement over his question about the Macedonians, etc.† But I don't think it is funny; I will be very glad when it is over, for he can be so ugly and mean that it is not always easy to stay relaxed; and one slip of anger or a wisecrack and I could be in considerable Dutch.

Bill Waymack was on the stand this morning; made a fine impression, I believe. He got off into international control, and I was worried that it might get pretty deep, but he managed to get out of the holes, and to give a feeling of candor and openness that a more prudent attitude might not have given. He got one off for the books. Senator Johnson made a speech about how we had to economize; how much waste he had seen at Oak Ridge (how he knew it was waste wasn't explained, but I am sure his constituents would like the speech); and then he asked, "Now will it be your purpose to cut expenses to the bone?" Bill said the usual things about making every dollar go as far as possible, etc., and then said, "The difficulty, Senator, is that in this field it's hard to know where the bone is."

We are having fun kidding about the figures of speech employed by our boys. Sumner [Pike] drew a picture of a prehistoric man first seeing fire, and using a burning stick to chase his enemy over the hill, thinking that this was the only use for fire; today we use it in steam boilers, etc. Well, the picture of that gentleman urging his naked pal over the hill with a flaming torch gave us much fun. And Lewis [Strauss] added his. Asked how close we should be with the Military Liaison Committee, he said, "We ought to live in the same suit of clothes."

† On the first day of the hearing, McKellar declared that "Macedonian scientists" under Alexander the Great had been the first men to try splitting the atom. He then proceeded to give General Groves credit for discovering the secret that had eluded mankind for 2,000 years, and asked why Groves had not been left in charge of his discovery. (McKellar was not a member of the Joint Committee, but had been extended the unusual privilege of asking questions.)

JANUARY 31, 1947
HOME

McKellar didn't bother me at all this morning. Everyone gave me credit for holding my temper, but I don't really deserve any. I was more relaxed on the stand, looking up at him as he peered at me, than I have been awaiting it for these several days. The newspaper boys have invented a new expression: "The patience of Dave." But this will go on for days and days. The old boy will wear everybody out; the other members of the committee are terribly fed up already, and wondering how they are going to stop him. It will be rather a disgrace to the Senate if he holds things up for a couple weeks with this sort of stuff.

First press conference this afternoon: introducing Colonel McCormack, our wonderful new Director of Military Applications. Secretary Patterson came, at my invitation. Told me he was considering appointing General Groves to the Military Liaison Committee—what did I think? I was flabbergasted and asked time to consult my associates. An hour or so later he called to say it had already happened. This is pretty bad; it will start the whole civilian vs. military issue all over again. Let's hope something happens to save us somehow.


FEBRUARY 2, 1947
SUNDAY AFTERNOON

Last night I went to the Radio Correspondents' Annual Dinner at the Statler. I had a good time and an interesting one. The "good time" was due largely to the entertainment, which was excellent: Paul Whiteman leading his orchestra in Rhapsody in Blue, which is still sure-fire; Abbott and Costello in a terribly zany but side-splitting sketch about baseball (who is on first base, etc.); "It pays to be ignorant"; a beautiful singer, Patrice Munsel, an operatic singer who had more than a voice; and best of all, Henry Morgan giving out with a wonderful line: a report of the people to "labor," i.e., Congress, etc. This he did without script, and it was wonderfully well received. A more intelligent audience than at the Gridiron dinners, I would say, generally.

The interesting part was due to the fact that I sat next to Edward R. Murrow ("*This* is London . . ."). He talks with the same distinctive accent he uses in his broadcasts. And a man of great comprehension and a wide spectrum of understanding of the world these days— particularly the relation between European culture and the United States. What he said about TVA was moving: "Ernie" Bevin had asked him questions about it for two hours. To many people in England and on the continent, rather fed up with United States speeches, TVA is a living symbol—and at the moment the only concrete evidence of what they had always thought of as the "American dream." I talked atomic energy to him some, too; said I was against the idea of building up a big press section and of taking or requesting a good deal of time on the air, etc.—that the educational work ought to be done by existing educational agencies and not the Government—the schools and universities, the press and radio, the churches, etc. He was agreed on this. Said he would organize a small group of leading radio commentators with whom I could talk things over whenever I felt ready for it.

Baruch phoned me last evening. He was going before the committee Monday to tell them what a "bad boy you are." Seemed quite friendly. I always wonder what he has on his mind when he calls, because often he doesn't say. This time I judge it was to say that—or rather put me on notice that—he still didn't like the idea of Herb Marks, and that General Farrell would have been better than Wilson. But we joked back and forth—I try to keep our conversations on that plane. He said he believed Austin (Senator, that is) would not permit the Russians to get atomic energy sidetracked by the general disarmament talk, and that is encouraging, for it would be a great mistake.

This Sunday morning our General Advisory Committee met with us again. It was rather dramatic, for it began by their formal request for certain very highly secret information needed in their work. I had General Brereton there, and said the Commission had agreed to supply the information, within a plus or minus 20 percent, and asked General Brereton to comment; he concurred. Then I stated that the information was to be imparted by word of mouth, by Bacher, and no notes were to be taken. The staff was sent out and the recital made, in the huge, three-story-high, paneled conference room with its long table.

Although everyone, almost, that I saw at the party last night, and at a cocktail party at the Phil Grahams beforehand, said I had "done noble" in my passage with McKellar, it keeps running through my mind, and I experience a certain concern about resuming it tomorrow. I am sure that the outcome will be confirmation and general approbation of the way I am handling myself; but I keep "making up" questions in my mind, and then, in my imagination, answering them. This does not let go and is a nuisance. I feel somewhat more strongly than I wish I did a resentment against the kind of printing and reprinting that newspapers give the sort of terrible smear stuff that is going on in Clapp's hearing particularly. And it does have a bad effect; not one that cannot be lived down, by any means, but it doesn't help. I am inclined to think, though, that on the whole the attacks on me by McKellar—because everyone knows the kind of a boy he is—do me considerably more good than harm.

I wish I could tell now—while it is fresh in my mind—just how one feels when he takes the witness chair, with the room rather tensing and sniggering about it; or the feeling one has under the Old Man's rather baleful look as he leafs through his papers and begins to ask questions, questions that usually are speeches directed to the news-papers, and which when I answer make him quite impatient—that not being what he wants. This hearing is quite different from the usual ones with him, however, in this: that the chairman‡ will protect me if the Old Boy won't let me answer—his past habit—so I can take my time and divide the questions up—he usually puts two or three questions into a single one, and with an assumption or two in every one—and answer them or deny the assumptions. The record reads very well—a good stenographer—but chiefly it reads well because I have this assurance that the chairman will give me a chance to say my say without harassment.

President Conant called me aside at the recess of the General Advisory Committee meeting this morning. "Carroll has told you that I was upset about what you said in your testimony about the release of the Smyth Report. I have read your full testimony and I continue to feel the same way about it. What you may not have understood was this: that McMahon's question to you was part of the line of the dissenters among the scientists in the Manhattan Project, led by such fellows as Szilard. Their purpose is to discredit Bush, Groves, and myself for the conduct of the work, and since they can't criticize the results—because the bomb did work—they concentrate on such things as the Smyth Report. You didn't realize that McMahon had set a trap for you with that question. Now you did say that 'it may have been necessary,' but your answer nevertheless supported their efforts to discredit us. I don't think that was your purpose at all. After you are confirmed I suggest you make a fuller statement making clear what I believe to be your purpose and clearing up your statement about the Smyth Report."

I was really quite astounded by this. And I said so; I had no idea that there was a feud of this kind so deep-seated that it would disturb the president of Harvard in this manner and for these reasons. He didn't discuss the problem of security I was trying to make clear, and when I started to discuss it, was not interested. But I suppose there is a great deal of painful history back of all this, history that perhaps I should have been aware of before.

But I still think that even with this it was right to blow the top off the "security" myth.

‡ Senator Bourke B. Hickenlooper had become chairman of the Joint Committee, following the Republican victory in the 1946 Congressional elections.

FEBRUARY 4, 1947
AT MY DESK—7 P.M.

McKellar moved me deeply today, and was responsible for my getting off, quite spontaneously, a statement of my democratic faith, an attack on witch-hunting, and an exposition of what democratic liberties mean, that must have been effective. Senator Bricker, Senator Knowland, McMahon, and half the press table shook my hand fervently; the best statement of the democratic faith they had ever heard, they said. So the half-despair I felt last night has again been changed to hope.

FEBRUARY 5, 1947
AT THE DESK (5:10 P.M.)

I have heard the expression "He awoke to find himself famous." Something like that has happened, quite incredibly, to me, as a result of my spontaneous combustion yesterday afternoon at the hearing. There is all kind of extravagant talk about my statement being like something from Lincoln, etc., and the airwaves were full of it last night, every commentator, I am told. Glad I had the guts to do it.

FEBRUARY 9, 1947
SUNDAY

The Overseas Writers organization has phoned urging me to speak at an important gathering on March 4: Senator Austin, Gromyko. I have declined. This is no time to be appearing to compete with Senator Austin in the international situation. The kind of fame my words about democracy and the individual have given me, momentarily, is a dangerous thing. I must not only remain, genuinely, humble, in the mental attitude of the man whose job it is to serve, not the man on the make, but I mustn't encourage a spiral of publicity that will make others uneasy about me, jealous, or uncertain about my disinterestedness. Publicity and talking too much: I hope that like liquor and other heady things, I can take notoriety with good sense and restraint.

The ways of the human heart and the things that go on in the recesses of the mind are strange and mysterious. My experience this week is a notable example.

Last Sunday I was so exhausted I slept off and on during most of the day, and 14 hours that night. Monday I went to the hearings, troubled by the turn of events about military control (the appointment of General Groves under peculiar circumstances, the pounding the committee had given me on the subject) and rather apprehensive about what Baruch would say to the committee. I knew he would not come out against my confirmation, but beyond that I was none too confident. His testimony condemning complete civilian control, his towering praise of General Groves, the covert attack on Wilson by the staged (with Senator Johnson) endorsement of General Farrell, the committee's "executive session" with Baruch from which we were pointedly and not even too courteously excluded, and then the ordeal of being summoned by the old gentleman, and being forced by my duty to listen to his "explanations"—all of this hit me very hard. (The fact that Baruch was really helpful, on the basis of my assertions of confidence in Wilson, in getting Hickenlooper to call witnesses in Wilson's favor did not, at the time, make this experience any more savory or less unhappy.)

This was the state I was in, then, when I went home Monday night: very weary, rather discouraged, fearing that this would be the way things would go from here on out, with the military cutting the ground out from under us, and the committee harpooning us, telling us who our staff should be, criticizing us for our failure to get things done, and condemning what we did do—an intolerable and impossible situation. And on top of it all, the constant threat of "Red" scares, witch-hunting, spy charges, alarums about leaks, and charges that we had, deliberately or carelessly, lost "secrets" that never really existed in reality. And behind it all the picture of Senator McKellar, hateful, succeeding in creating suspicion against me, and receiving the hearty praise of Baruch before the flashing photographers' bulbs as the climax of the hearing.

I slept badly. I did what I very rarely do any more; had a time of near-panic inside; had a feeling that I might not be able to stand up, nervously. Recalled, for the first time in a long time, the near-crack-up I had in the early months of the TVA, and the exhaustion period during the Morgan row. I was glad that morning came, and yet apprehensive of the day, and that is rare for me these days.

The morning (Tuesday, February 4) was rough; I felt depressed and tired; my back had been kicking up badly again, and I lay down for two five-minute periods to ease it up. I lunched in the rather dismal Interior Department cafeteria, having to stand holding my filled tray for ten minutes because there were no tables. At 1:45 we started for the Hill. I was to go on at 2:00.

I sat back in the audience in the rather small hearing room, the Finance Committee's regular room. President Conant was called, was photographed, told the committee about Wilson, made a good impression but not a very strong one, I feared. McKellar furnished a bit of comedy by asking the distinguished scientist if he had heard of the bomb before Hiroshima, whether he knew that the Macedonians had tried "to split the atom." Conant said some fine things about me, about others of the Commission. He left the witness chair. The chairman called my name.

I pushed my way through the chairs, almost back to back, of the press table, moved the swivel chair away and put a straight chair in its place, put down my manila envelope, nodded to the chairman, and turned to my left to face Senator McKellar, looking down at me from the height of the "bench" that curves in a half-ellipse around the "victim."

I recall feeling relaxed, the inner cautions against losing my temper or composure at anything the Old Man might say apparently functioning. I used to have a sense of repugnance and in the earliest days even of dread of the ordeal; none of this now. I looked the Old Man full in the face. Not a pretty sight, really, but it somehow made it seem easier. This was about a quarter to three or so. A question about TVA ammonium nitrate, how much a ton. I thought I knew the answer, but I knew there was no reason to "recall" something so specific and then discuss my recollection—no, I didn't try to remember such things. A question returning to the birthplace of my parents, a question he had put on the Friday before. Over the weekend I had tried to locate the paper on which Dad had put the names of the villages where he and Mother were born; Helen couldn't find it at home, and Miss Reames hadn't had time to locate it in the office files we brought along from Tennessee. But by consulting a map at home last Sunday, Pressburg I knew to be the city near which were these villages so that I had written into the transcript—"the vicinity of Pressburg."

The Old Man pressed me on this. I felt trembly inside, with disgust at the meanness that he wasn't quite able to expose fully—only by this snide pretense of interest in knowing where my parents were born. My reply had feeling in it; I was dangerously near anger. He dropped it, and I relaxed and had myself in hand. But I was now aroused, a kind of smolder, far from anger or temper, but some emotional tempo quite different, but definitely emotional. Then, with a pleased look on his face, glancing out at the audience and half-smiling as he put the question—the cat just before the mouse is cornered—the generous complacent look when the victim is about to be taken in hand: some taunt about being leftist—Communist.

The stenographic transcript shows that I talked for several minutes, that what I said consisted of sentences that had subjects, verbs, predicates, that began in an ordinary, rather formal fashion, and marched on to a conclusion, that there was a pattern of word order and tempo. But I was not conscious of sentences or form or sequence at all. I remember a signal: Don't just deny; affirm. I remember that I didn't look at him, but squared myself away directly to the table before me, that I looked down and what I said seemed to me talking to myself. I wasn't conscious of a committee, and it was so silent, not a sound except my voice, rather low and without emphasis, going on. It was in me, and I was getting it out. McKellar and the hearing were a long, long way away.

I paused, sat back in the chair, unfolded my hands, said, "This I deeply believe," and sat silent. It was dead quiet, and I now was conscious of the quiet. Then a voice from the bench, before me, on the left of the chairman: Senator McMahon in a solemn voice saying something in praise of what I had said. More silence, and I was becoming self-conscious and fidgety. Then the press table, the audience—I could hear sounds and remembered that they were still there. And then McKellar, looking at his papers, asking a question.§

Later, when he tried to goad me into an attack on Russia I remembered feeling that something so cheap I wouldn't do, and saying something about being willing to be lynched by this hysteria, but what I felt was partly within me and partly a sense that people now understood things better.

When the hearing was finally over—perhaps 4:15 or so—I stood to pick up my papers, and Senator Bricker motioned me to the bench. His eyes were warm and friendly—this man that was sometimes pictured as a fascist figure, and whom I had heard sneer at the President at the Gridiron dinner. He shook my hand: "Don't be too troubled about this slur about your parents; let me tell you a story about a naturalization meeting I spoke to as Governor. My people came to this country in 1710 . . ." and so on, a lovely, gentle story out of the Mary Antin, Carl Schurz tradition, a good tradition. Then the young, athletic Senator Knowland, grasping my hand in his terrific one: "That was the finest definition of democracy I have ever heard in my life; I congratulate you," pride in his face, and friendly. I felt embarrassed, fussed. The newspapermen were crowding up (I later learned it was to get copies of the transcript of my eruption) and said quite kind words: "If it helps any from an ordinary newspaperman," etc. I joined my fellow Commissioners. Lewis said, "That was history; the tide is turned." They were all deeply pleased, and very quiet.

I phoned Helen from the office, saying the hearing had gone all right; I wasn't trying to understate, I just felt good about it, the contrast with the day before. I knew she would be worried, for I had been so whipped down and dubious about being able to stay on, just the evening before.

We, Helen and I, met at Helen Douglas' for dinner, and had a

§ A transcript of my testimony is reproduced in Appendix B to this volume.

pleasant, happy evening; went home early. (The radio was full of nothing else during the evening, but we didn't know it, nor did it occur to us to try to listen—it was just a good day's testimony.) Even when I saw the way the Washington *Post* had handled the testimony—a big double-column bold-face quote in Al Friendly's story—I didn't feel that it was anything more than a good turn of events. I read the quotes at breakfast; it moved me, just the reading. Baruch phoned at eight o'clock; "Now you are doing better."

And then came the telegrams, the telephone ringing all morning, and on the following morning the *Times'* of New York leading editorial. Then came some of the most remarkable letters; the theme that appealed to me the most was in the letters from people I have never seen or known: "You have said what we feel but haven't been able to say." They are wonderful letters. So many refer to others who have defined democracy and say it ranks with them—Lincoln, Jefferson, Tom Paine. I am not sap enough to take this seriously or literally—though the praise in such terms from men like Chester Barnard, etc., not given to extravagance, is wonderfully gratifying. But it came at the right time—when hysteria was on its way to a frenetic pitch, and in a setting made to order—the voice of sanity and the appeal to reason from the pit of the inquisition.

FEBRUARY 10, 1947
OFFICE

At the conclusion of the hearings this afternoon (Dean Acheson, John Lord O'Brian, Walker Cisler were witnesses with an almost full attendance of the committee), Martin Agronsky came dashing up to Senator McMahon and myself. He said there was a report in the Senate Press Gallery that Senator Taft would oppose my confirmation. When I got back to the office, the ticker carried the report that the Republican Policy Committee was considering the matter; that Senator Wherry, Republican Whip, had made a statement opposing my confirmation and urging other Republicans to join, and that Senator Taft would make a statement tonight.

I telephoned Clark Clifford to pass this word on to him. He said that after my call to him this noon he had had a brief talk with the President. He asked me if I had any thought in my mind at all of giving up the fight. I told him that if the President felt at any time that to continue to keep my name before the committee would result in embarrassment to the President, in his relations to the Republican Congress, or in any other way, Clifford was authorized to tell him without previously discussing it with me that I would ask that my name be withdrawn or agree completely with the President's withdrawing it. I said also that I had considered what I would do if the Republican Policy Committee asked me to withdraw my name in the interest of not continuing this controversy.

Clifford said there was only one thing he wanted to know and that was whether I would be willing to go through with it. He said that the President had said to him and asked that he say to me that he was in this fight to the finish; that he was in it if it took 150 years with all the effort and energy he had; that if they wanted to make an issue of this matter, he would carry the issue to the country.

I said the only thing I wanted to be sure of getting clear to the President was: that there is no occasion at all for the President to feel that on the merits any point has been made against me; that the Communist charge or the charge that Communism had gone on in TVA was completely cleared up in the record—a few people in minor positions admitted being Communists, but the vice chairman of the Dies Committee appeared, loudly protesting the charges of Communism in TVA. Furthermore, the press of the country, with the single exception of the Patterson-McCormick papers, has been right down the line in an amazing way and my mail on the basis of my Tuesday's statement has really been beyond belief.

He said all he wanted to know was that I would stick.

FEBRUARY 11, 1947
IN THE SENATE HEARING ROOM

Arthur Morgan is testifying. "That voice" weaker, but the same hesitation in speaking, the same vagueness. This is where I came in. "Dishonest"—the word comes again.

FEBRUARY 16, 1947
AT HOME, SUNDAY

What a week!

I can't spare the time from resting to record it now, even in outline. But it has been a sore trial and yet an exhilarating experience, too.

Sunday night, last, came the first suggestion to the public (though I had heard it predicted as "in the plans" for two months at least) that a real fight was ahead on my nomination. Until then it was just more of the McKellar business, which was a nuisance, but actually an asset to me, etc. Then Bridges of New Hampshire let loose with a blast—an old enemy of the TVA and a low-grade private power spokesman—i.e., spokesman for the lowest of the private utility crowd. On

Monday Acheson, O'Brian, and Walker Cisler, utility executive of Detroit, testified; they were there not because of me, but to clear the record, we hoped, regarding Herbert Marks. Then Wherry, the Republican Whip, a rather noisy and vigorous but not too highly regarded man, cut loose with an attack on me.

The report I had last Friday night that Taft was about to come out against me revived; it was definitely established that he was opposed to me, but whether he would work to bring the Republicans into line wasn't clear. Lewis [Strauss], who had thought he had Taft's early assurance that there was nothing to worry about, was greatly upset, saw Taft, came back with nothing to cheer us up; but no "statement" from Taft, as had been predicted, came along. But it was now clear that a determined fight to defeat me was on. Demands that I withdraw my name began to appear from such men as Congressman Cox of Georgia. The Patterson papers and Hearst began a violent barrage.

On Tuesday night I talked to Helen Hiett of the *Herald Tribune,* and five minutes later Mrs. Reid called me, in the most sympathetic and understanding terms. This would be a major mistake, she said, and a tragic failure by the Republican Party. On Wednesday morning the *Herald Tribune,* leading Republican newspaper of the country, carried a vigorous lead-editorial, "The Test," written by Walter Millis, and making a broad issue of national policy and Republican policy of my nomination. The *Times* of New York had a comparable lead editorial. It was evident that a terrific fight was on.

It didn't look good either. The press throughout the country was extraordinarily favorable, even to the smaller papers, but the country was taken quite by surprise; everyone had assumed that there was nothing to it—that there would be nothing except the usual McKellar rowing. My words about what I believe had stirred a remarkable reception through the country, and beginning in the magazines. The lag between public understanding and the facts of the situation within the Senate was one that might not be overcome. Organizations began trying to reach their members, to get the situation to them, to get letters to the Senate. The Senate leadership on the Democratic side was preoccupied with other things, and did nothing. On Thursday the President stated flatly that he had not the slightest intention of withdrawing my name, and denied the charges that I had Communist sympathies, etc. The radio was full of the subject, chiefly favorable.

Anti-Semitism as part of the opposition began to be somewhat clearer, though it had been there all the time, as we who attended the hearings could see so clearly. Now the big boys' pressure became more visible, the fertilizer crowd, and the power people—some of them at least. The Communist smear having rather discredited itself, partly because of its chief sponsor, the ground was shifted: though not a Communist, if there is a "shadow of a doubt," why select such a man for the most serious and critical body in the country? He is a New Dealer, the country has rejected the New Deal in favor of the Republican Party—why should we have any New Dealers appointed to a vital position? Atomic energy will have great consequences upon business; we should have a man who isn't an "enemy" of business and the private enterprise system. Etc., etc.

Thursday was my "low" day. I had worked hard the night before on the telephone, getting the word around, and answering calls; there were so many things to follow. Arthur Morgan had been on the stand all day and the day before, and this was a distressing experience for me, partly just pain and partly the shame and sorrow that a man could be so filled with hatred and nourish it so long.

I went to see my old friend, Deke Parker of the Scripps-Howard papers. The fire had gone out of this onetime crusader against the Ku Klux, the "young man" of old man Scripps. Cautious, worried about his failing health, what Roy Howard would say. I became a bit worked up—the first time—and warned him that the first victim of this kind of irrational and debased attack might be such a fellow as I am, but before long it would be the newspapers, the bankers; that unless the "stable elements" stood fast at a time of hysteria and fear, they could hardly expect other elements to do so; I told him of the march of 20,000 "fundamentalists" on their radio station in Knoxville, goaded by crass hysteria preachers. (While I was talking with him a call from Miss Reames: "The ticker says that Senator White, Majority Leader, has come out against you—says you can't get along with Congress.") Parker gave me a long explanation of why they hadn't taken an editorial position, and referred, defensively, to the fact that they printed Tom Stokes' columns favoring me. He took notes, but I felt that nothing would come of it; friendly, but not wanting to appear to weaken their stand of opposition to Russia, the New Deal, etc. (It turns out that I was not correct in this; the Washington *News* had a friendly editorial yesterday.) When I left, I was very weary and heavy of heart. I returned to the office for more telephoning, more reading of letters stacked up high from all over, warm, friendly, and excited.

That night I had a spell of jitters—could I stand up under this, nervously, until it was over? It might be weeks. I looked bad—never had I had such dark caves under my eyes.

Friday night I had a kind of spiritual experience that one can hardly write down for other eyes to see, but one I shall never forget. And after that, I slept. Saturday morning I got down Grandma Lamb's◖

◖ My wife's mother, Alma McCluer Lamb.

Bible. I opened it at the place where there was a note from me she had put in the Bible, a typed note thanking her for a Christmas present to me: a set of Sandburg's *Lincoln*. At this point, in Isaiah:

"I the Lord have called thee in righteousness and will hold thine hand. . . ."

And across the page in Chapter 41, the tenth verse:

"Fear thou not: for I am with thee: be not dismayed, for I am thy God: I will strengthen thee; yea I will help thee, yea I will uphold thee with the right hand of my righteousness."

She had marked two passages: the opening verse of the 42nd Chapter:

"Behold my servant whom I uphold; mine elect in whom my soul delighteth. I have put my spirit upon him: he shall bring forth judgment to the Gentiles.

"He shall not cry nor lift up, nor cause his voice to be heard in the street.

"A bruised reed shall he not break, and the smoking flax shall he not quench; he shall bring forth judgment unto truth.

"He shall not fail nor be discouraged, till he have set judgment in the earth: and the isles shall wait for his law. . . ."


Mr. Baruch has just called. He is being most helpful, I really believe. He says Saltonstall and Lodge have acted for me. I hope this is true. If it is, then Baruch's prediction that the nomination will be confirmed by a minimum of 10 and possibly 25 votes would seem to be correct.


A really high point was Nancy's atomic Valentine, which gave me great joy, for its lovely spirit. What pride and satisfaction there is in such a child.

A tormented person needs just what I have had: inner strength and friends and loved ones. These I have, and therefore I will come through.


I certainly can't complain that my nomination fight is going on without the public knowing about it, or having the press against me. And today the most friendly radio comments. Raymond Swing gave it his entire time this morning, a beautiful statement; Shirer gave it half his time this afternoon; this evening Drew Pearson finished his program with a strong plea that the people write their Congressmen. And everyone is making it a very broad issue, so that if we win, it will have been a victory of consequence and helpful in getting the work going; if we lose, at least I will not feel the country didn't hear what is going on, and my prestige will hardly be dimmed.

Talked to my grand old Dad today. He is home. Doesn't bother him, all this tumult, he says.

Slept 12 hours straight last night, and getting as much rest today as I can; this will be a tough stretch ahead.


FEBRUARY 23, 1947
AT HOME, SUNDAY MORNING

This has been *another* week!

Last week, at this time, I was quite worn out, but composed. All day the radio commentators devoted themselves to support of my nomination and discussion of the issue: Swing, Shirer, Pearson. But the outlook did not seem good. Furthermore, I was troubled greatly that though I might squeeze through with the necessary majority, the margin would be so close that I could hardly expect to be effective on the Commission.

This beautiful, bright morning—outside the snow covers everything and cardinals are brilliant and lovely against the white—this morning things look much, much better.

In between this Sunday and last, though, I have lived a good many years, packed in close. I won't repeat the record here, but just the highlights, and how I felt and feel about those top occurrences.

First: I got a notion of how determined and ruthless are those who are fighting me when, on Tuesday morning I think it was, without any notice I heard the chairman call "Mrs. Mead Leitzell," and heard the little thin voice of a typist and stenographer of mine of almost twenty years ago telling the committee from a prepared statement about how she received checks from Commerce Clearing House for me, while I was a member of the Wisconsin Commission.

The point of her testimony wasn't clear, as she spoke, but on questioning by the chairman, who seemed a bit puzzled, she explained that receiving my "salary" (as she called it) was contrary to Wisconsin law. No one asked her how she happened to come (later she told newspapermen that it was "at the instigation of the Hearst papers"). Indeed, it didn't make any particular impression, though a friendly Milwaukee *Journal* newspaperman asked me about it later. I knew that what I had received during that period wasn't "salary," and that the arrangement was entirely proper and regular. But her appearance did worry me a lot, for it gave me an idea of the fine-tooth comb with which "they" were working over my past to search out any possible basis for criticism, or innuendo.*

Another incident that troubles me—just to get in the "subjective" side of this story—occurred on Monday. My friend, Paul Williams of Richmond, came over to me just before the afternoon hearing began. Father O'Connell was sitting at the committee table next to McKellar, while awaiting the opening of the hearing in which he, the Father, was going to tell about the Catholic Committee of the South award to me. "Father O'Connell," said Williams, "wanted me to tell you this. Senator McKellar called a man over to him a moment ago and said to him, 'The *Daily Worker* is endorsing Lilienthal; isn't that magnificent news!' Father O'Connell thought you ought to know this."

For an hour or so I felt very bad; Helen said afterward she thought —she was there that day—that something was wrong, that I looked drawn and worried. By God I was. For this was just the sort of devious tactic the Communists would think of and just the thing they would enjoy for the confusion it would create. I thought to myself, "Well, that will just about finish you." But later I stopped worrying and began thinking—this while the hearing went on in the standing-room-only hearing room. Somehow this move should be anticipated and discounted in advance.

At the time I didn't doubt that it was going to break any time that afternoon. I kept watching newspapermen who came in, to see if they weren't bringing the report to the press tables, which would, I thought, be immediately astir about it. When someone brought a note in to one of the newspapermen, I had a bad turn. I wrote Joe Volpe a note, telling him of the O'Connell report, and asking him to telephone Miss Reames, to ask her to locate the attack made on me and on the State Department Report, contained in the *Daily Worker,* about the time of my Press Club speech; a good memory is a help. . . .

But nothing developed that afternoon. I worried about it some that night, along with other things. Next day the articles were located. I talked briefly to Senator Hill about the possibility of just such a coup. By afternoon he issued a statement, predicting *Daily Worker* or Communist "endorsement," and calling attention to their previous op-

* Commerce Clearing House was the publisher of the legal reporting service on utility regulations I had developed and edited in Chicago. When I accepted the Wisconsin appointment, I did no more work for the service, but for more than a year continued to receive payments. These were primarily to reimburse me for the continued use of my Chicago office until my lease expired, and also to compensate me from current earnings for my past work in building up the enterprise. This arrangement was expressly approved by Governor La Follette prior to my appointment.

position to me. *That* was pretty well spiked. But for a couple of days it was a troubling thing, ranging through the back of my mind. And the Commerce Clearing House thing woke me up one night. So one goes from trouble to trouble; but also from good event to good event.

The high points of the week both came on Friday. At the opening of the morning session Senator Vandenberg, in a deep, resonant voice, said he had received a communication of great importance from an outstanding American. He then proceeded to read a letter from Karl Compton, not only endorsing me, but expressing in strong and non-tactful terms the "disgust and disillusion" of the scientists at the spectacle of the Senate fight. And at the close of the hearings Chairman Hickenlooper read a telegram from the chairman of the Detroit Edison Company, Prentiss Brown, favorable to me and denying that they were opposed to my confirmation. This will probably develop as the definite turn of the tide, for it was taken to indicate Vandenberg's attitude at this stage. He had been friendly ever since the "working over" he gave me on the first day of the hearings on the Military Liaison issue.

That day also saw the biggest gun of the opposition fired. I was at my desk about 6:30 that evening when Miss Reames, frowning and angry, came in and put before me a yellow ticker message: Senator Robert Taft has come out against my confirmation.

This was a kick in the teeth, for I thought he would wait till the committee report reached the floor. Lewis came in, looking very dejected, and saying, "Dave, I have failed you." What he meant was that he had felt that his long friendship with Taft would have held the Senator in check—indeed, at one time Taft had told Lewis that there would be some opposition from Jenkins of Ohio and, of course, McKellar, but that after a couple of days that is about all that would happen. I didn't believe that then, but Lewis apparently did, for he looked as blue as bluing. I said to him, "Well, this means I can't be confirmed"—and that's the way it looked to me as the next section of the ticker came in indicating that the Taft statement was a violent one, on all counts. Lewis disagreed; "It will split my party," he said. "Let's keep up the fight and split the damn party." Of course, these were the words of emotion, but at the moment they reflected his strong feeling. "We'll go into business together; I guarantee you'll make a million dollars in three years." And went out, looking most downcast.

I put my feet up against my desk and felt sunk, for about five minutes. Then I came to life, and haven't felt low or in any doubt of the outcome since. I talked to Bob Duffus of the *Times* and Helen Hiett of the *Herald Tribune*. I read the Taft attack and saw how vague and vulnerable it was. Helen came in. It had begun to snow early in the day, and by this time was snowing like all get-out. We had decided to stay at the Hay-Adams, not go home for the night. What about going to *State of the Union?* she asked. By this time it was nearly eight. We picked up Herb Marks and Joe Volpe, who phoned his wife, and at eight o'clock, we, with Miss Reames, were sitting on stools at a drugstore eating sandwiches. I was in fine spirits again, and vastly enjoyed the play.

Emotionally, the summit of the week came Thursday. A procession of businessmen from the Valley took the witness chair. In a simple, unpretentious way, extemporaneously and with a depth of sincerity that was not lost on the committee or the press, they told about progress in the Valley, about Dave Lilienthal and how the Valley people felt about him. Joe Lane and L. J. Wilhoite of Chattanooga were terribly impressive. Joe Volpe, a very self-contained and controlled fellow, said to someone, afterward, "As I listened to these men I could feel a lump in my throat." I felt enormously proud, and homesick for the Valley, and occasionally weepy. It was like attending your own memorial services though, at times—a strange and not a pleasant kind of experience, that feeling. But I think for the first time Vandenberg and Hickenlooper got a bit of understanding of what TVA was about. I really don't think they had much of an idea before.

Another emotional experience was the appearance of Henry Hart, whose "letter" was a principal prop of the McKellar case.† At times it looked as if it were Henry Hart whose "trial" this was. I had forgotten how he looked; had known him only slightly. He was the very picture of every man's youth, of every man and woman's children: youthful idealism, the conflict between ideals and realities. His candor, his good looks, the contrast with the ugly old McKellar. The whole room was caught by the drama of it. Helen noticed the hard-boiled eggs at the press table, looking moved and touched. Afterward, Marshall McNeil said, "That was something. He had a lump in my throat." Marsh was thinking of his own son, I suppose, as I was, and my own youth.

Saw Van Bush at the Cosmos Club. Friday a week ago he had met with the full Senate committee—this was the "secret" meeting that the newspapermen guessed was for the purpose of asking me (or the President) to withdraw my name. He said he told them the grave consequences of the delay and uncertainty caused by the fight. He must have talked pretty plainly.

† Hart was an idealistic and religious young man who had joined the Communist Party in 1937, when he was about 20, became disillusioned, and left it 18 months later. At that time, he was a minor TVA personnel employee. The "letter," which purported to record Communist activities within TVA, had a mysterious history. Hart denied under oath having written it, and the question of whether it ever existed was never satisfactorily established. It was dated in 1939 and was supposedly seized and photostated in 1940 by a Dies Committee investigator in a raid on Communist headquarters in Birmingham. Neither the original nor photostats were produced, however; merely mimeographed versions.

FEBRUARY 28, 1947
AT HOME (NOON)

Quite a kick in the teeth. A few minutes ago Volpe called to say that the Public Works Committee in a surprise meeting had voted on Clapp's appointment, turning it down 7 to 5. I felt very bad to get this very surprising news. Had I permitted TVA to become subject to wrecker politics, after all the hopes and accomplishments that have been poured into it?

Later reports from Miss Owen indicate that there was apparently some connection between the sudden action of the Public Works Committee and the fight on me, but just what are the reasons, etc., aren't yet known. She felt that it was by no means hopeless, and that TVA has been in worse spots before. But it is tough to contemplate. She just called again to say that McClellan of Arkansas, whose vote could have produced a tie, said he voted as he did because it was "just too much power to give Dave Lilienthal, atomic energy and TVA." Of all the ridiculous alibis for voting with the Arkansas Light and Power Company! He had previously told the Democrats he was voting for the nomination.

I came home yesterday afternoon about four, half sick with an earache and plain fatigue. Got a long sleep—picked a good time for it.


MARCH 1, 1947
AT HOME

Yesterday was another "low"—comparable and perhaps even exceeding the Monday when Baruch testified. The Clapp rejection was just the beginning. Then came word that the committee had decided that open hearings should be resumed so I could be questioned about the Wisconsin commissionership matter, the charge that I had violated the law and ethics in receiving money from Commerce Clearing House while I was on the Commission. McKellar had circulated a letter to every member of the Senate drawing six inferences about this, and, so the word to me indicated, the committee felt that the matter should not go to the floor with the record in a fuzzy shape. As Clark Clifford said this morning, "That is the only place where there was anything that could be remotely described as moral turpitude; so it would not be unreasonable at all for your supporters on the committee to want to have it cleared up even if they accepted La Follette's statement,‡ as I did."

‡ Former Governor La Follette notified the committee that he had known of and had fully approved of the Commerce Clearing House arrangement at the time he appointed me to the Wisconsin Commission.

But it got me down. For I could foresee insinuations, ugly cracks because I couldn't remember every detail, etc. Even worse, I feared that McKellar would begin another filibuster in the committee, calling witnesses all over the place, and thus requiring me to call some, and this would go on and on. I was mad because of the Clapp business, which seemed outrageous, and mean politics, and disgusted at the prospect of another long period of hearings. I was concerned that I would have to start a new series of side excursions in the hearings, which could be used to arouse vague doubts and add to the "shadow of a doubt" theory that is being used as about the last resort of the opposition.

Joe Volpe and I met with Dean Acheson and General Osborn at about 5:30 in the State Department. Osborn, a huge man, was General Osborn during the war, head of the Army Special Services (education, entertainment, etc.). General Marshall picked him the other day to become Austin's deputy in charge of atomic energy matters—the place previously occupied by Baruch. This session lasted an hour or so. Then we returned to my office, where we spent another hour drafting a statement concerning the Wisconsin matter for the Monday hearings. Helen and I sat down to dinner about 8:30.

I was badly agitated and low. How long could I take this? There is a kind of torment about it that is difficult to describe. One hates to think that he hasn't full control, that he is losing his perspective, that his determination and guts may be waning.

I did not sleep well, although I took a pill. But somehow I will make it.

Carl Matson of the Cleveland *Press* called to say that the whole Scripps-Howard outfit was pulling for me, that many people in Cleveland were really working at it, that the betting all was that I would come through.

The thing that sustains me is that I simply cannot let down the people, the wonderfully decent people, who count on me. This is a very real thing to me right now, one of the few things that are real.

This morning Helen and I discussed what I should do if, being confirmed by a close vote after a bitter, ugly floor fight, I had to face the same thing all over again in 1948. Would it be better to resign now, immediately after confirmation, so that the work would not have to be disrupted again in '48, or to try to get it going and then announce several months before new appointments would be due (August 1, 1948) that I would not accept reappointment?

These are the things that go on in the mind of a guy in a tough and important spot.

Reading from the Bible, which I have come to do more and more in recent years, is one of the things that helps. And efforts to draw on strength from beyond myself.

MARCH 4, 1947
AT HOME

Old Man McKellar didn't look so chipper; not at all. Sitting up there on the end of the horseshoe-shaped dais he looked anything but triumphant and sure of himself, the way he looked just a month ago today, in that same room when he was "playing" with me about "your leftist views." That day seemed very dark, when I took the witness chair, but it turned out to be the turning point, for I finally turned on him and got out of my system the statement of my beliefs that hit the country hard.

But today he looked old and fuddled. He had a bad day yesterday, lost his temper, got really mad at my quips, shocked the committee with the ugliness of his attacks. He had insisted that he had other questions to ask. The committee voted to give him this morning, and that was to be absolutely the end. I was set for a full morning of it; I guessed that about 11:45 he would start a wholly new line of questions or subject, and then when he was cut off would howl to high heaven that the committee was trying to protect me, to hide something that the country had a right to know, etc.

He started reading a question; it was a question he had asked me yesterday, and I said so, suggested that he go down the page—these absurd questions written out for him and he hardly able to read them. The questions were pretty much the same as yesterday. He asked a question about this "unprecedented flood of letters" that all Senators had been receiving in my behalf, was that something my propaganda machine was responsible for?§ A question about international bankers supporting me, a question about CIO supporting me (which gave me a chance to say that TVA was an almost entirely AFL outfit). A silence. He didn't like these long answers in which I made a good record continuously better. A last question: Did I know Justus Schlichting, president of the Commerce Clearing House? I pulled myself together—was this something new?

Then: "That is all the questions I have, Mr. Chairman."

Senator Knowland, presiding, didn't lose any time. The open hearings are adjourned. What a relief. The long ordeal was coming to its end.

The first closed session was held this afternoon. It was rather

§ The Joint Committee's tabulation of letters and telegrams showed 2,604 in favor of confirmation and 445 opposed.

disheartening. Given over entirely to criticizing us for our salary scale, departing from that prevailing in the Government generally. Two and a half hours of just this. Vandenberg didn't say a word, but I thought he was pretty disgusted. Millikin said, "What is there about this undertaking that requires special legal talent, what is there that isn't just routine?" Hickenlooper went after us, time and time again, about the disturbing effect these above-$10,000 salaries would have on other Government positions. We didn't do too well by our case, and Carroll Wilson's first effort as a witness was, understandably, not too effective.

After 2½ hours of this, and nothing else, I felt pretty discouraged. But as I thought about it my courage came back. We have a job of education to do; the country must be made to understand, as I think it can be, that this is a special and terribly complex undertaking, and that we must have unusual latitude to work it out. If we can persuade the public of that—and with the press we got during this fight I don't see why we can't—then Congress will come along.

The hearing yesterday was under the Klieg lights. I was apprehensive: I didn't know whether my statement about the Wisconsin thing would be met by taunting and sneering questions, whether the questions would lead into all kinds of things that could be made to appear ugly. It went very well indeed. McKellar gave up quickly along that line, the other committee members seemed to be little interested beyond the statement I had rather carefully prepared. Then the old man went off on a remarkable, but for me wonderful tack: that I was the darling of the "magnates." I had a chance for a number of cracks that brought laughs but not disrespectful to him, and this for the first time made him bull-mad. He roared, the veins on his forehead stood out, his eyes were red and looked tiny and fierce as he came at me time and again. The *New York Times* leading editorial this morning was headed "Outrageous is the Word," a title taken from a remark the press overheard Vandenberg make at one stage in the attack.

Yesterday I had an interesting 45 minutes in my office with Ed Murrow. I talked to him about two troublesome matters: (1) My concern that the technique used in the attack on me would become standard practice, revealing a terrible state of public mind beneath the respectable surface; and that I felt that the commentators, the press, and all those concerned with stability in the community must expose this danger—that this was more important than the immediate issue concerning my nomination. He confessed that his experience abroad confirmed my fear that this was an ominous thing. (2) Was the damage done by the attack—and that which will come in the next ten days or so as the nominations are the subject of a floor fight—so great that in the interest of the atomic energy program I would have to resign, after being confirmed? He is a very thoughtful fellow, and an impressive one. It is wonderful to feel that there are so many men of this caliber who are glad to visit with me about matters of this kind, and who will go to bat, if they can find some way to be helpful.

MARCH 8, 1947
AT HOME, SATURDAY

Life is just one "crisis" after another. I marvel that I don't fall apart. Must confess I did have a temporary case of fright this morning—about an hour—but I have it in hand now.

But the story really goes back to late yesterday afternoon (Friday).

Thursday afternoon we appeared again before a closed session (but by no means secret, I would guess) of the committee. FBI reports on certain people were discussed. One young lawyer had written into a passport application some amendment—something to the effect that he would defend the Constitution "according to the dictates of my conscience" or something of the sort. There was a statement by some unknown "informant" that the same fellow had suggested getting something into evidence by a roundabout way. Someone else had a brother who was a Communist. This created an extraordinary furor: Senator Bricker couldn't understand why the minute such reports came in the people were not gotten rid of immediately. Senator Knowland, Chairman Hickenlooper showed agitation. I didn't enjoy it, and neither did my associates. We could see how use would be made of such items to spread fear and how it could get the whole question out of focus.

But yesterday was a relatively good day. The committee had announced a meeting for the morning and that it expected to report the names out. The word was that there might be a unanimous vote, favorable to the nominations. I had four hours with Palmer Hoyt, publisher of the Denver *Post,* whom I had asked to come on, some two or three weeks before, in a long telephone conversation. We talked about my theme question: How can we awake the country to what atomic energy means, short of hysteria? Bill Waymack was in the discussion much of the time; there was good talk, reassuring, impressive. The importance of what I had undertaken to do, Hoyt's confidence that I could do it, the illumination the chance to chew things over with him had given: all these things helped.

The ticker was brought in; the committee had not voted after all. They expected to Monday. Some Senators wanted more information. This was disturbing, somewhat. I called Senator McMahon about another matter, hoping he would tell me what was wrong, if anything.

He did. They heard Van Bush urge speed, etc. Then when he left, Bricker exploded. He had decided he couldn't vote for me. He couldn't understand the reason for some things: Why did we have this man from TVA who had this "bad" record; what about this man with the Communist brother? What about these widely varying reports about another man?—ranging from the highest praise to such strong condemnation. Were disloyal people being "infiltrated," etc.? He wanted time to think it over further.

I sent for Volpe, Wilson, and Marks. Volpe said the newspapers already had the report—a man from the *Herald Tribune* had it, wasn't going to use it, didn't seem much news to him. But this meant that the Hearst papers would certainly spread it all over. These "confidential" FBI reports, were they being leaked, would they be spread on the public records, without a man having a chance to defend himself against the charges of anonymous "informants"? There was some pretty excited talk. I found myself becoming calmer by the minute, and offhand—a strange thing that happens to me when other people get rattled.

That night I talked to a man who had spent the evening with Hickenlooper. He found the latter fair, considerate, not too disturbed; still hopeful of a favorable vote by Monday. So after a disturbed evening I went to bed thinking, "Ah, now I will have a restful weekend, so I can stand what comes next week, whatever it may be."

But this was not long-lived. At eleven o'clock this morning a call from our security officer, Jones. J. Edgar Hoover had sent me a long report on an important scientist: his brother a former Communist, his wife had had radical associations, in her first marriage. Why did Hoover pick this particular moment to send this along, the man being one who had been connected with the Manhattan Project from the outset?◖ Was this part of a scare campaign? The air would be filled with this sort of thing. Could hysteria be avoided? Would we be so troubled by it ourselves that we would become so cautious, so unwilling to take necessary chances that the work would be stalled?

Called Van Bush. He appeared in a closed session yesterday morning. Said the committee had heard some strong stuff from him before, at the time when things looked bad because McKellar had really made headway, and they wanted some of this "on the record" so it could be used in the floor fight. Bush seemed optimistic. Apparently he had heard rumors about the subject of the FBI report that Hoover had sent to me today, for he asked about it; said he and General Groves had known all about that, had decided it was no reason not to use the man, and had never regretted it. This made me feel somewhat better.

◖ This was Robert Oppenheimer.

Tough going, this business. But if it is important to the country and the future of our children and other people's children, then I mustn't turn soft, and above all I mustn't get rattled.

It has been so long since I have thought of normal, wholesome things, like things growing, and the troubles of everyday people, that it is no wonder, perhaps, that I am not entirely in focus. But this surely will be over one of these days, and then a little holiday, and then back to the daily "crisis" or two. I am sure I shall toughen up—already have, in fact, and will be able to take it. Inside of me I am really pretty tough and plenty stubborn, I hope.

MARCH 9, 1947
AT HOME, SUNDAY

Since the first of November I have been deprived of one of my greatest joys: out-of-door activity, exercise, riding, walking. That damn back picked a very poor time to go haywire. So yesterday was a kind of landmark. Nancy and I had a walk in the woods, through the snow, with [our cocker] Penny gallumping hither and thither in great excitement and flopping of long, red ears. It made us think of Palos days, when Nancy was a baby, a round, roly-poly, little girl, and we went for walks on the "kement kapavement" as she called it; and I took a stick and drew pictures of Kathleen the Elephant and others of our private menagerie for her entertainment—and mine. As we were plodding through the woods, Nancy broke through the snow crust with a strange sound—beneath was a pretty good-sized slab of tin, which was startling for the moment. Said she, in the spirit of the occasion, "A Pooh-trap for Hefalumps." It brought back Milne and Palos and her childhood. I can remember her at four, but not her father then, very well.

Last night Helen and I were dinner guests of the Acting Secretary of State, Dean Acheson; the other guests were George Kennan and his wife. It was very pleasant. Dean had shown me some of Kennan's long and thoughtful dispatches from Moscow, where he has spent some five years. Very influential man, really, just by the power of his analyses and the fact that he has had perhaps as good an opportunity to observe Russia and the Communist politicos as anyone in this country. He is back now, and rather full up with Russia, to teach at the War College. Dean says he has induced him to come back into the Department of State to help in setting up planning and research.

A quiet, rather academic-looking fellow, about 40, I should say. Bald, slight, not impressive except for his eyes which are most unusual: large, intense, wide-set. Perceptive man.

Dean spent a good deal of the time bubbling over with his enthusiasm, rapture almost, about General Marshall. He has admired him for a long time. But to work with him is such a joy that he can hardly talk about anything else. I am delighted about this, for Jimmy Byrnes' erratic and often thoughtless (as well as sometimes just plain inept) administrative and other ideas had about driven Dean crazy. Marshall has put great responsibility upon Dean. Partly because he trusts him, I have no doubt, partly because Marshall would have been completely sunk if he had done anything else, and partly because Marshall has neither the excess of energy nor the interest in detail that would permit him to get into administration of the department. But it has made a new man of Dean, and this is a good thing for the country right now.

This was a particularly good time to have an evening's talk with these two men. The President—Marshall having gone to the foreign ministers conference in Moscow—has determined to take a stand to "aid" Greece, as a counter-Russia move. It is an historic change in American policy, and where it will lead, no one can tell. It may be the end of the bipartisan political support of our foreign policy, for one thing, for I somehow can't imagine the Republicans under Taft and Martin going for it. It may mean that we should have to take similar measures in Hungary, say, or France, before long. It will divide American opinion in strange and unforeseeable ways: Thus, Senators Pepper, Taylor, and Murray, and Helen Douglas, old Congressman Sabath, called on Dean yesterday late, and raised Ned about supporting the imperialism of Britain, etc. These are what we call democratic liberals. But it looks like the same kind of confusion about liberalism that got Henry Wallace so far off the beam in his letter to the President of last July—what is called the "sphere of influence" letter.*

Kennan is anxious that the President does not play this Greece business up too much, so that prestige isn't too deeply involved. And apparently he believes what I have tried without success to get over in my limited way, that "standing by" a country is *not* simply a matter of money. I recall my trouble making Sam Rosenman see this regarding China a long time ago now—"Why, Dave, we've loaned them 250 million dollars—what better way could we show them of our concern and support?"

The same thing is going to happen in Greece. What they need are graphic demonstrations of democracy in action, of technical aids and skills applied to the building up of their country. I gather Kennan has some such idea, for as we were seating ourselves he said something

---

* The letter, critical of the "get tough" policy toward Russia, was made public in September of 1946, shortly before Truman forced Wallace to resign as Secretary of Commerce. One of Wallace's points was that Soviet influence in Eastern Europe was as justifiable as our own in Latin America.

about wanting the Greek aid supplied by an "authority"; and then decided that might arouse antagonism.

I want very much to have some long talks with this fellow, for I want to know more and more about Russia. He is the first man I have talked to about Russia who seems to have the facts that support my essential thesis: that Communism isn't what Russia stands for; it is rather simply a political machine with vested interests, and a political machine that intends to stay in there, and do nothing in respect to the rest of the world that will weaken their hold on the Russian people; who might as well be beaten by the outside world as be beaten by an opposition within the country, better perhaps. I have learned a good deal about Russian politicos by seeing how Tennessee and other tough guys act when they are in.


MARCH 15, 1947
AT HOME, SATURDAY


Courage: What is it? Isn't it the capacity to hang on? I have thought of it, on the few occasions when I have thought of it at all, as something active, a positive action of some sort. There's a good deal of comment these days about my standing up to bullies and hatchetmen, and the editorial writers and commentators and the writers of letters to me use that word "courage." If it should be applied to this thing, then all it means is just that quality of hanging on, of not giving up no matter what. Which is quite a different thing than I had always thought of: the soldier fighting his way across the bullet-torn field, etc. But mostly courage is a kind of just going ahead regardless of consequences.

Spent all this Saturday working like the very devil, instead of resting as I should have perhaps. Dictating an article for *Collier's* to a writer on their staff, Lester Velie. First time I have tried this particular method: I would talk along, he writing it down, prompting me when I would get off the track, listing new points, etc. He will write it up, I'll go over it, and see how it works.

I am trying to make one point: that atomic energy development is more important as a stimulus to the imagination, an awakening force, than are any of its foreseeable applications—electric power, medical, etc. This is fundamental to my notion of how we will survive our Congressional difficulties; unless the people, the press, the radio, keep the light on atomic energy, it will go the way of a routine Government operation, bogged down, subject to the small potatoes of Congressional piddling. This simply must not happen. The way to prevent it, if it can be prevented, is an appeal to the public imagination, a series of such appeals, through every medium of communication.

If my energy will hold out, I believe this can be done.

MARCH 16, 1947
AT HOME, SUNDAY

A year ago we were meeting at Dumbarton Oaks. The final chewing over of our report on international control was going on, the report was receiving the blessing of the Acheson Committee. We were skeptical about Russian acceptance, of course, but not hopeless by any means. We had discussed that rather vaguely, for it did not seem likely to any of us on the Board of Consultants that our report would be taken very seriously within the State Department.

We were quite wrong about that latter, of course. The report has had a remarkable course. That day—it was a Sunday, too—Acheson had been told that Baruch had been named United States Representative; we didn't know this, any of the rest of us. Then began all sorts of things, in which "relations" with Russia have grown steadily worse, or perhaps what one should say is that it has been recognized, openly, how far apart and antagonistic are those relations. Until a year later, a year after we talked seriously about a world accord in which an international agency would build atomic energy plants all around the world, including Russia, the air is full of dispute and discussion over Truman's bold proposal that we (not the United Nations but the United States on its own) move into Greece and in effect rebuild it, and protect it from Soviet coercion; or perhaps more realistically, see to it that Russia does not control Greece, whatever that may take, including atomic bombs.

All this reminds me of the moving letter I received about a year ago, from Athens, written by a group of Greeks. Greece needed what the Tennessee Valley had—a kind of agency that would enable the Greek people to build upon their resources. Greece is poor, we are told (the letter said), but our reply is: no poorer than Tennessee ten years ago.

The letter emphasizes the thing that bothers me, perhaps will bother most people about this Greek move. Are we supporting democracy —which is our purpose—by the measures we are adopting? Or are we going to make people, here and abroad, cynical about our democratic purposes? If we could have afforded Greece technical help, along TVA lines a year ago, at far less cost than the $250,000,000 now proposed, what then? No one can be sure; but it would have been a far better setting for a contest of ideas if in the final analysis the contest is one of ideas, and a far better setting if the contest should prove to be one of force.

I can't help thinking about my present responsibility, in all of this, and none too comfortably.

MARCH 19, 1947
AT THE OFFICE

Luncheon with Baruch at his hotel. He is here, he says, because "they" want him to testify before the House Committee on Foreign Affairs about the President's Greek-Turkish policy. He is full of doubts about it. Why? he asks. Why now? What is the whole policy, if there is one? I gather he has them worried, for his public position on a matter of this kind could be quite influential.

I said: The question is not whether Communism should be stopped, but how? How do you stop Communism? There are many things that must be done. One of them is to preserve and increase our own strength here at home. Another is not to overextend. Another is not to put all our faith in the making of loans, technical aid, etc., and depend on demonstrating in our help what democracy can do that is better than what Communism can do.

The Old Man is a tough baby; it is interesting and very useful to see how he refuses to take any answer for granted. "We have to go into Greece now because England is out of dollars. Who said so? How do we know? Suppose we don't. Then what? How many troops does England have in Palestine? 100,000. What about them? Suppose they say they can't keep on in Germany, then what do we do?"

Well, of course, anybody can think up questions, but he puts these things in a dramatically sharp, tough way that is worth observing.

MARCH 23, 1947
AT HOME

Last week was distinguished and rather unique in my recent life: I did not have a single day of worrying and anxiety. I got mad about the continued leisurely delay in beginning debate on our nominations; I was unhappy over the fact that we cannot recruit our staff because of this uncertainty that the delay imposes; I was a bit disgusted to see how that great statesman Robert Taft is playing cheap precinct politics with the atomic energy program; I got terribly tired so that I went to bed Thursday night at 8:00 and got up 12 hours later—but at no time during the week did something come along that had me scared, anxious, and having to hang on to hold off being upset. This is about the first time since late January, which gives some idea of the kind of life I've been living.

Having worked hard all day on Saturday the 14th on the *Collier's* piece, I rested Sunday and was able to work a rather short day Monday and Tuesday. Wednesday at breakfast I sat down with Velie of *Collier's* on the article; it turned out surprisingly well, but I spent several hours (pieced in between seeing people and many phone calls) redrafting, trying to keep it informal, conversational, and therefore readable for the wide audience of a public weekly—not too easy a trick on such a subject.

The President got back from Key West Thursday, and I spent 45 minutes with Clark Clifford. He asked if a release of an executive order on procedure for ridding the Government of Communists would have a bad effect on our debate. I said I didn't know, but whatever the effect they should go ahead and release what they had in mind. I read the inter-departmental committee report: presents a procedure fairer than the Un-American Activities Committee at least, but rather ominous in some respects nevertheless. In effect, it makes service in the Government subject to the risk that some malevolent or crazy person may accuse you of being leftist. The accusation, for most people, in the present temper of things, would be so injurious, however the hearings came out, that it might prejudice their chances of employment in the Government or elsewhere. In practical effect, the usual rule that men are presumed innocent until proved guilty is in reverse.

Some mention was made of Baruch; I asked Clifford if he knew that the old gentleman was rather emphatic in his doubts, if not opposed, to the President's Greek-Turkish recommendations. Yes, several Cabinet members had told him they had spent four or five hours talking to the old boy last night, and Harriman thought "he was beginning to come around." The chief trouble, Clifford said, was that the President hadn't consulted Baruch. He was advised that he should, but he decided against it. "He said, 'I'm just *not* going to do it. I'm not going to spend hours and hours on that old goat, come what may. If you take his advice, then you have him on your hands for hours and hours, and it is *his* policy. I'm just not going to do it.' The President said we have a decision to make and we'll make it." C. was amused by this, but admitted that it was causing some members of the Cabinet who depend on the old boy some considerable time and sweat. The story about the President's comment interested me because it was so human; one of the few things a President can enjoy is to decide whom he will consult.

Lewis went to the dinner Forrestal gave Wednesday evening for Baruch; Patterson and Harriman there. When Forrestal called Lewis, he said the purpose of the meeting was "to grease the old boy." They really work at it, too. Everyone does. Everyone, apparently, but the President, who says he just won't. But Baruch is a very shrewd, hard, realistic man in these matters.

Osborn, Austin's new deputy on the Atomic Energy Commission of the UN, called to ask us to begin working with them up there. Bacher will go up Monday to talk things over. This should be interesting. And somehow, despite Gromyko's heated rejection of the whole plan in his speech the other day, I can't believe it is by any means futile to continue to seek understanding, nor that it is hopeless.

I had planned to get away right after the vote on the nominations, since I am traveling on reserves of energy these days. But late Friday "Casey" Jones of the *Post* here phoned to urge me to become the banquet speaker (with Van Bush) for the American Society of Newspaper Editors meeting on April 19. I begged off, but it was obviously a great opportunity if I could measure up to it. For these editors, most of them, have supported me in this fight in an extraordinary fashion, and they are ready, or could be made ready, to continue to help in the even more difficult times ahead—more difficult because less obvious, less dramatic. So after talking to Bill Waymack, who thought I ought to do it by all means, I accepted.

It excited me quite a bit getting out on the kind of limb where I am under close and hard-billed scrutiny (if their liquor of the early evening has worn off). As Doris Fleeson said to me at a dinner party at Senator McMahon's that evening, "You have been built up by the magnificent way you have handled yourself in this business, until you have the tough break of being practically an angel—a hell of a break to have to try to live up to *that*." This was partly her natural high spirits, but there is just enough truth in it to make one pause a bit.

Next week, surely, the debate will begin, though I notice this morning that the Republican conference has put it off again until mid-week, which could be Friday.

MARCH 28, 1947
AT HOME

In the Senate one of lower Delaware's courthouse boys, a sallow, hollow-chested man, Williams by name, is denouncing me and TVA. He was preceded by Ohio's pride, John Bricker. (Helen left for the Hill, at my suggestion, to be on hand for the resummation of the leisurely debate, and I am here by myself trying to rest.) I have just seen a copy of the form letter Senator Brooks of Illinois is sending to people who write in approving me; it is a kindly little piece—like hell. And this goes on, week after week; even if I am confirmed, as I suppose I will be. the same story goes on. Small potatoes. So this is one of those moments that must come to everyone in public service when he asks himself, "Why do you go on? Why not chuck the whole business?" I gave myself my own answer: I can't let people down now, when despair and cynicism are so widespread. But so far as joy and satisfaction for me is concerned, there will not be too much of it. Actually, I suppose the reason I stick is that I'm not a quitter, and I'm not this now. But it does wear pretty thin at times—and this afternoon is certainly one of those times. This debate will be even worse than the hearings, I suppose.

David is coming home tomorrow: that will be grand. He has made a wonderful beginning in his work.

MARCH 29, 1947
AT HOME, SATURDAY

I must get over this "low" feeling. Largely fatigue, of course. Fatigue plus the rankling anger of the attacks by John Bricker yesterday. I will have him and his following and his kind pursuing me with their piddling criticism and witch-hunting minds as long as I am on this job.

This I must remember: (1) if I set out to get the support of the John Brickers of this country, I can't hold the confidence and support of the people who really count; (2) if I worry about the criticism and ill opinion of the John Brickers, I will not be able to do that solid piece of work which is the only justification for taking all this punishment.

Remember these things, Dave.

APRIL 3, 1947
AT HOME (9:30 P.M.)

We walked into the President's office at a few moments after 5:00 P.M. I told him we came to report what we had found after three months, and that the quickest way would be to ask him to read a brief document. When he came to a space I had left blank, I gave him the number; it was quite a shock. We turned the pages as he did, all of us sitting there solemnly going through this very important and momentous statement. We knew just how important it was to get these facts to him; we were not sure how he would take it. He turned to me, a grim, gray look on his face, the lines from his nose to his mouth visibly deepened. What do we propose to do about it? He realized the difficulties. He spoke of the outrageous situation that had developed in the Senate, but he felt sure it would soon be over, and in our favor.

Then at 5:12, by the clock on the President's desk, Charley Ross stuck his head in the door and said, "The Senate voted to reject the Bricker motion. I'll get the vote in a moment."†

I was rather struck dumb and my forehead became damp. I had felt weak all day. The last word I had had was that "the absentees may determine the result"—this from Senator Morse at noon. The vote, Charley said in a few moments, was 52–38—a 14-vote margin, greater than anyone thought possible.

It was another dramatic episode added to a long line of them in this overdramatic business.

We shook hands, said our good-byes. The President was rather subdued and thoughtful-looking—his customary joke on parting was missing. Then, in that rather abrupt, jerky way of talking, he said, "Come in to see me any time, just any time. I'll always be glad to see you. You have the most important thing there is. You must make a blessing of it or" (and a half-grin as he pointed to a large globe in the corner of his office) "we'll blow that all to smithereens."

I phoned Senator Vandenberg, who had made one of the greatest speeches in the history of the Senate, so we are told, a speech that probably greatly affected the result. He was pleased to hear from me, said that he never had any doubt about me after the first few days' testimony. Then he said, "Well, Dave, for seven or eight weeks I have been seeing a lynching bee, and I just thought I wanted to separate myself from the lynchers."

The last ten days have been the worst I can remember. Very tired, low, difficult to maintain perspective, agonized by the prospect of weeks of "FBI" investigations and butchery and wanting nothing so much as release, and yet seeing that there was no way out except to go through with it. And now this, which is a considerable victory.

APRIL 4, 1947
AT HOME

Trying to rest today: pretty tuckered and with three important speeches to write this month.

Attended two meetings last week of the so-called Executive Committee on Disarmament, of which I am a member. This consists of the Secretaries of State, War and Navy, and the Chairman of the Atomic Energy Commission. Yesterday, just before going to the White House, there was an interesting and important meeting concerning the course our Government representatives (Senator Austin and his Marshall-appointed deputy, Fred Osborn) should take in the forthcoming renewed discussions of atomic energy control in the United Nations.

† Bricker had moved to recommit the AEC nominations. The defeat of his motion made it fairly clear that I would be confirmed.

The subject matter is too critical to permit writing it in this journal, of course, but with one thing I was considerably impressed. That was Senator Austin's remarks to the conferees. In his soft, bland, pleasant voice, he said, "I think it is a mistake to take an attitude of defeatism about whether the Russians will agree to our proposals; it is a mistake to guide our course with the thought only of putting them in the wrong because of their refusal to go along with the rest of the world on our proposals. We should approach this matter with optimism and hope, or no good can possibly come out of it. It is a mistake to take the position, 'Here it is; take it or leave it.' "

He said this in a way that may have sounded like fatal naïveté to some present—it obviously did to more than one. But there was something about it that, properly balanced and checked, seemed rather good. I think he is quite wrong in his stated belief that the Russians have made progress toward the essentials of our proposal, simply because Gromyko said an "international act" is necessary. But with a quite skeptical deputy, Osborn, and a more than skeptical Acheson, Forrestal, and Patterson and a quite unsanguine Lilienthal around the place, this attitude of determined confidence, so obviously sincere and deeply felt, seems to me quite right. Austin is a stubborn man, in his own way; he is stubborn on the idea that agreement can be reached. While for the predictable future there is no evidence whatever, so far as I see, that such will transpire, perhaps it is a good kind of stubbornness. The United Nations represents a great step forward, a very great step, he says, and it is our only hope for peace.

I was concerned that they might try to "draft treaty provisions" instead of trying to work out descriptive language of what an international agency's functions should be, how it would operate, and the reasons that support this kind of agency. I gather this latter idea was accepted, though it was contrary to Austin's and Osborn's initial idea.

David and Nancy both heard the last day's debate in the Senate yesterday. David was quite excited by it, and Nancy said she had no fingernails left. In the early part of the roll call the opposition had a 16-vote head start on us—and that must have been a bad moment for them.

APRIL 9, 1947
AT THE OFFICE (4:30 P.M.)

In ten minutes the Senate will begin taking the final vote. The bitterness continues to the end—or is it just another "stage"? Flanders made a terrible statement, and there was a full-page ad in this morning's

*Times-Herald* against me (directed to the members of the Senate—said the "life of our country is at stake"). God! It has been a long, hard row.

APRIL 13, 1947
AT HOME, SUNDAY

Wow! Fourteen hours' sleep. That sets a new record. And it gives some idea how clear-through tired I am. The final vote was a good one; and that is over and behind me.

I *did* survive, and according to Dr. Ecker's rather thorough physical exam last Tuesday, really none the worse for what is considered to be one of the toughest ordeals of the kind anyone can remember.

According to every rule of sense we should now be on a cruise, resting up for the punishing days ahead and recovering from the punishment. But not so. In fact, even the long weekend away from home didn't materialize. And this morning I find myself making notes for the American Society of Newspaper Editors speech for next Saturday night. I must be a tougher article than I ever supposed, or just a plain damn fool.

I haven't done much journal writing lately; there just didn't seem any extra energy and time. But let it be recorded again that the first week of April, the days preceding the vote of April 3, were the most horrible I do believe I can remember, so that the actual vote of confirmation was somewhat of an anticlimax though very good to taste. That business of being in a box, of delay and delay, of FBI operatives going all around inviting ugly remarks from every anonymous ill-wisher, and no way to chuck it—that was a nightmare of nightmares. And the consequent barrage of ugly and mean words on the floor of the Senate and in the press, even up to the last hour before the final vote last Wednesday; this was trying in the extreme.

The last-minute excitement was an effort to bring Nancy into it, something I had expected. It came within an ace of coming off, then didn't. Nancy, it was reported, was coming to work for me in the Commission. It was reported she was with the "left-wingers" in her United Public Workers Union, etc., etc. Two newspapermen were hot on the story. When they learned she wasn't working for me, that she had resigned from the Labor Department, they gave the story up.

The yellow ticker tape was brought into me at about 5:10 last Wednesday. "Confirmed." And then, only a few minutes later, the vote —50 to 31. A good vote. I had thought, at a rather optimistic time early in the fight, that if there were no more than 30 adverse votes that would be quite a victory. Counting the absentees who were paired, the vote would have been 57 to 38.

(And this makes it pretty clear that Gordon will come through, perhaps quite handsomely. Which puts me in mind of that awful black Saturday when the astounding word came in that the Public Works Committee had adversely reported on Gordon and disaster for TVA was added to my other worries.)

Wednesday evening Helen and I went to a DePauw dinner. I had refused to have pictures taken at the office; thought the college reunion idea much better. And so it proved to be. Newsreels, old Jim Watson,‡ President Wildman, the whole thing all together, with Helen getting a taste of that sort of thing with a vengeance.

Thursday morning the Commission did a newsreel; then a call on the Senate and House chairmen of the Joint Committee; then an important Commission meeting; and reading of sheafs of congratulatory wires from all over. The funny movie-cast colored Western Union boy met himself coming and going with his chest filled with these wires; furnished amusement to everyone.

Sweating over the newspaper speech. If I were a bit less tired, it might come more easily; or if I didn't try so hard. But that's me.

This evening we are going to supper and an evening's cruise on the Secretary of the Navy's yacht. The town of Norris and my garden and no shave a long way away.

Spring has come, quite suddenly, and this place is beautiful.

## (LATER: 10:15 P.M.)

Senator Vandenberg and I were sitting in the fantail (is that the word?—all right then—the back seat) of the Secretary of the Navy's yacht. "Dave, I don't see how you could do it, week after week, keeping yourself under control under that outrageous performance. What keeps a man in public service with that kind of provocation? The price is just too high."

He talked about how he thought he had "Bricker away from Taft"; how a 9-to-0 committee vote would have ended the whole thing; how Bricker was on the lookout for some "excuse" to go the other way;§ how McKellar would have none of him any more (Attny. General Clark put in that McKellar hasn't spoken to Senator Connally since the committee vote).

But what he said that was really interesting was on another subject, and it was one that Vandenberg was full of: Henry Wallace. Looking Clark and Forrestal firmly in the eye, he said, "The President can have

‡ U.S. Senator from Indiana, 1916–33, and a DePauw alumnus.
§ The committee's vote on my nomination had been 8 to 1, with Bricker opposed.

me on his team in foreign affairs, or he can have Henry, but he can't have us both."

Clark said something about that being too hard on the President; that his remark about expecting Wallace to support him in 1948 was just put to him at a press conference, etc. This didn't put Vandenberg off a bit. "I think what Wallace is doing today is one of the worst things that has happened. It will confirm Molotov's notion that the country is divided on foreign policy. I looked into Molotov's face for 210 days and I know something about him."

Later he said, "You know, it is a terrible thing to think, but I am beginning to be afraid that there just isn't any room in the world for both Moscow and Washington. Awful thing to say."

I said that was the thing that was most troublesome; that our experience with Russia was running up against some ideas we have held too firmly. One was that *any* dispute can be amicably adjusted if the parties, as F.D.R. would say, "were locked up in a room and told to stay there until they reached an agreement." It was this that made it so urgent to keep ahead in atomic energy. If both the United States and Russia had bombs . . . well, was that a thinkable situation?

After buffet supper we saw the movie *The Late George Apley* with its digs at Boston society, while the grandson of Henry Cabot Lodge, the present Senator, sat on the floor, as I did, a few feet away, and his tall wife next to Helen. I thought they laughed even more heartily than anyone else at the rather tough ribbing.

Also present, as they say: Mrs. Davison of the Red Cross; Senator and Mrs. Tydings; Admiral Towers and two couples from the British Embassy whose names I missed.


APRIL 20, 1947
AT HOME, SUNDAY

General Eisenhower pushed his way toward me, giving me a knowing look, his head tilted forward in that characteristic way he has when he is serious. He shook my hand firmly. "I want to congratulate you on what you have said." Then, moving close and speaking in a low, intent voice, he said, "But what is more important I want you to know I am on your team—I mean I am on your team." I was flustered and murmured something about thanking him and saying I would be honored to be on his team. He looked at me closely with that "You know what I mean" look and said, "You can count on me."

This somehow seemed the high point for me of a happy and successful event—my speech to the American Society of Newspaper Editors at their banquet meeting. This was held in the huge banquet rooms at the

Statler last night before 1,100 people, editors from all over the country and Washington dignitaries of press and Government.

Last Sunday, just a week ago, I had no speech, although this I knew to be, as Palmer Hoyt of the Denver *Post* said, "the most important speech of your life." I had been brooding about a central theme for quite a while, the theme that I am hammering away everywhere on, i.e., the vital importance of this atomic energy program to the American people, and the responsibility of the press in respect to the dissemination of information and ideas about it. But making it hang together was getting nowhere.

A couple weeks ago I had gotten the idea that something graphic as a place to begin would help and I thought of a cylinder of uranium I could hold up—had dictated a nuclear primer around that idea. But this was far from a speech. I was very tired—the reaction from the confirmation fight. We thought we would go away for the weekend to rest, but Helen wasn't well—flu—and that didn't pan out. I worked a bit at it Monday last, but still it seemed punk. Then Helen took a hand. She read what I had, said I had a good speech idea. Then Tuesday morning at breakfast we talked about it some more and at the breakfast table I started to write in shorthand. By noon I had it, and from there it was just a matter of polishing.

It was a good speech, right for the audience, and right because I had thought about it enough and written and rewritten enough until it was part of me. That's the greatest trouble with a ghost-written piece— it isn't something you've lived through. I read it over for emphasis perhaps five times Saturday morning and afternoon, so had it well in hand.

There is a thrill in holding a great audience in such a setting intently through 30 minutes. The upturned faces caught, intent (I watched them; "That audience hardly moved, the whole while," said Justice Jackson afterward), some thoughtful, some with their heads cocked as if a bit puzzled, some rather taken aback at this dramatic and oratorical effort. This latter amused me some, for this was my first speech in Washington to an important gathering in all the 14 years I have been in Federal service and a number of men—Chief Justice Vinson, Attorney General Clark, etc.—remarking about it afterward were obviously surprised that they had a speaker on their hands.

Hoyt may have been right: this *was* an important occasion. And it couldn't have been better timed—coming so close on the confirmation fight which made me so well known, and having in it so many revealing things about the kind of person I am; the kind of ideas I really have as contrasted with the many assertions and reports about this strange animal.

I got special satisfaction out of it because Helen had done so much to pull it out of me. We can do this sort of thing again, and it is good to renew a practice we started married life with when I would write my articles at home at night and have her criticize and shape them up for me.

As we came in to go to our seats I noticed Senator Tom Stewart at a table in the back. How he must have fumed at my references to the fight, to politics, and how it must have puzzled him to hear the applause that I got which was fervent and that the audience gave when Van Bush spoke of me so warmly in his own speech that followed.

This is all quite a new life. Where in Heaven's name I get the continuing energy for it I don't know, but I suppose I am rather hopped up with excitement somewhat as one would be if he used drugs.

I had thought I could just barely last until a holiday in February. Then things went on and on and April seemed the last limit. Here I am still going strong, and without any vacation and not a good prospect of one for some time. It isn't sensible, but it is good to know that I can manage.

Last Wednesday I went to see the President, with the Secretaries of War and Navy and Admiral Leahy, the President's Chief of Staff. This was an off-the-record, unannounced meeting to present the President with a letter the four of us had signed regarding production of weapon material for the year. I have written a top secret memo about the meeting and won't include it here. But it seemed rather fantastic, my being there, and yet I used the occasion to push ahead with ideas as if such meetings were something I had been engaged in for years. I do have a lot of what that DePauw sophomore chapel speaker, Cush Hoke, years ago called "self-confidence in myself."

A long session Thursday with John Taber, chairman of the House Appropriations Committee. He is a kind of bear, but he was very cordial, pleasant—and, I thought, puzzled about me. I told him of the danger of "loss of security" if we really testified in detail concerning our financial needs, and yet how wrong it would be not to disclose the facts. I proposed that he select two or three veterans of the committee and have us tell them the facts. "It isn't right that we do not make you fellows share the full responsibility by getting the whole story to you. If we don't, you may not appropriate the money and that may be very serious." He was at the dinner last night, and we had a pleasant chat along with some of his home-town friends. One of them said, "When they hear back in Auburn that John Taber has introduced us to David Lilienthal, it will cost him a thousand votes." I laughed and said, "Well, John Taber is one of those rare Congressmen who can afford to lose a thousand votes and never miss them." This seemed to amuse the old boy.

Met a great many new people last night as well as many I've known for a long time. Senator Knowland introduced me to Jones of the Sacramento *Bee*, a long-time friend of TVA. I met the editor of the Portland *Oregonian;* of Spokane's leading paper; Clarence Streit (*Union Now*); Howard of the Cleveland *News;* Virginus Dabney of the Richmond *Times-Dispatch* (for the first time—and what a fine-looking man he is—as fine-looking as he is a fine person, though younger than I thought); the Ambassador to the Netherlands; Canadian Ambassador Hume Wrong, just back from a visit to TVA.

This afternoon I leave for the Tennessee Valley for the first time out of Washington since we returned from the Western trip about November 20. This is a record for me—not traveling in all that time.

There was quite a flurry of excitement during the week about Nancy. There have been recurrent rumors, by way of telephone calls from newspapermen "hot" on a story, that Nancy was going to work for me at the Commission and that there would be attacks on her for being a part of the "left" in her United Public Workers Union local. She wrote me a little memo of the facts—very clear and good—and we got the facts to Senators lest it be brought up in the debate. It wasn't. Her day for resignation according to our agreement came along and I thought it was all over.

Then last Tuesday Congressman Busbey of Chicago got up in the House and said Nancy, a Communist sympathizer and leader, etc., was going to work for me in the Commission. The papers had to carry it then and they started calling Nancy. The *Star* sent a photographer and reporter and there was an interesting story. It bothered me, but actually it was a good story. "My father thinks one of us working for the Government is enough." She didn't agree but let the old fuddy-duddy have his way. No, she wasn't going to work for the Commission. For a while it was quite all over the place and may come again. Nancy is very low in her mind; her job gone; and I rather guess some emotional rough spots in addition. Willson Whitman is going to write a biography of me for Henry Holt and Nancy could help on that and there are other things I need done and that would be good experience for her until she decides what to try for next. There are considerable disadvantages, too, in having a too prominent father who is in controversial matters, especially if you yourself also have firm convictions and those are controversial. As Nancy said in her interview, "Anyone who is sympathetic or believes in labor unions is called a Communist these days. I don't think it is fair." Indeed it isn't.

I hope I don't let the virus of Russiaphobia bite me, too. I want to hammer away at the things they do that we shouldn't do; but to emulate them or the bloodthirsty Russia-haters in the process of contesting

Communistic ideas would be a sad fate; but it could happen to me, for perspective in this highly charged atmosphere is difficult.

APRIL 27, 1947
AT HOME, SATURDAY

General Eisenhower spoke to a small meeting of the Secretaries of War and Navy and the Joint Chiefs of Staff and their planning staffs on Thursday or Friday of last week. General Groves was there, to talk to them about atomic weapons development, etc. General Eisenhower "went out of his way" (so our General McCormack reported) to comment enthusiastically about my ASNE speech.

Choosing that particular place and with General Groves there seems rather significant. I hope to have a long talk with Eisenhower about this whole business before long.

Clapp was confirmed by a close margin on Thursday evening. Helen and I celebrated. What a relief.

It was a hard week, and I worked most of the day, Saturday, on my speech for New York next Thursday.

Saw Secretary Anderson to start getting the research agencies of the Agriculture Department working with us. This will be helpful in many ways.

Driving work through the Commission is a drain. We are not well organized yet, not by any means, and I want to abstain from doing things myself that the staff should do, though I could do it better at this juncture. But we move. We really do.

Some very delicate policy questions are under way. Let's hope there are no leaks. I would like to write out some of these things as they develop—and I am having a lot to do with getting them rolling—but it is too risky setting them down even in a code. It is an exciting life and tiring, but I can't think of anything I would rather do.

The meeting at Oak Ridge last Sunday was all that I could have hoped—indeed, it was better. Everybody turned out to the evening meeting. I was "piped" to several other halls than the school auditorium where I appeared "in person." Dashed off the speech in a few moments, standing up in a vacant office on the fourth floor of the New Sprankle Bldg. in Knoxville—dictated to Miss Brown. Then I extemporized the rest and it worked all right. If I had recited the multiplication table, it would have been all right. They just wanted to see me and know that something like certainty might be their lot for a while.

After I spoke it was my plan to hang around and talk with people. I got, instead, a bobby-soxer rush. The bald Frank Sinatra is what I looked like in a series of crazy photos, me with my bow tie, gleaming dome, surrounded by kids rabid for autographs, poking a piece of paper at me. It was fun, really, and gave all of us some change.

APRIL 30, 1947
PUBLIC HEALTH BLDG.

I am sitting in a joint meeting of the Military Liaison Committee and the Commission. We are talking in the most impersonal and objective way about things that concern the lives of men in a quite terrible way, and perhaps as well the whole prospect for peace in the world in the next decade. Too bad I can't write these things out—they are fascinating and horrible; but oh, so impersonal, as we discuss them.

MAY 5, 1947

At our initial meeting with the Joint Congressional Committee this morning in the District of Columbia Room, Senate side of the Capitol, we noted with some alarm that the door leading from the hearing room to an adjoining room consisted of a drape and a couple of swinging saloon doors. Later on when some of the more important projects of the enterprise were discussed, this travesty of security gave us the creeps.

Wilson described the project, using a map as a prop. This seemed to go quite well. In executive session Senator Johnson and Senator Millikin raised the question of fixing higher prices for the uranium content of ores for the Colorado miner. Before long this led into a discussion of raw materials. We told the committee that their assumption that domestic ores would meet the problem was wrong. Likewise about Canada, and we were soon in the middle of the Belgian Congo. At this point, the question being pushed, I read the statute which directs that the Commission should keep the committee currently and thoroughly informed and said that that required the disclosure of classified matters as it was secret and involved international relations of a delicate character.

There was some alarm expressed that England is getting half of the Belgian uranium output and some surprise at learning that Great Britain and Canada actually had had men participating with all four feet in the development of the bomb itself, during the war. Senator Connally said that then you mean that England knows how to make the bomb. The answer is certainly "Yes." I explained that we had been concerned that the Joint Committee and the Foreign Affairs Committee had not previously been informed of our agreements with England and recommended that they learn of these basic agreements directly from the Secretary of State and the Under Secretary. This apparently they will do. We tried to impress upon them that this was obviously very secret information and should be handled accordingly, although I must admit that that open door with swinging saloon barrier seemed a sample of how little actual security we can expect. And yet I am completely persuaded that we cannot operate on a reasonable basis with the Congress if the Congress does not receive information that is classified.

I plan to write a detailed memorandum on the Joint Committee hearing in this aspect as soon as I can.

Commission meeting at about 3:00 to partake of a terrific cake made by a top secret formula of Bill Waymack and with his hands. This to pay off a confirmation bet of some kind.

In fine, free-wheeling fashion I got to discussing a favorite idea, namely that we should have a group of distinguished men study the problem of security in the light of our traditions of civil liberties and the need for the sustained confidence and active cooperation of the scientists. I made more headway this time in making clear why this seemed a good idea. Some names were mentioned—notably John W. Davis, Charles Evans Hughes, Sr., and Herbert Hoover. Lewis Strauss will talk to Davis about this idea and I asked Bill Waymack to act as combination recording secretary and draftsman of formulated ideas.

We have had drastic steps taken in hysteria in peacetime and hysteria in wartime that threaten civil liberties. Witness Lincoln's suspension of habeas corpus and the Palmer raids after World War I. But this time it is not only civil liberties but our position of leadership in science that could be swept away by a wild nightmare of fear leading to drastic and dumb limitations on scientific men and standards of "personal clearance" that are impossible and that assume that scientists can function behind barb-wire compounds.

We have a great responsibility to keep this from getting to the point where no one can do anything about it. The fear in the eyes of the committee last week as they looked on a map that showed 30 or 40 universities participating in this project was all the warning I needed. A tidal wave of hysteria could wipe out our scientific program and our sense of freedom in rather quick order as the months go by and the fear that Russia has made progress.

MAY 7, 1947

A meeting to hear a report from men just back from South Africa. Discussion of uranium and gold. General Smuts; leaching; black labor; geology.

Commission's first meeting was on October 28, 1946, and that is over six months ago. During all that time we have not had a disagreement that could not be resolved. I have yet to put a matter to a vote, although there have been motions made which I blandly disregarded, waiting until the discussion made it clear that no motion was necessary. There have been matters on which we did not agree but which I kept plugging and pushing and polishing around sometimes over a period of several weeks until an answer agreeable to everybody developed. This has not involved any splitting of differences, but an actual development of consensus that arises out of the discussion and out of the points of difference.

How long this record can be continued God knows, and it is sometimes a very strenuous thing to manage, but it is worth all the work that goes into it and is a record from which I get very great satisfaction. The warm personal relations and mutual forbearance as well as the fun that the Commissioners get in working together are perhaps as much a result of this process of developing agreement as they are a cause of it. In fact, I think clearly the personal relation situation which is so good is result rather than cause. Back-slapping and joviality will not produce results of this kind, but the good feeling that comes about from finding a way of bringing one's mind into harmony with other minds of five men coming to be welded into a special unit. This creates a good feeling that is very precious and very useful.

Saw Congressman Thomason and discussed confidentially the matter of his succession on the Joint Committee.◖ Said he would discuss it with Rayburn and McCormack. It looked like seniority on the Military Affairs Committee would determine it. I recommended a cross membership with the Appropriations Committee, but that seemed to present too many problems in connection with the Military Affairs Committee seniority.

At the Commission meeting yesterday it was the opinion that when any member, including the Chairman, was away for any more than a day or so, no matter how important matters are, they should not be deferred for his return. Should go ahead and act with those present.

MAY 10, 1947
(ABOARD SS CIBAO, 2ND DAY OUT OF BALTIMORE)

Feel quite pleased with myself at the moment. I stood the long strain, with no visible damage, physically or otherwise, and here we

◖ Thomason resigned his seat that summer to accept a Federal judgeship. Lyndon Johnson took his place on the Joint Committee.

are actually at sea, on a holiday, which while only a short one (11 days or so) will nevertheless give me a real breather. There were times, particularly in the early days of the work (back in November and December, for example) when the old fear that I had "burned myself out" in that TVA job would come back and worry the hell out of me. I'm over that now, and believe if I set a pace and learn how to worry about the right things, that I can manage very nicely.

We have had a following sea most of the way since we left Chesapeake Bay, and last night it was a beauty, with great rolls that sent everyone crashing to the decks and made breakfast this morning rather an acrobatic stunt. Still rolling heavily. *Cibao* is a brand-new beauty of a ship, but she is small (less than 5,000-ton), and though her ballast tanks are full, she is without cargo, so we toss. The weather has been cold, with wind. Is still quite cool, though we must be off southern Georgia by now. But by tomorrow it will doubtless be fair and hot.

Read bits of *Two Years Before the Mast*. There is considerable grumbling among shipmen, both on shore and on shipboard, about how arbitrary the union is about crewmen, overtime, etc. Quite a contrast to Dana's time. Makes one feel somewhat less sympathy with the undoubted headaches of ship operation.

The ship is a freighter headed for Puerto Barrios, Guatemala, for a load of bananas to be put into the refrigerated hold and sold on return for a pretty penny, as the market is very good. We expect to go to Guatemala City and Antigua, being met by the Fruit Company's representative and an automobile, we hope. So the ten days will seem much more than that. But it will be good to get back—even the second day out I feel that, though I am in that somewhat fallen-apart stage of resting after a long pull. Quite in contrast with other vacations, when I was exhausted and rather depressed—that being the first reaction.

We are the only passengers aboard (though there is a Fruit Company port steward here on a sick leave), which makes it rather good for this kind of trip.

MAY 18, 1947
SS CIBAO, SUNDAY

It has been a good holiday.

But it is no longer possible for me, if it ever was, to call a period of time a vacation and not see what is going on, to puzzle over it. The disembodied spirit of the true "tourist" is not for me, apparently.

Thus, the "picturesqueness" of Guatemala. It *is* that. And we had a wonderful opportunity to see a great deal of the life of the people in a very brief time. The Indians gathered at the numerous little stops along the railroad where we sat on "sidings" by the hour; the Indians; West Indian and other Negroes and just mixtures who carried the bananas to the conveyers to the hold all night long and most of the day; the men driving the bullock teams; the Indian women trotting along the roads, a baby on their backs and a big load on their heads. But it is pretty seamy, really. Hard to take the very "picturesque" stuff—human beings straining up a hill carrying a pile of wood looking just what they are—beasts of burden. Passed a baby funeral—how many of them there must be in all that dirt and disease.

I was struck by one note. On board ship, in talking with the manager of the Fruit Company's plantations in Guatemala City, the same story. Labor. Even the coffee plantation owners on their way back to the States complaining about the Indians not being satisfied with 50¢ a day, even the house help. The company's representative at their town, Bananera, talked with great feeling about Communism spreading from Moscow and Mexico City and "social legislation" (apparently largely a matter of limiting hours of work, according to his story), but he was full of strong feeling. The Government officials, if they really wanted to help the people, he said, that would be one thing. But they don't; they line their own pockets and make it impossible for employers to produce. To hear this sort of thing in the United States is bad enough; but to find the same concern here in this country that does not have a single industry of any consequence is strange indeed. And among the ship's officers, their feeling about "the union" and its "high-handed" way of picking their crews and even stewards . . . Only a depression will cure it, they say. As one man put it, "Apparently the only way you can get along with labor is when there are two men for each job—and the sooner that time comes again the better."

The railroad trip to Guatemala City was an experience. We were in a small Diesel-driven car owned by the Fruit Company, nicely equipped with a small observation lounge, beds, lavatory, galley and refrigerator, air conditioning, etc. With a crew of three and a steward along, we went through Indian villages, plantations, and deserts, a tiny oasis of comfort and gadgetry in a world of insects, poverty, and wildness. A curious feeling.

MAY 21, 1947

The code names amuse me no end.

"Tube Alloy"—the official British name for the bomb project and then in a solemn document another—honoring a movie queen—"Myrna Alloy."

Today we solemnly discussed "operation paper-clip," which relates to what in hell to do with the "liberated" German nuclear scientists. Let them go and Russia will "hire" them. Bring there here and the U.S. scientists will raise hell.

Another code that is worth recalling is "alarm clock."*

MAY 25, 1947
AT HOME, SUNDAY

Returned to the office Tuesday morning, May 19, and had a heavy week.

Dictated the speech I make tomorrow in Chicago and using it in its first-draft condition. Don't like to do this—not taking adequate time for revision and polishing—but there simply isn't time and the draft a member of the Information staff prepared for me wouldn't do even as a basis.

Condon, Presidentially appointed head of the National Bureau of Standards, notified Berkeley he expected to visit there in a few days; the security officer out there asked if he could be "cleared" for all parts of the Radiation Laboratory. His file was sent to us; it is an FBI report that is full of all kinds of stuff, allegations of those interviewed about Condon's reliability, discretion, judgment. He was recommended by Henry Wallace [in 1945, when Wallace was Commerce Secretary], and much is made of this in the report.

What to do? We answered the particular request by a specific clearance since there isn't much at Berkeley to worry about—fundamental science, most of it. Pike said if it had been Los Alamos he would have felt differently. Strauss was for saying that we hadn't had time enough to consider the matter—which is true enough. Waymack and Bacher felt that such a refusal, however put, would precipitate a row that wasn't worth having in view of the things he could see at Berkeley. I thought it a close case, but thought the specific clearance a wise interim conclusion and ultimately we all agreed on this.†

But the case illustrates the terrible power we are wielding. If later we conclude to deny full clearance, then without opportunity to be heard, without confrontation, and largely on the basis of the judgment of some anonymous people that they don't "trust" C., etc., we destroy his standing in his profession, despite the fact that he was

* Code for a design for a super A-bomb.
† The Commission gave Dr. Condon general clearance the following July. (By that time he had become much publicized because of loose attacks made on him by a House Un-American Activities Subcommittee. He was firmly supported by the President and by the scientific community, and continued to head the Bureau of Standards until 1951.)

appointed by a President and confirmed by the Senate. This is a new idea of justice to me. The worst part is that we will feel impelled to do these things rather than "take chances" or subject ourselves to criticism for having taken chances, and thus decide very important matters affecting people and events on a basis of caution, not justice.

Not long ago Wilson dismissed a man with a fine record of public service because he appeared to have denied that he had ever objected to military service, or something of the kind. The man was stunned, and it may be that his career would have been ruined as well as his peace of mind. Later, Wilson reported that he, Wilson, had made a mistake on his facts and admitted his error. But suppose he hadn't; suppose he hadn't been the kind who is willing to acknowledge an error, what remedy would the poor fellow have?

Visitors from Belgium this week. The ore business is a fantastic aspect of this whole business.

We got our new Magnavox and are enjoying it immensely.

Appropriation hearings again. Taber and Wigglesworth and the entire subcommittee. I refused to permit the submission of a tabulation demanded by Wigglesworth, showing our projected administrative organization—figures and numbers of people—as of June 30, 1948. There was utter scorn about it, but I insisted that since it would be simply a guess at this time it would amount to misrepresentation. I knew they would use those figures—something they could get their teeth into—to hammer on limitations and restrictions, or to make fun of. They will anyway, but at least they won't have figures submitted by us to work on.

Probably a unique appropriation here. Asking for more than 500 million. What will be in the record is almost nothing. The committee itself refused to look at secret tables we had prepared, but I insisted on it; then we withdrew them. But the secret tables contained large lump sum amounts—140 million for this, 200 for that. The committee members were baffled, and we admitted frankly we didn't know how to present a budget when (a) we didn't have a set of books showing costs, since the Army's Manhattan District didn't have or keep any; and (b) to disclose details would be to breach security.

So, it was quite an experience. No telling what they will do, though I doubt if they will do much butchering. May try to find some way to defer giving us much money. This will give the appearance of cutting the budget and keeping us on a string. I objected to this, as it would impair our position with prospective contractors.

I sympathize with the position this puts the members of the committee in, with their colleagues, particularly since no one trusts anyone about atomic energy on the Hill.

Just before we left on our vacation the secret agreements came up in a meeting with the Joint Committee; came up in a perfectly natural way.‡ I said as little about it as possible and yet insisted that, highly secret as it was, it was our duty to see that they knew about it; and asked that the State Department be called upon to give the underlying documents and terms. This was in accordance with a prior understanding with Acheson. They were considerably shocked to learn that we have so little in this country in the way of raw materials.

While we were away Acheson did appear. Connally and Vandenberg, I understand, were considerably surprised by what they heard. The amazing thing, however, is that it hasn't been in every newspaper all over the place. I am sure the Republicans will be cooking up something to make something of the discussions, but how it happens that it hasn't been blurted out or in a column by this time—several weeks now—is beyond belief.

MAY 27, 1947
AT HOME

Wilson reported to us this morning the negotiations he has been having with Monsanto Chemical Co. (Messrs. Queeny, Rand, Charley Thomas) have broken on this issue: the Co. insisted that the core of the new program for Clinton Lab, the high-flux reactor, be built at St. Louis or Dayton where their operations are, and thereby become part of their operations. Apparently they were sure we would recede. But this business of putting very expensive facilities at or within a big industrial property so we are tied to them, in practical effect, was accepted by Groves on the insistence of General Electric in the case of Knolls Lab at Schenectady, and we had to swallow his commitment. But we don't intend to do it ourselves.

Furthermore, the scientists have been very restive under the Monsanto arrangements and the work hasn't been well conducted. We are ready to go with them if they would design the new reactor—a major research facility of incalculable importance—and build it at Oak Ridge.

So what to do?

Wilson reported that yesterday, in my absence, the Commissioners having heard this story had authorized his opening negotiations with Du Pont to see if they could be induced to change their decision to get out once the war was over—this involved [the operations at the plu-

‡ This is a further reference to wartime agreements with Britain and Canada for the joint development of the A-bomb, including a provision still in effect for dividing the uranium ore from the Congo. Vandenberg later made an issue within the Government of one of the agreements—the U.S. pledge not to use the bomb without British consent.

tonium plant at] Hanford. Then there was the possibility of Standard Oil Development Corp.

I didn't oppose this, directly. But I called attention to the fact that if Du Pont accepted Monsanto's place, we would become part of Du Pont rather than the other way around, for a big industrial concern of that magnitude is a kind of world in itself, has its own way of doing things, and could hardly be expected to change its over-all management policies because of a contract we would have to plead with them to accept. Furthermore, it would involve public policy questions: people would be afraid that this great new possibility was to become part of the Du Pont area of domination. Similarly with Standard Oil, though perhaps to a lesser degree. Furthermore, was there any evidence that the malaise the scientists felt at Oak Ridge in working on fundamental research under the management of an industrial concern engaged in profit-making was going to be any better under Du Pont?

Then, a remarkable thing happened. The force of this point, put largely in a deprecatory way and by way of "question-raising," was felt at once. Strauss said: What about having the men who run the Clinton Laboratory—the scientists, etc.—organize a corporation—the Clinton Nat'l. Laboratory, Inc., he called it—and we would enter into a contract with them? They are the people we would expect to do the work, anyway.

This led to an excited discussion all the way around, and I could see that the Du Pont idea would have hard sledding in the future. How this magic took place is hard to tell. But when we arose from the discussion (in which the possibility of turning to Kellex, a specially organized technical corporation not related to general consumer activity, was explored) it was clear that we had had a real adventure in joint thinking.

Each man said, "That was a good discussion."

Called Baruch for his "counsel": should I cancel the engagement to speak to the United Nations' Working Committee next Monday?

Told him Darwin, Chairman (Great Britain) of the United Nations Atomic Energy Committee, asked that I appear before committee. Agreed to. Now I'm not so sure. Calling for his counsel. He said, "You must go. But tell them you can't discuss organization in any detail at all until they decide what they are going to agree to in the way of international agency." He talked at some length—criticism of Osborn's position, saying that all these discussions should be eliminated unless and until the Russians decide whether they are going along. (This apparently is what Osborn referred to as Oppenheimer's position.) I said I thought Osborn's position was that it was a matter of good faith and good relations with the other nations that required these continued discussions. Baruch said he didn't think that was the case.

He said we ought to offer to organize Europe and Japan with the Russians, or if they didn't come along, to do so without them.

He said he didn't see how I could decline to come when invited. Urged me to visit him when I am in New York.

At the outset, he spoke highly of my speech of yesterday at Chicago, particularly the point that there was no secret that could be locked up in a safe.

Then I called Senator Hickenlooper, and he came to my office (this coming to my office, of course, was his proposal), and I asked him about the same matter. At first he was doubtful; he later said, "I wouldn't advise you not to go. It might be construed as a discourtesy, and the invitation to you was logical and appropriate." I emphasized the incident because it shows an increasing awareness on my part of the importance of conferring with others about such steps—this must become a habit.

Benjamin Fine, education editor of the *New York Times,* came in for a few hectic minutes at six, to ask me some questions about a piece he is doing on education and atomic energy. I launched into a favorite subject of mine: that this whole issue of atomic energy is the greatest example and test of education as it is in a democracy—something I want to do some thinking about, and this was a good way to stir me up on it. I am amazed at my ability to improvise at the end of a long, tough day, on a subject like this. And judging from his note-taking, and his comments, it seemed to make sense to him.

In the same day here, a project to look into the scientific and military possibilities of radiological warfare—a pretty subject; preparation for a conference with the Civil Service Commission tomorrow; a talk with Miss Brown about my journal and how we can incorporate portions of the documents into it that will make it more complete; a telephone talk with Congressman Thomas of Texas about appropriations and Senator Aiken about my appearing as a witness for the St. Lawrence Waterway—he is finally getting hearings on it beginning this week. I begged off, unless later they need me.


MAY 29, 1947

Monsanto's withdrawal from Oak Ridge now an accepted fact. GE situation: can't they possibly shorten period for redox?§ This is very

§ An improved process pioneered by Glenn T. Seaborg for separating plutonium from uranium, and uranium from its fission products for reuse.

disturbing because raw materials supply is thin ice. Not willing to accept that as best that can be done.

Commissioners spent long time jointly correcting minutes. Hard, dull job, but they buckled down to it, though if it had taken another half-hour would have had revolt on my hands! Wonderful good will all along.

MAY 30, 1947

Met with General Advisory Committee—a really distinguished group of men.◖

Our problem in getting waste recovery and redox in time we want—GE won't promise earlier than 3⅓ years. This is bad.

(A thought: if the President's Cabinet were made up of men who in general philosophy of administration and policies had the distinction and brain power of this group!)

Here is a request—a demand that entire Eighth Air Force be "cleared"—thousands of men—for atomic work so they could function. Wow! Complete information security with all the whole Air Force "clear"! What a change from the day when Groves wouldn't even inform the top military forces.

JUNE 1, 1947
AT HOME, SUNDAY

Had a long talk with David last evening. Outcome, directly, of his having me look at his Philosophy final examination questions. But he has been developing ideas about the world rapidly lately, and this was obviously quite an event: telling the old man how he feels about things. Essentially, his point is that the major question for a young fellow is "the ethical one": am I going to live to "gouge and fight my way through to help myself along" or is there something else? That is "after all, the whole question of what to do with yourself," said he. He repeated the speeches he had made on the subject to bull sessions at college.

He has developed wonderfully. His shyness and brooding seem quite gone. There is great energy and understanding in the boy and a kind of balance that is remarkable for one of his age and temperament.

We exchanged a few words, early in the day, about his immediate future. I asked if he had a particular professional line in mind further

◖ Oppenheimer was the chairman, and the membership included such scientists as Conant, Fermi, Rabi, Seaborg, Lee DuBridge and Cyril Smith.

than he had previously. No. I said it didn't really seem important whether he did or not; the thing to remember is that if he is learning about himself, how to analyze things, how to express himself, the rest will come along when the time requires. And I have long thought that there is rarely any "occupational" problem for the plainly superior young person—there is always a place for that kind wherever they go. It is the mediocre who have to plan their course carefully and make highly specialized preparations.

He returned about midnight Thursday night. After we were sound asleep the phone rang like mad. We dressed and drove to Chevy Chase to get him. He looks a bit thin and worn, for he has worked hard. And effectively, too.

He received postal cards about his marks: English, A minus; Philosophy, A minus; History, B. His French mark has not yet come, but he expects at least a B. Those are some marks for a "transfer" student at Harvard who has been away from study for a year.

Spent two hours or so with the General Advisory Committee yesterday (Saturday) afternoon.

Robert Oppenheimer summarized the committee's views on the questions we submitted to them for their opinion, in an hour's statement that was as brilliant, lively, and accurate a statement as I believe I have ever heard. He is pure genius. Even these great brains joined in the amazement and delight we all felt with this wonderful piece.

We are at odds with the committee on the issue of a large central laboratory for program work (principally reactors). This is partly philosophical and abstract, I fear (I dislike the idea of a large lab and so does Bacher), but partly because of the administrative difficulties it presents to a new and untried organization at the beginning of its trials. The withdrawal of Monsanto Chemical Co. may affect this proposal, though, for it leaves us more or less free to put the first new research reactor, a high-flux one, at Argonne or some such central place.

Tuesday I make another speech to a group of "opinion-influencers" —the Dutch Treat Club in New York. All the speeches I have made since confirmation have been to such groups: the American Society of Newspaper Editors; magazine publishers on May 1; Inland Press Ass'n. at Chicago on May 26; and now this one. Each speech contains the same theme: the importance of the public knowing, and the responsibility of the press, etc., to do the job of public relations and public information.

All of this is getting me onto a limb. For we are not equipped to develop the liaison with the press, etc., that such a policy as I am proposing requires. Why then do I persist in proposing a broad program that we are not in a position to carry out on our part?

Because it is a basic notion of mine that it is only when one deliberately puts himself out on a limb that he gets anything done. Thus in TVA I took a public position on decentralization, on the world-wide implications, etc., before I knew at all fully what this meant or how we would come through. By being on the spot, by my own voluntary and deliberate action, I had to come through—and pretty well did, both in act and in further statements of the philosophy.

I have applied the same idea to a number of things around the Commission. Where I have yielded to the cautious who want more time to think through the implications, just nothing has happened. No one has been actively studying the matter because the pressure isn't on. So, instead of making headway because of deliberateness, nothing happens.

I may extemporize myself out of public life with this method some of these days, but it is a firm policy of mine and I take great stock in it.

The other day I described the job we have undertaken in some such language: "What we are trying to do is to repair the front wheel of a bicycle and ride it at the same time."

JUNE 2, 1947
NEW YORK CITY

Tonight Helen and I had a new experience coming under the heading of excitement. We had just seen a show, and (whistling the best of the tunes, as people do, coming from the theater) we wandered out to Broadway, just as I saw ". . . ienthal says" going round the corner of the Times Square Building, in running lights, followed by something I had said this afternoon at Lake Success to the United Nations Working Committee. Helen had seen somewhat more than I, on another side of the building, and we waited around a while hoping it would "come on again"; but gave it up and decided we had had as much fun as the situation afforded anyway.

The show was *Finian's Rainbow*, and here, too, this was something "special." Yip Harburg visited the TVA and our home shortly after the 1944 election, as I recall, and just before (or after) his *Bloomer Girl* appeared first on Broadway. He said he was hoping to find some material for a musical play in the Valley, about which he was deliriously enthusiastic. When I heard about his new play, I understood it would have something to do with a valley and the South; but it was only after Nancy saw it a couple of weeks ago that its closer connection with his visit came to me. Actually, it had a great deal to do with us: the Senator was McKellar; the thought that the soil and resources of the region are the "gold" of the people; even Oak Ridge. We enjoyed it very much indeed.

I had gone through a considerable period of worry about my statement at Lake Success. When Osborn reported that the British delegate, Sir Charles Darwin, and the others had extended the invitation, I accepted without much thought about it. But as the time grew nearer, and Gromyko took a healthy poke at the American proposal, and Senator Taft and McKellar made ugly remarks about my forthcoming appearance, I began to realize this wasn't something to be done casually. I asked Marks, Volpe, and Frances Henderson to give me an outline; but nothing came of this at all.

So I went to Osborn's office this morning with some pencil notes, by which I hoped I could thread my way through an afternoon of discussion without injuring his important work, which he is carrying forward with considerable gallantry and the deepest earnestness. (So concerned had I been about the harm I might do by getting drawn into things that I should stay out of that I called Mr. Baruch and conferred with Senator Hickenlooper last week. Both, however, thought I should go, as to decline might well be offensive, but thought I could stay out of harm's way.)

While Osborn, his staff, and I were discussing the matter this noon, I learned that it was planned to give the press a copy of the transcript of my remarks immediately after my appearance. This bothered me some and worried Osborn a lot. Then we were told that the newspapermen were insisting on being present. Then the news release insisted on taking precedence. Everybody forgot about lunch, and I had to raise Ned in order to get a sandwich before we started out to the United Nations headquarters.

When we got there, I found one of the largest and most cosmopolitan news and photo groups that have ever swarmed over me—the foreign press is, of course, generously represented, as well as the American.

The theme I decided to stress—in its "lesson" value, though definitely not in volume of words—was that the purposes of the United States Commission and of an international one were quite different. The U.S. Commission represented national rivalry; the international agency an end to national rivalry. Hence, it was our purpose to maintain and increase the lead of the United States, whereas the international agency, if established, would take over all aspects of national agencies' activities in this field that related to weapons.

But I didn't realize what a sensation my bearing down on this point would make; showing how little, really, these men and the country understand the issues, broadly, in this matter.

The radio in the taxi on the way to the theater and the front-page stories in the *Herald Tribune* and *Times* indicate that the statement did a useful thing, without harming anything. And a day later Osborn was using my word "fraud" and approving and following up on my statement.* So what might have been quite bad seems to have come along well.

JUNE 7, 1947
AT HOME

Thursday of this week was one of those bad days when I wonder why in the name of hell and good sense I am willing to have anything to do with so ugly and insane an enterprise, much less accept chief responsibility for it.

These days usually have to do with cases where we are called upon to decide upon "clearance," that is, to play God and decide on ex parte evidence of FBI detectives whether Mr. A.'s or Mrs. B.'s loyalty, character, or associations are such as to justify permitting them access to Commission work and facilities—i.e., "restricted data." Most of these cases do not reach us, of course, but the tough ones, or the *causes célèbres*, do.

Thus, there was Thursday the case of a man and his wife who had been employed for the Brookhaven Laboratory, and then for four months have been sitting around, uncleared, while their friends wondered, their income was cut off and future clouded. The recommendation was that clearance be denied. Sounds simple enough. But scientists in the field of physics who have been passed upon that way—well, it's like a police record. Except that in the case of a police record the Constitution declares that you must be told of the charges against you, be confronted with the witnesses, but permitted the right to call your own witnesses to be heard in open court, to cross-examine, etc.

None of these things appear in these cases that come to us. These young detectives of the FBI talk to a lot of people, and the reports are abstracts of what they say about them: hearsay, most of it opinions. These files sometimes are volumes—100 pages. This is called "derogatory information."

We have been talking for a long time about the necessity of setting up review procedures that will make these things less arbitrary. But thus far, because we have been pressed with so many other things that seem more urgent, little progress has been actually made. We did have two able lawyers in from the outside to study some of these cases with

* I had called any international system to protect against clandestine nuclear activity a "fraud" that was not based on international cooperation; Osborn used the word more bluntly, to describe the Soviet atom control proposal.

a view to recommending how to go about providing decent evaluation and review. But as things now stand, the fact that ten years ago a scientist contributed to the defense of the Scottsboro boys, or believes in collective bargaining or the international control of atomic energy—such things as these are solemnly reported and regarded as "derogatory information"—and the sum total opinions of anonymous informants that a man doesn't have good judgment may lead to a star-chamber summary determination that may effectively end his career and make his whole life unhappy.

Well, this process makes me sick at the stomach—a lot more when I find myself part of it than when it is operated against me.

On the same day there was the appearance of two articles by J. Parnell Thomas, the irresponsible chairman of the Un-American Activities Committee—in *Liberty* magazine stating that Oak Ridge was just crawling with Communists, and that there was nothing but a fence standing between saboteurs and the plants; the other that Russia could get all the information about the atomic bomb she wanted, and was doing so, by copying patent applications. Such a disgraceful performance does make me a bit vomity. But I suppose it would even if I wasn't on the more or less receiving end.

And then we discussed our joining with the War, Navy, and State Departments at their initiative—actually the initiative of the security officers of the War Department with Patterson's active support—in securing legislation authorizing the Chairman of the AEC (and the Secretaries) to dismiss any employee summarily. I hate this sort of thing. It is only permissive, but it confers the kind of power that is bad for the best people, which includes us. The discussion about it didn't make me happy at the kind of business I was in, where such powers are probably necessary for emergency cases. I recalled vividly how we did approve the summary dismissal of a man at Wilson's recommendation late one day—and then two weeks later Wilson came to us to say that he had been mistaken on the facts.

Then we had a discussion of the proposed exportation of radioactive isotopes to foreign countries for research. As we analyzed this proposal I could see a bit more clearly what the future, the immediate future at least, appeared to hold out for the world, and this made me low as a duck's instep.

I was opposed to the idea of sending the isotopes abroad because I couldn't see how it would further the policy of bringing about international accord on control of atomic energy. So long as we are in an atomic weapons race it is only sense to do everything we can to slow up other countries in their efforts in this same direction—or so it seemed to me at the time, coming fresh from Lake Success as I did.

Then I projected for the Commissioners what that policy could and probably would mean, a policy of delaying others. It certainly meant a stringent control of machinery. Thus dredges and steam shovels may be more important to Russia's efforts, at this uranium mining stage, than almost anything else. Similarly with large electrical installations, necessary for isotope separation plants as we know them. And as the argument is carried forward, you see that *anything* that builds the economic strength and industrial productivity of European nations that are now or may fall within the influence or domination of Russia may shorten the period when Russia may have atomic weapons.

Then what happens to international trade, and that part of our own commerce that depends on foreign trade? What happens to a doctrine of aiding and assisting in the restoration of Europe, which Truman and Marshall are pressing these days? Will we not lose what friends we have abroad?

So radioactive isotopes, which could aid fundamental research in France and Sweden, say, and perhaps add a bit to a restoration of the international fraternity of knowledge, set off a train of thought that leads to a bitter isolation, and something more aggressive than isolation. How far we can go, and how quickly, if we do not find a way of improving this international tension.

Late in the day, along about 6:15, came another variety of messiness—this one rather dramatic. By this time I was so weary that this business didn't upset me, as it very definitely did my conferees; in fact, I was rather objective and flavored the story as it came out. It appeared that a former staff sergeant in charge of accounting for materials, etc., on his discharge in March of 1946, walked off with a number of what he called "souvenirs." These included documents from the first atomic test, at Trinity (Alamogordo), and other documents. As a souvenir collector he was a beaut, for as they were shown to me by the security officer who had recovered them, via the FBI, my eyes boggled.

This was a bit ironic, for having read Representative Thomas' recommendation that we keep the atomic energy development in Army hands "to safeguard the secret," we find that this young soldier walks off the premises, in Army hands, with hot documents.

I shall talk to Hoover about this situation Monday and urge him to press hard to find out, if possible, how many people have seen (or perhaps copied) the documents. But that there will be fumbles of this kind is inevitable, I suppose. How much of this sort of material is wandering around the country, taken away by the many thousands of former Manhattan project employees, God only knows. A year from now, or even now for that matter, it will be different: then the responsibility will be right smack-dab on me. What is there that can compensate one—I kept thinking on this low day—for such a damn-fool job?

And then there are the horror stories. It is good copy for magazines to print stories about what an atomic bomb will do if it drops in the middle of New York City or Washington, or how the world will be destroyed or two-headed children born (mutations) as a result of radiation, etc. And when such stories come from military men, or doctors, that causes all sorts of hell.

Well, we had a discussion of what to do about this. It is not pretty conversation: the idea of trying to suppress discussion doesn't fit into my temperament or background one damn bit.

I thought what we needed was to agree on a policy: that horror stories do not further intelligent action. This has been a theme of mine for some time and I made a strong point of it to the Dutch Treat Club in my off-the-record talk Tuesday. We should discuss the reasons for that policy openly, with the country. We should show the scientists who talk this way how quickly some terrible measures of suppression, violation of civil rights, etc., could follow if vast terrors were aroused by such horror stories.

Then, too, when there is a difference of opinion among scientists as to a technical point concerned with horrors, that fact should always be stated. Thus, Dr. Stafford Warren, a fine physician and radiology expert, made a speech the other day that the explosion of 500 atomic bombs of the type now known would destroy every living thing on earth because of accumulated radioactive effects. There are others who seriously disagree with him on his premises regarding radiation effects. He should, at the minimum, state that fact.

As to the Army people, we ought to press the reasons against their issuing horror stories, but not try to gag, or have them gagged by official action—so it seems to me. And voluntary censorship by the press in this country is virtually impossible and probably wrong to attempt. Our only hope is public discussion, and for us to select the subjects for discussion and also control the supply of facts about so vital a matter—that is something that is wrong in any hands.

But, as I say, this isn't too happy a subject matter for one's daily work.

It isn't all that way by any means. But there is enough of it to justify setting down the course of "one of those days."

JUNE 8, 1947
AT HOME, SUNDAY

The Dutch Treat luncheon speech went quite well: one of those rising ovation things at the end, which, for this gang of hard-shelled and overpaid lads, is pretty good. This was the first AEC speech I have done not wholly from MS—most of it was from notes or impromptu.

I get a kick out of seeing "celebrities" still. And the place was as full of them as Shakespeare is of "familiar quotations." F. P. Adams, the "Information Please" gent, came up to see me, full of warmth and cordiality that is quite contrary to his radio "character" on that program; Hu Webster, the cartoonist; Roy Howard, worried about the American proposal—"Why can't the Russians agree, and then three years later when they know everything say 'thanks' and withdraw and make a bomb?" It is evident that he has never read our report or the Baruch speech. Hugh Baillie, head of UP, with a crew haircut matching Gene Pulliam's (the Indiana publisher) and Kent Cooper of AP. James Melton, the singer, full of enthusiasm about how radio programs can help in "your problem" (I had insisted that it wasn't "my" problem but theirs, but never mind), and Rube Goldberg, a fabulous name for me, with a long neck in a blue shirt. John Golden, the producer, who made a big point of speaking to me afterward; H. V. Kaltenborn, a much more attractive man than his somewhat arbitrary voice and statements by air would indicate—wants to organize a radio commentators' luncheon, etc., for me to speak to the commentators. Clarence Budington Kelland, the author, who introduced me, and gave me a good opening to call him (in return for his ribbing me in the club's tradition) "Mr. Mc-Kelland." And Lowell Thomas, Frank Crowninshield, Walter Davenport, etc. Will Hays, the movie czar, looking startlingly youthful (he must be the age of Helen's Uncle Gayl), full of promises to help (about which I am most skeptical).

Spent an hour after the meeting at our offices in the Empire State Building—a noble view we have, too. Stopped to meet a number of the people working on raw materials—some of them unique (and a few years ago nonexistent) kinds of experts, as in uranium, thorium, Russian economic geology, etc. I have a long-time practice, from TVA work, of always stopping to meet the stenographers, file clerks, guards, etc., and apparently this caused quite a fluttering, for it was evident that it was not expected, but I think it was appreciated. Anyway, it is what I enjoy doing and I shall continue to do it.

Then, in a dash, to a party arranged for me many weeks ago by Ed Murrow of CBS, at his house. A tough customer of CBS, a prematurely white-haired man, Church, impressed me because he questioned practically everything I said. Good guy. Louis Fischer, a solemn-looking bear of a man: "What difference does it make whether the people know about atomic energy or not—what practical difference?" I think I told him. Quincy Howe, who recalled my efforts to dissuade Newton Arvin many years ago from his collectivist views. "You haven't changed in your position," says Howe. Lyman Bryson, Richard Hottelet, fresh from Moscow, youthful, a bit naïve and soft, I thought, but I understand a very good reporter. Russell Davenport, an enigma as far as I am concerned, who said he had come up from New Haven especially to see me but with whom I had few words. Joe Barnes, foreign news editor of the *Herald Tribune,* thoughtful, sober fellow, who said he had never seen any news lose its standing as rapidly and completely as that about atomic energy had in the past twelve months. "Unless there are orders from the front office, if it is about atomic energy it goes way back"—but who said what I had to say about the issue of free inquiry, and a number of other things I said, "was exciting—why don't we hear about *these* things?"

Davidson Taylor, all shy, grave, a CBS executive. A keen young fellow from the *New Republic,* co-author of a recent best-seller on China —can't recall his name, but an able fellow.†

Then dinner with my brother Ted (in for a shopping trip and looking fine) and the long train ride home, talking most of the way with Trapnell‡ when I should have been resting. Got in about 1 A.M. Up again at 7:30 A.M. for a hard, hard day at the office.

More about the trip to New York.

Helen and I got to the hotel Sunday night about 9:00; had late supper and went out for a long walk along Fifth Avenue. Great pleasure, really, for it was one of those spring nights and there are few things we enjoy more than a rather aimless walk of this kind. (I am quite determined that by one means or another Helen can go on more of my trips; we were apart because of my travels far too much in TVA. Being in New York together twice in a month, as this time, breaks all records for us, I believe.)

Monday morning I went over to Mr. Baruch's apartment, just off Fifth Avenue about 67th Street. He has sold his big house on Fifth Avenue for a little apartment, he had told me, which latter consisted of an enormous jernt; in the servants' wing, six bedrooms and baths, etc. He was having his hair cut when I arrived; as Miss Novarro showed me around the place and let me into his bedroom where the shearing was taking place. He sat there looking like a little boy, a cloth around his neck, and that stiff, upright position that a kid takes when the shears are snipping at him. He has the twinklingest eyes, when he is amused, of almost any man I have known, at any age.

He was in fine form (that morning he was to be given still another

† This would have been Theodore H. White.
‡ Acting director of the AEC information office.

honor—the Cardozo medal or something of the sort—and this seemed to set him up particularly). In any case, he gave me a good demonstration of the "personality" and eloquence that have made him such a figure; that and the compulsions of a tremendous ego.

He is quite intemperate about the British. They are going the way of Germany and Russia and Italy—"die for dear old fascism"; "suffer for the Fatherland and Hitler—rah, rah Princeton; rah, rah Socialism." That sort of thing, delivered with great gusto.

A very flattering portrait in oils of his dear friend Winnie looked out at us—Winnie *without* his paunch and whiskey complexion, incidentally. And Woodrow Wilson, an austere portrait, done at the Paris Conference. These two, and his father, are B.M.B.'s great heroes.

His violent feeling against the British features his thoughts these days. The Socialist Government could account for it alone, I suppose, especially since it substituted for his friend Churchill some strangers. I rarely saw a man who was more *personal* in his political and economic judgments. He kept up a running fire of critical comments about the British. This has some importance in my work, for he skirted the matter of our relations with the British in the atomic energy business: were we still dividing raw materials, etc.

He said we must not let any machinery go abroad that the Russians (or anyone else, I recall) could use to further their atomic energy efforts. I pointed out that this matter will include such diverse things as steam shovels and electrical power generators.

He seemed to be quite friendly and interested in me, as a person, this time. He spoke of all the honors that were being proffered to him—some of them he couldn't accept because they meant travel "that will knock me out; and I don't want to be knocked out"—an honorary degree at Washington University at St. Louis, for example. "Well, these things will be coming to you, too; people will come to respect you very much. That is bound to happen. The only trouble is, you ought to have money; you ought to take time off—how old are you? 50? Oh, 47. Well, you ought to take time out right soon and earn a lot of money. I was born at a lucky time when a fellow could earn a lot of money, taxes didn't take it all, and now I can surround myself with beautiful things." He waved to the contents of the large drawing room. Chinese furniture, lovely, of course, and so on. I thought to myself, "This isn't stuff a fellow can put his feet on." This part of the argument about having money didn't sound very persuasive. If he had said, "You will burn yourself out in a few years at this pace, and then no one will want you, and then where will you be for a living?"—that would have impressed me.

An important and most interesting hour with Admiral Kirk, our Ambassador to Belgium. Nothing could better illustrate the potential hazards to world peace that will come, and are coming, from an atoms arms race. I remember when our board was studying this matter, it was Joe Volpe's guarded statements (responding to my questions) about competition for raw materials throughout the world that opened my eyes—it was, I believe, then that it occurred to me what should be the theme of the report: the elimination of national competition in this field because that competition was *itself* a cause of war. This is re-enforced almost every time we look at the world raw materials situation.§

Kirk's dispatches from Brussels have been a great help in the past months.

A year ago I was at Salt Lake City—the Utah speech. So much has happened I can hardly believe this is only a year.

I have felt a considerable nostalgia the past few days—acute—this doesn't happen often. Have been rather tired, too—the reaction from the intensity of the days since we returned from the trip, and particularly the two days in New York. But I can sleep like mad—12 hours last night—so I am all right.

JUNE 12, 1947
AT THE OFFICE, THURSDAY

(Meeting with the Secretary of State, General Marshall, New State Department Building, June 11.)

The fabulous young officer, General Carter, dark, bird-like, said the Secretary would see us; it was 12:15 "on the nose." He met me as I came in (followed by Bob Bacher, Lewis Strauss, and young General McCormack) and asked me to sit in a corner of a leather sofa, at the right of his chair; this was in a corner of his long, narrowish, and beautiful office. (But it doesn't compare with the offices in the old State Department Building.)

I had met General Marshall, rather casually, during the early days of the war, while he, Hopkins, and Admiral King were waiting, one noon, to see F.D.R. His was a stern and concentrated face and figure, in my memory of that brief meeting. (This was—to fix the date—when the President was trying to persuade George Norris, who had just been defeated in the Nebraska primary, to accept some kind of assignment in the Government.)

But the Marshall of yesterday seemed quite different. For one

§ Belgium at the time controlled the largest source of uranium ore, in the Union Minière mines in the Congo.

thing, now quite relaxed, very free and with a twinkle in his eye, even when we were going to the point of the matter we were there to discuss. Youthful-looking in color and demeanor. And with not one sign of tension or worry. I am not sure whether this is good or not, considering how much there is to worry about.

(Which is a good place to interpolate a story McCormack told afterward. During the worst days of the war, young staff officers—he was one of them—were assigned to "sit on the old man's telephone" through the night, sleeping on a cot in the General's office, and if the calls for the Chief of Staff seemed important enough, to put them through to him at his home. It was in one of those very low moments— right after Tobruk, the African debacle. The telephone rang and he answered. "This is Major McCormack." "This is General Marshall; how are things going?" Before he could think, he said, "Jesus Christ, General, don't *you* know?" He was thinking, of course, of the whole sorry state of the war, for us; but all the General had called for was just to know whether there was anything at the office he should know about before turning in. A good story, and it was well told.)

I started off with our mission. From a technical and production viewpoint the Commission had decided on project T.❡ Since it was an important activity with broad implications it would require the President's approval. I had discussed it informally, on April 16, with the President, the President's Chief of Staff, Admiral Leahy, and Secretary Patterson and Secretary Forrestal, and again with Leahy on June 10. Our purpose today was to state to him the need for the project (which must be handled on the highest level of secrecy, at this stage particularly, as possible) and to secure his views. The reasons for needing project T I stated rather simply. To carry it out required perhaps nine months of planning, so if the project were to be carried out by the summer of 1948, an early decision on policy was necessary.

Why did I think that the Department of State had an interest in T? I answered that T might be construed by other nations in a way that would affect his (Marshall's) work as Secretary of State. Other nations would, of course, know about it, for the fact that the project was to be carried out would have to be made known at some stage.

Why did it take nine months to get ready? We thought that time could be shaved, and there were good reasons for wanting to cut the period; but that was the best figure that our staff would give at the present time, for these things took a great deal of advance work.

Where would T be undertaken? Outside the continental limits of the U.S., on an island in the Pacific probably. Why? The alternative,

❡ The atomic weapons test series at Eniwetok.

within the U.S., would create considerable fears and concern, possible damage suits, and general public relations problems.

Outside the U.S., T would create more problems for him. We could see why this would be. The time would be very important (it was clear that he understood fully why we had informed him and sought the views of the State Department). If it were in November, or just before November when the meeting of Foreign Ministers is scheduled for London, or immediately afterward, this would probably be unfortunate. He smiled quietly as he said these things.

We had covered the essentials in very short order; I handed him a ¾-page letter summarizing it, which he read, saying this would be useful as a basis for discussion with his advisers; they would think it over and let me know.

I was prepared to leave. But the General's memory had been stirred by this talk and he began to talk, and the next half-hour was one of the most interesting I have ever spent.

"There has been a good deal of discussion about whether we were justified in using the atomic bomb. There is one point that was missed, and that, frankly, we missed in making our plans. That was the effect the bomb would have in so shocking the Japanese that they could surrender without losing face. One of the things that appalled me was the cost, in casualties, of an invasion; that was set for November. Even an ill-equipped force can cost terrible loss to a landing party. To get to the plains would have been a very costly operation, in lives. We knew that the Japanese were determined and fanatical, like the Morros, and we would have to exterminate them, almost man by man. So we thought the bomb would be a wonderful weapon as a protection and preparation for landings. But we didn't realize its value to give the Japanese such a shock that they could surrender without complete loss of face.

"Stimson wrote a good article about it, but he generously took a greater share of the responsibility than was fair. But what he said as to the considerations that were weighed is entirely true. But we missed one of the most important consequences."

At this point Lewis said that he had thought Stimson had said one thing that might better have not been said at this time, as a possible security breach; namely, that we only had two bombs at the time we told the Japanese they could expect a whole series of these things if they didn't surrender. That, in view of the disclosure now that we only had two, might make us out as bluffers, which in the future might make our statements subject to discount.

The General looked at the ceiling and said, "No, I don't think so." Then he talked about the schedule as he recalled it. That up to the time of the invasion (November), the schedule called for a total of twelve, three for each of two areas related to landing (he said nothing about how the radioactivity would affect our own forces). Knowing the situation, we all looked a bit incredulous, particularly Bob Bacher, who told us later, with his boyish grin, that "We would have had to hump to make such a schedule"—meaning, when translated, that such a number could not have been ready.

This then led Marshall to talk about the argument that the use of the bomb was not humane. He disagreed with that; it had actually been humane because it shortened the war and made it unnecessary to exterminate the Japanese. And then he went into a discussion of the use of poison gas. He had definitely favored the use of gas—he called it gas—not poison gas. "We were all ready to use it on some of the islands." After the terrible losses at Iwo Jima he was prepared to use gas at Okinawa; just sending in enough to force the inhabitants to move into a remote part of the island and to keep the troops in masks. If they were in masks for a week, they would be so weakened that the invasion could have been accomplished with little loss of life. He described this technique in some particularity. No mention of the fact that international law forbade its use. He didn't argue that it was justified but only whether it would be effective in accomplishing the result without such terrible losses as the island invasions occasioned.

This I thought rather striking—this matter of not referring to the international covenants about gas. And he spoke with such gentleness (which is the way he always does—a soft, husky voice and soft features), yet he was talking about great military operations and his conclusion that gas should be used.

So, of course, I said, "This is very interesting, in respect to atomic weapon control, for the Russians support their position that an international prohibition against the use of atomic weapons is all that is necessary upon the ground that this is the way poison gas was banned from warfare. The argument seemed to me fallacious, for a number of reasons, but this is the first discussion of the use of gas in this war I have heard that throws some light on the effectiveness of banning a particular means of warfare."

The General's candor is remarkable and he met the question head on. "The reason it was not used was chiefly the strong opposition of Churchill and the British. They were afraid that this would be the signal for the Germans to use gas against England." Then he spent some time indicating how exceedingly vulnerable the British are, compared to ourselves and others; how well they realize it; how they worry about it; how it affects their attitude in international dealings; how important it is for us to try to understand their feeling.

This opposition to gas in the Pacific was before the V-2 bombs use, he said.

There was one delightful story about General Groves.

"There was a great deal of difficulty persuading them on the Hill [Congress] to put up all this money on a gamble, and one that they had to take our word for. I always had had trouble getting appropriations for the Army, and to get this much money on something that might not work wasn't too pleasant. One day General Groves asked to see me. I was writing at my desk, and I asked him to have a seat until I finished; it wouldn't take me more than five minutes, I explained. Gen. Groves was living way up above ordinary mundane affairs" (he said this with a chuckle that we were in a position to understand and relish) "so he sat there while I wrote away. Then I turned to him and asked him what he had on his mind. It was this: there was a process that he was sure would quadruple our output, but it would cost another hundred million dollars, and would I sign a letter so he could go ahead. Well, I said, a hundred million dollars is a lot of money. But we had already spent almost two billions, and that seemed a good bet—another one hundred million to increase the production four times—so after a few minutes' discussion I signed the letter for a hundred million dollars.

"Then I said to Groves, 'You may have wondered why I kept you waiting'—Groves is a very serious man about himself, and he took this very solemnly. 'Well, I was writing out an order and a check to Burpee'" (he accented the final "ee") "'for flower seeds to the total of $3.94.' Without batting an eye Groves said, 'You don't need to apologize for keeping me waiting; it was perfectly all right,' and got up and walked almost to the door before he turned around and gave some sign that he got the point of my remark about keeping him waiting on the hundred million while I wrote out a check for $3.94."

Last night I went to a dinner meeting of the Business Advisory Council of the Department of Commerce, something set up early in the New Deal and still functioning. Marshall was the speaker. Said it was his third speech that day, but he looked as fresh as he had at noon, and spoke, without any notes, quite easily and at length. Spoke first about the department: it needed only minor organizational changes. Spoke of Acheson's going as a sad loss, and when he said Clayton was to leave in September (which is news), there was a groan from the 40-odd men around the table.* Then he spent almost an hour talking about China. He told of the difficulties, the suspicion between the Government and the anti-Government groups, chiefly Communist. He

---

* Acheson resigned at the end of the month to return to his law practice; Clayton, under secretary for economic affairs, resigned in October.

emphasized how the Generalissimo simply does not know what is going on; that the Government Party is organized from the top down, whereas the Communist is a grass roots from the bottom up organization with the strength that gives them public support; that Chiang Kai-shek has some of the most incompetent military men Marshall ever saw around him, but he won't dismiss them because they are old military classmates of his. And so on.

"I have tortured my brain and I can't now see the answer."

Well, it was quite a day of "Marshall." Fine human being. Whether he, or any other human being, can do much to straighten the world out in our time is open to real question. So far as our work is concerned, my sentiments were those I expressed as we left: "Mr. Secretary, it is our hope that as a result of your labors in the next year or so you will put us out of business, at least out of the business we have been talking to you about this morning."


JUNE 13, 1947
AT HOME

This noon I went to the National War College, where amid quite some ceremony Herbert Swope presented a bust of Mr. Baruch to the War College, which they accepted with great acclaim. The way these things are staged is a tribute to the school of men who want to take no chances about what happens to their name after their death; they take care of it while they are alive and can arrange it personally. Actually, the old boy has done his country very great service and he should be honored for it in every way. I would prefer for myself if these things were somewhat less "managed" and arranged, however. But that may be the counsel of perfection.

Then the Secretaries (Marshall, Forrestal, Patterson, Harriman), General Eisenhower, Admiral Nimitz, and a few others had lunch (an elegant luncheon with Virginia ham) at the home of the Commandant, Vice Admiral Hill. I sat at a little bridge table with General Eisenhower. He is a relaxed man and full of energy and talk.

Admiral Hill made a big point of urging me to speak to the War College in November; which I shall do, of course.

Got something of a blow today. House Appropriations Committee reported out our bill. It took care of us on money and had only one important fly in the ointment: limitation on salaries above $10,000 except for those authorized by statute. This was discouraging, though not wholly unexpected. It is hard enough to make headway in recruiting without adding this sort of handicap.

An amusing exchange about "worry."

I was standing outside the War College, main building, talking with Leon Henderson, who is now head of a private research agency and making a lot of money. General Marshall came down the steps and stopped to talk to us.

"Look at this fellow," I said, pointing to Leon. "Out of public life, nothing to worry about."

"Hell," said Leon, "my business is worry; doing other people's worrying for them."

"What worries me," rejoined Marshall, "is that I can't worry as much as I ought."

JUNE 14, 1947

Admiral Leahy reached me by phone at noon today, while I was on the Hill, with the following message: that he had taken up with the President on their trip to Canada the matter which I had taken up with the Admiral in regard to T and that the President "was all for the idea in principle," but that he would want to talk to the Secretary of State, Secretary of War, and Secretary of the Navy about it.

I reported to Admiral Leahy that we had visited with General Marshall on the matter. He asked if Marshall expressed himself. I said he had reserved judgment until he could consult with his assistants and then would let us know. Admiral Leahy said he would suggest to the President that he see General Marshall and get his view.

JUNE 15, 1947
AT HOME, SUNDAY

Little Penny has been very sick all week. It has made us all pretty sad and anxious. I see her, so thin and weak and sometimes apparently about to go, and I think of all the fun we have had; see her digging like mad, her tail and hind legs stuck up, and then practically disappear into a hole—how much this always amused us. And her "hunting tail motion"—that special quick flutter she reserved for bird or rabbit scent. And how she always resembled Wrong-Way Corrigan by picking up a rabbit scent and dashing off in full cry heading wildly along the trail where the rabbit had come from. And so on.

Helen is so sweet and tender with her, putting her in the study and sleeping in there so she can look at her during the night. But it is getting to be a strain on her, and if Penny can't live, it might be more humane to have the vet put her to sleep—which is the way we cover what we mean, which is to kill her.

The vet says she has a bad heart, and these spells are heart attacks. She hasn't eaten a bite for days now and simply won't have anything to do with food. She may have some malignancy inside, too, the vet says.

Well, it hangs over us all. She *is* old—will be 13 this summer—which at the ratio of 7 to 1 is the equivalent of 91 years for a human being. So we shouldn't be surprised that old age is taking its toll of her. But when she peps up she is so endearing and yet so helpless that it wrings your heart.

This is rather rough going these past days.

Yesterday we began the day with a meeting between the Military Liaison Committee and the Commission, with Groves present. Efforts were made to smoke him out about the "top Government official" who was the source of the scare stories about theft of secrets at Oak Ridge. He denied having talked with the *Times-Herald* but admitted he talked with Representative Thomas (of the Un-American Activities Committee) and always talked to newspapermen—and gave notice he intended to continue to do so.

Late in the day we—the five of us plus General Brereton—called on Patterson and told him it was no longer possible to work with Groves. We put it very strongly but without temper, I thought. Surprisingly, he didn't blow up, was very philosophical (as he said, he could afford to since it was we who were having the trouble) and said we should wait a few days to see what the Congressional investigations about the Oak Ridge stories amounted to.

About 5 P.M. Brien McMahon called to say that the Joint Committee was about to go into session to hear one of their dopey investigators report that he had been to the University of Chicago and had learned from our survey up there that 300 documents were missing. This was a stingeroo. Called in Tom Jones (a security officer) and learned that this occurred in 1945, under the Army. But, of course, no one will bother much with that. It will start the stories all over again.

It's hard to sleep and hard to toss all this off. Growing feeling: the temper of the country and the nature of the job are such that I am beginning to wonder if we will ever get on top of it. Yet TVA was in a mess for the first four years and I finally got on top of that. But we don't have the atmosphere for work here.

JUNE 16, 1947

Major General Fred L. Anderson called on me today and I spent almost an hour with him. He is with Joint Chiefs of Staff Planning.

He talked to me about a problem that is being discussed; he came to see me on the suggestion of Admiral Nimitz. The problem is what should we do in the event the efforts in New York for international agreement are a demonstrable failure by autumn.

I threw out a few ideas about this, but this is not the purpose of this note. It is rather to record what he ran into in England. He had just returned on a secret mission, his name not on the manifest, civilian clothes, etc. He reported that British military people were quite bitter because they felt that this country through its knowledge of atomic energy development could if it wished help England to solve its fuel problem via atomic energy; that we didn't do so despite the fact that the project during the war was carried out on a partnership basis.

Although a professional soldier, you could see that this feeling had rather shaken him. I said that it was an illusion that atomic energy electricity was just around the corner, that this was quite untrue and we had said so repeatedly. He said it would do a great deal of good if the Commission were officially to make such a statement. At the end of our talk about other things as he left he looked at me in a gravely concerned manner and again urged that we do something to explain that the British were not being kept from atomic energy tomorrow. I reported this to my associates.

J. Edgar Hoover just called to say that after checking into the matter he sees no reason—from the standpoint of the FBI—why the Commission may not report to the Joint Committee, in executive session, the Luft case. I had raised this question with him in a visit on Monday, June 9, thinking that such a report might prejudice current investigations. This is the case re: missing records traced to Alexander Von Der Luft.†

JUNE 17, 1947
AT HOME, TUESDAY

When I got home about 7:15 P.M. I was plenty low. It was one of those days that take the heart out of me; which means I have had too much of the legislative branch. What the hell: why should I work so desperately hard while these thin top-soil boys make it impossible to do a job?

Talking to Wigglesworth, as narrow a man as one can imagine,

† Von Der Luft and another soldier had taken some classified documents as "souvenirs" from Los Alamos in 1946, when they were Army sergeants there in the Manhattan project. The story caused a stir in July when it was printed in sensational form by the New York *Sun* and the Washington *Times-Herald*.

about the necessity for discretion in fixing salaries to attract good men was one cause of my low state.

An afternoon before the Joint Committee was the second: such self-assurance and superficiality and just orneryness. A thick-headed committee "staff" member told all about what was wrong with physical security at Oak Ridge; one trip and he has all the things that are wrong. And a long, tense day of appointments all through.

But after a good dinner and the wonderful atmosphere of this place that is home, and a rousing series of games of horseshoes with David and I feel all right again. At least I feel I can carry on despite such messy experiences as this. I am determined, however, to carry to the country, in some fashion, how we are expected to do a big and important job and then are hampered by such absurd limitations as we do experience. But the price of public service—and the test of whether one is fit for it—is ability to absorb just this kind of punishment—for that is just the word for it.

Actually, I am having a wonderful time—the most exhilarating kind of experience, and I *ought* to be made to pay for it somehow!

Had lunch with Frances Perkins in her office at the Civil Service Commission. She told some amusing stories about the Civil Service Commission.

We talked about "Henry" (Wallace), who spoke here last night. Said the politicos among the Democrats wouldn't like to admit it, but actually they were worried about the inroads he was making. Huge crowds all over the country who actually paid admission to hear him. "They may have to run him for Vice President yet," she said. I can't imagine such a thing myself. His speech last night—I heard it by radio—was in excellent voice and delivery. A plea for peace is always a moving thing; it made an impression on David, quite evidently. But Wallace is actually just as full of the "or else" attitude toward Russia as everyone else; it is just that he draws the line of 54-40 or fight at a different place.

Well, I feel better getting these things off my chest. Of all the things I most prize as accomplishments, this ability to write shorthand ranks high on the list. In a few minutes I can write what would take quite a while on the machine or in longhand.

JUNE 24, 1947
AT THE OFFICE

This has been a rather bad time. Tossed around last night and feel on the low side, despite a good rest over the weekend. A feeling of discouragement (I wrote that first "despair") that is hard to throw off.

When I stop to analyze it, it comes down to anger about almost everything I must do that relates to this Congress. Helen reminds me that it took years of hard, patient, and uphill work before there was even a handful in Congress who understood TVA and had confidence in what I was trying to do. And this problem of atomic energy is even worse—more complex, more filled with emotional, even hysterical, content. But I have had a hard time shaking off the feeling the last week or so that it is quite hopeless, that it will not improve, and "why in hell" should I have to put up with it? I think about just how I will state, next spring, that 15 years in the Federal service is enough, and stop play-acting.

Part of this is nothing more serious than injured pride, or wounded ego or something of the kind. This is because of what appeared in the report to the House of the Appropriations Committee. I had parleyed around with Taber about how we could avoid disclosing secret data to the members of his committee that he thought (and frankly said) couldn't be "trusted" (meaning they would talk, not that they were disloyal, of course). I thought it was all agreed to. They were all worried about our putting top secret information into the hearing record. Then when we didn't, their report made it appear that we had put in no worthwhile information at all. Wigglesworth, on the floor, made us out a bunch of dopes who didn't know what we were doing.

I talked to Everett Dirksen of the Appropriations Committee (member from Illinois, and, I believe, a kind of friend) about this this morning and have written a memo to the Commission about it which follows.

This is about what I said, and reported to my Commission colleagues.

I said I felt we had been quite unfairly dealt with by the House Appropriations Subcommittee; that the committee through the conference we had with Mr. Taber, its chairman, had expressed most concern about the wisdom of submitting detailed secret information to the committee in view of the fact that, as Mr. Taber put it, there are men on his committee that he didn't think were trustworthy and who talked too much; that after our first hearing, on that basis, much of the broad outlines of the program were described but little classified information supplied; that we came back with seven or eight top secret documents that analyzed what we proposed to do and how much it would cost, though not setting forth, as it would be impossible to do realistically, the exact number of people that the Commission or its contractors would require for these broad and experimental programs or for vast construction work still in pre-design stage; that at the second hearing we had the distinct impression that the committee preferred not to receive this top secret information; that two members of the committee, Mr. Thomas and Mr. Phillips, expressed considerable concern even about the non-classified breakdown, to say nothing of the other very revealing program analyses and top secret tables; that it was to a considerable extent because of the insistence of the Commission that the committee examined and read testimony off the record and with the reporter excluded on these documents. Nevertheless, the committee's report to the House stated that they had been unable to get an adequate picture or to get adequate analyses and breakdowns of our program and what we proposed to spend the money for and made no reference whatever to the extensive off-the-record testimony submitted. This I said to Dirksen I felt was taking unfair advantage of the Commission inasmuch as it would be difficult for the Commission to defend itself and such statements would inevitably impair public confidence and Congressional confidence in the Commission; that the committee should at least have referred to the fact that substantial and extensive off-the-record tables and testimony were presented covering the program, and that these tables, while the details could not be guaranteed because of the nature of the program itself, would present a broad and comprehensive picture of what the Commission proposed to do.

I got this off my chest because it has been bothering me considerably. I said something of the same thing to Senator Hickenlooper yesterday morning when I discussed with him the necessity for a Joint Committee series of meetings with the Commission. I stated to Senator Hickenlooper that if the Congress expected us to maintain security and at the same time expected detailed knowledge of the Commission's activities and plans, then in all fairness and decency the Congress must accept responsibility for maintaining security of such information, which will be highly classified and highly important, or it should explicitly decline to hear such testimony and put the full responsibility on the Commission. Having made a detailed presentation to the Congress as we had to the House committee and then have no reference made to that fact in the committee's public presentation and statement on the floor giving the impression that the Commission is providing no information will destroy the Commission's standing and make its task impossible.

[NOTE: *The following was written June 24, 1947, and filed with my Journals as "contemporary evidence" of how I felt about my job.*]

The author of the following piece holds what is probably the world's worst job. It is not only full of nightmares and horrors; it is a job that needs every "break" in order to succeed, and yet starts out with two strikes against its success. The Atomic Energy Commission is expected to carry out a highly complex managerial and technical undertaking, on which the world's future may depend. [And yet] the worst imaginable way to get a complex technical job done at the present time is to have it done by the Federal Government, at a time when the conditions of Government service have dropped to the lowest level within living memory.

If anyone could have possibly imagined some way to do this job except through government, it would have been set up that way. But through a whole year of Congressional conversation, no one could imagine turning this terrific power over to a private corporation. So if it was to be done, it had to be by the Federal Government. And because of the hazards of atomic energy, because of its close relation to national defense, and because there was no chance for profit within the immediate future, it was turned over to a Government commission, as a tight Government monopoly.

The making of atomic weapons and the development of the potentially vast beneficial uses of this new force—these are not routine jobs, like collecting taxes or garbage, or making automobiles or adding machines. This calls for the very highest order of scientific and technical skills, and the ability to supervise and manage a pioneer undertaking. It requires the best managers and scientists and engineers the country has.

But men of these qualifications are busy at their own work, in industry, in the universities, in private undertakings of various kinds. What does the Government have to offer them to induce them to stop what they are doing and join the Atomic Energy Commission's work? If we were in a shooting war, they could all be had, as they were before. But the incentives to work for the Government are very slim at the present time. Industries have had their fill of breaking their necks to do a good job, as many of them did during the war, and then have some irresponsible politician in Congress denounce them when it is all over— when the ships have been built, the trucks delivered on time, the war won.

Scientists—what incentive is there for them, upon whom this country is absolutely dependent if we are to keep our military pre-eminence? Well, the Atomic Energy Commission can assure them absurdly low salaries, the good prospect that they will be investigated and humiliated with personal abuse by noisy demagogues, and that they must work under conditions of secrecy and often of isolation in dreary Government towns.

And what about able young executives, whose services are needed more than all else—for management is the essential ingredient of the entire atomic energy enterprise? They will be working for the

Government—either directly on the Commission staff or as an employee of a Commission contractor. And at the very time when so much depends upon the success of a Government enterprise which may be the nation's chief defense, Government service, one must admit candidly, has become the least attractive form of human activity. The temper of Congressional debate, the attacks on the motives of such superb public servants as Dean Acheson and Will Clayton, has reached a new hundred-year low—and worst of all, the addition of impossible and unworkable red tape by recent legislation of Congress.

The chance of success is therefore not more than 50-50.

(SUMMARY OF CONVERSATION WITH CLARK CLIFFORD AT THE WHITE HOUSE, 12:00 NOON)

I called on Mr. Clifford at his request. He first asked me how things were going, whether I was glad I had finally agreed to take the job, etc. Then he said there was another matter that might cause some friction that he wanted to discuss. He said that the President, even though he is President, has certain "practical problems." Occasionally he has to find a place for someone. On a few occasions, he thinks it was three, Matt Connelly, the President's secretary, has sent a chit over to us saying that the President knows Mr. "A" and he is very good and is there a place he could fill in the organization? Matt has reported that not a thing has been heard from any of these chits, though the President has recommended these people. This was causing some friction.

I started to bristle at this and said that the fact that the President considered these people as problems meant that they were political problems; that the President's judgment of their qualifications would be very important because he is a good judge of people, but that the fact that it was the President who recommended them—"Now I want to get this straight, Clark—doesn't make and will not make one bit of difference; I don't want to sail under any false colors about this."

I was about to go on in this vein arguing an abstract question when Clifford was interrupted by a telephone call. When he was through, I said, "Clark, what do you think we should do in these cases?" He saw that I had my stubborn mood on and said, "Now I am in my work for no political reason, just as you are. Politics don't mean a thing to me. All in the world I want you to do is to see that these communications are answered. If the man recommended doesn't meet qualifications, or there isn't any appropriate place for him even though he is qualified, just let Connelly know so he can get off the hot seat."

This seemed reasonable enough and I let it pass by saying that I hoped we understood each other about political appointments from any source, but of course every recommendation should be acknowledged and the result communicated and if we had failed to do so I would talk to Mr. Waller‡ and see that it was corrected.

JUNE 26, 1947
THURSDAY

Our first successful, really successful, meeting with the Joint Committee on Atomic Energy. Very carefully planned in advance, even to holding it here at our office at 9:00 in the morning (and almost full attendance, including Vandenberg), and close attention through two hours and more of discussion. It takes the kind of careful preparation, rehearsal, criticism of method in advance, etc., to do a job of this kind.

I led off by stating that our assumption, our idea of what the country and the Congress expected of us, was that we maintain and increase the pre-eminence of this country in atomic energy development and atomic weapons; that this required maximum production and uninterrupted production and an increase in production of fissionable materials. That there was trouble and danger on this score, and that although it involved important secret information it was our duty to inform the Joint Committee of the facts and particularly of what we were doing about it. Then Wilson explained the Hanford process, the troubles there; then Zinn of Argonne National Laboratory did a whale of a job explaining the basic scientific situation of neutrons, which produce other neutrons, fission products, and heat, and how each of these affects the problem. It was a great job of explaining.

Then solid, substantial-looking Harry Winne told of the industrial and construction plans.

This took about two hours, and only two members left, and there was the closest attention.

Vandenberg, who sat next to me at the head of the table, asked me if the situation would be improved if our arrangements with the British regarding raw materials were "rewritten," and after thinking a bit I said, "No." That story Acheson told them is working on him.

Our purpose was to impress the committee with the difficulty and seriousness of our problems so they wouldn't be too impressed with silly rabbit-chasing side issues, as they were recently when one of their staff creeps reported to the committee about plant security at Oak Ridge: such gunk as, "You could plant a mortar 1,200 feet away and blow up the plant."

But the highlight of the meeting wasn't something serious but quite otherwise. We had set up a mouse trap demonstration of an

‡ AEC personnel director.

atomic chain reaction—traps set with two black rubber corks on each set trap. A "neutron" cork tossed in set off the whole, to everyone's amazement. Vandenberg jumped a foot and everyone was delighted. They will remember that. In fact, it appears that there will be much photographing of it. Hickenlooper came all the way up to the office Saturday—the day after—to be photographed while the thing was going off. "If you set that up in the Senate, you would get 100 percent attendance at a Senate meeting," he said.

We propose to follow this with two other meaty confabs. The purpose is not only to inform the committee but to give them a sense of the complexity, the magnitude, and the importance of the central problems we are sweating with and therefore to minimize and cut down to size the kind of piddling details that otherwise become the subject matter of such meetings. The initial one was very successful. (Unhappily, John Bricker, who could have used some of this, was not present.)

JUNE 27, 1947
AT HOME

David "took off" a week ago to see the country. No papa-paid de luxe expeditions for him. He had the $65 he had left from his college funds, an old battered handbag, *and* his thumb. In short, he proposed to cross the continent by hitchhiking, which he did. We had a few postal cards from Ohio, St. Louis, Idaho (he had to take a bus through Utah as a "state cop drove me off the road"), and then (as promised beforehand) a wire that he had arrived in "Frisco" in six days. Also the jubilant news that he had won a sixth of a Hudson automobile! He and five other students decided they would gang up on a Planter's Peanut contest; divided the dictionary up among them, and sent in answers to some kind of "word" contest that represented mass production of some sort. And in the first contest one of them (representing all) won; they think they are going to win all the other Hudsons too, I guess.

Quite a boy.

As for Nancy: she set off for Cambridge and Radcliffe last Tuesday, there to take a six-week course in book publishing and magazine techniques—not the writing but the publication side. Then she would launch a new career, her father having "kicked her out" of her one as a Government economist. Yesterday we had a letter from Miss Willson Whitman in New York: "Your daughter at the moment is having luncheon with the managing editor of *Collier's;* Friday she has an interview at *The New Yorker*." Not a word to us about these rather grandiose ideas.

As Helen says: "She figures that if she has to start in all over again she might as well talk to the top as to the employment office." Well, God bless her, I hope her everything good for her independent and sweet self.

(NOTES ON A MEETING AT WHITE HOUSE, JUNE 27, FRIDAY, 3:30–4:00 P.M.)

I was the first to arrive for the meeting; Brig. General McCormack with me. We were ushered into the Cabinet Room. Looking out on the garden we could see the others arrive, coming through the walk beside the swimming pool and the rose garden, a walk I remember for so many reasons. First was General Eisenhower, with that springy, short stride of his, so familiar to so many over the world, with a young aide alongside. It was rather like a play, watching them come without their seeing you. Then came Admirals Leahy and Nimitz, two very self-assured-looking old men.

General Eisenhower chatted with me a while before the others came. Apparently Bush had told him I was considerably disturbed by the treatment we had received from the House committee and the general difficulties of carrying this kind of load under present political conditions. I referred to the fact that I had been forced to cancel our luncheon engagement (which he had called me to fix) because of a Senate appropriation hearing. He said, "Don't let those fellows on the Hill worry you too much." I expect we will talk about this further when I see him Monday at luncheon as we now plan.

Patterson was the last to come, a grim, humorless, intense-looking man, punching his steps out of the air before him. We were sitting at the end of the Cabinet table. We rose, in the middle of some laughing remark Eisenhower was making about the British expression "the Admiral's Club" (meaning cautious men, I recall), for the President had come in through the door to his office next door. I was closest to him and so violated seven kinds of protocol by shaking hands first.

He took the chair at the end of the table, nodded to me and said I had a matter to present; that he knew about it and thought there was only one thing to do but, of course, he wanted their views. "Will you state it?" he said, rather solemnly to me. So I did.

"Our technical staff are unanimous in the view that T . . .§ The reason is a rather simple one." I stated it (the reasons are set out in memoranda to Leahy and Marshall and had best not be written down more often than necessary). "The Commission believes this is necessary, as soon as arrangements can be made. That is about the size of it."

§ This was a deliberately incomplete reference to the proposed weapons test at Eniwetok in the Pacific.

The President turned to Marshall, who was sitting in a relaxed way in a large chair away from the table. "I agree that it is necessary, of course," Marshall said. "The only concern I have is the time. It would be awkward if this occurred right before or right after the meeting in London in November. That may be our last hope, that meeting." (Marshall said this with the one-sided half-smile he has.)

So there was some discussion of time. Eisenhower suggested April 1 as a "target" date; I said I would prefer February, and the hope that it will occur by March or April. We don't want to go along much longer this way, any longer than we can help.

Where? Patterson asked why couldn't it be at [Trinity in New Mexico—i.e., Alamogordo] as before. Eisenhower strongly opposed to any place inside the country. Would spread fear, etc. He was firm about this. I said that at [Trinity] would require elaborate super-atmosphere investigations that take time.

Could it be done secretly? It was before, says Patterson. Everyone agreed that it was unlikely that in peacetime that would be possible. There should be no fanfare, I said, nothing like last summer,⊄ absolutely. Nimitz said, "It should be entirely an American undertaking; no foreign representatives."

I said that, of course, this required the cooperation of the Army, Navy, and the Commission, and what we needed was a decision to go ahead on the particular plan, including time and place for the President's later approval. "Yes," said the President, "and then we will check further with General Marshall."

There was a disposition to discuss details of where—at sea, and where, how it could be covered up and the world told about it afterward, etc. The President would patiently bring them back. Then he looked at his hands and said: "What I must decide is . . ."* He decided it and told Patterson, Forrestal, and myself to work it out. The meeting was over.

JUNE 28, 1947
SATURDAY

Dean Acheson leaves the public service Monday. I spent 45 minutes with him this afternoon. He looks very, very tired; said he is "all tired out; the last month has been exhausting. Bob" (Lovett, his successor) "is next door and he comes in every five minutes. It is the right way to

⊄ A reference to the Manhattan District's 1946 bomb drop at Bikini Atoll, heavily publicized and witnessed by many foreign observers, journalists, Congressmen, and others.

* That is, whether to authorize the tests to be carried out.

do it, but it is terribly wearing." Yes, I agreed. The hardest part of my
job I thought was the constant necessity, as part of the job and an
essential part, to keep every member of the Commission at the same
place, as nearly as possible, in understanding, information, and push
them to participate and join in discussions and decisions. (And it is a
hard chore, believe me; though since my fellow Commissioners have all
the good will in the world, it has no ugly side to it.)

I raised the question about a test. The decision had been made to
authorize us to go ahead at the White House meeting, I told Dean. (He
had been asked to advise Marshall about it, but they apparently had
never gotten around to talking it over, so when the President called
the meeting—at my instigation, through Leahy—Marshall went ahead
on his own. That's what happens to "staff work" when a man has more
to do than a human being can get done. Pretty theory though.)

Dean strongly advised: (1) against any announcement prior to the
event itself. Otherwise, other countries will want representatives, the
AP and UP, etc. Go ahead and do it and try to say nothing about it in
advance. (2) If the Air Forces are in on what is up, those publicity-mad
fellows will have it all over the press in no time. I said I would take this
up with Patterson as a special problem.

As to the effect, he thought it would be used by the Russians to
win sympathy in various parts of the world: a threat, etc. Nothing much
could be done about that. I suggested that perhaps it might have a good
effect, as a sobering effect, on the Politburo. He doubted that; more of
this later in this interview.

He was strongly in favor of an unhabitated place or at sea in an
unhabitated area; this will have to be looked into.

Then I brought up the proposed press release about the huge expansion of plutonium production at Hanford; it was the submission of
our release to him for "clearance" that precipitated this meeting, really.
We had prepared a statement that would have been quite a story: gave
some idea of the magnitude, 40,000 people in a new construction camp,
etc. He feared this would scare the American people into thinking we
were about to have a war; would sound like saber-rattling to other countries; would make the British think we were putting into effect industrial
applications and leaving them out in the cold. In other words, he wanted
as simple and limited a statement as possible. So I agreed and said we
would cut it down.

But I was curious as to why he worried about saber-rattling. Why
would that be bad, in terms of the Russians and the negotiations in
New York? Would statements from us showing that we knew we were
in an atomic arms race and were going to go places be harmful or helpful
or have no importance? Have little importance, he said (and apparently

a bit taken aback by the question). Unless they are absolutely out of their minds, the Politburo will carefully avoid war, he said. They will move in, through international brigades and such methods as they had used in Hungary, in Czechoslovakia (this latter startled me; but he said they were expecting this almost any time), and they would "pull the plug in France" any time they wanted; what kept them back was fear of civil war in which they might lose, with de Gaulle winning. They will see to it that the "so-called Marshall Plan" will fail, and then they can point to its failure and capitalize on the further disintegration of Europe. But not war.

I said, was it clear that if they were as ruthless in Czechoslovakia as they had been in Hungary, that such a move would be like the sinking of the *Maine* and arouse this country, particularly since our people thought we had enough atomic bombs to win a war very cheaply and quickly? No comment; he studied this quite a while. Perhaps it would help to calm them if we showed we meant business about atomic weapons; perhaps it would. He thought quite a while, and then said, "But even if that is sound, the way to impress the Russian political mind is to *understate* what we are doing." The thing to do is to go ahead and do things and say little. And that, too, might be the best way to impress and give confidence to the people of this country.

We talked about our relations with Britain and [uranium] raw materials. I told him Vandenberg had shown evidence of grumbling about the disclosures he, Acheson, had made to the Joint Committee concerning division with the British. He, Vandenberg, had asked whether our situation would be improved if those arrangements were "rewritten." I had said, "No." But it worried me that they—that is, the Joint Committee members—might bring this matter up while things were going on in New York. Furthermore, I wondered if the Joint Committee realized that antagonizing the British might make our chance of getting South African materials [that is, uranium as a by-product] from the gold fields more difficult, and that was very important to this country.

No, he didn't think they would bring it up. Vandenberg didn't like the agreement, but he didn't think they would endanger the New York proceedings by bringing it up between now and fall. I hope his estimate is right. Probably is.

What do we do if, come September, Russia says "nothing doing" on the Commission's report and plan? Do we let the UN Commission dissolve? "That would be a shock to the world." Do we try to continue discussions? That would tend to a loss of Britain, France, etc., who never did like the American plan very much anyway and would begin to break away from it. He asked me if we had restudied our problem— the Board of Consultants' report—to see if we still felt that international operation was essential, that being the heart of the opposition to it from Britain, etc. I said we would do that, but I couldn't see what prospect there would be for protection against clandestine activities without that element.

Had I heard about the British counterproposal, now held up as a result of Marshall's message to Bevin? Yes, I had. It wasn't good at all. He hadn't heard of the Conant alternative, whereby power development is forsworn, and hence not part of international development and operation, and everyone agrees to raw material international control and limiting themselves to non-dangerous research. I had heard of this from Bacher, who didn't care for it, but did hear that Oppenheimer was rather in favor of it. Conant's reason for putting this forward was that since it was obvious that Russia wouldn't agree to our proposal we must find something else that they might agree to, and this might be it. I said it didn't sound like much protection, and he looked very dour about it.

He said, with a troubled, almost tortured look, "It is very secret indeed, but the British are almost out of dollars. The way things are going, unless something can be done—Clayton is in London now trying to work something out—in a few months they will have exhausted about all but $500 million of the British loan of 7½ billion." I must have looked quite startled, for he sought to reassure me that something may occur to help. I asked if this situation might make it worth their (British) while to consider changing the allocation of ore so we would be buying and paying for the ore? I pointed out that we could use it because we had the plants, but they can't, perhaps for some time. No, he didn't think there was a chance of that. We had offered sometime back—I suppose this is the Combined Policy Committee he was referring to— to have us buy it all and hold it in this country subject to later allocation, but they would have nothing of it.

The talk was quite impersonal, except as he saw me out. He said that he and Alice wanted Helen and me to come to the "farm" when they returned from Canada and a rest. I didn't say anything about how I felt to see him leave the service, or how much I had enjoyed working with him; I think he appreciated the fact that I just walked out without anything of the kind being said, since it was understood.


JUNE 30, 1947

[*These notes were made of a closed session discussion at the Pentagon, joined in by scientific and top military leaders. The discussion, one of several, was part of an effort to convey to military chiefs the import of the new weapons; this was significant because though the atomic bomb was developed under the aegis of the Army, Groves kept*

*all but a very few military men completely out of it. They had to learn
about the weapon that changed all war plans and ideas of warfare long
after the weapon appeared.*]

1. Ships at sea and bodies of troops are in general unlikely to be
regarded as primary atomic bomb targets.

2. Passive defense, dispersion, concealment (and above- and be-
low-ground protection), practical for relatively small facilities; is im-
practical for urban and industrial areas.

3. Would depopulate vast areas leaving only vestigial remnants
man's material works.

4. Value of surprise increased with every increase in potency of
weapons; with atomic bomb surprise achieves supreme value.

5. Defend against imminent or incipient [acts of war].

6. Aggressive act or imminent or incipient acts redefined so standing orders by C-in-Chief for prompt and effective retaliation should another nation ready any atomic attack against us.

7. Atomic weapons most effective device for propagation of panic
and fear over national areas; hence most effective strategic use of the
weapon will involve mass scientific and social behavior patterns which
in the past have been given little consideration.

JULY 1, 1947
AT THE OFFICE

Last night heard on the radio the first ambitious effort to portray
the good side of atomic energy. It was an outgrowth of talks I had
months ago with Ed Murrow of CBS. An hour-long program called "The
Sunny Side of the Atom." A noble beginning, I thought.

JULY 5, 1947
AT HOME, SATURDAY
(LUNCHEON WITH GENERAL EISENHOWER MONDAY, JUNE 30, 1947, IN
HIS OFFICE AT THE PENTAGON)

Our conversation covered a wide range of subjects but the most
interesting follows:

"After you spoke to the newspaper editors last April I told you at
the head table you could count on me. I meant just that. I understand
Groves, and I know what a problem he is. He is a problem for us over
here, too. He was a czar during the war, and everything is a comedown
for a man of his type. Yes, it is true that he has a lot of enemies over
here, because of the way he rode herd on everyone during the war.
There are ways of getting things done that don't require humiliating

people and making enemies of them. Say, I know what I am talking about; I worked with Montgomery! And Patton was much the same. But we got the good out of them without hitting them over the head. I had the authority to run over them rough-shod. Groves will never understand about these things; he was that way before he was put in charge of this atomic project.

"Let me make this clear: we put him on that Military Liaison Board for two reasons. That it didn't seem wise to antagonize those people who think he is the last word; and in the second place we ought to use him as long as he has anything to contribute; ought to pump him dry. But if at any time he causes you trouble, let me know, or just say a word to General Brereton and we will take him off. Hope that is clear.

"Let me make a suggestion: call him in once in a while and ask his advice about something inconsequential. Kid him a bit—keep it light. That's what I try to do when he comes in here with a face as long as this. I say, 'Do you think I like sitting at this desk, after being in command of twelve million troops? Why, sometimes I would like to push this desk over and walk out of here and never come back. But I don't.' And so on. Make him feel he isn't the only one who has things that don't please him. He is always thinking people are slighting him, nobody wants him, etc."

I interpolated somewhat, saying that we had genuinely tried to make things easy for him, realizing that he was in a rather difficult position, but nothing we did seemed to help.

"He says the Commission apparently did not want his advice," Eisenhower said. "Well," I broke in, "when we were first appointed, he told us that we were to consult with Col. Nichols, who represented him; Nichols explained that Groves wanted to get out of all this as quickly as he could. So we did consult with Nichols. Now he is sorry for himself that we did as he told us to—in a not too tactful way, I might add."

The most important part of the discussion related to our relations with the British. I brought up the fact that it was evident that the feeling of the British concerning their partnership with us on raw materials [uranium ore] was of great importance, because they had an advantage in dealing with a portion of the Commonwealth where large opportunities for such raw materials existed. They felt that our denial to them of exchange of atomic information was harsh and unfair.

He started to pace up and down, his hands in his pockets, looking down at the carpet and then out on the Potomac. "The British blame Groves for that"—and we were back on Groves again. "They insist that the agreement that was made the same day as the Attlee-Truman-King decision was drafted in part by Groves and that he led them to believe that 'cooperation' in that document—a secret document—meant exchange of engineering data on the construction of facilities. Groves takes the position that what they wanted all along was not to help in making a bomb but to learn things that could be used after the war, and that their whole participation in the project was for that purpose from the very start.

"This the British deny and point to the record. That record was, they say, that the British had made progress toward an atomic bomb, that the question was whether the work should not be carried on in Canada because of location; that we talked them into a full partnership, the work to be done in the United States on the condition that the advantage of the British's early start should be retained by the British and not lost as a result of the decision to join forces in the United States, rather than locate the British effort in Canada.

"They realize that the McMahon Act forbids you to exchange information or supply new information, but they blame Groves for going around behind their backs and having that provision against exchange of information put into the McMahon Act, even pointing to the line which singles out 'industrial uses,' which shows on its face that whoever got that line inserted had the background which only Groves and two or three others had. They feel he has overtraded and are deeply upset by it. When you consider that they led us in radar and jet propulsion and made it freely available to us, and still lead in a number of other military fields—the British are very good in engineering, you know—you can see how they feel and how costly it could be to us.

"The two countries that believe in a Bill of Rights ought to stick together. They do believe in a Bill of Rights, and whatever form of social organization they feel they have to go for in order to make their economic machinery function, they won't give *that* up, and that is the real test. There isn't anything you can do about it; it's in the law, though it might be possible to construe it to cover only new information uncovered by you since the McMahon law was passed. But it would make them feel better if you talked to them candidly about it."

I said they felt that our position was ungenerous and smacked of overtrading, though with the law as it stands, of course, there isn't anything that can be done unless and until it is changed. If things go as they now are, a change in the law may be wise.

"The British know most of what we do, don't they?"

I pointed out that they had a British scientist at Bikini who actually gave the final signals for detonation, and helped with the final assembly.

We spent a good deal of time discussing AEC's troubles in recruiting able men from industry. He suggested that we call a conference of ten or a dozen men from the largest corporations and tell them they had to give us some of their best men. He almost rehearsed this meeting right there and then. I felt to myself that the emergency argument requiring them to lay down what they are doing would sound better if the General of our Armies had not just announced that he was leaving the Army to become head of Columbia University. As to that, he said it was clearly understood with Columbia that he was to give just as much of his time to public service as was needed. He said a number of industries tried to get him to take jobs paying high salaries ($200,000 a year and that sort of thing), but he declined because it didn't fit into what he thought was the right thing to do or that interested him. He intimated that Columbia had offered to pay him more than $25,000 but that he had demurred to that.

A curious circumstance. He began our conversation by referring to a belting the Chicago *Tribune* had given him as an "Anglophile." I commented that I had been used to this line as a former resident of Chicago and reader of the *Tribune*. But in the South it was quite strange: the highest percentage of Anglo-Saxon population in the country. Strong for intervention in favor of Britain—destroyers to Britain, and so on. And yet an anti-British speech would get great applause, almost as if the Revolutionary War had just been fought. Senator Stewart's retelling of the story of the British officer who whacked Andy Jackson as a boy for not cleaning his boots, as ordered, and making the story sound as if the incident had occurred yesterday and by God no Britisher could order us "to shine his boots, etc."

"Well, I am very familiar with military history, but I didn't remember that story."

I said it was a school-history story and may not have occurred, but it is quite a familiar one. But when he said that, I began to wonder if I had been mistaken. (Helen looked it up in Marquis James' biography of Jackson, and, of course, it is there. Curious thing. Don't know whether to write him and give the source or not!)

Just before our luncheon I popped in to see Patterson on a hunch. Urged him to help us maintain secrecy on [the Eniwetok tests] at least until the preliminary studies were out of the way; in other words, not to inform the Air Forces, who will make a show of it if they can. He took this piece of rather straight talk very well; in fact, he agreed. He sent for Eisenhower (whose office is next door), and we talked it over further.

Last Wednesday evening the Commission members (minus Bacher, who is at Los Alamos) came out to dinner with us. I made a stiff Tom Collins and then we pitched horseshoes—this being a middle-aged "athletic" event I've gone in for out here. They obviously didn't think much of the idea but humored me. But after playing a bit they had such fun that we played three full games and they wouldn't have quit then but it was 8 P.M.

Last Monday Carroll [Wilson] spent an hour talking to the Commission about "where we stand." He was very frank in pointing out what he had *not* been able to do, and this had a fine effect on the Commission—as Bill says, "It takes quite a man to stand up and discuss his inadequacies." What he had not been able to do was to get staffed as he needs to be, either by a field manager at Oak Ridge and Hanford (where they are very badly needed) or a director of engineering or of security. It is hardly Wilson's fault, of course, though it was characteristic of him to take the blame.

It is difficult to get men to give up what they are doing to work for the Government these days, and that is evident all over the Washington scene. Whether we will have to resort to the dollar-a-year and emergency line—as I proposed—or whether a little more time will work this out is hard to say. But unless things improve in staff within three months our "reservoir of good will" will certainly be drawn on rather heavily. The high standing of the Commission—and that it certainly has—and the patience with us will not last much longer. We will have to produce results.

JULY 9, 1947
WEDNESDAY

One of the most serious aspects of "What next?" in the international negotiations is on the question of whether the nations that went along with the Baruch proposal as of December, 1946, would still go along as of today; and whether they are discouraged with the prospect that even if the plan were adopted the United States Senate would ratify it. This may be a very important factor.

In a curious way the debate on my confirmation served to chill the hopes of those in the other nations that the U.S. Senate would really go along, even if Russia did agree to the American proposal.†

Continued excitement about the "stolen files."‡ Patterson called to say that they would issue whatever statement we thought necessary

† The opposition to my confirmation included two elements that would naturally raise doubts about the Senate's attitude toward ratifying an international control plan: first, sentiments in favor of giving the military a stronger voice in atomic affairs; and second, suspicions that an international plan would weaken the power position of the U.S.

‡ The newspapers had broken the story of the 1946 document thefts from Los Alamos.

because "I don't want you blamed for this." I said I had spoken to Edgar
Hoover about it and he urged that a direct statement be made. Patterson
suggested that if Hoover would make the statement that might be the
best way to handle the situation. I conferred with Lewis and Sumner,
who agreed, and then called Hoover, reading a statement we proposed
to make and then said both Patterson and we thought it was more appropriate for him to make the statement, since the FBI recovered the
documents. He said this was agreeable, I read our draft, he said he
would call back if they made any substantial changes in the statement.
Our purpose here is to avoid making any statement at all. If his statement does the trick, that will be all to the good. But, of course, the
Hearst and other parts of the press will go right on charging us with
laxity, helping Communism, etc. And a jumpy country will give such
stories considerable credence.

This office is a mess of people walking around in somewhat of an
amused dither. The wires are hot with stories of "stolen documents."
We take it with considerable humor. Partly due to the fact, I suppose,
that it was while Groves was in charge that this happened. The comments, however, are that this shows that a civilian Commission doesn't
know how to maintain security, etc. But it is as exciting around here at
the moment as if we had located a flying saucer.

JULY II, 1947
FRIDAY

This has been quite a day. Most of it has been spent in excitement
over the New York *Sun*–Hearst–*Times-Herald* campaign on "stolen atom
bomb secrets."

At noon I had a telephone talk with J. Edgar Hoover. He said that
he had talked to Attorney General Clark. He said that it was unfortunate
that there had been delay in a decision about whether to prosecute the
two Los Alamos ex-sergeants; that if there had been prompt action this
story would not have broken in the way it did. The Attorney General said
he shared my views and has issued orders that the men are to be
prosecuted. I pointed out that we had been confused as to what the
position of the department was and who spoke with authority; that one
statement said there would be prosecution, another person that they
were studying the matter, etc. Hoover was rather contemptuous of the
lack of decision and said that he now believes that the matter was
clarified and that action could be expected. He said he understood it to
be my view if action is to be taken it should be promptly and vigorously.

Then he tossed a minor bombshell. Day before yesterday Von Der Luft, one of the men, left the country. The FBI had no warrant, so couldn't hold him. The story was that he had gone to Nova Scotia to pick up a sailing vessel and bring it to his home in Penn. This was the sort of thing that would happen if leaks about a case got out as they did through the Joint Committee in this case. Now the fellow wasn't within our jurisdiction, and while he thought the Canadian Royal Mounted Police would grab him, it might be complicated.

Hoover said that a rumor had come in that an eminent scientist had disappeared completely.

Later in the day, about 2:25, I had another talk with Hoover. He said that his Canadian office is trying to locate Von Der Luft, who apparently is with his father.

Then he spoke rather vigorously about the harmful effects of press stories such as have been running in making his job and ours more difficult, the danger of disclosure of information. I told him we had in mind the preparation of a public statement on the subject condemning such irresponsibility and suggested that he might want to join. He didn't commit himself but did discuss what such a statement should include, including a reference to voluntary censorship. All of these conversations were quite cordial. He was especially firm in his remarks to the effect that these stories were intended to be critical of civilian control when as a matter of fact these things had occurred during Army control.

I had several conversations with the Attorney General. He said that because there was so much feeling on this matter he thought "maybe" we ought to take action, leave it to the courts, and the judge could give a suspended sentence. "They will keep on hollering about it until they find out who it is."

I said our position was the whole question turned upon this question: Will a prosecution serve the purpose of deterring further occurrences of this kind and help preserve security? If there is a kickback because these boys appear to be obviously innocent of evil intent, then a prosecution would probably not serve as a deterrent but otherwise. On the whole case I thought an arraignment, arrest, indictment, a plea of guilty with a suspended sentence and a stiff lecture from the bench might have a quite wholesome effect in that innocent but careless people would take these things more seriously. He said that while Von Der Luft had left on Monday he was sure that he was not trying to escape. I said that they should go ahead, and he said, "Edgar will pick them up."§

§ Von Der Luft was, in fact, given a suspended sentence. In the next few months, three other ex-soldiers were arrested by the FBI, also for having taken classified "souvenirs" of their Army service at Los Alamos.

JULY 12, 1947
SATURDAY

This morning's *Times-Herald* had a double-line, eight-column banner about a former Communist working on the atom bomb; namely, Frank Oppenheimer.⟨

Joe Volpe told me that last evening a Major formerly at Oak Ridge and now with Groves' Special Weapons Branch, had visited him and Tom Jones. The Major asked two questions: (a) When did the Commission detect the loss involved in the two sergeants' case? (b) Who was responsible for the period of delay between the discovery and the present time? They told him that on the second he would have to consult the FBI. Then Volpe asked the Major that in view of the fact that he was at Oak Ridge as recently as May, what did he know about the alleged disappearance of documents? The Major gave Volpe an arrogant look and told him it was "none of his damn business."

I called General Brereton to call his attention to the *Times-Herald* story, which he apparently had not seen. He said he agreed with my position and that he would talk to Groves on his return Monday and ask him frankly whether he was the source of information and whether the story correctly quoted him.

I said we had no desire to muzzle anyone; on the contrary we wanted to un-muzzle these people who hinted that they knew of violations of law but did not assist the Commission by providing the information. General Brereton was most cordial and in agreement with our position. I said that I hoped he would take the matter up with the Secretary. He said that the Major's call on us was doubtless attributable to the fact that General Groves was meeting with the Secretary of War on the matter of the sergeants' case.


JULY 15, 1947

When the conference report was considered by the House, Congressman Cannon, the ranking minority member of the House Appropri-

⟨ Robert Oppenheimer's brother. In 1949 Frank Oppenheimer made a public statement that he had been a member of the Communist Party from 1937 to 1941, but quit long before his employment on the Manhattan project. He never was an AEC employee.

ations Committee, commented on the $150,000 appropriation to the Joint Committee as follows (*Cong. Record* of July 15, p. 9109):

> An appropriation of $150,000 is made for the Joint Committee on Atomic Energy. This is the committee popularly known as the Watch Lilienthal Committee. The sole duty of this joint committee is to look over the shoulder of the Atomic Energy Commission. We got the idea from Soviet Russia. In the early days of the Russian Revolution a political commissar was appointed for each regiment. He was a snooper set to watch the colonel of the regiment and his staff. Much of the credit for the debacle of the Russian Army in its disastrous war with little Finland was laid to the meddling of the political commissars. If any untoward influences affect the administration of the Atomic Energy Commission, it will probably be due to the meddling of the political commissars appointed to watch Lilienthal and it will cost us this year $150,000. They wanted a quarter of a million dollars to start with. It would be difficult to estimate what they will ask when the witch hunting really gets hot.
>
> We have innumerable commissions and agencies in the Government. But this is the first time a committee of Congress has been appointed and financed to watch one of them. In order to carry out completely the program of our Russian prototype we should appoint still another committee. Stalin appoints committees to watch committees and then appoints committees who are to watch the committees who are watching the committees. Now that we have a joint committee to watch the Commission, we should appoint a committee to watch the joint committee. And finance them with $150,000 to start on. The system has endless possibilities.
>
> Mr. Speaker, economy, like charity, begins at home. If we had put our investigators upon this bill as we did upon the other supply bills, if we had required our investigators to follow out every expenditure here and make an analysis and a report, as we did in the departments downtown, it would make very interesting reading.

JULY 17, 1947
THURSDAY

Left the office with some aches and sor-ish throat on Tuesday evening. Decided I'd better stay home yesterday. Slept 13 hours, straight, Tuesday night; two hours in the afternoon (stayed in bed all day); and 13 hours again last night. So I must have been rather tired with all these excursions and alarms. Result: sore throat seems much better and the world looks better, although the rumors and skulduggery continue.

JULY 19, 1947
AT HOME

Night before last we were fast asleep when the telephone rang and rang. Helen rolled out; I could hear her repeat the usual formula, rather sleepily: "No, no, he is not here. No, I don't know where he can be reached." Then a long silence. After a while she whispered "in a loud voice" something about a secretary to a professor at Columbia, so I could decide whether I suddenly *was* at home. Then she came in looking quite disturbed. The woman told her it was most urgent. Can't wait until morning. She had instructions to deliver a message to me of the utmost importance. "Asked me how I could possibly take the responsibility for keeping her from delivering the message. Also asked where she could reach Professor Einstein."

Well, it sounded screwball, of course. But I went to the phone, since Helen was obviously rather upset, and said, "What the hell do you mean, calling me at this hour?" This didn't bother the lady at the other end. "Yes, I know, it is too bad, but it is so urgent and so terrible that I can't tell you over the phone. I have instructions, etc., etc." I asked her name; where she was; why the professor didn't come himself. (The answer was good—"He is working at the laboratory!") Could I reach him there? "No, probably not." She gave her name. She had a room at the Statler Hotel, but she was phoning from a booth because she "knew she couldn't trust her hotel room phone." She had been given instructions about that, too. Well, I told her, yes, I would take responsibility for not seeing her, and hung up. But that wasn't the end of her. I asked Miss Brown to get a security officer out to see what was up, and this business kept several people up more or less all night! She disappeared from her hotel room, and to make a long story less long than it might be—at 4 P.M. yesterday I was told she was in the mental hospital.

This is quite a job, this one!

JULY 20, 1947
AT HOME, SUNDAY

I am so proud and happy about David that I could almost burst my vest buttons—if I had a vest, and if it had buttons! It is such a joy to observe his enthusiasm—just a moment ago, looking up from *Wind, Sand and Stars,* he said, "Hate to finish it." Then I said, "Let me have it a minute." I started to leaf through it to a favorite passage. "You mean what he said about machines and sailing vessels?" That was it. So I read it aloud and we grinned with appreciation. And yesterday we played horseshoes, dividing two matches, and laughed and kidded and whooped over ringers, two of which he made for me by driving my shoes over the pin with his pitches.

And again this comes over me (as it has many times before since he was born and turned out to be such a real-for-sure boy), that if I had not had just such a boy, to be proud of and to watch grow into a good man, I would never have gotten over the sense of being deprived of a joy—a great joy. Nothing else in the way of satisfactions could quite have taken its place. I think I have felt this more than most men for a number of reasons, one of them being the fact that I practically raised Allen, so much younger than I, as a son rather than a brother. But this feeling about a particular kind of son is really quite deep in me.

JULY 21, 1947
AT HOME

This was the first really good day we have had for a long time. My anxiety over the Joint Committee hearing was dispelled. I started off with the statement about test, guarded and lived with all these weeks. (It was fun to see the eyes of our own staff people pop who had not been permitted to know about all this.) This went very well, I thought—quietly put, but I thought they were impressed and persuaded.

Then I read our statement about security conditions under the Manhattan District, and any hopes that "Army" control was the solution of security problems must have gone right out of the last one of them. And no reaction of anger that we are attacking Groves. And then young Brown of our security force took up the points, one by one, admitting errors freely (which is disarming and gives a good impression of open-mindedness), explaining changes we had made at the suggestion of their investigator or our own survey. It was a good job. When he told of the 17,000 blueprints unaccounted for, there were some jaws that dropped visibly. "How many did you say?" "Good God!"

I believe we are developing some confidence in this committee, and that is very important—most important. And Hickenlooper seems to be growing, working hard, and trying to be helpful, trying to make our job possible.

They are calling General Groves for next Friday, they say. If he appears, there will be fireworks and a busy weekend—perhaps. For he will, for once, have some things to explain. They will have him on the defensive. After sniping at us, sneering at us and running us down, he may find this will be a somewhat different role. We have taken all the kicking around we intend to take.

For two weeks, almost daily, we have tried some new form of public statement. Our friends kept saying, "How long are you going to take this beating? When are you going to answer?" But what we had to say never quite seemed right to me, always seemed defensive and not in keeping with our great responsibility. Now I am glad we did hold our fire and reply before the committee by taking the offensive as we did today. At least it so seems at the moment.

As I came into Secretary Patterson's office—it was six o'clock this evening—he stalked over to give me his abrupt handshake and warm little smile. "Judge," I said, taking a chair, "there is an expression that has been used formally so long that it has almost lost its meaning. But in this case I use it in its most literal sense. I have come to pay my respects—and I mean just that." And I tried to tell him how much it had meant to me, as a public servant, to observe a man of his complete honesty and directness, when all around us here there is so much guile and deviousness and maneuvering.*

He was quite pleased, and like the really modest man that he is, started talking about me, to change the subject. From the beginning he saw that I was a "fine example" of a fellow who not only had good ideas but "knew how to get things done" and so many of the people in Washington—good, sincere people—were hopeless that way. "When you say something will get done, you can count on it."

I switched back to him, but he abruptly renewed his expressions about me. "You have a terrible responsibility, but you are getting it done. That job is in good hands. Your appointment was the best possible one the President could have made—better than the others he was considering first—I have said that to Bush, Conant, Compton, all of them. You have had a kind of experience no one else has, that this job needs. No one but such crackpots as Parnell Thomas or hopelessly political fellows as Taft will deny that, and the people are with you. And you have a very warm friend at the White House; you know that, don't you?"

More talk back and forth. I shook hands, said we would want to see him from time to time. "You can count on me," he said. "I don't say that in any idle way."

---

* This was a farewell visit. Judge Patterson's resignation had been announced on July 18; his successor, Kenneth C. Royall, was sworn in on the 24th.

At the door I turned to see him standing by that big desk, his eyes moistened, the old Indian, and then he said, in a moving way I shall never forget, this (for him) remarkably emotional sentence: "I thoroughly believe in you."

You can't let a fellow like that down, really.

JULY 29, 1947
AT HOME (EVENING)

Had quite a blow today. The General Advisory Committee drafted a statement that, as written, not only discouraged hope of atomic power in any substantial way for decades, but put it in such a way as to question whether it would ever be of consequence. This pessimism didn't come from nobodies, but from a top group—Oppenheimer, Conant, Rabi, Seaborg, etc. I can't believe it is true. Not that the difficulties and uncertainties don't exist—of course, they do, and that I knew before. But I don't believe that anyone can see ahead so far as to say that those difficulties are of such magnitude. But there was the statement, and they were bound to issue it. For a while I felt they would, and if they did in that form, it would have been interpreted to mean that atomic energy is actually just a matter of military weapons and little more. Which, to go with the situation we saw enacted in the Pentagon this morning, might well have finished off the rather fragile life of civilian direction of this project.

They decided to postpone the statement long enough to get some criticism of it from other scientists, which is all to the good, and to give everyone a chance to size up the situation.

Actually, a properly worded statement deflating the atomic power *overoptimism* would be definitely in the interest of the Commission; and this was their purpose in proposing it. The Commission is being criticized for not making satisfactory progress in developing power, and this is attributed to our incompetence, or antagonism to industry, etc. There was still another political reason for their proposing the statement, namely, that foreign nations think we are keeping them from early atomic power to meet their terrible fuel problems. It is curious how political reasons motivate scientists and savants, though they would be surprised if you pointed it out to them, and probably deny it. Wishful thinking—which so largely characterizes political thought—is no monopoly of politicos or ordinary men.

I started the day by being in the midst of more brass and braid than I have ever seen together, I expect. It was not a very edifying exhibition. Arthur Compton, it seemed to me, was lending himself quite uncritically to the military way of analyzing things, which seems routine and uninspired and lacking in the great perspective that is required.

The Navy said the atomic bomb wouldn't be used against ships, and if it were, there was little change in structure that would do much good. The Ground Forces say it wasn't much of a weapon to be used against deployed troops. Wouldn't affect ground operations particularly. The Air Forces wouldn't change their ways of doing things. So that leaves the civilian as the only one affected, and there was no one there to talk about him the whole morning long. Even soldiers and sailors weren't boys and men, but "personnel." Hitting a potential enemy (which now calls for a declaration of war by Congress) becomes "anticipatory retaliation." The whole thing seemed quite unreal and stuffy.

I am quite tired and run ragged. We need top staff terribly. Apparently at last we have a manager for Oak Ridge—an excellent fellow by the name of Franklin of TWA, and a good prospect for Admiral Gingrich as Chief of Security and Intelligence. This may be the break we need so badly.

Real fame at last! Appeared in a comic book serial. Posterity, here I come!!

JULY 30, 1947
AT HOME (EARLY MORNING)

I ought to record that yesterday afternoon we had our first less-than-unanimous decision. It was 3 to 1; actually 4 to 1 with Bacher's position known, but he was absent. Case involved "clearance" of a couple at Brookhaven.

I used to say that the picture of a public character on the cover of *Time* or *Life* was the "kiss of death." It was a portent of an early, very early, demise so far as public standing was concerned.

I pointed to Leon Henderson, who reached this distinction and a couple of weeks later was "through"; and even poor old General Weygand, acclaimed thus as a great military genius, and a few weeks later both he and his Maginot Line in disgrace.

Well, I now have a chance to test the theory, for a rather stern-looking Dave Lilienthal appears on the newsstands all over the country and South America on *Time*'s cover. The article itself, thanks to the better standing I have attained with *Time* since the time they ran my photograph on the same page with one of the Communist, Eisler, and linked them with a common cut-line, plus the important fact that the story was steered through by Frances Henderson, is a good one in almost every way. It doesn't make this entirely a one-man show (which it isn't, but which is the usual journalistic line), and it doesn't contain any of the digs and ugly twists that *Time* delights in.

General Groves attended the Military Liaison Committee meeting today. We anticipated a big row, as he had put two matters on the agenda that looked like appealing for a fight. I wasn't misled by his apparent good nature, for he does not respond to anything, we have found by bitter experience, except sternness and stuffing things right down his throat. When he tried to change the subject—at which he is very skillful—I kept sticking his nose into the thousands of blueprints that were unaccounted for. His Navy colleagues particularly enjoyed the session.

AUGUST 1, 1947
AT THE OFFICE

It was one minute to twelve today. I was talking with Stu Syming-ton, who should be the new Secretary for Air.† General Spaatz stuck his head in the door, looking very pleased, and said, "Those were the B-29s; right on the button." He referred to a roar over the Pentagon that had rushed over us a moment before. It was the planes that had just made a new record from Tokyo. This, by the way, is Air Force Day.

AUGUST 4, 1947
AT HOME

Some light on this job is thrown by the kind of things that happen that give a ray of hope, that seem to make it a good day. Today I had a long talk with Dr. Fisk, our Director of Research (a remarkable young man), in which we considered the possibility that there wasn't a lot of uranium in the world, in rich deposits, and that low-grades would be so expensive to handle that it wouldn't be worth the trouble. I said, wouldn't it be wonderful if we could take what we have in the way of plutonium, etc., and dump the stuff into the sea, and know that no one

† The act creating the new Department of Defense had just been passed; Symington did become the first Secretary of the Air Force. (Navy Secretary Forrestal became Defense Secretary.)

else would find enough ore to bother with? We both beamed. We would be out of business and a lesser nightmare could be substituted for this one.

As he left I took a sheet of paper he had been writing things on during our conversation, and hardly thinking about it proceeded to burn it up in a large ashtray. What a strange kind of business this is.

Today I had presented to me for signature the first detailed direction regarding the test, and I confess to a strange feeling, to be issuing directions on so fearsome a subject. I'll get used to it, perhaps.

Sumner [Pike], Bill [Waymack], and I had lunch this noon with a new member of our Joint Committee, Lyndon Johnson of Texas. He is an able young man, definitely liberal, and shrewd, full of savvy, and a great break, for that committee can make or break us.

He gave us good advice about getting the Joint Committee and the appropriations people to take visits this summer and fall, and to "develop" Forrestal and Symington. He has a great enthusiasm for Symington. Tells a story of how Symington flew down to some Texas shindig and could do anything—make cooing speeches to the farmers; eat barbecue with the ranchmen, make a speech about Czechoslovakia to a Czech group.

Johnson told of a luncheon with John Rankin and how he spent most of the time bragging about me, how I had remade "that country down there," etc. "I said, 'Well, I hear he is domineering.' 'Domineering? That is that damn Ickes talk; only one I ever heard say such a thing. Now let me tell you about that hound, and how he tried to take TVA away from us, etc., etc.' "

Johnson said, "You darn near ruined the state of Texas with your confirmation. Old Man McKellar hasn't spoken to Connally since. Curses him out in public. At a dinner the other day, with a lot of Senators present, he was asked to speak. Got up and said, 'I see there are some men here I used to consider my friends,' (Connally and George stiff as pokers) 'but they aren't my friends any more, so I'll just sit down.' And thereupon he did."

Spent an hour this morning—the Commission and I—talking with Dr. Parran and some of his staff people of the Public Health Service. I felt a bit funny at the thought of welcoming him into his former office, but he was gracious enough not to mention it, and none of us did.‡ The discussion was friendly and may later be profitable. The Public Health Service is reassured, I think (at least this I hoped for), that we intend to carry out our work cooperatively with them as we did to such a large extent in TVA.

‡ The AEC had taken over the Public Health Service building for its offices.

AUGUST 5, 1947
AT HOME

The Commission started a meeting this afternoon at 2:30 P.M.; at 7:20 P.M. we broke up. And this was the second long meeting of the day.

This afternoon's was punishing as hell. And again, the worst part of the job, in wear and tear on the soul: the passing on FBI reports about people. There is an accumulation of these, men and women who were in the Manhattan District and who have been reinvestigated. There are really no cases of "disloyalty." These are usually cases of people who have a mother or a brother or wife who is, or is reputed to be, a Communist or the equivalent, and the "evidence" to confirm these conclusions is only some FBI agent's rendition of what someone has said, or a conclusion from some very flimsy, thin stuff indeed. And so we sweat and agonize about the injustice to these people by such a travesty as our examination of these files must be. And against this is the risk that some of these people may indeed turn very bad or that the whole project will be badly hurt by ballyhoo and prejudice aroused over these cases if we "clear" them; or by a feeling that we are spending too much time and energy on such matters because of our concern about individual justice, while the major interest committed to us suffers—as indeed it already has.

It is heart-warming, though, to see how these associates of mine act in such tests as these: how humane, balanced, decent, sensible. This is most reassuring.

I have been somewhat concerned about my personal financial situation; trying rather vainly to find out just where I stand. The figures indicate that for the first six months of this year actual expenditures have about equaled, perhaps exceeded, my salary. Helen remarked tonight, "Sometimes it makes you mad—you have to worry and grieve about your work, and then are so poorly paid that you must come home and worry about your income. It somehow doesn't seem right."

Friday I called Clifford to tell him that we of the Commission were concerned about certain paragraphs in the Joint Chiefs' report on the test at Bikini, which had been submitted to us before being made public. We felt that these parts of the report would reopen the military vs. civilian issue. He said the President did not know of the report (although Leahy is a member of the Joint Chiefs) and asked, "Do you mean the Joint Chiefs plan to release a report without getting the President's approval?" I told him that it was definitely my impression that the report would be made public soon; that just that had been said at the Pentagon conference, and we were being "hurried" to give our approval to those parts indicated for public release, our approval being related to the question of restricted data. In fact, if we had not stalled, it might well have been released by this date or later on, August 6, the anniversary of Hiroshima.

I said I would send over my copy, a "top secret" document, and urged him to read it.

In the meanwhile, we are considering a letter to the chairman of the committee, Dr. Karl Compton, in an effort to call attention to the facts about how poorly military control of atomic energy had protected the national security since the bomb was dropped.§

I spoke to Clifford again this afternoon. He said he had read the entire report and had called certain parts to the President's attention. The President, he said, was "outraged"—that is Clifford's word. Clifford opined that things were pretty warm on the subject over there, and that he believed the Joint Chiefs would themselves decide against publication of any of the report.

Tomorrow we take off for the West. I am so glad to get away. A change of scene should help.◖

SEPTEMBER 3, 1947
AT HOME

Working at home; outlining my lecture to the War College which I am to make September 5, and trying to write a first draft of the Crawfordsville [Indiana] speech, which I have been worrying over far more than I am justified in doing.

Have been rather tense and having difficulty in sleeping, etc., since returning from my trip. Part of this may be concern over the first internal rift within the Commission ranks. Tonight a message from the President will be read to the International Cancer Congress at St. Louis stating that the Commission will make radioactive isotopes available to foreign countries. L.S.S. [Strauss] opposed the idea from the first, and after weeks of discussion and inaction I concluded that we would have to vote on it; the result was 4 to 1. He took the position that he

§ A Presidential advisory committee headed by Dr. Compton had that summer proposed the Universal Military Training system, arguing that the threat of atomic war had made the old mobilization method obsolete.

◖ This trip, from August 6 to 27, was chiefly to visit the atomic installations at Los Alamos, Berkeley, and Hanford.

wanted to indicate to Lovett why he thought the State Department should disapprove. This could be bad business so far as acting as a Commission is concerned, for it might well lead to what the rest of us could properly construe as efforts to obstruct decisions of the majority. I am far from happy about it.

I wish it had been feasible for me to take several weeks' vacation, completely, this summer. But I will make the grade if I am careful. It looks like I have a lot of speech-making to do, and I always take these hard, though that is perhaps one of the reasons they often turn out rather well.

SEPTEMBER 9, 1947
ON THE TRAIN BETWEEN NEW YORK AND WASHINGTON

Luncheon meeting with the top *Life* staff this noon; it went very well. To most of the others' surprise, apparently, Henry Luce came and I sat beside him during the 1½ hours. I continue to be amazed at my self-assurance under the circumstances of talking "from the hip" with such a group. I made some points that seemed to interest Luce greatly; he would look rather puzzled, say, "That's an interesting idea that hadn't occurred to me," etc., and then pick at it, or ask me to carry it further. Particularly he seemed struck by my statement that our competition, and decisive competition, with Russia may not be with bombs but by our relative progress in science and technique. My point was that a police or closed state can't get good scientific results compared to ours. The reason is that we encourage men to take chances—i.e., do things that may not work, and they discourage that. (Because if you turn out to be wrong it goes badly with you.)

I bore down on the "Crawfordsville" idea that I am working out for my speech, and said that *Life* ought to lend its expository talents to the job of making atomic science seem clear to the general public. I was definitely put on the spot about this by Luce, with many questions, but I think the answers (impromptu, I may as well confess) sounded pretty good to me and I gathered seemed all right to him.

Met with Mrs. Ogden Reid, Geoffrey Parsons, chief editorial writer, and Helen Hiett, at the *Herald Tribune* later in the afternoon, and Helen H. and I had quite a visit about my Herald Tribune Forum speech next month, and a lot of other things.

Parsons must have been responsible for the line of editorial attack on me and TVA years ago, particularly bad during the Morgan row and the investigation. But after some talk he turned to Mrs. Reid and said, "I like this fellow." Helen H. said afterward that this was quite a triumph of complete conversion.

With the visit and lunch at the *Times* yesterday—which was hardly exciting, but useful perhaps—this was a good two days. We spent the weekend at the Sulzbergers' at Hillandale, their place in Connecticut. Restful and plenty of swimming and good food and quiet.

Had a visit with Mr. Baruch this morning; John Hancock was there, which turned out to be fortunate. B. said he wanted to make it clear that he had not taken a position about the exportation of radio-active isotopes, as indicated in some of the stories, and which had troubled me rather. But you could see that he didn't like it. I told him that the facts simply did not warrant concern over sending such materials abroad, and Hancock agreed. I doubt if B. will kick up any fuss about it, not now at least, though if I fall into disfavor he may bring it in as an item of his case.

We did talk about some important matters concerning raw materials—this was at his insistence—and its relation to the Marshall Plan. This made sense to me and fits into plans we have under way.

SEPTEMBER 19, 1947

General Brereton advised me that he had a discussion with General Eisenhower this afternoon. General Eisenhower had advised Brereton that he, General Eisenhower, would probably relieve General Groves of the Armed Forces Special Weapons Project Command. The question he wanted advice on from us was whether leaving General Groves on the Military Liaison Committee would be workable and agreeable.

General Brereton recommends that we do so, believing that it has a chance to work. I stated that the minimum was the removal of Groves from the Special Weapons Command. I said I would consult my associates on the other point and was agreeable to accept his recommendation on it.

SEPTEMBER 25, 1947
AT THE HAY-ADAMS, WASHINGTON (ONCE AGAIN)

The barn-storming expedition back to Indiana was highly success-ful, and what is more, gave me great satisfaction, personal satisfaction.◖

All the worrying about the Crawfordsville speech—and I really worked and stewed about it—was paid for by the feeling I had, as I delivered it, that this really expressed my convictions in a way that

◖ On September 21 I was in Michigan City for my parents' fiftieth wedding anniversary celebration; the following night I gave my speech at Crawfordsville, on the Wabash College football field, and on the 23rd spoke at my alma mater, DePauw University, at Greencastle.

people understood and to which they would respond. It was quite a business: a fellow who a week ago was dragging himself around after the flu, standing up in a football field, temperature 39 degrees, and holding an audience of 3,500 people so they hardly moved during the whole performance. Maybe they were frozen solid, as Helen suggested, but anyway it was quite something to see this crowd hold onto every word. I was glad that I had spent as much time as I had on delivery, though my hands were so numb I could hardly turn the pages during the last part of the speech.

Then I repeated the business to the radio (CBS) before an audience in the Wabash College chapel. This was a very happy business —a good place to speak and a fine, friendly, and active audience. I had poured lots of coffee (heavy with sugar) into me to keep up the energy. Those who heard me on both occasions said they detected no signs of fatigue in my voice—this had worried me, for Sunday night I was rather quite worn out.

But the most satisfaction of all I got out of the trip was in speaking to a DePauw college audience that packed Gobin Church, including the choir loft, kids sitting on the floor, etc. This was real fun. And a real moving experience, for it was one generation to another—in fact there were a number of youngsters who came up to speak to me afterward who are the children of my Delta U classmates—Red Chandler's daughter; Warren Cooke's son; "Spin" Llewellyn's son. And Nancy and Helen there. I talked extemporaneously, and it was relaxed and a joy; and the jokes and pleasantness established a bridge between us that nothing else can do.

My parents' golden wedding anniversary was a very happy occasion, filled with the exuberant spirits of those "Lilienthal girls"— Aunt Hermine being 80! Mother was charming and lovely; we all forgot the crisis of the day before when I had to put on a real act to get her to change her determination not even to wear the ring Dad had bought for her and had engraved, etc. He was quite hurt, of course, and I was so provoked. She didn't want jewelry, she wanted a home, etc.—a quite bad performance. But all this was forgotten as hordes of people and more relatives than I have seen in a coon's age came in. It was true that the side-attraction of seeing the notorious David had something to do with the number of townspeople, as Ted suggested; but the whole business was fine.

Then Dad [and my brothers] Ted and Allen drove down to the Crawfordsville business and apparently got a big kick out of the furor— which was complete with the Governor, a band, much flashbulb, radio, etc. Dad was introduced three times in one evening and he made a big hit. He seems in wonderful health and is a very impressive man.

Helen and Nancy stayed on for a few days and I am staying in town.

David was a sensation at the reunion, of course, with his great height, his wonderful smile, and fine manners. He left for Cambridge by air Sunday night. I shall miss him. Particularly I shall miss our walks at night. We broke down the reserve between us and talked about everything under the sun. He is a great boy; I can't see how I could possibly have a son who more nearly fills my ambitions for a son. He has matured and seasoned a great deal and should make a fine, balanced, effective man.

SEPTEMBER 26, 1947
AT THE OFFICE (6:15 P.M.)

I have been greatly concerned about the danger of a bad rift in the Commission, after all my months of working to create solidarity great enough to withstand the inevitable differences. For the moment this seems to have been averted, though I am still not too sure.

L.L.S. [Strauss] felt very strongly, and emotionally, about the export of isotopes as a research tool. He told me he wanted to talk to Lovett, to try to get the State Department to reverse its position. This shocked me, but I felt the consequence of objecting might be worse than the risk taken by his seeing Lovett. I don't think, actually, he sensed at all that this was no way to treat his brother Commissioners.

The President made the announcement; the *New York Times* had a story that L.L.S. had dissented; we managed to keep from discussing that phase of it; and it appeared to go off as "that's that." But I did not reckon on how strongly he felt.

When I returned from the Indiana trip day before yesterday, Bill Waymack told me that L. had asked him to his apartment for a bachelor dinner. He proceeded to urge him to change his position, L. saying he was going to press a motion of revocation for Commission action. L. asked W. to read a statement of reasons why the action was wrong and should be revoked. Bill said it contained nothing really new and was a strained piece of advocacy, not an objective analysis. He said he put it pretty strong to L. that this would wreck the Commission's harmony if he persisted; that he thought the future and integrity of the Commission were more important than this particular issue, and urged him not to carry it on.

While they were talking L. had a call from Forrestal; he put him off at that time saying he was engaged but would see him the next day. He said to Bill, "That was Forrestal. He wants to talk to me 'about this foreign isotope matter.'" This really upset Bill, this business of campaigning with the Secretary of Defense against the Commission. He said he had told L. that "While we are discussing matters within the Commission, we are like this—" and he held out his hand with five fingers outspread. "But when we have reached a conclusion, by whatever vote, then we are like this"—and he closed his fingers except for the pointing index finger.

Bill reported that he and Bob Bacher were keeping in close touch and that L. had been working on Bob, too.

I dropped in on L. yesterday afternoon to tell him the latest on the Groves matter. He had been rather subdued in talking with me at Commission meeting, and both of us showed we are having difficulty. He himself is very sensitive to moods and was obviously worked up. So as I told him my story he said he still felt we are wrong about the foreign isotope matter; what did I think of his submitting this paper for the Commission's consideration; and handed me what was probably the same paper Bill had seen. He said he had shown it to Bill, "But I must confess I didn't shake him, and to Bob, who said, 'Yes, it ought to come to the Commission.' " I read it, rather grimly, I expect, found it filled with strained statements and the wobbliest kind of argument, not the balanced sort of thing he is capable of. He could tell from my face how little impressed I was.

I said I wanted to tell him frankly that I had been very much worried. He said he supposed he was completely out of my good graces, and he thought the best thing for him to do was to resign. I said that was absurd; but that it was essential that he realize how dangerous and fatal to everything we are doing it was for him to oppose Commission action *outside* the Commission. I said I had strained to develop a kind of family feeling among the Commissioners so we could deal with each other on an intimate, relaxed basis and thereby, when the time came when we could not agree—which was inevitable among independent men—we could disagree without in any way losing each other's respect or affection. But that would be destroyed completely if any of us carried our disagreement outside the Commission and sought to obstruct or build fires under the Commission. This was pretty strong meat, but it was necessary, and I said it with the patience and calm that one would use with a friend, and he is just that.

He was agitated, said I was a saint, etc. I tried to turn it back to the issue of what is permissible and what is not, remembering that it was because A. E. Morgan did just this thing that the break was inevitable. But this time I had a man to whom I could speak, and that never was true with A.E.

So I said, of course reopen it with the Commission (of course, he had already done so, to individuals, which he recognized), but it was fatal to our relations to do so outside. I didn't mention Forrestal, but he said something about calling on Forrestal, but I wonder if he was being completely frank about the purpose or content of the talk, for he said his purpose was to tell Forrestal that it was not true that we deliberately avoided notifying the MLC of our proposed action.

He said he had talked to Admiral Parsons of the MLC, without success, and mentioned talking with Herbert Bayard Swope; I gathered it was Swope who told the *Times,* though this is conjecture.

He said, "No, I'm through with it. I will forget it, or try to, though I am still not convinced I'm not right." He said some more about how terrible he felt. I said, "Don't criticize yourself that way, you just didn't realize what you were doing." He turned and grinned in what seemed a very genuine way and said, "No, I'm old enough; I knew exactly what I was doing." Which I believe is about the size of it. But the ethical implications are different for men of differing experience.

I doubt that he will be able to drop it entirely; but here's hoping.


OCTOBER I, 1947
AT HOME


These are *good* days. And since I have usually done a better job of journal writing when I am glum, I would do well to record some of the good times, too.

The work of the Commission is really moving now. We have finally landed a Raw Materials Director [John Gustafson], a good man, I gather, from industry, from Newmont Mining. This means there will soon be some competent person who can organize that important and rather neglected sector, and relieve my worries on that score; for it does trouble me that though we have recognized this from the very first meeting as a major chore requiring new techniques entirely, we have done precious little, compared to its importance. My repeated urging that we get a distinguished and hard-boiled industry committee for raw materials and one for industrial engineering is bearing fruit and we shall have both of these very soon now. That means more work for me particularly; these advisory boards add a great deal to my work for they are acting at a level that requires some attention from the Commission. But this will be a comfort and interesting, these two committees.

We expect to have a Medical Director very soon, too. With the appointment of Salisbury as Information Director last week, the roster of key posts is about complete. Boy, oh boy! What a difference this should make.

Another thing that makes me feel good these days is the grand reception the Crawfordsville policy got—almost without exception. It was risky. There was danger it would badly and openly antagonize the military. There was danger it would be considered as "giving away the secret." So far very little evidence of anything but a sense of relief through the organization, and praise outside.*

Today I completed the second major speech of the fall "campaign": the one for the Detroit Economic Club for next Monday. This is not well written, but I have managed to hit timing extraordinarily well, by a bit of luck and foresight. And I gather it will serve a number of useful purposes long urged on us, at the same time appearing to follow up the Crawfordsville policy of telling the public what they clearly have a right to know.

My relations with the military continue good. This morning a conference between the Commission and Lt. General Hull, who has been named in charge of the supporting military forces concerned with the [Eniwetok] test. We plowed through and decided things that were troubling him with a dispatch and direction that obviously surprised, and I assume pleased, him. This is going to be a huge and important operation, and it will be organized, I am willing to bet, much better than "Crossroads"† in a number of important ways.

This week we will be talking with people just back from Africa, and next week entertaining and negotiating with an important Belgian about uranium. We met with the General Advisory Committee. I got *Life* started on what may be an important educational effort to make atomic energy understandable to the American people, a direct result of the visit with the Luce and the *Life* staff in New York recently.

*And* David writes in fine fettle, the weather is sharp and bracing, and all in all I am enjoying myself. And since this journal has, as I have said, seen so many pages written in discouragement and even near-despair, it is good to write when one is so full of heart.

This is despite the fact that the news of the world grows increasingly bad—or perhaps it is more accurate to say that we are now seeing the facts more clearly. The worst of all, of course, is the performance of belligerence and plain bad manners the Soviet representatives and the press are putting on. This can't go on indefinitely, surely. And what do they think all this will get them? It is puzzling and not happy. And Europe is going to be in a mess for a long time, with the Good Samaritan being blamed, as so often, because the help isn't

* The Crawfordsville speech criticized the notion that atomic energy was too "technical" or "secret" for public information and discussion, calling this idea "plain nonsense and dangerous nonsense."

† The Bikini bomb test of the previous year.

enough, or prompt enough, or something, rather than blessed for being willing and able to help at all.

OCTOBER 3, 1947
AT THE CONFERENCE TABLE AT MY OFFICE

We are listening to a report by men just back from the interior of the Congo. The people who just preceded them were a lady from the League of Women Voters and the director of the Committee on Atomic Information, talking about public information by the medium of county fairs. And before that the General Advisory Committee, nine distinguished men. What a fantastic job this is!

OCTOBER 7, 1947
EN ROUTE, BY PLANE, FROM DETROIT

The industry speech yesterday noon at Detroit was well worth the effort, the rather considerable effort of writing the darn thing, and the trip. For it was a very large overflow audience, and cordial and friendly. I didn't do as good a job of delivery as I can and sometimes do, but the interest held throughout, to my surprise and delight. I no longer worry about whether the essential facts about the atom can be explained reasonably well, to lay audiences.

Met a great many people at a reception prior to the luncheon (this was the Economic Club) and also after the speech. These included old college friends, such as "Spin" Llewellyn, now in charge of distribution for General Motors, a very successful and attractive man; Warren Cooke; Bob Trees; such figures as S. S. Kresge (who said he came from the Poconos to hear me) and his son and grandson; Kettering, and a considerable number of automobile and other executives. The policy of the speech went quite well.

When I realized (or thought) that the statement of the speech would not make much of a dent so far as the daily press was concerned, I decided Sunday that the way to save the day was to announce an industrial advisory group at Detroit, thus giving a news angle on which to hang the speech. Trapnell was against this; thought it would blanket the speech, and there was the objection that the panel was not quite complete. But it turned out to be the right thing to do. It gave it a Detroit flavor, in Detroit; pleased Parker, chairman of the advisory group, and I notice gave it the lead and spotted the speech story in the page-one *Herald Tribune* story.

Last evening a dinner was given for me at the Detroit Economic Club. This was intended as a way of acquainting influential people of the community with our problems, in a way that couldn't be done in a public meeting. I learned a good deal about the limitations as well as the value of such sessions. K. T. Keller, Chrysler's dominant figure (short, bull-necked, a highly successful man in all things mechanical and therefore a Detroit hero), did not think much of anything I said, and said so. Life is pretty simple to a man whose great talent is in finding ingenious ways of repeating the same operation millions of times. They built Bofors guns and 26,000 tanks with parts that were so nearly the same that they could be interchanged freely. And he understands the kind of men who work in a shop or who design such gadgets. Beyond that, he is rather impatient of ideas. Looks just like a Hollywood casting director's picture of a hard-boiled automobile executive.

He told a story that throws light on his point of view as well as upon the spirit of Army administration. He was visiting at Oak Ridge during the war. Noticed some Negro women—almost immobile, slowly sweeping a porch. Remarked that they weren't getting much work done. He was told that they were worth what they were paid to have them on the place, but for another purpose. It was explained that the project had to use a good deal of Negro male labor; that Knoxville was quite a ways away, and there weren't many Negro women there. To keep the Negro men on the place they had to import women and they had to appear to be doing some work. Later Keller said he passed a place with a stockade around it. This was where the Negro women lived. Why the fence, since they were there to "help the morale"? "Oh," he was told (all of this rendered by Keller with amusement, of course), "we brought them; but what they do on their own, that's none of our business."

What a contrast to the TVA way of doing things, to TVA construction methods. This is just the old lumber camp method. But the climax to this tale was Keller's clincher, this part dead serious. "That's a good case of the Army way of getting things done; practical, no foolishness." This tells a lot about what we inherited at Oak Ridge. It is not surprising that what TVA inherited from the Army at Muscle Shoals also had a non-human, cynical quality to it, and the contrast with the rest of TVA, the part we built, continued. A. E. Morgan did a vast deal to set that new way of doing things, even though he did it, or went at it, in a paternalistic way.

Keller said, "What I object to is all this publicity; why don't you get the ballyhoo stopped about the future possibilities and all that stuff? I won't do any more work for you because of this publicity."

This rather shocked the others, and made me angry, a luxury I don't often indulge in. I let him have it: During the war you could tell the newspapers and the writers what they could say or suppress them entirely; at least that is what the Manhattan District did. But don't fool yourself, you can't do that now, and let me warn you not to try it.

He got red in the face at this and my belligerence, and said he would give his opinion and then go home. Which he did: We should train men to make atomic bombs, train enough of them, and let the rest go. All of what I said about industrial participation, and about the necessity for a vigorous and dynamic development that would attract and hold people—nothing to it.

I don't think he made too much of an impression on the others. But I was glad he said what he did for I must be prepared for this type wherever I go. It also made it plain that the close relation between atomic research for weapons and for peaceful uses is not well understood; otherwise many of the things Keller said he would have seen to be nonsense.

Conant told me the other day, at a General Advisory Committee meeting, that he had urged his alternative to the Acheson-Lilienthal proposal in a talk to the War College. This morning there is an account of Cavers' (of the Harvard Law School) proposal, along the same line: a prohibition of development of atomic power reactors, and confining all development to research. This is trying to put the genie back into the bottle. It is against the whole spirit of science, and as Bob Bacher says, "This is the way of the Middle Ages." Besides, the proposal puts a premium on clandestine activities, which methods give the Soviet kind of government an advantage over us.

OCTOBER 10, 1947
AT HOME

Slept from 8 last evening until 9:30 this morning, and am spending the day at home. Pretty tuckered.

Good day yesterday. President Harry Mitchell and Arthur Flemming of the Civil Service Commission (Miss Perkins was out of town) said that they would support us in our conclusion that the Atomic Energy Commission should be exempted from Civil Service completely for at least three years. This will relieve us of the many troubles and scars of a fight to establish this against their wishes, or without seeking their support and cooperation. Back of this are months of staff preparation and study, consultations, etc. But actually it would have been as easy to secure this result without all that report writing, etc.; the important point was to put it up to them that we did not believe we could dispatch our terrible responsibility in any other way, and asking them not to make our job more difficult than it was. Until the very last few minutes before the meeting with them the personnel staff expert was still talking about arguments to make to the Civil Service Commissioners based on reasons relating to personnel administration, etc.

This is what experience gives us; I knew that only a *broad* issue would be likely to get the result we wanted without unfriendly hangovers. This morning I wrote a warm personal note to Mitchell and Flemming; I hope this particular issue—which still must go the rounds of the Joint Committee, the Budget Bureau, etc., etc., *ad nauseam*—is behind us.

The test matter is up again, because it is necessary to say something publicly about it lest it leak and seem like an ominous bit of clandestine activity, fitting into the pattern of Soviet attacks at the UN Assembly and overseas. It was therefore not surprising to learn today that after securing approval of the things that needed to be said—and these the minimum—staff people in the State Department have objected and I must see Marshall and Lovett and try to find some acceptable course. It is not feasible to have a test without some public statement; and a test is essential to the present program.

I have been party to a blunder, and the very kind that I should be expected not to make. As follows:

Some weeks ago I recommended that we form an Industrial Advisory Panel, to advise on increased participation by industry in atomic energy activities, both in reactor design and in other ways. This was partly to offset the strong academic tinge (partly the change from Monsanto Chemical to the University of Chicago at Clinton National Laboratories), partly because good industrial advice on research would be definitely useful.

A list of names was suggested to the Commission; among them James Parker, president of Detroit Edison Company, and as executive secretary of the group, Walker Cisler, also of the Detroit Edison Co., now AEC consultant on other matters. I said that of course it wouldn't do to have two Detroit Edison men, and that one or the other should be dropped. Marks made the point that Cisler would be the effective man, that such was needed, etc. I said that perhaps that was the case, in which case Parker should be dropped.

I decided on the Detroit trip to announce the membership of the committee, to make the story of my speech more effective and spot news; when the list came to me, both Parker and Cisler were on it. This meant that despite this objection they had been invited and there seemed nothing to do at the time but announce it that way, though I should have known that whatever the consequences I should have either withheld the announcement or secured a change. I didn't, and this was a blunder. Why did I fall for it? Doubtless because I have become somewhat less aware of issues such as this through which I lived so long (and also perhaps because I did like to believe that no such issues continue to exist, since they are a "distraction" in my present work).

I thought about it a bit the day after the announcement was made, and rationalized by saying that the Commission's job was to protect the public interest, whereas this was intended to be a private industrial representation. But that was pretty thin, and I knew it.

Today Cap Krug called to say that the public power people were greatly disturbed by this. The committee was dominated by a private power company, and that Cisler particularly was strongly anti-public power. I didn't defend it much; said that it had been recommended to me by Marks and Warner and I hadn't given it the thought that I should have. He suggested a strong TVA man on the group, proposing DeMerit, TVA chief power engineer. I countered with Wessenauer (TVA power manager), and he said that would be perfect. I told Wilson about the situation, and he called Wess and will call Clapp.

I reminded Wilson of my objection at the Commission meeting; he said he found upon inquiry that both Parker and Cisler had been "approached" before the Commission met, in other words that my hunch about prior commitments had been right. I told him we would have to ask Cisler to retire in favor of an AEC employee, to act as secretary.

I think we will pull out of this all right. It is an *ad hoc* committee, to explore the problem of industrial participation. I should not have shot the thing off in Detroit so hastily. The addition of Wess, etc., will help in this particular case.

But another thing Cap said is important. He said that people looked at this "NAM Committee" and wondered if the benefits of atomic energy are going to be held up to protect the investments of industry, like the Bell Laboratory, etc.

It is so easy to fall into a way of thinking that goes on around me, and I must be on my guard against it. In my anxiety to eliminate fear of the Commission by industry (which is unwholesome) it would be utter folly to go to the other extreme; not only folly but completely against my whole record of 20 years, and an unwitting sell-out of the people who trust me or have no one else to look out for their interests.

So this is a lesson, and a warning, and one that comes before any serious harm has been done, I am sure.

Met much of the day with the Advisory Committee on Medicine and Biology, a grand group of men, with a chairman who is really a great well-rounded man, Dr. Alan Gregg. I am gradually getting the feel of the subject and find it terribly interesting. But if our Advisory Committees continue to meet on Saturday and Sunday (last week the GAC), my seven-day week will become a fixture.

The test matter is stymied; Forrestal and State both in doubt. Discussed it with Clifford a bit this morning. It should cause grave concern, for it could cause quite an international disturbance. But we must fish or cut bait about it.

It is just a year since Clifford came to the White House—slightly more, and about that time since I first met him. He said an interesting thing. Before he came here he always thought that what he wanted was to make a lot of money, to have a big house and lots of servants. He says he will never be content with anything as unimportant as that now, after what he has experienced in the last year. Making a lot of money seems rather irrelevant. I believe he thinks just that. The things that are going on in the world that he has seen at close range are now too much a part of his life to forget completely. He had a lot to learn, but he was the kind of man who was capable of learning.

OCTOBER 15, 1947

At Lewis' suggestion I telephoned General Eisenhower and told him that I had had a talk this morning with Army Secretary Royall and that what he told me bowled us over here, i.e., that Groves stays on the Military Liaison Committee; that he, Eisenhower, had been so candid and forthright with me in this matter I thought I owed it to him to tell him how we felt.

He said that the Joint Chiefs came in to see him yesterday about this matter. He said, "I told them how I felt about it, as I explained to you the other day, but the other members said that we just couldn't do that. That we would be in an indefensible position if we didn't use him, as he is the best-equipped man in the Armed Forces, and we couldn't stand before the public," etc., etc.

Continuing quoting from my notes of what Eisenhower said: "I am only one member of this group. Understand that actually the AFSWP [Armed Forces Special Weapons Project] works for the Joint Chiefs of Staff. I am only one of three, so I placed my views before the other two and they took it under advisement with the result that you know. They were quite willing to remove him from the MLC, but when it came to the other spot they said they couldn't remove the one man who knew anything. Their contention was that the MLC was the point at which the Commission had contact with General Groves." I broke in to say that this was a misconception, as I believed he knew, and that we were building toward an impossible operating situation.

He said, "I have always believed in being honest and straightforward with all the people I deal with. I was prepared to do what you know I said I would do, but the others took a different view, and that's the score. It is a very puzzling situation and I don't see what can be done about it. Although the Army provides the services, this weapons project is an operational thing which lies with the other services. Any man who believes in cooperation as I do will be very much disturbed about this situation."

I thanked him for telling me the story as he saw it and said that the Commission is giving it serious thought and would probably carry through on it; that it was an important public issue and had to be carried through. After some amenities this was the end of the conversation.

OCTOBER 16, 1947
AT HOME, THURSDAY

I have had two kicks in the teeth this week.

Yesterday morning from the Secretary of the Army, and the Joint Chiefs. For further details see the memorandum copied "as an appendix hereto." Quite a blow to think that General Eisenhower would back down so easily. Well, live and learn.

The second was from Hickenlooper, a big bawling out Tuesday from four till six. Got me so disgusted and mad during the first bitter scolding that I almost lost control and told him off, in a way I would have enjoyed but regretted. Although things improved as we went along, and there was some point in some of his complaint, the whole thing made me rather sick; literally, too, for my inards (which almost never misbehave) have been rather out of sorts ever since.

But there has been one pleasant experience. The speech for the Herald Tribune Forum has been an enjoyable thing to work out, for in the course of thinking it out (this has been going on for weeks, now and then) and putting it down on paper—typewriter composition this time—I think I have developed my ideas of the *relation* of moral purposes and moral principles to economic activity. As a result, I think I have "said" something; but I may learn quite otherwise. These "philosophic" speeches rarely get much newspaper attention, and when they do (as Wallace's "The Century of the Common Man" that was such a sensation a couple years ago), they often turn out to be flashes in the pan. This may be an exception. But it has been good to work on it; even if nothing further results.

It is good to be in the middle of things where the stimulus to write things like this is so natural.

I worry at times about whether my health will stand up to what I have to bear, the constant pressure, the snarling and troubles and all the neck-breathers, but we must find some way of keeping happy. But if I can "take it," it certainly has a lot to be said for it.

(MEMO OF MEETING WITH SECRETARY OF THE ARMY ROYALL, 10:30 TO 11:15, OCTOBER 15, 1947)

Secretary Royall had asked me the night before to come to his office in the morning; hence this meeting.

He said that he and General Eisenhower had discussed the problem of General Groves; that General Eisenhower had been of the opinion that since the Commission is so firmly of the opinion (and Mr. Royall added, "with some basis") that General Groves was not in harmony with the Commission, he should be relieved as head of the Armed Forces Special Weapons Project.

Secretary Royall said he had told General Eisenhower that he strongly disagreed with that recommendation. He said that he had had a great deal of dealings with General Groves during the legislative period of the present Atomic Energy Act and that they were in agreement as to what should be done; Royall added that he, Secretary Royall, had drafted the May-Johnson Bill which was later replaced by the McMahon Act; that he thought this was a mistake and that he and General Groves had been right. He said Groves was the best-qualified man in the Armed Forces for the Special Weapons Project. He said that the direct personal contact between Groves and the Commission was through the Military Liaison Committee and that his idea was that Groves be replaced on the MLC but definitely retained on the AFSWP. He said after he had discussed it with General Eisenhower, General Eisenhower agreed with him.

Secretary Royall said that back of his conclusion was the fact that a great many people in the country had confidence in General Groves, and with justification, and that they would raise a row if he were relieved from the AFSWP. He then asked me what my view was.

I said that I would, of course, take his views back to my associates on the Commission and after we had discussed it would express a Commission viewpoint. I pointed out that the decision about who should be designated by the Armed Forces for the particular positions of responsibility was entirely for the Armed Forces to say, and the Commission would certainly not seek to arrogate to itself any part of such decisions. But I said it is also plain that the Commission is responsible to the

President; that if conditions of cooperation with the Commission were lacking in the Armed Forces, particularly in the critical nexus between the two—that is, the AFSWP—I did not see how this already difficult job could be successfully discharged and that if that were the case it was our duty to say so to the President.

I said that any implication that this was merely a personal disharmony was quite erroneous; that the situation as we had pointed out as a Commission to Secretary Patterson months ago was this: that the country had decided on a civilian Commission and the President had selected five men to administer that law; that the Commission was entitled to have everyone in the Government proceed on the assumption that a civilian Commission was responsible, and that this particular five-man Commission was responsible and that therefore everything should be done by the Armed Forces and others to facilitate atomic energy development on those assumptions; that General Groves had not accepted those assumptions—that is, he disagreed with the law and he had no confidence in the men named to administer the law, and furthermore conducted himself in a way that carried out his fundamental disagreement and opposition to the Commission.

Secretary Royall asked for an illustration. I referred to the incident at Sandia Base which General Brereton as well as Mr. Wilson had reported; namely, that General Groves, speaking to officers of the AFSWP, had crudely disparaged the Commission's representative at that critical point of contact, namely, Captain Tyler, and had said in effect to the officers at that point that it wouldn't be long until the Commission's mess of things would throw the whole business back in the Army's hands.

I pointed out that this was not a single instance, that this episode was known to General Eisenhower and to General Brereton and its consequences were still being felt; further making the point that this was not a merely personal difficulty, a matter of "incompatible temperaments."

Secretary Royall said that he knew General Groves was difficult and that things had happened that were wrong but that he would see to it that he kept within bounds.

I said I would report to my associates, but that I would remind him that Secretary Patterson had said the very same thing but even more emphatically and that General Eisenhower had said the same thing a long time ago; but that it was not a matter of the surface of things, but rather that General Groves' honest convictions were that the Commission was no damn good and that he, General Groves, knew all the answers, and that he regarded it as a kind of sacred duty in his various capacities to prove his point. I said further that I had no doubt that if the Armed Forces felt so inclined they could destroy the Commission's effort to make this project effective. Speaking for myself, I felt the country was entitled either to civilian control under the McMahon Act with the full cooperation of the rest of the Government or, on the other hand, it ought to put General Groves in charge and then everyone ought to cooperate with him, but that we could not have it both ways.

Secretary Royall said that he had not intended to tell me the following but thought it appropriate to do so; yesterday, not at his initiation, the three Chiefs of Staff met in General Eisenhower's office and discussed this matter. They reached the unanimous conclusion that General Groves should continue as head of the AFSWP. He said, of course, if the Secretary of Defense disagreed, then, of course that would be another matter, but that this was the way things stood.

I said in view of the representations the Commission had made to Secretary Patterson and to General Eisenhower, and the known facts about General Groves' antagonism and opposition, this appeared to me to be a vote of no confidence by the Joint Chiefs in the Atomic Energy Commission. Secretary Royall disagreed with this statement, but I expressed the opinion that I could not see how, with all the background of months of what I termed a "disgraceful and intolerable situation," the decision of the Joint Chiefs could be construed in any other way, but that I had great respect for Royall's contrary opinion. I said the matter would be taken up with the Commission; and said if they had another view I would of course go along with it, but that it seemed to me that this situation was heading for disaster and that I for one did not propose to be caught under a disaster without the country knowing that an important issue was at stake. Secretary Royall became quite troubled at this; said he did not see there was any issue, that it was simply a matter of selecting a man for a military project whom they regarded as best qualified.

He said of course Secretary Forrestal might not concur and thereupon put in a call to him, suggesting that perhaps I should talk to Secretary Forrestal. I said that perhaps the whole Commission would want to talk to Secretary Forrestal. After talking with Forrestal he said that Forrestal wanted to explore the matter for a few days; that thereupon he, Forrestal, might want to talk to me about the matter further, and urged against going to the President with the issue. I made no comment except to say that if Secretary Forrestal wanted to meet with the Commission, of course we would do so. Mr. Royall again urged the Commission not to "trouble" the President with this matter, but I made no comment on this.

I said I hoped he understood clearly this was not a merely surface matter of personalities; I told him that the Commission had recommended General Groves' promotion to a lieutenant generalcy; that we had spoken at a luncheon of his great accomplishments and his patriotism; that we had done everything we knew how to make the situation workable, but a time comes when no self-respecting men, especially men who have taken on such terrible responsibilities, can have any other course open to them, and still maintain their self-respect. I think he knew how strongly and deeply I felt about this issue.

OCTOBER 23, 1947
NEW YORK
(AT THE WALDORF, I A.M.)

All my work on the *Herald Tribune* speech, all my fussing and rehearsing its delivery, and all my misgivings about saying the same old thing—there was an extraordinary climax tonight. For at the end of a long evening of speech after speech—hours of it—I picked the audience up—I could see it almost from the first words, and we went along together, and at the end an ovation, the kind where the applause goes on and on, you stand up and acknowledge it, and then it goes on. And this under the auspices of the conservative *Herald Tribune,* in the Waldorf Ballroom. So of course I felt quite wonderful about it all.

After the speech we came up to Mrs. Reid's suite, and this was an interesting session. Nancy, who was at the proceedings, came too, and was most attractive. This job-hunting has done her worlds of good. She really has something, that gal. I had a long session with Clare Luce, which I was able to break up by saying, "Would you give a young girl a big thrill—she happens to be a daughter of mine?" This startled Clare. Carl Sandburg; Henry Luce; Bill Robinson, business manager of the *Herald Tribune;* Geoffrey Parsons, chief editorial writer; Jennie Lee; and Barbara Ward, the economist, of England—was a good party.

I was interested to see the contrasting reaction of the audience to me and to Eric Johnston. He is a very polished and attractive man, and he made a good impression. But he does not seem sincere—the glamour boy.

Perhaps it is just as well that I am a rather ugly mug, mangy with baldness, for people don't stand back and say, "He is giving us his charming profile."

I am now convinced that I am about as good a public speaker, with as much to say and an effective, persuasive, emotion-inspiring way of saying it, as there is in the country. This may be partly the effect of three Scotch and sodas; but one should be honest, and this was a real test—this sophisticated audience. If I don't make too many speeches, and only when I really have something to say, this can become a great asset to important things.

Thurman Arnold preceded me, with a very good, fresh, original statement—in considerable contrast to the rather stuffy speeches of Benjamin Fairless, president of United States Steel, and Senator Flanders (who sat next to me on the platform, he having raised nasty hell about me on the Senate floor). Arnold got a fine reception, but as we left he said, "Of all the speeches yours was the one that wowed 'em."

I have learned quite a bit from this, I hope.

Senator Ives was on the program, and I liked him. Partly, perhaps, because he spoke very warmly about being "glad you are in the job you are in."

OCTOBER 31, 1947
BUCKHORN INN
GREAT SMOKY MOUNTAINS NATIONAL PARK, TENNESSEE

This has been a wonderful week. For the first two or three days I was asleep or in a coma most of the time—a really complete relaxing and getting over the too tired state I had gotten into. (It was this, I think, that accounted for the strange chill-and-fever business that hit me the day before we were to leave.)

The weather has been beyond dreams—brilliant, crisp mornings, with the mountains green and dark, then the sun growing warmer, and lying out flat on the porch feeling the sun on one's face—really grand. The last two days we have been taking hikes and tomorrow plan another.

Yesterday I phoned Washington; found that Marshall wants a meeting with Forrestal and myself to determine policy. A courier arrived this morning with two top secret documents. These I sat out in the sun and studied until noon, then went to Gatlinburg and phoned Wilson again. Will leave here Sunday, meeting in Washington Monday and Tuesday on this matter, and then I hope to return to finish my visit at Oak Ridge and Norris.

There is something quite extraordinary in thinking and turning over in one's mind the kind of issues these documents present, while out here in this peaceful, lovely place.

One thing I have been more than ever determined about is that I so arrange my life that 15 minutes for a walk in the morning, or a swim in the afternoon, or a rest at noon, or a week away every two months or so, becomes as much a part of my schedule as some relatively unimportant conference or speech or such a matter which, when set, I always manage to find the time and energy to take care of. If I don't establish such a rule, and let almost nothing break it, this job will get me down, or in any event I will simply not be able to bring to it what it really requires— that is, a physically and nervously fit person.

So I shall go back with high resolutions in this direction. My back seems quite well again—I am climbing about for the first time in a year, without any ill effects whatever, so that horseback riding would seem in the picture again.

The devil was sick, the devil a saint would be—it is the old story. But I simply must take this seriously and make definite plans in the office—put these rests and bits of recreation down as firmly as any other part of my program.

NOVEMBER 6, 1947
NORRIS, TENNESSEE

This *is* a red-letter day indeed!

For I rode Mac again, the first time in exactly a year, almost to the day. He was beautiful, and my back seems to be quite all right; my legs felt it, of course, but just the muscular soreness you would expect. To be able to walk without limit and to ride again—two things that the experience of the last two weeks shows that apparently I can now do again—this is like being pardoned and set free again.

Visited with Dr. [H.A.] Morgan. What a sweet, wonderful old boy he is, and his continued enthusiasm is simply amazing. He is no more articulate and no less hazy, to me, than before; but no more so. And this never bothered me before and doesn't now.

Knocked on the door marked "No Admittance" and walked in to see the TVA telephone girls, who were always so nice to me, and friendly, and of course they were pleased. The elevator operators; Bernard Foy and his library aides; Menhinick, etc. I made the rounds. The "topside" boys were away—at budget hearings in Washington. Didn't see Pope; he was away whenever I called.

NOVEMBER 7, 1947
NORRIS

Another ride on Mac, and he was full of his old steam. His bad eye is now white and plainly blind; but for that he seems every bit as good as ever, and my horsemanship is no worse.

I am going to begin in a modest way doing something about that craving of mine to raise beef cattle. Ernest Smith has taken on more land near his stables, and I am going to put up the money for two Polled Hereford heifers, calves six months old, registered. He will raise them and try to build a herd. It will give me something to interest me, and then if I can, and when I can, I would like soon to have a farm, say 100 acres or so of pasture, and really go in for cattle. But this is a way to play with the idea—and see some cattle of my own if only two—while thinking it over and trying to figure out how I can manage a more elaborate scheme. Ernest would make a grand partner, for he is terribly interested, works very hard, and is learning.

## NOVEMBER 14, 1947

President Wilson Compton came in to ask me to deliver the commencement address June 5 at Washington State, and receive a honorary degree. Told him I couldn't promise now, but it has its points, since the Hanford undertaking is one with which we ought to identify ourselves more closely.

A stocky, well-set-up man, rather different in appearance than the other brothers Compton.

## NOVEMBER 15, 1947
### AT HOME

We may be over the worst of the crazy hysteria about "loyalty." The President's statement to the Loyalty Board just assembled (*months* after his executive order) reflects the better state of public sense on this subject and a far cry from the terrible state of affairs that reached a high in the hearings on my confirmation. The bad public reaction to the State Department's dismissals without cause, and the bad press J. Parnell Thomas got on the Hollywood investigation are other indications. The President could have done a world of good if he had done something like this at the time of the executive order. But I am not in a very good position to criticize, since within the Commission we did not know quite how to be effective in dealing with our own problems, and it was really only because of Herb Marks' grumping and Sumner Pike's tough good sense that we did not go off the deep end.

I am troubled about Nancy. She still does not have a job, and though we haven't heard from her for some time, the prospects are apparently far from good.

David writes full of vigor and intensity, chiefly about his do-or-die efforts to "make" the *Crimson* editorial staff.

Am wearing "reading" glasses for the first time; this is just a way of saying that middle age has really hit me and that soon I will have to agree with Dr. Leach and put on the cursed bifocals, official badge of decrepitude. And the fatigue I experience after long days—while actually borne better than I did ten years ago—I take also as a personal affront.

Brought Penny back from the vet's this morning, where she has been in durance very vile for three weeks. My, but she was a happy little dog. So were we.

Congress begins the special session Monday. This does not mean a particularly better time of it, by any means. But we are so much better staffed than when they left that it certainly should be manageable; even with the rash of important speeches I have to write and deliver.

NOVEMBER 17, 1947
AT THE OFFICE

Lunch with Eric Johnston, at his plush office here. His Spokane firm is bidding on electrical work at Hanford; it amused me to see the way in which he spoke of this. He told me he was recommending that the ten writers who refused to testify before the Un-American Committee be fired. He is troubled by the issue, and I didn't pour oil on his concern, pointing out that whereas in the case of the Commission the danger of a pro-Communist in our ranks was rather obvious and fairly direct, in the case of a writer or actor in the motion pictures, the danger was remote rather than direct, at worst, whereas the danger to free speech, etc., could be considerable.

He is an attractive fellow, more so privately than when he wears his public personality, which is a bit too self-conscious for my taste.

A good session with Senator Hickenlooper late this afternoon, quite in contrast with the painful "going over" he gave Joe Volpe and me when he returned from Europe. I handed him a goals report—with charts, etc., which he had requested. We explained that this was a very "hot" document. This led to a two-hour discussion in which I made and remade this point: it was for the committee and *not the Commission* to limit the scope and character of the information it furnished the committee, and that the Commission was entitled to a statement of policy by the committee justifying our limited reporting. We batted this back and forth, but in the best of spirit. He asked us not to send this report until he had a meeting of his committee, at which he would ask them to decide what the hell to do with it.

We recognize that we are feeling our way along a difficult course. For the Appropriations Committee will probably not be nearly so sensitive to such considerations, and a [security] break is a break, wherever it occurs.

One point we made this time that we had never been able to make "stick" before, i.e., that it is not enough to say that "we do not want technical details," which does not meet the security issue, though of course everyone could wish that it was that simple. For many of the matters that foreign agents would want most of all are neither technical nor details, but broad generalizations about the status of things, the troubles, the needs for the future, and the reasons for the vast new construction activities we are starting. The very fact that we are asking for huge sums of money ( ¾ billion for next year plus a supplemental appropriation of many millions to finish this year) will require us to give an urgent reason.

This process of trying to find a way of complying with our duty of informing Congress, and of keeping them worrying about the same things we are worrying about—it is tough. I think we made some headway today, in that I believe the committee will be pushed into taking responsibility for determining how far we should go in keeping them "fully and currently informed."

NOVEMBER 18, 1947
AT THE OFFICE (6:45 P.M.)

Bill Waymack presented each of us Commissioners with undershorts, decorated with red ants and a scorpion (drawn for him by Ding Darling). This was to mark the first year of our existence as a Commission, i.e., November 13.

I am about to complete my speech to the American Education Fellowship in Chicago day after Thanksgiving—it has been something of a job, and is spotty in quality—too discursive.

Taber called me this afternoon. Wants to put someone in the organization to straighten us out and show us how to run things, I gather. Another set of "helpers" and we are sunk. Said he and Wigglesworth will come down to the office tomorrow and "We will see what you are doing." I get along personally with the old boy, but he has a task that is so tough I don't see how he stands it. He looked tired and harassed, too.

Lunch with Dean Acheson. He told me of his experience with Herbert Hoover on this new Government Reorganization Commission. He said he didn't see how any man could be so wrong about so many things—how to go about a job, people appropriate for things to do, etc. —as Hoover has been, and recited some of them.

When Marshall first came into office, he said to Acheson, "I have had a visit with Baruch. He says there are people in the State Department who are frustrating the Secretary. He is an old man, and needs a good deal of flattery and attention, but he is a good man, and this troubles me. Who are they?"

"I pointed to myself," Acheson said, "and said, 'Your Under Secretary.' 'Oh, no,' Marshall replied, 'Baruch has a high regard for you; he told me so.' "

Acheson continued: " 'Well,' I said to Marshall, 'you try this out on him. Ask him directly about me.' The next day he said, 'You're right.' I told him the reason Baruch distrusted me was that I had objected violently to his appointment by Byrnes as the United States delegate in this atomic energy matter in the UN, and that I had insisted on the publication of our report. I did both of these things, and for good reason.

"One day Marshall said that 'Really Baruch was all right if you knew how to handle him. For example, he was determined to get his bust in the War College. This wouldn't do; we only have Napoleon, Alexander, and Caesar in there; didn't even have Pershing in. So I salved him up and that was that.' The next day I went into his office with a card, saying, 'Read this.' It announced that the War College invited him to attend the unveiling of a bust of Bernard Baruch. 'You certainly know how to "handle" him,' I said. 'Yes,' said Marshall, 'and to top it off, it seems I am going to make a speech at the unveiling.' "

We discussed British-Canadian-U.S. relations at some length. He is a solid man, with a great instinct for what is essential and what is off the beam.

NOVEMBER 19, 1947
AT THE DESK

David's 20th birthday!

Just talked to a young fellow sent to me by Bill Donovan.‡ A weird story, brought in from eastern Czechoslovakia (the Carpathians) by a Jewish rabbinical student, and purports to concern Russian efforts in atomic energy. Turned him over to Admiral Gingrich.

NOVEMBER 22, 1947
AT HOME

Worked at the speech for the American Society of Mechanical Engineers this morning, and putting the finishing touches on the one for the education gathering next Friday. Believe the latter will be a real addition to the "line" on public education.

Then went to the office (yes, this *is* Saturday!). Commission spent an hour discussing our CPC position.§ I have to be particularly careful

---

‡The wartime director of the OSS.

§ The CPC—the Combined Policy Committee—was formed in 1943 by the U.S., Britain, and Canada for joint policy supervision of the A-bomb project. For some time, the British had been pressing for fulfillment of what they considered about this for the other conferees do represent their departments; whereas I must act as spokesman only for what the Commission has already concluded is the position they believe in. With this in mind, and because I know of [Strauss'] reservations about cooperation with the British, I emphasized that what we were agreeing to looked in the direction of abandoning the position of "going it alone" and toward cooperation with the British. No one doubted this, although I expected a stir.

Our whole effort—this is the same matter that was sent to me by courier while we were at the Buckhorn Inn—is to lay a factual basis for discussion. The State Department staff people, Kennan and Gullion, keep pressing for a broad approach—something that smacks of an alliance. I shall do everything I can to discourage and prevent this; it is not the way to approach this matter. I was quite successful last time, as the record shows—complete minutes were written and agreed to— and I hope to be equally successful this time.

Then we lunched, as Lewis' guest, with the General Advisory Committee. This was quite pleasant. I talked to Conant about his War College speech on international control. He said I shouldn't worry, he didn't plan to talk publicly about it, and anyway this was no time to propose anything in this direction, anything at all. He certainly is right about that. I told him that this morning I had found occasion on which I could make clearer my view about the Smyth Report—this will be the Engineers speech. Although I am going to incur some disapproval, it does seem right that I should say that the purpose of that report, to make information available, and helpful in guiding American public opinion, was a necessary and proper one.

This subject of secrecy was brought to us by the committee as we met later in the afternoon. They felt it was hampering our scientific progress badly. I said there was no disagreement about this so far as we were concerned; but that they must not underestimate the difficulties in making headway and still retaining public confidence. The trouble is that unless the public knows more, they cannot understand why secrecy is so largely an illusion and a hobble. So it is a circle. We discussed criteria of determining whether information should be kept secret—not scientific information but, say, how we stood on numbers of weapons, as to which there is a great misconception in public thinking.

The General Advisory Committee will make some kind of report to us on this. It was interesting to see that what concerned them is just what concerns me now: that an intelligent and panicless public opinion

to be our wartime pledges of complete atomic information exchange. Here and in the next three journal entries (written with deliberate vagueness at the time), I refer to our efforts to clarify the scope of the existing information exchange to meet, at least in part, the British requests.

cannot be expected unless there is more information, and non-technical information, to a considerable extent.

### NOVEMBER 24, 1947

Conference: Lovett, Forrestal (looking pretty worn, I must say), Bush, Wilson, Marks, Gullion, Arneson.

Lovett began with a reading of a dispatch reporting on a Belgian Communist paper. It was a story—quite lurid—that the bankers in America had exposed their hand. This had reference to Vandenberg's statement that before the Marshall Plan was passed the United States would insist on Belgium's uranium—and went on from there.

Then followed a very impressive recital of how the State Department feels about negotiations on our problems of "cooperation" with the British, and a revision of the Commission's proposed redraft of the position to be taken.

### NOVEMBER 25, 1947

Commission met this morning. Got unanimous approval of the position that we are to take with the British by approving word for word the statement.

### NOVEMBER 26, 1947

Just got home from one of the most remarkable experiences a man ever had. From 5 until 8 P.M. we were at Blair House with Vandenberg, chairman of Foreign Relations, and Hickenlooper, while Lovett and I (with assistance on facts from Carroll Wilson and assists from Dr. Bush and Forrestal) presented a proposal that, if it results in agreement, will present a new course of basic policy in the world. It has been months and months in coming. To my great surprise it was received almost without question, in every essential. The thing we thought would cause the most trouble didn't raise a ripple hardly—the matter of [supplying the U.K. atomic technical] "information."

I don't know when I have been more pleased by anything than two things Vandenberg said. As he poured himself a drink before we began (he had just come from being through the test vote on Emergency Foreign Aid), he turned to me and in quite an animated way said, "Do you know, getting into the middle of your confirmation fight did *me* more good throughout the country than it did you." Wasn't that a gracious, generous thing to say? (He told me how worried his son was as to how he was going to vote, and when he finally told him, the son said, "Good; I was worried about that.")

The other thing he said I can't write in full; but he said, "As far as 'information' is concerned, I here and now give my proxy to David Lilienthal and to Van Bush for anything they think is the thing to do." Boy, that really was something! It indicates that at this stage at least Herb [Marks] had overestimated the difficulties on this score and that Lewis was considerably wrong in his estimate.

But on certain wartime agreement provisions Vandenberg was very strongly opposed indeed;◖ but it only makes the general course of our proposed policy all the better.

(I wrote Sen. V. a letter, longhand, next day, on his remarks, and got a grand reply.)


NOVEMBER 29, 1947
ON THE CAPITOL LIMITED, RETURNING FROM CHICAGO

Arrived in Chicago yesterday morning to find snow. Seemed rather good, too.

Luncheon with Bob Hutchins* at the Electric Club in Insull's old hangout, 20 North Wacker Drive. Made two proposals: (1) that we experiment with pure research projects which industry and Government jointly finance, perhaps on a sliding scale with industry gradually taking larger share; (2) that we rig up a stiff-shirt occasion at which I can speak *for* industrial-financed pure research and deplore the tendency to have Government do it all. I have thought about these two moves a good deal, and while they have their difficulties, they both appeal to me as being right—consistent with my theme—and in the interests of the country. In any event, if then industry fails to come in, it will not be because they weren't urged.

Hutchins still puzzles me. He is amusing, very handsome and impressive, but somehow there is a streak I cannot quite understand in so experienced and hard a customer. He seems to like to build up logical oversimplifications, as a college senior might. Russia, for example. There is no secret; there is no defense. Hence, we should do nothing that would cause Russia to fear us and therefore be likely to use the bombs she soon will have against us. I just declined to chew it over; too much work and too risky. But his simple assumptions and his notion that we are dealing with fixed factors reminded me more of a college debate than a serious discussion among men who have decisions to make.

◖ This refers to the wartime U.S. pledge not to use the bomb without British consent.
* Chancellor of the University of Chicago.

The speech last night (to the American Education Fellowship) went well enough—in fact, it was quite well received. But the group did not seem important enough for a major speech to educators. There is one thing about it that I was quite glad about, though; it was a gesture, a public expression of my liberal beliefs to balance, or clarify, the fact that I have been doing a lot of talking to and associating with extremely conservative and "respectable" crowds. I do so much want to be independent and self-sufficient—in a special sense—that I can go where I please, talk before whatever group I please. This "crime by association" hysteria that is going around these days gets even me once in a while—at least I find myself too cautious about it.

Started the day very early this morning, going to the University of Chicago and visiting the Argonne Lab with the Industrial Participation Group. Met Isaac Harter, a rather fabulous man, the brains of Babcock and Wilcox (from whom TVA bought so many waterwheels), and Robert Wilson, chairman of the board of Standard Oil of Indiana. The group left for Hanford. Listened to a very complex discussion of the chemical recovery process business—I find that each time I hear it I find it somewhat less difficult, somewhat less bewildering. But I am uncertain or vague still about some elementary things—e.g., is there enriched uranium in the Hanford pile?

Spent yesterday afternoon with Ted. He is a wonderful man, so good, so pure of heart and kind. Very much like his Dad. Doesn't seem very well, though. "I love him like a brother" is a phrase made for how I feel about my brother Ted.

It was a difficult afternoon in one way. For the Joint Committee was meeting in Washington to raise hell about some people we had "cleared." At last, about 5 P.M., Joe Volpe called to say that they had been at it all day long; that Gingrich had done a good job; and that the concern of the committee as they went through the cases was to acquaint themselves with the cases, because they expect J. Parnell Thomas to blow off about it, and to warn us against taking on a burden, a public relations burden, by cases that could be exploited by our enemies.

The notion that the military vs. civilian issue is settled grows more and more untenable. Groves is hard at it, of course; but it goes way beyond him. My feeling is that somehow we had better postpone and temporize, avoid a big row for a time at least, but we may not be able to. The "custody" [of weapons] issue may be the detonator.

Robert Hutchins told me of an hour and a half he had with Forrestal and Bush, just before he called on the Commission on October 7. He said this was the first time he had ever seen either of them. He thought Forrestal was a positively dangerous man. As to Bush, Bush scolded him for encouraging people to believe that atomic energy had industrial uses—and this bored Hutchins—said he was too old for scolding. Said he was shocked to notice how both Forrestal and Bush cussed me out, to him, although they had never seen him before: "Why does Lilienthal make such speeches?"—this must have been the Crawfordsville one, though I am not sure—encouraging hopes from atomic energy.

Hutchins said their whole point was that it must be kept in the public mind as a weapon—this would insure military control. "I used to have industrialists come to ask me about the future of atomic energy; but I have discouraged them, so now they rarely do"; this he attributed to Bush. I take these statements of Hutchins with a certain qualification for interpretation, but I do remember how Bush bawled me out for the Crawfordsville speech.

NOVEMBER 30, 1947
AT HOME, SUNDAY

The leak on the Pacific testing operation has come, just as I felt sure it would: a dispatch from Honolulu, AP and INS. They agreed to hold it up for 24 hours, and we are making a release tomorrow, with Marshall's concurrence. The General Assembly adjourned last night; it was Marshall's fear that if the announcement of the test were made while the Assembly was in session, the Russians could use it as a sounding board or as a basis for some dramatic move. Now he fears it will have the same use in London at the Foreign Ministers Conference.

These fears seem to me exaggerated, though I am sure that if I were in his shoes I would have them, too. But we can't avoid such things if we are in an arms race. It is extraordinary, though, how freely the Armed Services make the most bloodthirsty statements about their preparations, with no one so much as raising an eyebrow.

Just called Hickenlooper to tell him about it. He had been queried by an INS man and told him nothing. He said the Friday meeting on "clearances" had gone well; everybody laid things right on the line, got things off their chest, but "no one got mad." He suggested that perhaps the committee should later next week issue a statement on the whole subject to "take the edge off J. Parnell Thomas if he blows up" and to reassure the public that the Commission was on top of these things, and that the record was a good one. Such a statement should be discussed between the committee and the Commission and drafted jointly. This is a remarkable attitude and bodes good for the future.

DECEMBER 4, 1947
AT THE DESK

Newsreels this afternoon here in the office on the Eniwetok announcement,

After I finished my talk to an auditorium-full, at Wharton School in Philadelphia yesterday afternoon, Dean Balderston said he overheard one student say to another, "Boy—that's better than what Wig and Mask ever put on in here." (This was on the stage used by the college dramatic society.) This seemed to amuse everyone—this remark.

It was a good show, the speech, and though I was terribly tired before I began, it disappeared as I got up. I said, "President McClelland," and just then a little dog—cur out of the alleys, it was—came rushing down the center aisle, barking in a high voice, madly. I grinned and went right on. "My canine friend," sez I, and as the laugh died down, went on to include Dean Balderston in the salutation. The dog began again, rushing wildly up the other aisle. "You can't fool a dog," I said. The dog quieted down and we were off. Later, Balderston said three people told him that from the time I included the dog in the introduction, "the audience was his."

The speech itself, largely extemporaneous, dealt with atomic energy as a problem in business management.

The evening meeting with the big shots of the Sunday Breakfast Club went much better than I hoped for—it was quite informal—and the questions went on and on. The questions showed a number of important illusions, chief among them about how many bombs we have, and that we now have a much bigger one.


DECEMBER 6, 1947
AT HOME

Returned from my trip to Philadelphia to face several hard days. Long session with Phil Murray, Allen Haywood, Wagner, and others of the CIO, and the Commission, etc. Murray said they were prepared to call a strike at Oak Ridge, if the negotiations for a new contract with Carbide did not work out. They insisted on our directing the company to include in the contract a broad arbitration of terms provision. I warned Murray that this was in effect compulsory arbitration. He said this wouldn't be a precedent, that the unusual conditions surrounding this operation set it off, and that since the men didn't have the usual privilege of striking (since public opinion and the national interest would be against it) some outside board or arbitrator must be set up.

Apparently they object to *our* writing the contract. I feel pretty sad about the way this is going; after our good TVA labor experience and record. But there we dealt directly with the organizations; here we have contractors, and what a difference this makes.†

Yesterday from 10:30 A.M. until 1:20 P.M. we were with the Joint Committee. Attendance was about half the committee—but Vandenberg was there throughout, Millikin, Knowland, Cole, Elston, among others. Lovett and I told the story we had told at Blair House. There was not a peep of criticism, no blow-up, no hesitation to approve the program [of information exchange with the British]; or, more properly, to tell us to go ahead with the negotiations. So all the worrying about it was actually misplaced. They accepted the idea that this should not be explicitly tied to economic relief to Britain—though, of course, the two cannot be wholly separated in reality—and this I thought was very good.

An important milestone, this.

Spent the evening last night with John Gunther. He is doing a second volume of the *Inside U.S.A.*, this one about Washington, but will not write it until after the election. Told me of a three-hour visit with Eisenhower yesterday noon: delightful stories. John is sure that Ike is running, and hard. But he found him a delightful man, which he is, and with great gaps in his knowledge but very quick to learn.

John and I had a wonderful steak, in his suite. I took the bone, wrapped it in paper, and brought it out through the swank Mayflower lobby to take home to Penny. This rather shocked John and may be the first time that anyone ever carried a bone out of the Mayflower. But Penny certainly appreciated it.

[*Following are some rough notes I took at the December 5 meeting with the Joint Committee:*]

*Lovett:* At certain levels of research and development there are fields of information that in the opinion of qualified people can be safely and reasonably exchanged with the British to our advantage, advantage of our national security.

In the meantime must give some information ourselves.

A journey over Thousand Islands begins with the first step. This is a first step. An entity in itself.

And this is not a matter which can technically be involved in European aid—a separate operation.

We feel hesitant to go forward with comprehensive program unless committee feels it is the proper approach.

†The CIO local did authorize a strike against Carbide & Carbon Chemical Corporation, our Oak Ridge contractor, but later in the month agreement was reached on a new contract.

*Vandenberg:* First I think you have clearly stated the interpretation that is put on the first of these secret agreements.

I don't recognize that [British] veto [on the use of the bomb]; a war agreement. Also recognize that so long as anybody can make it appear to be a valid agreement, it can be source of desperate embarrassment. Horrified and have been since I learned of it. Vitally essential wipe that off beyond any dispute, though I deny continuing authority of the agreement.

Raw materials matter must be separated from economic aid to Britain because you cannot expect on a question involving national interest England will deal with you on a trading basis. Separate this one so long as you settle it before we settle the other question of economic aid.

Beyond that, believe you are on the beam. Don't need to worry about kind of information you will exchange, so long as Dr. Bush and Mr. Lilienthal are on the veto end.

*Vandenberg* (as he was leaving): We are worrying here this morning about a factor [uranium ore] that can interrupt our production of atomic weapons. We also read in the paper that CIO can interrupt production. I would like to see this committee have bare-knuckled story of that situation for that is something we can control, and if we don't control it we ought to resign. Utterly vital that something be done about this raw materials situation. I hope they will proceed with our encouragement and blessing.

Statement of conclusion:

*Hickenlooper:* Let me summarize:

1. Stockpile of materials in Britain would be in ultimate danger [of capture by Russians].

2. Cancel and eliminate agreement re [British veto on] use of X.

3. Cooperate with British in acquisition of materials in South Africa.

4. On exchange of information, there are certain areas of information which do not go to the top flight or ultimate information of bomb manufacture.

May we assume that it is the consensus of the committee that the procedure and objective discussed here is, in the opinion of the committee, a proper and desirable approach and we have no dissent? (There was no dissent.)

*Millikin:* I do not think we have jurisdiction. We expect State Department to clear this up. We reserve the right to criticize what they do.

*Lilienthal:* We would not initiate discussion with the British at all if this committee believed not compatible with the law.

*Millikin:* No suggestion here that you do not proceed to discuss these matters as proposed.

*Vannevar Bush:* In general I believe security of the U.S. can be advanced by appropriate interchange with the British in fields where we are both working, and I believe that would not in any way involve interchange with them in fields in which we alone are working. Those fields in which we alone are working go to the heart of this thing, as you gentlemen now know.

## DECEMBER 9, 1947

Frightfully tired. Decided couldn't "take" the National Planning dinner tonight, so came home. Thank God I didn't fall for the "just talk five minutes" bait. My last piece of work was at State—preparation for the meeting of CPC tomorrow. Lovett was supposed to be here; as we gathered Gullion came in to say, "Mr. Lovett has just returned from all day on the Hill. He asks to be excused. He is dead tired; is going home to bed." Kennan looked sad and said, "It has been ghastly. I'm afraid if he ever goes to bed, he'll never get up."

If you want a cinch, just work for the Government!!

## DECEMBER 10, 1947
### AT THE OFFICE (12:30 P.M.)

A great triumph!

Late one day last week, talking over the troubles about "clearances" we decided to ask Dr. Frank Jewett of the National Academy of Science to head a "loyalty" board. I suggested Justice Roberts, then agreed he probably wouldn't serve. Saturday this bothered me; I called Monday and asked the members to reconsider and let me call Roberts. I did; he has just been here; I did a good job of presenting our need and he accepted at once, and will organize a board.‡ This may save this Commission, and we may contribute an important by-product to American institutions. He said the President had put all sorts of pressure on him to have him head the National Loyalty Board; he refused because the executive order setting it up wasn't decent and didn't provide an American way of going at such problems!

## DECEMBER 14, 1947
### AT HOME, SUNDAY NIGHT

Have been in bed the last two days most of the time, trying to shake off or ameliorate a sore throat, with how much success tomorrow will tell.

‡ Other members: Karl Compton, Joseph Grew, George M. Humphrey, H. W. Prentis, Jr.

Very considerably worried about Hutchins' article in the *American Magazine* of a week ago. I read it with amazement and incredulity. Such poor taste, in its tone, and so shockingly wrong in facts and inference!§ And here I had been trying to understand, and gain his confidence so the partnership the Commission has with the University of Chicago would have a chance to succeed. At this point I talked to Robert Oppenheimer, to get his advice as to what position I might take tomorrow when I see Hutchins—at his request. He advised against blowing up. Said: "These were old, warmed-over subjects; are Chancellor's issues, but they are not people's issues." Good advice.

DECEMBER 16, 1947
IN THE CAPITOL LIMITED BEFORE PULLING OUT FROM CHICAGO
(4:30 P.M.)

I was certainly dead right about the importance of making this Farm Bureau speech today (even though I took a risk of getting plenty sick—in fact, this morning I was running a fever, feeling like hell and my voice sounded like something in a well), for it was one of the very best jobs I have ever done, beyond a doubt.

The audience was terrific, to begin with—the ballroom of the Stevens jammed, the galleries three tiers up, and 500 people standing up in the back. 4,500 people from all over the country.

At first my voice troubled me; than I got warmed up and while husky, I wasn't conscious of it. And though I hadn't been able to read the manuscript aloud even once, as I am accustomed to, I hardly needed to glance at it. This in spite of the fact that I had terrific lights in my face from the newsreel cameras.

The tempo of the speech, its cadence, and the dramatic and intense interest in the subject made the audience an exciting thing to work with. They were pretty well in slumber through an excellent but quite unexciting speech by Warren Austin, who preceded me.

The props worked beautifully. The black cylinder of uranium was worked in better than ever. And the "demonstration" of radiophosphorus worked to a charm. I held the little mike up, and when my "assistant" (as they say in vaudeville) put the counter probe against the poinsettia (and I couldn't remember the name of the damned plant—calling it

§ The article predicted quick and revolutionary benefits from the peaceful uses of atomic energy, e.g., "Most human ailments will be cured as rapidly as they are diagnosed," and "In a short time, atomic energy should be the cheapest energy the world has ever known." Hutchins warned that a world government must be established "within five years" to avoid the catastrophe of atomic war.

"this fine Christmas plant") and a few peeps came out, I said those were very few, just normal cosmic rays and so on, and perhaps a little more than usual because of the nearness of the vitality of "President Ed";◖ this went very well. Then the radioactive plant just raised Ned with clicking, so much that I couldn't be heard over it. This is the first time I have tried anything as elaborate as this—and I didn't know, of course, whether the damned thing would work or not. A fuse blew out— all sorts of casualties. But it made the subject seem real.

It was wonderful to see how profoundly moved these people are when one talks about eliminating this as a weapon, putting it to beneficial uses such as agricultural research. I added a conclusion, reverting to the note of "service to humanity and the Kingdom of God," and that audience seemed to merge into a single picture, a great many people, but a unified presence, you might say; and it was like uttering a benediction.

Considering how punk I felt, to have this come out so wonderfully well is satisfying and exciting. These farmers are solid and not excitable people. But their applause was startling; and then as a body they rose and stood applauding till I got up, etc. A great experience.

I am beginning to get onto my part of the job, the most important part for me to do.

(ON THE CAPITOL LIMITED, 5:30 P.M.)

I have had about half a pint of Old Granddad; and a better medicine for a cold, or whatever bothers you, I can't imagine.

Old Granddad and Abner Dean's wonderful new book of drawings— *What Am I Doing Here?* This should be read with bourbon, and bourbon drunk with Dean. What *am* I doing here, indeed!

DECEMBER 18, 1947
AT HOME

Before me is a book across whose jacket is my name. This is the Whitman biography of me. I have just run through it. I might as well admit that it is quite an affecting experience, to see this book—something I suppose I thought might happen to me someday when I was an old crock and done for, but not now, while I am still in the thick of it.

Yesterday I was told that Henry Luce has suggested me for the *Time* "Man of the Year." It will, of course, be George Marshall or someone who really is.

◖ Edward A. O'Neal, president of the Farm Bureau Federation.

DECEMBER 21, 1947
AT HOME

Have been ruminating a good deal lately (what with time to do so, traveling on trains, and sitting up in bed, snuffling through an interminable cold in the head) about the theme of diversity. This I touched upon, with just a gesture, or pointing, in my *Herald Tribune* speech, and to some meager extent in my book. But I should like to do a full-length article or even book, about it.

The theme, as I see it now, is:

1. The Lord, our Creator, established diversity as a basic principle of His handiwork:

No two cells, animate or inanimate, are identical.

No two individuals, or trees, or storms or sunsets are identical. Diversity, variousness, is of God.

2. To live in harmony with God's word, as written in His handiwork, we must accept and encourage *not* likeness, but diversity.

3. Diversity is an affirmative virtue, or state of being.

4. You and I are different—your color, your ideas, your religious beliefs, disbeliefs or unbeliefs, etc. It is not that I tolerate your differences from me and from others—for tolerance is passive, patronizing, negative.

5. Diversity is a law of life, to be developed, gloried in.

6. Diversity is a principle in support of freedom. If I demand that you be as I am, then I seek to take from you your Creator-given characteristic of being different. If I disapprove of your different ways—you are too loud or too Republican, i.e., different from me—I am in effect seeking to impose my pattern upon you.

7. Diversity is a safeguard against this impulse to make others conform and adopt my way. Tolerance is a weak fare, for it says I will allow you to be different; diversity says you and I are different, because all matter is different, and it is not a moral virtue in me to permit to exist what is natural and of Creation.

8. This theme has its applications in economic enterprises, and in Government—we should encourage diversity in institutions for making a living, and in institutions for maintaining order and safety. These institutions should begin with the premise, *not* that diversity is error, but that it is right, and to be encouraged.

Nancy has a job—and "in the labor movement." She got home yesterday; David arrived the night before (morning, it should be; he phoned us at 12:40 A.M. from the station).

She got this job with the Interunion Institute (of which I had never heard before) quite by accident, which is so often the way these things happen that it probably can hardly be called accident any more. But it was important to her that she got the job through her own efforts, and without any help, directly or indirectly, from me. The fact that it is an economic research as well as an editing job, and for a labor publication, was something of an accident, but since that is what she has wanted to do (though reluctant because she felt it might embarrass me) this helps her morale greatly.

Is not the worst fact about modern scientific weapons—notably the atomic bomb—the effect they have upon moral concepts, those patiently built, fragile steps out of the jungle from which man has emerged?

For centuries men have fought wars. But these were fought within certain rather well-defined ethical line-fences. I don't mean only those international rules of warfare embodied into some law, international law. I mean the fact that warfare was something like a game, a competition, and the presence of ethical limitations and standards was always recognized. An unarmed man was not to be shot. A man who put on the uniform of the enemy had stepped over the line, and could be simply dealt with, etc., etc.

Then the Italians bombed villages of the Ethiopians and expressed pleasure over the sight; everyone recoiled with horror. The Germans obliterated an area of Rotterdam; this was a crime, for it wiped out the notion of an individual adversary. The V-2s were directed against anyone who happened to be there, not against a "military target," i.e., an individual adversary.

Then we burned Tokyo, not just military targets, but set out to wipe out the place, indiscriminately. The atomic bomb is the last word in this direction. All ethical limitations of warfare are gone, not because the *means* of destruction are more cruel or painful or otherwise hideous in their effect upon combatants, but because there are no individual combatants. The fences are gone. And it was we, the civilized, who have pushed standardless conduct to its ultimate.

Most of the talk about the bomb relates to the danger to the world, in a physical sense. But isn't the real danger to civilization to be found in the recognition that warfare is no longer conflict within limits imposed by morality, but without limit, without moral containment?

CHRISTMAS DAY, 1947
AT HOME

The "cold" has turned out to be a rather substantial illness; apparently I had the flu or its equivalent, for I have the characteristic exhaustion. And my whole body is sore to the touch, this being a kind of poisoning that grippe gives, or the lymphatic glands fighting it out with the flu bugs, or some damn thing.

It is unpleasant, unhappy, and disgusting. It's two weeks since this "cold" began; I usually get rid of them in a week, and this one is still going strong. So I am rather in for it. Will have to cancel my early January speeches, apparently, and probably the one for next Tuesday.

I thought I would "get away" with that trip to Chicago; but as usual, I am not one to get away with much.

It is not time wholly wasted, however. I have been reading: Sir Osbert Sitwell's third and second volumes (in that order) and enjoying them enormously (*Great Morning* and *The Scarlet Tree*). Just why, I can't quite tell, for he is clearly not the kind of person I would enjoy being with. Too refined. He writes so wonderfully, for one thing. I have enjoyed watching for the words I either (a) don't know at all or (b) recognize in a nodding acquaintance way, but could not define or use myself. Putting them down on paper, and looking them up, something I haven't done for a long time. I really enjoyed this, in a special sort of way—as a change from my skimming sort of existence. A throwback to earlier days, too.

I plan also reading John Addington Symonds' *The Life of Michelangelo;* and probably some more chapters in the *Travels of Marco Polo.*

There are troubles to think about, too. The plan to have the University of Chicago take over Clinton Laboratories has gone badly sour. After six months they have not yet been able to induce anyone to assume the directorship of the lab, and the feeling that Oak Ridge will never be a very creative place for important development work, i.e., reactors, grows into more than just an opinion. Carroll is facing up to it; talked to me at length twice and tomorrow they will come out here so the Commission can reach some policy decision. The alternative he is considering is moving the high-flux location to Argonne, and emphasizing chemical development at Clinton, with Carbon & Carbide taking charge of that, as sole contractor.

Despite wobbly legs and not-so-good feeling I "presided" over the Christmas tree distribution of gifts this morning—a rite of this household for so many years. David, who *used* to be the squealiest (and the earliest, gosh blame his rising habits), is now rather scornful. But we had a good time. Nancy wrote a poem to accompany Helen's gift to me of the wonderful wood carving (squar' dancers) I had so much admired at Norris. The poem was very good. I gave Helen a violently raspberry-colored silkish padded coolie jacket, which will look funny on her as she carries wood in and does other chores! It was silly, but I couldn't find what I wanted (a house-coat) and the Jelleff's salesladies just carried me off my feet.

But of course we did have a tree—small and *not* festooned with my favorite strips of tin foil, for I wasn't up to that last night, but definitely—it wasn't like the old days, of course, when the kids were little. But it is so good to have them home, little or big.

DECEMBER 29, 1947
AT HOME

The past two days have been very difficult. Partly physical, of course; perhaps largely so. For the hangover of my illness is with me, with a vengeance. After one is in bed a week, even if not very sick, it is tough getting going again. And I began this illness rather badly worn down.

But what has been rather agonizing has been a spell of corrosive worrying, of an intense troubled state of mind about the kind of burden of responsibility I find I am carrying, and must look forward to, if I continue for another several years.

My doubts and agonizing were set in motion by two amusingly different kinds of triggers. One: Frances Sorenson, not having seen me for years, called yesterday, with the Richbergs. "Do you have to worry all the time about the atom bomb and all that terrible thing?" Agreed that I did. "Well, how long has it been since you have had such heavy work—it's been 15 years, hasn't it?" Yes, it has been that long. "Well, it does seem that you could let someone else worry with such heavy chores, and step out into something easy, or easier, and more money." It was simple and direct; but there was a lot of sense in it. The exhilaration and overexcitement of these things; how long does it continue to be sensible, and when is it just romantic nonsense (in terms of an individual) and overgrown vanity?

The other trigger: I opened the life of Brandeis (by Mason); it begins by reference to the fortune he left; some 3¼ million dollars, earned in law practice for all kinds of prosperous corporate activities, etc. Mason justified this: Brandeis felt it was important that he have "independence" so he could carry on his work in the public interest—a not unfamiliar theme. But it got me, at a rather worn-down moment, thinking about how vulnerable I am, in a security sense. I should know better, and in my saner moments I suppose I do realize that, if I continue to have decent health, I can go out into something and earn a living for ten years more certainly. But I am not like a fellow who leaves an active law practice, to which he can return. And the financial pressure on me does not let up: Nancy now has a job, after six months, but I wouldn't bet on how long it will last. Dad is needing money, perhaps as much as a thousand a year from me. Vacations have become essential, so wearing is this work, and that costs dreadfully. In spite of the highest income I have ever had, in dollars, the amount left over after the year I would guess would be quite small.

The grating on raw flesh that is the worst, though, is the increasingly grim outlook for peace, the increasing likelihood of war; and that means the increasingly important role of our work directed toward what could be the greatest destruction of human life in the whole history of mankind. This is a prospect that I can learn to face, I am sure, as one does almost anything. But it does not include the requisites of a reasonable or desirable way of living. All my impulses are against it.

I talked most of the afternoon with Herbert Marks about this today. He is sure that the prospect is very grim, the chances that Russia will change her course not substantial—that is, change enough to avert the conflict from which war could or perhaps necessarily will result if this country is to survive. He is inclined to be over-sour about things, and sometimes I suspect him of taking some pleasure in dark outlooks. But one must face it: two locomotives are heading for each other. The atomic bomb may be the decisive factor, and there may not be much time—a matter of years, less than a decade probably.

If this were all, it would be bad enough. But the business of carrying on these next few months while a political campaign of great ferocity is being waged around, and perhaps over, us, and the amount of irritation we must put up with—add that to everything else and it is not a happy prospect at all.

I do feel I have good qualifications for this sort of business, for once I get into a row I lose my softness and become tough and long-suffering, getting up and dusting myself off and going in for more. And a great many people do have confidence in me just because I do have such strong compulsions *against* the crude use of force—the very part of the job that I despise the most and that grieves me may be a rather important part of my qualification. For if one were crass and calloused about it, the thing could be pushed along to a bloody destructive crisis before the last hope was exhausted. And hope is terribly important; hope, and the imagination and faith and endurance to build on whatever turns up that will support one's weight.

DECEMBER 30, 1947
AT HOME

I "lost" ten million dollars today. Paper profits, mind you! That is to say, I lost something I never had. And I must say, I took it—have taken it—the way I should have, that is with considerable laughing at myself.

The facts: Ten days ago I learned that Henry Luce was in favor of naming me as *Time* magazine's "Man of the Year." (I know so little of these things that I didn't even know there was such a thing, the gent's face appears on the cover of the year-end issue, and there is a special article, etc.)

My retort, of course, was that that would be quite wonderful, but after all this is the year of the Marshall Plan, and this would take some explaining.

While I was ill I freely admit that I daydreamed somewhat about this prospect. It would have been great, and helped solve some of my Congressional labors. (I also recalled my conviction of years ago that to have one's picture on *Life* or *Time,* etc., and to get an inordinate amount of personal publicity, was what I called "the kiss of death" to a public figure. The reason was that great publicity aroused jealousy, enmity, etc., and prevented doing a good job of certain kinds. And I could point to General Weygand, kicked out a week after a big spread and picture in *Life;* Leon Henderson about the same, etc.)

Well, today Miss Henderson told me that it was to be General Marshall; but that I continued to be Luce's candidate to the end; that one of the editors who was there said he made an "impassioned" speech to support his view; that it took a secret ballot of the editors, etc.

Well: it would have been fun. But after the initial disappointment I must say my perspective returned. Partly, I think, because it really doesn't make sense. I am doing all right, at the moment, but not *that* all right.

My illness is on its way out, but I am still not all there. Spent some time today at the office—first time in more than a week—and made headway on the report on labor policy, bringing staff arguments into agreement.

This labor problem is a troublesome thing for me. I know that normal collective bargaining isn't possible, perhaps, but I hate to get in a position of appearing to admit that no unions is the answer, which is the tendency.

NEW YEAR'S EVE, 1947
AT HOME

This certainly will rank high among the years "Lilienthal will-long-remember."

It has been a year of pain. Physical pain, of a kind I have never known, week after week and month following upon month. That bad sacroiliac, that from November of last year until September hardly gave me a decent day, and at times, particularly during the Congressional investigation, was quite terribly painful, and a nerve-racking kind of pain. But it is good to go through such an ordeal, in a way, because now I know it can be done.

There was another kind of pain, a mental anguish and agony, the result of two things. One was the long period of being smeared and subjected to indignities and overexposure to public gaze. There were days when this hurt so much that when I fell into bed at night, knowing I would repeat it all over and over again as I tried to get some sleep I would say, "Well, I can't take another day of that; and I won't." But the next morning I would start it all over again. I could; and I did. And it is good to know that you can be beaten to the canvas time and again, and get up and come back for more; even have enough presence of mind and reserve left to avoid losing your temper or composure, outwardly at least.

There was another kind of pain; and this I have felt as much during the past few days, convalescing from the flu, as any time during the year. That is the pain of contemplating the grim aspect of my work, concentrating as it does on the development of an instrument for the annihilation of human beings on a scale and in a manner that would make Sherman think his definition of war was a great understatement. With all my natural impulses so strongly against violence, physical violence, and with little background for such a gruesome possibility as this, there are times when it comes over me that it is just too much to carry on my soul. The pain that I get from this is acute and shocking, the pain that comes from considering how horrible the world would be if it turned out that my handiwork would be turned loose in a wholesale act of destruction. The impulse to run away from such a responsibility, to enjoy life and forget this whole business, rises at times.

I know better, really. I know that it is better that one who feels as I do should have a hand in this business, as a deterrent to the kind who rather likes the idea of the biggest act of killing in all time—making Attila the Hun seem a piker. And I know that the more successful we are in our present urgent, feverish effort to make this enterprise extraordinarily efficient and progressive, the more chance there is that we can buy time during which Russia will reconsider her tragic rejection of sense, not only in spurning our proposal on atomic energy for war, but rejecting every other effort to work out a cooperative world. And if, in the end, there is nothing left, however hard we try, and persistently we urge Russia to "join the world," nothing left but a choice between the domination of this country by the tactics now being used in Eastern Europe, and used before by Hitler, then it will be far better that we did

Above, President Truman with Lilienthal and TVA Director James Pope (at right) in 1945 at dedication of Kentucky Dam. Lilienthal was still TVA Chairman at this time. A year later he was appointed to head the new Atomic Energy Commission. Below, he is congratulated by Gordon R. Clapp, his successor as TVA Chairman.

Leaders in the wartime development of the atomic bomb, and frequent figures in Lilienthal's Journal entries: above, Dr. J. Robert Oppenheimer with Albert Einstein (Photo by Alfred Eisenstaedt, *Pix Incorporated*). Below, left, Vannevar Bush (*Wide World Photos*) and Major General Leslie R. Groves (*U.S. Army*).

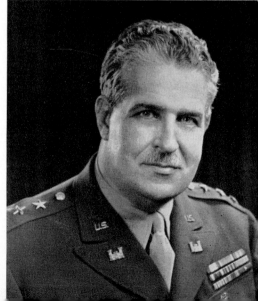

The U.S. proposal for international atomic energy control was presented to the United Nations in 1946 by Bernard M. Baruch (above, left). With Baruch are, from left, Warren R. Austin, U.S. Security Council Representative; Herschel V. Johnson, Austin's deputy; and John M. Hancock, Baruch's associate. The proposal was based on a plan worked out by a State Department consultant board headed by Lilienthal and reviewed by a special committee of which Undersecretary of State Dean Acheson (below, with President Truman) was chairman. (*Wide World Photos*)

Senator Kenneth D. McKellar of Tennessee (above) vigorously opposed Lilienthal's confirmation as AEC Chairman. Below, he listens to testimony favoring the confirmation from Chester I. Barnard (left), president of New Jersey Bell Telephone Company, who had served with Lilienthal on the State Department consultants' board. (*Wide World Photos*)

At the 1947 Senate hearing on confirmation of his nomination, Lilienthal faces questioning by McKellar (back to camera). (Man to left of Lilienthal is official stenographer.)

PERHAPS THE WISE CHOICE LIES BETWEEN THE TWO

A cartoon comment on the confirmation hearing by Berryman of the Washington *Evening Star* (the original drawing, inscribed by the artist).

"Lucky Boy! We're Going To Let You Work For Us."—Herblock in *The Washington Post*

Another view of the hearing, with Lilienthal at extreme right. Senators are, from left, McKellar, Tom Connally, Richard Russell, Chairman Bourke Hickenlooper, Arthur Vandenberg, Eu-

Above, the Atomic Energy Commission, 1947. Around table from left: Carroll Wilson, AEC General Manager, and Commissioners Sumner T. Pike, Robert F. Bacher, Chairman Lilienthal, Lewis L. Strauss, William W. Waymack. (*New York Times*) Below, Henry D. Smyth (left) and Gordon E. Dean, successors to Bacher and Waymack in 1949. (*Wide World Photos*)

Much of Lilienthal's time as AEC Chairman was spent explaining atomic energy to the public and to Congress. Above, demonstration of chain-reaction principle, with mousetraps being set off by rubber corks, shown to Senator Hickenlooper (left) by Lilienthal and T. S. Chapman of the Argonne National Laboratory. (*Wide World Photos*) Below, Lilienthal greeting members of audience after speech at Oak Ridge, Tennessee.

Inspecting the University of Washington's new cyclotron are, from left, Lilienthal; Dr. Raymond B. Allen, university president; Dr. Clinton L. Utterback, laboratory director; and Fred C. Schlemmer, manager of AEC Hanford Operations Office.

Three major figures of the 1945-1950 period: from left, Secretary of State George C. Marshall, President James B. Conant of Harvard University, and General Omar N. Bradley, at Harvard graduation ceremonies, 1947. (*Wide World Photos*)

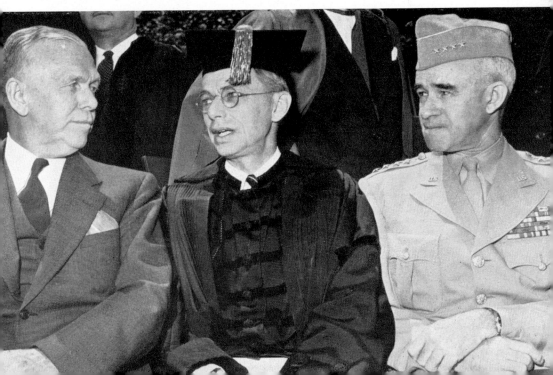

At the June, 1949, hearing of Senator Hickenlooper's charges of "incredible mismanagement" in the AEC: Lilienthal is at table at left, with AEC General Manager Wilson (smoking) and Joseph Volpe, Jr., of AEC legal staff (at Lilienthal's left). Facing them at right are members of Joint Senate-House Atomic Energy Committee

"You Got Him Strung Up Yet, Boy?"—from *The Herblock Book* (Beacon Press, 1952)

Government leaders in July, 1949, prior to a closed meeting on atomic energy relations with Britain and Canada. From left, Lilienthal, General Dwight D. Eisenhower, Senator McMahon, Secretary of State Acheson, and Secretary of Defense Louis Johnson. (*Wide World Photos*)

Lilienthal and General Lucius D. Clay (right) receiving 1949 Freedom Awards, presented by Mrs. Eleanor Roosevelt and Defense Secretary Johnson. (*Wide World Photos*)

Lilienthal with Senators Connally (left) and McMahon at hearing in February, 1950, on the case of the atomic spy, Klaus Fuchs. (*Wide World Photos*)

David and Helen Lilienthal, with their son, David, in 1947.

Lilienthal leaving the AEC building at the end of his last day on the job,
February 15, 1950.

our work here well, than that this country and what it stands for shall disappear.

I console myself with this, and believe it to be true. But the agony is there, having to live so intimately, every day and every night, with such companions as these thoughts.

I will remember the year for its pain. But it has also been a year of high exhilaration; of the most pleasurable and satisfying kind. On many occasions had the feeling that I was fully alive, at the height of such powers as I have, and putting to their best and highest use the talents I have as these have been developed in a rather rigorous and intense school of experience.

This exhilaration I felt most, I believe, in some of my speeches, beginning with the speech to the banquet session of the American Society of Newspaper Editors last May. It was the most famous audience I had ever faced, I suppose—the Chief Justice at my right, General Eisenhower, etc. The fun I had, just high excitement, from such experiences as the Crawfordsville football field speech, or the following morning to that wonderful bunch of youngsters at DePauw. Or the Herald Tribune Forum, and the American Farm Bureau at Chicago, or the Engineers at Atlantic City.

Almost as exhilarating—although much more agony and groaning, too—has been the writing of these speeches, trying to develop a theme, pounding all over the place trying to find the right opening.

There has been exhilaration, too, in seeing a floundering, mediocre organization change into something quite remarkable. To see a staff come into being, develop a spirit and drive and cohesion. That's really an exciting business.

Well, it has been quite a year.

1948; bring it on!

# IV

# THE ATOMIC ENERGY YEARS

# 1948

NEW YEAR'S DAY
1948

I keep thinking about the view of American life I outlined—perhaps hinted at—in the Herald Tribune Forum speech. If I had the time, I would like to do a book, or a series of articles, about it. Very timely: We can withstand the tension of these coming years only if we are relaxed about what we have; don't get gouging each other over meaningless issues. The sort of thing I heard Henry Wallace do the other night, organizing his third party, is one sort; rather spectacular, but there are others just as serious though less easily recognized.

What we do is to choose that way of doing things that *works*. For "works" we have certain rather definite measurements. "Works" in the sense that it increases the sum total of individual elbow room, as well as increasing the standard of living for more people. Thus, in the Tennessee Valley, what "works" is Government sponsorship and direction, up to a point, encouraging and giving impetus to private and individual things that follow upon the essential governmental beginning. The other way did not "work."

There is an additional aspect. As "private" business gets bigger, as more things depend upon it, it loses its power, in the sense of arbitrary power. This is not because there is a "law" that imposes such added responsibility. It is because it is recognized that this vast power over the lives of others carries with it, in the very nature of things as they are in the American ethical climate, a kind of responsibility. Is this paternalism? (When I said all this to David, he gave me a sharp look, and

[ 278 ]

asked this latter question.) *"Noblesse oblige?"* I don't know that it takes words, tags, to explain it.

I read that in the past two years the New York Telephone Company, a monopoly, installed two million phones—the second millionth was the occasion for a celebration noted in the *Times* the other day. This private monopoly turns out to be the best way to get telephone service, the best way ever devised by all odds. Why does the company take such pains to satisfy its customers, who have no effective recourse? Is this just "preventive public relations"? I don't know what to call it, but the fact is that a huge enterprise, legally a monopoly, has worked like hell to perform a great feat in the way of supplying service.

We usually say "competition" is the reason for such feats of enterprise. It wasn't in this case, and in many others. Not that simple, or at least there is no single answer. We look around and find, by trying, a way that produces the result we want, and don't worry about the formula.

You can say this is a public utility, and there is a legal "duty" to supply service. But no legal duty will put in two million phones in two years! Nope, that doesn't explain it.

We don't put too much emphasis on such arbitrary things as "ownership," i.e., that a public utility should be owned by the public. Not at all. Any great service affecting many people—such as manufacturers of refrigerators—must be conducted in a way that delivers the goods, does the job.

Isn't it important that we stopped this chatter about our "system" as if it were monolithic; for such apparent dogmatism does not present our way in its most favorable light, and exposes it needlessly to *argumentative* attacks?

This needs more thinking; but there is something to it.

JANUARY 2, 1948
AT HOME

Clark Clifford phoned me today, with "a request that I realize is unusual." He was working on the State of the Union message. This is perhaps the most important period in the history of the country, as Congress returns; perhaps the most important in human history. So the message of the President will have extraordinary import.

He was searching for a note that it needed. (This was somewhat in keeping with his rather disingenuous explanation to me, when discussing an atomic energy speech by the President, that leadership in a democracy requires that the President "capture the imagination of the people.") In the course of searching around he came on a speech

I had made to the Herald Tribune Forum. He would read me a paragraph, which he did—something about our faith being in men, not in economic production. If the President said that, it would be widely heard and considered. He couldn't very well lift the words exactly, though that expressed about what he thought the situation required, just the tone, etc.

Would I undertake to rewrite the paragraph so he could consider putting it into the State of the Union message? He would have to have it by tomorrow morning if it were to be helpful.

Yes, of course, I would try it; which I did this afternoon. Not a finished product, but it could serve as a beginning. And actually it would be helpful to those things I believe in, in the world, if some such idea should get into the message and into our policy. It would furnish quite a contrast, too, to the quite cheap tone most of the Republican leadership are bringing to this Great Debate.

The chances are, of course, that the draft will not be used at all; I can't, frankly, picture Harry Truman actually saying the heroic things I wrote for him to say.

The atomic energy fireside speech by the President has to be deferred until there is an opportunity, which seems right to me; too many things brewing right now.

Offered honorary degree from Syracuse today; will probably decline. And an invitation to make the commencement speech at University of Virginia in spring.


JANUARY 4, 1948
AT HOME

We have been having a tough time of it. A week ago Wilson brought a group out here and told us that it was the unanimous conclusion of the staff that the University of Chicago arrangement for Clinton Lab and the high-flux reactor just had no chance of succeeding. That was Friday; the transfer to the university from Monsanto was to take place on the following Monday! But we authorized them to go ahead and find some way out. It was rapid-fire and rough. The people at Clinton Lab engaged in fundamental research felt they had been double-crossed, for we proposed to have Carbide & Carbon operate the lab (what was left of it, i.e., minus the high-flux reactor), and this caused great anguish, not only among the chronic complainers but quite generally.

Scientists do not feel that fundamental research can successfully be carried on by industry; they felt this way about Monsanto, but even more so about Carbide. There is good ground for this feeling. But our efforts to meet this by utilizing a university, Chicago, had been a complete failure; after four months they still had not been able to persuade anyone to take the directorship of the lab, and the outlook for success was so dim as to be an almost foregone failure; and this is what the General Advisory Committee had predicted.

We will probably ride out the storm, but it will be bad, particularly if we cannot find some way of carrying on fundamental research other than by industry. This may turn up.

JANUARY 7, 1948
AT HOME

Some very good news yesterday: Dr. Ecker, concluding the first general examination I have had since last April, gave me an enthusiastic bill of health, despite my long stretch (four weeks) of the cold bug and the feverish weeks of overwork preceding it. My weight has gone up from 176 in April, 1946, to 183 yesterday, the highest it has ever been. He doesn't want it to go any higher, and I don't either. Lack of exercise is the chief trouble. My blood pressure is beautiful, and hasn't changed a particle since he first examined me in March, 1936. I continue to have a very slow heartbeat. "Like Justice Brandeis," he said—Brandeis was his patient all the time he was in Washington. He told me a good Brandeis story. He advised Mrs. B. that a bit of a drink of whiskey would do the Justice good. She was a bit surprised, but said she would see that he got it. He asked later how it went. All right, she thought. How much does he drink? "Oh, I give him a *teaspoonful* each evening."

Got mad as hell over a call from Donald Dawson, administrative assistant to the President. "We must place Miss ———; I am asking you to help. Will you?" I asked whether she had applied, etc. Yes, she had been interviewed; everyone had been nice to her over here but no job. "It will take your help." He said again that it was a case where "we," meaning the White House, just had to place her.

I asked why. That stopped him, but only for a moment. "That is a matter for our jurisdiction," said he. I was getting mad, against my promises to myself not to. So I said I would look into it; if there was no work for which she was qualified, or if there was work, but there were others better qualified, that would be that.

I find that she, upon being interviewed, explained that "Matt Connelly is planning my career." I am telling Dawson nothing doing. Makes me sore.

We met at Blair House at 4:30; and the long year of uncertainty about British-American relations was ended and a new chapter begins.* It was most undramatic and unimpressive; anticlimax, actually. The housekeeper couldn't even find a green cloth to cover the table around which we gathered, much to the State Department boys' distress.

But the hours before this were torture, for the meeting had been set without our knowledge, and the Commission had never formally gone over much of the ground. So I kept the session going right through lunch—I read aloud some of the documents—there weren't even copies enough for us to have one each, or to study in advance—with my mouth full of sandwich. I never felt more ashamed of the internal working of an organization. But it came out all right in the end, and I suppose that is what counts. But such close sailing.

Sometimes I marvel that we get anything done at all. Operating with a five-man board, the Chairman with no authority to make decisions or bind the Commission without discussion and approval of a group—this is a terribly difficult thing. I believe it is worthwhile, but compared with the problem of a department head or administrator it is an agony, and terribly time-consuming.

One of the nicest things about the whole business is a remark of Vandenberg's that Lovett related to me. Lovett had gone to report the agreement to Vandenberg and Hickenlooper. V. was enthusiastic and most complimentary. Then, according to Lovett, he said, "And one of the best things about it is that it will make things easier for Dave Lilienthal." I prize that man's confidence.

The President's State of the Union message today did include some of my stuff in his opening and closing. Lilienthal on Truman: on him, how does it look? I have my doubts.


JANUARY 11, 1948
SUNDAY NIGHT, 6 P.M.

Worked all day Saturday and today on my speech for the New York State Publishers Association for a week from Monday. These seven-day weeks are great stuff!

The Oak Ridge business is still in the balance. Met with Bill Pollard, Gross, and Seitz of the Oak Ridge Institute, representing the scientists of the lab, and believe we made a little progress.

---

* This refers to a further step in the very limited post-war cooperative arrangements on atomic energy between the U.S., Britain, and Canada. Under the revised arrangement, the U.S. obtained a larger portion of the Congo uranium ore supplies; there was a clarification of the non-weapon areas of technical information which the U.S. agreed to share with the other two nations, and a wartime pledge by the U.S. that it would not use the bomb without British consent was terminated.

This awful taking of depositions goes merrily on.† No matter what else goes on in the rest of the world, these measly little lawyers go right about their ant-like trade. Lord! So I must let everything else go and go back to face this pale-faced, bloodless meaninglessness. McKellar never made me so mad.

## JANUARY 17, 1948
### AT HOME

Helen and I had dinner last night with Ed Murrow and his wife, and with them Joseph C. Harsch and his wife, and Richard Hottelet, both the latter being also part of the CBS stable of news commentators.

Ed is one of the most impressive men I've ever known. Now that we have become rather friends, the kind of formality he had with me has given way to a relaxed manner, and we hit it off very well indeed. He has a kind of fire and intensity that most editors and radio-editors don't have. He is a man completely absorbed in the business of *observation,* i.e., a great report, *but* with a kind of passion about what he sees in the world, and a viewpoint about it, that makes him not only a rare specimen among his rare species, but a delightful human being and a most useful one.

He spent an hour and a half the other day with Eisenhower. The fact that Eisenhower is giving so much time to such men as Ed and John Gunther (and doubtless to a whole line of such avenues to public opinion) lends color to their unanimous verdict that he is "running for the Presidency as fast as all get-out." Ed was taken with the warmth of Ike. When he greeted him, he made him feel, "Ed, I've been sitting here for months just waiting till I could have a good long talk about all this just with *you.*" Eisenhower is unlettered in economics and politics— this is what Gunther had said. One thing he said led Ed to say to him, "General, you can't say a thing like that." (What Ike had said was, "When I read about those fellows at Oak Ridge even thinking about a strike, I want to reach for my gun.")

Ed is to introduce me to the Radio Executives Club luncheon on the 5th, and I asked him what sort of thing I should hit; I am rather drained of ideas. Be critical of the radio industry, he said. They're used to having advertisers, etc., raise hell with them, so it will be nothing new. The newspapers and the radio have done a terrible job on atomic energy, he said. Tell them what you've just told me about the great interest through the country in this grass roots movement to understand this thing, etc.

† At this time, a group in Illinois was opposing the AEC's condemnation of the Du Page County site for the Argonne National Laboratory.

My throat kicked up badly Wed. night, and I felt rather discouraged, with a radio broadcast ("Family Hour") Sunday night and
this rather important speaking occasion at Albany Monday night. It looked
as if I was headed for another cold. In some desperation I called Dr.
Ecker; he said penicillin lozenges might help. I took them, stayed home
Thurs., and whether it was that or something else, the sore throat was
almost gone Friday and today seems about normal, normal for me in
the winter being a red throat, but one that works and doesn't hurt.

JANUARY 22, 1948
AT HOME

The trip to Albany, N.Y., was uncommonly successful. Not that
the speech was in the first rank, compared to some this fall and
winter. But I got rather well acquainted with a great many people,
which I enjoyed, had a long visit with Governor Dewey, which is important, and on the whole did something effective on the central
problem: getting increased public confidence.

The speech to the publishers had its moments. I began with some
stories which surprised them, as my sober reputation and the weirdness
of my job had preceded me. The speech had a lag in it, that I feared, esp.
as it was preceded by some rather dramatic stuff. Then I had a break.
In the middle of a sentence there was a big commotion at the end of
the speakers' dais on my right, and then a great laugh. A little goggled
man (looked like the fellow who is always secretary-treasurer of such
organizations, if you know what I mean) had been squeezed in on the
dais, but just; and he was pushed or fell (as the coroner's verdict says)
right off the platform. He picked himself up, covered with confusion.
Well, that stopped the show; and when I could, I said, bowing deeply
to Governor Dewey, at my left elbow, "May I call Governor Dewey's
particular attention to the fact that no matter how strong the planks,
it is very important not to fall off a platform." This was well received.

Then I went on ahead, and just when I got to another slow spot,
another break. The light on the lectern went off; it had been temperamental before. This left me with about as much light to see my MS
as you'd find in my right pocket. I put on my glasses and peered and
went along, when I noticed out of the corner of my eye that the
Governor of the State of New York and Presidential candidate was on
his knees fiddling with the electric cord on the floor, trying to fix the
trouble.

I said, "Governor, don't bother with that gadget. I'm one of these
Tennessee hill boys and I've just gotten used to shoes; I don't believe
in these modern gadgets like electric lights and TVA and such; but if

you've got a pine knot around here, be glad to have it." This seemed funnier to the audience than it was, partly because it brought the disappeared Governor out from under the table, and very red-faced he was, too.

He traded seats with the president of the Association, Dapping of Auburn, and sat at my right during the long dinner, and talked with the greatest animation and intensity. He asked me about TVA: was there anything to the flood benefits; what return did we make—and when I just gave up on figures he said, "Oh, well, why should I ask you for these details; you're not an Army Engineer with all these figures in your mind."

(LATER: SAT., JAN. 25, '48)

(Had terrific snowstorm last night, and it's going on like billy hell now.)

To continue about Dewey and Albany.

Dewey said Al Smith was the greatest N.Y. Governor; knew the state government inside out. He could look at an enacted bill presented for signature and know everything about it.

I wanted to explore Dewey's ideas about public administration, so I opened by saying he had impressed me with his efforts to get highly qualified men. How does he go at getting good administration: make a survey of the state government, etc.? No—he was very positive and cocky—never. Get good men and then never see them again; don't bother about details. "Why should I give a hang about highways and state police, etc?" Then he launched into a prideful and impressive story of how he got a very fine physician interested in taking over the mental hospitals of the state—100,000 mentally ill to work on, etc. His interest in this subject, and pride in the standing of N.Y. State in the field was curious, and it is evident that he does keep up on such matters.

He says we have got to have more power, and that means developing the water power not only of St. Lawrence, but the Far West. But what about irrigation? That doesn't make much sense: we're going to be overproducing food in five years and then these millions of new acres will be a curse, etc.

What did I think of Bill Douglas? (I didn't answer directly; frankly, Douglas seems to me considerably overestimated.) Dewey went on to say they went to law school together—that was my impression. Almost went into partnership. When someone said this to Douglas, he is reported to have said—or perhaps it was Dewey who said it—that by this time, had they become partners, one would be suing the other for an accounting!

He made a good deal (while he was being introduced by the chair) of the fact that "This is my speech," this being notes written on a program for the dinner. He began with a good deal of relaxed chitchat, about my troubles with the stand (which was especially made, and belongs to *him:* "Built for a man exactly five feet eight inches tall"). Then he said, quite elaborately: He was delighted last year that he and the only Senator from N.Y. (a reference to Wagner's long illness) were in complete agreement on the confirmation of Mr. Lilienthal—Sen. Ives being for the confirmation. He made a corking speech—super-confident, vigorous, telling the publishers they ought to be supporting him on his stand against further state aid for education, etc. When he sat down, he looked a bit startled and red-faced and whispered, "Was I too rough with them?"

JANUARY 23, 1948
AT HOME

Saw Clark Clifford at the White House late this afternoon. He was late to our appointment. As he came in he had a copy of the Washington *Star,* just out, with Eisenhower's statement that he would not accept a nomination. "When this news came along, the President asked me to come in and talk about it. He read the statement aloud to me and then I read it aloud to him. Then we talked awhile about what it said." I thought this was an amusing touch. He, Clifford, seemed pleased by the news. So are the Republicans, no doubt.‡

I talked to Clark some about the problems of reappointment of the Commission. It is quite a long way off, and yet Marquis Childs talked to me about it this afternoon, so people are beginning to think of it, so we should, too. Clark will explore the question of whether it would be a good thing to send the names in quite early, while Congress is still here.

JANUARY 28, 1948
WEDNESDAY

At 12:15 today the full Commission and Wilson saw the President, and handed him our report. He said he was glad to see the production figure on number of gadgets, but was more interested in what we could do to insure that he never again would have to order the use of these weapons. "It was a terrible decision to make," he said.

‡ It was generally assumed at this time that Eisenhower was a Democrat.

He referred to the new Army Chief of Staff, General Bradley, in connection with some reference to General Groves, and then he made this priceless remark: "General Eisenhower was in here this morning. I said, 'General, your statement was kind of bad on me because it made it certain that there is no way of my getting away from this desk.' " The amount of confidence in this sentence is *something*—as well as being disarming.

FEBRUARY 2, 1948
AT HOME

Saturday I was boiling and steaming. General Groves again. This time he objected to inclusion of some things in our report to Congress. I told Trapnell not to waste time discussing it with him. The objections were an almost perfect caricature of what is known as the "military mind."

Then, this morning about 10 A.M., came the word: General Groves has announced that he has requested retirement, to enter private business.

This indicates that the confident expectation he and his crowd had that we would be out in six months, as John O'Donnell and the Hearst press predicted when I was confirmed, those hopes have gone flat. This business of not having Napoleon sitting on Elba while his crew waited for "the Day"—that at least will no longer be our trouble.

Last week was a very good one in almost every way. I felt very much alive. On Monday and Tuesday morning stayed home and wrote a speech for the Radio Executives Club, and knew I had a good one, too. Kept polishing and working at it all week, at times. Sent a draft to Ed Murrow, who called me Saturday to say that he and his wife thought it was "magnificent," but that I should crack out even harder in criticism of the radio industry and the obligation they have to do something about atomic education, and education generally. It surprised me; if he feels that way from within the industry, it must be bad. John Crosby's article in the January *Atlantic,* and one by Rolf Kaltenborn in the *Saturday Review of Literature* tell of a constant sourness about the decay of the "promise of radio." So I am hitting this theme at a good time, anyway.

We got out our report to Congress last Friday; quite an impressive story. We are making progress in getting this thing organized, and in holding public confidence. There hasn't been a bad break, publicly, for quite a while.

Wednesday we all went over to see the President, and had a number of good Commission meetings—nothing spectacular, but they all are good evidence that we are working together in a satisfying and happy way.

FEBRUARY 7, 1948

Robert Oppenheimer told me this afternoon that early last month Bush, Conant, and he had gone to see Forrestal and insisted that Groves must get out. That while they were discussing it Royall joined them and agreed. Thereupon a paper was drawn up making this firm.

The Russians are putting the pressure on the Belgians to try to get ore from the Congo; during discussions at Moscow on commercial agreements in late January of this year the Belgian delegation even gave some encouragement to the Russians as to 1949. This is going to be something to worry about. Something more to worry about, I should say.

P.S. Feb. 17: This was reported in press dispatches (*N. Y. Times* Bureau syndicate) a few days after the above was written.

I have before me a document marked "Top Secret." At the bottom of the cover is the ominous statement, "This document contains restricted data within the meaning of the Atomic Energy Act of 1946; its transmission or the revelation of its contents in any manner not authorized by that Act is prohibited by law." Jail for you, me boy.

The attachment is a letter from the British Supply Office here in Washington, and the letter is marked "Top Secret," accounting for the cover being so marked. That is, it is British Top Secret, too.

It is dated January 21, and is a memo which sets out in full an article by Terence Clarkson, Capetown, *appearing in the London Daily Mail* for January 19, headlined, "Smuts plans to give U.S. atomic head all uranium from Rand."

Except for this reproduction of the newspaper article the letter simply calls attention to it, says, "Nothing is known about the above article," and that inquiries are being made.

Top secret? God!

FEBRUARY 8, 1948
AT THE HAY-ADAMS, WASHINGTON, SATURDAY

(How many times I have written such notes as these on Hay-Adams stationery—as I am now.)

The trip to New York was filled with new and good experiences.

Helen and I saw two shows: *Man and Superman,* with Maurice Evans, the Shakespearean actor playing Tanner, and an excellent cast; and *Antony and Cleopatra,* the Shakespeare version, with Katharine Cornell, who was magnificent—though the play dragged at the end, to my taste. We went to the Murrows—Ed and Janet—for dinner, and to *Man and Superman,* and then afterward to the Stork Club for a drink.

The dinner party was unusual, in that our host, and now my good friend, was not present in the flesh; but at my suggestion we had a radio put in the dining room and heard his 7:45 broadcast while we ate at his board.

This was also unusual in that the gent who sat at the head of the Murrow table in the absence of our host "in line of his duty" heard his host's voice talk about "David Lilienthal came down to New York today and told the radio executives, etc.," going on for a substantial part of his broadcast to quote from the speech I had given that noon, a speech which he had "gotten me into" in the first place, and which he had read in draft and criticized for me a few days before.

This was, in all, an interesting kind of experience. One of the guests, Lady Reading (the Dowager Marchioness of Reading, to be exact, and widow of the great law lord), said afterward that there I sat listening to this discussion about David Lilienthal and never moved a muscle of my face.

Russell Davenport and a lovely young woman, Mrs. Collins, a cousin of Janet's, were the other dinner and theater guests, and of course Ed joined us for the theater. Davenport has become rather cynical; "disillusioned," he says, and makes wry remarks. He and Marcia Davenport have been divorced. He feels, I take it, that he came so close to making Wendell Willkie President that it was probably a mistake of his that accounted for it, and of course the politicians would say so at the time, and just this week the project of Henry Luce's to put out a new magazine devoted to "values" was deferred, which probably means abandoned. "I'm a jinx," Davenport says. Poetic fervor has a way of turning sour, and when it does, it is plenty sour.

The high point of the visit was, happily, the speech Thursday noon. It was a remarkable audience, so I was told, and certainly the head table was a reflection of this, with heads of networks (though not Paley, who is in Florida, or Stanton or Trammel), Hugh Baillie of UP, General Sarnoff, who sat on my right, Mrs. Basil Bass, wife of my classmate at the Law School, who is executive editor of the *Ladies' Home Journal,* etc. I had the fiendish television lights in my eyes—two great headlights that shut off much of one's contact with one's listeners, which is difficult for me, for it is the audience's response that gives me my cues and stimulus.

But it went very well, despite this. My voice was as good as it ever is, and the timing was about right, not racing as I sometimes do, and not overstressing, vocally, as I did the first time or two I went over the speech out loud with Helen. There was considerable comment to me and even more to others, retold me, about the impression I made as to technique and voice. John Daly said I had the best stage presence in America; and such things were repeated to me last evening at the Radio Correspondents dinner here at the Statler. A vice president of one of the networks last night said, jokingly, "What an announcer that voice would make," and that I could make a lot more money than fooling with the atom (this was supposed to be funny). Whereupon Ed Murrow broke in to say, "Stay off him; I have him under option."

On the content of the speech the reaction was close and even intense attention throughout; but what they could *do* was what bothered, or what they said bothered, them afterward. Last evening I was told that several networks had meetings that very evening (this Murrow had predicted) to see what programs they could work out, etc.

The *Herald Tribune* reporter, a young fellow, not well informed at all, asked me what kind of information the radio should furnish the people. He said the same thing in his story. This irked me, I freely confess, but not so much that I didn't realize that this sort of needling is good for me and for my work. The radio people were left without any idea of what "information" they should pass on to the people. As if this were something one could answer in a 27-minute speech.

But in one respect the effort was a real success: it did arouse a sense of responsibility and an interest in doing something. Whether this can be stimulated and developed, followed up, etc., that is a real question. It is particularly difficult to believe that very much will come of it because *there is no specific issue.* It isn't as if military versus civilian control, or political interferences were live public atomic issues at the moment. And without them, a straight public education effort—sans bomb and sans international action, etc.—is a most difficult thing to carry out through the medium of commercial enterprises like radio and newspapers.

I have certainly started something, though, and it is already far more successful than I had dreamed, even if we do not make another single bit of progress. This is temperamental with me. I deliberately get myself out on a limb, forcing a big issue to be made, and this keeps up not only my own efforts, and makes me a better protagonist, but it does get things moving, by contagion. But since my sights, actually, were relatively low to begin with, it is rare that I feel even a limited accomplishment is a loss or waste, and I am rarely cynical or bitter about failing to gain everything that I say, publicly, I think ought to be achieved.

In this case what I set out to do has already been accomplished. I wanted to attract attention to the importance of the work of the Commission, so we would not be under a blanket where our throats could be cut without anyone knowing what is going on; I wanted to protect us against being hurt by the Joint Committee hazing; I wanted to establish a prestige for the Commission that would help to attract good men to the work because the work was generally recognized as being of great importance; I wanted to increase the measure of public confidence in the Commission and in me; I wanted to fight the hysteria about secrecy and "loyalty."

These were some of the things I had in mind, in the first *Collier's* article last spring, and the speech to the American Society of Newspaper Editors. Those things have been accepted to a remarkable degree, actually. I think we will make a rather good try of the vastly more ambitious effort I have launched—a general nationwide education effort. This will be most difficult to sustain. But we already have made gains that, if never added to, will be very considerable indeed. This, I think, is the sensible mental attitude in such matters, as contrasted with the perfectionist.

(Continued at the office, Sunday P.M. following a lengthy session with the General Advisory Committee. This has been one of those seven-day weeks—we worked all day yesterday, and convened again as a Commission at 1 P.M. today.)

Wednesday evening John Gunther gave a dinner for me at the Century Club. Those present were Archie MacLeish, who was very friendly; Hamilton Fish Armstrong of *Foreign Affairs;* Albert D. Lasker, who surprised me by being a kindly-looking, rather humble-acting man (I expected an advertising tycoon à la huckster, I guess); Harry Scherman, inventor of Book-of-the-Month Club; Clifton Fadiman, very short, to my surprise, very bright, a man of great sincerity and feeling about things but almost no experience—that is the way he struck me; Geoffrey Parsons of the *Herald Tribune,* warm, friendly man, but quite definitely dated; John Hersey, tall, young, very earnest and thoughtful—not the brilliant type I would have guessed from his remarkable writing; a Professor Somebody-or-other, a friend of Gunther's, a teacher of science at Columbia, pleasant but very quiet; H. V. Kaltenborn; Stuart Chase was absent—snowbound.

We began at 7:30 with drinks and broke up at 1:15 A.M.—really quite a long, long session, talking continually about atomic energy. Of course, a good deal was quite philosophical—the effect of secrecy on democracy, etc. Gunther was very good as a host and "chairman," for he tried his best to keep the discussion from going off on speculation about the Russians' motives, etc., which is so common a way of wasting time, and we were able to talk a good deal about what AEC is doing and why. But whether any good will come I don't know.

Friday noon I was guest at lunch at the Williams Club of the radio news analysts, sitting at a square table. This was quite good. Present were Kaltenborn, my host, Ed Murrow (who impresses me more and more the oftener I see him, for his sagacity and independent way of looking at things); Larry LeSueur, a very intelligent young man; Vandercook, the man with a full beard, an oddity therefore, verbose and inclined to take more than his share in asking questions; John Gunther, eager and proud of me as his friend, who speaks with an enthusiasm that is wonderful, though sometimes not accurate or penetrating; Quincy Howe, who seems like a professor of political science, but whom I like greatly for his earnest good will and lack of smart-aleckiness; Ned Calmer; George Fielding Eliot, big and beefy, who said not a word, hardly, the whole time, and what his reactions were I couldn't understand, except to an illustration I gave of how absurd military secrecy can become at times—well, there were 16 of us in all, and the others I don't remember.

## FEBRUARY 9, 1948

Had lunch with Sir Gordon Munro,§ at his invitation. He said it was to get better acquainted; that he was returning to England for a few weeks and I might have something on my mind I might want to transmit, through him. Entire time spent in sociable conversation, of no particular consequence though pleasant enough, with the following exception: I urged that we proceed with dispatch in getting things done re exchange of information between U.S., U.K., and Canada. He was agreed about this.

## FEBRUARY 11, 1948
### AT HOME

I had a visit with Henry Luce, on my New York trip. He had read my radio speech and was apparently considerably impressed; seemed to see more clearly and to be much more interested in the theme I

§ One of the British members of the Combined Policy Committee, which directed the limited cooperative program on atomic energy between the U.S., Britain, and Canada.

broached first to him and his *Life* staff at luncheon back in August. He strongly urged me to speak at New Orleans next April, at a big shindig *Time* is putting on there devoted to the theme: "The Future of Freedom." I said I would think about it.

It was an interesting visit and one in which we attended closely to what the other said. But I wasn't prepared for what I learned about the impression it had made on Mr. Luce, which I learned through his Washington man, Robert Elson, and from Miss Frances Henderson, formerly of *Time* here, now of our staff. It seems he thinks I am quite all right; is so persuaded about the atomic education matter that he is considering becoming chairman of the National Committee on Atomic Education and supporting it financially (it is about on the rocks) and is definitely in my corner. (I must make sure that I stay in my *own* corner.)

This is all to the good, for he has a tremendous sense of timing—he wouldn't be grabbing on to the atomic energy issue if I weren't right in thinking it is ripe, and that the line of public education is right. And as an ally he can be enormously helpful.

I am about persuaded that I ought to make the April speech, though it is a burden; for having made a hit with the *Herald Tribune* one (he called it a "minor masterpiece"), this one must be down the center of the fairway, too.

FEBRUARY 12, 1948
AT HOME

Told Elson, of *Time,* that he could tell Luce I would speak at the New Orleans Forum in April. *Time* today had my radio speech (well handled indeed) as the first-page story—about a column or more, with a new and life-like picture of me (i.e., an ugly phiz, but one that looked human, in contrast to so many of my photos). And I am agreeing to meet with the entire *Time* news board, for an evening down here. They will put me over the jumps, make evident the soft spots in my big idea, and make me deliver. This is very much to the good.

A crisis today. Back in July Andrew Lang, a *New Yorker* writer, spent several days wandering around the offices. (He had written a piece about the State Department Board of Consultants—not a bad piece, but nothing terrific and far from perceptive.) He caught me very late in the day—it was the same day, as I recall, that I talked to Frances Henderson when she was gathering material for the *Time* piece. I had talked in a spirited way to her about the crucial issue we had—of developing great force, as a means of buying time to develop the conditions of peace. When I saw Lang, I talked just as freely to him as to Frances, whom I could trust, forgetting that I had no such basis for confidence in Lang's treating what I said to him judiciously. I hit upon a phrase: Where we are, here this late afternoon in this building in Washington, in the offices of the United States Atomic Energy Commission, this is the center of reality. All else is shadows and unreal— meaning the international discussions going on all over.

I thought it was a good phrase, but apparently he thought it was even better. For today the boys received his manuscript for a *New Yorker* piece (and also a chapter in a book to be published in July), which he entitled "Center of Reality." He quoted me in a way that sounded like the worst saber-rattling jingo. The worst line was, "We around here are a group who are grim but satisfied." And then, too: "No foreign minister in the world can keep the atom out of his thinking." In other parts of the piece there were some quotes and tales (about security, etc.) and about our Congressional hearings that made us seem smart-alecky and most unattractive. But the quote of me was the worst, in terms of its being quoted throughout the world to show a bloodthirstiness, etc.

Much pacing back and forth. Salisbury (the interview took place before he became information director) was fit to be tied, and so was Volpe, who was quoted in a most unbecoming way. Should they try to kill it, by an appeal to *The New Yorker*? Of course not. That would be even worse than the effect of the piece as it stood. I recommended they ask Lang (who they say is most friendly and admiring) to modify the quote of me enough to put in the idea he left out, and that he thought he still had in, i.e., the purpose is to find a way to peace. Well, we shall see. We are due for some episode—things have been going along too beautifully of late!

[*The following are notes for a possible speech or article.*]

1. Science, physical science, brings changes in the physical world, in the environment of men.

2. These changes in man's physical environment have been very rapid, often bewildering, quite complete, etc.

3. Atomic energy is one of a series of such results of physical science.

4. We say: Science has gone too rapidly. It has progressed more rapidly than the social sciences, the science of man's behavior, and his institutions.

5. The social scientists say: You should support the social sciences, the study of man's behavior, so that social sciences can keep up with physical science.

I have felt for some time that there is something phony about this, but I have never quite located the error.

Have I got it now? As follows:

1. The changes brought by physical science, by a physical scientist, result from a discovery or experiment he performs on his own.

2. But the changes by which social institutions accommodate themselves to these changes are not changes wrought by individuals at all, but by men as a group, by the people.

3. One set of changes can take place in a laboratory. They can be studied there by physical scientists, and affected by physical scientists.

4. But the changes in human institutions are not affected by social scientists at all. They merely record changes that have occurred, or predict ones to come, or analyze the facts, etc.

5. The changes in one case are affected by scientists; in the other *by the people,* and not by the social scientists.

Doesn't this put a broader foundation under this hooraw I am putting on about "the people must know" about atomic energy? We can turn to the physical scientists for changes in physical matters, but for changes in our institutions it is the people themselves who make them.

And—here is the nub of it—since science, and the changes it brings, is the most important single fact of our time affecting our institutions, it is the people—and not the social scientists or anybody else—who must understand the world of science, since it is that realm of facts that is the most important single factor in the change of social institutions that is under way.

Science is not the only thing the people must know, of course. But it is one of the most important. And it happens to be a wedge by which other, related fields of knowledge and understanding can be made interesting and *relevant,* terribly relevant. Without that sense of terrible relevancy public education is quite impossible.


FEBRUARY 14, 1948
AT HOME, SATURDAY EVENING

Helen and I have just finished a game of rummy; a pleasant, relaxing afternoon, with the very first touch of March in the wind and the blue, blue sky. This has been a hard winter; more snow and ice and cold than I can remember; more, I guess, than since we left Wisconsin. But the buds of the dogwood trees, as I tromp around in the remnant of snow, these will soon begin to swell, and the forsythia can't be far away.

This morning attended a meeting of our Advisory Board on Biology and Medicine. We discussed the Commission's decision to support cancer research with $3,000,000, and to give isotopes free for cancer research. Yesterday, in preparation for the meeting, I read in a number of books on cancer and radiation effects on living tissue. It is hard, uphill going, trying to understand enough about these things, but I do not find it impossible, and the more one gets of the lingo and the way of expressing things, the better the going becomes. It is just as well that I don't know too much, for I am much less likely to get mired down in the details, and much more likely to be able to express it in language that other ignorant laymen like myself can understand.

I refuse to believe that anything cannot be made clear, in its essentials, to the average laymen, if it is stripped of all but its central meaning.

FEBRUARY 21, 1948
HOME, SATURDAY

Gen. McCormack just called to tell me that a Russian warship (or ship) was watching us at Eniwetok, about 20 miles off. He told me this by phone, so it was told in code and without detail. State and Forrestal have been told. Not unexpected, of course, and no doubt they and some underwater colleagues will be with them from now on. We have issued a public warning covering a large expanse of water, but I gather they have a right to sit there and learn all they can. But we must be careful and not provoke anything or make a misstep.

A week or so ago Bill Waymack talked with me, in confidence, to say that he had been thinking about things and had reached the tentative conclusion that he would not wish to serve beyond August 1, when our terms expire. He will soon be 60; apparently not in the kind of robust health he has always enjoyed, and the load of our work is very heavy and wearying. He says he puts his heart into whatever he is doing and feels that way about the Commission. I pointed out that for us to break up the team would be a blow, and to do it right in the middle of a campaign summer would be construed in political terms—the same thing Marsh McNeil had said to me when I said I had doubts about my own desire to go on, with 15 years of Fed. service behind me, beyond some appropriate stopping point. The thought of losing Bill is bad; I urged him to think about taking the one-year appointment.

Then yesterday Bob Bacher came in to say the same thing: he wants to get back to physics, and this would seem the time to do it. I said much the same thing to him. But to lose these two, and have to build a team all over again is not a happy thought. Well, we'll see. I advised Clifford that he'd better get a decision on reappointment from the Pres., so we could begin to think about timing and program.

FEBRUARY 23, 1948
MONDAY

What is wrong with this thesis:

The discoveries respecting atomic energy will almost certainly result in an advance in civilized life.

If it were not for its usefulness as a weapon, this would seem a rather obvious proposition; obvious, that is, to everyone except the few who distrust all machines and therefore all knowledge, actually.

My point is that every new knowledge raises a question of its net worth; in the case of atomic energy we have such a huge addition to knowledge about our environment, such an increase in our control (consequent on the knowledge) over it, and chief of all, such a *stimulus* to more understanding, that the balance of useful or beneficial will almost certainly outweigh the non-beneficial or destructive. But we see the latter more clearly than the former, so this cannot be proved nor even too clearly seen at the present; it is speculative, but not wholly speculation.

The thesis really is an effort to state the accretion of this knowledge as a *positive good,* a position that would even now seem reasonable if the scientists had not (ironically) underlined its bad side with such vigor, picturesqueness, and skill at a time when no one else knew enough to weigh their arguments; and when they, the scientists, were driven forward by a notion that their vehemence could effect political changes—that the amount of change toward supra-national government was in direct proportion to the vehemence with which they said this was the only way out, as a consequence of the facts of atomic energy's destructiveness.

I have written Mom and Dad at least once a week, these past several years; in fact, since Helen's mother died. And having a very acute feeling about our own children, now they are definitely "gone" makes the letter-writing to the folks more relevant. I remember when I left such things entirely to Helen—as Dad always did to Mother for his own mother. Just getting mail from the kids, even if they don't have much to say, is a treat; it's the first thing I ask about when I get home at nights. And when David left last time, I really felt quite badly; irrational, but true.

Last night Winchell said the big guns that got rid of Landis and Eccles were moving up to get me, when my term expired August 1.

He had the date right, which is a novelty—I mean having any fact straight—for a columnist of his variety.⟨ About the getting rid business, time will tell.

FEBRUARY 25, 1948
AT THE COMMISSION TABLE IN MY OFFICE

The red-cheeked, handsome young Commander is giving the monthly "oral" report on the state of "the stockpile"—the number of weapons, the various kinds, the components. The room is empty except for the Commissioners and General Jim [McCormack]. This is information of the greatest importance. The "numbers" represent what I once called "the center of reality" in the world. (This morning's paper told of the Communist accession to power in Czechoslovakia.) My office, this "monthly report," is a peaceful scene among very peaceful men. To me nothing could be more dramatic than the contrast between the quiet questions and impersonal answers, and the implications of it all.

Bob Bacher: "I don't know much about explosives . . ." as introductory to something he has to say. *He* doesn't know about explosives!

FEBRUARY 26, 1948
AT PRINCETON, NEW JERSEY,
IN THE OPPENHEIMER HOME (II P.M.)

Tonight I sat just that far from Einstein that I could have reached out and touched his shoulder, and watched him as he listened (gravely and intently, and at times with a chuckle and wrinkles about his eyes) to Robert Oppenheimer describing neutrinos as "those creatures," and the beauties of physics. I arrived for my visit at Princeton just as the Oppenheimers were off to the last of four lectures,* with President Dodds presiding. I didn't understand all of the lecture, not by any means, but it is a mark of my headway that I actually did understand quite a little. And I thought of Genesis, and the deep impulse of man to explain his world.

FEBRUARY 27, 1948
PRINCETON (10 A.M.)

Great excitement! A few days ago at Berkeley they found (or think they have found) that the big cyclotron is producing mesotrons

⟨ James M. Landis was not reappointed to the chairmanship of the Civil Aeronautics Board when his term expired in 1947; Marriner Eccles was succeeded as chairman of the Federal Reserve System early in 1948, but continued on the board of governors as vice chairman.

* This was the Vanuxem Lecture Series, which Dr. Oppenheimer delivered on atomic physics.

"by the bushel." These had been available before only from cosmic radiation. The amount of real excitement that goes on over this is a new experience for me to observe.

I have sat at Einstein's desk, in a little cubby office that he prefers to his big one, and listened for a half-hour while Niels Bohr talked to me, walking back and forth.

Earlier this morning I had more than an hour with Einstein.

Discussed with Robert [Oppenheimer] the question of "what are the alternatives—what should be the course" assuming as we must the failure of the Lake Success efforts [to agree on international atomic control]. Told him of Kennan's general thesis. Robert doesn't place too much importance on the Marshall Plan, though he is ardently for it. Goes much deeper than that. No reason to believe that because Marshall Plan works, and Western Europe on its feet because of our material help, this will make Stalin willing to talk sense about atomic energy or perhaps anything else.

FEBRUARY 28, 1948
AT HOME

The House Appropriations Committee on Deficiencies (which includes the senior members of the House committee) heard us again today.

I was struck with the increasing confidence these men show in me, and take the pains even to express in so many words. And since this includes hard-boiled Republicans who would hold my TVA background and appointment by F.D.R. and Truman against me in the ordinary course of events, this is puzzling but worth recording.

The chairman, John Taber, continues to be respectful as well as courteous, thoughtful, and consults with me about the course of the hearings. Congressman Robertson of North Dakota came to me at the table and said, "No one on this committee understands this, or ever will. We have just got to have someone running it that does understand it and that we trust. Thank God we've got you in there."

I get accustomed to taking politicos' words in a special sense, liberally applied with salt, but he continued in this vein. They are all obviously troubled by the whole thing, and by their inability actually to understand it, as well as their fear about it.

A huge and roaring character from Wisconsin, Keefe, with great piercing eyes and a fierce manner, was perhaps the greatest surprise.

He asked some good questions about the relation of our work in medicine, etc., and that of the Public Health Service, whose appropriation he handles as chairman of the subcommittee.

Carroll did a good job of replying, after which Keefe motioned me to come into Taber's adjoining office, shook hands with me warmly, saying he had never met me before, but wanted to say that "I want you to know that you are doing a really great job, a great job." We discussed cancer research somewhat; then as I returned to the hearing he repeated the statement about doing a good job, etc.

One member of the committee is Rep. Engle. He is a short, tousle-haired little man, noted for his terrific blasts against the military, as chairman of the Armed Forces Appropriation Subcommittee. The reports of his cussing out of generals right and left, and making mincemeat of full admirals, are legendary. But when I interrupted Kelley (our N.Y. operations manager), to prevent him answering a question I thought was risky in a security sense, instead of exploding Engle was very respectful, and afterward was very friendly, I thought. Cannon, ranking Democrat, whom I turned down last year when he wanted me to speak in Missouri, and who is rated very acid, stopped me as I was leaving Thursday and said, "God be praised, we've got you in there."

Politicians use words differently than other mortals; this I know. But after making all allowances, this is still very encouraging. Of course, Wigglesworth will continue to be sour, no matter what.

It is rather startling how a rugged experience will affect one's appearance, the face particularly. I have noticed it particularly with Carroll Wilson. He has had a terrific year, and it has written itself all over his features. He no longer faintly looks like a young college professor. (And what a great job he is doing, against terrible odds. His testimony before the Appropriations Committee of the House Thursday, and again today—Saturday—was a thing to see.)

Seeing the change in Carroll, I just took a hard look at me, and it certainly has written itself on my phiz, too. My chin and mouth especially seem to show the rough time I have had, and the sometimes quite harrowing sense of grim responsibility. This was underlined by having Helen show me, just a minute ago, a group picture she ran onto taken when I was in my third year at the Law School—this would be 1922 or 1923. Not only youthful, and with a full complement of wavy hair, but with such a carefree grin as you never saw.

The other change I note particularly is around the eyes. I never had dark places under my eyes, unless I had been going very hard, and then this would disappear after a night or two of sleep. Now the pressure has stamped itself in dark places, and in the morning especially a most unflattering kind of rocky look around the eyes; and a sort of depression clear down to the cheekbones.

But I keep a good color, a remarkable good ruddiness even though I haven't been in the sun for a long time (except for an hour today, a most unseasonable Saturday afternoon).

Although I do get frightfully tired, and have a lot of accumulated fatigue, I am really quite well; I mean I feel well, can stand long strain, and if I could be sure of a full month of rest this summer, should have no permanent ill effects of this tremendous job of getting this job rolling.

And it *is* rolling.

But returning to personal matters: I am in the pangs of changing glasses again, and probably forced sooner or later to the bifocal indignity that I seem to hate so.

MARCH 1, 1948

Well, the "low" that usually follows a high or plateau has arrived. I refer to our appropriation hearings, which went on all day today. Taber found an item of road maintenance, etc., that he saw was high, and then said that showed that probably everything we did was a "mess" and didn't show good management. Later he went on, building the story he wants to report, that this even raises questions of our good faith, etc.

None of this was barking, but it made us feel pretty low and sore and to hell with the whole goddamned business—that sort of feeling. After working so hard, then to have such a throwing of ugliness over the whole thing. Well, if ever men tackled a tough one, this is it. I thought: God pity General Marshall, having to show the light to such minds.

MARCH 3, 1948
AT THE OFFICE

Was handed a dispatch from the Navy that a plane had definitely sighted a submarine (complete with a snorkel, whatever that is) near Sandstone.†

MARCH 5, 1948
AT THE OFFICE

Have just come from a visit with Taber, who sent for me. I said to him, "Mr. Taber, you worried the hell out of me the other day."

† Code for the Eniwetok tests.

This amused and pleased him enormously, and he settled back to a half-hour of ruminating, in which he opined Marshall didn't know what he was doing, that "We might need some of that stuff you are making," and many other gems. Extraordinary; here is a man who as things stand today has more to say about world affairs than any member of the Cabinet.

MARCH 6, 1948
AT HOME, SATURDAY

Helen and I went to a reception for Gen. Omar Bradley last evening, at the War College. He is an impressive-looking man, but of such a gentleness that it is hard to believe that he commanded more men in the field than perhaps any man in history. A soft, studious face; but I gather a man of great force and decision.

Then I went to a dinner at the office of Secretary of the Army Royall, with the following: Forrestal, Symington, Sullivan (Secy. of the Navy), Don Carpenter, new head of the Military Liaison Committee, and Col. Nichols, who succeeds Groves.

For an hour the talk was about the Negro, and discrimination, etc. Symington is indignant about the extent of it, and how we all lie about it. He says we can talk a lie, but we can't live a lie. He is a corker. Royall, North Carolinian, is proud that his state has done so well; says the President shouldn't back down on the civil rights row, but shouldn't stir it up any more. It's all a matter of "timing," he says. Forrestal says go ahead and improve things, but don't talk about it, nor brag about it beforehand.

But the purpose of the gathering was to weld closer together the Commission and the Natl. Military Establishment. When asked what I thought was the most important need, I said to improve Sandia, where the AEC and the military must fit closely.

Royall then said something interesting. He said, "We're moving that way. We didn't do it as fast as Dave wanted" (a rueful smile) "but we got that done. I went out myself to look at Sandia, and I saw it was a mess, just as Dave said, and something had to be done."

When I came into Royall's office, he was asking (and later we all explored the question): How long would it take to get a number of "eggs" to, say, the Mediterranean? The idea of using them, Royall said, disturbed him a great deal. Symington said the American public was completely misinformed about how quickly we could go into action and what we could do. And so on; it was a rather grim hour of this kind of talk. A small table in a big room, in a big empty building overlooking the Potomac and the City of Washington. A small table with small men, all of us; but what such small groups can do to tear the world apart. Holding it together—well, that's another story.

I got much, much too tired this week, and had a rather tough go of jitters; too much strike threat at Oak Ridge, appropriations, spy scare stuff from J. Parnell Thomas (the Condon smear, a disgraceful, outrageous thing), too much in one week, on top of working hard too long without fun. All these men I was with last night have had holidays in the West Indies, play golf, etc.

Thursday evening, the 4th, spent with the *Time* editors, who came down from N.Y. especially. Did some good, I think, but was made terribly difficult and elusive because the manag. ed., T. S. Matthews, sees everything about it as a moral question, or in any event, reduced simply to "Do we drop the bomb on Russia; when do we do it, before they do or now?" I tried to tell him that these were not necessarily the alternatives at all; time could change the picture. But though I tried to describe the work in general, he wasn't impressed that it was relevant. Alexander, asst. manag. ed., I think I made headway with (he said, "I feel better about atomic energy now"). Fuerbringer, ed., national affairs, and Ways, foreign news, were quite good. I'm told *Time* has another cover of me on the way. Is this the Kiss of Death?

MARCH 11, 1948

Talked to Secretary Royall and Col. Nichols outside the President's office; they said they didn't know what the meeting was about, that Royall hadn't asked for it.

The President said he had before him the recommendation of the promotion of Col. Nichols as head of the Armed Forces Special Weapons Project, that he wanted to have a talk with us before acting on it. "I don't want another General Groves incident." Royall injected to say that he saw after his trip West that that situation was as I had said it was, quite impossible.

The President said, "I want it clearly understood before I act on this appointment that this is a civilian-run agency and I thought I ought to say this to you directly. It requires cooperation between the civilian and the military, of course." Nichols said, "You can count on 100 percent cooperation." I said, "You have a team, Mr. President."

Talked to Clifford about the expiration of our terms and the future steps to be taken.

MARCH 21, 1948
CAPTIVA ISLAND, FLORIDA, SUNDAY

Back again on Captiva. We have only been here a few hours, but we already seem rather settled down. We both need it; I particularly, for I came as close to exhaustion recently as it is well to get. What saved me was a cold that began last Sunday; this is nature's way, I guess, of laying me out with something not serious so I don't get something really bad.

I had managed to pull out a speech for the Boston Chamber of Commerce (for the 18th—it is hard to believe that I was speaking in Boston just a couple days ago), and then Tuesday I had fever and felt pretty bum to count on any such venture as that. Wednesday I called Dr. Ecker, who told me I was *not* to go, that with that kind of throat, and so tired, I stood a good chance of getting "a really lively bug"—of which there is a good deal going around. This sunk me, for I knew they had made elaborate preparations; and besides the thousand-dollar fee was really needed—without it I didn't quite see how I could afford a holiday.‡

I phoned Charles Luckman; no, they couldn't put someone else on at this date, etc.; they would cancel. Then he asked, would it help if he sent the Lever Company plane for me? This worked out beautifully. I left that evening (Wednesday), got to Boston and in bed by 9:30. The next morning I felt considerably better, my voice still far from clear, and I made the speech—with no ill effect. In fact, it went quite well, with enough half-humor and enough simple information plus suggestions of policy to make a better speech than I thought I had when I finished putting it together.

David heard the speech, from a seat in the gallery of the ballroom. Then, after my brief press conference, we had a visit. When I learned that his spring recess was so near, I said, "Why don't you drive our car down to Captiva and join us there?" Then I phoned Nancy, and David urged her to get a week off and make a family party of it. It was so good to hear him talk to her, in that easy, affectionate way they have between them. And next morning we heard from both: they would be down. This elated us, and we can hardly wait.

This morning we saw Herman Dickey, who took them "pin-fishing" when we were here for that long stretch in 1939, and we had a good "reminisce."

The Commissioners (minus Bacher who is in the West) saw the President for 15 minutes last Friday afternoon (that would be the 19th). This was a meeting I had been urging on Clark Clifford, to settle the question of whether the President wanted to reappoint us; and in this way prevent if possible any member of the "team" declining to accept

‡ In the AEC, I sometimes accepted article and speech fees, which was a legal and common practice among Government officials. I had not done this in the TVA.

reappointment. This is the first step toward meeting the question of what happens upon the expiration of the terms of all of us next August.

The President came right to the point (I had urged Clark to have him bring up the question himself). "I think you fellows have done a damn good job, a very good job, and I want you to go right on. It would be a bad thing if any one of you didn't go right on. My idea is not to send up your names until Congress has gone home. I am afraid if I send your names up now—you know, those fellows up there don't like me very well—they would refuse to confirm. If they would, I would turn around the next day and reappoint you for the full terms."

I spoke up to say that we had all talked it over and had the idea the nominations should be made soon, rather soon. This project was in bad shape when we took over a year ago, and it was now on rather solid ground. The reason it was in such bad shape was chiefly uncertainty, uncertainty as to policy and uncertainty about the real authority of the people ostensibly in charge to make future commitments and decisions. We felt rather strongly that the project, in the interest of the country, couldn't stand another such period of uncertainty. But there should be such a period if we served under interim recess appointments.

The President listened intently to this, which I said in a rather strained tone, I fear (I certainly wasn't relaxed). He looked tired, as I have hardly ever seen him, and under strain, though his voice was just the same soft, friendly one. He had been through a *week*. He decided to make the far-reaching statement of policy about Russia that was embodied in his Wednesday speech to Congress, and then that night in a speech in New York.§ The Southern states have been pounding him like all get-out, and even such friends as Sparkman had been saying he should not run for re-election to keep the Democratic Party from being "cut to ribbons," etc.

Well, he said, he hadn't decided definitely against making the nominations now; he just thought it would save a big row. "What would that bird from Memphis do?" I assured him McKellar would certainly fight, but that would be a help. This amused the President. The opposition that counts will come from others. I didn't mention Taft, but it was he I had in mind.

I went on to say that the President was on strong ground: he had made the nominations without any politics in it, and we had operated in that way all the way through. The country was entitled to have atomic energy treated that way; if there was an effort to stall acting on the

§ The President had accused the Soviet Union of planning to subjugate all of Europe (this was only a few weeks after the Communist coup in Czechoslovakia), and declared that the U.S. would support free nations everywhere.

nominations, it could only be for political reasons—the hope that they would have another crack at it if they should elect a President in November.

The President rared back. "I wanted to avoid putting you fellows through a fight. I believe you" (looking at me) "like a fight." And then he laughed.

There was a suggestion—I think I made it—that the senior member of the Joint Committee be called and told what the President had in mind doing, and why. Vandenberg was mentioned in this connection. The President leaned over his desk, speaking to Lewis [Strauss], and said, "Vandenberg is one I do get along with fine. He is the one Republican I would trust in this chair; I wouldn't trust any of the rest of them."

Lewis spoke of the idea that had been broached of the Congress amending the law to extend our terms until next February, say. Lewis said he thought it was a pretty good idea, on first blush, but since then we all believed it was wrong. The President said that would be bad.

Then Bill Waymack spoke up, in one of the best statements I have ever heard him make. He said he first wanted to speak for Bacher, who had specifically requested him to make certain things clear. He, Bacher, had left his work—physics—seven years ago. He wanted to get back to the laboratory and teaching. He wanted it understood that he didn't want to serve beyond August 1. At this, the President interrupted to say that would be very bad. Right now that would be construed politically. Bill went on to say that Bacher was willing to carry on for another year with the distinct understanding that there was no moral obligation on him to continue longer, even though the term to which he had been appointed was for longer than that. He wanted further to say that he was completely devoted to civilian control, for a number of reasons, not the least of which was that it was the only way to develop our military potential in this field. Bill did a beautiful job. Then, he said, "Speaking for myself, I agreed to serve until August of this year, and have no obligation to go on beyond. In years I am the oldest member of the Commission; in every other way I am the youngest." He, too, wanted it understood that he would continue long enough to get the Commission on solid ground and over this hump, but then he wanted to be able to resign without any moral commitment of any kind.

I was glad we had this said, because my point with Clark had been that this meeting was important, early, because these two men had spoken to me, and it was bad to let the situation jell.

The President said, "Well, we can work those things out later."

I brought up the question of custody [of the atomic stockpile]. Yes, he said, the military had spoken to him about it; looked as if they had a point. I said the important thing was that he understood that the decisive question was the policy question, the question inhering in the matter of the weapons as offensive weapons and hence different from the usual. He said we should talk about it at some other time, and agreed that before he acted we would talk to him further. "I certainly don't want to have to use them again, ever," he said rather ruefully.

(Now I have these notes written I'm going to forget atomic energy and return to beachcombing.)


(Oh, I almost forgot:)

"I have an idea," I said to the President, "that I thought might provide continuity, and minimize and perhaps eliminate a fight at this time. I tried it out this afternoon on my colleagues, and frankly they didn't go for it; but I thought I might try it out on you just the same.

"The opposition was chiefly directed against me; that will be true this time as well. If I should be appointed to the one-year term, at my own insistence, then a year from now, more or less, the opposition could finish me off, if things turn out their way in the intervening months; in any case, they could try the case again at a time when it would not involve the entire Commission, as it does now."

The President said that will just make another fight in a year. The other Commissioners grinned, that I hadn't made any more headway with the President than I had an hour earlier with them. Their reaction had been, "It would look like throwing you to the wolves; it would be a sign of weakness."

I'm not so sure. Perhaps one reason it still appeals to me is that in another year I would be glad of a chance to bow out and get going on something else. I am pretty fed up with that phase of public life that involves dealing with Congress—I always get low about appropriation time of year. I can hardly think of any work I could be doing that would possibly be more interesting; but the price for that, when it comes to the Congressional end—both appropriations and such messiness as the hysteria over secrets, "security risks," etc., is a good deal to pay after 15 years.

Well, I guess we will just play it by ear and see what happens. With the state of the world as it is, this seems about the most that anyone can do.


This is a wonderful place to let the world go hang. The beach is almost deserted, the weather lovely, and I can snooze whenever I feel like it, which at this stage is a good part of the time.

MARCH 25, 1948
CAPTIVA, THURSDAY

The children arrived yesterday morning, while Helen and I were at breakfast. Helen saw the car and let out a yip of excitement, and in a second we were out there greeting the kids. How happy we were—and are. We have been drinking it in—having the kids again, here where we remember them as youngsters. Just a mile or so away is the place we stayed for two months while I was getting over undulant fever. David remembered how we used to play catch in the yard, and how one hot day he keeled over. I remember some unpleasant things, but without any inner flinching: the time I had a cave-in down here, after the excitement over my reappointment in 1936, and the ugly terrors of undulant. Ah, well, when a horse—or a place—throws you, you must get right back on. Go back to the scene of the crime, and all that sort of stuff.

Last evening I turned on the radio to listen to Ed Murrow. A neighbor had brought over their radio, saying that they were sure "the children" would want one; the "children" weren't interested in the least, both being engaged in earnest reading. But like a dope I felt we should show some sign of appreciation by playing the thing. I know better, of old, but I thought this wouldn't matter, this time. Ed said, "Senator Bridges said today that the country should return atomic energy to the military; that this was one of the most important issues facing the country"—words to that effect.

Up until this time I had been doing a wonderful job of forgetting everything—the Marshall Plan, the coal strike, John Taber, and atomic energy in all its parts. But this damned sentence stuck in my mind like a sand burr. My face showed it at once; Helen remarked on it. I tried to recover my insouciance, but it just wouldn't come. Then I would say, "Well, by tomorrow you will have forgotten it." But I slept badly, for the first time since we left, and Bridges and all the rest paraded through my dreams.

This morning I resolved I would get rid of it; it was simply unthinkable that I should waste a single moment of this almost too-good-to-be-true vacation with Helen and the kids by any such inability to throw off something of this kind. But it is an incident out of a long series. I remember so many times when something of this sort—quite unimportant things in themselves—would touch a spring and set me off. In this case the occasion is particularly stupid, for Bridges was against the transfer to the Commission, was an early antagonist to my confirmation, in fact I think was the first in the series that culminated with Taft's opposition. True, in our sessions with him on appropriations he seemed to have mellowed, but actually I knew better than that.

The circumstances here for forgetting things—not an easy thing these days—are almost perfect. We went "shelling" this morning, to Sanibel. This always makes Helen so happy, and it is nice to see her enjoyment of wandering slowly down a beach, looking down and occasionally picking up something, generally to throw it down again.

On our trip down we thought we were to take a train at Tampa for Fort Myers. It turned out there was no train, but a bus. We left Tampa at 5 and arrived Saturday night at Fort Myers at 11:30. Two hours were spent sitting by the side of the road—a quite deserted stretch—between 8:30 and 10:30—because the bus had broken down. I gathered it wasn't the first breakdown, as it was an old antique. The Fort Myers paper, Sunday, reported that the guy who "bosses the scientific marvels of the 20th century" couldn't do anything about a balky bus. I was provoked at first, but it got to be rather interesting. Two jolly, plump women, about 35, made a joke of the whole thing. One lady was a caricature of the worry-wart, and so on. We were amused, because the preceding day I had been with the President, and the day before in the lap of Lever luxury.

MARCH 27, 1948
CAPTIVA, SATURDAY

What a perfect family holiday! Never thought it was to be for us again. Here we are, just the four of us, living together in a house to ourselves, on the beach, shelling on Sanibel, swimming, rummy in the evenings amidst the uproarious kidding and laughing.

Yesterday we revisited the "Chadwick" cottage, where we spent six or seven weeks when I was so "shot." We roamed the Sanibel beach, I starring by the most absurd luck, by proceeding to pick up a rather nice lion's paw in the first few minutes of play. Today David and I are going fishing with Herman Dickey and Fred Herzog, in Herman's boat.

Sunday Nancy flies, in a seaplane, to Tampa (she takes off right at Randall's dock just a 100 yards from our cottage) and then flies through the night to be on hand for work (we hope) Monday morning.

It is difficult to imagine four people who enjoy each other more than this family. And in all sorts of moods. The fun Nancy and Helen get out of talking about clothes and shells and Shelley in rapid succession. David has matured a great deal. He asks me questions with a hard gleam in his eye: "What about Vandenberg? What are the chances of MVA? What about Dewey?" and on and on.

A great day of fishing. I brought in four large redfish; two of them quite large, nine and ten pounds, the others about five each. A fifth, the first strike, was even larger. I worked with him for what seemed a long time, a really spectacular business of runs and jumps, this great, beautiful fish dashing this way and that, visible 35 feet away through the dark water against sand bottom. Herman grabbed the leader and swung the red in, but he hit the side of the boat in the process and with a wild leap was off.

We didn't have a strike, not one until after 3—we started about 9:30. It looked like one of those days you run into in fishing, and no one caught anything but trout for some time. Then going through a mangrove pass I got this big one. The next move through I got a whale of a strike, and landed him, and then on our very next pass through, the third, also large. This is the way fishing is. Although three identical spoons were out, side by side, Mr. Herzog got not a strike, and David caught a six-inch grouper.

The sun was very hot and the reflection from the water all day has given me a lulu of a face burn. My ears feel as if they were little torches burning merrily, and my cheekbones are pillars of fire. David looks boiled, too. If I don't blister from this, I'll be pretty lucky.

MARCH 29, 1948
CAPTIVA

What a happy time we are having! This morning we tore off to Sanibel Island, right after breakfast. David and I aren't too keen about "shelling," but Helen enjoys it so completely that last night he and I thought up the trip because we could just see her poking down the beach, absorbed and happy. The storm (we had quite a blow last evening and night, turned into a northeaster, rather cold) had thrown up the shells in great shape, and many people were out, digging in the heaps. One very dignified gent who stayed at one spot, with a little rake, spoke to me in considerable amusement at himself. "Digging in the city garbage heap," he said, "even have a rake so I can spear a piece of hamburger."

There was great excitement on the shore, a woman suddenly the center of a circle, all agog. She had, of course, found a junonia, the prize leopard-spot shell. The word spread, like the story about a fire in a small village. People who had talked to people who had talked to the lucky finder would tell and retell the story: "She was just standing right there, and the tide washed it in to her feet—to her feet, mind you!" and so on. I found a beautiful, though small, lion's paw, a rarity, the other day; just walked along and saw it, nothing dramatic about it.

But it is fun. The surf was high and quite wonderful to fight. And Helen and I fished from the bridge—but not long. No mail from Washington; I had expected to have to work on my National Press Club speech today, but the suggestions from the staff didn't come, and this gave me a good excuse to defer the evil hour.

We put Nancy on a tiny little plane, at the dock last night. The wind was going like sixty, the weather was stormy and overcast. I wasn't too happy about seeing her off, but thought it important not to decide it for her. Helen was uneasy, too, but we said nothing. So it was very good to get a wire at noon today that Nancy had arrived in New York on schedule this morning. The holiday has certainly been a success.

I have been having a good deal of fun with water colors on this holiday. The paints the Tobeys◄ gave me almost a year ago. I did almost nothing with them at home—tried it, but as I obviously have no talent in this direction, and no training, it didn't go well. But I brought them along, and took Barney's advice just to slap on the colors to please myself. I discovered things—such as how to make one mountain in a landscape seem far beyond another. Then I tried wild colors, and yesterday made a remarkable fish, flourishing with oranges, yellows and violets (which strong colors seem to appeal most to me). Quite absorbing.

APRIL 8, 1948
AT THE DESK

I have just blown my top. The military do not want to announce that the [Eniwetok] test has been held, until it is all over. I object on the ground that the Russians will know, and so will everyone except the American people. I do not want to say much, but the fact should be stated. I haven't been so riled in a long time. Ostriches, sticking their heads in the sand, are intelligent compared to such.

APRIL 10, 1948
AT HOME (SATURDAY—AND A BEAUTIFUL DAY IT IS, TOO)

I found that actually very little had transpired during my two weeks' absence (it is a week next Monday since I returned).

a. There was a flurry caused by Senator Wherry introducing a bill to return atomic energy to the military, based upon the argument that we are in an "emergency." This, I gathered, backfired, even Wherry admitting this. He stated it was not intended to be a reflection on the Commission. He told Miss Henderson he certainly didn't want to get

◄ My cousin, Beatrice, and her husband, Barney, both artists (Barney being also a *New Yorker* cartoonist).

into another fight with David Lilienthal. Bridges' comment in this direction turns out to be a rather tentative question, put to Secretary Royall, who said this was no time for any change, so far as the military was concerned.

*b.* The House Appropriations Committee gave us every last dollar of contract authorization we asked for, and wrote a report "admonishing" us to proceed with research with all speed, and absolving us from responsibility for the inadequate state of finance and cost records; this is in contrast with the nasty dig at us last year at this time, and the general predisposition of that committee to raise hell with everybody.

*c.* The row over the President's order directing executive agencies not to furnish committees of Congress with confidential files—which upset our relations with the Joint Committee—was still going strong on my return. Negotiations with the Attorney General and the White House, we urging that we be exempted from this order because of the special legislative relationship we have, and the certainty that a bad row would result, ended successfully, but with a close call.

After we had finally persuaded the Attorney General (this I did by telephone Thursday morning last) that he should yield his last point, I called Hickenlooper. He told me that he had talked to the President by phone shortly before, and that the President was sticking to his position. This report turned out to be right, as I confirmed by a call on Clifford late Thursday afternoon. We presented Clifford the completed agreement between the Commission and the Attorney General. I told him of the reported talk between Hickenlooper and the President. "Perhaps I better check," he said. Which was wise, for the President had told Hickenlooper that "You fellows run the legislative branch and we will run the executive"—all friendly enough but firm. The Attorney General was with the President, and it was talked over and settled.

Wednesday evening I attended a dinner given by Bob Lovett for the Belgian delegation: the Prince Regent, a stooped, colorless young-old man; Spaak, Premier, a big beefy football center with huge owl-like glasses, and their party. Included Sir John Boyd Orr, the international food man, who looks as if he had walked right out of a waxworks; Spaatz, with whom I had a lively conversation and who admits that Washington is too much for him ("Can't take it" says the air commander who could take anything in the field); Taymens, counselor of the Belgian Embassy, who looks something like Spaak would if Spaak weighed 100 pounds less. Lovett was wonderful as always; easy, witty, friendly. Had a good talk with Admiral Kirk, our Ambassador at Brussels, about the Congo, and a business trip to Katanga this summer. Says Spaak has the Communists (about 10 percent of the seats in Parliament) backed up and no troubles. At Kirk's urging I talked to the Prince Regent for some time and with Spaak. They are going to TVA on this trip; that and Pittsburgh are the things they want to see, and it is evident that TVA is the cause of their looks of appreciation at me, and not atomic energy. Which is the way I would wish it, actually.

Taking things much much easier, and will try to continue this way. I am rather deeply tired, and ten days' rest won't do the trick; I must continue to live differently, somehow. This constitutes chiefly (a) not considering what I am doing as being quite so terribly important, hence not considering myself quite so important; this takes off a lot of tension, emotional and otherwise; and (b) not getting involved (by seeing people, etc.) in so many things that then must be continued. I am not taking on any speeches or honorary degrees, save only the University of Virginia commencement address in mid-June, and cleaning up a commitment at Manchester, N.H., the 19th. I may go West to see AEC things, but will try not to make any formal speeches.

My speech to the National Press Club on the 6th (last Tuesday) went very well indeed. Crowded—about 100 men standing—and excellent response. I spoke from notes only, rather sparse ones at that (which is risky, but worked), and had 30 full minutes of questions, which I handled with no particular nervousness, declining to answer some, including one or two about Dr. Condon, and weapons.

I am thinking more and more about the time when I undertake some different kind of work. When that will be and what it will be, I don't know, of course; but it is rather comforting to think about it, and to find that it is a not unpleasant prospect. It doesn't panic me by any means to consider leaving public service—though this may not be possible or appropriate for some time. I find myself more tired of this intensity of worry and excitement than I realized. The answer, as it now seems, is either (a) diminish the intensity or (b) plan to do something less exacting in this sense, of which doing considerable writing and traveling seems the most attractive prospect at the moment. I have a wild notion that two years spent going around the world, reporting on countries that are establishing themselves on a new basis would be great fun, a fine way to make the break, and sufficiently profitable to pay for the travel, etc., at least. Mexico, Burma, England.

The war feeling, the anxiety about the future, continues unabated. Recruitment has picked up; a draft law, that would, or might, put David and lots of other youngsters back into the service is quite certain to be passed in a matter of weeks. The President's stock is very low indeed; somehow I wonder if this is permanent, as is assumed. He doesn't seem to give a hang; he is going to be President as long as this term lasts, come what may.

Speaking of anxiety: Thursday we visited the German art treasures, at a special showing, at the invitation of the director of the National Gallery, David Finley. It was a great delight, really. Present were Justices Reed, Frankfurter, and Burton and wives, and, among others, Madame van Kleffens, wife of the Ambassador from the Netherlands, a very charming and delightful young woman. We saw many of the pictures together (many of them by Dutchmen and many of them about Holland).

She said, "We have just had a letter from an uncle, a most unexcitable and matter-of-fact man, living in Holland. He asked us, quite seriously, to consider how he might evacuate his three children to America or somewhere. This was because of his fear of the Russians. You do not realize how near they are to Holland and to all the West of Europe. This is from a man who went through the underground opposition to Germany. He also said, 'If this happens again, I am not so sure that it would not be better to join with whatever conqueror comes along.' "

Her expression, while telling me this, was something I shall not forget.

(LATER, 11 P.M.)

Half an hour or so ago I stopped in the middle of a rummy game with Helen with a decision made that has been troubling me for some time. The decision (it seems very clear that it *is* final, so far as I am concerned) that when the President announces my reappointment I will state that at the end of another year it is my firm intention to return to private life. I can say at that time (presumably within the next two or three weeks; sooner, I hope) that the work is now well on its way; that in another year it should be well begun, and that I can therefore, properly, do the thing I want to do, namely, leave public service.

This is the time to take this step, while things are going well, there is no fight on, yet it will give me almost a year to consider what to do next.

It is about time I did something that was in *my* interest. This seems clearly to be of that character.

I ought to see Wilson and the Commission members, and Clifford and the President promptly about this. And I ought to talk to Vandenberg about it. When I go to Cambridge next Monday, I shall talk to Conant about it.

APRIL 14, 1948
AT THE OFFICE (1:50 P.M.)

Just finished a long session with Don Carpenter, new chairman of the MLC, and the Commission to try to solve the disputed question:

should a public statement be made about Sandstone [Eniwetok]? The military and Van Bush were dead against it, as helping the Russians acquire information by filters. We were firmly for it because we are sure they will know anyway, and the American press will feel we have let them down. What kind of cooperation can we be expected to receive in the future if we let the American people hear of this through Reuters, etc.? I said last night that if the release were not made, it would be because the military stopped us.

Things looked very bad for an hour of this discussion—in fact, just about zero hour—and then I came up with the idea of providing 72 hours' leeway (which it is agreed will minimize the usefulness of filter results) but cutting down that time by giving the word to the press some 24 hours in advance, with a press conference to emphasize the importance of not breaking the release date. We have no idea that this will work (and it does put the announcement the very evening before the Italian election!), but it seems the best we can work out.

(LATER, 4 P.M.)

While I was in a meeting an hour ago Commander Ashworth of the MLC brought in a written note: "Word has been received of the arrival of a bouncing baby boy according to expectations." This is wonderful news.*

(LATER STILL, 6:15 P.M.)

Carpenter called to say that he thought he had authority to speak for the Defense Secretary; turns out that all three of the department Secretaries and the Chiefs of Staff disagree and object to any public release. Boy!

APRIL 17, 1948
AT HOME

The conflict between self-interest and detached, unselfish service to one's fellows and the principles in which we believe: this goes on, I suppose, in most men more often than we suppose. The reach for the stars; the gravitational pull of making a living and having the luxuries and the fun and the freedom from immediate worry that we seek by "tending to our own business" and making money.

Had a violent session of this, this morning, as I went over the figures of income and expense of last year. The figures aren't well set

* This referred, of course, to the success of the first of the Eniwetok test series.

up to reveal the ultimate facts, but it's clear that in spite of our modest way of living in this luxurious city (Helen has a woman in one day a week!) I don't appear to be saving much, if anything. The children cost $2,000 last year, and travel about the same, but I had an income of more than $22,000. How people manage who make much less is more than I can figure. Maybe they don't.

But in any case, it underlined the decision to get into private life, where (a) probably the income would be greater, and (b) where the pressure might be less. Helen says the trouble may be I'm trying to save too much—more than insurance—at a time when we should be enjoying things that cost, such as travel; that I should assume my income will not be less and probably more for the next 10 to 15 years. But about such things I am very cautious and pessimistic.

We are going ahead with the test release for Monday. And Tuesday the President will probably send in the names to Congress. Then we shall see what we shall see.

The attached broad-tape† appeared with a remarkable coincidence; we waved it at Secretary Royall and those who opposed our basic notion that the way to get maximum security is to say a minimum and then hold the line; the wrong way is to assume there will be no leaks, and when they come, to blame the press for them when it is usually from within the government. This story certainly was a good and effective point-maker.

But even more remarkable as a demonstration: Hickenlooper said that a reporter for INS called him at 6 P.M. Wed., saying he had a story that he had on the wire at five—would Hick. confirm it, etc.? Of course, he wouldn't; but it does show. And Thursday the N.Y. *News* and the Wash. *News* called to say they understood we would have a news release between four and six.

The American Society of Newspaper Editors is meeting. The Seymour Committee Report, read yesterday P.M. at a meeting I attended, was pleasant listening, and showed the fruits of my speech of a year ago.‡ In my case, it appears to be true: It Pays To Worry. Van Bush made the conventional defense of military secrecy, extended to peacetime, which was nice-sounding, but I thought Hanson Baldwin and Nat Finney punched it full of holes, in particulars.

† This was a United Press story from Honolulu dated April 15 that began: "Military sources believed today that the first phases of atomic tests at Eniwetok Atoll have been completed and that they probably involved the use of a guided missile."

‡ The editors voted the next day to commend the AEC for its information policy, and to set up a special program to train newsmen to handle atomic energy information.

I'm making the Western trip week after next if all goes well. Leave for the long deferred Manchester, N.H., one tomorrow. See Conant in the morning.

APRIL 18, 1948
AT HOME

The President did a dramatic thing, and a very successful one, last night at the ASNE dinner. He read one of those deadly dull speeches over the radio, and "read" is the word. Then off the air he spoke "off the record." He talked about Stalin, Potsdam, Molotov when he and M. both lived at Blair Lee House, when Truman was first in office, but lived at B.L. while the Wh. House was being redecorated.§ He spoke fluently, with deep feeling, almost passion, and courageously: he attacked the big Air Force idea with great force. The important point was that he took the editors quite by surprise, and by storm, and everyone said: Why wasn't that on the record? That is what the whole country should hear.

Went to the party with John Taber and Wm. Dapping, our host. Taber was most friendly and even jovial. At table he noticed that a man across the table asked to have the rolls passed to him, though there was a whole plate of them right under his nose. I said, "He probably asked to have an economic survey made as whether there were enough rolls, rather than just trusting his eyes which told him there they were." This kept him chuckling for ten minutes; it wasn't that good, but he thought otherwise. He said he knew more about labor than anyone on the Hill, had studied it thoroughly before he came to Congress. "The answer is not the Taft-Hartley law, but to tell these fellows if they don't behave we'd repeal all the labor laws. That's what is needed."

Anna Roosevelt Boettinger, and handsomer than I remember her, was there last night. How Truman's incredibly bad radio style must have pained her.

Helen and I have a tough problem. She is alone too much, out here. For that reason I've tried to keep travel down to a minimum, though I can't do this indefinitely. She would like to have people drop in, to have friends as she did, and we did, in Norris. She inclines against joining things in Bethesda. Writing is difficult, for doing the housework takes so much time and energy, there isn't the chance to get absorbed, so

§ Molotov, then Soviet Foreign Minister, was a guest at Blair Lee House in 1945, en route to the San Francisco United Nations Charter conference. This adjoined Blair House, then the President's temporary residence.

important in her kind of writing. I'm so tired most of the time after a long day, and need rest so much, that going out much is hard for me. I've had such a lot to worry about, and what I do is so absorbing, and there is so little of it I can talk to her about, or want to for that matter, that we don't share common interests quite as much as we did in TVA.

I've noticed her troubled state about this, and a certain sensitiveness that isn't like her. So this morning I brought it out and said we must do something about it, however drastic, before it brought trouble between us. She is so sweet and so fair; it troubled her, because, she says, "I don't want to be that kind of wife"—meaning, the one that doesn't fit into the life work of her husband, and do what serves that work. But this is too much for her, and frankly I don't give a damn what happens to the work, I'm not going to let it ruin everything for us. But we must find an answer to it, and before long. I stand on my decision to get out of public service, though that won't solve all these problems; it would help, though.


APRIL 20, 1948
EN ROUTE, BY PLANE, BOSTON TO WASHINGTON

A wonderful visit with David was the chief advantage and the outstanding event of this trip. The ostensible purpose: to speak to the Manchester Forum at Manchester, N.H.

As we drove to Boston last evening David really "opened up"; I can see that we have made great headway in overcoming the father-son inhibitions and tension. He talked about himself, and this is important, with a rush of words and a candor that shows that he can unlax with me in the way that Nancy has with Helen. It is difficult to say how happy this made me. I watched his fine, sensitive face, in the half-dark of the car as we drove along, and it was almost as if I were there, in that corner, myself, 30 years ago, and yet with the strange advantage of knowing what I know (and how little I know) and with the rare joy and pride of a father. It was, too, like a friend unburdening himself. David and I have had many talks together—over the years; and notably last summer in our nocturnal walks across the golf course near our house in Maryland and on the beach at Captiva. But there wasn't either the irritability that was sometimes so marked when he suspected parental "judgment" nor the "touchiness" and shyness about some things.

He told me, more clearly than before (partly because I was frank to tell him when I didn't "get it" or pressed, by asking questions) of his own analysis of himself. This is a difficult thing to do, from one generation to another, and particularly difficult across the generation to your own parent. I never was able to manage it with either my father or mother.

He *struggles* with his limitations—which he recognizes as limitations of temperament. He is retiring; he sometimes "goes to pieces"—these are his analyses—when he gets angry or sore, and becomes irritable and snappy, and burns up and would like to fly off the handle. What occasions this: not "social injustice" and that kind of impersonal thing, as in the case of Nancy and discrimination against Negroes, for example. No, he was emphatic about that. It's when someone kids him in a way that wounds or hurts him and he can't take it calmly. Personal things. (Later, it developed that some of these furies arise when someone's show-off attitude incenses or disgusts him, and that girls have so acted as to make him steamed up and tell them off for being such fools.)

He fights with this. When he was little, said he, he could take it out in a tantrum, kicking his heels on the floor, as he did. Now he tries to talk himself out of it. I urged him to walk away from it, literally—going for a walk, go to a movie, take a swim, and not fight such things directly, for this is too wearing, and may even intensify what is at the bottom of it. What *is* at the bottom I wouldn't suggest, but it doesn't matter too much, perhaps; it is better for him not to brood about causes, anyway.

When I said this sounded familiar; that I too had a low boiling point, lacked certain kinds of self-control, did not suffer fools gladly, etc., and this is still strong, he looked at me, in the half-dark, with an expression of incredulity and intense interest. But I am so self-assured! (He had seen a good case of this in the way I handled questions after the Forum for an hour.)

It has been my hunch right along—as it was last year—and against the view of most, that there would be a fight against my renomination, in the Senate. It was for this reason that I proposed the one-year term idea for me, as a possible way of averting the tumult, and the danger of no confirmation, and a disastrous interregnum.

At the present writing it looks, suddenly, as if this is just what we are headed for, in a big way.

When I got back to the office this afternoon, Taft had left a meeting of the Republican Policy Committee saying the Repubs were considering not approving any of the President's nominations: apropos the word yesterday that they were going to be made soon.

At about two the White House told the press the names were going today; Hickenlooper called to see the President, and the nominations were held up. H. left; the word went out—the names go up at once.

I called Clifford; he reported back that Hick. had told the President that if my name were sent for the one-year term, he thought he could salvage the nominations of most of the Commission; otherwise not. The President said No, and Hick. left with no comment to the press.

Carl Levin of the *Herald Trib* told me that he called Taft: "The Pres. has sent up the names of the AEC." Taft's first remark was, "What are the length of terms for each Commissioner?" "When I told him Lilienthal for five years, through the next Administration, the silence was terrific. That's what he was thinking: what term for you."

Elmer Davis started the ball rolling with talk about playing politics with atomic energy, and I expect Tony Leviero of the *Times* to say the same tomorrow. I see the President at eleven.

APRIL 21, 1948
WEDNESDAY

I had a meeting with the President this morning from about 11:30 to 12:00 noon. The President looked worn—as I haven't seen him look since I have known him—but his spirits actually were excellent. He made some reference at the outset to the fact that he had discharged his responsibility as President in sending these names up (this had occurred the day before with the furor about Hickenlooper's call, etc.) and that it was now up to the Senate to discharge its responsibility. (I got the impression that he meant that this is what he had said yesterday to Hickenlooper; though Hickenlooper says that he, the President, simply listened and did not make this comment.)

I wisecracked by saying, "Mr. President, you kidded me the last time when I proposed a one-year term for me by saying that this would only produce a fight a year from now and that, by golly, you thought I rather liked a fight! I want to return the compliment." Beyond this nothing was said about the nominations.

I presented a letter approved by Forrestal and myself that (when approved by the President) becomes AEC's charter for the year as to production, etc. The figures were left blank, and we asked the President to fill them in in his own handwriting as Wilson ticked them off for him. Then I gave him some word about the way the tests had gone. He looked interested, but it was evident that the loose news talk about "new bombs 1,000 times greater than those at Nagasaki," etc., had taken the edge off the word about what actually happened at Eniwetok.

I had planned to talk to him about peacetime applications and had had a little session, just before going to the White House, with Dr. Johnson and others going over possible items of this kind. The fact of the business is that my purpose was to have something to say to the newspapermen about what I had talked to the President about, as I have learned that coming out time after time with nothing to say does not endear you to the press and is actually a wasted opportunity, as the big mahogany, oval table in the lobby of the White House is the best sounding board in the country. But, as I introduced the subject and made the point that of all men he who had given the word to drop the first atomic bomb had the greatest interest in the beneficent possibilities of the discovery, he was obviously moved and his interest was immediate.

He was behind in his appointments, which is unusual over there, but he listened for what must have been twenty minutes to a series of these things. He said, "I want you to tell that to my little doctor over here because cancer is his special interest." Then I went on to talk about wheat rust and how irradiation can help it, etc., and suggested again a speech along these lines to the country.

I told him what a tremendous impression I thought his speech to the ASNE had made because it was so earnest and he was so obviously talking from knowledge and conviction and that I hoped he would talk to the country that way from time to time.

In the outer office the former Ambassador, Lord Inverchapel, had a familiar-looking little man with him whom he introduced to me as the Duke of Windsor. This makes two kings in the same month and neither of them a very impressive manifestation. The Duke of Windsor (he will always be the Prince of Wales to me) was full of conversation, but just what it amounted to I did not get.

When I opened the door from Matt Connelly's office, the press boys let out a sound that must be something like a mob about to take over, so I went into my plan of talking about peacetime applications, which I doubted would divert them very long and we would soon be in the middle of the political row over the nominations, the Knowland Bill,◄ etc. Not at all. What I had told the President about cobalt as a substitute for radium in cancer treatment made an immediate impression and I could see that I really had a story. In fact, it was such a good story that almost no questions were asked about the nominations and even prodding on the test was brief.

I phoned Senator Hickenlooper at about 9:30 A.M. I said I wanted to see him to make a further report on Sandstone, on results just received and to discuss when and how the report should be made to the full committee. He said he would be glad to see me; he wanted to talk to me also about "this other matter," which I construed to mean the furor about the nominations.

When I saw him at about 12:30, he was extremely cordial. I gave

◄ A bill to require FBI investigations of all future AEC nominees, and also providing that the investigation reports be made available to the Joint Committee.

him the high spots of the report. As to hearings, he wanted to talk to Congressmen Cole and Price after their return before deciding the nature of the report with the full committee. This would be Saturday or Sunday, he thought. He would call me next week. I reminded him that I had made plans for a trip to the West Coast for next week but said that I had twice before deferred the trip and I would do so again, if he thought I should.

"No," he said, "don't do that, you can't make any plans if you have to drop them every time a committee matter comes up; but we won't have any hearing until you return. There was a little criticism, but not much, when you were absent before."

I repeated that while I was reluctant to do so I would certainly follow his advice about deferring the matter. He added that it would take a good deal of discussing anyway to decide when and how to put forward this information, which he recognized as being very hot and touchy, and since I was going to be back at the end of the week, he said, that is the way we would leave it.

Then he began on the matter of the nominations.

He said that what he had to say had nothing to do with personalities whatever, that he was trying to look at this whole thing in the interest of the country and the atomic energy program. (And it is my opinion to a remarkable degree he believes he has done so, and I believe that he seriously means to maintain just that standard.)

On Monday there was a newspaper story in the *Herald Tribune* intimating that the nominations would be forthcoming this week, with certain references to possible terms of office, etc. That same morning a broad-tape was brought to him stating that Charley Ross had announced that the nominations would be sent up this week, though the announcement did not include any reference to the respective terms of the Commissioners.

When he got this word he called the White House for an appointment. This was about nine o'clock in the morning. "Eventually," he said, at eleven o'clock he reached Connelly. Connelly explained that the President had a speech on Cuban independence at noon and the opening ball game that afternoon, that it would have to be on Tuesday morning, and that he, Connelly, would call to fix the exact hour, on Tuesday.

Hickenlooper said that he had in mind discussing with the President the prospects of confirmation of the present Commission. He said he had talked to four quite influential Senators. Three of them had been for my confirmation last year; one had been against. Each of them favored the idea presented by Hickenlooper to them of a one-year term for me; no reference was made to the varying terms for the other Commissioners. He did not name who the four Senators were. The Senator who was in opposition said, "I'll go along on one year, but no more; that is, if the term were for two or three years, nothing doing."

He explained rather elaborately his sole purpose was to avoid a controversy at this important time and to get confirmation through with a minimum of friction and time and thus avoid any political row or injury to the work that controversy about the nominees would produce.

At this point I broke in to say that he need not stress the point that his proposal was not an expression of lack of confidence in me, either personally or for my work; that I felt it necessary to tell him that I had myself thought about this problem a good deal; that I had the same strong desire to see that a controversy was avoided and continuity assured; that I fully realized that for good reasons and some bad reasons I was the focal point of the attack and opposition; that the unwillingness to confirm an appointee of what might be an outgoing President, while it had no proper place in a perfect world, it is evident that the five-year term would inevitably raise the political hackles of a good many Senators; and furthermore my personal desire, for compelling reasons, was for an opportunity to return to private life under honorable conditions; that is, without running out on a responsibility.

I said that I had made this suggestion, after discussions with my colleagues, directly to the President on March 19. I said that it was obvious that the President did not consider this a good idea inasmuch as he had in making the appointments followed the usual custom, providing the longest term for the Commissioner designated as Chairman and in this case with the longest period of Federal service.

Senator Hickenlooper, resuming the thread of the chronology, then said that later Monday reporters came to him with word that Senator Taft, emerging from a meeting of the Republican Policy Committee, had announced the intentions of that committee to "slow down" on passing on all Truman's appointments. Hickenlooper spoke emphatically in saying that at no time had he been consulted on this subject; that if Senator Taft had the Atomic Energy Commission appointments in mind he certainly had not intimated that to him prior to this policy meeting, that he had no knowledge of the policy meeting until it was over. Furthermore he was most emphatic that newspaper stories asserting his visit to the White House was a result of Republican political pressure on him were completely without foundation.

On Tuesday he heard that the White House had handed out the list of nominations, that they were to go up that noon to the Senate when it went into session. He again called the White House and said he wanted to discuss the appointments with the President before they were made. Whereupon he learned that the mimeographed announcements were withdrawn from the press room and shortly thereafter his name was added to the list of the President's callers for the day, for 3:15 P.M. This of course created considerable interest.

At 3:15 he saw the President. The President repeated his previous expressions of personal friendliness and cordiality. Senator Hickenlooper said that he told the President of the importance of avoiding a controversy, and that while he could not guarantee or assure that under any circumstances the nominations of any of the Commissioners could be confirmed, he believed that the very best prospect lay in naming me for the one-year term.

At this point he again digressed to assure me that this was no personal reflection. He went on to say that he knew that three of the men now considered as likely Republican nominees would almost certainly reappoint me at the end of that year if they became President.

He said to the President that his proposal for a one-year term for me had no politics in it whatever, that it was an effort to avoid any injection of any political issue and to permit the nominations to go through his committee on a more or less agreed basis and through the Senate in the same fashion, in the interest of atomic energy and security. He said the President listened to everything he had said, but he did not indicate whether he agreed or disagreed. Hickenlooper made quite a point of this, feeling apparently that the President should have told him what his position was, since, as events indicated, he had at that time firmly made up his mind.

Hickenlooper said he went through the waiting newspapermen saying he had no comment whatever and drove his car back to the Senate. He had hardly gotten into his seat when he heard the presiding officer announce that the nominations of the AEC members had been received from the President. This irked him considerably; apparently immediately after leaving the President's office the President directed the nominations to be sent and the press men had the releases again almost before Hickenlooper had returned to the Senate. This he regarded as a discourtesy to him.

He said he didn't know what would happen; and at no time did he discuss the Knowland Bill and the FBI investigations at all.

I said that my position was obviously a difficult one. I would not have made the proposal if I didn't believe it had merit. For my part, I thought there was enough merit in the idea that the Chairman of this unusual Commission so closely related to military security and military defense at a time of international strain should present his resignation to an incoming President as a matter of course, just as the Secretary of the Army would do, although the statute did provide for fixed terms; that is, there was no legal obligation to transmit a resignation but a good case could be made for the propriety for such a move. But none of these possibilities are open to me now, for I am responsible to the President, and personally very loyal to him; furthermore he is the President of the United States in a tough period, and having heard my suggestion and rejected it, I am bound in every way not to weaken his position by anything I do in that direction.

Hickenlooper had at no time stated or suggested directly or indirectly that I ought to do anything in the interest of avoiding this controversy that would weaken or question the position the President had taken. The whole tone and content of everything he said was on an impersonal and high plane.

APRIL 22, 1948
AT HOME
("AFTER THE RUMMY GAME")

A long talk with Clark Clifford tonight. The first portion about the success of my meeting the press yesterday, after the talk with the President, and how more things like that could happen; and fewer politicians on the President's calling list. Then, how to do something about the President's radio talks: this apropos the wonderful speech he made extempo last Saturday night.

We went over the developments concerning my reappointment, like a couple veterans who had won one campaign and had no intention of losing the next. He quite evidently doesn't share my belief that Hickenlooper is genuinely interested in the atomic energy program. As to my proposal to the President that I be given a one-year term, he said, "The President and I talked that over quite thoroughly. If a Commission is a success, it is because of its Chairman; if it is a failure, it is usually because of the Chairman. If the President (ascribing it to 'health' or anything else) were to give the Chairman of this Commission the shortest term, most of the people in the country would believe it was a mark of loss of confidence by the President in you, and therefore in the Commission he had appointed."

The cobalt radium story certainly went over big; best thing on peacetime applications yet, for unlike the power story it is here and now, and it is something that touches millions of people directly. It is not really "news" either; that is, it has been known for a year; but the setting, and the way I described it, and the fact that we were in the news for other reasons (the test, the nominations) all combined to make it. A release "by the Commission" isn't worth much.

APRIL 23, 1948

Worrying about political interference with our research program, and having Congressmen pass on what kind of research is important—

usually insisting that it be "practical"—I was struck with the following dispatch:

[*This is an excerpt from* Pravda *of March 3, quoting a warning to Soviet scientists issued by Kaftanov, Minister of Higher Education.*]

"The oblivion of a certain part of scientific intelligentsia to the very important principle of the Party nature of science results in deference to bourgeois science, to the acceptance of the idea, foreign to Soviet society and the Soviet man, that science is a non-party and supra-class matter. . . ."

APRIL 24, 1948
AT HOME
(VISIT WITH SENATOR VANDENBERG, APRIL 23)

The Senator hollered out of the depths of his office, as he heard me greet his son and secretary, "Come in, David," and then, with that youthful grin he has, "Well, it is a funny world." "Yes, it is, but it takes a rather broad definition of the word 'funny.' "

He waited for me to begin. I told him much the story I had told Hickenlooper on Wednesday; i.e., my concern about continuity and momentum in the work; the plain fact that the fight, if there was one, would be focused on me; my pride and satisfaction in the progress that had been made, and how bad it would be if there were another period of uncertainty such as a recess appointment after a deliberate delay would produce.

He said he had just come from a visit with Hickenlooper, whose position was summed up when, as he left, he asked Hick. pointblank, "Would you vote to confirm Lilienthal?" The answer was "No, not for a five-year term." Hickenlooper's position is that he simply will not, personally, go through such an experience as he had last year with those long hearings (that *he* went through; I thought that was a strange way of putting it, since I thought it was I who "went through" them). Hickenlooper was sore at the President for the "treatment" he got, referring to the incident Hickenlooper referred to Wednesday. Hickenlooper takes his position very seriously, Vandenberg said, and although it was plain that Vandenberg didn't think Hickenlooper was a ball of fire in ability, he was chairman of the committee and had given it a lot of time.

I said that was true, although unfortunately most of the attention of himself and his staff had been on personnel clearance matters and sleuthing. "Yes," said Vandenberg, grinning, "that is about the level of Congressional intelligence," and with a wink indicating that Hickenlooper fitted at about that level.

Then, laying the groundwork for "mediation" (as I inferred, and I suppose correctly), he said:

"David, I am in your corner. I fought for you last year; nothing I have discovered since would cause me to change my opinion in any way. But I want to say candidly, that if it comes to a point—I hope it won't—where I must choose between a break with you or a break with Hickenlooper, I will stand back of Hickenlooper."

I liked this candor. And as a Presidential possibility (and I am sure he is definitely that), this was both candid and necessary. But what it meant to me was that in Hickenlooper's plans he must figure on Vandenberg as one who will not let me be butchered.

Hickenlooper had an idea, Vandenberg said, that he, Vandenberg, thinks may have merit; what would I think of it, if I could say, offhand? It was that the committee say to the Senate that there had not been time to judge and appraise the work of the Commission during the year since we were definitely installed; that therefore the terms be extended another year, or until spring of next year, at which time the staggered terms would begin. This would avoid a row, provide continuity, etc.

I said the scheme had almost as much objection as the idea of recess appointments; it would be noticed that the Republicans wanted to appoint their own Commission and that therefore the present Commission would have no standing in the interim adequate to carry on their responsibilities.

No, Vandenberg said, it doesn't compare with the recess idea, in that respect.

I said it depended somewhat on how the report on such a bill were made. What grounds would be asserted for not approving the nominations, in the way the law allowed? If it was for a political reason, or to avoid a row (which is another way of saying the same thing), that ought to be said frankly, for the country would be smart enough to see through anything else. Hickenlooper had said to me, time and again, and made quite a point of it, that his suggestion of a one-year term for me was no reflection on me at all, etc., from which I assumed that although he didn't like this and that, by and large he did not feel that we should be thrown out because we weren't doing the job; if he did, if he thought we weren't competent, he should say so, and then there was no excuse for our staying in office beyond our present terms; the names should be withdrawn and new ones proposed and confirmed.

Vandenberg said Hickenlooper had complained about the Commission, and about me. "I tried to pin him down about what it was that he didn't approve. He was pretty vague. He mentioned the cases of 22 scientists who he thought should be fired right away, yet we had fooled around with it for months and months. But as I listened to this

I could see that he had been sitting there in his office, boiling over these little things. So I said, 'Bourke, you'll have to do better than this to make this stick.' "

Then I really opened up. I said that I would have thought a great deal more of Hickenlooper if he had not poured over me all this guff to make me feel that he was for me and for our work; it would have improved my opinion of him as a man if he had told me the things he thought were wrong, so we could respond to such criticism, rather than pretend. If the proposal for a one-year extension were accompanied by a report or statements that the work was inadequate, or even that there had been inadequate time to judge whether we are any good or not, we would insist on being heard, and heard publicly, and that would bring out the fact that not once has Hickenlooper or the Joint Committee consulted or secured the appraisal of the various advisory committees on the quality of our work.

I rattled off the names of these committees, and Vandenberg perked up. He took down the names, and the chairmen. How would it be if I got Hickenlooper to ask these committees for their opinion? Would their letters be good enough to append to a Senate committee report?

I said I felt sure they would; but in any case, they would show that any vague criticism would have to be documented.

I got rather warm under the collar at this point. I said that as to the personnel clearances, Hickenlooper was terrified of Parnell Thomas and his criticism of the Joint Committee, and was prepared to outdo them if necessary; that for my part I knew enough about the institutions of freedom and how they are undermined that I would be God damned if I would start lynching these poor devils just because Hickenlooper or anyone else didn't have the backbone to insist on decency in these things; that we had asked Justice Roberts and a distinguished and conservative board to review these cases, and despite Hickenlooper needling we would not hurry Roberts in any way. I really blazed.

Vandenberg took this with a grin, and, I rather think, with some appreciation. I mean every damn word of it. Vandenberg recalled that it was to prevent a lynching that he had stood up for me last year. "I was worried about Hickenlooper last year; I didn't know until the vote was actually taken where he would be." This is interesting, especially since I, like the absurd creature I am at times, have been building Hickenlooper up wherever I can, urging Ernest Lindley and others to name him for the Collier's Award, etc.

Vandenberg said Hickenlooper was also annoyed that Pike—"He has no use for Pike at all, for some reason"—was given the next longest term, and that Waymack, whom he doesn't care for at all, was renamed.

When I warmed up about Hickenlooper's vague criticisms that he might use as a basis for urging that we not be confirmed, Vandenberg said (a bit alarmed that he had said too much about Hickenlooper's views), "Now get this straight; I should have been more explicit"— meaning, that is a bad line. Hickenlooper would propose to turn in a report that would not reflect on the Commission; just say that there had not been time to judge fully as a basis for permanent appointments.

I said that the country would understand that this meant either that something was wrong (otherwise why not pass on the nominations?) or that the Republicans wanted to name the Commission and this was a way of accomplishing that end. I said again that if the committee proposed to judge the Commission, they had better provide for an opportunity for the Commission to be heard, or we would yell like hell.

Commenting on the President's "treatment" of Hickenlooper, Vandenberg said the President is on thin ice from morning till night because he is surrounded by fellows who have no sense of public relations.

Then he told me how, at the signing of the European Recovery Bill "the President took me aside, gave me one of those Missouri smiles and said, 'Van, I've got some fine news for you.' 'Do you think I can stand it, Mr. President? What is it?' 'I have persuaded a man who is just the very man in the whole country to take the Administrator's post for ERP. Took a lot of persuading but I finally managed it.'" (I thought, of course, that the President had been in consultation with Vandenberg all along on this.) "'Well, who is this paragon?' The President beamed and said, 'Dean Acheson.' I batted my eyes and said, 'Mr. President, I hate to do this, but I must tell you that if you nominate Dean Acheson, I shall be compelled to oppose his confirmation and I know the Senate will reject the nomination. Dean has fine qualities and I am personally fond of him, and there are many posts he could fill with distinction. But throughout the discussion of this measure, the Senate and the country was assured that the Administrator would be a big industrialist. This would be letting them down and it would be rejected.' I felt sorry for him. He looked just completely let down and troubled. Later he appointed Hoffman, of course, and I think Hoffman will do a job. But this shows you how utterly inept they are up there."

I mentioned the Knowland Bill. Said I didn't object to FBI investigations, of course; but AEC nominees should have a legislative investigation; that is, open and no "confidential informants," or it would be a slaughter. I don't know that I made my point, but it was worth trying.

He returned to the proposal for an amendment extending all the terms for about a year. If this were accompanied by a statement that would not reflect upon the Commission, he thought it might be the best way. In the meantime he would try to get letters written to the advisory committees. I should relax and see what comes.

I then went down to see Hickenlooper; talked first about our labor program. At my urging, we decided to make another effort to avoid a drastic program of making strikes illegal and setting up Commission fixed standards. I feared this would take away from management so much that we would, in a brief time, lose contractors who had national business interests, and force us to use engineering service outfits. This might result in a strike and the plan was for us to say to the unions that in our opinion the Carbide Co. had not been arbitrary or oppressive in the position they have taken. I hate this, but it seems the better of the two alternatives. The staff was rather disappointed, and perhaps they may be right, that this will not do the job. But they have worked out the details of a broader scheme and this we are sending to Hickenlooper for the committee's advisement.

Then I said I had talked to Vandenberg at length. I didn't tell him what we talked about, just that we went over it all. Hickenlooper gave me some more of his speech; said he had been pestered by news men all day; he didn't know *what* to do; he had the bill to extend the terms in his desk; had had it there for months; hadn't decided what to do; wanted to do that which would further the interest of atomic energy, etc., etc. Oppenheimer phoned while I was there, to urge that Hickenlooper assemble his committee to meet with the General Advisory Committee. Hickenlooper, right off, said he couldn't get more than three or four members to do this, or it wasn't worth doing.

So here (where?) it stands. I leave tomorrow for the West Coast.

Turned on "Meet the Press" last night, just before it closed, to hear Taft's voice saying he sure was against Lilienthal as Chairman of the Commission, etc., and Doris Fleeson pursuing him, both talking at once. I am glad he comes right out with it.

I called Clark Clifford this morning to report that I had had a talk with Senator Vandenberg and since I am going to be away for a week I wanted him to know about it.

From the talk and a subsequent visit with Hickenlooper I learned that what they are thinking about now is to get an agreement on a bill to extend the terms of all of the Commissioners for one year.

Clifford said, "I hope you did not agree to that! That is a compromise in its worst form, and we shall be unalterably opposed to it. I should think you fellows ought to walk out if they do anything of that kind." For him, he was quite upset at this prospect and apparently angry that Forrestal had accepted a Universal Military Training "compromise" which will eliminate the issue. He said, "Here we have a real issue, and it should not be obstructed by any such stuff!"

I told him that I had not accepted any such idea; that I had suggested to Vandenberg (who is not yet committed to it) that it is only slightly less desirable in terms of the atomic energy program than the proposal for a recess appointment, which is hopelessly bad.

Later I phoned Arthur Vandenberg, Jr., and asked him to tell his father (1) that if the Joint Committee opposes doing anything about these nominations next week in view of my absence, I very much hope the Senator can see to it that public hearings are held in which the Commissioners can express their views; and (2) I reminded him that the Knowland Bill had been reported out without the Commission being given an opportunity to be heard—hence this precaution; and (3) that the proposal for an extension of the terms for a year—after an opportunity to think about it—does seem to me to introduce an element of uncertainty to an undertaking that needs certainty, and that it would be preferable just to reject the nominations. I told him I just wanted the Senator to be clear on that. As a Presidential nominee, I am bound by the decision of the President, and that decision is that the Senate act upon a five-year appointment.

APRIL 27, 1948
SAN FRANCISCO

Breakfast with Paul Smith, the wonder-boy of West Coast journalism, at his house overlooking the harbor and the world, remarkable place right on the brow of Telegraph Hill. Redheaded, "natural," and apparently very friendly and understanding. Talked labor, atomic energy, and all in between.

About the row precipitated by Taft's opposition and the nominations, he told me of being next to Congressman Carroll Reece at a dinner here a year ago when the confirmation fight was on. Reece said to them, "I sat next to J. Edgar Hoover at a dinner recently and he said, upon being asked about Lilienthal's record, 'Of course we have investigated him, as we do all public figures. He is a dangerous man.'"

Smith wrote Hoover a personal letter repeating this and asking if it were true; that is, if he was correctly quoted. Hoover replied in writing that he had not, but that perhaps some things he had said might be tortured into such a statement; that the investigation of Lilienthal did not reveal anything that would support any such statement.

Quite a pretty little story, particularly since it appears that a fight is again in prospect.

Later (May 5): Asked Hoover about this story. He had never talked to Reece about me. Sorry the President hadn't sent my file to the Senate; "It was all favorable."

I have just returned from the Neylan* dinner across the street at the old brown Pacific Union Club. An oval table of 32 men about as conservative and full of achievement as one would expect to find in that number, in a new country that already bows to status.

Met Governor Earl Warren for the first time—talked to him at length over drinks before the dinner. He told me, with none—but *none*— of the politico's unction when doing something he ought to do in any case, that the newspapermen today had asked him what he thought about Taft's position on my confirmation, and he had told them what was "obviously right," that he opposed it. (The headline in the paper I have just opened is "Warren Supports Lilienthal Confirmation.") This was graciously done. (By the way, this is Number Four in that class of Presidential hopefuls who have said this same thing in the past few days—Dewey, Vandenberg, Stassen, and now Warren.)

But what made the most favorable impression upon me of this soft-voiced man was his great interest in TVA and in the problem of water resources in his state. I have a feeling that if he saw that only public multi-purpose projects could meet the state's obvious needs, that is what he would be for. I said it was important to think in large terms in a state that had gained three million people in a few years. As he bade me good night he said again that he would like to talk over the whole problem with me before long. His earnestness in listening to me tonight—he leaned over the table and was intent to a degree—made me feel that here was no ordinary politico, but a sincere and devoted public servant.

Neylan was in good form. He said something as we talked before the dinner that stuck. He had gone to Sacramento when Hiram Johnson came in on a reform ticket. He spent six years there, until he was 32, in fact. Then he had a terrible attack of grippe, and got to thinking about how his family would get along if he lost his health. "It came over me there is nothing so terrible as an impecunious old age," and he left public service determined that such a fate wouldn't be his and his family's. He inquired, "Do you have a competence?" I said no. "How old are the children?" etc. I felt uncomfortable and a kind of fool. "But you hate to give up the power, don't you?"

He introduced me to these 30 bigwigs in a way that I didn't suppose would ever happen to me, frankly, in such portals. "I met Mr. Lilienthal only once, for several hours' talk last summer. I confess I have never before been so impressed with any man as I was by this

* John F. Neylan, a leading lawyer, was a regent of the University of California. The chief object of my trip was to work out a revised arrangement for the university to continue its contractual supervision of Los Alamos.

encounter. In the months that have ensued I have had no reason to change my mind."

The speech itself went quite well; sufficiently informal to fit the occasion, and rather informative, on the whole. The men were friendly, of course, being my hosts, but as Russell, vice president of the Southern Pacific, said, "I got a real picture of David Lilienthal, and not the kind you get from newspaper accounts."

As the party broke up and we left the table and drifted out, the handshake and the squab all over, I spoke to the uniformed waiters and said what a fine meal it was and how I enjoyed it; and then stopped and shook hands and thanked the pale-faced man in charge of the dinner, a minor functionary of the club. I felt the sense of surprise this occasioned, and a look that said: "This isn't done" from the guests. To hell with it; I felt that way and that privilege I still have.

Later (May 6): Baruch phoned this A.M. Some people in from S.F. had criticized him for his "support" of me last year (*his* term), all enthusiastic, from having spent an evening with me, etc.

His advice: Don't get drawn into the political ruckus; be above the battle; say you will serve two days or two years or five years "if you are able"—give yourself an out. After the election, they'll be "imploring you to stay."

Well.

MAY 2, 1948
HOME AGAIN, SUNDAY

Incidents in my West Coast trip that seem, at the moment, most interesting and worthy of remembering:

1. Driving up Laurel Canyon after midnight, with the lights of Hollywood way down there, to the very top of the canyon, and seeing the inside of a windowless concrete blockhouse, that stands behind heavy fences, guarded by ex-marines (who looked startled and came out guns in hand when we—our local chief of security and I—drove up at this weird hour).† Across the road and all around, the homes of Cary Grant, etc.

2. The business of being protected by never less than two security officers wherever I went, not excluding Mike Romanoff's restaurant, and with two cars following me wherever I went.

3. An afternoon, or part of one, at [my cousin] Dee's house on

† The film record of the Eniwetok tests was being processed here. It was then highly classified; hence the heavy security precautions.

Friday afternoon; that would be April 31; with interesting talk and reminiscence and a visit on Appian Way, on the gallery overlooking Hollywood, on a very clear sunny day, with three sky-writers "drawing" RITE TIME and then a clock, with smoke-hands showing that it was 5:25.

4. The ride with Ernest Lawrence down the coast highway, from Berkeley. That drive must be one of the most beautiful experiences in this country. Mountains to one's left, crowding in, the highway cut in their very side; the Pacific far below, on the right, white and full of momentum across the jagged rocks, blue and white-capped away out yonder toward China. The light on the rocks, especially in the early morning, is beyond belief. We stayed Wednesday night at Highland Inn, which I remembered before, and drove about looking at houses and flowers, the houses including Robinson Jeffers', where he wrote most of his poems, such as "Point Lobos," which one can see, of course, as one stands and looks out to sea.

MAY 3, 1948
(TELEPHONE CONVERSATION WITH CLARK CLIFFORD)

I told Clifford I called, upon my return from the West, just to check in.

Clifford: "The President is determined to see this thing through; I have never seen him more determined about anything."

DEL: "Our position here is clear enough. The President has made his decision and we are bound by it."

Clifford: "I trust that no member of the Commission and no employee will say or do anything that could be construed to mean that he favors this compromise, for that would be to let the President down."‡

DEL: "Yes, you can count on that. Our course is clearly just to keep our mouths shut and saw wood, and see what happens."

Clifford: "The President believes strongly in this Commission, and he sees no reason why he should not stick to his position, right on down the line to the end."

DEL: "Well, if you are referring now to a possible veto, I suggest we just wait and face that situation when it presents itself, but not before."

Clifford: "That's right."

‡ On April 30, Hickenlooper had introduced what amounted to a compromise on the reappointments—a bill to extend the terms of the Commissioners by nearly two years, to June 30, 1950.

MAY 7, 1948
AT THE OFFICE (6:10 P.M.)

Our efforts to secure hearings before the Joint Committee on Atomic Energy on matters that are really important are bearing fruit. But in a way that makes the whole basis of the Joint Committee and their big talk about how seriously they bear their responsibilities seem a bit ridiculous. Yesterday, for example, during most of the session only Hickenlooper was present, and at the most only two or three even put their heads into the room. Today was almost as bad. But we are making it clear that many things have been done, and making a record on that.

The rowing about the appointments continues on its merry way. Why it is still news I don't know, but it certainly is. Vandenberg has plunked for a two-year extension; he told Ed Murrow that it is the President who is playing politics. Taft keeps the pot boiling (he started it off) by saying a one-year extension is all he will stand for. McMahon had a press conference today and quotes various scientists as saying the extension idea endangers the project.

If it had not been for Taft's frank avowal (*before* the appointments were made at all) of political reasons for not confirming the Commission, then the two-year extension idea would not be bad, actually, if coupled with a committee report explaining that more time was required before making long-term appointments. And from my personal viewpoint, to have a two-year terminal facility is rather a good thing. But now a row is almost certain.

MAY 9, 1948
AT HOME

After many attempts over the past six weeks I managed to see J. Edgar Hoover on last Wednesday.

Told him that my misgivings about the foreign intelligence on atomic energy, expressed to him a year ago, had been confirmed and more. Furthermore, the connection between domestic intelligence—his job—and foreign intelligence was so close and intimate I didn't see how his work in this country could be effective if foreign intelligence weren't improved.

I was pretty emphatic. Told him that unless things improved—we now have a Dr. Colby working for us who is to check into the caliber of present "sources"—I thought the President ought to consider some drastic change in the setup.

This was partly "for the record"; it was also intended to advise him that he could not rely upon help in his domestic investigation and sabotage protection activities from the foreign intelligence setup as it now is.

He said one thing that I remembered as being interesting and rather remarkable for a large-scale detective. (He insists FBI is not a police agency, but a fact-finding agency. There are some men now in jail or plugged full of tommy gun bullets who might find the distinction unimpressive.)

We had discussed the danger of oversecrecy and lack of criticism— I brought this up. He said that a number of years ago George Norris had made a four-hour speech in the Senate, condemning the Bureau for violation of civil liberties. The information was wrong; "He had been misinformed by a newspaperman he relied upon, a rat," said Hoover with disgust and finality. "But it did us a lot of good, even though it was not justified. For it put us on our guard against violations of civil rights during the last war—and I don't believe anyone would say that any such violations occurred during the whole of the war."

Went to see Clark Clifford yesterday morning about 11:30. Told him I thought from the standpoint of the Commission it would be a mistake for the President to veto the Knowland Bill. (This amends the Atomic Energy Act by directing the FBI to make investigations of men nominated by the President to be members of the Atomic Energy Commission, such reports to be made to the Senate committee.)

My reason was that the veto would be the beginning of a campaign of innuendo against the Commission: that they had something to hide, etc. I pointed to the fact that the President's refusal to let the Thomas Committee see J. Edgar Hoover's letter about Dr. Condon, Director of the Bureau of Standards, was being used most effectively to build up a case against Condon beyond what the letter possibly could. (I gather that the letter does contain criticisms of Condon, but that it reports that there is no evidence of disloyalty.) (Later in the day Condon asked the President to make the letter public, because of the way the refusal was being used to blacken his name.)

I said further to Clark that the President, in my opinion, ought to send a message to the Congress accompanying his signing of the bill or returning it without his signature but not vetoing it. The message should point out how badly the legislation could be abused, and how it would undermine the whole idea of public discussion of appointments, etc.

He broke in to say that "As long as I am here I shall raise my voice against approving or the signing of any such bill. It is part of an attack by the legislative upon the executive branch, a grave violation of the separation of powers," etc. I was surprised and rather taken aback by the vehemence and obvious strong feeling this quite equable fellow showed about this. Later I got more light on this: apparently all the appointments to Hoffman's ECA organization are being virtually directed by Taber or Vandenberg, and all through the Government there is this taking over by Congress of strictly executive functions.

Well, this really disturbed me. I haven't examined the decisions, but I can hardly believe the constitutional question is so clear; in fact, I should think it would be doubtful. But the unwisdom of opposing FBI investigation—as a short-range matter—seems clear. For it puts us in a most difficult position. But perhaps we are there in any event. This makes it possible to plague us, and smear the lot of us, or any other nominees, for FBI reports record any gossip or rumor or vague stories that may be floating around, and yet when contained in such a report, in the public mind they take on real weight.

Then we discussed the Hickenlooper bill to extend the terms of the Commission until June 30, 1950. It was evident that this, too, was headed for a veto! The President plans to speak to various legislative leaders, Clark said, and try to defeat the bill. But I don't see any chance of that, with Vandenberg for it as he has said he is; and this means another veto.

I didn't argue the question here, at all, for the bill hasn't yet passed. But it makes the outlook pretty complicated, I must say. It isn't as if the President had about him men in Congress and in the White House or in the departments who were good at planning such fights, and carrying them through. On the contrary. He goes into these things with very little staff work, and little consultation.

The drop in the President's prestige is one of those remarkable phenomena of politics and public opinion that are hard to fathom or explain—or do much about, apparently. People are restless, dissatisfied, fearful. They want someone who can "take over" and solve everything. Truman is just a man, a likable, courageous, stubborn man, but just a man. So away with him. Well, the substitute will quickly prove to be just another man, and perhaps a pretty sorry one at that.

Clark invited Joe Volpe and myself to go into the White House garden to witness a ceremony—"going to give the President an award." It turned out to be the Collier's Award to Senator Barkley and Congressman Christian Herter, and a surprise award to the President to top it off. After the presentation, before the newsreels, etc., and a felicitious speech by Barkley, Bill Chenery of *Collier's* and Eric Johnston who was chairman of the Award Committee asked me to join them at luncheon. I said I might do it. So I returned to the meeting of the Advisory Committee on Medicine and Biology (discussing effects on humans of fissionable materials, i.e., the Hiroshima casualties, etc.) and went to the Carlton. To my surprise this luncheon consisted of perhaps 40 people, a quite interesting group. And shortly after I got there who should come in but the President and Marshall.

There were speeches all over again, by Herter, a long and amusing one by Barkley, and then Johnston called on previous winners of the award, Bob La Follette, Mike Monroney, Jesse Wolcott. Marshall said a few vague words, Johnston and President Crowell of *Collier's* spoke.

Then I heard Johnston say, "And now we will get what might be called an atom-view; I call upon David Lilienthal." This is a hell of a thing to do to a fellow, and if I had had even a few minutes' warning I might have found a single sentence or two. As it was, I found myself on my feet, addressing the President, half his Cabinet and a rather good audience (Josephine Roche, Cong. Walt Horan, Elmer Davis, etc.). What I tried to say was that to one whose responsibility was the administration of laws the importance of high standards in the legislative branch was very clear, though not often recognized. I paid particular tribute to Barkley. I am rarely caught quite so un-laxed, and its chief importance was that Johnston should have thought it appropriate to call on me.

I was quite impressed with Herter, whom I had never seen before. Tall, patrician-looking, with a kind, thoughtful, rather humble manner. A good selection, I thought.

In the evening Helen (dressed in a beautiful all-white long dress that was very becoming indeed) and I (dressed, if you must know, in a dinner jacket that looks very much as if I had worn it when I graduated from college) went to a dinner party at the Dutch Embassy. This was thoroughly enjoyable. The food was delicious, particularly a soft shell crab course, covered with roasted almonds, and a filet mignon that was out of this world.

The company was good, though the ones I was most interested in talking to I didn't get much chance to visit with, namely Madame van Kleffens, with whom I was smitten when I saw the German art treasures in her company, her quite beautiful sister, and Herschel Johnson, the new Ambassador to Brazil, a stocky, businesslike-looking man. I told him a good Brazilian story, which I had just heard from Dr. Alan Gregg: the one that winds up, "In Brazil we use the printed word for only two things: poetry and politics." Also the story about young Cesare Lattes, a Brazilian scientist we admitted to Berkeley and who helped establish that the cyclotron was producing mesons.

I sat next to Mrs. Houghteling, formerly of Chicago, a daughter of Frederick Delano, Roosevelt's uncle. The Belgian Ambassador, the almost movie-like Baron Silvercruys, sat next to Helen; it was a curious mixture, as Washington parties are so often. Talked at length with a very impressive young woman, a Mrs. "Garry" Norton, he a former Chicago and New York businessman, now I gather in the State Department.

## MAY 14, 1948
### AT HOME

The final package [at Eniwetok] was opened at 2:04 (our time— actually 6:04 "yesterday") this afternoon. I was very worried about it; the hardest and most important. At about 3:15 Gen. McCormack was outside; I was in a meeting and he came in and we proceeded to my little side office. The message was good, very good. We shook hands—a year of strain we had seen through. I told him how wonderful he had been to assign his deputy to get the big kudos. And that's that.

Two and a half hours with Sen. McMahon: what should he do Monday when the committee takes up the extension-of-term bill? This is tough.

## MAY 15, 1948
### AT HOME, SATURDAY NIGHT

Have developed what I trust will be a genuine public relations coup —partly luck, partly skill in these things after years of practice. It is something I have been working on for quite some time, and look forward to the zero hour with relish.

To wit: The Commission will call on the President Monday at 11 A.M. Shortly after we leave, the President will issue a statement: The Atomic Energy Commission has reported the conclusion of three tests, highly satisfactory; the President has approved a plan for steps to take advantage of the new knowledge gained in the tests. The President has commended the cooperation between the military and Commission forces.

This will be the most effective thing, as I thought it over, that could possibly happen for public opinion concerning the effectiveness of the Commission—it is told, not in argument, but in spot news of things accomplished; it ties the President into the Commission's work, so his nomination of the Commission is, by direct inference, based upon its accomplishments, with which he is familiar. Finally, it says that a program, close to the national security, is under way and with the direct inference that politics should not be permitted to interfere with it.

This is one of the biggest of such public relations setups I have had a chance of devising, and I get considerable fun out of doing it.

The amusing thing is how it clicks on timing. One of the reasons I urged the President to push the nominations ahead was because of the chance that the tests would be coming along about the time the nominations were considered. But I didn't, of course, dream of such timing as this: that the very morning that the Senate committee will take up the two-year extension "compromise" bill, the announcement about the completion of the tests will be made.

After working out the details of this with Clifford this morning (and snoozing on the couch in his office when he was called out to see the President for 14 minutes—"Lilienthal sleeps in the White House," it says here) I lunched with Senator McMahon and Rep. Holifield of California, and discussed the Monday hearings. I advised against their demanding hearings; they went over the accomplishments of the Commission, and my strange behavior in saying to people that I didn't want more than a year more of this business.

Then I called Helen and we arranged to meet at the Zoo. We had a wonderful time—I knew no one could reach me by telephone amid the ammonia-scented precincts of rhino house. The place was jammed with kids—by the millions—and I had fun until, in backing out of a parking lot, I locked bumpers with another parked car and had a helluva time getting out without getting a ticket. Then Helen guided me, with great skill, to a place on Audubon Terrace, to see a house that is for sale. And though the house is not modern, the location is beautiful —a stream gurgles through the place, it overlooks Rock Creek Park; it is quite impossible to believe that it is three minutes from Connecticut Avenue. So we talked, Helen quite excited, about how it could be made over, and whether we could possibly afford anything like the $38,000 they ask for it. If my plans would just jell!

MAY 18, 1948
AT HOME (10 P.M.)

This morning is Atomic Page-One Day.

1. The announcement of the Eniwetok tests.

2. The story on the two-year AEC term extension bill being okayed by the Joint Committee.

3. The action of the UN Atomic Energy Commission in terminating what we started so hopefully two years ago: the quest for international control.§

The coincidence of timing of (1) and (3) is rather dramatic, for our purpose in (3) was to put an end to an arms race.

§ The UN Commission voted 9 to 2 to suspend its attempt to reach agreement on an international control plan, and to ask for new instructions from the General Assembly.

Yesterday morning at a few minutes before eleven o'clock, we entered a White House cluttered up with (a) the world champion ice figure skater, a long-necked, lithe maiden, more accustomed to being gawked at than we were; and (b) some kids from the Italian Relief, accompanied by proud and squat mamas and papas; and (c) Margaret O'Brien, the movie child star. The amount of that kind of circusing that goes on is really a crime.

After greetings, the President began at once to say that he had vetoed a bill we were interested in (meaning Knowland's bill requiring FBI investigation of AEC nominees) though he knew that "You fellows would have preferred to have it signed," but he had to call a halt on invasion of the prerogatives of the President.◖ We, wisely, "sat mute."

Then he went on to say, "I am being accused of 'peanut politics' in sending your names up. It is hard to keep politics out of things during an election year, but we can't let it get into foreign policy or this thing. And I haven't paid any attention to politics and neither have you. I didn't inquire into your politics when I appointed you and I'm not interested in them now."

He looked at us rather sternly, his jaw set and then added, in his curiously thin voice, strangely high for so stocky a man, and added, "So this will have to go through to its logical conclusion."

I understood, and I am confident my associates understood, that this meant he would veto the two-year extension bill that even at that moment was being discussed by the Joint Committee in their meeting on the Hill. But again we didn't utter a syllable (our way of doing or not doing things, as a unit—that is, seeming so often to have a common sense of what an occasion calls for, and their willingness to let me set the pace or call the turns, is quite a remarkable thing about this six-man team).*

So the President broke abruptly, turned to me and said, "But you didn't come in here to talk to me about this."

I began with a lame joke: "We noted, Mr. President, that we have followed a great ice figure skater. We are not as attractive, but we do know something about skating on thin ice." To which Lewis [Strauss] added (as if anything was needed to be added to *that*), "And we don't cut so good a figure either."

I said that we wanted to make a complete report on the completion of the tests, and to propose a general plan for the future for his approval; that these were not ordinary weapons, not ordinary ordnance matters at all; that in a real sense they were symbols, and a matter on the highest possible level of policy, about which the Chief Magistrate

◖ Truman's veto of the Knowland Bill was narrowly sustained by the Senate.
* The five Commissioners and Carroll Wilson, the general manager.

for all the people, the civilian Head of State, should be kept informed, and should make the decisions, rather than have them made by us, as technical matters, or by the military as military matters; that whether the subject were whether the weapons should be made at all, or their custody, or handling, this was for the President. Then I asked Bob [Bacher] to go into his act.

He repeated the substance of what he had previously said to the Joint Committee—some color about what a sight it was (the President interjected, "I wanted to go out and see that") and then what the tests indicated as to our weapon position.

The President rubbed his hand over the back of his neck; I knew just how he felt. "Why, that's enough to wipe out a good part of the world. If we could just have Stalin and his boys see one of these things, there wouldn't be any question about another war."

It is far from that simple, of course, but he looked hard at me as he said this, and the weariness in his face, so marked these days, was rather painful to see.

Bob stated that to take advantage of this new information from these "radical" tests, certain things needed to be done. I then formally asked the President for his approval to do them.

He looked very troubled. "Of course, I don't like the idea of such things at all. I gave the order for the others, and I don't want to have to do that again, ever. What I hope you will work hard at is the peaceful things about it, not the destructive. But until we are sure about peace, there's nothing else to do."

I said, "Mr. President, you couldn't have picked a less bloodthirsty six men if you had tried for a long time. But this is a job we had to do, and we have done it."

"That's why I believe in a civilian Commission," he said. "I feel just like you do about it. But we have this to do, and you have made fine progress. As to your plans, that seems to be the thing to do; go right ahead."

I said there were several other things we wanted to report on: an experience that Strauss had, in respect to medical uses; organization matters to be reported by Wilson; and our pressure on fundamental science. So I asked Lewis to tell his story of the progress respecting leukemia and radioactive treatment of cancerous goiter he ran into at Montefiore and Mount Sinai Hospitals in New York. He said he thought the President would get some spiritual satisfaction, as we do, from such stories. He told them well, and simply, but by this time it was 11:20 and the President was beginning to get fidgety, as we could tell sitting right next to him. Then Bill Waymack broke in with a story he ran into at

Ames, Iowa, of radioactive materials being used, in tests, on seven farms of the Iowa State Agricultural School.

The President had done his part, by this time, so I got up, we shook hands and started out.

I stopped as we all stood by the door to say, "Mr. President, when you first spoke to me about this job, I said the law was an administrative monstrosity and I didn't see how five men each with an equal voice could possibly run a huge enterprise of this character. But the wonderful part is that we get along so well together, and enjoy and respect each other so much, that my worries on that score have disappeared and I just want to tell you how well that part, that human part, is working out."

He replied, "I told you that poor men couldn't make a good law succeed, and that good men could make even a poor law succeed. I appointed good men."

With 15 minutes' preparation I went over to the Labor Department to state the Commission's views on the labor dispute at Oak Ridge—the maintenance men engaged in the Laboratory at X-10—to the President's Board of Inquiry. On one side of the big table were the representatives of the Carbide Co., a very hard-boiled and rather antediluvian chemical corporation (as to their ideas of labor policy); on my right were the spokesmen for the unions, most of them from the local. Opposite me, at the far side of the room sat the President's Board: my old friend John Lord O'Brian; Dean Balderston, of Wharton School; and a young, fine-looking fellow, the third member, Stanley F. Teele, associate dean, Harvard Graduate School of Business.

I read from a statement that had been agreed to by the Commissioners, a rather dull and overcarefully phrased thing. Then I was asked a question that gave me a chance to amplify extempore. With my long record as a pro-union man, and the fine labor record of TVA, it wasn't easy to say flatly and bluntly that we stood behind the contractor, but looking at our whole responsibility that seemed the only thing we could do.

Scott, local union spokesman, made a speech, in the form of a question: "What would the little people at the plant think of the Commission that was supposed to be for all the people banding together with this powerful corporation that didn't need any help, they could get along all right because it was powerful," etc.?

I told him I had lived in the Tennessee Valley a long time and hadn't met any "little" people—they were just people, and fine people. We weren't banding with anyone. This was *our* contractor.

What struck me, as I left the hearing, was rather pleased surprise that I hadn't felt inclined to soften the blow, or be on both sides, but faced up to an unpleasant duty, when the test came, despite the fact that this particular company's labor policies, or rather, the *way* they approach human relations seems so gauche, tactless, and even worse.

MAY 19, 1948
NEW YORK CITY

Luncheon with Mr. Baruch (he now calls me "m'boy" and "David," but he seems much too much of a "figure" for me to respond with Barney) at his apartment. Almost two hours.

He warns me *not* to talk to anyone about my worries about the future, and particularly not to so much as hint that I will resign or quit over any particular circumstances that may lie ahead.

"You are in a wonderful position. There is nothing else quite like it in the world. In two years you will probably have made great progress in peacetime applications—these things sometimes go very rapidly once the ground has been broken—and then they will plead with you to stay on. Then you can have your pick of almost anything there is, and will make all the money you will ever need, if at that time you feel you want to leave this work. But you may find at that time that you don't want to allow the fruit to be picked by someone else, and that you will stay on no matter what. So just don't let them make a political football out of you; and that you can help prevent by not saying anything about what you will do if this or that is or isn't done about these appointments. They can't get along without you now; you are the one who has the competence and the experience and they know it." (By "they" he implied the Joint Committee.)

I told him that I really would have a financial problem, because the value of our savings has declined so, and the value of my insurance likewise in the event I die soon.

"Don't even think about those things for the next two years. You are in the best, most strategic place in the world, and if I were you I would starve before I would give it up right now. And when the time comes for you to go into private business, there will be no trouble—let me make a deal for you. The important thing is that you show no anxiety or pique or irritation over what is going on now, maintain your dignity and go ahead with your work.

"The people of the country now have gained confidence in you, in your competence and your wisdom. Just keep that and your personal problems will not amount to anything. I have confidence in you, and I feel rather responsible for you, so you must remember that." (This was half-joking.)

He asked me no questions of the sort he usually does, questions that showed a concern that we are letting something slip. He seemed greatly pleased by my report that things were going so well, in weapons and other things. "What you have done is to create the balance for peace at a terrible time."

What could he do? Should he talk to the President? I thought so, with the thought that it might keep the President from going way out on a limb and saying publicly that he would veto the two-year extension bill, and then he might have to do it. I told him how terrible it would be for the work if Congress left without either extending the terms *or* confirming, i.e., recess appointments. He got this at once.

He was in high spirits and sparkling health.

I felt grateful to the old boy, for he restored my perspective to a remarkable degree. I said a visit with him was like going up on a hillside where one could see more clearly the relation of one thing to another, after having been down in the valley too long. I meant just that.

Tonight I dine with Henry Luce. Tomorrow two speeches, behind closed doors—the Calvin Bullock Forum, a Wall Street thing, and at quite a private dinner at the Council on Foreign Relations. Friday breakfast with Bishop Oxnam, and later a session with Rafferty and others of the Carbide & Carbon Chemical Corporation. Quite some variety.

(LATER: 10:30 P.M.)

The dinner with Henry Luce was quite something. I broached my idea of a trip around the world—as a journalistic idea—the purpose of which would be to report on the effect of the rapid coming of the machine upon life—the real inner life—of the peoples of such nations as India, China, Latin America, etc. This he caught in three sentences. "It is a great journalistic idea," he said, banging the table.

I introduced the subject—I had written that I had something on my mind—by referring to TVA. How I had seen a region part of which had had no effect of science and the machine whatever, and bang, in ten years it was in the middle of it. This had given me a chance to observe the effect on people, on the spirit of men, on the richness of life. I observed that what is essentially an American thing—rapid industrialization—is the important fact in many parts of the globe where it represents a sudden change.

I had two interests: one, to see what was actually happening as a result of the spread of the machine, the American machine; and two, to try to counteract the idea, harmful to this country, that the machine is all there is to the American idea, when in fact that is but the surface, and the substance is an idea of which the machine is only a peripheral manifestation. "Ye must be born of the spirit" is a phrase of Jesus, somewhere, that somehow seemed relevant.

This, to use his own expression, set him off. He got quite excited, and at times incoherently so. He told me of his boyhood days in China, seeing Chungking when it was a country backwoods; then, later, as an adult, when it was strung with electric lights. What effect does this miracle of lights have on the people? was the question he asked. His conclusion was that it was accepted at once, and had very little effect.

He told me of his plans for a change in the magazine *Fortune*. It fit beautifully into the thing I have tried to formulate about our "business culture."

Then he returned to the idea of my trip; I had said I had suggested it when it looked as if I would not be in the atomic energy business much longer, and thought of this as a fine way of spending the interval between a long stretch of public service and going into business. Now it didn't seem that I would be free for that for a while. He said, "The important thing about your idea is that the man who makes the trip must have a special qualification for it; he must be able to sense these things. It all depends upon who does it. You are the only one who has had just that experience, so it looks as if it would have to wait for five years."

Then he rared back, literally, and said, "This would make a tremendous thing to do to recover our lost ground in Asia. The trustee for the world of this new scientific marvel, atomic energy, the builder of TVA, goes to India, Burma, and China. He is accompanied by half a dozen news correspondents from this country, and we send along our best man—I know just who he would be right now. You visit Hangkow, etc., and at each place you visit the university, talk to the students. You are the exponent of the third of Sun Yat-sen's three points—for TVA is the American example of that. The Chinese recover face—the atom chief comes across the sea to sit down and talk with them. Marshall flubbed China and Asia; this is a bold way to recover that. It would be a world sensation, and do great good."

Well, it went on like this. Two months would do it, two months taken off of atomic energy, and well spent. He said he couldn't talk to Marshall or Lovett about it, because he had been panning them so about Asia. I said: no, I wouldn't talk to them about it myself; would look as if I were promoting myself for something. He asked: Could he speak to Charlie Merz of the *Times* about it? I said I didn't see why not.

MAY 20, 1948
ABOARD AMERICAN AIRLINER, HEADING HOME (3:45 P.M.)

If the *variety* of things that happen to me in a 36- or 48-hour period happened to most people in as many months, they would say they had a rather exciting and varied life.

*Item:* At 7:30 A.M., a bishop (Oxnam), in fact, *the* Bishop of Protestantism, for breakfast in my room, to talk about the moral problems of mass weapons, and what the faiths could do to clarify those moral issues that I face personally, and that we as a nation face.

*Item:* At 10 A.M. to a house (filled with Renoirs and such) on Beekman Place on the East River, supporting its own pathetic little tree —a tree being the supreme luxury of Manhattan Island, by a special irony (since a tree almost the poorest man in a small town may have for his own).

Here I visited, to his obvious pride and pleasure, with old Albert Lasker, who made millions and millions inducing the American people to buy this and that kind of soap and cigarette. And his wife, much younger, perhaps 45, attractive and smart, and greatly worried about the old boy's heart, a recent development.

He got "worked up," telling me of his idea about what we should do to let the people know about the beneficial applications of atomic energy, and his wife warned him. He brought out of his wallet a couple of slips of paper, and read from them: his doctor's orders. "Number 6. *No* conferences." But this he felt so strongly about that he was violating instructions. "But, dear, you need not talk so fast," his wife said, looking at him anxiously, as indeed I did, not wanting to have the old boy keel over right before my eyes, and his face getting ruddy and his eyes glowing. You could see why he had been such a salesman, even this white-haired old boy, for as he warmed up, it was like an old fire horse.

He was present at the Council on Foreign Relations meeting last night, and drove home with Wild Bill Donovan. "You know Donovan. He's no sentimentalist. Rather hard, as a matter of fact, rather hard. But you would have been quite surprised to hear what he said about you. There are lots of men who are brilliant, lots of men who have great brains. But *purpose,* purpose, that is what you have in a rare way, and it moved Donovan to say some rather remarkable things. Purpose, that you either have or you haven't. Brains you can be born with, and brains you can develop. But purpose is something that a man makes, builds himself." (As he said these, and other things, he acted as if I wasn't there at all.)

He reminded me of the long evening at the Gunther party at the Century Club last winter. "A terrible waste of time." Could he be blunt?

Well, he told me I go about this the wrong way. "Don't ask people to do something for you; tell them of the interesting things that are important to them, and they will know what to do about it. You go around making a speech here and a speech there, but they will wear you out and is just piddling. Get 200 or 300 together—like the National Health Conference recently held in Washington, sponsored by the Security Agency. Needs someone from the outside to organize this, and at private expense, etc."

I said this was the way to do it. But people get enthusiastic about such an idea, make a move or two, and then the continuous momentum is lacking and it falls. I have made up my mind that I am not going to encourage starting anything of the kind unless there is a good prospect it will be continued—it requires not a sudden big push, but continuity. All this talk of private financing, and of the public-spirited citizens like Cowles, or Roy Larsen or Cass Canfield, who, like William Jennings Bryan's "volunteers," will rise like the growing corn—to hell with that.

Frankly, I think nothing will come of it.

*Item:* To the offices of the Carbide & Carbon Corporation, to see Rafferty, one of the geniuses of the modern chemical industry, synthetics, plastics, bakelite, synthetic rubber, etc. A long-headed man, sitting behind an ugly carved desk, most of the fire that made the company quite obviously burned out of him, but now and then a glow fanned into flame, for a moment, by something I said or that we discussed.

You could see that he hardly believed what he had recently been told: that this New Dealer had "told off" labor to its face, and before the company (this is the Oak Ridge dispute, and the hearing before the O'Brian Board of Inquiry last Monday), but I told him again that what we wanted was that they should feel that these plants were theirs, and that they should put their best brains to work improving the processes, making them simple, cheaper. I told him that the notion that 235 was a bad second was disproved by the tests. Then he called in Felbeck, a clumsy man about human relations, but a great chemical engineer and development man; Winans, their labor relations man, a fuddy-duddy given to details, and wrapped up like a mummy in the traditions of an earlier day of labor relations.

Rafferty's comments about labor were really priceless. A movie scenario; a burlesque or caricature. He told me how they began the plant at "ho-m-me," he said, in a sentimental way, at Charleston, W.Va. No unions at all, never had, didn't have them now. Pickering—heavy-jowled, looks like a frustrated Shakespearean actor, who is their "most effective labor relations man"—got his start at Charleston. Came to Rafferty with an idea of lending "the boys"—the workmen—money when they needed it. And what a fine idea this turned out to be. And picnic grounds. And then, so help me God, Rafferty folded his hands

before his face and said, "Just one big family." Fact. So corny that in a
script it would come out, bang.

But in this particular dispute, Carbide, the contractor, is "our"
son-of-a-bitch, to quote the old story. They will try to break the strike,
if it happens, and the way they will do it will grind my soul, and
threaten my reputation as a labor man.

*Item:* Lunch, all by myself (and more's the pity), at a French
restaurant I just wandered into on 55th Street, Le Gourmet. But *French*
French. Like a movie short, the whole thing. And after a wonderful
Martini (at lunch, mind you), a delicious lobster bisque, a pork chop
with a long French name, and *two* pieces of pastry, all with a huge
goblet of red wine—I was quite mellow and to hell with bishops, advertising giants, *and* chemical engineers.

MAY 23, 1948
AT HOME, SUNDAY

To the office this morning, Sunday, 9:45 till 12:45, to open and
attend first meeting of a panel on a new military use of the atom
[radioactive materials], its potentialities, possible defenses, methods of
detail. When this was first mentioned months ago, it hit me in the pit of
the stomach so hard that I was almost sick; ordered the memorandum
by which I was to direct the beginning of the preliminary study returned
for redrafting to make it somewhat more endurable. But that was months
ago, perhaps nine or ten. This is something we must find out about, get
the facts, and face it. This morning that sick feeling hit me only once,
when one of the technical men, a physician, said in the most dry and
toneless way, "The problem divides itself into a number of questions:
What do we want to do to people, (a) kill them, (b) etc.?"

The panel includes some outstanding men: E. O. Lawrence, Alfred
Loomis, Dr. Noyes (who is chairman), Dr. McLean. One of the subjects
that came up concerned one of my special interests: the bad effect, from
every point of view, of super-scare public statements, of which there is
a wonderful example in the current *Harper's Magazine*. Dr. McLean,
quoting from this article, said that the statements in the article were
wrong "by a factor ranging from 1,000 to a million."

I commented that we are, by these things, developing a panic
possibility beyond anything the Russians could produce if they worked
ever so hard. And people who are (a) less well informed, (b) regard
human life as expendable in a way we do not, and (c) more stolid by
nature would have a considerable advantage over us, on the psychological side of warfare. I insisted in a big, belligerent voice that the military
give us the facts about biological warfare.

Dr. McLean told me afterward that though he is on a consulting panel for the Chemical Corps (which has jurisdiction, in part at least, in this field) he has been able to get only a little information after trying to get it for a year. But I made clear that I would insist that we have some general measurements, comparative in nature. I suspect (and Dr. McLean volunteered a confirmation of these suspicions) that the Chemical Corps is stimulating the rash of scare articles along this line to support its claim for appropriation support.

Ernest Lawrence talked to me on our Western trip about his recently developed friendship with Col. McCormick, the Chicago *Tribune* Bertie, and his wife. He rarely goes through Chicago without being a guest at their country place. Ernest said to me today that he had talked to McCormick about my approval of the idea that he, McCormick, make a trip to see part of the Commission's activities at Hanford, Los Alamos, etc. Ernest recommends (that means he more or less assured McCormick he would "deliver") that I plan to take the trip with McCormick. I said I would write him, asking about making arrangements. And perhaps visiting with him beforehand to describe the work, in general. But the trip seems carrying things a bit too far!

After the Council on Foreign Relations speech in New York Thursday night, Cass Canfield, chairman of Harper's, asked to see me, and we went to the Savoy for a drink. He urged me strongly to do a book [on atomic energy]; if I found it was quite out of the question, then he said we ought to consider my doing it with some professional writer, and said he felt sure Stuart Chase would be interested.

Talked to Helen about this at some length, as we drove in to a party Mark and Biddy Childs gave last night. Decided I would try to develop an outline of chapter headings sometime before going on our vacation this summer. It is important to do the book if I can possibly make it. The TVA book was the most important single thing I did for TVA; or for me, for that matter.

MAY 25, 1948
AT HOME (EVENING)

Spent an hour and a half with the Director of the Budget, Jim Webb. He is "greatly disturbed" by the way in which the armament program "has run away." The President made his speech on March 17, pointing out the danger to the country, and how we propose to meet it. But every branch of the services began an all-out drive for appropriations that totaled 25 billion a year. Even the Maritime Commission wanted to recondition every vessel. And the speeches and pressures, he said, mentioning Symington and General Kenney, to scare the country into believing that anyone who wouldn't go along with these plans would be responsible for a catastrophe. (Hanson Baldwin told me this morning that he is convinced that the crisis of last spring—the Berlin business—was a wholly Washington crisis.)†

Webb was really steamed up. He had just come from a meeting at the White House between the President and the Chiefs of Staff—Bradley, Adm. Denfeld and Gen. Vandenberg. "Forrestal has lost control completely. The President gave directions to the services, but it turns out that Forrestal is so bulldozed that he wouldn't even distribute the President's directions to the services. Instead of Forrestal calling the Chiefs in and demanding that they indoctrinate the lower echelons, the President today had to deal directly with them, and gave them letters which contain the severest reprimand I have ever seen delivered, and in writing. It is a sad situation, and very disturbing."

You could see that he was in great distress. And no wonder. He said, "With that kind of situation, the idea of turning over custody of atomic bombs to these competing, jealous, insubordinate services, fighting for position with each other, is a terrible prospect."

Steve White of the *Herald Tribune* was in today. Banged away at me for the way in which the area of know-nothingness about atomic energy activities is spreading. He asked me to confirm the report he had, quite evidently from some reliable source, that conferences were going on between the military and the Commission concerning the custody of weapons. Was it true or not true?

I knew that if I confirmed it the military would raise Ned, and no purpose would be served by opening the door, which would then have to be closed. So I said, "No comment." He said he believed the *Herald Tribune* would have a strong editorial condemning the idea that so important a matter of public policy should be determined by a handful of men, without public discussion. I agree with him. But how are we going to get out of this circle of vetoes?

MAY 29, 1948
AT THE STATE DEPT. BLDG.

Talking about South Africa. Strange things: The United States is, of course, the place where world's gold price is determined, and quantity of production. And gold determines the life of South Africa. Gold and uranium are physically inseparable. Now old Smuts has just been de-

† This may refer to the spring of 1948, not 1947. At this time, disagreements over Berlin between the Western powers and Russia were building up—but the crisis that led to the airlift was not reached until late June.

feated in an election, by the Nationalists, anti-British, highly nationalistic crowd. Now what? Lovett presiding.

JUNE 2, 1948
AT HOME

My speech at the "High School Graduation for All America" program went fairly well last night, at Gettysburg. Beautiful drive over.

Worked today on the University of Virginia commencement address.
Finally decided against two outlines I had prepared, and wrote half or
more of another version, which went quite well, in a semi-ironic mood
I rarely try any more.

Tomorrow I face the AFL Executive Council on the Oak Ridge
business. Revised a proposed statement for the President to send to
Congress. This took a good deal of "doing," for it is a difficult issue at
a difficult time, and it is possible he may not go along.

There is a good deal of labor criticism of me since the Board
of Inquiry meeting, when I made it clear I was definitely supporting
the company. But it is one of those issues where, once you have
crossed the river, there can be and should be no looking back over
one's shoulder. I have some trouble with our own labor staff people on
this score—a bad business.

Appropriation hearings concluded yesterday afternoon. Wigglesworth gave me a chance for a moral victory; that is, a victory over
myself. He was as petty and sarcastic as anything I have run into for
quite a time, concluding the hearing with "some questions I would
like to ask Mr. Lilienthal." I met them with "speeches" for the record
that he didn't like one bit, but which hushed the hearing room down,
and the other members listened intently while Wigglesworth tried to
stop me—unsuccessfully.

But the important thing was that neither at the time nor afterward—the latter being my usual trouble—was I angry or resentful or
"burning up." If I could just take that attitude about Congress and
that miserable side of this business, I could be much more effective—
and happier.

Nancy was home over the Memorial Day weekend, and so was
David, who left yesterday for New York. Mr. Baruch just phoned to say
that David and his friend had arrived at his apartment, and "They are
not going hungry, and tonight they go to *Finian's Rainbow*. And what
a fine boy, a fine boy; tell his mother she has a fine son."

Long talk with Nancy as we walked back and forth on the lane
that leads to the highway. Her job with *Labor and Nation* folds sometime in June; six months' experience it was, and rather good for

the purpose, but she isn't sorry that it will be over, I gather, for the job leads nowhere and the experience from now on will be repetitive. Then what? I asked her what it was she wanted to do most in the world. To work somewhere in organized labor. "Well," I asked, "is this just something that appeals to you, or do you feel rather strongly about it, for it is a difficult course, particularly for one who isn't born and brought up in a union or 'working' family, and on top of that, being a woman in union circles is no cinch."

She was very quiet about it, as is her wont, but she looked at me firmly and intently and said, "Maybe it's idealistic, but it is something I am quite sure about. That is what I want to do more than anything."

I told her that so far as I was concerned, that was all there was to be said; the only things to discuss now are how best can this ambition be furthered. After all, I had the same kind of ambition, went to law school for the express purpose of becoming a labor lawyer, and got into Don Richberg's law office for that reason. So I was hardly in a position to try to dissuade her on grounds other than workability of the idea. And as for "idealism," I believed in that, and thought there wasn't enough of it in the world.

I urged her to get over the idea that she could not let me try to help her, to the extent of asking friends of mine to talk to her about her hopes. She has been very extreme about this. I think she will look at that differently now. She thinks perhaps a labor newspaper might be something she could do and would enjoy. I suggested a number of people to talk to: Morris Cooke, Clint Golden, Isador Lubin.

She looks terribly young, though she is now 23½—at which age I was beginning law practice and about to be married.

Her weakness is lack of aggressiveness, particularly "in person." She realizes this, and tries hard to do something about it, but it is so hard for her, talking to people who are new or older. Poor kid. Her strength is a very orderly mind, very logical and intelligent, a good talent for writing and editing, a lovely, sweet, balanced temperament, nice appearance, an excellent voice.

She seems much too tired. New York has been a strain on her, and she doesn't care for it. I urged her to spend August with us at Martha's Vineyard.

JUNE 3, 1948
AT HOME

The election at Oak Ridge was overwhelmingly against the company.‡

‡ The union voted to authorize a strike on 24 hours' notice.

From eleven until one today I was before the Executive Council of the AFL. A long table, with hard, firm-looking men lined along it, and in chairs through a large room. Old fuddy-duddy Bill Green (who was 20 minutes late, while I waited) presiding, and looking very puzzled.

I put it to them with everything I had: I was responsible to 145 million people of this country to keep ahead in atomic development and I was determined to back and keep those industrial contractors who could do just that, come what may. I didn't run away from any questions, and when George Googe, with whom I had gotten along so well in TVA, put the really mean one to me, I stood up to reply, with my dander slightly up. The question, of course, was: "If the men strike, will you evict them from Oak Ridge and will you back the company when they bring in men from other plants to keep the plant going?"

I said, "George, those plants must be operated, and whatever it takes to do it, that's what we must do."

It was a grueling experience. I never thought I would live to see the day. But it is a part of a hard, mean, but fascinating job.

And in the afternoon—variety is the word for the atom—we spent three hours with the Industrial Advisory Group. The least effective Advisory Group we have.

It is raining hard, and remains cool—thank goodness. David is probably on the high seas by now, en route to England. Bless him.


JUNE 5, 1948
AT THE DESK (6:35 P.M.)


Pretty tough going. The General Advisory Committee has just told us how greatly we have disappointed their expectations. This they attribute to the form of our organization, with our emphasis on staff officers at Washington (rather than line executives, as they want) and the decentralization we have put into effect, with regional officers given broad functions.

The fact that very successful organizations operate the way we have set things up, as well as the way they recommend, does not faze them. All the complaints about slowness of decision, too little delegation of decision, and all the rest of the kind of things you always hear about any organization were brought in.

We certainly have a wealth of advisers and watchdogs. What we need is some help in getting able men, and able men can run *any* kind of organization.

I feel pretty *low*, frankly, but I will pull out of it.

JUNE 9, 1948
AT HOME

The brickbats have really been flying. Got back this morning from the Harvard Law School reunion to find a violent Appropriation Committee report (as expected) with a whale of a cut in our administrative expenses and a great bawling out about "general extravagances" and so forth. Rot. Also to find myself "no longer the worker's friend" and denounced by resolution of the employees in the Oak Ridge strike situation, against our confirmation, etc. This is indeed something new for me. After the beating we took from the General Advisory Committee plus this, and Carroll dead on his feet with fatigue, I ought to be low, particularly since I have had two nights in succession traveling on the sleeper. But though the Oak Ridge thing hurts quite a bit, I don't seem to be too upset.

The Law School reunion was a surprise, a pleasant surprise. I had about given up the idea. Little afraid of seeing how much these men I knew when they were 23 or so had changed. And I with them. But Helen rather insisted on it. And I don't know when I have enjoyed an evening so much.

I found that 25 years had not changed things as much as I had supposed. This was, of course, a group of rather successful men, some of them quite so, and that makes a difference.

When I was in Law School, I was on the shy side, and though I did quite well in the annual examination, I said very little, and I doubt if I ever volunteered, as the more aggressive men did, nor was I a teacher's favorite, to be called on when things were lagging. My respect for the Law School and its prestige is simply enormous, a kind of religious awe. So it meant more to me than I can quite explain to be singled out of the entire class. There were to be no speeches from the class, Jim Nicely, our president, said, but of course they wanted to hear from the most distinguished member of the class, and one of the great men of the country. At this point I realized I had a speech to make, and began pulling my thoughts together. Then he went on to say that he had wondered how to introduce Dave and had finally hit upon a quotation from Montaigne, which he then read, a long passage, describing a man such as I doubt ever did live, such redoubtable talents and character did he have, but certainly they had no more relation to me than to Mickey Mouse.

But of course it was very impressive, and to have the class rise and applaud for a long time, etc., meant more than it has on the many other occasions when nice, glowing things have been said. And the reason goes back to the humble position I always felt I had in the class, despite my marks in the second and third years. And to ice the cake, Dean Griswold later said, "David Lilienthal, who for my money is the finest public servant of our generation, and I say this who am no New Dealer, in fact I was in Washington under the Administration of Herbert Hoover."

The high point of the evening, on the side of conviviality (which was pleasant and not overdone on the alcoholic side), was Jerry Smith. He is the only son of a distinguished wealthy family, and a character right out of *The Late George Apley*. He stutters, in an aristocratic, good-humored, unself-conscious way, and his account of how "at the age of 44¾, and in my condition, I was d-d-drafted" was side-splitting. His tale made *Private Hargrove* seem pale by comparison.

The following is full text of the AFL resolution adopted at mass meeting Tuesday, June 8:

Whereas the workers of X-10 (Oak Ridge National Laboratory) do hereby go on record as opposing David Lilienthal for any reconfirmation as Chairman of the AEC because of his open support to a vicious contractor in our lengthy labor dispute. Lilienthal's statement that if the X-10 workers strike the Commission would order Carbide to operate the Laboratory shows clearly that he is no longer the worker's friend. We further condemn him for his implied strike-breaking tactics. Therefore be it resolved that we respectfully request our various international unions and the public to oppose Mr. Lilienthal and his fellow Commissioners' reconfirmation to the Atomic Energy Commission as being too small in stature to assume and carry out the vast responsibilities necessary to protect our national interest and welfare.

JUNE 16, 1948

IN THE OFFICE, WEDNESDAY (8 P.M.)

The last days—I fondly hope—of the 80th Congress are drawing near. Helen is now in the Senate gallery, in the hope that at tonight's session there will be some kind of decision about the future of the Commission.

Senator Lucas, the Minority Whip, phoned this noon. He said he had been asked to agree upon a limitation of debate on the bill to extend the Commissioners' terms for two years, and was disposed to say to hell with it: bring the bill out and vote on it when they got ready. He said that when the people of the country realized what the Republicans had been up to, later in the summer, kicking atomic energy around, they would be aroused about it, and that it would prove a very important political issue. The question he wanted to put to me, though, was this: Would recess appointments injure the defense of the country?

I told him the members of the Commission had thought about this whole situation a good deal, and only yesterday had reached the conclusion that of all the possible alternatives the very worst would be recess appointments; that this would result in a deterioration of the enterprise that would be very difficult to take; that this would without doubt seriously affect the security of the country.

This sobered him a great deal, and he said, "That was what I wanted to know about."

I went on to say that whether the recess appointments came because the Congress had failed to act on the nominations, or because the President vetoed the extension bill after it was too late for anything else to be done, i.e., after the adjournment of Congress, the result of injury would be the same.

I later learned, from Hickenlooper, that Lucas and the Democratic Policy Committee had declined to agree on a time limitation; but Lucas apparently was not going to make a terrific and long fight, for he told his office (Hollis informed me) to throw away the hour-long rough speech and substitute about ten minutes.

About midnight last night McMahon called me. He was in the Senate cloakroom. Vandenberg had approached him a few minutes earlier and asked him to agree to an hour's total time on the extension-of-term bill. He had declined, but said they would consider a five-hour limit. This was unsatisfactory to Taft. What would I think? I told him that recess appointments would be very bad indeed, as I am sure he knew, having seen this project go through a period of uncertainty before. I referred also to the dangers in a Presidential veto, should the bill be passed. He said he recognized the situation, that a pistol was at their heads, and that he would not recommend Presidential veto himself.

What will happen is still quite uncertain.

I was greatly angered this morning, to the point of blowing my top for the first time, really, for quite a while. The goadings of the Joint Committee and their staff, and a feeling that they were all part of a pattern of driving us to distraction had me down. A letter had been received demanding the firing of our new Director of Personnel, for no damn good reason. This invasion of our responsibility, if continued, would make it impossible to get good men or keep them, and would drain our energies to the point where failure of our administration and discredit to us all would be certain.

Then there was a "demand" for a copy of a preliminary draft

report by the Industrial Advisory Committee, and this made me mad, as it would be impossible to have advisory groups if their working papers were being pawed over. And this afternoon came another letter about our security organization.

Losing my composure and filled with disgust about all this was not surprising, perhaps. But fortunately I did nothing irrevocable about it; indeed, before it was all over I phoned Hickenlooper to say we recognized that there were deficiencies, and were trying to correct them. He was not sharp at all (Volpe having told him I was about ready to throw the whole thing in their face may have helped), and I arranged to see him Saturday and let him talk himself out—which will require considerable time.

The commencement speech at Charlottesville was a good kind of experience. The academic procession down the quadrangle and into the amphitheater was really a beautiful thing, and marching out, at the head of the procession with President Darden, was a rather moving thing. The speech itself went quite well, better than I could have expected. The student audience, usually very restless at such times, was remarkably attentive. The irony I had developed into the speech, the effect of which was saved by Helen's criticism of the heavy way I had planned to give it, was quite effective. I have noted editorials about the speech in the *New York Times* and the Washington *News* and the *Star,* and rather good coverage. And the *New York Times Magazine* plans to use it in the issue of Sunday a week. So I guess it was worth the trouble and fussing that went into it.

Helen and I spent the weekend with the Lewis Strausses at their farm near Culpeper. It was very pleasant indeed, with a chance to swim, and good company. Their son and brand-new and lovely daughter-in-law added considerably to the enjoyment—a very attractive pair, quick of mind and good fun.

Sunday morning I was called to the phone to be told that early that morning, after 50 hours of continuous sessions, the Oak Ridge labor trouble had been settled and an agreement reached. This was a great relief.

We got back from Charlottesville at 2 A.M., and I had to get up early Tuesday morning (the 15th) to finish preparation for appearance before the Senate Appropriations Committee, in our effort to restore the reductions made by the House. It was an open hearing, and went quite well. Senator McKellar, looking a thousand years old, came in, looked very glum as I testified, and before long left without uttering a sound.

I had dictated the statement before leaving Friday, and it had some revisions by staff. But when I saw the state of things in the committee,

I concluded that to read the statement—a departure from my usual practice but one I thought necessary under the circumstances—would be wrong, so I read a bit, then extemporized and got through without a great deal of apparent difficulty with the committee—though time will tell.§

I had taken the precaution of calling on Senator Bridges before the meeting, and was again struck by his apparent respect, and certainly his clear concern about the atomic energy work. Busy as he is, he appeared at the subcommittee hearing and asked "friendly" questions; i.e., questions intended to elicit good replies for the record. I believe we will be relieved of the worst part of the House's action, though of course it may not stick in conference at the last minute.

The TVA won an important victory, though again it may not hold, when the New Johnsonville steam plant, which has become a national issue of public and private power, was put back into the appropriation measure late last night by vote of the Senate.

JUNE 17, 1948
AT MY DESK ( 1 P.M. )

Call from Hickenlooper at about 9:50, for some 15 minutes. Said the extension bill is coming up, perhaps at eleven, and had something he wanted to say before that time.

Spent some time saying his interest was solely in the atomic energy program, etc. "If you feel that this two-year bill won't work, then I am through talking. But if you feel that it can be workable, and at this point it seems to be the one solution for best interests of atomic energy, then I have this to say.

"I would like to have you write me a letter saying that, which I could use if I thought it necessary, in the course of the debate."

He went on to say that Senator Lucas was planning to "make a Roman holiday of this thing" expecting to make political capital of it, and attacking hard. If he or anyone else does that, "I don't have to sit there and take it, and I won't. It won't do anyone any good to have dirty linen washed in public, on the Senate floor, but some of our men on our side, who will go along without saying anything if the fight isn't made rough, will certainly let fly. I thought such a letter from you would stop such a row."

I told him as to the letter, I could not write such a letter, and I didn't think my associates could, though I would advise them of his request, for the simple reason that the President, our immediate superior, has taken a public position against the extension bill, and a strong

§ [Note of July 17, 1948]: It was successful.

one, and that precludes our taking any other position without his approval, regardless of the consequences.

I said there was something I could say to him, and that he could quote us on, namely, that recess appointments would be very bad, very bad indeed.

Helen has just called from the Senate gallery to say that the bill hasn't yet been called up, and that they are still working on the farm bill. Time is growing short, though Hickenlooper said definitely that the bill would be brought up and passed before the session is over.

5:30 P.M.

I think I have some light on this secrecy problem.

We were told that the trouble with us is that we do not have an adequate "policy," or indeed any policy at all; that this procedure and that procedure is wrong; that declassification is awkward or muddled, etc.

Some of these things are true.

But the difficulties do not really arise from such things. The fact is that the essential ingredient is a kind of desperate courage on the part of the members of this Commission, a willingness to stand up against fear and fear-begotten emotions that have swept the country, and that are being inflamed by almost every event, and by reactionary forces.

I believe this is a group of nervy men; I have never worked with any better. But our courage and willingness to stand up to the consequences of a bold and sensible (but easily attacked) program will be wasted unless we do one thing—and this is the second part of my "discovery." To wit: we must come out in the open with the things we do that require this courage, and not continue to do them behind closed doors, with only the Joint Committee, etc., knowing of them, and only the Joint Committee to answer before.

An illustration:

The National Research Council has been delegated by us the responsibility for selecting promising men for fellowships which we provide out of public funds. These men will go to universities with generous stipends. They are not our "employees" in the technical sense or any other, so as a matter of law do not come within the "investigation" terms of the Act.

One of the young men recommended for a fellowship, it develops upon a file check, was a member of the Communist Party, and may still be—for purposes of this illustration assume that he still is. The question is: should he be denied the fellowship because of his political views? If he were to have "access to restricted data," clearly he would not be accepted, not "cleared." But he does not. It is true that one of the purposes of the fellowships is to provide trained men who may later work on "classified" projects; but not necessarily.

Wilson admitted there was some difference in the staff, but he himself was strongly of the view that this should not bar the man from a fellowship. The Commission, remembering how the Joint Committee sleuths and its chairman and others react to anything like this, knows they would have a fit, and so will Rep. Thomas, etc. But we agreed that we should go ahead.

Now here is where my "discovery" comes in.

I recommended that we make this story public, on our own initiative, perhaps by making public a strong letter to the National Research Council, stating all the facts and our reasons for refusing to countenance the idea that political acceptability should be a criterion in our public support of education. The thing has no limits if we do not stand at this point. But if we did this, and only the Joint Committee and their staff gumshoes knew about it, we would be hammered and hell-raised and chawed at, with no one able to come to our side. As it is, I think we will get a lot of hell-raising (if we are still here), but the strength of our idea, made public, can be tested against the strength of the opposition, and the strength of our friends against that of our enemies.

I have taken another step in this general direction. Whenever a paper comes to me with a classification mark "Secret," etc., I ask, what is there in this paper that requires that classification? I insist that the burden should be on those who classify, instead of the other way around, as now.

Some of these things are bad habits, to a large extent. But all the administrative devices in the world won't take the place of the essential; to wit, a courageous willingness to stand the gaff.

JUNE 18, 1948
FRIDAY

Talked to Wilson, Fisk, Williams, and Waller about my idea about secrecy; the necessity of finding some way out of the increasing morass we are creating, and by the necessity—the foundation necessity—for guts on the part of the Commissioners as a condition precedent to getting things done.

This was welcomed warmly. Fisk said it would have a good effect all through the enterprise just to know that such things were being said.

I thought it would be worthwhile reversing some of the silly things we had previously done—such as the "security" fence around the cyclotron at Berkeley—put there because a Congressman, Van Zandt, had complained about lack of one; and the condemnation of large additional acreage near Oak Ridge because that Teeple of the Joint Committee staff said a man with a *mortar* could use it as a base from which to fire upon K-25!

This morning we met with the Military Liaison Committee, a full-dress session [on custody of weapons]. I told them we would not agree to a joint recommendation to the President, as this would not allow him adequate freedom in which to make so vital a decision, a decision that might well disturb the conditions in the world even more than they now are. We also disagreed with their recommendation on managerial or technical grounds, principally that it would adversely affect development work we were carrying on, and because they would not have the present capability to discharge the responsibility.

This was done very solemnly indeed, but without heated exchanges of any kind, and with expressions on my part of respect for their opinions and their motives.

I stated that I thought a decision on turning over custody of weapons to the military was not an issue that could or should be decided without a public statement. This will create a row, but nothing was said at the time.

JUNE 19, 1948
AT THE OFFICE (5:50 P.M.)

An hour and a half ago—according to a report from the Senate gallery—the Senate began debate on the two-year extension bill that determines the immediate future of this Commission and its work—and the immediate future of yours truly. Helen is there, taking it all in. She has been going up and listening through hours and hours of talk about tobacco, the draft, and the beginning of Glen Taylor's short-lived filibuster, so her perseverance has been rewarded. And some of the things that are said will probably make her pretty mad. Although, having gone through the debate on confirmation, I guess she has heard *everything* about that terrible husband of hers.

Spent the afternoon writing down ideas for chapter headings, etc., for a future book on atomic energy, the one Cass Canfield has been urging on me.

I have about made up my mind that it would be foolhardy to try to write the book while I am working so hard to make this thing go. It is the kind of thing I could do in a few months if I had nothing else to do and would serve as a good way to make a transition, when I'm through here, whether that is soon or some two years off; further, I could write with much greater freedom if I am out and with a much surer touch. Also, the book, if it was real good, might make quite a bit of money, which I could use after a Government salary for so many years and which I couldn't keep now, or wouldn't feel I should.

Tonight I go to a dinner at the Pentagon given by the four Secretaries of the Military Establishment for General Hull, and to hear a report on Eniwetok. The other day we saw movies and heard a report from Capt. Russell, who was in charge for AEC at Eniwetok. Frankly, I am fed up with hearing about the tests, having had about enough of them in every way. But we have to go through with this. Hull is a fine man, and when I phoned General Bradley, Chief of Staff of the Army, the other day to tell him how highly we all regarded Hull, I spoke with a good deal of feeling and generosity because I felt that way about it.

But this big bang is something I will be glad to take for granted from here on out.

JUNE 20, 1948
AT HOME, SUNDAY (2 P.M.)

Congress adjourned last night (or more exactly this morning at 7 A.M.), and among many other last-minute chores the two-year extension-of-term bill was passed without a record vote and with only desultory debate. None of the red-hot fireworks that had Hickenlooper disturbed the other day developed. In fact, Lucas didn't even appear on the floor during the debate.

Whether the President will veto it now is hard to guess, though I don't think the chance that he will fail to do so—in view of what he has said—is less than 50–50. At the moment I feel we should strongly urge him to let it become law.

The impulse to turn my back on the whole business recurs. This is partly good sense; partly going through sessions with the professional military (as last night and Friday morning); partly just plain fatigue. But right now I wish I could get into a rather settled view, a view that I will make up my mind to "stick it out" for the two years, come what may—or *almost* "come what may." A good deal will depend on who the Republicans nominate next week. If it should be Taft, obviously I couldn't serve under him, even though he might hesitate to ask for my resignation. But if (as seems likely to me) it should be Dewey or Vandenberg, certainly Warren or Stassen, then whether the Republicans win, as appears fairly sure, or Truman (as might happen in spite of the present outlook), "stick it out" for two years seems like a good idea.

The reason I feel this way is that I see now that I must devote myself more to administration, must give Carroll and his business a lot of close attention and help. If I do this, six months should improve things a lot, and if I only spent, in that effort, about the time I felt I had to give to speeches, conferences, etc., about "the public must be informed," a great improvement can be effected. The chance is very good that we can make substantial progress of the kind one can see and appreciate during that time. As Baruch says, "You have gone through the hardest part; why let someone else come along and pick the almost-ripe fruit from the tree that you tended?"

The meeting last night at the Pentagon was dull, and I violated protocol and left before the Secretary of Defense and to hell with protocol. Perhaps 30 high-ranking officers, two of the three Under Secretaries, members of the Commission. It was intended to honor General Hull and the civilian scientists, but particularly to be a sop to the scientists.

What troubled me was the way in which both Froman and Bradbury (of our Los Alamos Laboratory) took with the same kind of keen enthusiasm as any strategic bombing general the glorious progress made and the fine things that lie ahead in the tests they hope to hold two years hence. I don't object at all, in the least, to expressions of satisfaction that the job to be done (since it appears inescapable at the time) is being pushed and done well; but that there should not be even a single "token" expression of profound concern and regret that we are engaged in developing weapons directed against the indiscriminate destruction of defenseless men, women, and children, the fact that it does not appear either necessary or appropriate for these men to call attention to that—this bothered me.

I talked to Major General Kepner, who was in charge of the tactical bombing in Europe and who went himself, in a fighter, on twenty German missions. Even he felt troubled, saying that he met a German whose town he had obliterated who asked him, "Why did you destroy my town?" and Kepner answered that he did it and under the same circumstances would do it again—but you could see that he recognized that there was a problem. But there was no other recognition of this the whole three hours I was there.

Froman told the story of an "overzealous security man" that is worth remembering. This lad was so anxious to keep a check on films made at the Eniwetok test that he wasn't content to see the outside of a can of film; he opened it, and that wasn't enough; he measured it foot by foot to see if it checked with the amount supposed to be there. As a result he exposed and spoiled the whole can of film, part of "Zebra."

I have an additional angle to the rotating public service idea. It is this: that I should propose that elected officers of the Congress—Senators and Representatives—should be limited by constitutional amendment (as is proposed in the case of the Presidency) to not to exceed, say, twelve years' tenure. This would keep the Congress refreshed with men closer to the stream of ordinary life; would end the terrible evils of seniority power in the only way I can ever see it ended.

Don't get much of a personal sort written. The fact that my shorthand notes—the way I write these journal notes—are transcribed by the girls in the office is somewhat restraining about personal things. (This I am doing myself, on the machine at home.)

Last night there was a terrific storm, high wind and then a dash of hail for a half-hour to top it off. With a tin roof and all things were merry hereabout. The "sun-deck"—a tin dish that covers one end of the living room—has its water-exits stopped up, and it fills up, so that just before he left David and I did a big bailing job to dip her out and spill bucket after bucket over the side. This morning Penny woke me early barking, about six. I let her out into the murky after-storm morning, came into the study to see how the rain had operated on the sun-deck. Sure enough, full of water to the brim. So I rolled up my pajama legs and waded out, with a bucket and dipper, and half-asleep, and started bailing in a big way. Not long after, I was conscious of company. There was Helen, in a pair of shoes, mind you, and her nightgown, swishing a broom and pushing the water around, histing her nightgown with one arm, sort of. This not working—that is, not too well—just as earnestly as could be she put the hem of the gown between her teeth, and in this rather unusual condition—that is, for bailing—went right ahead with her labors. We must have been quite a pair.

We are just back from seeing Spencer Tracy and Katharine Hepburn in *State of the Union:* a terrific wallop at politicos just before the convention which opens tomorrow. But what specific does such a picture do, besides add to the people's presently large dose of skepticism about politics?

JUNE 21, 1948
AT HOME

These are notes I made today, at home, while trying to find some way out of the quicksand of the secrecy policy.

1. Re-examine whether classification hurts common defense, etc., more than helps it, in various broad and specific categories of information, both technical and non-technical.

2. To whom should Gen. Mgr. delegate final decision on clearances—

Division director, in consultation with Security and Personnel Director.

3. "Security risk."

What does this *mean*? Depends upon what is regarded as "security."

4. The *cost* of maintaining secrecy in its effort on:

   a. slowing up technical work;
   b. harassment of administrators;
   c. in darkening areas of public policy discussion requiring facts;
   d. in increasing problems of "clearances";
   e. discouraging recruitment by contractors and Commission.

5. How much classification (non-technical, largely) is there that is justified chiefly to avoid public discussion, or possible lawsuits (contamination) and other *non*-defense reasons?

6. To what extent, and in what areas (technical and non-technical), is secrecy justified on anti-sabotage grounds?

7. What is the particular justification for the pass, visitor escort, and high density of guard system in Washington Central Office? Why not non-AEC guards (i.e., Public Building Administration employees)?

8. Quantities:

   Volume of Secret and Top Secret.

   Increase in number in 1 year, 6 mos.

   How many could be declassified?

9. Engineering "secrets."

   How important to defense *are* they?

   How costly to keep them classified?

JUNE 23, 1948
AT HOME (10 P.M.)

Helen and I have just heard the nomination of Dewey, and his speech of acceptance.

The acceptance speech, delivered in an "oratorical" manner, which makes him seem remote, had nonetheless a note that is quite in contrast with the Martins and Byrds and Brickers. It is such a relief, such an infinite relief, that we don't have to face the prospect of the sort of thing that a Martin or Bricker could have meant, and that on international matters both the platform and the candidate represent the best of the party, not its worst.

As to the effect of the nomination on atomic energy development in the near future, on the Commission and on my own plans. From this point of view, next to the election of Truman and a Democratic Congress, the election of Dewey certainly improves on any other possibility, not excepting Vandenberg. It is interesting that by a kind of accident I had that visit with Dewey in Albany back in January.

Called at the White House this afternoon and talked to Clark Clifford about the President's action on the two-year extension bill. I explained the Commission's present position as being that recess appointments would be very, very bad. Instead of the fire-eating talk I feared, Clark said rather resignedly that he thought, offhand, that the thing to do was to approve the measure. If the President thinks otherwise, he will give the Commission a chance to discuss it further with him. I think, though, that it will not be vetoed.‡

I also mentioned the weapons custody matter, saying that I could see no justification for forcing a decision on the President at this particular time, since emergency action could be taken as things now are.

JUNE 25, 1948
AT HOME

Yesterday, late afternoon, Robert Oppenheimer phoned me from the West Coast and talked at great length.

The burden of his call was to express his "great sorrow" for the grief he had inflicted on me and the blows to our confidence in the future which the General Advisory Committee had administered. His explanation was this: For more than a year worries about some of the things we are doing or not doing had boiled and boiled. They did not speak of them—chiefly security and organization—feeling that our difficulties were so great that to make too much of a point about these errors or omissions would appear to show an insensitivity to the very real and towering difficulties we faced. But finally they thought the cork should be lifted from the bottle, and when it was, what bubbled out was not a balanced statement, an evaluation, over-all, of the job the Commission had done or our capacity to improve what had been done, but only the negative things.

The fact is, he said, without exception all nine of these men have great confidence and affection for the Commission and faith that we can make the improvements that they feel are so important. As to their apparent ignoring of the atmosphere in the country and the world in which we must necessarily operate, and over which we have no control (or at least, they are beyond our immediate control), these, he said, were not referred to, and in retrospect this does appear to be unfair and insensitive.

‡ Truman signed the bill.

On the whole, he was firm in saying that what the committee said was just what it believed, about deficiencies, but that if what they had said would undermine the confidence of the Commission in its future ability, undermine its courage to go on, then it was a grave and disastrous thing that they had done, and they were full of regrets for this, this not being their intention and the farthest thing from it.

He talked at great length with Bob Bacher about this. I had said to Bob that the worst thing about the way they had presented their views was that it raised a question with me: *Why* (if the prospects of our being able to do what these men, our friends, expect of us, is so slim) *why* in the world should I, as an individual, tear myself to bits trying to do what is, in their view, rather beyond me; why not just give it up as a bad job? What personal motive is there for me? (And everyone, even the most disinterested, must have *some* personal motivation.)

The medicine they administered so crudely and cruelly is having a good effect since I recovered (with great pain, I freely confess) from the shock and deep distress of the initial experience. We are re-examining our organization. It has made it clear that I must be much more active in management matters, press Carroll more, give him more help in this direction (whether he wants it or not).

I have rather good hopes that with Congress out of our hair for a while we can greatly improve things by October. We must.

The Republicans have nominated Governor Warren as Vice President. This is really quite encouraging in a number of ways since it appears so likely that the Republicans will win.

Warren comes closer to being a progressive by his record (as on the medical care issue, a touchy one; and on publicly produced power, water resources, etc.) than any other Republican, and as contrasted with Stassen's talk about being a "liberal" whereas his record is ambiguous to say the least. Warren has really felt the heat of the battle.

The nomination is particularly interesting to me as it affects (a) the Atomic Energy Commissioners and (b) TVA. As to (a) he announced publicly that he favored my confirmation when I was in San Francisco last spring, and his closeness to Sproul of the University of California, I should think, would mean that in him I have, if not a friend, certainly a potential friend or better. His closeness to Senator Knowland (a friend of TVA) and Paul Smith of the San Francisco *Chronicle* is of considerable importance, considering that the candidate might have been Halleck or Bricker or such! As to (b) Warren is quite evidently open to reason about TVA and the TVA method. I recall with some measure of confidence that Knowland pushed strongly for the TVA steam plant.

Perhaps as important as anything about Warren, and Dewey too, is that being career public servants, particularly Warren, the importance of dealing decently with the public service, and of getting a good caliber of men in the administrative side of the Government is something that both understand and have done something about.

I have just read Hoover's speech to the Republican Convention. It received such a lot of kudos in the press that I thought it might have something. It makes me a little ill, with its rear-guard sourness, a sourness that the eloquent passages about "faith," etc., do nothing to relieve. As for his concern for the rest of the world, that means nothing unless it is spelled out. And his strictures on collectivism and denial that there is any "middle of the road" position (which would put the Post Office into private hands to avoid Communism!) are the mouthings of an old superseded man. I was prepared to be quite generous in reading it because he has been punished out of all reason, as if he were personally the cause of the Great Depression. But while I still feel there is no justice in blaming him for everything, this speech does nothing to reassure me that those who see things as he does have anything to contribute to the actual problems of the world as they are or that they will provide the protection against Communism we need.

JUNE 28, 1948
ON THE CAPITOL LIMITED RETURNING FROM CHICAGO (6:00 P.M.)

I ascended the Tribune Tower this noon, and was swept at once into the Sanctum Sanctorum and before The Presence, the Colonel Himself. His office is high-ceilinged, with papers scattered about the leather lounges, dark and Gothic. Col. McCormick was older-appearing than I expected but rather courtly, courteous in the extreme, and with no slight hint that I was one of the devils that for years and years he had been whamming vigorously, in "news" columns and whooping editorials.

Dr. Zinn, who accompanied me, and I were greeted not only by the Colonel, but with not a little exuberance by a waddling gallumping English bull, the kind that is terrifying to see but actually very friendly. (When we left for the Argonne Laboratory later, after luncheon, the Colonel put a chain-leash of huge links on "Buster," who pulled the Colonel along through the corridors where people gawked and guards straightened up, passed a double column of pickets—the Typo Union has been on strike since last November—and into his car, manned by the most obvious tough-guy driver-guard I have ever seen. Buster sat in the front seat with the driver, and stuck his ugly but much excited phiz around every so often. An *English* bull.)

We were the first in the dining room, which led the Colonel to remark, rather peevishly, that luncheon was at one o'clock (we arrived on the second!) but he never could get them to come on time, and just for that we would begin on our soup, which we damn well did! Then the rest drifted in, one or two at a time. Only a few of the names I got. Maloney, Orr, the cartoonist. It was quite evident that I was regarded as a rarity, as the sort of object rarely seen in that room, and they gawked rather openly. But I was especially struck by the fact that, for all their ferocity (i.e., the editorial staff and the business group who feed them raw meat, I have no doubt) in print, they were a very meek, washed-out, and middle-aged-looking bunch if ever I saw one.

I had hoped for a chance to talk to them in a little set talk, and I brought a map along which I showed the Colonel and hoped he would suggest that I tell them about the work going on in the various parts of the country. He himself seemed very interested and I got the impression he was quite set on making his trip around the various AEC installations upon his return from Europe. There were a few questions, some rather thoughtful ones, from the staff for me or Dr. Zinn; but it was evident that the Colonel regarded this as *his* party and show, and when he finished dessert (it was a prodigious lunch: roast, potatoes, beans, noodles, not a lettuce leaf), he rose and said we must be going on and without more ado we did. Which was too bad. But it has been my general experience that it is usually much harder to call a fellow an s.o.b. if you have met him, and since this went off so urbanely I felt that it was by no means wasted. Actually, if we get into trouble in Chicago about the Argonne Lab—and we may—I would feel much better able to pick up the phone and ask for a chance to talk over our problem, which is an important part of "public relations."

Zinn gave us a good talk: the whole subject of the Atomic Energy Commission is radioactivity and the measurement of radioactivity. Then he went on to show some instruments that do that, i.e., measure radio-activity. Then we saw (a) a demonstration of radiochemistry, precipi-tating, by centrifuge, a microgram of uranium, and preparing it to be "counted"; (b) a tracer demonstration, the kind pretty much that I did for the farmers last December, i.e., putting a rose into radiophosphorus and watching the stuff climb up the rose and even make the leaves "hot"; (c) lathing uranium metal; (d) the effect of beta radiation on white mice, who were developing some gruesome tumors—and so on. The boys evaded the problems of secrecy very nicely, so nicely that I doubt if the Colonel knew anything had happened.

The Colonel was very red-faced and hot—we all were hot—and either absorbed or something. I wondered if he was getting bored, but his tough-guy driver assured my security man that if the Colonel got tired of it he would just walk out; which he didn't. After several hours of this Zinn took him out to the atomic piles at Palos Park and I took off for my train.

(We are, at the moment, going through the Calumet region; the strange shapes, gray in the half-dusk. An ore boat is being unloaded, much the kind of ore boat I shipped on, as a boy, 30 years ago this summer.)

There were few touches of humor. Humor, or even response, wasn't easy, as the Colonel was very quiet and only partly communicative, except on the rare occasions when military matters, his "field," seemed pertinent. But there were touches. For example, it seemed to amuse the Colonel to the point of a real laugh (and he can laugh, and it is a rather pleasant sight at that) when, after the demonstration of the radioactive phosphorus in the roses, I said that there was, I was sure, a romantic twist to this whole thing although I couldn't quite figure it: "I send thee roses, radioactive roses. . . ."

And to me, this was funny: We were speaking of progress in technical matters and how people always assumed that what *they* had was the last word. He said, "I have just come back from the Republican Convention in Philadelphia. Among the things that happened to me there were elevators." (He feels that the forces of the New Deal and internationalism and Wall Street defeated him and Americanism at Philadelphia, as a very bitter *Tribune* piece by Walter Trohan this morning indicated; but this was the only reference to what must have seemed like a terrible thing to him.)

(And now Gary, the steel mills, the flambeaux, the rows of stacks— a familiar sight of my boyhood, and memories of my first row with "authority" in the presence of Captain Norton, general agent for the Gary Land Co. As a reporter on the Gary *Tribune*, I was tossed out of a meeting of the County Council of Defense at Crown Point for reporting what went on over there.)

(This may grow somewhat disjointed; how much of this is due to the fact that I have been treating myself to some Old Granddad that has been in my suitcase too long, I don't know.)

The high spot of the McCormick afternoon, to me, was the following: Zinn, earnest and intense, a fine and devoted scientist and a damn good salesman, was talking about the site plans for the new laboratory on the Du Page site. We got down to an artist's rendition of a front elevation. Fine, simple, said Zinn. "No Gothic." He went on vigorously, while I winced. "No Gothic fancy stuff. What we want is a building that is *useful*." And we had just come from the Tribune Tower, a Gothic skyscraper, with gargoyles, flying buttresses, and all the rest, and made much fun of by one and all because it was so fancy Gothic. The Colonel, however, didn't bat an eyelash! This was my favorite moment of the afternoon.

In the morning I spent a good deal of time meeting the staff at the Museum, where they are presently officed. It was evident that going around shaking hands with everyone, stenographers and file clerks and guards, wasn't the usual, and I had to keep reminding Tammaro* or just moving in without him. I enjoyed it and so did they. Terrible conditions of work for most of them, though, in rooms without a single window and often way down in a hall.

(The Northern Indiana corn will never make it "knee-high by the 4th of July" if what I now see is any criterion.)

JUNE 29, 1948
STILL ON THE TRAIN FOR WASHINGTON

Yesterday morning I went to Dr. Collins to have him check up on my nose, ears, and throat. He looked at a yellowed card (I swear it was discolored!) and said, "Well, considering that it has been 23 years since I first examined you, you have done wonderfully well." That card was made out in 1925 when I was not much older than Nancy is now! He found my hearing normal (in the lower ranges of normal); nose fine and, though irritated, all right, and nothing to do about it.

His office is no longer in the Loop, but in the Osteopathic Hospital on South Ellis Avenue. A new wing, modern and attractive, has been built onto the old hospital. We should take a picture of the old hospital, or get one, for there are few places in this world that have been the scene of events as important—and poignant—for us.

It was up those front steps that I carried a terribly ill Helen 25 years ago this coming November; it was there that I paced the floor waiting for the verdict on the blood test (no one ever waited for a jury to come in more anxiously, I do believe). They told me she had typhoid.

It was there that young, absurdly young Dr. Peckham came out of the delivery room, grinning, to tell me that I had a daughter; and three years later, a whale of a big boy.

But the time I remember most sharply, one of the most dismal of my whole life, was of stumbling out of the hospital on a gray November day, having brought Helen to the hospital so few weeks after our marriage, and setting off for our "home," the two-room apartment at 1647 E. 67th. I walked a block west to Cottage Grove Avenue, I think it was, with an ache inside of me that I can still recall (as I do as I write this) as painful as a physical wound could possibly be, and as I stepped over to get the streetcar, half conscious, I suppose, I slipped and fell in the

* Manager of the AEC Chicago operations office.

slime of a Chicago street. People looking at me on the way home; the opening of the door of the apartment, left just as it was when we took Helen away, her clothes hanging dismally in the closet, the remnants of the oranges I had been squeezing desperately for her (the doctor had said give her orange juice, so I plied her with quantities, this being the only thing I could do to help). Then going into the tiny bathroom and looking at myself, a splash of mud on my face, and the gloomiest look I had ever seen on mortal countenance.

An interesting thing, the long arm of coincidence. In the winter of 1927 I think it was, Mother was diagnosed as having cancer of the uterus. I remember Dad coming back from Billings Memorial Hospital one winter day so shaken by the news the Dr. had just given him that he sat at the top of the stairs, panting, completely gone. (We were then living, for the winter, in an apartment on the Midway.) Should they try X-ray, a doubtful recourse and protracted, or surgery, a difficult operation, long, risky? We all agreed Mother would never have the patience for treatment, so it was surgery. The doctor was well known, but he was receiving only what was a nominal fee. I was tapped for blood for transfusion, by a redheaded intern (whom Helen still remembers with indignation because he missed the vein and made quite a mess of my arm).

Well, the point of recalling this is that the Atomic Energy Commission of which that clinic patient's eldest is Chairman, is building a cancer research hospital, the finest and only one of its kind, costing 3½ million dollars, as part of the Billings Memorial Hospital group.

JUNE 30, 1948
AT HOME (EVENING)

We had our custody meeting this noon in Forrestal's office with all of the Commission, Carpenter, Dr. Bush, Secretary Royall, and General Nichols. This went on from 12:00 noon until 1:15; then luncheon together, when we were joined by General Eisenhower in civilian dress. He was affable as ever, but so much less impressive without that uniform that he wears so well, and those stars, that it was rather a shock, the difference in presence.

The discussion itself is not worth recording, particularly as we went over the same ground, practically. We insisted that the President should be free to decide the policy question and resisted efforts to box us in so that the President would find himself pretty circumscribed if he tried to leave things as they are.

Royall added something new, though. The shadows of the current troubles with the Russians in Berlin rather followed him around as he came and left the meeting to get the latest word. What he wanted, he said, was to have some broad policy questions decided. Will we use this weapon, if we are compelled to use force? Upon what kind of targets? And under what general circumstances? Until those questions are determined, in advance of an immediate occasion, other questions such as custody are not very important and those can be answered satisfactorily when the first questions are answered.

What struck me with these remarks was that it showed that the military have been *assuming* that they already have the answers to such questions, that they are the ones who answer such questions, since this is like any other kind of weapon. It illustrates the real cleavage here and an important one.

I pursued Royall's opening, for it enabled me to say what I believe is true, i.e., that to decide these broad questions through the device of an argument over technical custody is to invite confusion about the fundamentals. It is because the issue is one of policy, underlying policy, and not a question of technical custody, that so much of the arguing seems somehow beside the point and indecisive.

The purpose in having the meeting with the whole Commission was to insure that my colleagues didn't feel that they had not had a chance to say their say, in their own words. And they did. Lewis pointed out that the representations made by the military about their capabilities had been wrong, badly wrong, time and again—as in the case of storage. Bill made a good point about the effect of this move in "freezing" designs. Sumner, I thought, talked pleasingly but rather dangerously about the election-year political atmosphere in which this issue would be dealt, saying this was a bad time to raise it; I thought his point was dangerous because there were some who would then assert that a decision against the military would simply be a political decision by the President, which could be quite damaging.

Bush proposed that we tell the President jointly that *at some time* the military would be ready and able to accept custody, and that he decide now to direct that, jointly, a plan be drawn to be put into effect when they were ready. This was a neat boxing operation and I resisted it hard, saying that this assumed the answer to the policy question, leaving only the question of whether the policy *now* should be in favor of transfer and that this we would not do. Bush didn't like this a bit.

Forrestal obviously doesn't take the military position simon-pure, but he is impressed that unless the military are told that this will be their responsibility, they will not be on their mettle to get people, organization, etc., and make themselves ready.

I countered this by saying that this assumed that the division between civilian and military would thereupon assume a state of repose, with the line in that point accepted as a final line, whereas the fact was that so long as military and civilian operated together the military would continue to push for a shifting of the line, saying next that it would be better if those who had to use the weapons designed them, then when they got into that, they should make them, etc. And in each case they could make the argument that though they aren't yet capable of doing the job, they never would be capable unless they were told that such would be their function at some early date and that to be ready they must be told that they should get ready.

I said that it was certainly not a simple question, easily answered, whether the transfer of the atomic weapon stockpile to the military at this time would further the interests of the United States, for who could tell whether it would impair or destroy the Marshall Plan; whether it would retard or facilitate the improvement in conditions in Europe, etc.?

When we went to luncheon, General Eisenhower was there to join us. He spoke ruefully of the way he is being pushed around by his new job,† but said it wasn't so much his new job that was "getting me down as it is my past sins." He has 3,000 pieces of mail every day, he said. "It's got so I won't answer the phone at all unless the caller is an old friend and can identify himself as such. It will get better as soon as the Democrats meet and get that over, but still the load of mail is going to be heavy."

It was interesting to see his enthusiasm, which is quite evidently the key to his great popularity. For he is one of the least profound men, I might say one of the most pleasantly superficial men of great reputation and achievements, I think I have ever listened to. But the enthusiasm with which he talked about Columbia. He was kidded for sounding like a Chamber of Commerce secretary, and it was that kind of thing he was saying, the obvious, not thoughtful, but apparently quite sincere enthusiasm of a man who puts what he is doing right at the top. I suspect he also gets quite discouraged—has the ups and downs, in other words, that most people capable of enthusiasm usually have, yours truly included.

Tito came up; he is much in the news these days, having been given hell by the Cominform. Eisenhower said this illustrated the limitations of punishment, how after a time there really isn't much more you can do, if you rely on punishment.

Which reminded him of an experience he had when he was training a Negro regiment, years ago, made up of hard New York Negroes. He was giving them a tough forced march in the Kansas heat and it was very punishing. Lips cracked and bleeding; dust, etc. They began

† As president of Columbia University. (There still was a movement to draft Eisenhower for the Democratic Presidential nomination, despite his insistence that he would not be a candidate.)

to drop out, fifty at a time, just throw their rifles down by the side of the road and drop out. When hell was raised about this, and they were threatened with being sent up for insubordination, they said, "Fine; Leavenworth is a lot better than this."

Someone asked, "Well, what did you do with that Negro regiment?" Eisenhower dismissed this as of not too much interest, though I would have liked to hear more, for here he was talking about something he does know. "Divided them into companies; stopped the march; put on brisk short training hops; promoted competition between companies, etc."

He spoke with some vigor about Federal financing of universities. "I guess I am a strong states' rights man, but I don't want to see university education dominated by the Federal Government and politics and Congress." Of course, this is partly due to the fact that he is out trying to raise 170 million dollars for Columbia funds, and that he is using, to get private funds, the argument against Federal funds that Hutchins used: fear of Federal domination, etc. But it is a wholesome fear, and a warranted one, I think.

In the morning we had a session with Dr. Colby of the University of Michigan. We called him in to explore with the CIA and other intelligence agencies the whole business of determining how long it is likely to take before Russia has atomic armament. The thing that rather chills one's blood is to observe what is nothing less than lack of integrity in the way the intelligence agencies deal with the meager stuff they have. It is chiefly a matter of reasoning from our own American experience, guessing from that how much longer it will take Russia using our methods and based upon our own problems of achieving weapons. But when this is put into a report, the reader, e.g., Congressional committee, is given the impression, and deliberately, that behind the estimates lies specific knowledge, knowledge so important and delicate that its nature and sources cannot be disclosed or hinted at.

This would be bad enough were it not for a fact that makes it actually dismaying. That is this: at some future time the action of a President in ordering "anticipatory retaliation" by way of a terrible atomic attack may be based simply on intelligence reports of what others are about to do to us. If the integrity of the intelligence is not a great improvement over this sample, no one will ever know what terrible things could ensue that might have been prevented, that may have been utterly needless.

This morning I had phoned Clifford to say that we were having our meeting with Forrestal today and would he have any further comment on the issue? He hadn't been able to talk to the President about it but would try to before noon.

He phoned at 12:20, but by that time we were at our meeting. I got him back about 2:55 P.M.

He had presented the matter to the President. The President said, "As long as I am in the White House I will be opposed to taking atomic weapons away from the hands they are now in, and they will only be delivered to the military by particular order of the President issued at a time when they are needed." Clifford said he wasn't surprised but seemed pleased.

What should I do about it? Well, Clifford suggested I tell Forrestal that I received this message. I explained how difficult that would be. Said I would consult with my colleagues and talk to him further.

After thinking about it and talking it over it is clear that, though this is very encouraging, we must go ahead and see that there is a full presentation of the issue to the President, hoping he will make the same decision on the policy question, for it is evident that it is policy he is deciding it on.

An addendum to the notes about today's talks at the Pentagon.

Forrestal said again that the American public has a mistaken idea of the value of atomic weapons. In his view they are powerful but not decisive. Part of this comment is undoubtedly due to his smarting over the way Congress rode over him on the air-power issue, for he spoke with some scorn of the stories about planes taking off from Maine and flying over the Kremlin, whereupon Stalin would roll over and quit.

Royall had a somewhat different view. They *might* be decisive, he said. Both agreed, however, that these weapons were the best and almost the only thing we had that could be used quickly. And they didn't underestimate the healthy respect the Russians have for them.

JULY 3, 1948

Thoughts while plowing through a famous loyalty case. The file is now a foot high and I weighed it: 12 pounds.

Characteristics of these "loyalty" reports:

"Washington X, a reliable informant" or "who is considered reliable," etc., etc. Then: "Washington X declined to furnish a signed statement or appear before a Loyalty Board."

XY, "who possesses considerable information regarding activities in the Soviet Embassy, stated that he was personally aware that the ————s received invitations to attend the annual receptions held on Nov. 7 at the Soviet Embassy in celebration of the 'great Socialist Revolution.' The informant vaguely recalled that ————s were unable to attend the

1946 reception due to a prior commitment but he thought that they were in attendance in 1947."

Such guff to pay an informer for. Hell, half of Washington used to stuff themselves at these receptions.

"I remember (says XYZ) "that ——— disliked Xkoolooski and gained the impression it was because he was in sympathy with the Old Polish Regime. . . . She conveyed to me the impression that the present Government in Poland is better than the original one."

Suspicion, suspicion, supicion. And what an opportunity to gouge a man you don't like, one who has disagreed with you. Godamighty!

Informant stated that A and B (with whom ——— had "closely associated" as fellow-employees (!) had said thank the Lord someone is doing something against free enterprise. Then this priceless one: "The informant stated that he had never heard ——— express himself along such lines, but he felt he must know of the feelings of A and B about such matters."

And this from a fellow employee who joined a society ——— belonged to: "Consequent to my joining this society I noted a few lines in the Washington *Times-Herald* [not quite the N.Y. *Times* of Washington journalism! DEL] re this society which indicated that there might be some question as to this society. *Based on these, I decided not to continue membership* upon expiration of the one-year membership which I held." (My italics.)

Army told him not to go to Russia on a scientific "convention" junket. If he insisted, would stop him. Which they did.

"Professor ——— stated he decided to explain what he termed ———'s lack of discretion and tact. . . . ———, when an undergraduate student . . . took great delight in practical jokes which in one or two instances embarrassed members of the faculty who were in a position to influence ———'s success at the University."

"Confidential informant PDQ 606, a well-known scientist, advised that . . . ——— is the type of person who does not necessarily approve of everything because it is done by the Government." . . . Gee!

"Dr. A stated" that ———, "without being asked, went into a vigorous attack on the newspaper columnist Westbrook Pegler, during the course of which ——— bitterly criticized Pegler for his 'anti-labor policy.' Dr. A mentioned this instance to illustrate what he considered to be a 'tactless' approach on the part of ———."

JULY 5, 1948
AT HOME

I am simply aghast at the unfair way in which President Truman is being "judged," if the current lynch-law atmosphere can be called "judging." And the attitude of liberals and progressives, now whooping it up for Eisenhower or Douglas, is the hardest to understand or be other than damn mad about.

Truman's *record* is that of a man who, facing problems that would have strained and perhaps even floored Roosevelt at his best, has met these problems head on in almost every case. The way he took on the aggressions of Russia; the courage in calling a special session of an antagonistic Congress controlled by the opposition to put through an extensive program for the restoration of Europe; his civil rights program, upon which he hasn't welched or trimmed—my God! What *do* these people want?

If it is said that he wobbled on veterans' housing or Palestine or this or that, did F.D.R. never wobble? Don't be funny; F.D.R. wobbled through the Neutrality Act and Arms Embargo (isolation of the very worst and blindest kind); he wobbled on economic matters all the time, as in the 1937 stuff that assumed that the New Deal was no longer needed.

As for ultra-conservative appointments, if that is one of the charges, and there is plenty of support to this, who was it who put Forrestal and Harriman and Lovett (about whom they complain, foolishly for the most part) into public life in the first place but F.D.R. himself? Did F.D.R. ever stand up for public development of power, or human rights, or labor, essentially any more firmly than Truman? And who knows what Eisenhower would do on any of these issues! Bah!

It is grossly unfair. They say the people want someone else; that the people aren't for him. Well, who in hell but the Southern extremists and the perfectionist "liberals" together have created the impression (eagerly encouraged, of course, by the reactionaries and the Republicans) that the people don't have confidence in him?

That makes me mad and rather ill, these hounders of a real man.

This is a "holiday," which thus far I have been using to read a long report on isotopes which is to be the bulk of the July report to Congress. ("To Congress" is a kind of a joke, for it will be read by mighty, mighty few Congressmen, if any.)

What is the measure of a civilized man? There are, in every period, certain basic assumptions about this, and these assumptions are extremely important in charting the course of the present and the direction men take. It occurs to me that if we set out deliberately to establish as a measure of a civilized man, as a measure of that man whom we honor and respect most, *he who has a strong and effective sense of responsibility to others,* then we will make progress.

Whom do we most honor? In any particular time of history whom do we regard with the greatest respect? A great military leader; a very successful maker of money for himself; an artist, playwright, prophet?

As one observes how vulnerable to destruction our knowledge has now made us—this is a *new* fact in the world, *new* in a literal sense—one sees that the mark of a civilized man must be some quality that will help the world from destroying itself. He is most civilized who has those qualities and talents of leadership, by example and precept and character and ideas, that will help civilization to survive.

From this it could be said that the goal of education—education being perhaps the broadest of all social functions, and including the designation of *what is important*—the goal of education is increasing in public esteem the quality of responsibility to others, that being the quality which today stands between man's knowledge and man's self-destruction.

Perhaps I should try to expound this somewhere. The genius in science, the genius in music, the genius in securing power over others—that kind of genius is still of varying degrees of importance; but these are not the mark of the civilized man in his finest flower *for our world's present extreme need.*

On my Chicago trip I questioned Zinn closely about his visit (with George Weil) to England. They had been treated with great thoughtfulness and hospitality; a dinner was given for them at Oxford at which they met the leading British scientists. They proceeded with that part of their assignment dealing with "technical cooperation." But they learned, what was to them surprising and somewhat disturbing, that research was by no means all that was going on, and that while "reactors of natural uranium in which the power is not wasted" was certainly an objective, as indicated, there were under construction rather large-scale production plants sufficient so that in perhaps three years—well, a quite different situation would exist and all this thousands of miles closer to Russia and Russian-influenced territory than our own establishments.

Our agreement in January about "technical cooperation" did not forbid this. I checked the minutes and the discussions, and though the strategic considerations were undoubtedly discussed between Marshall and Bevin, what the British did was not a limitation on our agreement. Lewis [Strauss] urged that what Zinn reported was a new fact that justified a change in the future of technical cooperation; on a level of considerations pertinent to the State Department or Defense this might be true; but not, I asserted, for us. We had made a promise, and we must keep that promise, the only question being whether the scope of cooperation was within that agreed to at Blair House.

But these goings on are of considerable importance, very considerable. I am sure, reasonably sure, no one thought that this would be in the British plans, partly because of the very great diversion of men and materials involved, and partly because of the strategic hazards. So, I notified Marshall and Forrestal, and asked for a meeting with them tomorrow,‡ at the same time deferring a meeting of the Combined Policy Committee (with the new Ambassador Franks sitting in for the first time, as I understand) until Thursday.

JULY 7, 1948
AT HOME (10 P.M.)

The CPC meeting went off swiftly and without a hitch. Sir Oliver Franks, the new Ambassador of Great Britain, attended his first meeting. Quite youthful in appearance—actually in his early forties, I believe—soft voice, rather restrained manner, not "shy" as the feature writers say; at least in this small group he wasn't. Fine-looking man, and a considerable improvement, from my point of view, over old Inverchapel, who was through and done. I think less of the "career man" idea the more I see it, as a steady and unvarying diet.

Spoke to Franks as we broke up, about David, his enchantment with Britain; his consistent remarks about the "good manners" and "politeness" of all the people he meets; his pleasure in standing on the soil that bred the great poets and playwrights he reads with such excitement, as an English Literature "major."

Ambassador Franks and Hume Wrong, the Canadian Ambassador, suggested that the extent of U.S.–U.K.–Canadian cooperation now going ahead (with such benefit to good feeling among these nations) should be explained by way of a speech by me sometime, probably before the September meeting of the General Assembly of the UN. At that time the international control of atomic energy might well be debated, and such a statement as this should be made before that time to avoid the criticism that it was something clandestine and therefore evil. This would be an interesting thing to do.

I continue to get interesting mail about my proposal in the University of Virginia speech, and the article made out of it for the *New York Times Magazine*.§ The speech and article are another example of collaboration between Helen and myself in which we are succeeding better

‡ [Note of July 7, 1948]: We met yesterday with Lovett. They had anticipated this. It doesn't change anything; indeed, L. says it fits into foreign policy as enunciated in the Vandenberg resolution (virtually an extension of the Monroe Doctrine to Europe) and the plans for Western European Union now being discussed.

§ I suggested that every college graduate plan to spend a few years of his career in some kind of public service—a "citizens' universal public service."

than ever. I talk the ideas over with her, usually right after breakfast; then set out some kind of crude outline; go at the typing; then read the first four pages or so to her—in this case it was perhaps the first third of the speech; then see whether it is shaping up, in general; then go on and finish a draft; read that together; then polish it; and read it aloud, she taking notes which we discuss together; then when it is a finished product she listens to delivery, chiefly for tone and temper. In this last one, for example, for all my years of experience, I attempted a heavy "oratorical" tone to the opening pages, and this she criticized and urged a lighter, half-ironic tone, which, indeed, is the way I wrote it, and the way I first read it to her. Then when I have an article adaptation to make, we talk it over again, and she criticizes what I write.

This is working increasingly well; gives us things to do together, which, in appropriate moderation, is excellent for a marriage (and too much of which would have the opposite effect, I daresay) and yet does not introduce the agonies and frustrations of actually writing, i.e, composing, together.

JULY 8, 1948
AT HOME

A beautiful morning. And I have just been wished many more happy birthdays by a most attractive gal.

Lovett made some interesting remarks, day before yesterday and again yesterday, about the Berlin crisis. Such as: (1) The airlift into Berlin has reached 3,100 tons a day and can be increased. Compared it with the transport to China over the Hump. (2) "The Berlin issue will almost certainly come to a head in another ten days." (3) There have been a number of good breaks in the cold war: Tito and Belgrade; the Finnish elections in which the Communists went from the top to the bottom of the list; the Vandenberg resolution and the momentum toward a Western European military union with the United States supporting it. This also has a dangerous side, in that by the "peculiar workings of the Oriental mind" the Russians may feel they must make a stand and a good showing, and therefore push their advantage in the Berlin situation to the point where "anything could happen"; as, for example, picking a quarrel with France and "then the fat would be in the fire."

Lovett has a great talent for relaxed talk, with a flavor of irony. He gives one the impression of a man who knows what he is talking about, of directness, of not pressing logic too far. I think very highly of him indeed.

Was greeted with a "happy birthday" chorus from the girls as I came in the office this morning, which rather fussed me, as I have always pretended that I didn't have such things. But it was very nice to be remembered. Usually the only outsiders who remember have been the insurance company agents, with their form letters that have a somewhat interested sound, six congratulations for me and six for them, since the longer I live the cheaper I am on their books. And to top it off tonight Dad called on their newly installed telephone, and he and Mother sang "happy birthday" to me, which was very enjoyable. They seemed fine, Dad particularly having regained that vigorous voice.

Had the first dissenting vote today for a year, and I believe the third one in the history of the Commission, the second of any consequence actually. It was Lewis, who expressed "shock" and obvious strong feeling that we were ready to continue cooperation with the British after we learned definitely what their program in England is. The other members did not share his view, and since he really didn't have his heart in the original agreement it wasn't surprising, his dissent. But it was with considerable feeling.

The other day I had said that once a promise was made, as between nations in particular, it must be kept; that Mr. Hoover had said recently that the keeping of promises, even those you later regret or would like to avoid, is the very fabric of civilization; that I thought it would be unthinkable to be in the position where it could be said we were "welching."

The use of that word was unfortunate, I suppose, for Lewis remembered it even this morning, and it was evident that it bothered and perhaps angered him. He put the question in this way: "Surely it is not the policy of this Government to facilitate the production of atomic weapons by Britain?" I said that wasn't the question at all, but the fact that he did put it that way, and saw that no one would support such a position, showed how strongly he felt. He has been very willing to try to accept decisions that he would prefer not to make, but he couldn't manage this.

I have decided to try to be much more stern and "chairmanish" in handling Commission meetings, to cut off diversions, and to try to narrow the issues to those necessary for the matter in hand. Otherwise I simply won't have the time or energy for the organization work I feel needs my time and to which I can contribute a good deal. I applied this rather vigorously this morning to the disposition of the Condon case, which we passed on, after a year of its being kicked back and forth and round about, in about 30 minutes.

Had a report on long-range detection, based on monitoring of

Sandstone [Eniwetok]. Had one very encouraging fact about the success achieved in detecting the fact that there was a nuclear explosion, at far distant points, quite remarkable and far beyond our expectations. With the system working, everything except an explosion in a cave, etc., would hardly go undetected, and even some idea of its force at given distances. The travels of the radioactive clouds, dispersed to a width of several miles, around the globe, was fascinating. The story was told us by a meteorologist, in appearance the very caricature of the "professor," steel-rimmed glasses, etc.; apparently a very good man.

JULY 11, 1948
AT HOME, SUNDAY

Yesterday we had our first cocktail party; it was actually very pleasant, and I hope we shall repeat it this fall.

Jim Webb, the Director of the Budget, was here. He said, "I know that they are pushing that custody matter you mentioned to me some weeks ago. I talked to Marshall about it; I always go to him on difficult things. Don't tell anyone this, because his military friends don't like the idea, but he is against it, and especially is he against it now. And I don't believe the President will approve it."

I said that the more I looked into the matter, the more I felt it was a bad and troubling thing, that was being put forward for reasons that were not the real reasons. Webb said he would see the President Monday. Did I think that the thing to do was to have it delayed? I thought not. My notion, now, was that it would be better for the President to decide it, and answer the written communication from Defense, which put the President on the spot, with a "state paper" (as I called it); i.e., an impressive and well-written statement on the policy question. Would I prepare a memorandum for him, Webb, on the matter? I thought not, but I would be happy to talk over the points with him any time.

This is an interesting development. The Washington *Post* had an editorial on the custody question yesterday, and since we have not supplied the facts or arguments against transfer, it was a remarkably judicious statement, saying that civilian control was involved, which I now think it definitely is.

JULY 12, 1948
AT HOME

Lewis sent in a handwritten note: the issue in our Thursday session—continuing technical cooperation with U.K. and Canada, notwithstanding the information that U.K. was headed for [bomb material] production—was so important that he wondered if we shouldn't take it to the President. I asked to see him. Told him he was emotionally involved in some way (as a matter of fact, his hands were trembling most of the time we talked over our difference, and Bill W. says this was so at the Thurs. meeting). But he feels it deeply, and before we had gone on long it was evident that one reason was he feels Britain is "far to our left" and therefore may give "the secret" away to the Communists, "some of whom actually sit in Parliament." I said nothing doing going to the President, with an issue upon which four out of five of us are clear upon, and where State and Defense seem able to take care of any Presidential conferring.

I called on Lovett, 3:30 to 4:10. Said I thought we ought to lose no time telling the world of the cooperation with U.K. and Canada. I proposed, subject to his views, to go to our joint plant at Chalk River, Ontario, after which I'd make a speech in Ottawa on the subject, or weaving in the subject of the relations in atomic energy of the three nations. This is all right, he said; agreed with me that keeping it a secret would soon give it the appearance of something wrong. Only question was effect on the Berlin crisis, and the propaganda effect, in Russian hands. I said if things were tense in late July, when I plan the speech, I'd cancel the trip.

Told him Lewis felt strongly that we erred. He said L. is very active all over the place, criticizing this action, "as he did last December at the time of Blair House, and on the foreign isotope distribution." He said this is not good. "British Intelligence is good and they will hear of this stirring around and will begin to be worried whether once more we are all planning to let them down. See Forrestal and Bush, and get them to straighten Lewis out."

JULY 17, 1948
AT HOME

Thursday afternoon (15th) I visited with Jim Webb, at his suggestion, about the custody of weapons matter. He wants to present the President with some lines of thought about it. He thinks the transfer bad himself (though he admits he could be better informed) for the reason, if for no other, that the Armed Services are so hopelessly "out of control" under Forrestal and engaged in such fights among themselves that to add this "at this time" would be wrong.

He lays into Forrestal and brought out two letters from the President to Forrestal that were exceedingly critical. One was a long letter obviously written by the Budget Bureau; the other was a short and curt one from Truman and obviously written by him. Its concluding sentence was: "That is your responsibility." Webb says Forrestal just won't take responsibility; that he passes it all on to the President. "The President," he says, "is his own Secretary of Defense right now; he *has* to be because Forrestal won't take hold."

Webb spoke about the tenseness of the Russian situation in Berlin. Almost anything could touch off a fight and a fight that would mean war. The British have said that if the Russians operate fighters in the U.S.-British air corridor, they "will shoot them down." We are opposed to this. But a good many B-29s will be sent to England.

Thursday morning, following a talk by phone I had with Justice Roberts, we finally passed on the Condon case.◖ I would feel better about it—since it was I who insisted that we stop stalling, as, e.g., by ordering a hearing, etc.—if I were not ashamed of the fact that the case has been pending for a year, that is, that we could have prepared to decide it a year ago. On the other hand, there is some advantage, I suppose, in the fact that in that year another FBI investigation was had, which makes a rather strong record. Condon is not my ideal of a man of well-balanced judgment, but that is a long way from saying that he should have been treated wickedly, as the Thomas Committee has treated him.

Spent yesterday and today until noon with Archibald MacLeish. One of the pleasantest experiences I have had in a long time. And I had looked forward to it with considerable trepidation, assuming it would be very hard going and frustrating.

What we were doing was working out an article for *Life* which he has been commissioned to do and which he conceived, in form, as a "dialogue" between us. We lunched together (he, his fine son Kenneth, who is science editor of *Life*, and Helen) at my office some weeks ago. Then he sent me a kind of running account of what the article would be about, very general. This disturbed me, for I feared it would be so philosophical as to be not only meaningless but rather dangerous in its fuzziness. I gave it a good deal of thought and after talking to Salisbury, who was cautious as usual (which, in a way, is his function), I said the probable gain wasn't worth the risk. But on a hunch I talked to Frances Henderson about it. She thought an article was needed, that *Life* would treat it well, and I decided it was time I took some chances and wired him to come on.

Frances and Helen sat in the discussions. Frances is a very capable girl with fine judgment and considerable restraint in the way she

◖ The AEC gave Dr. Condon clearance for continued access to classified information necessary in his work as head of the Bureau of Standards. (Dr. Condon was frequently in the headlines in this period because of attacks made on him by House Un-American Activities Committee members, and his vigorous support by the President and fellow-scientists.)

expresses herself. I am hopeful that she will be able to help me in a lot of similar situations. It was she who arranged for me to lunch with the *Life* staff just a year ago (while she was still with *Time*), and this was the beginning of my acquaintance with Luce and increasing standing with his publications.

JULY 20, 1948
AT HOME (10 P.M.)

The one thing I have worked hardest to accomplish—because without it this job can become too unpalatable to be borne—is to cultivate a brother-feeling among the members of the Commission. Lewis' strong feeling about our action in the technical cooperation matter, and his vigorous dissenting statement, has had me troubled again as I was considerably troubled just a year ago about the exportation of isotopes. But something happened this afternoon that rather dispelled the dread that we might be faced with a period of "record-making" and fencing and coolness, that could lead to fighting each other on the outside and inside as well.

After an hour of our little private "executive sessions" we have each Tuesday just to talk together about whatever comes to mind, Bob [Bacher], just back from a holiday, brought up Lewis' statement. So we talked about it, and I fear I made it pretty serious. I stopped Lewis when he said that what we were doing was "giving the atom bomb to Britain" as being wrong and not a fair statement. This could have gotten away to something not very good, and hard to retrieve.

At this point Lewis saved the day by grinning broadly and bringing out a sheet of paper from his pocket, saying he would like to read a poem. Which he did. It was something Bill [Waymack] had written, ribbing Lewis about the harpoon he had thrown into us and particularly kidding about Lewis' introduction to the effect that he expressed himself badly, etc. We all laughed and to Lewis' credit let it be said he led the laughing and did it genuinely. It was a fine stroke by Bill, and good humor was quite restored. Then came a remark by Sumner, who was getting pretty fed up with the continued argument about something we had decided. He said, "It seems to me we have beaten that straw about enough." He didn't mean a pun on Lewis' name [pronounced "Straws"], but we all rose from the table in my office and called it a day.

Had a briefing on the current war plans, in case the Berlin emergency breaks out into war. The role of our work was deeply impressive and sobering, as various points on the map were pointed to and explained.

Tomorrow at 3:45 we have the showdown at least on the custody matter. The President will see Forrestal, Carpenter, and the Commission. I insisted on the whole Commission chiefly because it is an important event on which we have spent much time, although I know that Forrestal strongly preferred keeping it down to me.

Webb sent over a statement he proposed the President might make, and an analysis of the arguments pro and con, recommending our position. He saw the President today, and apparently the President's view still is to leave things as they are.

Decided today that come what may I should hold press conferences, on occasion, and plan one just before the report to Congress is ready for release. This is part of the campaign to try to "shed the veil."

The Berlin situation continues quite serious and all kinds of plans are afoot. We are having a kind of recital tomorrow so we all understand what would happen under any one of a number of circumstances, step by step, and to plan some "fire drills."

The reorganization work is nearly completed, and we expect to have a plan ready for approval this week. That is progress indeed.

JULY 21, 1948
(MEETING WITH THE PRESIDENT)

The President greeted us rather solemnly. He looked worn and grim; none of the joviality that he sometimes exhibits, and we got right down to business.

We were quite a crowd, the largest group I have seen in a conference with the President since the summer of 1936, when F.D.R. called a meeting to discuss power pooling; the first time, incidentally, that the President and Willkie ever met.

The crowd was my fault. Carpenter, speaking for Forrestal, wanted it cut down to me alone for the Commission. But he and Forrestal and Bush were to speak for the National Military Establishment. I said, no, if that was the line-up, the entire Commission should be present. As a matter of fact, if I had yielded, Forrestal would probably have had almost as many on hand as he did: the Secretaries of the Army and Air Force; Carpenter; his deputy and soon successor as chairman of the Military Liaison Committee, Bill Webster—and the Commissioners. We sat in a half-circle of chairs; I picked a straight little chair immediately in front of the President, with Forrestal at the President's left, his team between him and where I sat, and my friends next to me.

It was an important session, and a kind of seriousness hung over it that wasn't relieved a bit, needless to say, by the nature of the subject and the fact that even at that moment some terrible thing might be happening in Berlin that would put this group into the hands of forces that might sweep our desires and wishes away, while the tides of force took over.

I rather think it was one of the most important meetings I have ever attended.

Forrestal got a nod from the President. F. looked at me and said each of us had prepared a letter setting out our positions and the best way to start would be for me to read mine, and then they would read theirs.

The President wheeled around to look at me. I said I thought it would be better if the Secretary opened the discussion, inasmuch as it was the National Military Establishment that had made a proposal for a change in conditions as they now exist; that what we had to say would be more readily understood if it came as a response to their proposal. (This turned out to be a very important stand. It again illustrates the great importance of procedure, which is so large a part of the common law and the training and instincts of the lawyer.)

So Carpenter began reading their letter (2½ closely typed pages) without giving the President a chance to say whether he would like to sit there and have a letter read "at him" (and not even by the man who signed it, but his deputy), which I sure in hell wouldn't have, and judging from his reactions that was mistake #1 as far as they were concerned. When Carpenter had finished reading this document word for word, he said there were accompanying memoranda expressing the views of the Secretaries of Army, Navy, and Air Force and of the Joint Chiefs, and he set about to read them.

This was too much for the President and he reached for the documents and said, curtly and not pleasantly, "I can read."

Even a less experienced gent than I would have known enough at this point not to read aloud our letter to the President, so I began by stating that we regarded as the determining issues not the technical matters which were set out in our letter and which the President could study later. The real issue was a very broad one of policy involving the factors which the President would weigh in reaching a decision not as Commander of the Armed Forces alone but as Chief Magistrate. On these broad policy questions the Commission had little if anything to say except to state that we believed they were conclusive of the question.

It happens, I said, that the President of the United States, more than any other living man, has given thought to these problems of broad policy for three years; that the President has studied and thought about these issues since the time he ordered the first bombs dropped; through the discussions and fight for legislation providing for civilian control. (At this point the President interjected, with a little grin at me, "And we're still having to fight to save those principles.") I continued: he had been the sponsor of efforts toward international control. For us to feel we could enlighten him on the broad policy question "was like trying to teach grandmother how to spin." This brought a big chuckle from the President; and I could feel the temperatures among the defense establishment gents around me go down considerably.

I read the provision of the law that said the President "from time to time" could transfer weapons, under circumstances that *he* deemed required it, and that we believed that when and if the President declared such an emergency to exist, in his judgment transfer could be made effectively.

As to the Commission's own recommendation as to what should be done, we wanted it clear that we believed the the division of responsibility between civilian and military provided for under the existing arrangement had worked in the past; that it was working now; that relations between the military and the Commission had been harmonious; and that it could be made even more effective along certain lines set out in the last paragraph of our memorandum, which I proceeded to read.

I said that it was inescapable that there should be a division of responsibility in atomic energy, unless civilian control were completely abandoned—which no one had suggested; that the question always is where is the best place to draw the line dividing civilian and military responsibilities and functions; that the place the line has been drawn has been effective and can be made to continue to be effective.

I stressed the fact that we felt obliged to record our warning that a change in the present arrangement was fraught with risks to development and to maximum readiness; these were discussed in the memorandum which the President could read.

Having a strong feeling that the "Judge" was inclined in the direction of our arguments, I stopped at this point, taking up only perhaps three or four minutes.

Forrestal then called on Symington, Secretary of the Air Force. Symington's statement was simply beyond belief. Bearing in mind that this was a very solemn and important question of policy brought to the President in an atmosphere of tension through the world, he sat there and, I am sure to the consternation of his associates, talked about a visit he had at Los Alamos and Sandia.

"Our fellas at Sandia think they ought to have the bomb. They feel they might get them when they need them and they might not work."

The President looked at him hard and said, "Have they ever failed to work?"

"No, but . . ." and he left that one. "Mr. President, it is just like having some goods you manufactured, well, when the salesmen go out on the road with it, they learn about the troubles the customer is griping about, and that way you make it better. . . . I talked to some scientists at Los Alamos, and one fellow, I forgot his name, he said he didn't believe the law permitted the military to have the bomb, and I don't believe he thought we ought to use it anyway."

The President was giving this line of irrelevant talk a very fishy eye; at this point he said, poker-face, "I don't either. I don't think we ought to use this thing unless we absolutely have to. It is a terrible thing to order the use of something that" (here he looked down at his desk, rather reflectively) "that is so terribly destructive, destructive beyond anything we have ever had. You have got to understand that this isn't a military weapon." (I shall never forget this particular expression.) "It is used to wipe out women and children and unarmed people, and not for military uses. So we have got to treat this differently from rifles and cannon and ordinary things like that."

Symington went on: that "a Dr. Bradbury, I think that was his name, at Los Alamos, he thought we ought to have the bomb, but not now. Our fellas need to get used to handling it."

This went so badly that Forrestal took over. "As an old weaponeer yourself," he said, countering and taking a cue from my crack about "teaching grandmother how to spin," "you know how important it is to get used to handling a new weapon." Symington made one last entrance: "Yea, our fellas, they let them take out bombs without the hot stuff; afraid of a real bomb, I guess."

Royall, who was sitting there looking glummer and glummer, broke in: "We have been spending 98 percent of all the money for atomic energy for weapons. Now if we aren't going to use them, that doesn't make any sense." He said some other things, but this was a sample.

If what worried the President, in part, was whether he could trust these terrible forces in the hands of the military establishment, the performance these men gave certainly could not have been reassuring on that score.

He asked whether I wanted to reply. I said no. He glanced at the other Commissioners, who said nothing. I handed him our letter.

He said, "I will read these papers; can't make up my mind right off about a thing as important as this. I'll let you know.

"You have got to understand that I have got to think about the effect of such a thing on international relations. This is no time to be juggling an atom bomb around." He said this with a sternness and solemnity that was in marked contrast to the eager-beaver attitude of some of our friends.

He rose, and we all followed suit, and filed out.

As we all got into cars at the east entrance someone said, "Boy, oh, boy, how *Time* would like to have a photographer here to get *this* group." Forrestal said, patting my arm and grinning that likable grin of his, "Well, Dave, the amenities were observed."

When we got back to the building, the five of us got out of the elevator together. Lewis called us into a huddle. Then he said, "To hear those two lawyers buttering up the Judge. Dave says, '. . . teaching grandma how to knit . . .' and then Jim, 'an old weaponeer like *you.*'" At which we all burst into a big laugh that echoed down the corridor as we departed to our offices. The way we relieve tension by saying something funny is one of the saving parts of the job.

JULY 23, 1948
AT THE OFFICE (12:30 P.M.)

Jim Webb called at a little after eleven to say that the President had announced to the Cabinet this morning that he had decided the custody matter, and planned to issue a public statement. Forrestal took the decision fairly well, Webb said, but objected strongly to the idea of a public statement, questioning why it should be announced that he had been overruled. The President talked to him and Symington and reaffirmed his intention to issue the statement. Last night the President went over the statement as drafted by the Bureau of the Budget and personally revised it, just how I don't know, but will be able to tell.

The public statement is to be geared to the issuance of our report to Congress, which we now have sent to the press, will hold a press conference tomorrow morning, and the report and the President's statement will be issued together. General Marshall approved the statement, provided it was coupled with our report, and the exact text is now in process of being cleared at State and Defense.

This is a very important event indeed.*

JULY 27, 1948
AT THE OFFICE

I have been urged to accept a measure of "personal protection." Decided yesterday "to hell with it." As an indication of what is recommended here [are excerpts from] a memo from Frank Wilson, a consultant of ours, and for many years Chief of the U.S. Secret Service.

* The President declared that the existing civilian custody of atomic weapons would be continued. In his statement, he said: "Since a free society places the civil authority above the military power, the control of atomic energy properly belongs in civilian hands."

Because of the continued widespread publicity given to the Chairman and to the Atomic Energy Commission, it is extremely likely that mentally ill persons or others may endeavor to harm or embarrass the Chairman or members of his family. It is, therefore, advisable to consider appropriate steps to better assure his safety and the safety of his family. . . .

A small protection detail should be established by the Atomic Energy Commission. Agents of the detail should be trained in first-aid and jiu jitsu. . . . They should be prepared to quickly step between the Chairman and a potential assailant. They should be trained to function unobtrusively, to quietly persuade any mentally ill persons to leave the scene and only if absolutely necessary should force be used. . . .

Floodlights should be installed to illuminate the outside of the house and roadway where the Chairman resides. These lights should be controlled by a switch sunk in the roadway which will throw on the lights when an auto passes over same and by switches located at two points within the house. . . . Arrange for special inspection by the [telephone] company to discover taps or interference with the line. Ascertain whether the adjoining house is occupied and if not, who has access to it. . . .

It is suggested that an Agent in an auto follow the Chairman's auto when he is on the road after sundown. . . .

Agents on the detail should be trained to thoroughly inspect hotel rooms or other places where the Chairman may have important conferences so as to discover whether any listening devices may have been surreptitiously installed. . . .

When the Chairman is holding a reception and greeting a considerable number of persons he should, whenever possible, have his back to a wall to prevent persons from approaching him from the rear. When an agent is present at such receptions he should as unobtrusively as possible take a back to back position with the Chairman so that he can observe activities in the rear. . . .

JULY 30, 1948
AT THE OFFICE

What do you do about published estimates of how many bombs we have, considered of the highest order of secrecy? Drew Pearson said he knew, but didn't say how many. Nat Finney has made an estimate lately. The early practice was to discourage this speculation. Bill Waymack and I think that is wrong, both from a security position (the danger of bracketing the guesses or estimates by the terms of our reply) and because it looks like censorship.

Day before yesterday I called on Chairman Taber, one of the most powerful men in the whole wide world, with a terrible load of work.

With him were the ranking member of the committee and another senior member, John Phillips of California. What did we talk about for an hour and ¾?

A dipsi-doodle, as the mining boys say! Following is a memo I wrote about it, to my associates:

Chairman Taber opened the discussion of this matter by stating that there was something he wanted to take up with me that had been handled so badly that it had caused him to lose confidence in the Commission.

Referring to some letters before him, he then recited some of the circumstances of the Capt. Di Bella-Gigliotti matter.† He said that these people were well spoken of, had the confidence of General Donovan and of reputable people in California, and yet the Commission had been unwilling to deal with them except upon conditions that would have given away the secret of their invention. Furthermore, we had set the Italian secret police on Capt. Di Bella, and he was informed that the secret police had ransacked his home and questioned his relatives with the intent of "trying to get hold of what he had."

Congressman Phillips, who had in his hand my most recent letter to him on this matter, added to this indictment. He said that he could not understand why in the world we should have turned to the State Department to find out about this man; that we ought to know the State Department is no good; that they are filled with Communists and that since Di Bella had been against the Communists they would try to get away from him and into the hands of the Italian Government his secret invention. He said further that our position of asking him to disclose the method of his invention to us prior to an agreement with him did not look good to him. After having his house ransacked and after our treatment of him in the conferences (he did say that our representatives had behaved courteously) it was no wonder that Di Bella did not like the idea of secret patents as a protection inasmuch as it is well known that the Russians copy these secret patents every day.

Chairman Taber returned to the criticism of our unwillingness to give this invention a trial. He said he understood from Di Bella that this would not cost us anything, or anyway not very much since he was offering to make the survey at his own expense; and it could be set up in the United States and tried out and if they spotted uranium someplace, we could go there and see if it was there and then judge the results that way.

I said I would state my own reaction very candidly—and that this

† This man claimed to have invented a machine capable of locating uranium ore even though thousands of miles distant.

was based necessarily not upon my personal knowledge but upon the opinions of men with experience and training appropriate to the problem. All the mining and geophysical people said that this was a familiar kind of promotional claim except that it was extraordinarily fantastic in its form; that is, the claim that minerals could be exactly located thousands of miles away.

We had, however, not dismissed the matter without giving it the attention of experts both from the mining, geophysical, and fundamental physics side. I reminded them that Dr. Di Bella had suggested calling in Dr. Enrico Fermi, who had conferred at least twice at some length and whose conclusion I transmitted in the letter to Mr. Phillips.

I asked what beyond this they wanted us to do. If in their opinion we should spend public money or take further steps, then in view of the position of the three members of Congress interested, the Commission would consider such further recommended steps, but that frankly, on the basis of the matter to date, I would think that only a direction from them would justify such a course.

Both Mr. Phillips and Mr. Taber made it clear that they did not want to direct us to do anything. Mr. Taber said he did not see what harm there would be in arranging for them to come to the United States and test it out if it did not cost much money. But when I again asked him if that is what he was directing us to do, he said no, that he was not, but he did not see what harm it would do.

I pointed out that one of my colleagues, Commissioner Sumner T. Pike, had long practical experience in mining and exploration all over the world with the firm of Case, Pomeroy and Company and otherwise, and that he was well acquainted with a number of the most successful and experienced exploration people in this country; that he had doubtless run into claims of this sort many times and that it might be helpful to have him discuss the matter with the Congressmen, and if they thought well of it, perhaps for him to try it out on some experienced, practical, mining exploration people.

AUGUST 12, 1948
AT THE EPHRAIM ALLEN HOUSE, MARTHA'S VINEYARD, MASSACHUSETTS

We got here a week ago this evening: it was a misty-moisty day, cool and half-rainy and dark. We were met at the ferry at Vineyard Haven by Mrs. Henry Hough, who kept wailing that she was sure it wouldn't do, the house, but the Dillons said we loved roughing it, and that as an engineer the gasoline water pump would be just my meat!‡

‡ General Theodore H. Dillon, deputy chief of the AEC's engineering division, had suggested we take our vacation on the Vineyard. Mr. and Mrs. Hough were co-editors of the Vineyard *Gazette*; Mr. Hough's father, George A. Hough, lived in retirement near the house we rented.

That pump, down the hill, hangs over my days: when I get her going in par (which I have set as four trials), I come back from my liaison preening my feathers and all set up with tales of her little temperamental curves and how onto them I am; I sit down there in the pump house, amidst oil and the simply deafening pounding of her gigantic breathings, and watch the gauge with satisfaction. And then, as this morning, when she doesn't respond, and the gauge doesn't move a bit, and the priming valve doesn't produce the grinding, pounding sound from the pump that tells the tale of her taking "holt"—then I get a bit panic-stricken and low and wish to hell I'd never met the ugly bitch. We had a bad time this morning—she began to boil and I did likewise.

Nancy arrived last night, dropped out of the skies in a blinking, blinking plane. It will be wonderful to have her here (if I can produce the water!) and she gets such fun out of things, many things. This house, for example, is filled with strange mementos of old George Hough's life as a news publisher—New Bedford for more than half a century. Nancy's chortle—oh, for a rainy day to go through all these amazing books, large clipping books of the great cotton strike of 1890 at New Bedford, one of the first that was a sob-sister carnival, I gather, since the Boston papers at least took the textile workers' side, it was an evidence of what the clipping-book collector labeled in large letters on the outside: "Yellow Journalism."

We left Washington on Monday, August 3, about four (hence right on schedule fixed long before), our last act being the complex business of voting in the Tenn. primary by absentee ballot. I only voted for Kefauver, having no yen for Browning. But I felt it was largely a gesture; when lo and behold, we hear down here that he licked the daylights out of Crump.§

Which reminds me: back in about 1940 or '41 I drove young Albert Gore to the site on the French Broad where, after a violent battle with McKellar, Douglas Dam was rising. He walked out on a hillside overlooking the magnificent confusion of a big dam at that stage and what he said was: "What we are seeing is not just a dam; it may be more important still; the end of a political regime." A good deal could be said for this as a sound prophecy, all the more remarkable for the fact that at that time and for years afterward it seemed that they were going to "get away with" the attack on TVA.

Monday night we spent at Swarthmore, in an inn that would be

§ Estes Kefauver and Gordon Browning won the Democratic primary nominations for Senator and Governor, defeating the Crump-sponsored incumbents, Senator Stewart and Governor McCord. (They went on to win in the general election in November.)

impossible to get out of in a fire—what a place. Tuesday was a rather dreadful drive, and one I'd like to forget, through New Jersey, and more lost routes and wrong turns than I can count. That night we spent with Ed and Janet Murrow, in a log house they've bought overlooking the Hudson River hills, at Pawling. Governor Dewey [their neighbor] was overlooking his cattle about the hour we drove in, just across the next hill.

Next morning talked to Ed about my idea, should I step out or be forced by conscience or the Republicans to get out of the atomic business: a trip around the world, writing back an account of what is going on—the idea I broached to Luce some months ago. He, i.e., Ed, "got" it right off; said it was a natural, and that with a few telephone calls that day he could sew it up, so it would carry us around the world.

Ed said he doubted if he could continue broadcasting long; his contract was airtight, but if he kept talking anything except "hate Russia" he would be branded a dirty Communist. What I should do—it's badly needed and there's money in it—is to organize a small outfit to supply speakers through the country. He'd like to join in such an enterprise when he moves out of broadcasting. Well, one takes this only with salt, but it gives me some confidence to know there are things one can do, if he can't square public service with his own need for a sort of non-perfectionist independence.

AUGUST 17, 1948
THE VINEYARD

We've been quite sociable, all in all, something we don't usually go for on holiday.

The first Sunday we were here, we went to a "neighborhood" party for us by the elder Mr. Hough, and met the Sanborns—three attractive young married women, sisters, related—cousins, I guess—to the Straights (Willard, Michael, etc.). Thomas Hart Benton called the first day we were here. Frances Henderson was here from last Thursday evening till Sunday morning, to work with me on the *Life* piece (MacLeish) and my speech on cooperation with Gt. Britain and Canada, but being here added to the sociability; and Fred [Newton] Arvin came Friday night last and left this morning.

Last night we went to dinner at the Roger Baldwins, he of the Amer. Civil Liberties Union, and a most vigorous and intense man. There, too, were Jerry Frank and his wife, the Bentons, Geo. Hough, Sr. I spoke of MacArthur to get Baldwin going on the General, for whom he has a terrific and uncritical admiration; he sounds so uncritical as to appear naïve, but I may be wrong. He was disturbed that MacArthur's order forbidding collective bargaining and a strike by government workers would destroy the trade unions of Japan, since two-thirds of Japanese industry was or soon would be run by the Govt. and hence by civil servants, as he put it. I told him the ABCs of the TVA experience—in collective bargaining in a Government industry, and other things apparently not known to him, who is, I gather, advising MacArthur on such matters. The notion is spreading that the moment an enterprise is public, its workers must surrender that large measure of private right embodied in the term "collective bargaining" and the right to strike.

Judge Frank spoke entertainingly (and a lot) of Wallace, whom he knew well way back in 1933, etc. He said that at the time W. was giving some scientific impetus to the Weather Bureau, he was consulting Indian rain-makers, and while furthering genetics, consulting numerologists. Told more of the Guru letters business,ɑ which is incredible and depressing.

Haven't been resting the way I had hoped—still keyed up. Partly because the MacLeish piece is still on my mind—changes being negotiated, worked over with Frances, and a session set for next Sunday in N.Y. and then the N.Y. speech, which I wrote in a short day here, but nevertheless is in the mind. Also I got a bad back again day or so after arrival, and this is somewhat nerve-racking. But once I get back from the N.Y. trip things will be different, I'm sure. Reading not much; read *The Age of Innocence* by Wharton; enjoyed it greatly.

The pump is still a trial. Sunday she had me about licked—the primer wouldn't prime. Like the New Deal economic efforts, I need a primer for the primer. This I do by hand, opening the darned pump to do it, with wrench, etc. But I take a perverse, stubborn pride in overcoming my discouragement and making it work. Which to date it has.

Yesterday Nancy and I walked down to the beach, through the lovely sun-and-shadow-lined walk, took a swim and roasted ourselves on the sand; then came up the path and home. She is such a sweet and attractive kid. Said she thought she'd try to get on the staff of *Fortune*, which interested me as she had been unwilling to consider anything in which she couldn't agree 100 percent, a quite impossible idea and not effective. Labor is her intense interest. Last night at the party she spoke two or three times, with purpose and point, with a clear voice and assurance, and this despite the presence of not only older but rather distinguished or at least well-known people—the reason being we were at the time discussing labor matters.

ɑ This refers to some correspondence between Wallace and a group of religious mystics in the 1930s.

AUGUST 22, 1948
THE VINEYARD, SUNDAY

Don't know quite when I've crammed so much and so many satisfying and diverse things into 24 or 36 hours.

Left here by plane yesterday at ten, having spent the early morning hours trekking through the heavy dew down to the House of Assignation, the gray shanty in the wild cherries where that darned Gas Engine and I have it out. She was balky as hell, too.

A fine flight. Frances H. and Corbin Allardice met me, and from then, through luncheon in my room at the Waldorf (a lovely 22nd floor room overlooking the river), I was brought up to date on the speech, the grumblings and record-making of Hickenlooper on "technical co-operation," and the arrangements for the evening, which included, I learned, an impromptu speech I was to make at the Atomic Energy Exhibit opening.

Went over the newest changes with Frances, looked at a batch of mail she brought up with her (none of it that couldn't wait, fortunately, with a few exceptions), and then went to the University Club for a Comm. meeting in Sumner's room, with Bob Bacher, Joe Volpe, and Ev Hollis, which rather caught me up on the sore things that have been happening.

The only one that is bad is the case of a young fellow at Los Alamos, who has been there for years, who joined the Communist Party in 1943, and dropped out, he says, a few weeks later. Everyone at L.A. swears by him, and believes in him, and it's quite an issue. Wilson told them he would clear the man. But it is a bad case, and one that would disturb people no end. He's not an indispensable man, and he is in the document room, of all places; has been for months and months. Sumner and (rather reluctantly) Bacher felt there had to be some minimum standards, and this was it, and I agreed.

I learned that Lewis has been shooting at the Comm. conclusion in the matter of tech. cooperation with the British, and it seems clear to Sumner, who spoke without the least ill will, that he has been needling Hickenlooper. Hick called Forrestal, full of objections along the Strauss line, and H. and Vandenberg met with Forrestal and Bush on it, and apparently came away pretty well "answered."

H.'s letter was full of nonsense, stuffily put, but on the whole was simply the letter of a man who wants to be on both sides of a question at the same time, hardly the mark of a lion-hearted leader, and rather in character of that amiable, pleasant, and lightweight statesman. Apparently Lovett and Carpenter (Don, that is), as well as F. and Bush, stood firm on everything but an approval that through carelessness had been given Cyril Smith* to discuss with the British metallurgy of a kind probably not appropriate at this time.

I barely had time to get bathed and dressed before the six o'clock reception in the Sert Room, where I met Mayor O'Dwyer for the first time. As the guest of honor I really got hospitality and deference in a way that I don't know how to handle. I liked him at once—a warmhearted, very Gaelic, handsome man (he will be 59 soon, which is hard to believe). At dinner I had Trygve Lie, the Secy. General of the United Nations, on my right, and sat on the Mayor's right. The Mayor talked through the dinner, talked heartily and with feeling. His contempt for most politicians was notable. He made a big point that he was through after his term expired in 1949—wanted something less exacting at his age than the punishment of running for office. "You have to deal with men of the kind that you wouldn't let inside your house."

My story of how gadgets pursue me reached a new high at this point, and about the funniest of all. Bear in mind—this was an atomic energy event—the city on its fiftieth birthday looks to the future, symbolized by atomic energy, the newest gadget, the chief atomizer being the speaker, etc. Grover Whalen, the chairman, said, "Now we have just one minute and we are on the air coast to coast," and with that pulled the chain on the little light over the reading desk below the radio mikes. (He had just explained that outside, where we would soon be marching down Lex'ton Ave., the lights had been turned off to make it appear as it was 50 years ago.) His face became alarmed, he pulled the chain again. No light. The seconds ticked off. A man held up the cord from the floor in front of the dais table—a waiter had tripped over the cord and severed it.

So I was introduced and on the air, and it was really murky. I put on my glasses and set off. And then it happened—the darned solicitude. I was aware that someone was moving around and sure enough a tall candle was put next to the reading stand. Across the room came a waiter carrying another tall lighted candle. Darned if they didn't plant four candles alongside that stand, flickering and drooling and luckily not quite setting fire to my script. For some reason—perhaps the importance of the speech—I didn't fluff or miss, except saying "installations" for "undertakings."

The Mayor took over when I was signed off, to make a crack about the candles. A waiter kicked over the lights, this time; let's hope no one kicks over atomic energy, because if they do it will be worse than this.

* A distinguished metallurgist, then a member of the AEC General Advisory Committee.

Then came the big kick, and the most fun I've had in a long time. The Mayor and I were escorted out surrounded by some of the Finest, and soon I found myself in a boy's dream of fame: marching, on the right of the Mayor of N.Y. City, down Lexington Avenue, with 50,000 people cheering (not me, but the Mayor, of course) and *torchlights* (the street lights were off to simulate 50 years ago) and ahead of us a big band! Something.

Then the ribbon of the Jubilee was cut by an explosion set off by a split atom (the Whalen touch). We went around, did a television interview together, etc. And finished with a review of an incredible fashion show. This consisted of gangs and quantities of glamour gals, all so slim that it was hard to believe, walking down a huge curved runway dressed in the most beautiful and unbelievable clothes—this went on for an hour. The cracks passed between the Mayor and myself gave him a quite changed view of me, this was evident, and he was really good and funny. After which we went to his office, temporary, and the models came in for champagne. Stunning gals, definitely. I said I had to go to New York on business, to make a very important speech; and I wind up passing the time of day, or evening, with a flock of models, complete with champagne and the Mayor.

Well, it was a day, and my greasy overalls and that one-cylinder bitch I had wound up that morning would hardly have known me.

This morning, at ten, Archie MacLeish and Frances H. came to my room and we finished up the revisions on the *Life* piece, meeting a few objections or suggestions offered by *Life*. It appears that between the initial rather sour reaction of the managing editor and the "we are all now delighted" message from the same guy an event occurred: to wit and namely, Mr. Luce read the MS and then the boys knew whether they liked it or not; before that they had to play it safe. Very funny, in a way. . . .

Trygve Lie said only one thing of interest to me. He had read Baruch's 1946 speech two days before it was given. He said that the body administering control should be the Security Council, not a special body. He told B.B. that the Russians were suspicious, and to take it out of the Council would confirm their suspicions because it would deprive them of the protection of the veto. Baruch said he agreed. But it went in nevertheless, and that killed the chance of acceptance. Since B. agreed with him Lie said he understood that someone "farther up" had insisted on taking it away from the Security Council. I didn't tell him that since the veto and punishments idea was Baruch's strongest conviction about the plan, his interpretation of what happened didn't strike me as correct.

AUGUST 31, 1948
THE VINEYARD, TUESDAY

Sunday Carroll Wilson wired: would I come to Boston Monday to see Walter Whitman, with him, to try to get Whitman's "No" reversed, the No being his answer to our invitation to head the reactor development work. A C-54 picked me up yesterday at eleven.

We lunched with Pres. Compton and the Administrative Council of MIT. One question: how to answer the letter of the chief editorial writer of the *Christian Science Monitor,* who insisted that MIT's requirement of vaccination for smallpox violated the religious principles of his son, an applicant for admission, since they believed it was prayer and not vaccination that prevented smallpox. The medical people were all hot about the letter. Compton thought it wasn't a thing to make an issue about, since so few such were rec'd.

On being asked to say a few words, I said I had found, among technically trained men, a greater appreciation of non-technical matters involved in public administration than was usually assumed. Compton said he thought the student self-govt. policies of MIT helped give their students their first taste of such responsibilities. The dean of students seemed a bit discouraged about it, though: there are a few students who will respond, but most won't. MIT's function is not to teach the how of local government or international affairs, but only to encourage participation in such matters; and at MIT it is hard to get more than a very few to do so, so how make much headway in the post-college period?

After lunch we urged Compton to take an active position, urging Whitman to undertake our work. He responded well; thought it would be a great help to MIT, showing leadership in a new field, thought the difficulty was that Whitman was happy doing what he was, and didn't like the wrench of leaving to go to Washington.

Then we went to Lexington, to visit the Lex. Project† and Whitman. Housed in an underground building, air-conditioned, built as Fighter Control Center during the war. Whitman I had never met before: easy manner, friendly, relaxed, not an impressive-looking man, but with a talent for people, I gathered. My words to him I hope made an impression; he would very much prefer to stay out of it, if someone else, a younger man who would stick with it for ten years, could be found. Flew the plane (i.e., had the controls) part of the way back, over the Sound. Very lovely flight.

Very hot during the week; 99 at one time, and humid as everything. Terrible heat wave through the country and a hurricane on its way. I

† A study of the feasibility of nuclear-powered aircraft.

enjoyed the heat. Sunday we went to the ocean, some of the most exciting surfing I've ever done.

Saturday (or was it Friday) went for my first sail on salt water. In the *So Fong*, built in Hong Kong in 1937 for an American millionaire; 80 feet long, two-masted schooner, teakwood. Beautiful ship. Owned by a professor of biochemistry at U. of Chicago, wealthy Terre Haute, Indiana, family; in fact, the registry reads "So Fong, Terre Haute, Ind.," which is funny. With the sails up and full it was a wonderful sight and a lovely feeling; none of the noise and vibration you usually think of in moving over the water.

Big group of guests aboard, including an interesting man from Andover Academy faculty; the Nathaniel Eliases; the Thomas Hart Bentons; a woman chemist from the Argonne Lab, etc.

It now seems I can stay here until the 12th or so, though I may have to have much of my accumulated reading sent here to get out of the way before I return. We hope to hear when David's ship (from England) reaches N.Y. in a day or two; we guess about the 7th, and then hope he can come up here for a few days.

SEPTEMBER 5, 1948
THE VINEYARD, SUNDAY

Yesterday was our 25th wedding anniversary. Quite an event. We didn't quite manage to "celebrate quietly" for in the evening we went to "Miss Emma's" (Daggett) before-Labor-Day annual party and were quite convivial, with some 50 other people. Among them Max Eastman, a very handsome article indeed who lives here on a cliff overlooking the ocean, and Mrs. E., a Russian dancer, who paints. I told Eastman how much I had been affected by his *Enjoyment of Poetry,* which I'd read more than 25 years ago. He is one of these men who have sensitive feelings—and that's a great deal indeed—but no analytical powers. This wouldn't be so bad, but then they get swept into things, public affairs for example; so they go from one extreme of emotion to another, assigning "reasons" they have no equipment to develop.

Our social life has been more active than I would have imagined; indeed, were it not for Nancy (who loves to have a good time, and is gregarious, with all her apparent shyness) I'd say we had too much of it. But it has been pleasant and fun, and perhaps what I need even more than the extra rest. Thus: Friday we had a chicken chowder dinner with our neighbors, the Charley Nortons (he of the goats, and my Main Reliance when the pump gets temperamental). Thursday to a steak dinner on a cliff overlooking the ocean, with David Langmuir's mother the hostess. Wednesday night we dined with Nathaniel and Leona

Elias, at their home here, where we met General "Eddie" Greenbaum, and Mrs. G. He was a right-hand man of Judge Patterson's during the war and a partner of Morris Ernst. Mrs. Elias, who is a physician with the N.Y.C. health services, had her father, a wonderful old boy, prof. emeritus of zoology, U. of Kansas, McAlister Coleman, and Mrs. C. (also a physician). Went swimming with the Eliases and their guests.

Among other people we've met: the Henry Beetle Houghs, of course, of the Vineyard *Gazette;* John Henry Lewin of Baltimore, of my Law School class; a woman who gives her all to get sunburned summers here, winters in the Virgin Islands, a lady in her forties, I suppose, who talks right out of Hollywood, "dahling," etc., and a morose-looking husband and daughter, married, 22, with the kind of bad manners of the upper crust, so called; George Hough III, a nephew of Henry Hough, fine-looking, with the desire for independence in the newspaper world (he's a Wis. journalism grad, as is his keen young wife); J. Donald Adams, of the *N.Y. Times* book mag., a shy-appearing man of 55 or so; Mrs. General Walker, relict of the former Gov. of Panama Canal, an Army wife and child, and a spirited old gal indeed.

Have been doing some work; spent yesterday morning on a stack of correspondence, etc., sent from the office. Will continue this off and on during the rest of the week.

The painting is coming along a bit. Mrs. Norton has been very helpful. I've added some tubes of water colors, learning a bit about the use of shadows, some drawing. But it is slow and whether I'll keep it up is a question.

Found some remarkable books here in this old house, overflow of old George Hough. Among them a large two-volume work by George Kennan,‡ published in 1891 by the Century Co., entitled *Siberia and the Exile System.* In Vol. II, Appendix B, p. 484, "The Russian Press Censorship," contains some extraordinarily interesting and relevant material which I'd like to make use of some of these days.


SEPTEMBER 11, 1948
THE VINEYARD, SATURDAY

Our wonderful weeks on the island are about over. This is rather sad. And for the first time I can recall, I start back, not eagerly and impatiently, but with dragging feet. This is partly because we have come to feel so at home here, with many new friends (we had a neighborhood

‡ Distantly related to the contemporary George F. Kennan of the State Department.

party last night, of some 15 as fine people as one can imagine, of all ages), and partly, I suppose, because of the rigors of the future of my work.

We are so gone on this island that we are ready to buy a place here, if we could get one of the kind we want and could afford. An old place across the road, the Rogers house, seems about right, with a view, a considerable state of dilapidation, but a basis on which to work. But the owner, Mrs. Henry Hough, hasn't yet said she'd consider selling. But Helen has persuaded me, belatedly, I fear, that even if we can't manage a permanent "our-roots-are-here" place for the year round, we should have such a place right away for the summer holiday, which we may hope will never be shorter than this year, and will gradually become a five-month semi-active place, where I could write, etc.

The big event is: David is home from Europe. There was big excitement, sending wires and letters, and then Thursday early he arrived by plane. He had a tremendous experience, is full of good talk about it, wonderful to hear. Yesterday we went to the beach together; he told me he is rather sure he will try to be a writer, and while he is shaping up pieces he has done or will be doing, work on a newspaper. This is a fine goal, and a tough road, but he has at least as good a chance of making it as the average young fellow with similar ambitions, better in a number of ways. Nancy and I have had further long talks.

A wonderful sail Wed., with David and Nancy Langmuir, on the sloop *Star Dust*.


SEPTEMBER 12, 1948
BACK HOME AGAIN, SUNDAY EVENING

At four o'clock I was bidding good-bye to the family, on the Vineyard. Just a little while before, I had had my last swim, pumped my last pump, hung up my greasy gloves in the old pump house, driven the car through Mr. Norton's goats. Here I was, with a huge airplane and an Air Force colonel, captain, lt., and sergeant waiting to take me off. As I saw the last of the island, rimmed with the silver foam of the shore, I sat down at a table, opened a huge briefcase—and was back on the job after the longest, best holiday in years.

In two steady hours I had plowed through a mountain of letters, memos, and had answered all my mail of several weeks. Tonight I finished the entire stack of material, so that tomorrow I begin with the accumulation pretty well behind me.

It will be rather lonely here. Until Helen gets here this is just a house.

We have added quite a few family gags as a result of our happy time together, as a family. E.g.: Helen had scolded me, mildly but firmly, for failing to do or remember to do something or other, and said, "Dave, you just don't *hear* what I said to you, or this wouldn't have happened"—something like that. Nancy, in a mild voice, said, "But, Mother, if Dad had known what you were going to tell him, he would have listened."

SEPTEMBER 13, 1948
AT THE OFFICE, MONDAY (8 P.M.)

Jim Webb came to see me today. The situation in Berlin is bad, he reports. The Russians seem prepared to kick us in the teeth on every issue. Their planes are in the air corridor today, and anything could happen. "Anything—they might walk in tomorrow and shoot Gen. Clay." The President is being pushed hard by Forrestal to decide that atomic bombs will be used, but the National Security Council, Jim has reason to believe, will advise the President that there is no occasion to decide that question right now. "The President has always been optimistic about peace. But he is blue now, mighty blue. It is very hard on him, coming right now particularly."

Jim reported that the military, ever since the custody decision particularly, are spreading stories all over the place deprecating the Commission: It has no program for a submarine propulsion power unit; it is this and it is that. This kind of complaining is hardly news to me.

He asked: What about the idea of using r.§ to forbid areas to an enemy? Could it be used to block out the Russians as they have us blocked out in Berlin? No, I said, I thought not; that is, the idea had developed practical difficulties, and certainly couldn't be made use of in the near future, i.e., in a matter of weeks.

Put in a hard day, beginning at 8:30, and twelve hours later I am still here. Found a great deal of stuff on the desk to be read, and long conferences with Wilson and others to get caught up. Working on a speech to the American Association for the Advancement of Science, which I decided I ought to crash the gate to make, pointing to the peril we are in, because of general distaste for governmental service by scientists, engineers, and managers. I feel it is important to say this right now, *before* the Thomas Committee begins its messing about atomic matters, and because our inability to get Walter Whitman, Noyes, and others makes things look pretty bad at the moment.

§ Radioactive "dust."

SEPTEMBER 18, 1948
AT HOME, SATURDAY

A strenuous week. Beginning Sunday in the plane, working every night five running.

The speech to the AAA of Science Thurs. noon was a quick job. I got the idea a week ago yesterday, found the "spot" Sat., and wrote it Tuesday, with final drafting changes Wednesday night. Another successful collaboration with Frances Henderson, which more nearly fits my habits of work and need to do my own writing than any method I've found before, even better than writing them alone and then getting criticism. I talk it over with her, then she works out an outline. Then while she stands by, I start typing out the speech (this time I wrote the first few pages at home, and the rest of it with her at the office later when I came in), and I read a few pages with her, and make the changes the discussion develops as we go along. Then she takes it around for criticism, and makes the changes she approves, and brings back the product, indicating the changes and why.

The speech involved dangers not apparent at the outset, and those inherent in such a speech. The former was a fine speech by Truman, on Tuesday evening, lambasting the Thomas Committee fore and aft. That meant that my speech right after would be regarded inevitably as "political" because in line with his. But I decided to go ahead anyway.

Rep. McDowell of the Thomas Comm. labeled the speech political, and those newspapers who are now in the campaign or who don't read the full text will probably give me a scolding, along with the scientists. The *Post,* here, did a fine editorial this morning; and I hope the sum total won't be too bad. But among our organization and those we are trying to induce to come with us (Noyes is again considering the Dir. of Research, which he turned down recently) we hope it will have a good effect.

Dad and Mother arrived from Chicago yesterday, looking very perky, both of them. Dad is now 80 and Mother 74. He is quite over the heart upset of last winter, and Mother seems fine, full of spirit.

Last Wed. spent from 3:30 to 5:30 with Chairman John Taber, and a group from the Buffalo Machinery Co. This Co. is a reputable small concern. They have been sold the idea by some "inventor" that they have an "Atomic Power" plant, and have been lambasting us for years for not recognizing that they have licked the problem of converting atomic energy into electricity. They have pictures of their gadget, which is obviously a kind of gas-under-pressure device. But they say they put a "one-sixty-fourth of a grain" of "commercial diffused U-235" into this machine and get all this power out of it.

Well, every once in a while their lawyer, who looks like a typical police court type (he stalks around, shouts, proves things by newspaper accounts, and said I was "practically guilty of treason" for not embracing their work, when Russia might discover it any time), starts a campaign on a Congressional committee, or in this case on old David Harum John Taber. Taber was impressed with the Di Bella thing (the Italian's thing-amajig for finding uranium 3,000 miles away!), but on this one he began siding with our position almost at once.

But right in the middle of this, when we were trying to make plain to him that a fire and a nuclear reaction were slightly different things, he said, "How much is a grain?" Well, it's not a scientific term at all, and Dr. Ralph Johnson and none of us knew. So Taber sent for a dictionary and while he searched for it, said he did know once, when he was in school, and speculated about it. "Oh, yes, here it is—one-seven-thousandth of an ounce." And he grinned and was very happy. The casual circumstances that lie between having to spend weeks explaining why we didn't authorize a "demonstration" of this absurdity and getting out from under it with the hours we've spent, rather shocking but part of the game. He is going to have dinner with Chas. Dewey, head of the "watchdog" committee for the European Recovery program; and the same kind of casual, uninformed hunches will no doubt affect the life or death of millions of people in Europe.

But I rather enjoyed this experience. It shows I do have the patience, for my impulse was to say this was nonsense and walk out to return to really important things. But that would have stirred up Taber's indignation and impaired my usefulness with him. It is a hell of a way to run a railroad, but I don't know of any way to avoid the right of the lay representative to have his say and to review things, which somehow must be explained to him, however little time there is and however unwilling he may be to give it the time for study, even if he has the capabilities.

Wednesday I talked again to the War College. The question period was rather fun. And I gather quite successful. "Custody" and "military representation" on the AEC were raised and I met the latter by asking if he suggested that there existed a man or men who could "speak authoritatively for the entire military." Thurs. a long session with the MLC. Carpenter told me how bitterly du Pont feels about the smear of them after War I, and how they opposed his taking the Munitions Board chairmanship he now enters on.

SEPTEMBER 19, 1948
SUNDAY

Another chapter in the Technical Cooperation matter was written this last week. Came up in form of proposed letter to the Joint Committee, replying to an emphatic but on-both-sides-of-the-question (and therefore typical) letter from Hickenlooper, rec'd. while I was away. Our letter was objected to by Lewis, who thought we ought to say "Ooops, sorry," which of course we didn't.

Led to discussion of what we are doing, by way of policy. I said positions were possible and arguable, at the extremes: (1) We want to help U.K. and Canada as much as possible, things being as they are; and (2) we have a contract, we will try to give just as little as we can and still stay within the letter of our agreement, shaving each obligation to the absolute minimum.

I thought we had taken a middle course: Within the areas we had agreed upon we would try to be fully helpful, not treating this as a commercial transaction; if we took view (2) above, we had better stop the whole business as it would produce irritations and disharmony rather than anything really good.

U.K.'s Minister of Defense has in a very broad request that would put us back where we were during the war, and this will clarify things, perhaps. Genl. Lemnitzer tells me he spent all summer in London, going over, with the U.K., common plans of a military character, and this is relevant to our own problem.

The safety of reactors located near centers of population took up a good deal of worry and thought this week. The Schenectady GE intermediate [research] reactor was the immediate issue. Bill W. thinks all the newer types with uncertain characteristics ought to be built in a remote place, the desert, etc. This will slow things up a lot. We're to have a showdown on it next week. I feel this is carrying things too far for effective progress; if we were to locate gas refining and chemical plants only where they are "safe," none of them would be in or near cities at all.


SEPTEMBER 20, 1948
AT HOME, MONDAY

"What I want is to be independent and free." David, his great, long hulk dark against the faintly luminous sky, as we sat on a bench on the golf course across the road. This was this evening, resuming the evening walks we enjoyed so last summer.

He asked me what I thought he should do after next year, assuming he wasn't drafted. He didn't think it was worthwhile trying to plan too far ahead. "I'm not sure, real sure, that is, what I really want to do." Well, what are the various possibilities?

He listed them. A year's study abroad. A year in the Merchant Marine, for the travel and experience in another "caste" than the one in which he had been born and brought up. Going to journalism school; getting a job on a newspaper; getting some other kind of job.

As to a newspaper job, he isn't at all sure that he wants to go to the top of the newspaper game. But would it provide good experience and a livelihood while he was trying to establish himself as a writer of fiction? Well, a case can be made that newspaper work is bad for a writer, destroys his individual style, etc. What other way is there? Teaching, I suggested, perhaps. That apparently doesn't appeal to him at all.

As we made our way home he said there is one other thing we hadn't considered—that is security and an easier life. He told me, "Don't overlook the fact that you are an exponent, one of the leading exponents, of the success school, but there are quite a few people who don't believe it is worthwhile trying so hard to kick yourself to the top, who don't think it is worth it, and perhaps I'll find I'm one of those who don't believe it is worth it."

Getting some rather rough letters about my AAAS speech—half a dozen. None of them from anyone of influence, but an indication of the political atmosphere (referred to New Deal, etc.) and also of the ugly feeling about scientists these days. The editorial comment ranged from a wonderful one in the Washington *Post,* a personally flattering one in the Baltimore *Sun* but which missed the major point of my speech, to critical ones in the Philadelphia *Inquirer* and rather so in the Washington *Star* and Washington *News,* the latter two being papers usually quite friendly.

But the net effect is what is important, for I realized that this was taking a risk. And the net effect is that (a) the Thomas Committee issued a defensive statement; (b) the scientists feel that I have tried to protect them against the promised abuses of the new hearings by the Thomas Committee; and (c) in the future, if ugly things are attempted by the Hickenlooper-Teeple team, we have made our record early.

SEPTEMBER 23, 1948
AT THE OFFICE (6:30 P.M.)

Had interesting talk this morning with Admiral Gingrich, our Security Chief. He gave instances that show what a mine of fascinating stories there are around this show. Example: The Manhattan District had issued 1,800 copies of manuals describing just how to put the atomic bomb together, etc. There was no accounting for these, and Gingrich's people, beginning the first inventory, found that hundreds of them couldn't be located. Finally, they found all but one. They discovered that this one had been put in a safe and forgotten; that the safe had been sold as junk. They located the junk man and found that he had sold it; and finally located the safe. There, way in the back of the safe, was the last remaining manual.

In another instance a highly secret document had been mimeographed by the Manhattan District, and many copies distributed. But to whom? No record. They recovered many of these, but did they have them all? They noticed that the stencils came from a typewriter that had a peculiar figure 8; located the typewriter, and then the girl who had cut the stencils, and she remembered to whom the document had been distributed.

Had a report this morning from Dr. Colby, our new Director of Intelligence, a scientist. Looks like a movie version of such a combination scientist and modern spy.

A shocking performance by General Electric yesterday morning.

Winne (with a tough guy, name of Peare, their public relations vice pres.) said that the AFL was putting on an organizing campaign at Hanford, headed by Kenneth Scott, the fellow who took out after me so hard in the Carbide dispute. Muir, GE's manager there, was endeavoring to put the company's position before the men. This was: to discourage their joining any union, on the ground that this would only be against the men's own interest, and assuring them that the company would do everything for them that a good union could and would do. They had plans for worker representation on management committees, etc., etc. They were putting out a magazine or pamphlet, or series of them, about the evils of Communism and the strength of free enterprise, and this was part of the "educational work" about unionization. They didn't want to take the next step, to follow the "quiet talking to foremen and others," i.e., addressing the employees on the matter in open meetings, without "the Commission's blessing, or at any rate, without their acquiescence."

We were all flabbergasted. To listen to Harry Winne, who seems to me the most sincere and earnest of men, I couldn't believe that he didn't believe this was on the level; but it was patently a straight-out effort to prevent a union, and to create the kind of paternalism that in speeches they all berate. Lewis sent me a note: "Don't you think we'd better comment, else they go out thinking we agree by our silence?"

So I let Winne have it. In a polite way, I think, but I said flatly that this would be construed as fighting unionism, contrary to the policy of the country that the genl. principle was that employers and employees select their representatives without pressure from the other.

Oh, this wasn't pressure, just "education as to where their best interests were."

Bad business; a hundred big outfits are probably at this moment licking their chops preparatory to a big drive to get rid of unions.

Then we brought up their union at Schenectady, the United Electrical Workers, headed at the national offices by a bad lot. They wouldn't get rid of them unless we ordered them to. They are under contract with them all over the country.

I told Harry I believed myself that a pro-union position, promoting the idea of independent unions, was the best policy for management, and that we had made it work in TVA; but that even though we couldn't insist on that perhaps for GE, the other extreme wouldn't do at all.

Afterward, Peare told me "in confidence" that the Thomas Committee is all set to hold hearings in Schenectady, to expose the leadership of the local unions there as Communist; all of this very hush-hush. In this way the Communist tag will be used not only to get rid of the bad eggs, and some of them may be rotten as hell, but to add to the weight of a general drive to get rid of all unions.

They'll bring the whole edifice down, yanking on those pillars that way, and it will come down on their heads.

SEPTEMBER 25, 1948
SATURDAY

David has just left, returning to college. His senior year. I remember my own returns, almost 30 years ago. A fine young fellow he is. We had ourselves a horseshoe series, which he won 3 games to 2. Now he is gone again. But we have been very lucky this year: the four of us together at Captiva and the Vineyard.

Much excitement yesterday, because of a speech Dewey made in Ariz. Actually, as I read it, nothing much to get worked up over; not much different from the things I've said in the Economic Club of Detroit and subsequent speeches and was about to say in Chicago next Fri.◖ But it was construed to support a movement, now under way, to change the McMahon Act, which an article in the Wash. *Star* says has the support of Repub. leaders, even quoting Vandenberg to this effect. So it means I

◖ Dewey was urging that private enterprise be brought more quickly into the development of peaceful atomic energy; this was essentially the theme of my speeches.

must steer away from reference to industrial participation, etc., as such, lest it appear I'm debating with Dewey. It will be a relief when this campaign is over, for many reasons. The general "feeling" and the polls say it is in the bag for Dewey, though a recent set of polls say he is losing ground to Truman. But he'd have to lose one helluva lot to make much difference.

SEPTEMBER 28, 1948
AT HOME

Home all day. Helen ill, something very uncommon. So I cooked three meals (all of them scrambled eggs, bacon, and toast! plus salad and soup tonight). And how in hell did I collect all those dirty dishes, just two people? But it was pleasant to wait on *her*, for a change. She seems better tonight.

Clark Clifford called from Okla. City. Truman considering a speech answering Dewey on atomic energy. Fine spirit. Said they "had their second wind—few days ago about ready all of them to crawl in a hole and die. Encouraging signs, not a few of them." I'm not so hot about stirring up the issue, but perhaps I'm wrong.

Spent a long time on a sickening personnel security case at Los Alamos. This man joined the Communist Party in Berkeley in 1943, then dropped out. Tough case, and the lab people are all steamed up. These things tear me up inside: the gossip and horrid things in that file that for centuries we have been building defenses against. But we would shake confidence, I fear, if we had a former Communist at the center of the bomb factory's information.

The final version of the letters trying to get the United Electrical Workers out of Gen. Elec. went out.* Company rather mad because I said I couldn't see why they didn't do the booting. Phoned Charley Wilson, when I heard intimations that they (some lower-echelon guys, Boulware chiefly) were saying this was politics, etc.

Have been tuckered since a hard day Monday.

SEPTEMBER 29, 1948
AT HOME

What a day!

Most of the day was spent on the case of an artist who for five years has been at Los Alamos, and now it appears that back in '43 he

---

* The AEC ordered General Electric, its contractor, not to permit this electrical union to represent any employees at the new Knolls Laboratory at Schenectady. Union officers had refused to file non-Communist affidavits, as required by the Taft-Hartley Act.

signed a card making him a member of a Communist Party local in
Berkeley, a fact he deliberately refrained from putting on an employment record some time back. We overruled Wilson, and said he should
not work at Los Alamos. The laboratory people, including Tyler, the
tough Navy guy in charge of Santa Fe operation, are up in arms, and
five of them, heads of departments, came out to go over it with us,
with blood in their eye. Predicted that if the decision stands the lab
will suffer, badly, and you could see they meant it. 3½ hours of this,
on top of an hour on the same subject this morning, and more discussion ahead. Very bitter, some of the things that have been said, like
charging us with lack of guts in facing up to a hard fight.

Well, there probably is something in this. To me, it seems carrying
things a bit too far to ask the country to have confidence in us if we
accepted a former Communist at that particular spot, right in the
middle of important information some of which could be communicated
by word of mouth. But there is a good deal to be said on the other side,
since these highly responsible men take it so terribly seriously.

Helen much better. I had a fierce time this morning, cooking
breakfast and cleaning up after Penny, who picked this particular time
to display manners not appropriate to an old lady—or perhaps they
are to a very old lady. And then, right in the middle of that, and
burning toast, the damned telephone rang twice. So I've had a day!

SEPTEMBER 30, 1948
MORNING

Take off for Chicago this afternoon. Meeting with American Society
of Newspaper Editors this morning.

The Washington papers made a great deal of one aspect of our
letters on unions which have officers not reliable for the atomic
energy program, that is, the effect on the United Public Workers here
in Washington—something I had never thought about, actually. The
interesting part is that Nancy was a member of one of their locals
when she was in the Labor Department, and this fact was thrown up
against me by a Congressman from Illinois, Busbey, when my confirmation fight was on; it was also in that nasty *Plain Talk* article.
Nancy tried her best to keep the Communist issue from breaking up the
union, as she put it—and learned a lot about the tactics of infiltraters.
(That sounds like a phrase: infil-traitors!) She has such a strong sense
of loyalty to her friends and associates that this may give her a pang.

I have certainly had to do a lot of unpleasant things in this job.

OCTOBER 1, 1948
FLYING NON-STOP, CHICAGO TO WASHINGTON

This is one of those times when I *don't* feel "What the hell—why do I keep on doing this and taking all the grief and hectoring and no money?" In short, my speech to the Executives' Club this noon (which I didn't finish making notes on until eleven o'clock this morning!) went over big, and was great fun, actually. A large audience, place was packed, perhaps 800, and a good-looking, alive kind of audience. (The $350 won't hurt either, with my addition of Nancy and Dad to the roster, and David back in college.)

The speech demonstrated how much better it is, if I possibly can, to speak extemporaneously, as I did today, and how much skill I have gradually acquired in making the essential processes of nuclear reaction understandable.

From time to time I have wondered whether it was right for me to depart from my TVA practice of never, but never, accepting, or retaining, an honorarium for speeches or writing. I have been doing it in this job because I really couldn't make it otherwise, and because I know that the practice is not only legal (which it was in TVA, of course), but also accepted and common. The president of the club said they had Joe Martin, the House Speaker, the previous week, and when they gave him their check for $350 he said he was certainly relieved to have it, that a lot of these Republican outfits ask him to speak but they never say anything about paying him. So I am going to stop worrying about the propriety of it, providing I don't do it too often.

Had a very good visit with Wally Zinn and 25 members of the Argonne Lab staff, in the afternoon. They asked questions, and we talked things over for a couple of hours. A good deal of concern on two subjects: personnel security, and whether the reactor development work at the Argonne meant that basic research (which is the scientist's pet, of course) will be decreased in importance, etc. On the first I said there was no escape from the investigation as long as there was secret work, and that an investigator would occasionally put into the file stuff that was silly or worse; bound to. Also, I didn't see any end to the anonymous "informant." I thought it better to be on the pessimistic side rather than otherwise, considering what lies ahead. Other subjects I raised were how you make it clear to laymen, including members of an appropriations committee, *why* basic research, that has no particular "practical" application in mind, is so terribly important and should be supported.

A phone call from Col. R. R. McCormick. (I phoned him this morning, before he was in, and left a message for him, simply reminding him that we hoped he would take that Western trip to the installations. He phoned back.) He was very pleased, obviously pleased, to be called, and said he still had it in mind. A strange chapter in my acquaintances.

Saw quite a few familiar "old faces"—Oliver Williams, my life insurance man in the old Chicago days, Sim Leland, Dunc Lloyd, Tom Beacom, Zimmerman (Law School classmates), Bob Hutchins, Ben Goldstein and George Haight, Chris Christensen, now chairman of Celotex, formerly head of the University of Wisconsin Agricultural School. Some of the men at the "reception" before, and at the head table included Bob Wilson, chairman of the Standard Oil Company, on our Industrial Advisory Committee; Dr. Otto Struve, director of the Yerkes Observatory; J. L. Holloway, president, Crane Company; E. J. Doyle, president, Commonwealth Edison Co., James Nance, president of Hotpoint, Inc.; Dr. Hogness of the University of Chicago; Meyer Kestnbaum, president of Hart Schaffner & Marx (I felt like looking at the inside label on his suit).

OCTOBER 3, 1948
SUNDAY

Yesterday morning with the President's special commission on atomic energy labor problems. William Davis, chairman; Ed Witte of U. of Wis. (and friend since Madison days); and a Mr. Horvitz, a sharp and able-looking individual. Most of the time spent listening to Will Davis talk. Good, relaxed, sensible talk, but old man talk nonetheless. But happily he sees our viewpoint, isn't at this stage too attracted to the "easy answer" boys (compulsory arbitration, no-strike legislation, etc.) and knows the curves of such as Boulware, GE's personnel vice president.

I asked for recognition of two propositions: that we needed the active cooperation of the best of American industry, hence our principle that industry should make the principal labor decisions; but also (and this has been lost sight of) we need the cooperation of employees, *and* that the established and best way to secure that was through independent unionism carrying out collective bargaining of parties whose representatives were chosen without interference by either party.

Phil Murray let fly at me in the recent labor matter, but not too violently.

Did some gardening, and cut some firewood. Evening, went to dinner for the first time at British Embassy. Helen all over her bug, looking wonderful (in the apple-green evening dress with wide gold band around her middle; she's worn it for years, says this is the last time, but it is lovely and I'll miss it).

Sir Stafford Cripps the guest of honor. A small non-official dinner. Lady Franks told Helen this was a dinner, after many "official ones," to meet some of the "most worthwhile people in the U.S." Well, anyway, there was the ubiquitous Felix Frankfurter, drooling with Anglophilia, and looking more subdued (not a bad thing, as I see it); Frances Perkins; the Dean Achesons; David Finley of the National Gallery; Mrs. Dwight Morrow and Mrs. Dwight Davis; Mrs. Morrow's daughter (looking somewhat like Anne Lindbergh, her sister), her husband is connected with the Embassy; a John Miller, London *Times* correspondent; and of course Sir Oliver and Lady Franks.

Good talk with Franks; a "bit of business," over the coffee and brandy. Told me of his talk with Lovett, which I was to attend but was away or busy. Result: let things (new requests for tech. coop.) ride for a while. I emphasized the importance of a clear understanding of the *basis* of the cooper'n., what I said to the Comm. couple weeks ago. He said London was considerably disturbed by the way things had been going in this field lately.

Talked a good deal about the Labour program, which he had much to do with framing before they got it in. The young men are facing the future, not hoping for nor expecting that after this crisis we'll go back to the comfortable but dull times from 1900 to 1914, or before. Made much of the loss of so much of the older-brother generation, the men between him and his father's age (77), between him and Churchill. He is 43.

"Those men, who ought to be where I am, and others like me, they are dead, dead in the First War." A warm, eloquent, and very personable man he was as we talked, quite unlike the shy picture the press gives of him—which probably is fright of the terrors of the press.

After we "joined the ladies," Cripps grabbed my arm, vigorously and most unlike the austere picture of him, and the picture of British reticence, and steering me to a corner of the drawing room said he wanted to talk to me "for 16 hours." Then in the most cordial and charming manner imaginable, he told me what a lift TVA had given the English. 100,000 copies of the Penguin edition of my book sold; still selling. It is a moral idea, not merely a material one—and it "gives people happiness." What we need are more places in the world where these ideas are implanted and nourished. That's what I should be doing—organizing the friends of the TVA idea to carry it over the world—instead of "frankly, wasting your time, if I may say so, with atomic energy." Greatest achievement, monument of our time, etc., very fancy talk—and this from Old Austerity.

He smokes cigars and cigarettes hard, though his "food habits," as he refers to them, are as publicly pictured. Wears strange glasses, the top part is glass, the *lower* part cut out. Looked quite relaxed, well, ruddy, in good humor.

OCTOBER 9, 1948
RETURNING TO WASHINGTON FROM NEW YORK

Helen and I left Washington on the Congressional late Wednesday afternoon. Left in a flurry, signing a letter to Fitzgerald, president of the United Electrical Workers, on the run. (This I saw in the New York papers, a big "Lilienthal says . . ." etc., headline. How that letter was worked over along a line I suggested at a Commission meeting at 2:40 o'clock and signed at 3:30 was something.)

Went to two shows on our trip: *Make Mine Manhattan* (very good, wonderful dancing, fresh, and no smoking-car humor). And then Beatrice Lillie in *Inside U.S.A.* She is terrific, of course, and there were some good skits, but not as good as *Make Mine Manhattan.* The skit in which a hapless customer has to demonstrate the "atomic" pen that writes under water nearly had me in hysterics.

Highlights of the New York trip:
Visit with Baruch (accompanied by Helen) on Friday morning. He talked a good deal about his father, etc.—the "usual." I worked on him about the Vogt book, *The Road to Survival,* for which he wrote an introduction, and urged him not to go down that line in his opening speech to the Herald Tribune Forum. Told him that I wouldn't rely on the judgment of a man who exhibited such a view of the human race as did Vogt in this book. People like that certainly can't furnish any guidance for others, or for social policy. He liked this; that was what made the Russians so suspicious: they were not at peace with themselves, were unsure and so suspicious of others.

Spoke to the Book Publishers Lunch Club Friday noon, at the Yale Club. Most of the leading firms had their presidents and some editors present. It went fairly well, though not my best, I thought. It was very informal and rather personal. Whether any good will come of it is hard to say. I stayed away from recommending any particular course for the publishers. They think they have their troubles as it is; spoiled by making so much money during the war, I guess.

Helen and I had a lovely time together, but that is part of a different kind of account. I am determined that she shall be with me on these trips if I can possibly manage it. Besides seeing the two shows, we spent an interesting hour in the Museum of Modern Art.

Had dinner with Basil and Mary Bass, he a classmate of Harvard Law '23, she executive editor of *Ladies' Home Journal.* The other guests were the Goulds, the husband and wife team who head the *Journal*. It was a curious and inconclusive evening. They came quite evidently for the purpose of trying to find some journalistic basis for something on atomic energy. I tried every damn thing I could think of, but so far as I could tell the most that happened was that Mrs. Gould said at the end—this was midnight, "You have convinced me." I doubt if I did; didn't sound too convincing to myself, for that matter. Will try to interest them in covering the Cincinnati exhibit and program of atomic education.

Spent an hour with Bishop Oxnam, who had just returned to his office that morning for the first time since August. He is a power house, and is developing a practical judgment of tactics that is encouraging to see. But a peculiar thing happened.

I had suggested, months ago, that the Commission needed an advisory committee on the ethical or spiritual implications of atomic energy. How did we go about achieving this, assuming he agreed? We said we would think it over. I talked it over with Bill W., and we concluded that in any event the suggestion must come from the churches, and should be directed, initially at least, to information. This meeting I asked to discuss it further.

He said he had spoken to two groups, one small, the other 3,000 leaders of one kind or another, and they had derived a "tremendous lift" from the fact that a man in my position should crave the spiritual counsel, etc., etc. But my present suggestion, that *they* should initiate the idea, and that the church groups should name the committee, would take away from the idea its greatest inspiration, etc.

I said that I feared the precedent. Nothing was more important than maintaining the separation of Government and Church and the complete independence of the Church from anything that looked like playing up to or using the Church for purposes of the State, and particularly in matters affecting military considerations.

He didn't see this at first at all; said that he was especially concerned about the separation of Church and State (this was unnecessary for him to say, for he battles the Catholic Church on this night and day, fearlessly), but as I proceeded to discuss it, he began to recount instances in which Forrestal had "invited" Church leaders for this or that purpose, how they put on a great show for them, the same with the Navy, how shocked he was to find that the *assumption* was war with Russia, etc.

I told him how bad it was for the military or any Government official to pick churchmen for advisory committees relating to ethical or spiritual matters; that is, matters which are the concern of the Church, among others. Then he saw it, to my relief.

He will discuss the whole thing with Protestant, Catholic, and Jewish leaders and come up with something we can discuss further.

We discussed whether the Catholics would be able to join and make an interfaith matter of it. There is some question about this. The line seems to be that if it concerns only social welfare they can; if it is a Church matter they can't, because that would be an admission that there are other churches than the true Church.

A curious problem. I wonder if there is any parallel for it.

1. We protect the results of Sandstone [Eniwetok] with the greatest care. We report to the Congressional committee, and no leak.

2. We report to the country in the most general and guarded terms: "Weapon position substantially improved."

3. Gen. McNaughton of Canada, who has had no access to the results of Sandstone from us nor I feel sure from any source (e.g., the military, that is privy to the facts), says, at the Paris General Assembly of the UN, that the atomic weapons have been improved by as much as "one decimal place."

4. David Dietz, science writer, in today's *World-Telegram*, based on his version of McNaughton and our own general statement of "improvement," states *as a fact* that our bombs now are ten times more powerful than the first ones. This will now be repeated as if it were an official statement, most people forgetting just what their authority is for the statements.

5. If this is not the fact, i.e., the ten times business, what do those of us who do know the fact do about it? Obviously, we will do nothing. But is that the right course? To deny that it is true without stating what *is* true will not do more than give the Russians a chance to bracket the area of true-false. And so it goes.

OCTOBER 12, 1948
ABOARD A C-54, MILITARY AIR TRANSPORT COMMAND, HOMEWARD BOUND
FROM CAMP CAMPBELL, KY. (5:25 P.M.)

A trip to see a "demonstration." The impersonality of the whole thing amazes me. The "briefing" (in a weird setting of luminous blue lighting in a darkened room thrown on maps and charts that are blue in the darkness, with the "targets," etc. in color)—strange business, and I gather the standard briefing room procedure worked out during the war. As one officer said somewhere behind me in the darkness, "Seems like the old days, doesn't it?"

Conditions were "simulated," as they say, and even conditions of "personnel fatigue" for the engineer battalion boys were considered, tested, commented upon. (They did look tired, too.)

General Kenney, who until just the other day was head of the Strategic Air Command (four stars, and battles all over the globe), was the ranking air officer. A tough and not too bright-looking little man, full of politico talk about his "wonderful boys." My aide was young Col. Preuss, a very intelligent young fellow, thoughtful, well informed. We had a good talk about "what *is* peace," and about the criteria that have to be studied in determining what course we can take under the new conditions we face.

The "demonstration" itself was a pretty tame affair, of course, but it did make things seem more real. I was particularly glad to hear the explanation of tactics, under present conditions. My hunch was confirmed that no one is giving much thought to anything except the most effective way to deliver these gadgets as if they were just another form of blockbuster.

Sterling Cole, vice chairman of the Joint Committee, was along. A rather somber man, very good-looking, tired-appearing. Had a hard primary contest, and will have to do some campaigning, but not much in the election itself. Said he was pretty fed up: the cost of campaigning and of running his office, and nothing but hard knocks for it.

As we started to get back in the plane he said, "All of this effort and money, and only one chance in a hundred that it will ever be used." He didn't mean that this was the chance that there would not be war, but rather that if there should be a war, we would almost certainly not use atomic weapons. I said that it was my distinct impression that the plans were otherwise. The question of whether atomic bombs should be used, and if so at what stage, had so far as I could make out been jumped over, so far as military planning is concerned. Of course, it was for the President to decide, but the recommendation from the Joint Chiefs of Staff would be the only recommendation that would come to him. This seemed to shock Cole considerably.

I am more than ever impressed with the necessity for more thought about the moral and psychological aspects.

It was interesting to hear two soldiers, after a little discussion, say that the virtue of war was no longer apparent. Kenney and Nichols both showed grave doubts about where all this leads.

OCTOBER 20, 1948
AT THE DESK

John Steelman called. Apologized, but he promised McGrath he would call.† The Argonne Lab; an electrical contract was to be awarded

† McGrath, Senator from Rhode Island, was Democratic National Chairman; Steelman was the assistant to the President.

to Fischback & Moore. The University of Chicago decided to divide it between three contractors. McGrath "is somehow interested in Fischback & Moore." John asked: "Could I tell him that you don't think you can do any good but if you do get a chance you will?" No, tell him I can't and I won't.

OCTOBER 21, 1948
AT HOME, EVENING

Yesterday we had quite an experience. Word had come to me that four of our best men at Sandia, engineers, a physicist, etc., had a world-shaking idea so terrific that they could not impart it to anyone but me, about a weapon that would make the present ones, etc., etc. I said this was nuts bringing this to me; they should tell Bradbury, the lab director. No, it was either directly to me or they would go to Truman. It was so secret they couldn't trust anyone, etc.

Well, we decided that since they occupied such important posts we had better send for them. The young fellow who did the talking apparently was the sparkplug, a fine-looking man, about 30 I would say. We sat in a circle in my office: the Commissioners, Carroll Wilson, Gen. McCormack. After a lot of strange preliminary talk he read from a two-page typescript about the "plan." A hypothetical X, developed by a panel of outstanding scientists, supported by drawings, and other evidences that it was a reality, the documents to find their way into the right places. X would be so great as to prevent war.

Well, this lad talked on, not looking at us, his companion, a kind of plowboy type, nodding in eager agreement. They had "made it." They were telling their story in the holy of holies. All of us felt at once that what I suspected at first—and told Waller, who brought in the story, all in a tizzy—was quite true. The strain of working out there on the desert with these damn things had told on this fellow, and he had infected the others. He spoke mysteriously about a month or two being critical for getting the "plan" into operation. Why a month? The plowboy said brightly that Churchill and Marshall had said that there would be war in the next two months.

At the conclusion of his statement the tall lad, his eyes worried and strange-looking, said that the whole hope in the plan was the belief that fears of the uncertain could be implanted in certain quarters, fears such as we all have. When he said we "could now ask questions," I said, as kindly as I could (hoping to bust it loose), "What kind of fears do *you* have?" The answer was revealing, and I am sure would have been particularly so to the doctor who should have this fellow in hand. As Lewis said, "None of us will forget this afternoon as long as we live."

The tension had been so great that we did the thing that this group of men does almost every time we get too serious—and this is what saves our lives. We started telling stories—I told Louis Brownlow's about the paranoiac and the committing judge in the District of Columbia, and Lewis his about the sailor picking up pieces of paper, saying about each, "No, that's not it," until they handed him his medical discharge, at which he says, *"That's* it."

We approved a strong letter to the president of the United Electrical Workers today—I strengthened it up last night—and it will be released Saturday. We are on difficult ground, full of danger of abuse of Government power, and in apparent conflict with the principle I believe in so much that men should select their union representatives without interference. But I think we have handled it, by stages, in a way that avoids the worst aspects of a bad precedent. The Civil Liberties Union is looking into it, and I am getting a tanning from the UE.

OCTOBER 22, 1948
AT HOME

Forgot to record, I believe, that on the New York trip lunched with the Harper people and that Canfield said they would publish a book of my speeches. Helen is working on the idea, for if it is done as I would like—that is, not a miscellany or anthology, but more or less straight writing—it will take a lot of work, and she is the gal who could do a job on it.

Heard today that our effort to buy the Rogers house on the Vineyard was turned down by Betty Hough, but offered us a piece of land that sounds very interesting, and we may buy it. I would like to have some land on that island, and begin building a summer home there, right away.

OCTOBER 23, 1948
AT A MEETING OF GENERAL ADVISORY COMMITTEE

Talking about "raw materials." I recalled so well the dismal outlook described to us (the Congo mine flooded, etc.) just before we (the Commissioners) all went to Bohemian Grove a year ago last August. We were "out of business," as Ernest Lawrence said. Then I started, right there among the redwoods, to show that there were "things to be done about it." And that is what happened. Now we are looking at the figures again, and a report has just come in from Africa, a very good one as to the future. So it goes. A year from now I would guess the figures would look even more optimistic than today.

OCTOBER 28, 1948
AT HOME

Five days in bed. Am I tired of it! Sore spot in my throat during the night Sunday, and then the darndest severest attack of grippe bugs. Quite a lot of fever (to 102), which I think now has departed.

Helen and I voted today, here at my bedside.‡ At least, we marked our ballots: whether the Election Board will challenge them we don't know.

Had no question, of course, about marking an X before Estes Kefauver, or doing the same for Republican John Jennings. But I must record—though I may live to regret it—I did consider for a moment voting for Dewey. Not that I did; but my lack of enthusiasm for voting for Truman was strange, in a way, for I am one who was disgusted with the "liberals" when they attacked him before the convention. I have had nothing but good experience with him, from the day he called me in to reappoint me Chairman of TVA to the last time when he decided the weapons custody issue. But somehow the collection of faces in Washington these days has rather got me down, too. This is no basis for such a judgment, as I well know, but the fact that it was there for several moments shows how pervasive the idea of switching frying pans (if I may amend a maxim) can be. And even switching from one frying pan to another in the midst of some violent "cooking."

OCTOBER 29, 1948
AT HOME, FRIDAY NIGHT

My first day out of bed. Rather tough going. Worked with Frances Henderson for a couple hours on speeches, etc.

Reading a collection of spy stories. But the kind of things that come along all the time—as realities, if that be the word—make these stories seem less fantastic than they should.

Thus: tonight (or is it tomorrow night; the portentous exact date escapes me at the moment) tonight is the night of the "attack." What "attack," for the love of Mike? Well, FBI agents got hold of a letter, addressed to a certain box number in New Haven; the box holders (four students, I believe) turned it in. Filled with a lot of stuff, some of it could have been written by a reading of the Smyth Report and such; some of it did indicate knowledge of where certain things are located that should not be known. The date of the "attack" was October whatever it is. Full of dramatics.

‡ By Tennessee absentee ballot.

Are such nutty things taken seriously? You're darn right. Gen. Nichols came over, all hot and bothered, and talked to Lewis about it (who seems to rather enjoy all this sort of thing, while protesting its absurdity). And an alert is ordered, all over the country. I pointed out that this sort of indiscriminate rattling, if foreign agents knew it worked, would be used to get our goat, and after so long a time we wouldn't know what an alert was, when something important did come along. But Army minds live on the worst possibilities, all except sensible ones like Bradley and Eisenhower.

It turns out that on Sept. 10 there was an alert ordered, too, because two guys were overheard, in a restaurant, saying that the hour for sabotage had come, or some such stuff.

NOVEMBER 3, 1948
AT THE MORRISON HOTEL,
CHICAGO (10:45 A.M.)

Dewey has just conceded the election to Truman! And the Democrats control the Senate *and the House!*

This is the most remarkable occurrence imaginable. It is difficult to set down how completely out of tune with the sentiment of the people all the organs of information were, and how utterly wrong the politicians, including the Democratic ones, were. As I told Helen over the phone (she is in Crawfordsville, and jubilant), there were only two people who believed in a Democratic victory: Harry and Helen. She never lost her faith that Truman would be elected, never was budged by the polls, the wise guys.

My own "loss" of the election way back she paid no heed to: I always lose every election, ahead of time. Only the *Literary Digest* and I thought Landon would win; add Wendell Willkie to that list, for he told me, on the corner of the LaFayette Hotel in 1936, "This is how it is. It will be close; but Landon will win by carrying Ohio." So my own conviction (not just a hedge to save my feelings "in case") was completely in accord with that of all the wise guys (including Jim Farley, Elmo Roper, and what have you: add Walter Winchell, Marquis Childs, the Alsops, etc., etc.).

We have all known that the underlying trend of events was contrary to the indications of the 1946 by-election. But I thought the reaction would continue for at least two years more, and perhaps eight.

I went to bed last night, on the train en route to Chicago, about ten. Helen was outraged at the idea of my not being at a radio, among friends, but my arrangements made it necessary, and I really wasn't too interested. Seemed only a question of saving such figures as

Kefauver and rolling up a respectable opposition. But I got up very early—6 A.M., so I could find out something. The Chicago *Tribune,* at breakfast on the train, said "Dewey Leading Truman." This meant that at eleven last night the landslide hadn't occurred, otherwise they would have plastered it all over even their "home edition."

Then word trickled into the diner from some fellow whose ear had been glued to a noisy radio, who said (this was 7 A.M.) that the radio said all night long that Truman was leading; not Dewey. Well, of course, this was just some mistake. Then Eddie Brosnan, my security man, who is traveling with Bill Waymack and me, managed to get his radio working; and sure as hell, Illinois had elected Paul Douglas and Stevenson—this meant something. And Truman was ahead—by a narrow margin, but something. And it was clear by the time we arrived at the hotel that the House was Democratic. This meant a terrific current of popular expression. The words in the speech I make tomorrow at Des Moines (which I have been reading here in my room, as we wait for the noon train to Des Moines)—the words about the rude awakening that comes to those who don't understand that the people do their own thinking, that their over-all judgment is what determines the course of the country—these words took on a current importance.

NOVEMBER 10, 1948
AT HOME

The Cincinnati trip went well. The speech, at night, easy, informal from notes on a couple sheets prepared at the very last minute before dressing. A friendly audience, in a very conservative town, the home town of my chief opponent, Senator Taft. About the Atomic Exhibit which I went there to "unveil" I'm not so sure. Too complicated, too "expert," tries to tell too much. But it does give *focus* to the idea of public knowledge about the atom and the way in which it is being developed.

"Security" note. As I came down the hall of our building today I saw a burly fellow in workman's clothes chipping away at the marble step on the staircase. Seated *in a chair,* his arms folded, was a tiny half-pint of a uniformed guard, armed. One man to work and one man to watch him work. This "escort" system really is something. Today we heard a report that we are cutting down on the guard business. Getting rid of the dopey scare-mongers on Hickenlooper's staff (if that is what McMahon will do)§ will save this country millions of dollars

§ Democratic control of the Senate meant that McMahon would succeed the Republican Hickenlooper, as chairman of the Joint Committee.

and not harm security. Why didn't we buck it ourselves, and take the consequences? Well, with so many things to fight . . .

Hard Commission session this morning, that wore me down. Pressed hard, hard, all through the morning until 1 P.M., holding people to the point, pushing on, trying to move along by cutting off discussion, and "blowing up" on making personnel management an end in itself, and on the policy, which I believe we will succeed in having revised, of *not* according *applicants* for employment a hearing where they have been turned down on security clearance.

Lunch with Eric Hodgins of *Fortune* (author of *Mr. Blanding Builds His Dream House*). This is the result of Frances Henderson and my trip to the *Fortune* editors last month. *Fortune* has had quite a force at work on the story.

To Philadelphia tomorrow. Lunch with Justice Roberts, visit with the Goulds of the *Ladies' Home Journal,* then a shindig by the Golden Slipper Square Club, a Masonic organization entirely made up of Jews (or almost so). Sumner got me into this, and I am somewhat concerned that it might not be something I should be spending time and energy on. But it is perhaps a good thing for me to get out of the gilded squirrel cage, and there is a thousand-dollar check for charity that goes with it.

NOVEMBER 12, 1948
EN ROUTE FROM PHILADELPHIA TO WASHINGTON

The Golden Slipper Square award business last night wasn't too bad, though strenuous. For example, autographing—for a whole 40-boy choir, one after another, and a mob afterward—I would be there yet. It is a kind of ailment. I think they throw the autographs away. The etching (a portrait presented to me) not bad. But no more of these things than I can help.

But it is helpful to me to get away and see and talk to a variety of people. This serves to remind me that there is a very seamy side that, in my enthusiasm and natural hopefulness, I tend to forget, particularly when I am working with so fine a quality of men and women as I do here.

Breakfast with Federal District Judge Cullen Ganey, a Harvard Law classmate from Bethlehem, Pa. Active in Democratic politics in his county, and hence his appointment, by F.D.R., in 1940. He helped investigate the crookedness of the public utilities, back in 1932. Then he became local counsel for the utilities, though only on matters of no consequences, all the important things being done out of the Reed law office in Pittsburgh or the Mason firm in Philadelphia. He brought suit against the Bethlehem Co., who were pounding a lot of houses to pieces.

"Why, Cullen, what do you mean? You know how much we think of you. Why, only the other day at the club Mr. Grace was saying to me how much he thought of you." Then he was retained as local counsel. Not many lawyers with any independence, he says, and political corruption goes through the whole state. Union leadership very bad; drunks, tough guys.

Sat next to Chief Justice Maxey of the Pennsylvania Supreme Court, who talked and talked—I seem to invite these long discourses. But I found it interesting, and much easier than having to answer questions. Great libertarian, as he tells it, and he may be right. First judge I ever heard denounce the trial of Sacco-Vanzetti, for example.

Lunch with Justice Roberts. Seemed very friendly and very happy with his work at the Pennsylvania Law School. Brought him up to date about our "personnel security" criteria, etc. Wanted to be sure that he wasn't harboring some reservations or ill will about our handling of the Condon case, for example (where we departed from his board's recommendation that we do nothing until the Thomas Committee acted).

Said he thought we ought to be in better shape on the witch-hunting business with McMahon chairman of the Joint Committee. His low estimate of Hickenlooper was evident. What about their staff? He said he hoped this meant the end "of that fellow Teeple." "A zealot—had a zealot's face and manner. He would say to me, with a light in his eye, 'Did you know this?' 'Did you hear about *this*?' That is, things about the Commission. And he had Hickenlooper scared to death and wrapped right around his finger."

Almost two hours with the Goulds, editors of the *Ladies' Home Journal,* at their office. She is keen, quick, goes to the heart of her own preoccupation: will women *want to read* this particular article, piece, story? That is the ball as far as she is concerned, and she keeps her eye on it. Whether this is responsible journalism or not, and whether there is anyone who can really answer such a question—those are other matters.

They want—or think they want—me to do an "interview" with them on atomic energy. It might be very good. I'm willing to undertake it. Together with the article Eric Hodgins is working on, my campaign on the magazines is beginning to take hold.

NOVEMBER 22, 1948
AT THE OFFICE

Yesterday was an Important Day.

To wit: we acquired nine acres of land on the Vineyard, more or less; more or less land and more or less acquired, for we have yet to get a test shaft about water supply. But it was a grand and glorious feeling, Helen and I prowling over one of the most beautiful spots I have ever seen, complete with tremendous view of ocean *and* Sound, with two huge boulders and rods and rods of beautiful rock wall—and soon to be ours, a place for a house. Better late than never.

We flew up from the New England Council meeting before which I spoke Friday, in a funny little plane, four passengers and a big dog where two passengers were supposed to be. A terrific rain—southeast— made it impossible to see anything but fog from the top of what Helen thinks we should call "Topside" (because it *is* Topside and because we have a strong sentimental feeling about our original Topside in Tennessee). But Sunday was clear as all get out—and the view was simply wonderful.

We talked it over with Henry and Betty Hough and then with George Hough, a wonderful old man. Betty said $2,000, but you could see she hoped we wouldn't turn it down for price, otherwise she would be in the doghouse with both old Mr. Hough and all the neighbors who are set on having us. That seemed steep, a bit; I suggested $1,500 (which Charley Norton thought was too high), and the old man without hesitating said, "For Helen and David Lilienthal that is all right." Now if Charley's efforts result in our finding water for a well, we have something to plan a house on.

I pushed hard to get something done about this, at first because Helen, I think, needs to build a house, needs to have that kind of roots, even if it is, at first, only a summer place. But by this time (and this happens so often in this family) I am getting all enthused about it myself.

NOVEMBER 25, 1948
AT HOME

Was called upon this morning by the Ambassador at Large of the Union of South Africa, Charles te Water, together with the Chargé d'Affaires of their Embassy here, a Mr. Eustace. He said such extravagantly "generous" things about the "distinction" of meeting me, of the great achievement of the TVA—"the greatest accomplishment of our time," etc.—that I was actually fussed—and Sumner was greatly amused thereby. Their problem is their soil, he said. There is no soil problem, sezz I; it is always a problem of people. We talked uranium, too, of course, for we have negotiations coming along. Was urged to visit them —it would be nice, but somehow these trips never actually pan out.

Frances as an assistant is beginning to work out. I am almost completely freed of my mail, and most of my detailed reading of staff papers. After the speaking load lets up a bit I should think I will begin to get the full effect of long-delayed relief.

DECEMBER 5, 1948
AT HOME

1. The most important single issue we may have during the next ten years is our military program.

2. Important because of (a) amounts of our income involved, which affects prices, taxes (how spread, etc.); (b) strengthening of a conservative bureaucracy, the professional military man; (c) tie-up between that conservative group and business, who will spend most of the defense budget—"most?" well, a large part; (d) other reasons.

3. Atom bomb has a big bearing on this.

4. If atomic weapons change "style" of rearmament (e.g., minimize navy or large mass army or this or that), this will vex vested interests in this bureaucracy, and they hate it.

5. They can, and may try to, squeeze the atomic weapon into the pattern least likely to change their own ambitions, which are largely to build up their own bailiwicks as they were when they were at their height, i.e., at end of last war. (See Admiral Ofstie's candid Navy Day speech at Dallas.)

6. Secrecy about atomic weapons plays right into this game.

7. Some military people now playing down the bomb as "just another weapon."

*This has me steamed up.* I am likely to send off a trial rocket at Natl. Women's Press Club luncheon next Tuesday.

Enjoyed the Columbus, O., trip—to speak to the Ohio Farm Bureau convention—though I was ill through the whole thing. Some kind of internal epizootic that is going around hit me Sunday night, week ago (we went out to Frances' place in the country for late P.M. and supper— delightful place in what was once a country schoolhouse). Monday night on the train must have had fever—ached like the dickens. Had a good press conference Tues. A.M., 9:30 to almost 11. Good, hard-hitting lot, and we all enjoyed baiting me and watching me get out of it alive. One old-timer, Davis of Cleveland *Plain Dealer,* was really pitching. Heard afterward that he thought it was good show.

To Ohio State, to see Pres. Bevis, who had a group led by a Prof. Dreese, of the council of Argonne Laboratory. Campus swarms with students—slightly depressing, so many of them. Lunch with John Baker, whom I knew at Harvard Bus. School 25 years ago. Much taken with him; now pres. Ohio Univ. Very keen about Gov. Lausche, says I must come to know him. A man of convictions and principle, he says, citing as examples, two Repub. trustees of O. Univ. he appointed, though one was Bricker's financial backer.

By mid-P.M. I was feeling pretty rough, my insides definitely, and with fever. So got a doc, who said I had a "virus" (as if that explains everything) and said I mustn't think of going to the reception & dinner, but just at the time of the speech. I did, and did as good a job of a speech to a friendly, big audience as I can remember—talked in and out of the MS, for 50 minutes, and had fun and so did they.

I like farm audiences. I think I've got the way of making radiation seem simple and understandable—they followed me intently right through, and applauded so hard I had to get up three times before the next speaker, who was Murray Lincoln. Tall, Yankee drawl, fine sensitive head, great hand for talking with an audience. And he has led these Ohio farmers through 30 years, so they are different in their ideas than other farmers. It was wonderful to see how just one good man can do so much, if he has the talent and patience and integrity that leadership requires.

*Why is it* that there are so few genuine leaders in business? This is something I'd like to think about and write about. Really true. And yet business is our business—even this farm co-op is dominated by business ideas.

Rode back, by air, Wed. A.M. with Gardner Jackson. Now asst. to Jack Kaplan, head of Welch Grape Juice, as part of a deal whereby Kaplan intends to turn his business over to farm co-ops and the employees of the company. Fantastic tale: Kaplan son of a rabbi, South Boston, up from the streets, Cuban sugar, pretty rough and tough, now has this idea, but he is dealing with a realist, Murray Lincoln, who won't have the co-op take it without real control, and so the story rolls on.

I enjoy listening to Gardner—and he talks willingly and easily and well, so there's no conversational strain. Has no use for Bill Douglas, and agrees the Leon Henderson *et al.* crowd did a silly performance before the convention. Said Chet Bowles saw the Pres. last week, came away discouraged, lack of comprehension—I reminded him that the thing to do was not to complain that T. wasn't highly articulate as F.D.R. was, but to see that he had other qualities perhaps quite as good but different, and learn how to transmit ideas to him in a different way— e.g., through *people* whose ideas he would trust because he trusts them as individuals.

Somewhat troubled by organization matters in Commission. Shugg◖ very decisive, tough, and no fooling, but Comm. not getting as much of a look at policy or administration as we should; and some resentment

◖ Deputy general manager.

at Shugg's way of making changes with little or no discussion. But we needed a toughening up, and if it has swung the opposite extreme no wonder. But *I must stay home and dig into administration,* spend hours with Wilson and Shugg and others.

The problem is this:

The Commission must delegate most of management; otherwise no encouragement of initiative, and no time for public relations, study of policy course, etc.

So: in general, broad delegation and no interference in management by Comm.

*But: we are responsible,* and such delegations are no justification when things go wrong or can be questioned.

*And unless we know a good deal of detail,* policy guidance hopeless and in a vacuum.

*Problem:* How do a balance here?

Have a similar problem in our delegations to private "contractors," e.g., Gen. Electric.


DECEMBER 8, 1948
AT HOME

The talk to the Women's Press Club yesterday went all right—about a B average, I'd say. Weaved a bit in the middle part, but judging from the news reports I made my point—a dangerous one to do extemp.—that this is *not* just another weapon, etc., without making any vulnerable busts. Questions were not too clear; some of my answers likewise, but two or three went all right. I must try to stick to informal talks.

Critical point in Commission management, and relationship of Commission to genl. manager & staff; i.e., in function of Commission. About two years since we took over. Made a tremendous delegation, and almost had to. But we will become just a convenient "front," with no other function, unless we can successfully solve this dilemma: How can the Comm. give the general manager & staff enough final authority so they can move, rapidly and confidently, and still provide enough guidance and veto-capacity to make it possible for us to take full responsibility for the whole show, which by law we must? Saying we determine policy and G.M. execution thereof solves very little.

Had long session with Wilson, Lewis and Bob yesterday about it. Laid it down that either we must withdraw parts of the delegation, or be better informed and have more voice in the formation of policy and important action *before it has become so set that we can't take issue without discouraging staff unduly or actually upsetting what is an accomplished fact.* Suggested that in addition to approval of programs—

where Wilson has done a fine job of presentation—we must be in on new contracts involving novel or policy issues, and early. He will submit an attempted codification of existing contract practice, and summaries of all contracts so we can examine them and suggest improvements in future. But that isn't enough—must cover new contracts—and this takes some thought so it won't gum up the whole works.

Later talked with Fisher & Green, genl. counsel and comptroller: this by way of an additional way in which Comm. can exert more influence in shaping of policy and in keeping tab on how things go. They were very low in their minds: Shugg, new and tough Deputy G.M. (and toughness badly needed), has found that production and technical divisions have been underfed, compared with administrative, and in reversing it he may have overdone it; certainly has them upset. Don't want any backstairs methods of correcting these things; also need the broader and independent judgment of these two, directly to the Comm. So asked them to consider how they would phrase their independent and direct relation to Comm., apart from duties as head of service departments. This will give Comm. better surveillance, but if not handled carefully could make for friction instead of a better team. Worth trying.

Bureau of Budget figures recommended $194 million *cut* of our billion budget. I didn't bat an eye when Jim Webb told me this, saying he wanted our views, though only State and AEC had been given this privilege. Told him we didn't want a big deficit any more than he did, and we'd play ball; give us a few hours. Found that we could stand $150 with profit—we have a spoiled outfit—but more than $161 million cut would be dangerous. Told them that today—were delighted with attitude and it will pay dividends in future. Shugg said he was struck with confidence they showed in me and felt obliged to justify it to them.

Home today; still bothered with shaky feeling and some aches. Pretty tired.

DECEMBER 12, 1948
AT HOME

Thursday night Clark Clifford and I dined together here, with Helen (after drinking his version of a St. Louis toddy), and then he and I alone spent the evening talking.

I gave my diagnosis of Truman: a man who reacted *against* the words, the vocabulary of the intellectuals typical of the New Deal earlier period, the kind of line that Leon Henderson, Bowles, and Douglas would use. That he came out of the Middle West kind of progressivism, a kind of twentieth-century version of Populism—against Wall Street, the railroads, Big Business, etc., and hence he used the words and ideas of Teddy Roosevelt, Norris, Bryan, the elder La Follette, and could not communicate with the more recent progressives with their great emphasis on language that seemed to him highfalutin and crackpot. I said all this because I thought Clark's influence on the course of the President had been so very, very great because he caught on about this aspect of the President, and had found a language, a terminology, and an atmosphere in which the President could express those deep-rooted Populist, insurgent ideas.

Clark was greatly interested. He said when he first came to help the President he was called in for a talk, and said things that tend to confirm this general diagnosis. Some of these things go, or may go, beyond what I had in mind, and may confirm the feeling of quite a few liberals that Truman does not understand the world at all, and is no liberal by any definition.

At that talk the President had said: most of the people Roosevelt had close around him were "crackpots and the lunatic fringe" (Clark emphasized that those were the words Truman used). Truman said, "I want to keep my feet on the ground; don't feel comfortable unless I know where I am going." (Shades of the Truman Doctrine launched in Greece without any public debate!) "I don't want any experiments; the American people have been through a lot of experiments and they want a rest from experiments."

The President, Clark went on, doesn't like the words "progressive" or "liberal"—definitely doesn't like them. Helen broke in to ask, reasonably enough, what words *are* there then? Well, he likes to call it "forward-looking"—a "forward-looking program." He thinks *that* expresses it better.

But this—and other things—confirms my general appraisal.

Clark seemed tired and very thoughtful. He spoke in a worried tone —quite unusual for him—about the conflict within the President's own family about future policy, between the conservatives and the "forward-lookers." He said he was "tired, awfully tired; not physically, but emotionally, psychologically." Felt that the lift that came from doing new things, of learning, is no longer there. He spoke of the awful exhibition one sees around the White House of self-seeking, etc., and seemed rather depressed by it, not as if it were something new but that he was getting his fill of it. I was struck with the way he spoke of the dangers of being in the midst of such great power and influence, and its effect on people, adding, "Every once in a while I notice it in myself, and I try to drag it out in the open."

He asked about my present plans. I reminded him of my position, last April, when I said I didn't want to continue more than a year or so, that I felt for a number of reasons it was better if someone succeeded me and that I got some private activity during my fifties. I said I had no particular plans in mind, and that there was nothing urgent about it; that I would complete my present "enlistment," but sooner than that would be even better if it could be satisfactorily arranged.

Instead of chiding me, he proceeded to talk about himself, in a very personal way and at length. The upshot was that it was his thought that he get out of Government in the reasonably near future. Financial reasons were important—he had about used up what he had saved, and had a girl about to enter college. But he said, "If I returned to St. Louis, almost none of the rare experience I have had in the past few years would be of any particular value to me." I knew what he had in mind: he wanted me to comment on whether it would be proper for him to practice in Washington. I said of course he shouldn't go to St. Louis, that the fact that others had been greedy and not too principled in how they practiced law didn't mean that he needed to, nor would he. Later, in this same kind of discussion of our future plans he turned to me and said, "Perhaps we may do something together someday." I agreed that would be a pleasant thing to think about.

Actually, this, plus my considerable weariness these days and the aftermath of that damned virus thing I had at Columbus, led me to think again, and rather in particular, about my plans. A law firm here, with connections in New York, plus a "Celebrities Inc." a new kind of "lecture" bureau—supplying people of all kinds to talk, "radio-ate," etc., on public affairs; these are my present thoughts. The latter would contribute to building a business for the law firm. The law firm ought to make a big point of not touching anything it didn't believe in, nor any strictly "influence" business, and give much attention to clients who wanted public policy counsel as well as legal.

This could be made into something new and important and satisfactory, I believe.

Gridiron dinner last night one of the most enjoyable I can remember—perhaps since the one in which my troubles with A. E. Morgan was the *pièce de résistance*. Sat next to K. T. Keller, president of Chrysler. I joked about the night he walked out on our dinner meeting in Detroit a year ago. He was full of geniality (how much due to the way the election came out I don't know), and I really enjoyed him. He says that most business people are fooling themselves with figures of dollar volume. He is a machinist, really, with that kind of "things" mentality. So it wasn't surprising to hear him tell me that he looks only at number of units of cars, trucks, etc. Says the American people can only absorb 5 million cars a year for two years, so we only have at most another year to go at this rate. Putting out a new car in March designed for the motorist instead of the designer. Big gamble in such new models, he says.

Talked with Dewey before the shindig, briefly. He looked brown but rather strained—and why not? As we walked along toward the dining hall he took my arm, leaned over and said, "Well, there'll be no question about the length of your term now." I said I supposed not, and then thanked him for his hospitality at Albany of a year ago, and hoped I would see him again from time to time. The place was full of these guys who were to be so powerful in Washington for the next four years —according to *Fortune,* Kiplinger, *et al.*

Dewey's speech was without any trace of rancor, but it was hardly a masterpiece. How did he feel in the cold gray dawn of November 3? He told the story of the man who passed out at the wake, was put into the coffin, and then woke up: "If I'm alive, why am I in this coffin; and if I'm dead, how come that I have to go to the bathroom?" That's how he felt, he said.

Right at my elbow at the next table was Hamilton Fish and some other Republicans of that vintage. (Fish, the aristocrat, wearing gray sox with clocks and brown brogans with his white tie and tails!) As Dewey started, the man with Fish said, "Just a lot of words, so far"— rather sourly. Everybody applauded—not Fish. At another round of applause a couple moments later, Fish still sitting on his hands, looking daggers at Dewey. It was all he could do, apparently, to listen at all. There were a lot of Republicans there who were just like that—most of the congratulatory stuff came from the Democrats!

The President's speech was very brief, very quiet, lacking the customary bounce and tang, and he looked very somber. "I know there are a million men in the country who could handle the Presidency better than I can; but I happen to be elected and I am the President. I have got to have your help." Etc.

Had a moment with Frank Lausche. A very impressive man: youthful, good-looking; sense of strength, warmth, composure. Lyndon Johnson sat just one remove from me: they called him Landslide Lyndon (he won his Senate seat by 87 votes!). Met Stanton, absurdly young-looking head of CBS, who said Ed Murrow's history recordings were going great guns—100,000 printings so far. Don Richberg, looking pudgy and quite remote from anything in my life, somehow.

The practice is to call upon some of the guests—perhaps a dozen or so during the evening, "to rise and remain standing for a moment"— this preliminary to some ribbing of them, in a skit. Lyle Wilson, acting as master of ceremonies at this point, called out my name and that of Greenewalt, new president of Du Pont, and then as we stood called us "guardians of the peace of the world." That was all. No kidding or flick of the whip. And why that combination? I wondered if this was to pave the way for the "new Du Pont"—for Greenewalt as much as told me flatly that they were going to accept our proposition and come back into the undertaking. If this happens, my campaign in this direction will have borne fruit before I thought it would.

We had dinner Friday night at the Carlton with Edgar Sengier, head of the Union Minière, etc., Katanga, and his successor. It was a pleasant evening, for the old boy was in fine form. A new uranium negotiation is ahead of us, and the domestic price is being used to set the new price—which is rather tough. So we must continue to make him feel, as he has in the past, that this is more than a commercial transaction—that he is contributing to stopping Communism.

He told a fantastic story. At the time the war broke out he got some metals into ships to get them out of Belgium before the Germans could get them. Among them was 220 grams of radium. His mines in the Congo produced uranium for radium and since he had all the market could absorb for a long time the mines were abandoned, the machinery dismantled for other purposes, and this meant they were flooded. He had more than 1,000 tons of very high-grade uranium ore, in drums, in Brussels. He got this into a ship and sent it to the United States and stored in a warehouse—just any warehouse in New York City. One day Col. Nichols and "four other men" showed up at his office in New York (this was 1942) and asked him if he would reopen his mines—which would have taken a long time—perhaps a year or more. "Reopen the uranium mines," said Sengier, "you have a mine right here in New York City." And so we got started long before what might have been otherwise the case—at least on this scale.

The evening was spent in listening to stories, chiefly by Sengier and Lewis [Strauss]. I interjected the only serious note—since I usually try to remember why we go through these things. I said, "We have at this table a man because of whom many of the peoples of Europe can live without constant dread of being overrun."

Last night when I got home from the Gridiron the house was practically filled with lovely carnations from Sengier to Helen. She responded with a note making the point above, and I sent him copies of my TVA book, inscribed to a "fellow builder." He is to go to Oak Ridge—and, at his suggestion and my eager acceptance, to TVA. I urged him to see how TVA goes about the grass-cattle cycle, for it would mean everything to the Congo.

He responded with a longhand letter; part of it read:

My whole life has been devoted to the industrial and social development of Katanga, the mining district of the Belgian Colony, with a policy of putting the general interest of the country and the welfare of white and native populations above the financial interest I was responsible for.

The pleasure derived from such a policy turned out to be the most valuable dividend I received for my work.

DECEMBER 19, 1948
AT HOME, SUNDAY

No speeches and no set trips now for a month, praise be. And the children get home today.

This has been a rugged period, the past two months: I don't know how many speeches, trips to Iowa, Chicago, Denver, St. Louis, Columbus, O., and tough management problems. And two illnesses to get through and the election worries. And losing Bill Waymack by resignation.

The trip last week was rather a success.

Left Tuesday, by air, for St. Louis. Rough trip through rainstorms and uncertainty. Wed. morning called on Blakeley, new head of *Star-Times* ed. page, protégé of Bill Waymack's and a *very* impressive fellow, very tall, young (say 32 or so, I'd guess) and a power house. Why Cowles let him get away I can't understand. Then a half-hour or so at *Post-Dispatch*, with Kirschten (back from a spell with the *S-Times*), Rufus Terral, and a very solid fellow, Dilliard; then to Ben Reese, managing editor, huge bear of a man. Very friendly all around: puzzled about what they can do journalistically with atomic energy. "How can we 'criticize' what we don't know enough about to criticize? Isn't it just this: that we trust you and let it go at that?" And so on.

Then to the Mallinckrodt Chemical Works—does much of our uranium refining and metal making. Not too impressive plant, much handwork, dust, etc. But able men. Lunch with Mallinckrodt, son of the founder, a courtly little man of the Old School, whose hobby is ether. A whole story in this man, who kept notes for conduct of our little luncheon within his glasses case—the old kind with a stiff cover.

Then to Monsanto, to see Charley Thomas. Charley looks very successful and "businessman of distinction"-ish—the conflict between Charley the Teacher and Researcher, and Charley the Business Tycoon seems settled in favor of the latter, as I knew it would. But when he says his son at Princeton is "overbalanced" in favor of science and math, and wants to be a professor, he gets a glint in his eye, of pride and vicarious satisfaction. Human beings are the damnedest contradictory creatures. (And with my recurrent unhappiness about being a public servant and not a well-off lawyer or something, I lead the list of funny humans.)

Charley and I had little, really, to say to each other, but the circumstances were not good. Perhaps some other time, for he is very, very able.

A press conference: good questions, but I didn't think I did well—below average, but no busts. But it is worthwhile to have more newsmen exposed to the subject, and to know me better; we don't have a policy of news dissemination, so a press conference is just a social gathering.

St. Louis was unbearably hot: 75 and muggy and enervating. Denver was crisp and cold and clear—wonderful. Helen and I had the fabulous Presidential suite of the Brown Palace Hotel: complete with grand piano, etc. The Rotary speech (which I made from notes, re-written at the last minute) was one of my very best. My knees were still achy and shaky—a continued residue of the Virus X illness I had at Columbus—but I did a good job to a fine, responsive audience, and within the time limit, to the minute. A very successful informal speech is a rewarding experience, just as an experience even if what you say is bunk—and this was one I did enjoy.

Badly tuckered in the P.M., but had long session with Gustafson (raw materials director) and Volpe on next day's press confab. Found that the very *point* of the trip, as I thot of it two months ago, had been eliminated from Gustafson's statement (which in my rush I hadn't read, but had left to Frances to work out with the others)—to wit, that we thought the Colo Plateau's uranium resources were very small and rela-tively unimportant. Mystery: how did this happen? Gustafson and Thompson say Frances had taken it out, and they thought this repre-sented my views. When she returns, I must find out. Anyway, we hit it hard in the conference next day. But a statement of a "find" will get front-page billing; a moderate statement is lost. I get more and more puzzled by what is news.

Night: stag dinner at Denver Athletic Club, Palmer Hoyt of the *Post* as host. Perhaps 25 men, including the Governor, who is a dead ringer for the Hollywood version of a Western Governor. Tall, slim, big grin, weathered face, etc.

Press conference well attended, good questions, Gustafson heavy but impressive. *Post*'s report almost covered two pages.

Bad trip, by train to Chicago; very rough (over the wheels) and a party in the next bedroom. To Palmer House, for nice visit with brother Ted. He is brown from Fla., but very thin, worn-looking. A tough time, having a bad ulcer like that. Going to Billings Hospital next week. A sweet being if ever there was one.

Out to the Du Page lab site, where the place is filling up with Quonsets, which make fine workshops and offices, surprisingly so. I'm getting a bit fed up with the terrific appetite for funds of this side of the business. Flight home wonderful this time: three hours and level as a billiard table.

DECEMBER 20, 1948
IN COMMISSION MEETING

1. Dr. Bowman and Col. DeCoursey telling us what would happen to this building and its inmates in the case of an atomic bomb a half-mile away. Really makes your insides roll.
2. Dr. Shields Warren telling us about five "atomic cataract" cases.
3. Beryllium same thing.

DECEMBER 30, 1948
AT HOME

Have been working hard on organization matters, especially (1) better current reporting to the Comm.; (2) better presentation to Comm. on contracts, pending, under consideration, etc.; (3) making more effective the genl. counsel and comptroller functions, directly to the Comm. Tough going, but I feel some headway being made.

The *Fortune* article that Frances and I started last Oct. is out in the Jan. issue. Not bad and quite a colorful display. Won't hurt a bit.

Had a big press conference yesterday—capacity of our conference room and some of the best reporters in Wash.—partly because other news may have been scarce. Concerned the Industrial Advisory Report. Coverage indicates that when an industry group says Govt. is doing a good job, as they did, that ain't worth printing—but the effect over-all is to the good.

The effort to get out of the secrecy limbo (putting out nothing that is not vague and weasel-worded) is certainly paying off—though whether it is worth the effort of fighting against the inertia and the Manhattan District spirit of caginess I don't know for sure. *Time* this week had five atomic energy stories! I insisted on a press conference by Dr. Warren on the story, broken by Drew Pearson, of cataracts of the eyes by scientists working with cyclotrons—and he was glad to do it and it got good coverage. But it is uphill work.

Nancy leaves this afternoon, to go to her new job, as assistant to a management consultant who is doing a book on unions in the retail trade—an interesting job.

Offered an honorary deg. by Lehigh and, as I can use an old speech, will do it: commencement Feb. 6.

Clark and I talked further about our personal futures. He may have to pull out for financial reasons, fairly soon.

# V

# THE ATOMIC ENERGY YEARS

# 1949

Just back from a call at the hospital to see Cleveland Sullivan, my redheaded car-driver who came down suddenly a few days ago with appendicitis; when they operated on him, they found a tumor. When I was there to see him day before yesterday, his wife—they are about 30 —was pretty low, as they said they'd have to cut him open again, and didn't know if it was cancer. The doc said no cancer, so that was much better. We drove her and his mother-in-law home. Fine people.

Before that I went to a big party at the Carlton given by the Mark Childs for their quite lovely young daughter. Saw many of the most interesting people in this city, and it all made me feel better about the New Year under the Decision of the People of Nov. 2.

Vowed I'd not work today. But I did. Awful to have work that just steams you up so you can't get it quite out of your mind. Or is it so awful? Wearing, certainly.

Anyway, telephoned New Year's greetings and appreciation to Fred Schlemmer at Hanford, Tammaro at Chicago, Bill Kelley in New York, and Miss Brown at my office here; tried to reach Tyler at Los Alamos, he's away; and Jack Franklin, telling him I'd be in Oak R. next week, I hope.

Feel we've turned a corner, and things will be better. They couldn't be much tougher.

Wrote a memo to the Commissioners re information and secrecy.

In its draft form—I may revise it before it goes to them—it is part of my effort to get us in a position where we will really *do* something about this secrecy incubus. Now when we are being criticized, mind you, for keeping secrets—that's what it comes to—we are in a position for the first time to really do what I think we should do—junk a lot of this monkey-business. Felt this two years ago, but unless you have a good deal of public sentiment with you and understanding, it won't work.

First time I know of when a man set out deliberately to get criticized —the whole array of my speeches add up to that.

Still brood quite a bit about the future: daydream about just how I will announce my retirement, etc. Bad for me; should go on until the right circumstance comes and then do what I should do, and not fuss about it. But that's me.

Swung my ax mightily today, and worked around the place. Very nippy weather.

Measured David today, first time since Norris, when we had his various heights for ten years marked on the kitchen door—we should have taken that door with us. And he is *six feet five and three-eighths inches* in his shoes, and six feet four and three-quarters in his bare feet. Grown in the past year. What a boy.


JANUARY 7, 1949
MEETING AT OAK RIDGE


A year ago we were told it *couldn't be done:* industry could not promote basic research. Carbide had doubtful feelings about the "long-hairs." But we stood fast. Now—all lovely.


JANUARY 10, 1949
IN THE CONFERENCE ROOM (9:50 A.M.)


This is a large meeting on radiological warfare, about half scientists and half men in uniform. A crisp, brisk, efficient atmosphere. Compliment each other on "cooperation." But the subject matter!! Col. Cooney says "it has been very pleasant"—meaning the way people work together, but I keep thinking of all this energy on such a subject!

It may be (says Dr. Brues, tall, intent) that "you can monkey with the physiology of an animal" so it may be he can take more radiation.

Have just broken in to raise hell about making these things so secret that all you get are conclusions. This stirred things up.

JANUARY 14, 1949
EN ROUTE IN AN ARMY PLANE FOR ROCHESTER, NEW YORK
(7:10 P.M.)

Unbelievably beautiful out there. A full moon, and we are flying over the clouds! What a sight.

Yesterday had lunch with Ed Murrow, in my office. He described the outlines of an enterprise he is working on. (This goes back to our brief talk last summer at his place at Quaker Hill when I asked him what he thought would be the chance of my being able to pay for a trip through undeveloped continents by selling articles about it, and the general prospect of earning a living by writing, lecturing, etc.) At that time he said the possibilities were great for a service that supplied all kinds of material for a public that is hungry for facts and opinion and celebrities.

Since that time, he said yesterday, he is certain that such an undertaking has very great possibilities. He told about the great success of his record album, "I Can Hear It Now," which has sold, he said, more copies than any other record of any kind—and this after just a few months. He is doing one on Lincoln now, with Raymond Massey, and a similar thing to "soundistrate" a history book.

The interesting thing that happened was that he suggested that I might join in the enterprise, when I leave public service, which he assumed could not be before the end of my current term. He is sending me a paper summarizing the setup, which is now being worked on by two lawyers; and as to financing, he said he could get half a million dollars by two telephone calls.

This looks in the direction I would like to go. Independence, no big organization to be responsible for, and a chance to make some money—and work that would not be so intense and exacting over long stretches as this job.

Just before taking off, I spent half an hour each with Sam Rayburn, the Speaker, and the Majority Leader, John McCormack. Rayburn regaled me with stories about Truman and the campaign he put on—how people took to him. When he went out on that back platform, "He talked with them, not at them, he laughed with them. And when he introduced his family, instead of Dewey's 'I'm pleased to present Mrs. Dewey,' Harry would say, 'Would you like to meet my family?' "

The awe and respect in which atomic energy is held—and perhaps some of this is a certain respect for me, too—is manifested by the way I get treated in the outer offices of top political leaders these days. I did all right with TVA, but now it is really something. They get me in right away, etc. (I walked into McCormack's office without even phoning in advance.)

What I said to Rayburn was rather important.

1. He knows how important it is that private monopoly and big business not get a stranglehold on this new great natural resource, as they did in electrical power, etc.

2. But we must make use of industry in the enterprise. This gives them an inside track.

3. The real protection for the public interest under these circumstances is that the people, the public, know about the possibilities and about what goes on.

4. This requires that the Congress know.

5. The theory was that the Joint Congressional Committee on Atomic Energy would work hard at the job of understanding, and would, in turn, inform the Congress and the public.

6. Perhaps I was naïve, but I played the game according to the rules, and tried like the devil to make the Joint Committee machine work as it was intended.

7. The fact is that it did not work. Hardly anyone came to the hearings, or read the reports; they themselves issued no reports of consequence.

8. More than that, the JCC worked *against* the interests of keeping Congress informed, for most members, thinking the JCC was doing the job, paid no mind to the matter. (Sam said, "I never could get anything out of any of them.")

9. I would like to suggest that we try another route; that he sponsor the idea of getting together a number of Congressmen for informal sessions, at which I, and others, would explain what we are doing, in non-technical language, try to answer questions, etc., and hope that this would lead to greater public discussion by the members and better understanding of the opportunities as well as the dangers, economic and military.

Sam said he would be willing to bet that only a handful of members thought atomic energy was anything but a bomb, and that in his district this would be unanimous. The people don't know that this is energy, that this is something they can benefit from.

He said he had named Kilday to the JCC, in Lyndon Johnson's place, and what did I think of Henry Jackson for the other vacancy? I sang Henry's praises, and quite sincerely, as he is a hard-working and attractive man, able and liberal, and pointed out that the Northwest had no representation in the committee at all.

Had a kind of crisis during the week, within the Commission. Concerned a meeting Carroll [Wilson] and Volpe are attending at Princeton, to talk over where we stand and where we go on policy as to other countries, and in particular what next on policy re U.K. and Canada. Bacher and Strauss were rather upset that this meeting was being held without their knowing about it—or even had they known.

Bacher wrote a memo—in some perturbation—suggesting that matters of this kind were not management at all, but solely Commission matters. As an alternative he suggested that the Chairman handle these things directly, perhaps through someone attached to my office. Of course, Lewis did not care for the remedy, though agreeing on the complaint, and both Pike and I were concerned about moving in the direction of direct staff attached to my office. I dictated a memo, for Bob and myself, to delimit the scope of the proposed conference—which had snowballed in size beyond what was originally intended.

Then having gotten the steam let off, I warned that this was rather a negative attitude to take, that something needed doing and Carroll had proceeded to do it, and for us to sit around constantly and complain about initiative would try Carroll's patience perhaps beyond its load-bearing ability. This sobered Bob, who is one of the sweetest as well as one of the soberest men I have known.

I called in Carroll and Joe, asked them to write a memo setting these limits on their own initiative, so we don't lay a critical memo onto them and start that kind of record-making.

L.'s [Strauss'] attitude is one that makes me increasingly unhappy. My respect for him has suffered a considerable blow, not because of his *views*, as such, but the air of circumlocution. But I shall try to keep my patience and hold my tongue.

JANUARY 16, 1949
EN ROUTE HOME FROM ROCHESTER BY PLANE

The visit yesterday to the University of Rochester Medical School, where so much of our applied biophysics training goes on, was extremely interesting, only I didn't spend enough time. For I am in the process of learning a whole new language and a new way of looking at the world—with no scientific background and at an age when one doesn't learn utterly new things too readily.

But it was fascinating. We came into a room, brightly lighted. Cages of rats, and on a table, flat on his back, a bright-eyed dog, his legs tied back, a cloth over his lower tummy. Some of the white rats were lively, running up the sleeve of the young fellow who was explaining things. These were normal. Others were discolored, their tails looked red, and one was about ready to give up the rat ghost. These latter had been exposed to heavy radiation.

We went into rooms where dogs and rabbits were in chambers into which was being pumped beryl dust, terribly deadly stuff, from which some scientists may die because so little was known about the effect of its dusts.

I saw a gadget that atomized sodium chloride (i.e., salt) water into a fineness so great that when you put your hand over the "steam" it was dry. This device may play an important part in protection against bacteriological warfare, for it can penetrate, as a kind of antisepsis, an enormous area in almost no time. I saw a tiny bit of beryl, in a flask, and was told that this much, atomized, could render the entire building deadly in a few moments.

I saw little flasks in which liver antigens had been mashed in some way so that it was expected that they could be made to go directly into the liver of a rat (or another animal) as iodine goes chiefly to the thyroid. I saw a rat put under the Geiger counter to demonstrate how the radioiodine had concentrated in the thyroid, where it could kill cancerous cells—destroying such cells more quickly than other cells (the radiation affects *all* tissue, but the cancerous ones most of all because they are more sensitive and more rapidly multiplying). It was hoped that the liver stuff, to which radioactive materials could be added, might do the same concentrating stunt.

The men who work in these places interest me perhaps more than the things they are doing—the rats and electromicroscopes and the rest. An intense air they have. This is partly because the boss has come for a visit, but it is chronic and part of their make-up.

Another beautiful night, flying by moonlight.

It is an exhilarating experience and no mistake, rising and walking forward to speak to such an audience as I had this afternoon in the Eastman Theatre, filled to the rafters (two great galleries sweep in a great arc high above, and the vast expanse of the floor). I was told there were 3,400 people. It is apparent that my long years of speaking experience and a considerable measure of self-assurance have rid me of uneasiness or tenseness, to say nothing of actual fear of an audience of this kind.

I was asked by several people afterward how I felt ("now, honestly") as I began before such a throng. The question was prompted by the fact that Sumner Welles, an old hand, had said his knees were shaking and his hands were trembling visibly, when he spoke at the same place a few weeks ago. The fact of the business is that I sat, waiting my cue, with more than the usual composure (during my introduction I decided to begin quite differently than I had planned, i.e., by telling a story or two), and that it went more like a conversation until I established "contact" than like a speech. The speech I used (a wedding of the Herald Tribune Forum and an older one, plus extempore interpolations) was on the oratorical side, and I made the most of such an intent and large and warm audience. The response was one of those experiences that very few people, actually, ever have, and that cannot be described.

But it has been a rather punishing "weekend," for after the speech—which was quite an exertion—then there was the inevitable reception. I enjoy meeting people now—my old shyness and resistance this way have gone almost miraculously—but it is strenuous, nevertheless. Besides, I am trying hard to get names—to retain the habit—a very important one. The "party" was at the home of a Mr. Lowenthal, and I met a lot of very fine people, all of whom it was evident had been quite stirred by the speech. Among them was Tubby Moffet, a boxing pupil of mine in my DePauw days, looking rather pale and thin, he who had been such a terrific husky in those days, and his lovely wife, and son; Ned Ogden of my Law School class, a real prince of a man, and his wife, a very pretty little thing.

I began my speech proper by saying that I got an added pleasure out of participating in the 100th anniversary celebration of this Temple (Temple B'rith Kodesh) because therein was observed the faith in which I had been born, the faith of my fathers unto antiquity—this I added this morning, because it seemed a good thing, for since my college days I have been so inactive in religious matters that many people don't know I am a Jew. And while I don't like these people who make too much of religion, whatever it is, or become rather professional at it, it is just as well to speak of it when it is appropriate and relevant as it was today.

Soon I will be home. And another week begins, this time of work and festivities, too—Inauguration.


JANUARY 18, 1949

Helen and the Ambassador. She phoned: "May I speak to Lady Franks' secretary?" (This in re Sunday night dinner.) A male voice came on the line, no doubt some other secretary. "Lady Franks is away, is there anything I can do, Mrs. Lilienthal? This is Oliver Franks." Oh, gosh!

Luncheon for Ed Murrow given by Gammons (*very* bald) and Koop (medium, well-done bald) of CBS. Gen. Vandenberg said Berlin airlift is going to boomerang, because the Russian sector will be better off.

JANUARY 21, 1949
AT HOME

Yesterday—Inauguration—was a wonderful day, wonderful in every way. A brilliant day, the air clear and sparkling, the sun bright and warm (my face was "teched" with a burn before the day was over). But of course what was best of all about it was the President's great address, saying essentially the things I said in my TVA book back while the war was still on, about great development undertakings throughout the world, based upon a sharing of our technical skills and resources as an *effective* alternative to Communism.

Will it be anything more than a speech? I asked Clark Clifford this morning. No, he said, there wasn't a program ready, any more than there was when Marshall made his "Marshall Plan" speech at Harvard, but it was a good idea to jar the world with the idea and then see about a program.

I gather this is not strictly true, as some of the State Department people I saw this morning at Dean's swearing in,* who must have had a hand in the pronouncement, spoke of a 20 to 30 billion-dollar undertaking, utilizing the various agencies of the United Nations. But I fear this is pretty vague. But it is a great idea.

The day was full of delights. The people from all over the country: Western hats, and Helen Hokinson type committee members from the Middle West, and Hollywood characters, and the Beaver Falls, Pa., band, etc., etc. Great thing. The parade was the most fun I have ever had at a parade, and I forgot about atomic energy and everything else all day long . . . almost.

Gordon and Mary Clapp were our house guests and indeed are still here, and this was very pleasant. They are good company, equally unabashed about enjoying everything that came along, from drum majorettes and floats to glamour-guy governors.

Wednesday night Helen and I went to the Electors Dinner. We sat at a Maryland table—just why this classification I don't know. Governor Lane proved to be a very attractive and personable man, whatever kind of Governor he may be. The others at the table were apparently among the Democratic faithful (the state went for Dewey!).

The President always shows some new surprise in his new-found

* Dean Acheson, the new Secretary of State.

role of self-confident guy. His story about how he heard about how the election was going election night—mimicking Kaltenborn—was really so surprising that it caught everybody off guard. Very good and very funny and somehow, for him, right on the beam.

Dean's swearing in this morning, in the President's office, was very impressive—and would have been more so had there not been such a mad and terrific rush by the press photographers, who really "take over." The Cabinet, Felix Frankfurter, Alice Acheson and the girls and son David, all thrilled, of course. Dean was more charming than ever, which is a good deal.

Symington took me aside to say that "There has been too much of these speeches saying the bomb is not much account. I am making a speech for Brien [McMahon] in Connecticut in February and I want to talk to you and get your help. If they keep this up, they will do a lot of harm."

I said most of the attack along that line came from those who didn't believe in strategic bombing, in particular. He responded by saying that the new B-36—and then said something about its speed and range that is not generally known, or known at all for all I know, but since it may be classified I need not write it here. He is a rather impulsive fellow and I don't feel as much confidence in his judgment as I would like, considering the kind of post he holds, and I judge, will continue to hold.

Met so many, many people during the past few days, and tonight we are going to two more parties—the huge kind. Then I hope I can quiet down on the sociability. Actually, Washington would be a much better place if there were one-tenth the public sociability; but I suppose in that case it wouldn't be a capital city.

For example, among those I met, some for the first time, were: Jacob Potofsky, head of the Amalgamated Clothing Workers—with a Van Dyke beard, and his very attractive daughter—my count is that I shook hands with her three times in a brief encounter. And John Brophy, of CIO; Geo. Googe of AFL; Estes Kefauver and Gov. Browning of Tennessee; Mayor Cummings of Nashville; Leonard Lyons, the columnist; Will Rogers, Jr., and his attractive wife; McC. Martin of the Export-Import Bank; General Fleming; Sam and Dorothy Rosenman and their son Robert (just graduating from Harvard Law School); Lee Olds; Mrs. Donald Montgomery; Senator Broughton of N.C.; U. of N.C. President Frank Graham (who seemed quite intense about the Fulton Lewis attacks on him. He said, "I guess I've rather put you on the spot for me. The first time in my life I have ever answered an attack on me"—referring to his reply the other day to the Lewis attack); Senator Sparkman; and Cap Krug's dad, who came over to my office, telling me, "Now, you have always looked out after Cap; please keep on looking out for him," which somehow amused me.

JANUARY 27, 1949

Still no word about a new Commission member to succeed Bill Waymack, and yesterday another blow, or a blow earlier than I had planned. Bob Bacher and I went to lunch and he told me that he really must be through here by the first of May, although I had rather been hoping this could be put off till summer or early autumn.

This means we will have two replacements almost simultaneously and this presents very great difficulties. I called the White House and am to see Clifford and Dawson next Wednesday and try to get a little light on what happens. I am especially anxious that the appointments should not only be non-political, which is quite a trick at the present time, but that the men should command the respect of the country and be sufficiently intelligent and quick and hard-working so that we will not have to spend hours and hours, days and days, going over things that have gone before to give them background before proceeding to new decisions. This is going to be a rather tough row, I fear.

This has been an unusually varied week so far as Commission items on the agenda are concerned. This morning, for example, we started off with a question of appraisal of properties; in other words, a financial, accounting, and engineering matter.

Then we went on to a report from Dr. Bowers about beryllium safety measures, including a rather gruesome discussion of how beryllium attacks the lungs and what happens to the poor devils who get beryllium poisoning. It looks as if we will have plenty of trouble ahead in this respect if we are going to use beryllium a good deal. There is a backlog of lung injury in men who worked with this darn stuff without proper precautions that takes quite a long time to develop.

For one case there is the story of a scientist, one of the pioneers with Dr. Zinn at the Metallurgical Laboratory in Chicago. He worked with beryllium in the very earliest days of the war and now is about to die from a lung disease that has been slowly catching up with him. The day before, Dr. Bacher reported to us on the increasing number of scientists who have worked around cyclotrons and who are developing cataracts of the eye in various stages, most of them finding already a considerable impairment of vision.

This morning we went from beryllium, then to India and Brazil and a discussion of thorium. Brazil says any arrangements to buy thorium from them are unconstitutional, unenforceable, unwholesome, unhappy, and besides the price is too low! And from this we go on to Pandit Nehru of India and discussions with him about a thorium plant in India and from that on to South Africa, which wants a loan of a hundred million dollars for harbors, hydroelectric plants, steel mills, etc., and wants it tied up with our negotiations with them for uranium. And from that we go to the Colorado Plateau and so it goes, to the last item on the agenda relating to foreign intelligence.

Yesterday was equally diversified, starting off with proposed legislation in the New Mexico Legislature authorizing the formation of an incorporated community on the top of a mesa at Los Alamos with all the political ins and outs such a business always implies, going on to a one-hour, rapid-fire, around-the-country oral report of what is going on, which included an explosion at Hanford of a chemical variety (presumably or almost certainly) and a lot of other extremely interesting and extraordinarily diversified happenings here and there. The last item yesterday morning was one of the most interesting we have had in some time.

This was a report which I have been egging along for some months now on how we are doing on discrimination against Negroes and other minority groups in our operations, including those of our contractors. Waller, our personnel staff chief, made an extraordinarily good presentation, simply giving facts from here and there. The net effect was one of considerable shock on the part of all the Commissioners.

We found, for example, that the Commission's staff at Hanford never employs Negroes at all and refers all Negro applicants to General Electric, the contractor there. In this way the Commission's own record is that we do not fail to employ Negroes, because there are no applications! The General Electric Company's policy is to employ no Negroes either in the town operation or in the plants, with the exception of the construction workers who live in the construction camp of some 15,000 temporary structures, trailers, etc.

In the neighboring communities—bear in mind this is in the great Northwest and not in Alabama—of Pasco and Kennewick they have the rule that I thought was confined to a few North and South Carolina towns, that no Negro should let the sun set on him in either of these communities. Oak Ridge is not a whale of a lot better, and the situation in the Washington office is nothing particularly to brag about.

I have the impression that the Federal Government has probably the worst record of any in tending to discriminate against Negroes, especially against any opportunity for them to utilize the kind of education which they are now slowly being able to get.

The irony of this whole picture is pretty overpowering. For example, a great deal of public money is put into Howard University here in Washington to train Negroes so that they will be able to be chemists,

chemists' assistants, lawyers, and so on, but the same Government makes it very difficult for them to actually work at the professions that they have been trained in. We ought to represent ourselves to the world as a nation that is committed to policies of equality of opportunity among all men, but we should be pretty humble about the number of soft spots that there are in our own picture here at home.

(This is my first effort to dictate these journal entries on a recording machine. I shall be curious to see how it comes out.)

FEBRUARY 2, 1949

I have just talked to Strauss and Bacher, with Volpe present, about the latest development in the Graham case. This is an allegation by Fulton Lewis in his broadcast last night, in which he says that I did not tell the members of the Commission of the existence of an adverse report by George M. Humphrey of the Roberts Committee, and of the Roberts Committee's view unanimously that Graham should not be cleared.†

Both Strauss and Bacher remember my report on the meeting which I attended, as the only Commissioner present (they being at Sandia at the time), and Bacher recalls clearly my saying that I had asked each of the members of the Roberts Board if they had any question about Graham's loyalty, as distinguished from other characteristics which would affect their recommendations. Each of them had said it was not a question of loyalty, but that Graham was not a suitable or an appropriate person to be the head of a university or to be the head of an educational institution. I stated that I had said to the members of the Roberts Board that inasmuch as we had contractual relations with practically every university of any consequence or size in the country this would put upon the AEC the question of the suitability of almost all university chief executives; that we should try to avoid such a remarkable responsibility unless it were essential, and therefore had asked that the report be taken over by the Commission to see if a category of clearance could not be devised less broad than the usual Q clearance.

I have a distinct recollection of having reported the views of the Roberts Committee and will check further with Pike. After the discussion of this, Strauss said that he had had some conversations with Fulton Lewis in his office and on the telephone and with George Humphrey,

---

† The AEC had unanimously reversed the Roberts Board and had given clearance in December, 1948, to Dr. Graham, so that he could have access to confidential information in his capacity as president of the Oak Ridge Institute of Nuclear Studies, an association of Southern colleges (including Dr. Graham's University of North Carolina) engaged in research.

and that this was some weeks ago. As far as he was concerned, he still felt that the vote he gave in favor of clearance was right and he would do it again today.

Big day today. First open hearing of the Joint Committee. Four newsreel cameras, lights, flocks of news photographers crowded in front popping up and down while I testified. What surprises me is that I am so intent on what I am doing in answering questions that I hardly know that all this business is going on, although it is all packed into very little space, because the entire movie business takes place in the narrow space behind the desks of the committee members, ranged up there on their semicircular dais.

Senator Tydings did most of the talking—fully half, I would say. And between him and Connally (looking like an old, worn-out, and rheumy bull who once knew better days, but now could only bellow), I got what Fulton Lewis tonight called a tongue-lashing for including in our new semiannual report anything about weapons, or a picture of the model of a cyclotron! McMahon raised the question of whether the American public shouldn't know how many bombs we have in stockpile, so between these two extremes we had a real *issue* raised, one of the most important of all, the secrecy issue.

This is their preoccupation. I tried to present the difficulties of the issue, but without much luck. I must do my work by talking directly to the American public and not to Congress, except here and there, for it is only in that forum that we have a chance. Tydings' argument was so extreme in its implications that it surely will meet considerable opposition.

But what they are really laying for is to take us apart on the clearance of Dr. Graham, and I was all prepared on this. I had sent a letter to Senator Millikin explaining our position. Senator Knowland is apparently going to bat on that, too, and in Friday's closed meeting the fireworks will probably begin. If we can get it all out in the open, I don't worry about it at all; but these secret meetings are bad. Well, we'll see.

*Newsweek* has a feature piece on the report, with considerable about me, and a cover, and the coverage in the press on the report was very good. This attack on it will certainly make it a best-seller. But all the uproar will make the military even more uneasy about approving the release of information—which is where we came in.

Professor J. A. Campbell at Grinnell made a statement that the active parts of the bomb were between 20 and 30 pounds, and according to Campbell since "everyone knew" we were making one a week this meant we had between 200 and 300. His sole connection with the project was at Berkeley years ago.

International New Service asks should they or shouldn't they print a by-line article from this fellow along this line. Speculation, we are all agreed, we will not discourage, but what about an asserted statement of fact? If the facts happen to be right—and these are not right—and we do nothing about it, then what happens to the protection of secrecy; what of all this talk about "security guidance"? If the statements are inaccurate, then shouldn't we cooperate with the newspaper in not misleading their readers?

FEBRUARY 3, 1949
AT THE OFFICE

The meeting at Princeton last weekend didn't produce anything specific at all. This was a meeting of the American Trucking Boys, a third reunion.‡ Oppenheimer, Winne, Barnard, Thomas and Carroll Wilson, and myself.

The first morning we were together, which was Sunday morning, we talked about the following subject: What would we have done other than what we did do in our report of three years ago? This got off into such subjects as this: What is the effect on our report of such attacks as those contained in the Blackett book, *The Military and Political Consequences of Atomic Energy?* What is the consequence on our present judgment of what we did three years ago in the present tendency to seek to downgrade the atomic bomb? What about the "It's-just-another-weapon" argument which emanates principally from the Navy?

Oppenheimer got off a rather subtle and fine-spun discussion, the purport of which was that the "just-another-bomb" argument is meaningless because, of course, it is another weapon but the whole thing turns on how it is used and what the purposes of its use are. None of this seemed to me very fruitful or realistic. Indeed, the whole discussion about a kind of retrospective view of the report soon proved to be nostalgic but not very useful.

On Sunday afternoon I raised the question of what we should do next in terms of foreign policy regarding atomic energy. We had made a proposal, and it had had an extraordinary amount of careful discussion throughout the world and had stood up remarkably well. But it hadn't succeeded in its purpose; to wit, agreement.

‡ The meetings of our State Department Board of Consultants in January of 1946 were held in a tiny room in the American Trucking Association Building in Washington.

What do we do in the absence of agreement? The most immediate question in that respect relates to the fact that the British are going ahead on a rather ambitious program, and monopoly in this country will soon no longer be a monopoly, something we predicted, of course, in the report and everybody knew.

But what about our relations with the United Kingdom and Canada? Since this is still a classified subject except as it is reported in the AEC public report published Monday, I don't say much about our discussion here. But I did indicate in some particulars what the problem was as to our future relations with the United Kingdom and Canada. It was evident that this relationship, if it were broadened and returned to somewhat the form and intent and spirit of the wartime undertaking, would nevertheless not be a part of international control in the sense of our proposed plan. But time does not stand still, agreement has not been reached on control, and events have a habit of taking place. Developing from our relations with the United Kingdom and Canada are events that are bound to shape up and require decisions on the part of the President and the Secretary of State. That these further relationships in atomic energy with the United Kingdom and Canada are closely related with such matters and issues as are embraced in the pending negotiation and Senate debate on the North Atlantic pact seemed clear to everybody.

What we discussed is, of course, part of the context of things we are talking about here in the Commission. We had a discussion of it here today, a not too happy one for it is evident that there is going to be a good deal of fencing on the part of Lewis, who has not favored the cooperation, limited though it is, that has been going on and could hardly be expected to favor something more extensive. On the other hand, it is clear that the kind of in-between world in which we are living is a source of irritation to our friends and to us and worsens rather than improves relations with the United Kingdom and Canada, and something that worsens relationships can hardly be considered salutary at the present juncture of events and certainly can hardly be called cooperation.

I was especially impressed, and I am sure all the rest of them were, at how well we get along together. I don't know when I have felt a better sense of comradeship with men who are so different. I was especially struck, too, with how much more self-assurance I have than I had three years ago when we first met in that strange, bare, ugly, woolly-walled room on the seventh floor of the ugly American Trucking Bldg. at 16th Street and P, N.W.

Oppenheimer took quite a while to tell about Niels Bohr's proposal for a settlement with Russia, using atomic energy as a kind of catalyst. He gave some background on it of which I hadn't previously been informed. It seems that during the war and before the bomb was used Bohr had the idea that if he were sent as a kind of informal emissary to Russia to see Kapitza and other Russian scientists with whom he had had long and friendly and professional relations, this might mean something quite useful. The idea (if I understood what O. said) was that he would try to propose to the rulers of Russia, who were then our allies, via these scientists, that the United States and the United Kingdom "trade" their atomic knowledge for an open world. Or to put it another way, that we propose to the Russians that atomic knowledge would be shared with them if they would agree to open Russia and make it an open country and part of an open world.

Bohr did see Roosevelt and Churchill, according to Oppenheimer. Churchill, it appeared, was indignant at the whole idea and wanted a careful check kept on Bohr. Roosevelt earlier had given Uncle Nick, as Oppenheimer calls Bohr, to understand that he was very much interested in the idea and was friendly to it.

One of the nicest pictures I got on the whole trip occurred on Sunday evening at about dinner time. When he had been ill some two or three years before, Kitty Oppenheimer had made a kind of electrical thingamajig for their little son Peter. This they called "the gimmick." The gimmick consisted of a square board perhaps two feet on each side, on the face of which were a number of lights, buzzers, and other contrivances. On the underside were fuses and wires and switches and so on that made the gimmick operate. For days and days Peter had been asking his mother to help him fix the gimmick, which wasn't working. So she was sitting on the floor working over the gimmick, with Peter eagerly and admiringly watching her. Then she had to repair to the kitchen to tend to the cooking, with the gimmick still not working, although she had fiddled around with many wires and switches, etc., on the underside for an hour or so. At this juncture, Robert, looking very paternal and very loving at Peter, moved over and took his place on the floor where Kitty had previously been working with this mess of wiring. Harry and I were absorbed because here was the fellow who had put the atomic weapon together, perhaps the most complicated, subtle piece of gadgetry in the history of the world.

Peter rushed to his mother's side when she returned to the room. Robert sat there, cigarette hanging out of his mouth, looking down at this gadgetry and proceeding to fiddle around with the wires. Said Peter in a very strong whisper, "Mama, is it all right to let Daddy work with the gimmick?" This brought a gale of laughter from everybody.

FEBRUARY 5, 1949
AT THE HAY ADAMS (AGAIN) 6:10 P.M.
WASHINGTON

What a load off my mind—for a time at least! For just a half-hour ago the Commission (with one dissent) adopted a formula, and authorized me to go ahead with the next step in "cooperation"—the next important step in international relations in this field.§

This noon Helen, David, and I were having lunch together in the sunlight in our dining room at home. We were, actually, having an animated conversation about something or other, when an "idea" popped into my mind—or probably what is more correct, an idea that had been running around in the subconscious was brought to the top by something or other that was said.

I left the table—my family exchanging amused comments (the "there he goes again" sort of thing)—and wrote down the kernel of the idea, which was simply that this whole thing is a matter of welding our atomic sector into the whole total of foreign policy. After lunch I went up to take a short nap before getting ready to come down to a meeting of the General Advisory Committee (this is Saturday, but that has lost any meaning, lately) and with the Commission on this subject. But instead of napping I got out of bed almost at once, and pecked out a suggested resolution for adoption by the Commission.

When I got to the office, I revised it a bit in pencil, had it typed, and offered it. Pike and Bob accepted it at once. Lewis accepted the first part, but stuck on the real point. Instead of trying again to work out something that would be neither fish, flesh, nor fowl, I said, "Here we have a real difference and one that cannot be bridged. I will transmit your [Strauss'] statement to the American members of CPC, but let us vote this up or down." Which we did, therewith.

Tonight I go to the Radio Correspondents dinner, at the Statler, and in the morning to Lehigh for my "Science and the Spirit of Man" speech, and an LL.D.


FEBRUARY 7, 1949
AT HOME

Last week was a mighty active one; a visit to Princeton with the American Trucking Boys; a radio broadcast with Ed Murrow and a

§ This "next step" was to develop an American policy for a broadened program of atomic cooperation with the U.K. and Canada, more nearly like the wartime atomic partnership.

show in New York; the first public hearing of the Joint Committee for about a year and the first one, of course, under Senator McMahon's chairmanship; a closed hearing before the Joint Committee; the Radio Correspondents' dinner; and the week was topped off by a LL.D. at Lehigh and a commencement speech. Considering that this is about the fourth straight week in which I have worked at least seven days, this is quite something. *And a Newsweek cover.*

Oh, yes! I forgot the most important thing of all, namely that the Commission's semiannual report—and its only good report so far— was released Monday noon with terrific publicity coverage. The reason I forgot it, I suppose, is that the real excitement about it, so far as I was concerned, came in the press conference on the report which we had on the previous Friday.

I got a great kick out of the broadcast with Murrow. When he had heard that we were going to have quite a report out, he suggested that I go on the air with him in an interview. This seemed a pleasant thing to do, as an experiment, at least; and from my point of view, and I gather from everyone's, the experiment was a success.

I got into his office last Monday at about 4:30. The broadcast was to be at 7:45. Naturally, I would have felt more secure if we had had the thing all blocked out and perhaps partly written. But he was there at his desk in his shirt sleeves, necktie loosened and apparently the most relaxed man in the world.

We talked for quite a while, a half an hour or more, about his project. I mean, of course, the idea of a company to provide materials of various kinds, written and oral, film, etc., that we have been talking about before. He continues to be very enthusiastic about the idea; he is working on a film documentary proposal, to go along with the album of recordings that has been such a success.

Well, this went on for a while and I began looking at the clock with a little apprehension. Whereupon he sent for two assistants, one whose name I believe is Zeisman and another able-looking young fellow. We got talking about the report and this and that but nothing at all definite and nobody taking any notes or looking like they were getting ready to do a script. Then about 5:30 he said, "How do you like to work, by dictation or how?" I said that I had gotten used to the idea of a typewriter, so a typewriter was hauled in on a table for me, and he squared himself in front of his own machine; a kind of double piano arrangement. He pecked away at what turned out to be an introductory paragraph and then said, "The first question I want to ask you is what is the most interesting or significant fact about this report." I popped off spontaneously that it was that we could write a report at all of such dimensions, etc. And with this kind of informal business setting the tone the whole process was one of his asking me a question and my answering it on the typewriter.

Last Friday, I had a session at the White House concerning the replacement of Bill Waymack and the early replacement of Bob Bacher, who insists he must leave by the first of May.

Clark Clifford, with whom I discussed the matter alone first, handed me a brief file concerning a man whom Senator McMahon was sponsoring two years ago when the Commission was first organized and whom he is pressing for hard now. The fellow's name is Gordon Dean, a lawyer, formerly in press relations in the Department of Justice and formerly a law partner of McMahon's, now living in California. His file contained a brief note from Senator McGrath saying that he thought it was a fine idea that he should be appointed.

I told Clifford that I had always said that internally things in the Commission were fine because I didn't feel I had any business sharing troubles that he couldn't do anything about and that the President shouldn't be expected to do anything about. But with two new Commissioners and the end of my own tenure I hope not longer than a year from this coming June, I thought he ought to know that the selection of these two men was an extremely important one. I told him that we had differences that could be summarized as being involved in the issue of "isolationism," to use an oversimplification, and that we must watch out in replacements that we didn't make that division within the Commission worse.

I also pointed out that large business undertakings were an essential part of the atomic energy enterprise, but that it was also important to protect this great natural resource against being gobbled up by large business interests. This also is a relevant factor in the selection of successors to these two men.

I said there was a further consideration: that is, that under no circumstances should the appointee appear to be, or in fact be, a political appointee. I said I thought there was very considerable danger, however meritorious Mr. Dean might be, that his sponsorship by Senator McMahon and his background of association with him might be construed and indeed might in fact be evidence of a political appointment. I told Clark that I assumed he thought now as he did when he first talked to me about the Atomic Energy Commission, that there was hardly an activity of Government more important to our future and the future of our children and that therefore, whatever might be the practice in filling vacancies on, say, the Tariff Commission or the Federal Trade Commission, this Commission should be manned by the best people possible to secure.

When Donald Dawson came in, we got into some difficulty, for Dawson obviously had given some sort of assurance to McMahon about Dean. I don't mean that he had committed the President, but it was evident that he had given some kind of assurance that was troubling him. Seeing this, I suggested that to have two men at one time with no background for the post at all would be very bad; I pointed out the danger of Dean's appointment being regarded as being a political one and made the following suggestion. That we postpone considering who should be an appropriate successor to Waymack and make the first replacement (although it actually would be the Waymack replacement) that of a scientist, in anticipation of the vacancy in respect to a scientist when Bacher would leave.

I thought Clifford was sympathetic to this. Dawson, while very dubious, said that in any case it would be necessary for him to talk to McMahon and lay the cards on the table. I urged that Jim Fisk be the man considered at the top of the list for a scientific replacement, although I didn't have any idea if he could be induced to take the job. I also strongly urged Dr. Alan Gregg either for the Bacher post, if Fisk wouldn't take it, or for Waymack's position, and in any case that he should be seriously considered. I also recommended John Baker, president of Ohio University, without of course having any idea as to whether he could be induced to take the appointment.

I confess I was pretty worried by the whole set of things. Perhaps I have gotten spoiled, but it did seem to me that the basis of selection for this Commission should be an answer to the following question: Who is the very best qualified man in the United States, regardless of who his friends may be, for a position on this Commission? I don't think anyone would suggest that Gordon Dean, however fine a person and a young lawyer he may be, would quite fill that bill. On the other hand, I've got to remind myself that appointments to a Commission are the exclusive prerogative of the President of the United States and that the most I can do is to offer my views and not press them beyond the point where it is appearing that I am trying to have him delegate the appointing power to me.

I was somewhat relieved that both Dawson and Clifford observed that the President owes McMahon nothing so that it would not be a case of paying off a kind of promissory note.

This morning I was told that the President had asked me to come to see him, off the record, on Wednesday next at 12:15. I rather assume this has to do with the Commission appointment, and perhaps it will be the occasion on which he will tell me that he feels he ought to appoint the man Senator McMahon wants. What to do under those circumstances I don't know and am going to give it a lot of thought.

I'm not in my best condition for a difficult situation, for I have gotten more tired than I should and find it almost impossible to loaf or think about anything else.

My chief concern is about the prestige of the Commission itself if a man should be appointed who is not of the highest grade or whose appointment can be attributed to political motivation. As to Dean himself, I have the rather strong feeling that he may be at least as able as any of the rest of us, except in scientific matters, where Bob is obviously outstanding, and that his relative youth (I understand he is about 44) and his legal background may actually make him an addition to the Commission, with a kind of new look at things that would be very helpful.

The real concern I have, and it is a gnawing kind of thing, is that this is the beginning of a downgrading of the importance of the Commission by the selection of a man who has not demonstrated by his past activities any special qualifications for so important a post. Dawson said, "Well, did Waymack know anything about this business when he was appointed?" and made similar inquiries about Pike and Strauss. The fact of the business is that, except for my background in Federal administration and the State Department report, Bob is the only one who had any obvious qualification for the job.

The hearings before the Joint Committee last Wednesday were quite something. Four motion picture newsreel cameras, huge lights, flashlight bulbs, a very large press table, and general excitement. I waved the top secret quarterly report aloft to the grinding of the motion picture cameras and had it taken up to McMahon. This was slightly on the corny side, but it turned out that it drew attention to the fact that we had filed four of these quarterly reports with the Joint Committee before, and no other member of the committee, apparently, other than the chairman, Senator Hickenlooper, had ever seen the reports, much less read them.

The pay-off on this slight bit of dramatics came on Friday when we had a closed session devoted to the report. The session was remarkable in this: that for the first time in the whole history of the Joint Committee relationship we spent our time on what goes on behind the fences and no time on how high should the fences be. By this I mean something rather deep; namely, that our preoccupation with physical and personnel security, which nearly drove us nuts and ruined the beneficial value of the Joint Committee hearings before, was almost exactly reversed and we talked about the *program* itself. The mechanism was the reading aloud of a large proportion of the quarterly top secret report. While some of the questioning had the sharpness (and in the case of Bill Knowland, more than sharpness) that you don't like from anyone but always get in a Congressional hearing, it was, I think, without question one of the very best hearings we have ever had. A few more of these and members of the committee will really be coming to grips with the problems of the Commission.

But my hopes along this line are not too high. The attraction of witch-hunting, the fascination of taking up the case of some guy whose FBI report has something in it that conflicts with the political or economic prejudices of a member of Congress (and as Senator Vandenberg said to me, is on the level, the Congressional level), then we're off again to our usual haunts. We had expected the case of Dr. Graham and his clearance to be the main attraction at this closed hearing. I think it would have been except for the fact that Senator Millikin couldn't be present, since he seems to be carrying the ball, ably assisted, I am sure, by Hickenlooper and Knowland.

But no Dr. Graham appeared and we devoted ourselves for two and a half hours to a very interesting, though strenuous discussion. For these Congressional hearings are strained under the best of circumstances. You are constantly worrying that the answers you give or given by your associates can be made use of and twisted, or are incomplete or lacking in the requisite candor, etc. I was under considerable tension because Capt. Russell in answering a question did a very bad job of it, although I had anticipated the question the day before and we had had a rehearsal on it, it being a fairly involved proposition. Thereupon Senator Knowland said that a certain statement in the report was "misleading," which was a very bad word to get into a record unchallenged. We had quite a time getting a chance to be heard to straighten out what was admittedly an innocent bobble by Russell.

Jim Webb just called, returning mine. As follows:

Mr. Acheson and Mr. Webb had considered the problems presented by the relations with U.K. and Canada [on atomic information exchange]. It was recognized that the crux of the matter was that of fitting this matter into the whole picture of foreign policy. It was concluded that the U.S. members of the Combined Policy Committee themselves could not, in committee meetings, resolve and work out a recommendation for the President, in which these matters [proposals to broaden the existing program] would be fitted into foreign policy. Accordingly, the first step is a complete staff job, on the basis of which the Secy. of State could assume his responsibilities regarding foreign policy, and on the basis of which the other members of CPC could contribute consultative advice. In order that the staff work could be coordinated, and the whole task made part of the whole function of the National Security Council structure, the President will be asked to direct that Admiral Souers organize a staff made up of staff men designated by the CPC members. This may mean that no meetings of CPC will be necessary until the staff work is ready.

This sounds right.

I asked if I should send over our views and was told I might, properly.

FEBRUARY 9, 1949
AT HOME

Illegitimus non carborundum!

I have set this little classic phrase to music, in the last half-hour, and have thereby regained my sense of humor. The little ditty—too bad I can't write music—runs:

> Don't let the bastards wear you down.
> Oh, don't let the bastards wear you down.
> Don't let the bastards wear you downnn,
>     Tradeeadda day.

And so on.

But I did come home pretty much in the dumps—but to hell with that.

And especially I've vowed not to let provocation induce me to hate, or malice, or a sense of revenge, or other such sentiments. This is corrosive. I shall just try to keep my own composure, and return if not good for evil, at least patience for unworthy tactics.

Too much is at stake to take these things as personal triumphs or personal setbacks. And I mustn't give up my own principles of how a decent human being conducts himself simply because others depart from what I think are right standards. Maneuvering and backbiting is normal conduct in Wash.—my TVA experience (the latter part of it) spoiled me a bit.

Meeting with the President. My appointment was at 12:15, but I sat in the Cabinet Room from about 12:15 to 12:35 before Matt Connelly showed me in.

The President looked fine, somewhat heavier than I have seen him recently and quite white-haired, whereas a few months ago, when I saw him last summer, it was still rather iron-gray. He looks much more relaxed than I remember him last summer; those drawn lines from his eyes down across his cheekbones seemed to be considerably modified, partly because his face and neck are heavier than they were then.

I expected him to talk about the new member of the Commission and even perhaps to try to persuade me that the appointment of Gordon Dean, McMahon's boy, was the right thing to do. For this reason I was somewhat caught off balance when he began on an entirely different subject.

He began by saying that the atomic bomb was the mainstay and all he had; that the Russians would have probably taken over Europe a long time ago if it were not for that. Therefore he had to guard it very carefully. He was disturbed by a visit he had from Senators Tydings and Connally and he wanted to hear what my views were to see if we were all in agreement. He said they felt there had been too much talk about the bomb; they criticized the Commission and me for giving out too much information in our public report, and planning to give out more. He pointed to the *Times-Herald* of this morning, the headlines of which said, "Russians demand to know how many A-bombs U.S. has" or something to that effect.

I explained that I didn't think there was any basis for the President to be concerned. The report of the Commission to the Congress covering the period of the year's work referred to the test at Eniwetok and to the fact that this represented a "substantial" improvement in the weapon position of this country, using the adjective used by the President himself in his statement shortly after the Eniwetok tests.

I said that some of the newspapers had taken this language and blown it up to mean something more spectacular than that, but that this was the sort of thing that could happen with any kind of public statement. I agreed with Senator Tydings that there well could be too much talk about the atomic weapon, not because we would give away any secrets that way, but because I happen not to be a very bloodthirsty man and I don't like this side of the job and I don't see why we should bear down in talk about it, now or any other time.

The President said, "That's the same problem I have with the Air Force boys talking too much about the effectiveness of their new airplanes and so on."

I said further that at the hearings Senator McMahon had asked us to consider if the atomic stockpile numbers should be made public. Senator McMahon said he had not reached a conclusion himself and simply asked us to give our views or present the views pro and con on the question, and of course I said we would consider his views. From this Senator Tydings may have concluded that it was our intention to agree that the number should be made public, but there was certainly no justification for that in anything that was said at the hearing. Whatever our views were, we should certainly not make such figures public and that only one person would be authorized to do that and that is the Commander in Chief himself. I said this disposed of the principal point, but that there was another point that Senator Tydings made at the hearing and with this I must express my disagreement.

I said I thought that any effort to suppress or to conceal information that was *not* weapon information about atomic energy would lead us in a very dangerous direction. For example, the Senator had criticized the publication of a picture showing a model of a cyclotron which had no more to do with atomic weapons than the picture of an electron microscope. I went on to say that this could lead us into a hysteria of great danger; for example, the water courses and water reservoirs of the country would be very important facts in any future biological warfare, if that should eventuate. This might lead to a demand that all streams and water reservoirs be regarded as secret and all maps of them destroyed. There is no limit to which this sort of emotion could carry us until in our efforts to defeat Russia in the cold war we would be imitating Russia.

The President broke in to say, "Well, that is something that we certainly are not going to do, not as long as I am President." I think this rather disposed of that side of the question for the time being. It was quite evident that the two Senators, one chairman of the Foreign Affairs Committee and the other chairman of the Armed Services Committee, had really raised Ned and that the President felt it necessary to ameliorate them in some way.

The President then called my attention to a copy of a Modus Vivendi and said that it was necessary to get rid of certain agreements, but that those agreements had been entered into during the war by Roosevelt and others because it was not felt that Britain was a safe place for atomic energy weapon production.◖ He then went on to say that we have got to protect our information and we certainly must try to see that the British do not have information with which to build those atomic weapons in England because they might be captured.

I said this whole subject of our relations with the United Kingdom and Canada was one that the Secretary of State and Secretary of Defense and myself as members of the CPC would doubtless be bringing to his attention before long.

◖ The "Modus Vivendi" was the provision for a limited exchange of atomic information with Britain and Canada which had been in effect since 1948, at which time it had been agreed to drop the wartime partnership restriction under which the U.S. would not use the bomb without British approval.

I said that four years ago on the first of May, 1945, when he had been very new in his office, two weeks after Roosevelt's death, and the day on which the news came that Hitler had killed himself, I sat in the same chair in his office and heard him say to me that he was considering reappointing me as Chairman of the TVA. The only question he put to me was, "Do you think you could serve me loyally?" I told him at that time that I could, but it was based upon my rather incomplete and indirect knowledge of him gained through reading and hearing of his position as a Senator.

I said I now had a much better basis for saying that I had an increased sense of loyalty through observing his leadership in the last four years and that as long as I was in the public service I wanted to carry on my obligations in the way that he wanted them carried on. He said he had no doubt in the world about it and that he had brought this matter up only because he wanted to have a frank discussion of it.

I said that I had hoped he would discuss with me the filling of the two vacancies on the Commission; that the work of the Commission two years ago appeared to be among the most important things going on in the world because the fate of humanity might well be strongly affected by the work we did, especially in developing peacetime uses. The President broke in to say that was his great hope, that we would develop these peacetime uses and do so as fast as we could, and he believed that that was what we were doing and were doing a good job at it. But the whole thing turned on having a Commission that would function effectively, I said, and therefore I thought that the appointments for the two vacancies and perhaps others could be among the most important decisions that he, the President, would have to make in the field of atomic energy.

He didn't seem to have this subject in mind at all and said he had run over his time and would talk to me about it some other time but that he would certainly not be in a hurry and would talk to me further about it. I had tried to get the subject discussed, but it was apparent that there was no crisis about it and that was that. I know from talking to Dawson since then that he had thought the President was calling me in to discuss that very subject, but the question is still open.

After leaving the President's office I stopped to see John Steelman at his request. He had a memorandum from the President dated Jan. 15 which he had just gotten around to talking to me about. This memorandum indicated, as Steelman confirmed, that someone had been talking to the President and worrying him about our giving out information to the British, etc., etc. I said I would prepare a memorandum giving Steelman the background and the status of things and that the matter was on its way to the President through the Secretary of State and the CPC.

I said there was a difference of opinion within the Commission on this subject which made a handling of the discussion not too easy.

I especially emphasized that there seemed to be a notion that the British could be kept from making atomic weapons in one of two ways: one, by not telling them how to do it, and second, by telling them to stop doing what they were doing.

I pointed out that neither of these assumptions was correct. In the first place, the British know how to make atomic weapons, and indeed they had some of their best men at Los Alamos and at the Bikini tests. Second, if we were to tell the British that they must not carry on such a program as we thought was unsafe on the British Islands, they would tell us where to get off, since they are a proud and sensitive people and would regard this as conditioning our Marshall aid on political and military considerations of a kind that would be most offensive.

I don't know whether Steelman saw what I was driving at, but I am sure he did get the point that the British have a very large amount of knowledge in this field and that it is silly for us to act as if they did not.

This has been kind of a tough day. When I got back I learned that instead of having a meeting of the U.S. members of CPC on the question of our future atomic relations with Britain and Canada, someone has persuaded Acheson and Webb that the thing to do is to transfer this CPC function somehow into the National Security Council, and this will be a lot more wheels within wheels.

Whenever something can be handled in the Government in a fairly simple and straightforward method by existing machinery, someone always comes along with the idea of complicating it and making it a part of a bigger wheel and putting more and more complexities into it. I must say I get pretty fed up with this after all the time I have been in Washington. That was one great thing about the TVA; we would take a simple course if that seemed to be the wise one.

FEBRUARY 10, 1949

The President's special atomic energy labor panel met with us all morning. Will Davis, a wonderful, wise old codger; Ed Witte, whom I still remember fondly as that dog-trotting genius in the Legislative Reference Library in the State Capitol at Madison; and a keen and pleasant fellow, new to me, Aaron Horvitz. Their report makes sense, and I hope will save us much wear and tear. Never want to go through that tough spot I was in in the Oak Ridge dispute again.

Will told quite a story. The panel was meeting with a pompous man, appropriately called Boulware, vice president of GE in charge of industrial relations. An incredible man, full of himself. Goes about the country (e.g., at the New England Council meeting at Boston last fall) lecturing about how GE runs their labor relations by "selling American-ism" to their employees. These lectures are usually accompanied by loud noises from their plants, and costly strikes.

Well, he gave Will, who knows his way around in the labor field, a half-hour dissertation along this line. "I figure that labor relations are just like anything else in business . . . need business methods . . . has to be sold. You have got a product, just like selling flatirons. I was in charge of selling flatirons, and what did I do? I made my product attractive, I advertised, etc., blah, blah. . . ."

After a long line of this Will squinted his eyes at Boulware and, in that dry voice of his said, "Mr. Boulware, I guess I'm mixed up about your selling labor like you sell flatirons. I thought you were *buying* labor, not selling it."

The President's statement to his press conference yesterday—no bomb stockpile figures will be given out, Lilienthal never said they would be, and that the bomb is not a proper subject for discussion—has started a good deal of discussion, much of it pretty wide of the mark. McMahon doesn't seem discouraged—talked to him over the phone, explaining that so far as I was concerned this settled the question. What is the future of the Joint Committee's plans to discuss the issue? Well, I don't know.

I'm to see the President again on Monday at noon, presumably on the new members.

FEBRUARY II, 1949

All day long with the Advisory Committee on Biology and Medicine. Some pretty grim things, of course; some philosophical discussions about information and public opinion.

Bacher and I got a big kick out of a report on what is going on in Japan, where we have quite a sad business going on called the Atomic Casualty Commission, following the medical condition of the survivors of Hiroshima and Nagasaki. "Our chief problem," they tell us, "is hous-ing. We need to have a housing development." With all the troubles we have with housing at Los Alamos, rents at Oak Ridge, etc., all we need is a housing development in Japan.

Much talk about "pregnancies" and keeping track of the offspring. Which recalled to my mind the jargon of a young military officer talking about certain weapons and methods of dissemination, in which they refer to "parent" and "child" in re explosives.

I get a belly-full of this pretty quickly, and wonder, with Abner Dean, "What am I doing here?"

There are 110,000 people alive in Nagasaki, and about the same in Hiroshima, who were there when the bombs went off. Have them all on cards and will keep track of them.

FEBRUARY 13, 1949
AT HOME, SUNDAY

The luncheon at the Achesons was quite pleasant. Alice and I had a fine, cordial talk about her David (who is in our Legal Division, and has all the usual problems of the son of a prominent father, to which is added that they work in the same city) and about getting me started painting. "If you would just arrange with ———" (I have forgotten his name, but he was a painting teacher Alice called me about) "and take six or ten lessons, then you would be started off, and then you would have something very fine, as Mr. Churchill has, when you slow down." Well, she's right; why don't I *do* something about it?

Present: ten. The Prime Minister of Canada; the Canadian Ambassador, Hume Wrong; Jim Webb; Ambassador Steinhardt; Felix Frankfurter; Paul Hoffman; and Atherton, now on the UN delegation, formerly Minister to Canada.

Much taken with Paul Hoffman, with whom I had a good talk. Extraordinary eyes, very blue, with a light in them that gives him a youthful appearance. Soft voice, quite pleasant.

Jim Webb, looking very tired and intense, said that at a dinner last night Lewis Strauss said there was a "difference among us" and he wanted to talk to Jim about it. I said that we had agreed to transmit both the majority and minority Commission views to the CPC, but this business of shooting at one's brothers, which apparently was going on all over the place, made the rest of us feel that a principle was being violated. But I said, "Of course you should see him."

I said I would be away for a while, but I thought it would take that long to get the staff work on the CPC matter going. He said, "You don't need to be concerned about the move to put this staff work into the National Security Council; that was intended to enable the Secretary to handle the matter in accordance with the President's wishes, and Acheson himself suggested this."

Dean, Wrong, Atherton, and I got talking about Henry Morgenthau's funny practice of having a stenotypist present at every meeting or conference in his office, and this led to anecdotes about "Henry." Dean said, "The important thing about the Treasury during those 12 years of Morgenthau is that control of the banking system passed to the Treasury, leaving the Federal Reserve System almost meaningless. That wasn't Henry, it was Roosevelt, Henry being merely the instrument. What Henry did, and pretty well on his own, was to begin Lend-Lease six months before it was authorized—a kind of private Lend-Lease, and without this, which took a lot of finagling around, Britain might well not have lasted. The funny thing about Henry was that after he had helped Britain and Canada and they would begin to breathe again, something would come over him and then he would begin cutting them down —when they would get their noses above water because of his help, he would push their heads down again."

Dean told a long story about a correspondence he has been having this week with Scotty Reston, a *New York Times* man, and a favorite of Dean's. In a piece, Scotty had quoted some lines from a Charles Churchill about irony or satire. Dean wanted to know where they came from. Reston said, "Use some sweat and find out for yourself." So late one night, last week, he got out Bartlett, but no luck. Then he phoned Felix, who said, "Trouble is, you don't have the latest Bartlett, hold the phone, etc." This didn't work. Well, it was a long story, and the pursuit apparently gave him great pleasure. Finally located it. Churchill was born in the eighteenth century, and is little known, but Dean has been reading him, I take it, for he quoted another line that I imagine will soon show up in a press conference.

Dean's troubles will be not a little in his old field: the Senate. Tom Connally, who blew up at me week before last, is a prominent part of Dean's daily stint, for which God help him. He said he had told Connally, "Senator George is one of the most powerful and influential men in the Senate. How can we get him clear on this North Atlantic treaty? Will you do it, or you and Arthur Vandenberg, or shall I go see him? I'll do whatever you say." Connally had said, "There was something behind that remark. What was it? What was behind that?" And Dean had to spend an hour trying to assure Senator Connally that there was nothing behind it. This is partly the prima donna business you run into with Senators who have been there a long time, but it is, I would say, manifested by the inferiority complex sort of thing, because Vandenberg got such a terrific build-up.

FEBRUARY 14, 1949
(MEETING WITH THE PRESIDENT AT NOON. I AM DICTATING THIS AT ABOUT 2:30 OF THE SAME DAY.)

This was one of the most satisfactory meetings I have ever had with the President.

He said, "I want to talk to you about two fellows I am thinking about appointing to the vacancies on the Commission. I understand you will have a second vacancy soon. Too bad, too, about Bacher. He's worked out awfully well, hasn't he? I hate like the dickens to see him go. When will it be? About May 1 you say; well, that means we've got two of them right ahead of us.

"The two fellows I am thinking about are Gordon Dean and Fisk. What do you think about that?"

I said that in order to answer the question I wanted to go back to his original statement about the importance of the Atomic Energy Commission's responsibility. "When I first talked to you about this Commission, you said something that I didn't fully believe at the time. But as these two years have gone by I have come to believe them very much indeed, and everything we do is based upon their truth. What you said was something like this: the responsibilities of the men on this Commission are as great as any in the entire Government, and, in fact, in the entire world. At the time you said that, it seemed to me something to be pretty skeptical about. I don't think so any longer. And my first question in discussing the matter of new appointees to the Commission is whether we can proceed on the assumption that you still think the work of the Commission is that important."

The President looked me straight in the eye and in the most warmhearted and informal, and I must say pleasing way, picked up the ball at this point and ran with it for quite a while. He said, "That was right when I said it to you first and it is even more correct today. It is almost impossible for anyone who isn't sitting right there over the rat hole, as you fellows are, to realize just how important this work is and how difficult. It isn't only just important for us here, it's important," and here he looked over at the globe in his office (which he has a way of doing) and said, "it's important for everybody in the world and for our children and their children. It not only will affect the security of the country and is tied in with our military things, but it will affect health, and the industrial setup of the whole doggoned world."

With that assumption firm, I said I'd like to analyze the qualifications of Gordon Dean. For if the job were that important, then the standard of who should be appointed to the Commission should be "who is the best qualified man in the whole country for such an important responsibility; who can possibly be induced, persuaded, drafted, or shanghaied to serve." The President chuckled over this and said yes, that was it; he ruminated that he had an awful time getting the first group together. He thought they had done a fine job. That was his impression. He thought we had done all right. He had kept politics out of it entirely. And he wanted to keep it that way.

I returned to Gordon Dean. I said I didn't know him personally, but

I had inquired about him and examined his record. His experience was chiefly as a lawyer in the Criminal Division and the Division of Criminal Investigation in the Department of Justice. In addition he had had five years as partner of Brien McMahon in his law firm here in Washington. In addition to that he had been public relations officer to Attorneys General Cummings and Jackson and had served at the Nuremberg trials as assistant to Justice Jackson. This was the whole of his background. I said it seemed to me that he is undoubtedly a pleasant and reasonably able fellow, but that there was nothing in this experience or training which would justify the statement that he was the best qualified man in the United States for a position on the Commission. It therefore came down to this: his chief qualification was that Brien McMahon had sponsored him two years ago and was pressing hard to get him appointed now.

I thought the President might get angry at this blunt way of putting it. Instead, he chuckled, then laughed and, looking out the window with a big grin, said, "No, that isn't his only qualification. But I'll admit that's the chief one, at that. I don't want to do this to please anybody except the people of the country and my own conscience. The fact he is sponsored by McMahon shouldn't have anything to do with it." I said, "Well, Mr. President, it shouldn't, but I can't see any other basis for his being recommended strongly."

I went on to say that if it were important to appoint someone who would improve the situation of the President and the Commission in the Congress, then appointing someone sponsored by Brien McMahon was certainly not the way to do it. I got along all right with McMahon: we understood each other. But it was perfectly clear that if a man were appointed who was McMahon's representative on the Commission, this would antagonize the other members of the Joint Committee, who had a dim view of McMahon anyway; for example, Tydings and Connally, and instead of improving the situation on Capitol Hill, it would actually make it worse.

At this point the President broke in. He said he thought there was a good deal in what I had said. He was completely opposed to having anybody with "an inside track on the Commission." I broke in to say that we were all his personal representatives. "But that's a different thing," he said. "I mean in a personal sense, not in an official sense."

I had a feeling by this time that Gordon Dean would not be appointed.

He said, "There's something about McMahon—I don't know. Now I remember a debate in the Senate and McMahon making a speech. When he began I was for his proposition, but the longer he talked, the more I was against it."

I concluded by saying that since he had asked my opinion, it was my opinion that to appoint Gordon Dean would be a mistake and I strongly recommended against it.

"Well, let's talk about the other men," he said. So I told him about Fisk; said that if he could get him, he had the great advantage of not only being an excellent and a fine individual but a fellow who could start right off with a full knowledge of the enterprise, since he had been until recently the Commission's research director for a period of a year or more.

I then talked to him about Dr. Alan Gregg. I made two points about Gregg. The first was that a very great function of the Commission would relate to the protection of the civilian population. That on this matter Gregg had a very sound, sensible, wise viewpoint and that his wisdom would be greatly needed in the troubled times ahead. The second point was that he was a distinguished physician and an administrator of medical projects. That this would be understood by the country, if he were appointed, as recognition of the importance of atomic energy in the healing field and other beneficial aspects, and tend to counteract the fear and hysteria in connection with the destructive aspects.

I also spoke to the President about John Baker and Dr. Whitman of MIT, and handed him summaries about them, which he read and kept. When we finished this, I said, "Mr. President, do you have time to talk further about atomic energy and to hear some figures?" He seemed in a very relaxed mood, quite different from the other day when he was behind his schedule and I had difficulty in getting him concentrated on what we were doing.

So then we went ahead discussing atomic energy in a way that gave me a very great lift.

First, I read him the figures, which I had had prepared this morning on a tiny slip of paper with an elaborate code. These figures showed where we started on January 1, 1947, in terms of numbers [of weapons], where we were a year later, and where we were on January 1, 1949. He remembered what our assurances had been a year ago down to the last number, indicating a very retentive memory, I should say. Then I told him where we would be in numbers Jan. 1, 1950 and 1951. I then translated these from numbers into energy, and this energy figure for Jan. 1, 1951, is really something. His face was a picture and his eyes, enlarged by his glasses, as bright as I have ever seen them. "Boy," he said, "we could blow a hole clean through the earth!"

Then he said, "Wouldn't it be wonderful when Jan. 1, 1951, comes around, if we could take the whole business and dump it into the sea?" This gave me my chance to correct what I had felt sure was a misapprehension, for I had found it in so many places. "No," I said, "Mr.

President, that's the beautiful thing about it. All of this energy fabricated into weapons can be used without deterioration or loss for producing electricity and energy for many, many useful purposes, if only we can avoid war and getting into a situation where we are forced to use it for destructive purposes." This obviously pleased him a great deal. He grabbed the arms of his chair. "These are the things we want to do, to make the world better through atomic energy instead of wiping up the world with it."

Then he diverted to quite another subject. He asked me, "Have you read this book by this British fellow Blackett? I've read three reviews of it. He and a lot of people are making a serious mistake. When they think this is just another bomb, they are making a very serious mistake. I know that with what we have—" and then he proceeded to say what we were capable of doing in terms of wartime destruction, which I shan't write down here but which I shall never, never forget. And you can say that in capitals. "But this isn't just another weapon," he said, "not just another bomb. People make a mistake about that when they talk that way."

I interjected to say this is actually a man-made earthquake, a man-made volcano, and has to be dealt with in another way than with ordinary weapons. Besides it has all the beneficial possibilities one can dream of if we only can work it out that way. The President said, solemnly, "Dave, we will never use it again if we can possibly help it. But I know the Russians would use it on us if they had it."

From this we branched off into a discussion that I initiated in order to get another whack at the secrecy issue. I said we have got to assume that we are going to do everything we can to make these things useful for peacetime purposes, and never, never use them for war. Otherwise this job would hardly be bearable for a long stretch of time. But we must also recognize that we haven't yet answered the problem of war and peace and therefore our people have got to know more about radiation and atomic warfare, so if it comes, against us, they will be prepared in their minds and prepared in other ways. This presents the problem of dissemination of information. We've got to find more and more ways of having more and more people know. He didn't bat an eye, although I thought it might take him back to the discussion of last Wednesday when he said that he didn't want the stockpile figures made public under any circumstances and then on the following day in his press conference said that the atomic weapon was not a proper subject for public discussion!!

At this point we got back again on what wonderful things could be done with the energy uses of our stockpile of materials if used as energy rather than war. He said it would be like having TVAs all over the world. This, of course, was too much for me and I broke into a gigantic grin and said, "You can imagine how I felt, Mr. President, sitting out there listening to your Inaugural Address when you came to your Point Four."

At this point he rared back and began to talk with great enthusiasm and delight and understanding that indicates clearly to me that Point Four is not something that had simply been put before him; but he had thought about it a good deal. He talked in as dramatic and "visionary" a way as Roosevelt ever did. With another wave of his hand toward the globe over in the corner, he said, "I have been dreaming of TVAs in the Euphrates Valley to restore that country to the fertility and beauty of ancient times; of a TVA in the Yangtze Valley and the Danube. These things can be done, and don't let anyone tell you different. When they happen, when millions and millions of people are no longer hungry and pushed and harassed, then the causes of wars will be less by that much. Atomic energy fits into that picture just as TVA fits into that picture."

He said these things with great self-assurance and an enthusiasm that I have not recovered from since; and it has been several hours ago. I really ought to try somehow to see him more often, as these are things that need to be said to the world. Certainly they keep heart in a fellow who has as much grief and ugliness to put up with as we do here.

(LATER, AT HOME)

Frank Graham lunched "confidentially" today with McMahon and Durham, Congressman from North Carolina and vice chairman of the Joint Committee. Graham wants a hearing before the Joint Committee. "I want to get cleaned up," he said. Wants to delay it until after March 8, thank God, for I want and need that vacation I'm planning so badly I can taste it. Plan to leave the 18th!!!

I learned this from Brien McMahon. I called at his house on my way home (a home I left at about 8 A.M. and returned to 12 hours later). He's laid up with a case of just plain overtired—what a place this is.

Brien is still sore about what "Harry" did in stepping on his issue of making public "how many bombs do we have." I have a feeling that the Air Force boys may have already given him a general idea.

Symington makes me more and more uncomfortable: his speech at Norwalk about how far the new B-36 could fly with so many tons of atom bombs was a direct violation of the spirit of Truman's injunction of only a few days ago.

Very nice letter from General Bradley today about my Lehigh speech. He wrote: "I especially liked your pointing out that the choice between machines or men 'will not be exercised on a single occasion, surrounded by spectacle and drama. We will move from decision to decision, from issue to issue, and you and I and all of us will be in the midst of this struggle for the rest of our days.' "

Walter Davenport of *Collier's* in to see me today: wants me to write a piece on what Joe Public should know about the atom. May do it.

FEBRUARY 15, 1949
AT HOME

A visit with Bishop Oxnam. He was greatly disappointed that my original idea of an "Advisory Committee on the Spiritual Issues of Atomic Energy" or something of the sort had not worked out. I told him that the opposition within the Commission would have poisoned it somewhat, and I would have to be so careful and cautious while speaking *for* the Commission that the whole point would be gone. He said he had mentioned the idea to a number of others, and they had all been struck with it as a creative and original idea—that an administrator should thus openly recognize how important spiritual things were, etc., thought it would have had important international consequences.

He will think about getting a Protestant group together for me to meet with. Not much chance of *his* helping with the Catholics, whom he has been taking to task severely (and I think rightly) of late.

Last evening had a session with [Senator] Clint Anderson. Complaining about the fact that New Mexico contractors were not getting a look-in on work at Los Alamos. I managed to keep pleasant, keeping the discussion straight. Tyler answered most of the objections. I said there was only one subject that wasn't open for discussion: "Tyler here is as honest as my father, and that is as straight as I can make it."

When it was all over—an hour on the top of a hard day—Anderson said to me, "I have to do this for those fellows. Tyler is a fine man and they all trust him out there." But the complaints to Anderson just wouldn't stand up under the facts and a rather grim attitude that both Tyler and I took.

Talked to Bill Webster, chairman of the Military Liaison Committee. He has discussed the "technical cooperation" business with Eisenhower, Bradley, and about 18 others in the military and advises "substantial agreement." Talked also to Lew Douglas,* who says if it is approached in a trading attitude it will fail, but won't if we talk things over with the British as between equals.

The difference between the Commission and Strauss appears only to be a matter of "procedure"—do we insist upon the terms and conditions

---

* Ambassador to Great Britain.

*first,* etc.? But Bill Webster said, and very well, that the difference is actually fundamental. I said the reason it is fundamental is twofold, in my opinion. And those reasons are: Do we treat the British as men, with individual and national pride and dignity, believing in them and acting as if we did; or do we treat them as men unworthy of respect, whose pride and dignity is a matter of no more concern than it would be in any private deal? And the second reason is that Strauss' tactics are those of Henry Cabot Lodge and the League of Nations: agreeing "in principle" and then defeating by "amendments" or "conditions" or "procedure."

Appropriation hearings tomorrow morning. Have decided that instead of saying very little at the opening I will take a chance and give them a 15-minute "perspective" session. And shall see whether it does any good, or actually does harm. But it is a risk worth taking.

## FEBRUARY 16, 1949

Wonderful day for TVA:
a. The New Johnsonville steam plant won, decisively, in the House.
b. The Hoover Commission voted down a proposal to deprive TVA of some of its independence—the old Ickes business of "reporting" to the President through the Department of Interior.

We were before Appropriations Committee all day. I made a pretty poor presentation but with some good spots.

## FEBRUARY 18, 1949
ON THE FLORIDA SPECIAL HEADING SOUTH,
FRIDAY (8:15 P.M.)

A wonderful feeling!

Item: A whirlwind finish. (I love narrow escapes, if the facts must be acknowledged!) At 3:45 we were still before the Appropriations Committee, where we had been since Wednesday morning, and me with a wife already in Florida, by car, a reservation on a 7 P.M. train, and no energy to stand any changes in plans. But here I am on the train; and behind me a very successful week. Instead of feeling bitter and angry and "to hell with public service," as almost always after an appropriation hearing, I feel terrific. After a bad, bad start, it seems we really made a great impression on the whole committee; e.g., Cong. Case of S.D., a hard-shell Republican (though very hard-working and earnest and decent), after working over us hard all day sent a message to me after the hearings of the most complimentary kind. I had had the sense and the fairness to conclude the hearings with a statement of praise for the committee, and their response was about the same as would be anyone's response to a decent sentiment genuinely expressed.

(Such a contrast to Wigglesworth, *not,* praise God, on the committee this year, and what a difference, spiritually and every other way.)

Item: TVA did wonders this week.

Item: I am heading for a visit with my wonderful parents.

Item: I am to have two weeks of salt water and sleep and no crises, and shelling and some water colors and fishing—and with a clear conscience about leaving my work.

Item: I have had a very good dinner and my tummy feels like that of any well-fed animal.

Item: (I would put down, if I wasn't afraid it might raise a secretarial eyebrow in the transcribing of these here notes, that there is a very very cute gal across the aisle, and I must stop this nonsense because she has a conversational bent.) So it is: Item: (probably) zero.


FEBRUARY 19, 1949
EN ROUTE OUT OF JACKSONVILLE

Saw Marian Reames Gradick, her husband, and David, their bouncing boy. Marian ‡ is one of the world's best. For she takes things as they come, with a calm spirit. She had a hard time after her father died and her mother, crippled, had to carry on. It would have soured some people, but not her. I respect her a great deal.

The celebrity business has changed travel for me. I certainly could not get away with anything—not that I have any plans—for I am spotted right away. The Pullman conductor has just come along to ask me, "Where is Mrs. Lilienthal?" and to say some nice things about the job I am doing. A man who said he was "Riddick of Michigan City" spoke to me as I was coming up the platform at Jacksonville, and through the station people stopped and pointed to their neighbors. It is difficult to get used to; the lovely feeling of being swallowed up, when I leave my work, is now lost.

Invitations to speak keep coming in at about the greatest rate since I've been at this work, I believe. Run 15 to 20 a week, I would guess. Many of them quite uninteresting or unimportant, in a sense, but it all adds up to an expression of interest in what we are doing and what, in my speeches, I am saying these days. Accepted an invitation to receive a LL.D. from University of Wisconsin next June; this pleases me, somewhat in the way the same from DePauw did. Also, flattered (in a strange way, perhaps) by invitation to deliver the annual address to the Harvard Chapter of Phi Beta Kappa. Probably shouldn't attempt it, but because of David graduating and this and that it appeals strongly; to my vanity, I suppose.

‡ My former secretary.

About the happiest thing that occurred in a very, very full week was that Cleveland Sullivan, my redheaded driver, was opened up again and: no cancer! What a time he has had, and his sweet lovely wife— and all of us, watching his ups and downs day after day. Wrote him a note before I left.

And in an hour I shall see my dear old Dad and peppery Mother!

FEBRUARY 24, 1949
AT CAPTIVA ISLAND, FLORIDA, THURSDAY

The "resting" is going great guns. Slept like anything: ten hours at night, and at first three or four deep "naps" during the day. Was (and still am) plenty tired, but so long as I can let go completely this way there's no harm done.

Arrived at Daytona Beach Saturday morning. Dad met me, looking chipper as all get-out. Mother was cute, and looked so well. Hardly got settled, until there was a knock on the door, and Mother (appearing to expect a caller) opened the door to greet a strange young man, who turned out to be a reporter from a local paper (Greenleaf by name, a serious and obviously quite excited fellow). I was so amused: Dad and Mother had quite evidently not taken any chances about the newspaper hearing that I was in town—Dad had spoken to someone at the paper about it! The interview went along, with my trying to remind him gently that I was on vacation, in my parents' home, and he trying just as earnestly to get me to talk about something profound, or about international control, or something. The result was a mixture of hominess and international control rehash.

Helen arrived Saturday afternoon, having had a pleasant and leisurely drive down from Washington with Janet Murrow.

Sunday was a big day. Dad and Mother took us to the "promenade" and we had an informal reception that amused the hell out of us, and was pretty strenuous. All the retired people they see day after day came around to see the two-headed calf, to be able to say they had "shook the hand . . ." etc. And of course Mother and Dad were on top of the world. I don't think Mother has the faintest idea why all this fuss about her son—and an almost equal amount of fuss and public deference to her and to Dad—but whatever is the cause, she accepts it with the composure of Queen Victoria. It obviously gives them both great satisfaction, and this naturally pleases me greatly.

We reached Punta Rassa about four, the day being hot as the dickens. It was good to get back on the island, to compare the roughness of the shell road with previous years, to observe the increasing civilizing forces compared with our first trip here 13 years ago—and so on.

Went fishing Tuesday morning, with quite a little success and much fun. [My brother] Ted and Nell arrived early yesterday afternoon. Yesterday he and I out swimming were chased out of the water by two sharks who came right up to the shore's edge—there is quite a deep drop-off—their huge fins showing as they swooped here and there. Helen saw them and yelled for me to come out of the water. I looked to see what she was hollering about and saw these fins and assumed they were porpoises, so turned to look at them with interest. When she continued to yell and the fins came toward me, I got the idea and got the hell out of the water, and then followed them down the shore for a quarter-mile.

But we went back swimming today.

FEBRUARY 25, 1949
CAPTIVA ISLAND

Great day!

David wrote: "I have a job with the St. Louis *Post-Dispatch*." He said that "naturally" he was "elated" that the job-hunting proved to be so short. But I was more than elated: I was beside myself with a deep satisfaction and joy. Our son is launched on his life work, and under excellent circumstances. The *Post-Disptach* is one of the very best newspapers in the country, and Ben Reese, its managing editor, runs a paper that will give David just the kind of training he needs and will benefit most from; of this I am sure. Besides, it is a paper he can work for—as an idealistic and ambitious young fellow—with his whole heart, for it is genuinely forward-looking on almost every issue, has a great tradition, has produced great newspapermen in the public sense; all these things will bring out the best in a very likely youngster.

Reese's letter, from which David quoted, was cordial and friendly. It concluded by saying that if "you are anything like your father," etc. David realized that his father's good name was an advantage in getting him a job; he also realizes that this is nothing he can do anything about, and that from here on it is up to him.

He is to get $44 a week as an inexperienced reporter. He is lucky to be paid at all, actually, and to begin as a reporter rather than, as on the New York papers, as a copy boy.

MARCH 5, 1949
CAPTIVA, SATURDAY

The last day always comes. Tomorrow morning we leave Captiva after what has been one of the best breathers we have ever had down here.

I don't kid myself that 12 days of rest and recreation will make up for years of hard work, worry, intensity, etc. But it does help—helps a lot.

I now am quite determined that I shall set aside these breather periods, and real vacations, months ahead, and treat them as "firm commitments" quite as much as a speech or conference, or such.

Helen and I enjoyed being together with no "duties" on either of us. We "shelled" together—this consisting chiefly of Helen slowly and carefully examining the piles of shells, and finding them—and my walking down the beach—deserted except for the amusing birds, ducks, pelicans —and occasionally finding something. Matter of fact, I found a yellow pectin, quite lovely and rather scarce. Helen found three "fans," one of her special delights.

We saw more people this time than ever before. We were far more "sociable" here, in the Gulf View Inn. Then Jay "Ding" Darling, the cartoonist, called on us and we went to a party at his original "house on stilts" and met his wife and children; Mr. and Mrs. Koss of Des Moines, and their attractive boy, Kip. We spent an afternoon on Alice O'Brien's big boat going to Boca Grande. It was amusing to have two such "conservationists" as Ding Darling and David Lilienthal on the boat as guests of the daughter of such a forest tree-cutter as Old Man O'Brien, the lumber king.

Later:

Just came in from an all-day fishing trip with Herman Dickey (in his boat, a 30-foot guide boat), Fred Herzog, a retired Cincinnati businessman, and Willard Shuptrine, also a retired businessman, from Michigan. It was one of the most wonderful days of fishing I have ever had. I caught lots of fish—mackerel, the unbelievable fighting bluefish, and a huge redfish. This last we caught right off shore on a deserted little island up the Gulf, two of them at the same moment.

Stopped for lunch on a weird little island. I proceeded to strip and took a swim in the clear waters—fish visible all around me. Then a big lunch with beer, then back for a couple hours' more fishing and aimless talking, mostly about *other* fishing trips. They say: give the condemned man a fine meal just before his execution; this was a fine "last" day. Now we go to a sukiyaki supper (one of our neighbors here, a Mr. Philip Wootton, lived for 30 years in Japan and he is doing the preparation of this dish), and tomorrow early we pull out.

MARCH 9, 1949

In reading *Roosevelt and Hopkins* by Robert E. Sherwood, I came across the following paragraph [relating to the wartime atomic energy partnership]:

Churchill later cabled Hopkins concerning the discussion at this time, "My whole understanding was that everything was on the basis of fully sharing the results as equal partners. I have no record, but I shall be much surprised if the President's recollection does not square with this."

This is especially interesting in view of things that are going on at the present time.

MARCH 10, 1949
BACK HOME AGAIN

Events fly fast these days.

We got home last night about 9 P.M., I by train, Helen in the car, not only safe and sound, but having had a fine two days' drive, complete with seeing Beaufort, N.C., the Lee house at Stratford, Va., etc.

A letter from Nancy had come in, handwritten. "I told you I'd let you know, years ago, if it ever got serious with some young man" or words to that effect. Well, it had and it does and this is to tell you you're going to have a son-in-law—a philosopher and physicist who uses calculus in his courtship. No prospects, no job (he's getting his M.A. at Columbia this spring), and no money, but she recalled that some 25 yrs. ago another young couple had set off similarly. . . . And she is very, very happy and very, very sure that this time (contrasted with some earlier proposals from others) it is just right. And, "we're phoning you Wed. night."

I wasn't surprised, actually, for my impression of the young couple when we were in N.Y. with the Murrows was that this was more than another beau. But here it was. Helen didn't seem displeased; we both got a good impression of him as a man of considerable poise and nice-appearing. But Nancy only met him the first time in Nov. and she is so "deliberate." I feel all right about it: Nancy should marry an intelligent man, for she has a superior mind, and she is the kind of gal I think will make a good marriage; that is, make it work, and needs that kind of stability. But we know very little about the man (who is her age, exactly). But Nancy is marrying him, not Helen and I.

Then Nancy phoned—it was like a play. Helen was cute with her ("It's collect," she said when it came, with a wink). I said the traditional thing: "If this means happiness for you . . ." and also kidded. Nancy *is* growing up.

MARCH 12, 1949
AT HOME

This, approximately, is where I came in, 25 years ago. Except for bathing the baby, of which, praise be, there are none, though aged Penny provides the general idea.

Which is to say, I've just finished an hour and a half of house-cleaning. Penny's basement mess is my regular weekend pleasure, complete with a pail of soap-suds and broom to finish off with: she's an Old Lady now and can't sleep outdoors, and isn't in full control of her plumbing. After that, over Helen's protest, I pushed the vacuum over the house from stem to gudgeon; stripped to the waist, as I do it vigorously and shoving furniture around is work. Now if I had Nancy to bathe, as an infant, and a shopping trip for Sunday morning schnecken at the 67th St. Blue Goose grocery, I could swear I was still in Chicago, a cub lawyer earning $25 a week.

Helen didn't like my spending the whole morning at housework, but I don't like to see her do the same thing. . . . If I were vice president in charge of Fig Newtons for some company, we would miss this enriching experience. "Public service as a career, my boy, that's the thing."

Helen's work on the book of my views on democracy is coming along. She's read all my speeches, etc., and excerpted them around an outline or framework that looks good. We're talking to Canfield of Harper's about it when we go to N.Y. late this month. They don't know yet that our plan is that it be a book in Helen's name; this seems to me singularly appropriate, since the development of these ideas themselves, and the opportunity to pursue a course where such ideas had a chance to grow, owe so much to her.

The little things—how vastly important they are. Shaving, for example, something I've done almost daily for I don't know how many years. Always with a razor, usually Dad's original Gillette, but with changes through the years. First of this year I switched to an electric: a Remington Rand, in honor of their new vice president, General Groves, I guess. So now I begin the day in quite a different way than I have in more than 30 years.

While I was on Captiva I spent quite a bit of time with the paints— and vowed, of course, that I'd continue here at home. I have the time now, but somehow the itch to get going isn't there.

MARCH 13, 1949
AT HOME, SUNDAY

About health: my estimate is something like this:
Generally, better than for years.

Specifically: fewer colds, etc., last year than for a long time, and a great contrast to the period 1930–1940 when I had so much flu, with long post-flu exhaust'n. Last cold (it was grippe and a looloo), was about Oct. 10.

Nervous fatigue the chief problem. But I snap out of this when I let up a day or so. The cause is not so much long, hard hours, as the working under pressure, *driving* things through conferences or Commission meetings, or the strain of Congressional hearings, etc. Sleep very well when I let go—nine or ten hours a night, till I get rested, and can almost-sleep in naps. When I am too tired or intense about something, a not infrequent occurrence, of course, I sleep badly, i.e., wake up about two or so, etc.

Digestion disgustingly good—almost never have indigestion, lack of appetite, etc., despite usually working at luncheon and usually dining late, i.e., rarely before 8 P.M.

The sacroiliac back is about a thing of the past.

Due for general check-up, but score looks well, despite that next birthday: 50!

MARCH 16, 1949
AT HOME

Home today writing, or whittling, at my College of Physicians speech; trying to develop the theme of "balanced perspective."† And boy, do *I* need that commodity myself.

For Frances Henderson has just phoned to say that Mahon of Texas has taken out after us for "secret leaks"—a prod from the Air Force, I gather from a nasty letter from Symington recently—referring to the pictures in the report—pictures that had appeared almost four yrs. ago under General Groves! And Majority Leader McCormack put in that "highest levels" were concerned about an article in *Fortune* for Jan. in which "information valuable to an enemy" had appeared. This is what the Pres. put in handwriting on his note to me of Feb. 21 (about that date), and all in all it is a minor crisis. So now I'm tied to the phone trying to get the correct information to them.

Came back from Captiva to find a bad mess at Hanford: GE had exceeded its authorized allotment for expenditure on a facility by many millions. Carroll Wilson is, of course, gravely concerned, and I suppose I should reserve a lot of time to worry about it. We are investigating, but I've just shoved it out of my mind more or less

† That is, emphasizing the beneficial aspects of atomic energy, to balance the fear of the bomb.

till the whole facts are in. And Franklin is resigning from Oak Ridge. Ups and downs. Wilson is terribly tired.

Weeks ago, at Roscoe Drummond's for dinner, under the stimulus of tomato juice, his strongest, said we'd put on a seminar for Wash. news corps if they wanted it. They did. First session last Monday night, which I opened. Sumner [Pike] put on a tour de force—a Down East explanation of the atom. Well attended—four more to go. Should be great help, too.

March of Time did some shots of me "dictating" a speech to Martha Jane Brown yesterday. Had to throw the script together in a hectic half-hour—on secrecy, and is to appear next month and should certainly be timely, judging from today's "crisis."

Stirred around yesterday in some old old files—Wisconsin and before. My letter to Felix [Frankfurter], in 1920, asking to talk to him about my ambition, i.e., to be a labor lawyer. My letter to Don Richberg in 1923 applying for a job. Both letters long and terrible. David's are far better; less earnest, shorter, more to the point. This exhuming apropos Helen's work on the book about DEL on dem-ocracy, on which she has made admirable headway, I think.

A big shindig of little meaning (opening the gates at Oak Ridge‡) takes me there Sat. Spending more time on schedules—changing back and forth—than on many really fruitful things. Nuts to that sort of ceremonial. Like to be with people, but these planned jubilations are a bore.

Pretty tired. Especially considering I'm just back from a holiday.

Lunch tomorrow with Walter Lippmann, his request.

North Atlantic pact about ready: great event, but there are so many of them these days.

MARCH 17, 1949

Talked to Majority Leader McCormack a moment ago. Said at a meeting with the Democratic Congressional leaders the Pres. started off with an explosion about the *Fortune* article giving information to the Russians, vital military information about our atomic installations— McCormack assumed the P. knew what he was talking about. He seemed impressed with my explanation, but it shows how upset the Pres. really was.

Just heard that Carroll's ancient and beloved Rolls Royce (and their Ford) burned in their garage-barn last night. C. is low these days and this will be a bad blow indeed.

‡ Oak Ridge became open to the public, like any other town (with the plants themselves remaining fenced and guarded).

Joint Committee has hearing today on the "leaks" business—they are back on their natural level, to use Vandenberg's immortal phrase.

P.S.: The joke is on me about the Truman-*Fortune* business; if I hadn't sent a copy to him especially, via Clifford, because I thot it would please him, there'd have been no such explosion—!

Lunch with Walter Lippmann at the Metropolitan Club. Said occasion of his asking to see me was that he had to give a lecture at the Air War College on "War as an Instrument of National Policy." He wanted to put to them the question whether it was possible to frame a national policy regarding war without knowing two things: (1) how much damage could the Russians inflict on Western Europe if and when they had the atomic bomb; and (2) do we know when they will have atomic bombs in a quantity that would enable them to do these things to Western Europe?

I answered by saying that there were two difficulties in the way of a reply: (1) we ourselves are in considerable disagreement as to the techniques of the use of the atom bomb in a military sense; and (2) in my opinion our sources of information about Russian progress are so poor as to be actually merely arbitrary assumptions, and clearly no arbitrary assumption could be the basis of anything but an arbitrary conclusion rather than a rounded conclusion, i.e., a rounded policy.

The conversation covered a wide range, but a good deal of it dealt with our present troubles about atomic secrecy (added headaches in this field awaiting me, as I well knew, at the Joint Committee meeting that followed immediately upon the luncheon). He said that much of what was being said on this subject came under the heading of emotion and nonsense, and was dangerous. He thought Conant, or someone of his position should make a lengthy and well-rounded speech on the subject, and that this might turn the tide. What about the President making such a speech? It would be a fine thing, might stop the whole thing. But then, he said by way of after-thought, everybody would know that he hadn't written it and might not understand it. Yes, it is not unlikely that he wouldn't quite understand its implications, said I, thinking of the recent experiences I have had.

I told Lippmann that I remembered quite clearly hearing him speak at the Liberal Club in the Harvard Union back in 1922 or 1923 when I was in the Law School; that I now had a son who was a senior at Harvard. When he asked what he was interested in, and I told him journalism, he was very interested, and said, "I would like to have lunch with him sometime." I believe he meant it.

A wonderful letter today from Dean Griswold of the Law School, speaking in high praise of David's writings in the Harvard *Crimson* on the Van Waters case that had all Massachusetts stirred up. How happy such letters make me! David did do a fine piece of work, and his editorial comment on the way the Griswold investigating committee handled the case showed that he had not missed the great point of the proceedings.

Just returned from a two-and-a-half-hour session with the Joint Committee. The occasion was the criticism in the papers and on the floor of the House and elsewhere of our fifth semiannual report to Congress. This is a record that was played before and no new facts have been adduced. But it is evidence of a growing jitteriness in the country, reflected in the Congress. It is very worrisome, as a transcript of the statements made by Senator Tydings particularly will indicate. He referred to testimony by Dr. Karl Compton before the Armed Services Committee about push-button warfare and intercontinental warfare and 3,000-mile guided missiles. I question whether Dr. Compton realizes the effect of the statements he has made upon the stability of mind of a good many people in high places.

The hearing, however, went fairly well. I put into the record about 25 items showing that the Army had authorized and issued photographs, of installations. The relevance of this was questioned by Senator Millikin. I made the point that no discussion of future policy would be possible without knowing where we started from. Also, the chance of keeping the important *core* of secrecy inviolate depends upon not discrediting and making foolish the whole system of secrecy. The best way to make the whole system foolish is to mark and keep marked with "secret" stamps, pictures, information, etc., which have been distributed to every newspaper in the country and have been published again and again over the past almost four years.

At the conclusion, Kilday of Texas suggested that we ought to re-examine the Atomic Energy Act and by provision of law put into effect a secrecy policy that differed from the one the AEC has in effect. The whole thing is quite disturbing, and yet it is probably better to have the discussion going on, and a good forum in which it can be held, than to have no discussion at all, which was what was occurring over the many months before.

Hickenlooper made an attack on us—not so much in words as in the tone he used re the AEC press seminar which began last Monday night. He implied that the purpose of the seminar was not only to discuss the whole atomic energy program, regardless of security limitations, but that what we were doing was, in effect, propagandizing with the press and building fires under the Congress and so on. This was all by way of innuendo and inference. I was not too courteous in interrupting him to say he needn't have any such worries.


MARCH 18, 1949
AT HOME

Spent over an hour with Carroll and Carl Shugg yesterday, mostly on the Hanford overrun—actual costs far beyond estimates. It is a mess. But after asking questions steadily for 40 minutes I'm sure it isn't a scandal (unless a whole new set of facts show up). But it's nothing to be proud of either, by a long shot. General Electric is not equipped to do this kind of job and in the process of learning they have overengineered and badly, badly—underline, *badly*—underestimated costs. And been unresponsive to our efforts to control them.

Have had great trouble with my ears. The air trip to Schenectady Monday with a cold really fixed them. Mean.


MARCH 20, 1949
AT HOME, SUNDAY

The hearing of the Joint Committee last Thursday afternoon—2½ hours—didn't seem so bad at the time. But the next day was one of the lowest I have had in a long time. I must attribute this, in part at least, to the sense of almost despair the hearing gave me.

We were criticized, in the opening hearing of several weeks ago, for publishing pictures of installations—even of a model of cyclotron—in our report to Congress. Then, on the floor of the House this was repeated in a rather stiff fashion. Also the President's outburst over the map, etc., in the *Fortune* article. So I piled before the committee pounds of printed material showing that these and many, many other pictures and statements fixing locations of installations had been published hundreds and thousands of times, so there was no "disclosure." I was surprised myself how far this stuff goes—pictures not only of outside, but some inside pictures, aerial, etc. The Smyth Report of 1945 locates practically everything.

I hoped that this would be the end of the criticism. But Tydings went after me very vigorously—to repeat that it was bad, etc. Kilday of Texas, a new member, said they ought to consider amending the law to prevent such things. Millikin was very critical. To spend 2½ hours on such a patently silly business of putting the egg back in the shell was not inspiring.

But what came over me that made me so low, irritable, and full of self-condemnation I don't quite know. At one point I even decided that I had pretty well failed—that our management was sloppy, we had not actually advanced our program much in two years, and it was time that someone else tried their hand at what I hadn't been able to master.

Partly this is the result of being needled too much. I am going to put a stop to this "multiple needling," by which I mean having a criticism of how this or that is going made to me—usually raising the viewpoint of someone in the organization, i.e., an ex parte presentation usually as an aside and without giving the facts and supporting statements—and then *repeating* that needling from time to time until I am nearly driven crazy.

Most assistants yield to the temptation to do this, for their standing in the organization is measured by how useful they are to others to stick some idea of this sort into the boss' mind. This is usually done with the best intentions in the world, i.e., the "best interests of the organization," etc., though not always. If this is continued too long and too hard, the assistant loses all usefulness and standing. This is what happened to one man in State who badgered Acheson day and night, and got a great sense of righteousness out of doing so. Acheson told me that this fellow had become such a one-note dismal johnny that he, Acheson, never relied upon his judgment any more.

There is a strong tendency in this direction in the AEC, to the extent that my first day back in the office from Florida was a nightmare of confusion, a mixture of organization gossip and ex parte complaints from people in legal, accounting, etc., complaints about the Security Director, the Personnel Director, etc., all in a melange, and with no indication of what we *do* about it. This is good for me *once*, but it is the multiple needling that is bad, for this amounts to badgering. This, added to making a crisis out of everything—i.e., the furor over the criticism on the floor of the House about "leaks"—will drive me completely off my head, or, as I felt Friday and Saturday morning, lead me to conclude that this job is too much for me, and resign.

So I intend to limit needling to a single shot, and put a stop to the other form, pronto.

I am disappointed in the progress in a management sense. The place is not in the shape it ought to be, and nothing like TVA. But TVA organizationally was a mess at the beginning, and for years, and yet its essential vitality and drive pulled it through, and time and patience and thought and *mistakes* developed one of the finest, smoothest organizations in this country, I believe.

I simply must keep out of details of management, whatever transpires, for if I don't, I will crack wide open, and have to quit, or will be so worn down that I will quit in disgust. There is just so much perfectionism that an organization or a person can handle.

The "this is where we came in" feeling I get about security, and the continued bias against the Commission by some of the House members who wanted continued military control—this is something we must just live with, and wear out.

But I will get these depressed spells again—I would not be human if I didn't. And despair and utter discouragement and "to-hell-with-it" is an unforgivable sin, closely allied to one of mankind's chief enemies, cynicism.

Yesterday the opening of the gates of the town of Oak Ridge. Made a brief speech, returning to the attack on secrecy. Not much of a speech, but it has some good lines in it on the difference between secrecy and security.

Flew down with the Vice President, together with McMahon, Kefauver, Gore, Congressman Buchanan from McKeesport, Pa. (a white-haired Scotsman), and Noland, new member from Bloomington, Indiana, very youthful fellow, slight, looks like a kid, etc. The local committee of businessmen at Oak Ridge had gone ahead with this festivity despite our discouragement, and of course when they managed to get the Vice President, I had to go! Probably worth doing if for no other reason than getting Barkley's attention on atomic energy, even if briefly, and the chance to be with him for quite a while—I rode with him in his car to and from Oak Ridge and in his plane on the way home.

Barkley is absolutely one of the most remarkable men I have ever known. The span of his public service is indicated when I say that when I began the practice of law 25 years ago he was already chairman of the House Committee on Interstate and Foreign Commerce. The first work I did was on the drafting of what was known as the Howell-Barkley bill—now the Railway Labor law. When I referred to this, he remarked about Don Richberg, that he hardly knew a man who had changed more than Don, from a genuine progressive to an "extreme reactionary." B.'s language is usually so restrained. Could I explain it? No, I said, I couldn't; that though I had a great sense of gratitude, it made me sad to see how far against all his former associates and most of his former ideas Don had gone. (Where will *I* be classified 20 years hence?)

The celebration itself was a melange of politicians, atomic energy, and Hollywood "stars," in one of the strangest mixed omelets I have ever seen. Led by the movie actress Marie McDonald, who sat next to me on the platform, a pretty (but certainly not overpowering) young woman from Kentucky who confided to me that she is called "The Body" (for reasons that would probably be obvious in a bathing suit although not so in the suit she wore).

The place was crawling with a Hollywood contingent, complete with Master of Ceremonies, press and still camera boys, etc. They included a cowboy actor, tall and dumb-looking, who went big with the bobby soxers, Adolphe Menjou, a right-wing movie "statesman," and such. Marie made a beeline for Barkley and hung on, and whenever anyone with a camera of any kind was within range she grabbed hold of the old boy in intimate gestures of old friendship. And he ate it up.

At first it made me not a little gagged to see the Vice President of the United States so obviously made use of to promote the property of a motion picture studio and the personal ambitions of a nice enough young woman, but certainly no actress. But as I thought it over it was apparent that Barkley felt he got as much benefit out of it as he provided them, for the audience was, I would guess, at least as interested in the presence of the movie people as they were in the Vice President, and a lot more than the rather mangy lot of us public characters. But, as Barkley ruefully said as we started back for home, the photographer has become a national nuisance, and there seems to be nothing we can do about it but put up with it.

Martin Agronsky, the radio commentator, was full of amusement: Wouldn't you just like to see the report of a Russian agent on the opening of the atomic city? Moscow trying to understand it: movie stars and atoms all mixed up—what the hell *is* this all about?

And speaking of Russia: the plans for the program took an extraordinary amount of time and energy, but the final, the last straw came when someone from Washington called to say, "We have a call from the Soviet Embassy inquiring if the Russian Military Attaché may attend the celebration." (He didn't!)

Returned in time to attend the White House Photographers dinner at the Statler, as guest of Tames, the very good *New York Times* man. A rather good show of singing, comedy, etc. They showed the newsreel of the scene we witnessed when the President, at the Electors dinner in January, mimicked "Mister Kaltenborn." The President said he was asked how long had he rehearsed that impersonation. "Well, I didn't think about it till I was up there talking," he said. "Fact is, if I had thought about it in advance I couldn't have done it, and I couldn't repeat it now if I knew I were to be shot if I didn't; unless I was half shot." This was considered very amusing, but after the President left the presiding officer broke in to say that the President's remarks were off the record.

At my table was Jim Webb, and Szymczak, a governor of the Federal Reserve, formerly from Chicago.

MARCH 23, 1949
AT HOME

Still no word on successors to Bill and Bob, though I've tried to push along in that direction by calling the W. House.

The bill to increase salaries of executive officers does a beautiful job of downgrading the atom. The Pres. urged that the Chairman of AEC be given salary of Cabinet member in the new setup, $25,000; the bill as reported out of the Senate committee cuts this down two stages to $18,000, along with the Public Printer, Asst. Comptroller General, etc. Makes me a bit sick, not so much because of the absurd salary, as the way "the most difficult job in the Govt. aside from the Presidency," and all that bunk, is neatly made foolish.

Appointment of Frank Graham to the Senate (to fill Broughton's vacancy) set off the Graham hounds in full cry again. It is a lovely piece of irony. Fulton Lewis gave his entire time over to the Bricker speech cussing me out.

Finished the Physicians speech today in first draft. Not a great speech, but has some sensible stuff in it.

Read first two parts of Helen's book on my views of Democracy, this A.M. My reaction was enthusiastic, for she's done an incredible job of putting 15 years of my speeches into a fabric that has unity and direction. I think Harper's will like it.

MARCH 25, 1949
AT HOME

No one can say I don't get variety!

Started the day at the South Pole, complete with explorers; in the middle visiting a very history-conscious Senator; finished working with Frances Henderson on a speech about carcinoma and other medical matters.

Mr. Case, a Congressman from South Dakota, brought in one Commander Ronne, who headed an expedition to the Antarctic. Purpose: to get us to urge the State Department to insist on our claim to parts of the Antarctic, on the basis that there may be uranium in the vast land area at that pole, which Ronne called "The Unknown." (He had a stage Scandinavian dialect, and the usual jealousy, not disguised, of other explorers, chiefly Byrd, who he alleged had a mania for publicity and lack of interest in scientific aspects of exploration, and this Ronne worked in at every opportunity.) I agreed with his main thesis: you can't discount the possibility, though it would seem like one hell of a place to dig for anything.

Carroll said, "Is it possible for anyone to do any geological work in that country?" We had been looking at some photographs showing about the most desolate damn prospect you can imagine—bare mountain peaks sticking up from the most inhospitable, wind-swept wastes—chilled my blood just to look at the damn pictures. The explorer's face positively lighted up, enthusiastic and happy: "Ah, ya." Then he told about Dr. so-and-so, their geologist, who spent 152 consecutive days collecting samples in that Godforsaken country. "He luffs geology," he said, as an after-thought. Boy—he *must*.

I called on Senator O'Mahoney of Wyoming about our hearings; he is the new chairman of the Appropriations Subcommittee in the Senate. Suggested we come to his office someday and spend a couple hours giving him the background on what we are trying to do. Tried to interest him on the basis that here was a new technical development that might well be captured by large economic concentration, and this was the time to try to do something about it.

The sense of being what a Tennessee friend of ours called "a historical character," which is rather common among Senators, is particularly strong with him. He showed me a huge chair in his office in the Capitol: it was especially built because its occupant was William Howard Taft. He stopped to show me the old Supreme Court Chamber (a beautiful room); at one time it was, of course, the Senate Chamber, and once in 1940 during repairs to the present Senate Chamber the Senate sat there. He was given a seat which he found, on consulting the chart, had been at one time occupied by J. C. Calhoun. "When I was a schoolboy, it was said that I bore a resemblance to Calhoun, and my initials are also J. C." He laughed and was pleased with the story.

Bill Webster was in to talk to me about some classified matters. He gave me to understand that the situation within the Military Establishment is chaos and conflict and carnage confounded—and Bill is a pretty steady guy. The Joint Chiefs are at each other's throats, no decisions can be made, and even Eisenhower is discouraged and now ill. (I was invited to lunch with him, i.e., Ike, yesterday, but his illness prevented it. He has been ordered South for a rest.) Bill hopes a new Defense Secretary—Louis Johnson goes in Monday—will change the situation. I wonder. But I do wish him luck.

Bill tells me the Joint Chiefs and most of the seniors over there think the publication of information and pictures in our report to Congress was very bad—despite the fact that they had been published many times before. They are just as emotional and silly as anyone else.

There was some talk about what is sonorously called "the requirements of the Joint Chiefs of Staff." I said that so far as I was concerned there is nothing sacred about any of their pronouncements. They are made by men, and damned vulnerable men at that, and I doubted if their statement of their "requirements" for atomic weapons material had any background that would stand up under inquiry. I hit home on that. He asked to have another 30 days. I said I intended to have a showdown on these majestic pronouncements, but another 30 days wouldn't make too much difference.

MARCH 29, 1949
AT THE OFFICE (7:30 A.M.)

Put Helen on a 7 A.M. train to New York; she is going to a luncheon Janet Murrow is giving at her home for Mrs. Winston Churchill. This will be the nearest the Lilienthals will come to seeing the Churchills, and I am very pleased for Helen.

Yesterday was another one of Those Days!

We bought a home. We are slow, but if you wait long enough for us, we will do almost anything. It happened suddenly, actually, but Helen had been thinking about it a good deal, as a general proposition, and insofar as I give any thought to our personal affairs these days, so did I. But the house itself I saw only for the first time for perhaps 45 minutes Sunday afternoon; that is, the day before we bought it.

Its chief attraction is that though close in (it is just inside the District line, less than 20 minutes' ride from the office, and on a convenient bus line) it is located on about a third-acre that is quite private and isolated. A lovely garden, not unlike the one we were developing at Norris, and a sweet terrace. The house itself is small and very modest, the living and dining rooms being tiny, like ours in Norris were. But we had agreed that if we bought the place we would immediately enlarge the living room.

We didn't know our offer was accepted until 10:30 last night. I made the offer at about 5 P.M. and had to raise it a bit during the evening; it was finally $28,500. This is more than the house is worth, according to Dan Bell at the American Security & Trust, by $2,500, but what things are "worth" and what you have to pay to get them these days is a horse of another color.

I have been griping a good deal these days, and feel pretty unhappy about my work. I must snap out of this, and perhaps one of the ways to do so is to have more "normal" things to be concerned about; a home to fix up, and to get paid for, might help. More perspective and sense of humor would help, and mine hasn't been anything to brag about since I have come back from Florida. This is one of those "periods" that one must get through, and then look back on, and hope they will not happen again.

What the future holds has occupied perhaps too much of my thought. That, pretty largely, will have to take care of itself. I am admittedly pretty "fed up" with some of the things about public service; but there are damn few people who can enjoy the luxury of having everything hunky-dory in every respect about their work and their private life. I need someone to shake me till my teeth rattle to remind me that I am no exception to such a rule; that on the whole I have things much better than most people, and better than I deserve.

The March of Time picture was shown us in a preview yesterday. While it will probably stir up some silly talk about furnishing information to the Russians (though just what basis for this cry will be I am sure I can't foresee), it isn't bad. My sequence is not calculated to put any ideas into my head about my personal appearance! The first view of me is like seeing a mangy sunrise; to wit, the top of my head, leaning over a table looking at some papers! A later shot shows me dictating a speech about secrecy to Martha Jane. She is very impressive-looking, serene and handsome, and the background of the office quite plush; but honestly I was shocked to see how I actually look—one always has a picture in his mind of what he looks like. I didn't think I looked like, say, David, or my high school pictures, but *that* worn, drawn-looking guy, with the funny undersized mouth, is that me? Answer: it sure as hell is, and just after two weeks' vacation in Florida to boot.

Bill Waymack visited us yesterday. For a fellow who has had several months' rest and release from tension I must say he was a disappointment. He seems tense and not "let down" at all; and didn't look well, to my eyes. What a sweet and wise and warm man he is. I miss him like the very devil, and think we will have a hard time recapturing the spirit he did so much to make around here.

MARCH 30, 1949
ON THE TRAIN TO NEW YORK, WEDNESDAY

Bob Bacher saw the President this morning, following my suggestion to this effect. Told him what he already knew, i.e., that he must leave as of May 10, and the President agreed. But no light on successors, although Bob discussed the names suggested, plus Harry Smyth. B. got the impression that something was happening about this, but just what he did not find out.

B. said he made an opportunity to discuss secrecy for "60 seconds, but how successfully I couldn't tell"—the President had nodded as if in agreement.

B. said he made firmly the point that the scientific community was greatly encouraged by the fact that the President had dealt with the Commission and its work in an entirely non-political way. The President was emphatic in saying the Commission was non-political and would remain that way.

Very warm. Saw the cherry blossoms this morning, walked along the basin. They are incredible, and fully blown. A wonderful sight—"just like the pictures in the rotogravure."

The record re "secrecy" becomes more and more crazy. Let's hope my sense of perspective survives the ordeal.

Here is the latest (I almost missed the train because of it):

1. Monday morning there was a showing of a March of Time film, due for release April 15, on peacetime applications of atomic energy. Included in the audience were representatives of the military, Admiral Ofstie and Col. Hinds of the Military Liaison Committee.

2. At about 12:15 I called Clark Clifford about other matters. He had something to take up with me.

He had had a call from "someone from the military by the name of William Webster." It appeared that a film about atomic energy had been made, he said, by March of Time. The military had some question about it, and before deciding whether to clear it or not, they had brought it to Secretary Johnson, who said he didn't know enough about the subject yet, so he wouldn't clear it except with the President's approval. So, Clifford said, the President is going to see the film himself, probably tomorrow. What about it?

I was aghast. Passing the buck to the President of the United States on a thing like that, which is our responsibility, not theirs, and without our knowing of it. But I told Clifford that the film was about peacetime applications in which the President was so interested, that if *this* film couldn't be shown, then there really was nothing about atomic energy that the country could know; that there was a shot of Oak Ridge facilities that was made public by the Army with the President's approval four years ago; and I reminded him that I had sent the President a portfolio of pictures that had been released at that time.

3. I called Webster. He said it had been "garbled" as retold to me. That the President had not been asked to pass on the film, but that in view of the position taken by Tydings and Connally, and the views about our report to Congress of Bradley and Eisenhower (that the report contained "bomb target material"!), it was thought that the

film should be passed on to the White House "in an informal way, for informal guidance."

I was nonplused. Bill is a fine man and is doing a good job, but to have anyone describe sending a film to the White House for showing to the President as "informal"!

He said he hadn't known I was to be away this afternoon as he had planned to try to see me about this, rather than have me hear about it in this way. (If I had not called Clifford when I did, on another matter, I might not have heard about this yet.)

Last night, talking to the final session of the press seminar group, I went into this subject, saying that as an operating matter it is important that secrecy be kept sensible, that if it was made to look silly and a laughing-stock, in some parts this would discredit the whole system and make it more difficult to maintain the *essentials* in secrecy.

If the President, through this episode, stops this film§ (and it is quite likely, for it contains the same view of Oak Ridge and much the same map as he blew up about re the *Fortune* article), then he will be made to look foolish, for he himself, in 1945, authorized the widespread publication of these very same views, right after Hiroshima. And this will cause the further decay of respect in *all* secrecy.

In the seminar, Senator McMahon did a wonderful job before the correspondents, presenting the case in favor of disclosure of our stockpile. He had a critical audience and they went after him, but he handled it superbly, and did himself a lot of good, as I told him over the phone a little while ago.

APRIL 1, 1949
IN THE NEW YORK OFFICE

Our very interest in something that could be bought at any hardware store would have revealed an important amount of information and even something affecting defense.

APRIL 4, 1949
EN ROUTE FROM NEW YORK TO WASHINGTON

This has been an eventful few days. As Helen said, "I feel like Henny-Penny: the sky is falling!"

On the personal side, we had an evening with Sylvain Bromberger, our prospective son-in-law (and Nancy) and were considerably reassured. They seem very happy together, and I have never seen Nancy quite so happy. I am not "used" to the young man, of course, and his

§ He approved it.

field of the philosophy of science is so far beyond me that I am in almost as hopeless a situation so far as understanding what he is talking about as my Dad must have been about my interest in law or labor. But he struck both of us as an earnest, brilliant, and good-natured young fellow, and one with whom Nancy had (or could develop) great areas of common understanding. And they seem to have far more than an intellectual companionship. They had better have, or their marriage won't amount to much.

Then we spent an evening with the young man's father and mother. It went off very well indeed. Helen was wonderful; not a moment of stiffness or stand-offishness. Five minutes after we were in their apartment I think everyone felt at home. They are a cultivated family, with a good background, considerable courage (they left Antwerp and their cherished belongings practically overnight, when the Nazis invaded), and fine humor and faith in the right things.

Then we spent a morning with my Cousin Bernadine. She was in fine form—her first trip to New York in a long long time. We went back over everyone in the "family"; this was fun. She has mellowed a lot.

And we had a visit with Bandi Marton, who is shooting a motion picture on location in New York and New Jersey. He showed us pictures of the wonder-child, their Antonia, with Jarmila, and they both looked quite beautiful and happy.

Bandi and his friends Bella and Sam Spewack wanted very much to see us; so we asked them to come for a drink Saturday evening—and they stayed on and on and we all had a fine time—Nancy and Sylvain were there. The Spewacks have two plays on Broadway: *Kiss Me, Kate* and *Two Blind Mice,* and a third on its way. They spoke about my 1947 confirmation testimony—what they call "The Statement"—with considerable awe, and considering how sophisticated they are, this rather confirms that this particular business was good.

They asked us what we were doing that evening—would we like to see *Two Blind Mice?* So at 8:30 we were on the front row. Helen let out a little cry as we took our seats, for who should she be greeting but Helen Gahagan Douglas: Melvyn plays the lead in the play. The play was *very* good, though rather a busman's holiday, for it kids Washington and security; the Atomic Energy Commission is mentioned, etc. Helen D. took us backstage after the performance (the first time I believe I have ever visited backstage), and we had a little visit with Mel. "What are they doing to you these days?" he asked. Helen looks worn, and she seemed very quiet (which isn't normal for her), perhaps because it was Mel's hour.

Wednesday night (the evening of our arrival), we saw *The Madwoman of Chaillot*—a superb production. Friday night we went to

*Mister Roberts,* taking as our guests Ed and Janet Murrow. A terribly funny and rowdy play, but with a poignancy and meaning that made the obscenities just part of an honest picture of the life of a group of *real* people. It was very moving, and as well staged as anything I have seen in a long time.

This is quite a program. But it was only "the beginning."

For Helen got the plan, design, and content of her book accepted by Harper's, and publication for fall seems assured. She had two visits with them (Cass Canfield and Evan Thomas, a younger editor) and the four of us had an elegant luncheon in the Edwardian Room of the Plaza. (For the record of the future: this one lunch, with cocktails and tip, cost Harper's or Canfield almost exactly $25; isn't this shocking! And a lot of people in there eating and paying much the same; where in the hell does all the money come from?)

They were enthusiastic about Helen's title—*This I Do Believe*—and it will be advertised right away.

And to complete the "personal" things: We decided to buy the "New Topside" on Martha's Vineyard. This was the result of a visit with the Peter Mitchells, our neighbors on the Vineyard. He is a water engineer. His calculation persuaded him—and me—that a cistern was an entirely feasible way to secure a water supply for our home there, so the well-digging failure we had does not make it impossible to go ahead with that site, on which Helen has her heart set, as I have. So that is another event. "The sky is falling" indeed.

My speech to the American College of Physicians Thursday night went unusually well. I was in good form, took the precaution to "warm up" the huge audience in the beautiful Waldorf ballroom, and did quite a bit of ad-libbing, such as describing a chain reaction as "an atomic Pyramid Club"—a topical reference that will probably be unintelligible two years hence.

Had a pretty terrible experience when I first reached the hotel Wednesday. A call from Adrian Fisher. Appropriations Committee had called hearings on our $110,000,000 deficiency (i.e., supplemental) request for the next day (Thursday at 3:30 P.M.). He thought we were very vulnerable, for he could not find anyone who could explain precisely where the money had gone that made it necessary for us to have this much more cash to pay our bills than we had estimated we would; he was told it might take a few weeks to prepare the detailed explanation that would make an understandable answer to legitimate questions along this line.

Then came the sudden call for a hearing. I knew nothing much about the matter, because it was something that had been regarded as a management trouble. I asked Adrian (who was all atremble) what he thought I should do. Get on the night train and come back, was his suggestion. It might go all right; on the other hand, they might get through what he called "the thin veneer" and blow the roof off the Capitol, etc. I recognized that this might well happen, but said I wouldn't come back. It was a routine situation: simply funds to pay off prior contract authorizations. If it didn't go well, then there was time to ask for a recess to permit Carroll (who was on the train headed for Boston and the MIT celebration) and myself to get back and try to mend things. I would call the chairman of the committee and explain that I was away, etc. Adrian was very low and obviously rattled.

I talked to Shugg the following morning, found him quite steady, enlarged on some suggestions I had given him a few days before. But Wednesday night had been ruined! I didn't hear more than half the play, and slept very badly. Scared and worried and troubled. But a report that I got just before I went to my Physicians speech told me that Shugg had done a fine job of explaining the case, and even Wigglesworth had said it was the best hearing on the Atomic Energy Commission thus far!

Spent most of Friday in the AEC's New York office; a very interesting time. Hope to be able to write something about it, but it will take some code and ingenuity to get it on paper.

Had lunch Friday noon with the *New York Times* staff; Mrs. Sulzberger joined them. It was very pleasant. Gave me a chance to talk about the secrecy issue and the "downgrading" of the Commission.

They all had a good laugh recalling the time the *New York Times* printed a story one Sunday stating that there was report of a split in the Commission on the exportation of isotopes to foreign countries. "It was learned that Mr. Lilienthal was in New York, but efforts by the Times to reach him have been unsuccessful." At the time I was at the Sulzbergers' *home* in White Plains. This was August, 1947.

Arthur asked me, "How does it feel to live with secrets, etc.?" and Markel suggested that there was a good article for the Sunday *Magazine* in the answer to such a question.

Spent all day today at Brookhaven, my very first visit out there. Spoke to 1,300 people at three, and to a small luncheon group at noon. Made the point that they were partners with AEC, which I was able to make plain with some stories. An impressive building—the new pile— but I don't feel that the scientific development going on was as apparent, in the spirit of the people, as I had felt at Oak Ridge. Perhaps because my visit was so very brief.

One tends to spend too much time and attention on huge and dramatic buildings and machines (i.e., the pile) and not enough on people. And the people are the ones who are important.

At the new hospital I went in to see a boy, Billie McIntyre, a pale long-legged lad, desperately ill with a cancerous thyroid, being treated with radioactive iodine. That made "medical research" seem real, at last.

## APRIL 7, 1949

Very sad news. Hard to think of anything else, though I am going through the motions. A letter from Dr. Inge, in Knoxville. Dr. H.A. [Morgan] has a malignant tumor on the chest wall. I've asked our people to see if there is anything in the way of radioactive materials that might help, and it develops that there is such a chance. I shall go down to see the old boy in a few days. He has been a colleague, brother, and father, and most of the things that I know, or think I know, I have learned from him.

Robert Oppenheimer and Bob Bacher had lunch with me here in the office. As they said, they were here each as one-half of a Senator. By this they meant that I had invited Senator McMahon for lunch here and at the last minute he had to stay in the Senate for the ECA debate. Helen had gone through a lot of trouble to prepare a wonderful chicken salad, apple pie, etc., so these fellows, together with myself, ate the luncheon.

Yesterday the General Advisory Committee had two meetings of great interest to me on which I got a report from Robert.

One was the meeting with the President, which I had had a good deal to do with arranging. Apparently it went very well. The thing that struck Robert was the President's optimism about the international situation. He is not only optimistic in general, according to Robert, but rather specifically. This was rather puzzling. There doesn't seem to be anything in the outward picture to justify this. Nonetheless the President said that a year ago he felt rather low about the picture. Today he feels quite optimistic and even said that in two years he felt sure that there would be a general settlement with Russia. He went even further and said this settlement would include the outlawing of atomic weapons. He put this on the basis of "information available to me"—at least this is what Robert reported and he is a very good reporter.

The President went on further to say that he appreciated the great services of the members of the General Advisory Committee in getting the atomic weapons program thus far advanced, but that two years from now we won't have to work at it any more or ever again. This obviously puzzled the hell out of the nine wise men who make up the GAC and doubtless filled them with a sense of frustration.

The GAC meeting with the Joint Committee apparently went quite well. It occupied two hours, during which Oppenheimer did almost all the talking, something that was inescapable with so large a group as nine advisory committee members. He was considerably inhibited by the fact that President Conant feels rather strongly that the General Advisory Committee stay away from "politicians," and this extended even to a reluctance to have the committee go see the President at the President's own request. Nevertheless, Oppenheimer was able to discuss a good many things that will be useful in the future, such things as Joint Chiefs' "requirements" and what is or is not back of them, aircraft propelled by nuclear power plants, etc. There was full attendance of the House members and five Senators, including Tydings, which is rather good.

Returning to the visit with the President, Oppenheimer said he had stressed the fact that the GAC had been urging the Commission to make headway in releasing more and more information to the public in the interests of the best foundation under the program and the democratic processes in general. The President expressed approval of this and said, "I myself cleared the March of Time film for them." This sounds like a helpful countermove against the strong pressures of those who see things quite differently.

The President also said, "I just had a letter yesterday from Senator Tydings in which he recommends that custody of atomic weapons and production of weapons should be in the military." The President said to the General Advisory Committee explicitly that he had decided both of these questions and that they would stay decided that way as long as he had anything to do with it. And he went on to say that he believed firmly in the civilian control of atomic energy, and he had no reason to believe that he would change his mind in any particular. This is quite reassuring and I wish it were more widely known.

APRIL 8, 1949
AT MILITARY LIAISON COMMITTEE MEETING

Completely surrounded by stars and braid; [revised war plans have] increased [Joint Chiefs' atomic weapon] requirements "substantially."

[I asked:] Why? What assumptions have changed? More formidable rival?

[I added:] President is pretty optimistic these days; when he sees this [military request for expanded AEC production, we must have reasons ready]. [MLC member said:] General Eisenhower himself insisted that [such reasons] be in there [the joint Defense-AEC recommendation to the President]. [Eisenhower] doesn't want President complacent for a moment.

Some low humor about code terms: Brimstone; Millstone; or Happy Sunshine.

APRIL 9, 1949
AT HOME, SATURDAY

In two more or less half-days last week I sat down and whacked out the first run of an article for *Collier's*. The week has been full: Brookhaven Monday, a dinner party Wed. evening (Gardner Jackson's house, with Lowell Mellett, Arthur Schlesinger, Jr., Jack Fleming, Louis Bean).

Encouraging session with Shugg marked the week. As part of my effort to help improve management practices without diluting their responsibility I've arranged to see Wilson and Shugg at given times each week. Bore down with him on decentralization—my fears that our reorganiz'n. could work against it. Shugg impresses me more each time I see him in action. He is about my age, lots of vigor, can laugh heartily though usually seems rather solemn, can get in there and rough it up, which Carroll can't; isn't so intellectual and analytical as C., nor has he as great understanding of what goes on under the surface. His lack of verbalism is a strong point in his favor, in an outfit that naturally tends to preoccupation with abstract or intellectual argument. Chief trouble is with finance—getting a budget and accounting setup that really produces *the* figures, when wanted. But he'll get there. Excellent public servant.

Go in this morning to the final (I hope) session of the Davis-Horvitz-Witte panel on labor relations in our enterprise. They've come up with an inspired compromise. Our Commission session on it Wed. saw me at my best as a chairman—i.e., picking out the weak spots in a long, involved proposal, and proposing an accepted means of shoring it—in this case, a principle that the object of the plan is to strengthen contractor responsibility, not to substitute our decisions for theirs. If we'd had this before the Oak Ridge strike vote, I'd not have had to threaten to break that strike, something I hated and will never entirely live down, I suppose.

News at last on the vacancy appointments. Yesterday A.M. Dawson of the W. House phoned that the Pres. had decided on Fisk. Nothing about the second vacancy. I found F. was in town, and said that since it would be very difficult to persuade him, I'd better sound him out first. Bacher and I spent an hour with him. He had just (four days ago) bought a house in N.J.; he goes back soon to Bell Laboratories from his Harvard professorship to be third man in the setup, with Buckley soon to retire as pres., so for a man under 40 this is something.

Fisk was much surprised; said he had a repugnance for the public aspects of the work, appearing before Congress and making speeches, and felt not qualified for that reason. I didn't give up, of course, and after 45 minutes of why we all wanted him, he was obviously moved and shaken, asked time to think about it, said he would be willing to come down to see the Pres. I'd say the chances are not good at all. But he would be a fine man. Strong sense of duty, conservative type of judgmt. esp. for a young man.

Learned more about David last night in a couple of entertaining hours than I knew on my own in years. Two Harvard *Crimson* "colleagues"—juniors, Carswell and Simon—came by, using our house as a kind of "station on the underground rr" from Pinehurst, N.C., where they spent their spring recess golfing, to N.Y., where they are going today by car. David had left yesterday noon, for N.Y., to see Nancy, etc., after having put up two other lads earlier in the week. When our present guests came through heading South (we were in N.Y. at the time), they brought their sleeping bags in and unrolled them on top of the twin beds! We prevented this again by main force.

David has plenty of nicknames: Stretch, Dave, The Professor. He "carries" flocks of friends along in courses they can't be bothered to do the reading in, even the lectures. He disappears for a couple days; "We all know Dave is out writing some of those wonderful 'Brass Tacks' " —these being editorial page articles on Radio Serials, and Dies Committee, Education, what have you. How about dates, girls? He never tells us of any and we wonder if he ever sees girls? Oh, Dave does all right, they said, looking solemnly at each other, and recounting a blind date story of huge overstuffing on Chinese food.

They drank their beer out of cans, saying that is the *Crimson*'s unbroken practice. David had instructed us *not* to let any of the visitors know he had landed a job—so when they asked had he heard anything from the jobs he was seeking, we had to gulp something inaudible. Why this we couldn't figure. To make it easier for the others who were still trying to get a job, perhaps.

APRIL 11, 1949
AT THE OFFICE

Had an interesting two hours with Bob Duffus of the *New York Times*, who is going ahead on an article for their magazine on "How

Does It Feel To Carry This Kind of Responsibility?" He handed me an outline which I copy herewith:

BACKGROUND

1. The AEC security system—so far as we are allowed to describe it. The kind of thing that is secret and the kind that is not.
2. Anything Mr. L. has said publicly on the subject of secrecy and its limits. Committee testimony, if public.
3. How many people know *some* part of the secret? How many, at the top level, have to know it all?

PERSONAL

What happens when a candid and free-spoken man is obliged to take on the burden of such a secret?

*a*) His personal and social life. How different from the old TVA days? His play time, recreation, sleep.

*b*) His inner life—what does he think about? Does he worry? Mr. L. is obviously caught on a dilemma: he wants the public educated in all that it can safely know; yet for the sake of the national security he must guard some things with utmost care. Isn't this a terrible strain?

Yesterday planted flowers (peonies, and primula and iris) at our new home—our first *really* home.◖

AT HOME

*[Following are some notes on the "personal" part of the Duffus outline:]*

How do we keep the s.o.b.s of this world from making the same out of the rest of us, by the process of forcing us to imitate them while we try to prevent them from having their way? This is a problem that has long fascinated me. Hitler comes along, and to defeat him . . . etc.; now it is Russia. In an effort to fight off the form of know-nothingism, coercion, fear, and suppression they represent, we find that we are, here and there, increasingly imitating the very thing we hate, as a means of fighting it.

In my person I rather symbolize an effort to break through this old difficulty. For I am one who hates force and has no faith in military power as a *solution* of anything. But the devils of this world have no such feeling about force. Like Hitler before them, they gather force to their side, and would use it to enslave those of us who disdain power

◖ The house on Albemarle Street in the District of Columbia.

and force as a way of life. What do we then do? Run away from the consequences, default, and leave the field to the adherents of force and military power, thus avoiding soiling our hands with the dirty business?

I believe men like myself can devote themselves to the development of force and destructive power, and still retain a repugnance and a spiritual distaste for force and military matters. If this can be done, then for once the lovers of persuasion, agreement, and good will will be in a position to make use of these qualities, because the lowest common denominator, i.e., those who pin their faith on power, will know that we do not regard ourselves as "too good" to develop power, and develop it to use if we must—and yet *not* be poisoned by the very power we have developed—poisoned so that we have become like the very thing we hate and seek to protect the world from.

This is part of the difficulty that has puzzled me for so long: how do we make it true that the highest human common denominator, and not the lowest, shall prevail?

Jim Forrestal is in bad shape; went to pieces after leaving the Government about ten days ago. John Gingrich, our Security Director, went to Florida and got him, and brought him back to the Naval Hospital. Drew Pearson, who has been attacking F. for a long time, has continued what can now only be considered hounding, asserting last night that F. had been "out of his mind" for quite a while, and that some of his latest decisions should be re-examined for that reason. This is a shocking way for Drew to behave. I heard that at the Cabinet luncheon today the President "really let go" and gave Drew P. what's what; said that if he gets out in 1952 he intends to devote himself to evening the score with Pearson. Of course, this is just the thing D.P. lives on, and it does no good to feed him that way.

Talked with L.L.S. [Strauss] this morning, who is of course an old friend and associate of F. He said Jim had no resources—other than financial—except his work. Abandoned his faith years ago—he was born a Roman Catholic. He has no home life, no one to go to when things get rough. Even his "recreation" was actually a regime, squash racquets, to keep fit so he could go back and work some more.

Jim is in an acute state, at the present time, feeling that "they" are plotting to "get" him. He says he is a failure, that everyone thinks he is no good, is particularly sensitive about his part in the Palestine situation, which aroused the bitter enmity of many Jews who had always plugged for him when he was the fair-haired representative of conservatism in this Administration. I told Lewis I had become so ill with the kind of attacks made on F. that prior to his retirement I had written a strong letter to him of praise, etc. L. said they were collecting editorials, letters, etc., to show him as part of the therapy, to show him that he really isn't a failure.

There is something very modern in this travesty—the Irish immigrant's son, terribly ambitious, who gets *everything* the world can offer him—money, preferment, fame, power—and ends up with it all ashes in his mouth. A real product of N.Y. ambition.

APRIL 12, 1949
AT THE OFFICE

Last night Dr. Shields Warren called me from Knoxville to tell me about Dr. H. A. Morgan. There is no indication that the sarcoma in his chest will take a bad turn in the very near future. But there is also no way of knowing how long it will be; he is a very, very sick man. The radiation treatments by X-ray have not been given long enough to be sure they will be effective, but there seems to be a fair reason to hope. I told Dr. Warren that I would go down and see Dr. Morgan next Friday afternoon. This is all very sad indeed.

This has been another one of those terrific days. It started this morning at seven o'clock writing the concluding paragraphs to the *Collier's* piece, which I now have transmitted in rough draft to *Collier's'* representative here.

Had an extraordinary character in to see me today by the name of Boris Pregel. He is a French citizen, Russian-born, who has promoted all sorts of things in the atomic and the radium field for more than 30 years. Originally was a laboratory worker as a scientist in Madame Curie's original laboratory setup in Paris. He has been in all sorts of industrial promotions. He is the guy who owns the Caribou uranium mine on the Colorado Plateau. He insists that this is a great find, not of carnotite but of pitchblende.

Quite a promoter; he came in to recite a long story of the rows he had during the war with General Groves and a lot of other people. He gave the impression of a man who felt he had been badly mistreated and who wanted to know why it was that no one around here trusted him. I told him that he better just forget about the past. I told him there was no way of my insuring that people would trust him, that the best I could do would be to say that when he had any particularized and definite business with the Commission he would be fairly treated. When I went into each of these particular situations, the case pretty well disappeared. What he came in for, I'm not sure.

Dr. Warren had good news for me, though not surprising, from my physical examination at the Naval Hospital. They found nothing worse wrong with me than a slight cavity in one tooth. My blood pressure is still 130 over 80, which is about what it has been for 15 years and is quite satisfactory, similarly with the blood count, etc., so there's no excuse for that tired feeling except too much work.

Received a letter from Jim Fisk this morning saying "No thank you" and sounding very final indeed, so that's that. Suggested to the White House that they don't call him over there as it wouldn't be fair to the President. Went into action right away with Bob Bacher and we decided that Henry Smyth, head of the Department of Physics at Princeton, was the best bet and that he was fairly likely to accept because of his independent means and his situation in the university. By 4:30 this afternoon Smyth was here and I have just talked with him (it is now 6:20) and the "reading" looks rather favorable.

An extremely important thing happened in the Appropriations Committee's report on our budget request. We have finally persuaded them that reactor development—that is, power development—is a program of such importance that it must be coupled with and co-equal with weapons. This is quite an accomplishment. They spell this out in words that cannot be misunderstood in the report itself. While the significance of it will be slow to dawn on people, it is, I think, a real landmark in the history of this enterprise. More of that later.

APRIL 13, 1949
AT THE OFFICE

We (the four Commissioners) have just come from our first meeting with Louis Johnson, the new Secretary of Defense.

The first impression all of us got came before we were ushered into his office. The "characters" we ran into, or who were hovering around the outer office, were certainly not the kind you were accustomed to seeing when Stimson, and later Patterson, occupied that same office. They have the overfed, cigar-chewing, red-faced glum look that you see hanging around the courthouse and the city hall all over the country. The vultures who gather where there is dead meat (in the way of public contracts) and who think they know how to get a hunk of same.

This impression was not changed very much by what we first ran into when we assembled in his office. He greeted us affably, a tall, soft-spoken, relaxed man, big and as handsome as a bald man ever is.

I started out on a pretty serious plane, related to our visit with the President tomorrow on our annual rate-of-production "letter" with which we join with the Secretary of Defense. But he quickly took the subject to severe criticism he had "from the Hill," criticizing our conduct of Los Alamos.

There was a particular man who had raised Ned because he didn't get contracts for this and that. (I learned just a few moments ago that Johnson had told Bill Webster, MLC chairman, that he was prepared to shoot at us in public about this.) Webster broke in to say that the contractor was spending a long time this afternoon with Shugg, going over the facts about his various offers to "serve" us. Johnson said he knew the man over a long period; that F.D.R. had sent him on a mission to India at the time Johnson went years ago, that he was a very good man. Indeed, he may be, and I know it to be a fact that sometimes our selection of contractors isn't everything it ought to be. But starting out on this level didn't impress any of us. Sumner Pike looked as sad as a mortal man could.

I took this up. Of course, people who don't get contracts yell about it; that's normal. Los Alamos, "under the Army, had developed some messes," and we had a man there now, a good, honest fellow, who is straightening things up; that a Congressional committee had investigated the place as to such matters and had rendered a report that wasn't too critical; that the things they complained of were largely in the past tense.

When he talked about "numbers" [of weapons], he said some things in a rather offhand way that shocked us all. I got combative, and said flatly that in the past the Joint Chiefs had not been infallible, and therefore the basis of their reasoning was something we wanted to have before proceeding. He thought, I guess, that I was referring to military and strategic considerations, and until Bacher straightened it out, we were in something of a tangle. The inference in his remarks was that we were munitions-makers, who accepted requisitions from the military and asked no questions. Later he mellowed considerably.

Well, it was a picture of an able man who certainly feels his oats and is riding high. The amount of power he will shortly have, if the Unification Bill goes through, as it surely will (the way he is playing the Congressional game), is terrific. This will be a strain for democracy.

After the others left I stayed for a moment. There were vague remarks about working together, etc. Then he asked whether we thought the Russians would "stumble" onto the bomb. I said this seemed unlikely; that would be quite a stumble. He said, "But we stumbled onto it." This puzzled me. I said we shouldn't underestimate what they could do. He said the military was estimating that they might have bombs in a year; that they don't have them now. On this latter he put his hands in his back pockets (his vest unbuttoned, very democratic really!) and said, "Our intelligence is very good on this!" Really.

Lewis Strauss said afterward, "I have signed a report that I now regret. I signed a report recommending increasing the powers of the Secretary of Defense. That may be a terrible mistake."

Oh yes: Johnson said, early in the discussion, that on his recommendation the President had made a statement that the bomb will be used. He looked down at his desk at this point, as one might who was saying, "Aw, shucks, it warn't nuthin'. . . ."

P.S. Another Johnson gem: A unanimous military judgment of the Joint Chiefs is something the President *has* to follow.


APRIL 14, 1949

Meeting with the President, 12:00 to 12:20 P.M. The four Commissioners and Carroll Wilson gathered in the Cabinet Room while we waited for our appointment. We had ourselves quite a time; it reminded me of the earlier days of the Commission when we were in such a common stew of trouble that we had that as a bond between us. And the fine quality of laughing uproariously at our troubles and at each other came out again with its fine flavor; this is something that has been absent for a number of months.

Secretary of Defense Johnson and Bill Webster joined us in the Cabinet Room. We had time for only a few pleasantries when Matt Connelly said the President was ready for us.

Johnson made a great point of insisting, against my protestations and embarrassment, that I go into the President's office first. It was a pleasant gesture, but somewhat overdone. Rather than fuss about it, as one does about who shall go into an elevator first, I pranced in at the head of the list.

The President looked more worn than the last time I had seen him. He greeted us with considerable joviality. He said Clark Griffith, the owner of the Washington Senators, had just been in and brought him season passes. The President grinned over this like a kid. He pointed to a large handsome leather handbag on his desk and Johnson proceeded to open it and look at its contents. The contents were season passes. Johnson read, "Season pass for the President and party." The President said, "I only go to one game in the whole season and that's the opener." Johnson said, "Well, can't we be your party and go for the rest of the season?" And so on—Rotary Club humor.

At this point I handed the President an envelope marked "Top Secret." He proceeded to open it and began to read. The letter was signed jointly by Secretary Johnson and myself. It related to the approval required under the Atomic Energy Act, once each year, for production rates and weapon production. The most important figures were not recorded; they were to be reported orally.

The President read only a brief time and then put the letter on top of a pile on his desk, saying, "Well, I'll study that later. What I would like to know, Dave, is how are you getting along?"

I said some things about progress in developing the non-military sides of the work, referred to the Appropriations Committee's action in seeing, for the first time, that *power* development was on a plane of importance with weapons. Then I showed him a rough sketch, a curve, that showed how weapon production had improved since we took over, and from two tiny slips of paper discussed the stockpile figures with him, standing at his desk, our heads hovering over these bits of paper. I had prepared the pieces of paper so that certain items were on one piece, and figures (deliberately balled up by additions I had made, out of super-caution) on another piece. Johnson said, "Don't read the figures out loud."

I concluded by saying that our relations with the military had been good, it seemed to me, with almost no differences, and only two that had ever required the President's attention: the custody of weapons issue which he had decided last July, and the question of whether the military or the Commission should produce weapons, which he had decided when he turned the Manhattan District over to the Commission in December, 1946. (I said this latter because I hoped the President would comment—as he had to the General Advisory Committee the week before—that he had no intention of changing his position on either of these issues; but he let them pass and Johnson didn't rise to the bait either, rather to my disappointment.) I said I had no reason whatever to believe that the good relations between the Commission and the military would not continue, and in fact that they might not even improve under Secretary Johnson. Johnson took this without any expression on his face, but when I concluded, he said, "I agree with that, except that it is a lot better than he has said; they have done a hell of a job."

Then the President asked, "How about your supply of raw materials; I'd like to know about that. Are you out of the woods on that now?" I asked Carroll to respond, which he did with his customary lucidity, and great succinctness. (It was evident to me that the President must have been reading or discussing the paper on relations with the U.K. and Canada, and actually a few days later I learned that he had approved it.)

The President then paid his compliments to Clarence Cannon, chairman of the House Appropriations Committee. The President used some very vigorous and colorful language. The occasion was that in the course of the debate on the military budget ($15 billion in a single year!) Mr. Cannon implied that we had plans for dropping atomic bombs on Russia in certain kinds of planes and places—a belligerent speech. I gather it was pretty gruesome. This was simply Cannon's understanding of the war plans as they had probably been explained to him. (Subsequent events in the course of this visit with the President indicated that the word "probably" can be dropped out.) The President said that he had never heard of such a foolish thing as Cannon had done, and that in spite of the fact that he was his friend and that he was from Missouri. I am now quoting the President: "Just when I began to get a chink in the Iron Curtain along comes this sort of thing and destroys weeks and months of work. It is so maddening and frustrating."

As we left, Johnson said across the room to me, "It's a team."

APRIL 16, 1949
FLYING WEST

Saw Dr. H.A. in Knoxville yesterday late afternoon. What a man. He knows just what the score is with the sarcoma that has grown to such a size on his chest wall. And he has been in terrible torment for four days with bursitis in his shoulder. But he was not in despair; no self-pity; no resignation (in the usual sense); actually, he was gay, as we laughed and laughed over some of the terrible things we had gone through that seem funny now as we look back over them. He was just as full of that wonderful incoherent fire as ever, and would raise his head from the couch where he was lying to glare at me, or otherwise fix me with some point about the foundations of life. If ever a man illustrated his point that "the spirit of God is in man," he is that man and his is that spirit. His affection for me and appreciation of my devotion to him is very moving.

But what was most affecting was this: that though it is pretty clear that he is in mortal danger I left him without sorrow and dejection, as I feared I would. He is a man who is *ready,* and has accumulated the resources for such a time as this. I couldn't help contrasting his life of selflessness and domination by ideas with that of Forrestal, and of other men of intense *personal* ambition.

(FLYING WEST, BEYOND BOISE HEADING FOR RICHLAND, WASHINGTON)

This has been a day of grandeur, for we have flown through magnificent mountains when the snow was still deep upon them, and the air clear and sharp. It is now about an hour before sunset, so the slanting rays make the mountains particularly impressive.

We came through Weber Pass, into the great plain of the Salt Lake, and slowly circled into Hill Field at Ogden, Utah. When I dropped down through the trap-door by which one gets the hell out of this B-25 Mitchell bomber we're flying in, I was met by the Brig. General of the Air Force who is the commanding officer at the base, and newspapermen from Salt Lake, photographers, etc. Our pilot had sent word from Kansas City where we fueled and had lunch that we expected servicing at Hill— something about a transmitter. Hence the party. It gave me a chance to talk about the Idaho reactor, which still boils in Washington, where the Montana delegation is trying to raise enough Ned somehow to get us to decide to locate it at Fort Peck rather than in Idaho.*

Sumner gave me a bad turn by a free-for-all speech to a Bowdoin meeting at Boston night before last; I ran into it here with a request from the press to comment on what he had said. I had gone in yesterday morning to say good-bye to him. He was looking especially puffed around the eyes, as if he had had a rather rough time of it. As I started to leave, he rather sheepishly said, "I guess I put my foot into it last night at Boston." Then he showed me a copy of the Boston *Post*. It had a huge headline—whole layers of headlines. Pike was quoted as saying our monopoly could hardly be broken, that we were far ahead and would stay ahead, and then some quotes about the Russians not being so "cocky" if they knew how well off we are; that we are better off than most people think in the way of atomic bombs, etc.

I was so flabbergasted that I didn't dare read it, and went out. But I worried about it. For it was just the day before that the President had cussed out Congressman Cannon, in Pike's presence, for talking belligerently about atomic weapons, saying that such talk set back his efforts toward peace by months. The *Post*, of course, is a sensational paper, and doubtless colored what he said, but it was a poor subject to be talking about ad lib, right on the heels of the President's injunction.

But it will probably not cause any commotion, though if someone wants to annoy the President, a copy of the *Post* with that report would certainly do it.

(The shadows are beginning to darken the folds of the mountains outside. Terrific sight.)

APRIL 20, 1949
FLYING TO SEATTLE IN THE B-25 (5:45 P.M.)

Began the day by rising (by the cheery call of the incredibly energetic Mrs. Wilson Compton) at 7 A.M. Breakfast at 7:30 (we were

* In March the AEC had announced it would build a large materials-testing reactor at Arco, Idaho. Fort Peck, in Montana, had been considered as a possible site.

staying at President Compton's house—which is huge and almost a hotel). At 8:50 I began going about Washington State College, visiting with physicists, biologists, etc.; enjoyed this a lot—an able and enthusiastic group, especially a Dr. Biddulph, who is quite a different person when he is talking about the number of the elements within the cells of plant tissue. Radio-isotopes have here made possible a "profound" discovery about the pathway of elements, say phosphorus, within the morphology or structure of plant cells. Hard going for me, but terribly heartening and interesting.

Then at eleven we marched in to face one of the most beautiful sights I have seen in a long time. Six thousand young people, in the huge gym, the sunlight coming through the skylight illuminating their excited and interested faces. I had fun with them, in almost a personal way (though the setup for that kind of give and take was poor, because of the size of the place and the loudspeaker system). It was a very successful half-hour, and refreshed me as much as it seemed to interest them.

That kind of close attention is the greatest inspiration for a speaker —the faces all individual and distant, but absolutely motionless, almost as long as you choose, at intervals, to hold them that way. The actor in me really is pleasured by this, and the teacher by the feeling that my efforts to simplify the atom are "taking."

(The scenery today has been beyond belief; now, for example, flying over snow-clad mountains that you can almost reach out and touch.)

Then I left at once by air to Boise; met with the Governor, a relaxed, easygoing kind of man, Robins by name. Said he refused to organize groups to go to Washington to put on pressure. Said he didn't believe the Atomic Energy Commission would ever decide anything on the basis of politics. Apparently the Governor of Montana can't understand this yet; he had phoned Robins to ask, "What is the angle?" and didn't believe Robins when he said he didn't believe there was one.

(A snow below us now.)

Then back to Richland to let Fred Schlemmer† off and now heading for Seattle.

The big event yesterday was the Commissioners' meeting with the irrigation directors, who have been opposing our decision not to open added parts of the Wahluke Slope to irrigation and farming use (because we did not want to risk the hazard of environmental pollution from our Hanford operation).

† Manager of the AEC's Hanford works.

APRIL 21, 1949
AT THE OLYMPIC HOTEL, SEATTLE, WASH., THURSDAY

On top of that day yesterday I was out very late last evening with a very interesting family. The wife was very concerned about how strenuous my life is, etc., warned me to avoid people "who will kill you with kindness." They then proceeded to do approximately that. Didn't finish drinking until 8:30, eating a huge meal (which I simply couldn't finish) until midnight. People are nice but funny. All this concern about my health; I must be careful about a "coronary." "You remember so-and-so; had a normal cardiograph one day and dropped over dead with heart failure the next," etc., etc. "How tired you look; one *must* relax." And then merrily go on yak-yaking and keeping one up till all hours.

So I realized again that I had to be tough about it or no one else would, so today I am staying here in my room, getting a massage later, working on my speeches, and going to bed early, and I do mean early.

First time I came West was almost exactly nine years ago—in April, 1940. Only got as far as Hollywood, when I was laid up with a sore throat.

Well, today that trip and everything about it came back to me very clearly.

APRIL 25, 1949
AT THE CHICAGO CLUB, CHICAGO

I have flown a B-29, a Superfortress.

Well, it wasn't for long (though the young pilot urged me to stay on), but I sat at the controls, dipped the wings, rared her up, etc.

I am not surprised at anything that happens any more. But this one was more than usually unusual. We left Seattle last Saturday A.M., got to Rapid City, S. Dakota, in a hurry. After gassing up and having a bit of lunch at the Air Force mess hall, the starter wouldn't start her. While we were discussing how long it would take to replace the starter, Col. A. T. Williams, the C.O. of the base—a heavy bomber main base—said something about taking me to Chicago in a B-29. So we switched baggage and there I was, sitting in the Plexiglas nose, parachute on my back, strapped in tight as anything in the bombardier's seat. The take-off is always a question in these big big babies, but after we leveled off and went at our elevation of 10,000 feet it was nice and restful, and quite an experience.

I asked the pilot, a young fellow, Wachster I think was the name, did he like to fly (he has 1,000 B-29 hours, which takes not less than three years, and is a veteran). He looked out over the horizon, rather dreamily. "Sure do." Why? "Well, it's so peaceful up here." I looked at the Norden bombsight ahead of my knees, and all the switches and things marked "Bomb Salvo," bomb this and that, and was rather struck with his remark.

We got to Chicago after dark. Took quite a while identifying the airport we wanted—Douglas Field at Orchard Place, north of Chicago, a big military airport. But it looked much too small, and the runway, as we circled for it, seemed absurd—it was too narrow for this big bus. I was right up there ahead of the 20 tons that swooped down, lights blazing. A farmhouse and farmyard floated up toward me in the softest way—and then he let the nose wheel down and we scooted in as smooth and effortlessly as you please. I remembered the whole world ablaze with lights—it was an especially clear night—for hours afterward.

Yesterday, Sunday, I rested till noon, then went to the Chicago Art Institute. Enjoyed this enormously. Forgot how many good, very good, modern pictures they have. Remembered some of Helen's and my favorites, particularly statues we had seen together so many times when we were young. Lorado Taft's *The Solitude of the Soul, The Sower,* etc.

Then called on my cousins, Esther Szold, the Gildens, and a couple hours talking over beer with my law classmate, Mal Sharp.

I sure can "take it." At least if last Friday in Seattle is a fair measure.

As follows:

Up at 7:00    Work on notes for speeches, etc.
At 9:00    Conference with Congressman Henry "Scoop" Jackson, *et al.*
At 9:30    Press conference
At 10:30    Being interviewed, impromptu, for three different radio newscasts, seriatim, in the midst of the hubbub of a crowded hotel sitting room, flashlight bulbs, etc.
At 11:15    A 30-minute radio program, with Henry Casterson, Master of the Washington Grange, Jackson and myself, plus a moderator.
At 12:15    At lunch at Washington Athletic Club, attended by an overflow crowd, cross-section (at my request) that really *was* cross-section—Dave Beck of the Teamsters; Weston

of the AFL; the head of the CIO of the state; leading bankers, real estate men, liberal lawyers, etc. Introduced —and most extravagantly—by Mayor Devin, a Republican, I was told. Spoke for 15 minutes. Made a solemn kind of appeal to them to help us keep atomic energy at a high level of management and out of politics.

2:30–3:00    Rest!!

3:00–6:15    Trip to the University of Washington with President Allen, etc. Saw their cyclotron, still building, a pet of Dr. Utterback, and, best of all, spent a hurried and concentrated hour with Dr. Donaldson and his fine-looking team, who deal with aquatic life. Fish and more fish; irradiated salmon eggs, etc. They have been to Bikini each year, and now Eniwetok. Extremely interesting and intense man, Donaldson.

6:15    At the President's house, at a dinner for me. Met Bishop Bayne, of the Episcopal Church, a poetic and sensitive-looking young man, who comes here from New York and was the Chaplain of Columbia, I believe. Also the head of the China Club, an exporter, soft voice, a quality that was not too easy to square with his views, which seemed rather harsh. All for changing our relations with the Argentine, from which place he has just come. We should not kid ourselves: the Argentines *like* Perón, and Madame Perón, too, etc.

8:15    At Meaney Hall, an overflow crowd, people sitting in the aisles, standing in the back, etc. About 2,800. Mostly older people—surprised me, thought it would be largely students. Had a wonderful time, felt very relaxed. Talked for 50 minutes, and they held on remarkably. Talked very informally, used stories and cracks to ease things up. One of the most successful of my recent efforts with an audience. Particularly effective in getting acquainted right away.

9:45–12:30    A big "reception," way out on the other side of the city at the home of Dr. and Mrs. Quigley—I guess there must have been 150 people, the most varied kind of people, including Scoop Jackson's mother, who was born at Narvik, 150 miles above the Arctic Circle, and who says to him, "Henry, you talk too much"; to some very "swell" folks; and all in between. Had a good time, I must say. Great fuss made about my speech and this and that. One lady giggled, "How I pity this man's poor wife; when he gets home after all this to-do over him, she won't be able to stand him, he'll be that spoiled."

1:30    Finally got to bed. Then up at 7 A.M. for the homeward trip.

To go through that kind of day, on top of a lot of things that preceded it, and to return to some difficult work ahead is certainly some kind of test of stamina. I hope.

APRIL 26, 1949
AT THE CHICAGO AIRPORT

The long-planned party for me given by Tom Beacom (H. Law '23) was quite a success. About 25 or 30 men around a big table in the Chicago Room.

The important thing was that so "prominent" a group of men should have taken an evening to attend this kind of dinner. By and large, they're not the kind who would. Instead of my making a speech, Tom introduced the subject—and me—and his purpose, i.e., to give Chicago leaders a chance to become "acquainted" with a man who . . . etc.

Ran into two interesting bits of the past—the sort of thing you run into when people begin to consider you as one who has "arrived," etc.

One was from George McKibbin, a big political lawyer, once a candidate (Republican) for Mayor against the present Mayor. Said that back in 1933 Henderson of Antioch College came to him on behalf of A. E. Morgan, to ask about me. Says he spent two days "investigating" me, via George Haight, Kixmiller, and Barr, etc. He said, "Well, I'm glad I gave you a good report, now I've heard you."

The other comment was from Britton I. Budd, president of Public Service of N. Illinois. Said that about the time my term at Wisconsin expired in April, 1933, James Simpson, then chairman of Commonwealth Edison, spoke to the directors of the Associated Companies (C.E., PSN., Ill., etc.) about an able young man in Wisconsin by the name of Lilienthal. "Jim said we ought to take steps to get you back to Chicago, that you were going to be one of the leading lawyers of this country and we'd better get in on the ground floor. Then a short time afterward, and before anything definite was done, we read that you had been appointed to the TVA."

APRIL 28, 1949
THURSDAY

It is a bright shining day—and Helen and Dave own a home! Have just come from the title co. where we signed the papers, delivered the checks, and walked out the owners of a house in the District of Columbia. Happy day.

I think!

No, I'm confident this is right.

And the same day I'm sending a check that gives us title to a nine-acre tract on Martha's Vineyard. We don't do things by half, apparently.

Gave Mac away today. To the University of Tennessee farm at Oak Ridge. Well, all things come to an end, I guess. And it's absurd to pretend, when it has been 2½ years since I have really ridden him.

But it is an important event, nonetheless.

Will I ever again own a horse?

Penny still goes strong, running and racing along, but very thin, and sleeps a great deal. Over 15 years old! She's deaf (except to such a high sound as clapping one's hands sharply), but has all her teeth, and still looks like a young dog, except when she "folds." But something is wrong with her insides, so we can't bear to have her in the house any more, poor dear. We've had her at the vet's week on end, but no permanent recovery.

And speaking of vets, I have a wonderful story, told on herself by Mrs. Compton at Washington State.

This was at breakfast, mind you, and an early breakfast at that. She is full of energy and good humor, and bright-eyed, despite she is perhaps 57 or 58, and many times a grandmother.

"Everyone here is so intense and interested in his work, and nothing will do but Dr. Compton and I must go to all the affairs. Last evening we were strongly urged to attend an exhibit and social affair given by the School for Veterinaries. I was met at the door of the hall at the Vet School by an eager young man, all agog. This is the way he greeted me: 'Oh, Mrs. Compton, I am so glad you have come. Could I interest you in a demonstration of artificial insemination?' " She said it would be a new experience, but she certainly was interested.

My father and mother start tomorrow for California, he being 80 and she 75! Just like that. We were simply aghast when we read Dad's letter: he has been rather ailing lately. But they want so much to see Allen‡ and their grandchildren, and have become restless. Well, Helen and I worried about it a while and then decided that since there is nothing we can do to keep them from going, we should just make the best of it. Which we shall.

MAY 4, 1949
AT HOME

The news came tonight that agreement has been reached on lifting of the Berlin Blockade, the approaching end of the dangerous airlift,

‡ My youngest brother.

and the calling of a conference of ministers to try to work out the German problem.

Dean has had a simply incredible few months as Secretary of State. He is such a contrast with the cocky (as well as cocksure) Johnson. The difference between the two men is a vast one.

The first time I have seen Dean "to talk to" (as we say in Indiana) was last Wednesday. Jim Webb§ had invited me to lunch. We sat at a table in the small dining room used by the Assistant Secretaries, etc., and while we were attacking our food in walks the Secretary, alone, elegant in a new-mustache clip and a beautiful gray chalk-stripe flannel suit, three-button, very English (and also very 1922-ish!). He greeted me with the warmth and restrained humor that is his charm, and sat down with us. He looked very well indeed, quite composed, none of the strain and terrible irritation (almost to the fly-off-the-handle kind) I have seen him exhibit a few times, when he was working with Byrnes.

Jim told him that I had reported that things were going well with the atomic energy program. I spoke of headway in basic science, medical applications, etc., but very briefly. Then I said that I had heard that the President had approved the National Security Council Subcommittee's report on [broadening our atomic] relations with our former partner [Great Britain]. Jim had not yet heard this. Dean said in that solemn, slow, careful way he has when he is thinking *before* he speaks (the usual order with him—wish it were with me, more often!) "Yes," (long pause) "he wants to know just exactly how we recommend that we proceed next; just what Congressional leaders are to be approached, and when, and how."

He had spent the morning in a public hearing before the Senate Committee on Foreign Affairs, on the Atlantic Pact. Vandenberg had asked him a question; I gather it dealt with the procedure concerning admission of additional nations to the pact. The question: Was this something that could be accomplished by the President alone? "I knocked that one right out of the ball park," Dean said, his eyes gleaming with great pleasure, and illustrating by a gesture, "Right out of the ball park. I said I was happy to say that I was authorized by the President to say that such an admission of an additional nation" (if that was what it was) "was, in the President's view, a separate treaty requiring the advice and consent of the Senate. Vandenberg was greatly pleased that he had raised the question, and astounded but pleased to get a direct reply. So everyone was happy."

My talk with Jim Webb was not about anything in particular. I think he wanted to show his friendliness. I wasn't in as good a mood as I might have wished, until somehow the question came up of the

§ Under Secretary of State at this time.

Bold New Program (for technical aid to less-developed countries, "Point Four"). He said, "Isn't our whole problem to make democracy so attractive to the peoples of the world that it will have an emotional and spiritual appeal greater than Communism?"

Yes, I thought so, but didn't think that physical things alone could do this; it was largely a matter of how these "better things of life" he spoke of came to people—a matter of "how." And on this I had written some things five years ago that I believed to be still true and even more relevant now than then. He hadn't read my book; said he would, taking a note of its name. Later in the day I sent him a copy. But Jim is so busy, so harried, so tired, and so conscientious that I can't see how he keeps up with the day-to-day things. It is evident that Dean must leave much of the running of the department to him—for Dean is in the midst of international discussions and Congressional hearings all the time.

Dean said, with a twinkle, that he had returned to the making of furniture and such, had fitted up a wood-working shop in his home. Told a story about a pair of wooden brackets, for the holding of decorative china, that he had made for his wife, and was so pleased when his daughter-in-law spied them and described them as antiques.

Told Jim I didn't plan an indefinite tenure in my present job, but that I had no plans on the subject. I should not say much about this, but as a matter of protection there ought to be a few people in the Government who know that it can't be assumed that I will stay on this particular assignment indefinitely. I stayed in TVA several years longer than I was actually useful, and I don't want to repeat that.

Fred [Newton] Arvin spent the weekend with us. He is, in appearance and mannerism, the very picture of a college professor, in the stage version. But he is one of the world's best people. I have known him now for 42 or 43 years, which is a record for a friendship in these here parts. He asked me, in the nicest possible way, "Would you see any objection to my dedicating my book on Melville to you? I have thought about it from every possible angle; I can't myself see any valid objection. If you don't, I would like to do that." (This is a book he has been writing during his current sabbatical year, to be published next spring by W. J. Sloane as part of their "Men of Letters" series.)

Monday he and I (after I took care of some urgent things at the office) trotted along to the National Gallery. For one who has as little emotional capacities, so far as anyone can tell outwardly, as Fred has, he gets an extraordinary satisfaction out of viewing pictures. I suppose the intellectual understanding of great painting is perhaps as substantial as the more primitive reaction, which, I fear, is the sum of my own enjoyment—an enjoyment which seems to grow. It is a howling shame that such great pictures as those in the National Gallery should be here, day after day, and I see them so rarely.

Well, then I suggested we stop in the Smithsonian, which we did for a while. This is a quaint place. They have done everything they can to arrange and dispose of the various objects to make them as uninteresting as humanly possible, but despite this effort, the place is fascinating. Saw, high above us (and alongside the Wrights' first plane, now back here from England after a long and silly old man's squabble), nothing else than "Lilienthal Glider, 1894." Apparently one of the originals of Otto Lilienthal. Shaped like the wings of a great bird. The old boy broke his neck in one of them.

Later in the day, just to make a big thing of it, I went alone, for 15 minutes, to see some John Marin water colors at the Phillips Gallery. I suppose that will have to take care of "art" for a year. But I hope that once we live closer in, we can do this sort of thing quite often and easily.

Items:

1. *Collier's* accepted my article, on which I don't think I spent more than five or six hours, certainly not in the actual writing; and sent a check for $1,500.

2. Duffus of the *Times* sent in proof of an article based on an interview with me. Troubled me somewhat—by its emphasis on secrecy as synonymous with guards, vaults, etc. Worried Frances Henderson even more, and she was clear-headed enough and shrewd enough to catch some possible troublemakers in the article; between us we worked out language that would minimize or eliminate the difficulty; I am assuming she will persuade the *Times* to accept the changes.

Frances is exceptionally talented at matters that call for a critical faculty, and has a remarkable nose for potential trouble, all the more remarkable since she is young and without any public service experience except during the past year or so. She takes criticism from me splendidly, as a good assistant should, of course, not appearing to be supersensitive or taking things "personally," and always trying to improve on things. The volume of work in the Chairman's office has grown greatly, so that we need six people to handle it, and even so they will be working harder than I wish. But the office is a kind of nerve center of a huge organization, and is carried on, I daresay, at as high or higher a level of effectiveness as any place in Washington.

Read Helen's manuscript, *This I Do Believe*, through for the first time last Saturday. What a beautiful job that girl has done! It is the most creative piece of editorial craftsmanship I believe I have ever seen.

The reading even impressed me with my own words! Parts of it are still eloquent, and most all of it (the exceptions are few, and chiefly go back to 1933 and 1934) I still believe to be true and valid. Helen did not change anything; she did not put words in my mouth or change the sense of anything. She did a good deal of eliminating references that are too characteristic of speech forms, identification of a particular audience, etc. And the way she has assembled parts of a speech here and a speech there, and put it together so that it has cohesion and a unity—this is really something to see.

The success of her efforts make me think that the book could be a fairly important and influential one. What it needs is a more explicit theme, something that will tie together the various manifestations and illustrations of democratic action related or referred to. So I wrote some notes for an opening chapter that I hope will do this. And I plan to write an additional chapter or two.

The best thing about the book is that it has given us a common task, and an opportunity to express to Helen, rather explicitly and beyond mistake, how very much indeed she has contributed to the work I have been doing all these years.

She is altogether and beyond a doubt the most versatile and many-sided human being I have ever known, or heard about; and I doubt if there ever was anyone with quite so broad a range of great human qualities.

MAY 9, 1949
AT HOME

Since Thurs. noon (the 5th) have been working at home, writing on speeches, and thinking about the writing I should do on *This I Do Believe*—the title Helen has given our book (and Harper's have jumped for).

This is hard work, with agonies reserved for me that rival physical torment at times. But it has satisfactions that are full compensation.

It's been coming better than I feared. Getting going is still my chief trouble; which is to say, I go through the groans of getting the ideas tested, sorted out, and organized, through the device of the opening few pages, sometimes the opening paragraph.

Have a draft of half or more of the Harvard Phi Beta Kappa address done; took me the working part of 2½ days to do it, and the latter part then bogged down—or I did. But the tough stumps are pulled out or plowed around—and I'll put it away to simmer in the back of my mind—don't make it till June 17.

This morning the American Bookseller Assn. speech is at bat. Got

up early; after breakfast Helen and I and some coffee started trying
to find a theme, etc. She gave me the theme—I want this to have a
bearing on the theme of the book—and now I'm back before my machine in the study (having done 15 minutes of physical work in the
back yard: burying garbage, digging in the compost heap, stacking
cordwood as a break between). Now I'm going to stop this alibi for not
getting at it, and spend two solid hours here. Find that if I promise
myself I won't leave the machine or desk for two hrs. this makes me
stick out the low spots and get something written, however dismal, on
which to operate.

(11:40 A.M.)

At 11:15 I reached Donald Dawson at the White House, answering
a call he had put in to me perhaps an hour before.

"Dave, the matter of the appointments has about reached the boiling
point. All the checks on Smyth are now in, and the names will go up
[to the Senate] this afternoon."

"I see. You said names."

"Yes, Dr. Smyth and Gordon Dean."

"Thank you, Don. Good-bye."

So that's that. We will just have to make the best of what is clearly
a second—or third—rate appointment to a first-rate responsibility;
that is, the Dean business. I feel just as strongly as ever about the
unwisdom and bad precedent of having a former law partner of the
chairman of our Joint Committee put on the Commission.

But it was the President's decision and I had a chance to discuss
it with him—it didn't do a bit of good, it is apparent. But from now
on we must accept it, with good grace, and there must be no comment
"off-the-record" or otherwise about it.

And now, back to work.

MAY 11, 1949
MEETING WITH THE PRESIDENT (12:25–12:50 P.M.)

The President was reading our annual report to him as we [the
Commissioners] came in. And after greeting us with warmth, he said,
"I've been giving this a second reading." I said, "Maybe it would be well
if we sat quietly and let you finish your second reading"; but he put
it aside.

I said we enjoyed very much these visits with him and went out
with a great "energy release," to use the language of our atomic
weapons reports, every time we were with him. He smiled his biggest

smile and with a show of considerable enthusiasm said, "Well, I always enjoy discussing this proposition with you. It is the thing in the Government that I have most hoped for and am as interested in as any one thing that is going on—in fact, anyplace in the world. It has more hope for good in it than anything I know of."

Then he began speaking about China, and for five minutes he continued about China in an extraordinarily interesting set of observations. How he got off on China I don't recall. But what he said was that the "grafters and crooks" and their lot in China hadn't any interest in the millions and millions of Chinese who didn't have enough to eat; 2½ billion dollars had gone into China in recent years and, "I'll bet you that a billion dollars of it is in New York banks today."

"It's all for those grafters and crooks; rest of the people in China don't matter. General Marshall went over there and studied it for a year. He came up with a plan for two-thirds representation by the Nationalists and one-third by the so-called Communists and they turned that down. I say 'so-called Communists'—Joe Stalin says that people of North China will never be Communists and he's about right, at that. Well, nothing can be done about China until things kind of settle down." Then he used a wonderful expression. "The dragon is going to turn over and after that perhaps some advances can be made out of it. I had a couple tough Republican Senators up here the other day and I gave it to them hot and heavy and kind of pulled the rug out from under them. I haven't heard a peep out of them since."

He said there are great things to be done in China and it may not happen in our lifetime, but those are the things that will put the country on its feet and make something out of it. "Why, there is the greatest chance for a TVA in China you can imagine," (with that he gave me a great big grin and a large dose of his particular brand of charm, which is not inconsiderable) and ran on with an enthusiasm that I have rarely seen him equal.

I'd been sitting there absorbed and delighted but wondered how in the hell we would get back to atomic energy. Had this been Roosevelt, I would have known that we would never get back; for F.D.R. would either mischievously or deliberately pick up the ball and we would be ushered out without having had a chance to get any business transacted. Or if I had been a subordinate officer in a big corporation, I might have taken my life in my hands to stop the boss from going on about something we hadn't come in to talk to him about. But instinctively, I suppose, I knew here is a fellow who really has a sweet humility despite the quite terrible trappings of power all around him. So I grabbed the TVA reference to bring us back.

I said, "Mr. President, our increasingly successful effort to develop atomic power might within our lifetime do much toward furthering the headway of the Chinese people. There is less mechanical or electrical energy in China per person than anyplace in the world, and this is a measure of their poverty. Atomic power, once developed, probably can be set up without a complete system of highways and railroads, which wouldn't be the case with hydroelectric or steam power."

As I moved back to the atom he grinned and said, "Well, I guess you're right; we ought to get back on the subject," all of it with a kind of good-natured spirit that, as I say, probably wouldn't have happened if I had been Vice President in charge of Fig Newtons for the National Biscuit Company and he the President of that company.

But we didn't keep off the Bold New Program very long. I told him about the plans for reactors at Arco in Idaho and the negotiations with the Navy,◖ but very soon he came up with a big grin at a good joke he had on me and said, "You better let me know whether a TVA on the Yangtze is something we shouldn't bother with because atomic power will make it obsolete." I said that the thing about TVA that the Chinese needed most of all had to do with development of their land, and that was the part that interested him most, and furthermore I couldn't conceive of any kind of energy that would ever be cheaper than the natural flow of water. But he thought he had a good joke and said, "I certainly had you on the spot there."

He said that McMahon had been in a couple of days before and talked to him about the necessity of amendments to the atomic energy law; something about a change in the preamble and about repealing the provision about the terms that had been passed last June. "The Republicans thought they were going to reorganize the whole business," and at this his jaw kind of snapped. He said he thought it might be a good idea to change the terms to six years with a new appointment each two years or so. He said he didn't want to do anything about it until McMahon had talked to us about it and would we please give him our opinion about the proposals.

I brought up the subject of T.X. [future test], saying that the necessity for very long-range planning make it necessary that we know now whether he approved in principle; that we would, of course, come back to him later as we approached the date for approval or disapproval as to particular dates.

He said, "Yes, I think you ought to have them. The way the things look now I don't think there will be a question at all, but when the time comes there may be some negotiation on that we wouldn't want to gum up."

At this point he began to talk about the state of the world in the continued highly optimistic and excited note I had noticed before,

◖ The Arco site was an old Navy proving ground.

but even more specific. The T.X., apparently, seemed to bring this to mind.

"They've [the Russians] been waiting and expecting us to blow up. All of my information indicates that they're the ones who will blow up. They've got plenty of troubles, and as a result we're going to get a full settlement in Germany. This is strictly off the record." (He didn't say "secret" but "off the record," which in Washington is not considered a very strong expression—means "for background" usually.) "They'll try to mess around in Persia as they want to get in on the Persian Gulf and they'll needle us in China, but by the time T.X. rolls around I'd say that things would look a whole lot different. Things are 50 percent better today, I'd say, than a year ago."

I had arranged with Lewis that he raise the question of aggressiveness among the military men, especially Gen. Nichols, toward taking over design and production of weapons, but despite my signal to him, he rather faded out, and instead of talking about that he made a very friendly reference to Bob and this being his last meeting with us. The President gave Bacher a very indulgent smile and said, "We're going to keep strings on him. I have had a lot of fellows come in here and resign, a lot of them with no choice, but they almost all of them feel homesick and some of them come back and want to work for the Government again."

He told the story of Isador Lubin, former head of the Bureau of Labor Statistics, who came to him pleading to get back into Government work. "He said, 'I just can't stand it. I want to be where something is going on.' And Sam Rosenman sat on the corner of that desk just the other day and said, 'There is nothing to this business of practicing law; we make big fees but we don't do anything for the country.'"

I said that we had had a reorganization of Sandia (explaining what that meant) and would be coming to him for help in the way of a letter to a large industrial company, which I named, urging that they take on the work at that point. He said he would be glad to help in any way he could.

As we got up to leave, and still Lewis hadn't mentioned the civilian-military issue, which he had brought up rather vigorously in our Commission meeting and which I had asked him to raise (he explained later he couldn't find a place to put it in), I said, "Mr. President, we are determined to carry out your policy of an entirely civilian administration of atomic energy in all of its aspects. You have shown every sign of intending that that is the way it should be. I want to be frank to say that there are elements in the military establishment—not the whole of it at all, but strong elements—that don't agree with you and are pretty outspoken about it and are causing some difficulties."

The President drew himself up and practically sticking his chin into my face said in a way that was partly amusing and extremely impressive, "Well, I'm the Commander in Chief." His voice dropped at the conclusion of this quite illuminating sentence. I said that he had shown that very clearly last summer on the custody issue; that we didn't want to come running to Papa with troubles we could handle ourselves, but we might have to. He said, "Well, Papa won't hesitate to use the strap if that's what it takes," and his grin spread into a full-scale laugh.

On that encouraging note we left.

(IN THE CONFERENCE ROOM)

The scientific director of the Sandstone [Eniwetok] tests, before a lot of charts, a long and complicated statement on the tests. He talks in tenths of millionths of seconds, which is about as difficult to comprehend as the billions of dollars we spend are.

MAY 13, 1949
AT HOME (9:15 A.M.)

Starting to work on speech to the American Booksellers for Wed. Call from Jim Webb. He's going away for the weekend. "I feel all wrung out after these last three months. Want to try to get feeling a bit rested before next week, when I become Acting Secretary of State." (Acheson leaves for Paris then.) Then he laughed, the most wholesome laugh, and said, "The very idea is funny. I feel like a country boy from North Car-o-lina that had a load of hay fall on his head. The idea is ridiculous, of my being Acting Secretary of State!" I said that as long as he had that wonderful sense of natural humility and unaffectedness, the job was in good hands. Fine man.

MAY 14, 1949
AT HOME

Having a rough time last few days. Probably the onset of a bit of rough water.

About the AEC fellowship program. After a lot of thought and worry we decided *not* to ask for FBI investigation, etc., of those awarded the 600 scholarships for study in basic science, nor to insist that the National Research Council (with whom we contracted for administration of the program) do so. They strongly urged against it. Seemed to me an important principle was at stake, the extension further of this awful dossier system, beyond any necessity or security justification.

We felt sure there'd be a row about it, and Hickenlooper wrote a letter about it, to which I replied, oh, about last Jan., and asking a public committee hearing. No response. Then it was set down for a hearing last week. Hick. showed up long enough to say he was against what we are doing, but he didn't have time to listen to the evidence, as he had to go hear Henry Wallace testify against the North Atlantic Treaty. Ours being a closed session and Henry's one with photographers, I understood, but it made a record of how we had all marched up the Hill and then no one to listen to what we had to say.

Then, in interrogating Dr. Smyth day before yesterday, Hickenlooper let loose, and the same day Sen. Hoey, Cong. Cole, etc. Several of the scholarship holders were either Communists or "had leanings"— the new phrase. We saw we were in for it. In the meantime, beginning Monday eve. last my old pal Fulton Lewis, the radio boy, spent most of his time giving me hell: I had "opposed" Smyth and Dean, and my comeuppance was near; now this.

No secret data access being involved, the issue is at last the broad one: everyone who is the beneficiary of Fed. educational funds should be investigated and "cleared." Hick. put it that way, and that's what it comes to.

This becomes really serious. I got steamed up: phoned Charles Merz at the *N.Y. Times*, Elliston at the *Post,* here; Deke Parker of the Scripps chain; Ed Murrow; Albert Gore. (The House Approp. Subcommittee set a meeting for next Monday on it, meaning we are facing a "rider.")

My speech to the A. Booksellers Assn. for next Wed., which I have about completed, gives me a chance to wade into this sort of thing, and I hope what I've written, intended to use satire more than heat, will stay in.

Giving lots of thought to the differences, and relative usefulness, each in their place, of military management, and various kinds of non-military management; and particularly the reasons why this Commission should set up an island (or peninsula with a very narrow neck to the main body, the Comm.) made up of military men; i.e., men selected because of their training and status in the Armed Services.

Raised this with Carroll Wilson last summer apropos the change in organzn., esp. putting Los Alamos, etc., directly under Gen. McCormack and the Div. of Military Applications. Wilson, not thinking hard about it, has allowed McC. to staff that division entirely (except for minor posts) with men from the services, very good men, but with no particular reason for having military men in administration, research & developt., etc.

At several sessions this week, and hard ones, tried to make clear why this is in error. Partly, makes it too easy for Natl. Military Establishment to take it over: there in a package. More important, fails to distinguish between modern management of production, research, development, transport, etc.—things concerned here—and the kind of function for which, over a long period of time, military management has been found to be superior.

It should be the *function,* not the uniform or clothes a man wears, that should determine whether we put military men in a particular job—even when the object is to produce a military weapon, as that usually is a function for non-military organization. Used analogy: a brush fire gets out of hand on a farm. A group of men, informally and instinctively, organize in a military fashion to put it out; i.e., a maximum of authority, minimum of consultation, and emphasis on speed and urgency. The same group of men set out to plan the best way to handle the farm, from a production, etc., viewpoint. Here a quite diff. type of organzn. comes about—like our TVA soil-building community groups, with minimum of authority and max. of consultation, etc. Wilson and Bacher thought this analogy helped.

MAY 15, 1949
AT HOME, SUNDAY EVENING

Rough week ahead. Fellowship program attack. A hard fight to win, in the short term. Hard to explain to the public what is involved—looks simple—just don't pay good public money to educate a Communist. The ill effect on education, the evil of the precedent in that direction, takes some time and thought. And the "rider" on an approp. bill can go through almost without debate, and no veto. We start on this in the A.M., with the Approp. Committee, then in the P.M. before Joint Comm. (which is jealous of its jurisdiction, as Senate Approp. Committee wants next whack at us). Then the Senate Approp. open hearing Tues.

Begin my day at the office at 8:30 tomorrow—and dinner for Sir Gordon Munro* at night, so it'll be quite a day.

Met my new associate this P.M. and got an excellent initial impression. Gordon Dean. Looks older than I had thought, medium height, a bit of a paunch, good clear way of looking at one, no difficult mannerisms. Seemed thoughtful, judicious, easy. No touch of the politico at all. We spent most of the two hours talking over the fellowship thing— a good way to get acquainted.

* A British member of the Combined Policy Committee.

MAY 17, 1949
TUESDAY

This A.M. has established, I think, that we picked an organization that, despite faults, knows its onions. Bronk† is about as good a witness as the Joint Committee has ever heard.

MAY 19, 1949
AT HOME

Well, did I say this was going to be *rough*? What an understatement. It has been rough, hot and heavy, and rather a torment.

Haven't had time or energy to keep up day by day. Tired now.

Had to face the rough blast of emotional "outrage" over the granting of a fellowship to a professed Communist—one Hans Freistadt, young student at U. of N.C.—and with this unfortunate thing—it was the Natl. Research Council that actually granted the fellowship—had to fight off a bad precedent headed toward making all non-secret work of the Commission closed to all who, in Hickenlooper's gem of a phrase, have "potentially subversive or otherwise objectionable views."

And then another time bomb: a leak about loss of uranium oxide from Argonne, in the N.Y. *Daily News* and *Times-Herald*—this led to terrific jitters and excitement and last evening from 4 to 7:15 P.M. before the Joint Committee in a nasty session. Worst part is, the lab's property accounting procedures and our own are sloppy and lax.

I was before Senate Approp. this morning, and took the aggressive, with strong statement against Fed. interference in education. Had five questions at one time, and it was rough, but they handled me with gloves and began to see my point: that there *was* something to worry about—politically—in my assertions that this concerned freedom of education, etc. But it's a tough fight—after that day yesterday, then I went on to make a hard but very successful speech to the A. Booksellers.

Baruch just called: "Ride 'em, cowboy," he said. "With so much to cover you can't expect to look into every corner."

MAY 20, 1949
AT THE OFFICE (2 P.M.)

A very rough time this morning indeed. They feel they have me on the run, have tasted blood, and it will go on from here. Where it

† Detlev W. Bronk was at that time chairman of the National Research Council, which administered the AEC fellowship program.

will end, it is hard to say. Lowell Mellett, after the hearing, asked me if I was not the cause of a good deal of my own troubles, but just how I can mollify these fellows without giving up all sense of principle is hard for me to see.

I am a very troubled fellow today. That hearing this morning was mean, ugly, and even descended to insinuation, something I have not had to face for some time.

This fight differs from most I have had to contend with in the emotional excitement that surrounds the Communist issue right now. Dragging out the names, one by one, of these fellowship-holders about whom there is derogatory information is cruel to them, and makes it very difficult for us to get these issues heard in a reasonable and decent way.

MAY 22, 1949
AT HOME, SUNDAY

It is difficult to record my feelings, as I find myself in one of the most trying and unhappy crises in all my years of controversies. I try to believe that at the center of each vortex each one seemed too wild and twisting ever to survive and surmount, and yet I did, and the issue itself I faced in each case was resolved, with wide understanding. Thus, the charges by A. E. Morgan of "dishonesty," wherein I was hanged in public before the evidence was in—and in the end, such bitter critics as Dorothy Thompson, etc., changed their view. Thus, the row with Willkie. Thus, the AEC confirmation hearings, with all the weight of insinuations, charges, etc.

But at this juncture, these back-glances don't help much. The ache in the chest, the coming and going of emotions of fear and deep concern that I am impaled on an emotional issue from which I can hardly be freed come what may. Even a fear that this time I shall be so smeared by the general emotion as to mark me beyond help.

I know I lean toward overdramatizing myself and the events about me, and I have done this here, I suppose. I know there are many, many people who trust me, and respect the honesty and guts it took to stand up to this issue. And I know that few things of this kind can remain acute in the public mind very long at a time. If this lasts another week or two, that would be unusual.

Now we have called a retreat—agreeing to loyalty oaths—but that won't appease those who want to drive me out, and I know it. Nor will it allay the almost hysterical fear of Communism, change, ideas, science, etc., that underlies this. A historic pattern is woven into the course of things.

I slept 14 hours last night—from 7 P.M. until almost 9 this morning. I have a tough week to face next week. There is nothing to do but face it. This is the price of wrestling with such difficult issues as those involved in the atom and in freedom of inquiry. I recall now Chester Barnard's comment when he first heard of the drop at Hiroshima: "This is the end of our democracy."

(5:30 P.M.)

Another blow: Senator Vandenberg in a long statement to North American Newspaper Alliance gives me the devil, doubts if he would vote for me now, etc. My making the issue of the fellowship clearance business as one leading to interference with education seemed to make him mad; which means I have something there. But his statement was certainly a tough one to take. Must try to see him.

This is a tormenting business, and hard on Helen to boot, of course, for it's hard for me to keep from brooding about it—but I must snap out of it somehow.

Jim Forrestal jumped out of the 16th floor of Bethesda Naval Hospital this morning (the flag is at half-mast as we passed just now) and killed himself. Look, Dave, don't let this political fracas get you down. Take it as it comes.

Addendum: Joe Volpe tells me Hickenlooper has put out a statement listing my crimes (everything that isn't right is my fault, and the Commission's virtues are just happenchance) and demanding my resignation. It's that kind of a political fracas, and to the death, I take it.

MAY 23, 1949
AT THE OFFICE

Called about ten this morning, asking to see the President. To my surprise and delight Matt Connelly had me come right over, for a 10:30 appointment.

The President gave me his big smile and warm handshake. He knew what was bothering me. "Don't let this tempest in a teapot get your goat, Dave," he said. "You let it get under your hide and you'll get like Forrestal; no need to worry about it. There are a couple fellows up there running for the Senate in 1950, and they have to have something to get elected on, and they think maybe you are it. Reminds me of the story Senator Ashurst used to tell. He said a Senator was elected for six years. During the first four years he could be a statesman; the fifth year he was a politician, and the sixth year a demagogue. That's about the size of this."

I said what burned me up was that I should be the cause of adding anything more to his, the President's, burden. And he knew that if at any time he felt the burden was too great, he didn't have to request my resignation; it would be forthcoming on his slightest suggestion.

He waved all that aside, and gave me a good pep talk again. "You have done a good job and everybody knows it, and I know it. You just keep on doing a good job and don't let these fellows worry you too much. Christamighty, if I paid much attention to all the editorials in that stack of this morning's newspapers, I wouldn't have time for anything else. But I don't; and you shouldn't. Just go back and do your best, and this will blow over. Now you see if it doesn't."

I was feeling pretty tough at the time—it looked as if they "had" me for sure, in a ganging-up operation, and his words helped a lot.

(AT HOME, 9 P.M.)

Saw Vandenberg for 45 minutes late today—the evening headlines, eight-column, saying "Congress to investigate Lilienthal."

He began: regretted his Newspaper Alliance article to Hayden; didn't know it was to be used, etc. (Gee, he's just a novitiate!) Then said, hadn't any question at all about my personal qualities. Thought judgment bad on security matters. We must keep security. And my saying that barring Communists from fellowships had anything to do with education was wrong.

I showed him his latter point was wrong, if you based it on "no money to educate C-sts" where no security involved. He saw this, and said he was wrong on that.

Apparently first time he ever realized that the scientists saw security differently than he did, and that many of the moves I made had to be to retain their confidence and support in the program. "You aren't a free agent as an administrator," he said.

Thought he felt better about me by the time it was over. I can't help liking him, though a lot of people now regard him as a windy man with no convictions.

MAY 25, 1949

Call from Allan Kline. "Why in the world did 'Hick' do that? It couldn't be politics, for it is a fool thing to do, politically. I thought I would try to find out more about it, because for one thing I would like to get Hick out of a hole if I can."

(I thought *I* was in the hole, so from the president of the American Farm Bureau Federation this was interesting word.)

"He probably took some bum advice," Kline said, "fellows like Harrison Spangler."‡

(AT HOME)

Was on the rubbing table, at the "Y" the other afternoon—it was while all this ruckus was on in full swing. On my face, being kneaded firmly. Heard a voice say, "I would like to shake your hand, sir, and to wish you well." Very formal voice. Looked up to see a very erect, slender man, stark naked, gray hair in a wavy pompadour.

So I rared up, shook hands, thanked him, then asked, "And what is your name?"

"I am Admiral Byrd—and this is all a lot of Goddamned politics. I know. I've seen politics when I was in the Navy. You will come out of this all right. Good day, sir."

And with that he stalked off, stiff-legged, wooden sabots clattering, looking from the rear somehow like a penguin. Considering what his dear brother, the Senator, thinks of me, I enjoyed this considerably.

MAY 26, 1949
AT HOME

The awful nightmare feeling I have had to live with for the past two weeks is over. And suddenly, dramatically. It happened this morning, under the klieg lights (six newsreels and television cameras) and the biggest press turnout I can remember, in the huge Senate Caucus Room. I made my statement—improvised this morning, hurriedly, longhand notes, some of it I hadn't read over. Then Hickenlooper folded. My letter of yesterday had called him. You could hear the whole business fold, right there. The newspapermen enjoyed it, and you could hear Pete Edson say, clear around the room: "Why, the ————."

And then the radio has been going full blast, from which I learned that the President in his afternoon press conference endorsed our work, and me, warmly, and that pretty well finished it. And good may come of it, for we may get some light on the atom before the American people.

The turning point came yesterday morning. I called the office early to say I wanted a press conference; we needed to take some effective action, even if it would be risky. I couldn't stand just being pushed into a corner and being on the receiving end; wrong psychology,

‡ Republican National Committeeman from Iowa.

bad for the innards. I sat down at my typewriter here and pounded out a statement, intended to take the initiative, drive Hickenlooper to put up or make it stick. I wrote this in 40 minutes or so, then found that McMahon had blown up when Volpe told him I planned a press conference for the afternoon. Terrible—the forum should be the committee. I got him on the phone, said I agreed that the committee was the right place, but he hadn't fixed a hearing, was going ahead on such defensive things as Gingrich, the missing uranium, etc., and we *had* to get the whole thing into perspective, which is what I intended to do.

We were in a tangle, friendly enough, on this when Frances Henderson slipped me a note, "Suggest that we send a letter to him to release." I suggested this, he grabbed it. This was at one o'clock. I had not yet had a chance to proofread the rough draft of the "statement" I had been banging out. He said it must be up there by two o'clock, before they began their afternoon session with Gingrich, etc. I actually had that four-page letter revised, and Martha Jane, bless her heart, had it typed and on its way by two o'clock, and by 2:30 the letter was released to the press.

It took right away. It was the right thing, and the turning point. Joe Volpe was there, said the newsmen grabbed it and started for their office, one saying, "Now Dave Lilienthal is hitting on 12 cylinders again."§

What a wonderful relief. And how wonderful to find out, as I certainly have, how much people trust me and believe in me. And so sweet to see the relief for Helen. This has been tough for her, as well as for me. We worried about the house—here we had finally put much of our resources into a house, and then almost immediately the whole place seems to fall on me, with a chance that I might be discredited almost beyond recovery in this terrible hysteria, and perhaps with my health broken, too. The story of Forrestal's breakdown was in our minds, however we preferred to believe that the analogy was not appropriate. (A good many newspaper articles and editorials used the parallel, however, and actually I think this helped.)

I have had wonderful support from the good radio commentators such as Elmer Davis and Ed Murrow. Fulton Lewis' venomous and almost nightly attacks for a month have helped in steering support of the right kind, though it has also aroused terrible hatreds and suspicions.

§ In the letter I demanded a committee investigation of the total record of the AEC's program, not just the few instances where bad management had been charged.

MAY 27, 1949
AT HOME

Carroll handed me a yellow teletype broad-tape, marked "Secret" in big letters. I read its complicated text, then let out a big yell you could have heard over at the Federal Reserve: "The bottle, they've found the bottle!" The great uranium mystery was about solved. Quite a relief. This will finish flattening out the story. Now to find the "body"—the lab worker who emptied the contents into that disposal can, and was skeered to 'fess up to it.

An FBI agent was kept right along with the boys at Chicago while the bottle was pried open, a test made showing a few milligrams (!) of enriched stuff of the same enrichment as that which had been lost. We hope to get Wally Zinn to make the announcement, in Chicago, tomorrow afternoon, hoping it will be before J. Edgar dashes to Chicago and "finds" it. The FBI has the bottle here in Washington—why I don't know, unless it is to provide a dramatic "discovery" by J. Edgar.

He sent me an irritated letter this afternoon entitled "Loss of Uranium," complaining that uranium was "lost" at Oak Ridge and our security officer there had not reported it for two months; by then it was too late to find it, etc.—an ugly kind of "record" letter. Also he objected to the fact that our security force there had used polygraph tests (lie detector to you), whereas that, I gather, is the FBI's special privilege. The facts were that in the working of uranium, metal chips fell in a guy's *socks;* he failed to change his socks when he left, returned the chips in the morning, etc. Such a business to be in.

Beginning to get a fair amount of very friendly mail, moving mail, and some excellent editorial comment: this morning's *Herald Tribune* described Hickenlooper as one of the greatest statesmen to go off half-cocked. David called and gave me a fine talk; this was wonderful.

The Joint Committee met today; Hick. asked to have until Tuesday so he could prepare the indictment; having brought in the verdict on Sunday last he has not yet prepared the indictment. And I hear from Scoop Jackson that the Democratic members on the House side were kind of sore; their story was that during the 80th Congress we gave Hickenlooper the breaks, now we would do nothing for them—whatever that is. It is true we don't see anyone but McMahon, and we have to correct that, and soon.

I am by no means sure this committee won't side against me, or, in any event, engage in strictest censure of us. They are a very ordinary crowd, and we won't play their kind of political footsie. I don't much care, though of course I don't mean that literally. What I am concerned about is that the committee should vote to limit the investigation to specific "charges." On this, presumably, there will be a party-line vote, and if such characters as Kilday go off—he may—that would be a blow, but the country could be made to see what they are up to.

There is no use minimizing the bad impression that the last two weeks have made, particularly the fellowship-to-Communist business. And the stool pigeoning within the organization will probably continue, which won't help.

But I feel rather calm about the whole thing—perhaps too calm. And not mad, really.

MAY 31, 1949
AT THE OFFICE (7:30 P.M.)

Just before the battle, Mother!

Tomorrow morning Hickenlooper explodes his bombshell—whatever it is. Have been trying to figure out what it might be: mostly about security and clearances and the like, I imagine. It won't be pleasant, but I do feel the worst is about over.

Anyway, I am quite relaxed this evening. Got steamed up—deliberately—at my press conference yesterday, to make a point. Tomorrow I propose to be as calm as a mill pond.

JUNE 4, 1949
LYING OUT IN THE SUN, AT HOME

The past two weeks have been about as "crowded" (I believe that is the cliché) and full of torment and triumph as I can remember. I haven't been up to (nor indeed has there been time to spare for) the keeping of journal entries. A good deal of what happened, however, is pretty well reported, since most of it was hardly private or unobserved, being on the front pages of the papers and in the transcript of hearings, though some of the latter are still "executive" sessions, though not "classified" for the most part.

So just some of the items:

1. The lowest point, in my own feelings, I believe, occurred on Friday, two weeks ago yesterday. It was in the afternoon of that day, alone in my office, I realized we had to yield on the proposition that students must be investigated as to their affiliations and beliefs, and that this defeat, though we might make it appear a rather limited one (i.e., loyalty and non-Communist oath, as distinguished from "full FBI investigation and clearance" required for secret work), was actually

much more far-reaching and injurious for academic integrity than it appeared, for it would be difficult if not impossible to stop there.

I was low, with a feeling of how fear and hatred of an enemy can cause us to wound ourselves; and that a blunder way back the line (the fellowship board that admitted Freistadt) might cause a long succession of evil consequences. Having felt as badly as a man can, I called the Commission together with the staff and proposed that we take *action*, rather than just sit there, wallowing in our concessions about the fellowship program. When we rose from the table in my office, we had decided to require affidavits of all scholarship holders and announced it for Sunday papers.

2. But there were other very, very low moments. Another one that was a honey occurred in the executive session with the Joint Committee that followed, by a few hours, the sensational "exposé" of the New York *Daily News* and Washington *Times-Herald,* one of the most violent pieces of writing I can remember right off. It was difficult for Carroll and others of the staff to realize that this had to be taken very seriously, and that we must drop everything—things intrinsically more important—and get some good people at work on what we realized was actually a scare without adequate basis.

The Joint Committee was angry, scared, ugly. The facts appeared so simple—a bottle containing uranium not properly receipted for, etc. Then they proceeded to prepare a "public statement." Hickenlooper and Knowland served notice that they intended to assume the worst unless every possibility was excluded against that assumption.

This was too much for me. I said, "Criticize the Commission if you wish, as much as possible, but don't induce hysteria in this country. This is *not* bomb material, and you should say so, and it is small in any terms. If the people of the country find that the Congress is rattled over a seventh of an ounce of uranium oxide, what can we expect when the day comes when Russia has a stockpile of atomic weapons?" This calmed them down.

But I went from this session (which ended at 7:15 P.M.) to dress in white dinner jacket and make an optimistic speech to the American Booksellers, and then to bed to face another mean day on the morrow, with Hollering Homer Ferguson of Michigan, Wherry the Embalmer, and others at me tooth and toenail. This was a bad time.

3. It was difficult to get my mind off all the turmoil. Particularly was it difficult for me to believe that I would survive these attacks, in the sense that I could hardly remain on at the Commission, usefully, just because of the size and tone of the yelling, the innuendo and fear. Then I got to worrying about how I would make a living, me with practically no reserves and a new house just purchased in Washington

This was tough, but I pulled out of this after 72 hours of miserable doubts that took all I had to keep in decent bounds.

4. There were high points in the period, too. (At the moment I am in high, but rather relaxed, and reassured deeply by the events of the past few days.)

5. High point number one? Well, hard to say. But probably the reception my letter to McMahon calling for an "accounting of stewardship" got right away from the organization (whose back stiffened at once, for this was taking the offensive) and from the press. This I did as a kind of hunch, getting up early one morning and pounding at the typewriter, to provide a kind of draft for a statement I had in mind for a press conference. This letter (which was the way it was later used) changed my spirit entirely, for I was no longer "taking it" but taking the initiative and "dishing it out."

6. Another high point: When Hickenlooper finished reading his remarkable statement on last Wednesday morning, which simply said he would get the evidence of my "incredible mismanagement" together *later,* instead, as was expected of his statement of just two weeks ago, he would blow me out of the water with evidence long gathered and ready to shoot. He wanted to "confront" me with the "proof," etc. And then, under the klieg lights and television cameras and with a full attendance of the 18-man committee, he plops a short one to the infield.

7. Another highlight was day before yesterday, the second day of the hearings, when I had completely regained my composure, and made an opportunity for a touch of humor, kidding his expression of "incredible mismanagement." To be able to kid meant a lot, for it showed that I didn't take this too seriously, actually, and was beginning to make fun of the whole thing.


JUNE 8, 1949
AT HOME

Today was one day when indignation rather "got" me. I cut loose this morning in the hearing, trying to make plain how outrageous it was that "Mr. A." should not be given an immediate hearing.◖ We have them in a tight fix on that, and I bore down on it. Then this afternoon,

---

◖ This was a personnel case brought up by Hickenlooper, apparently part of an effort to show that certain persons were employed by the AEC despite "derogatory information" in their dossiers. Other committee members protested against the unfairness of this procedure; Mr. A. was never publicly identified, and no more such cases were raised.

seeing a stack of West Coast papers with wild headlines of the "charges" Hickenlooper has been making got me mad as the devil again. Furious at the injustice of permitting an investigation to run that way.

But I will overcome the indignation (or enough of it). On the merits, the investigation gets thinner by the day. The throwing out of spectacular charges which thin out into nothing—but the headlines have been made.

The house—*our* house—at 5126 Albemarle is coming along fine, and in no time at all we will be living in it. This is wonderful. I meet Helen there about every other evening to see how the changes are coming—and they look fine. She did a fine job of figuring out revisions that will make it a lovely place.

JUNE 9, 1949
AT HOME

It is a strange way to measure success, but now I watch the papers (and check the radio broadcasts), and the less there is about the investigation, the better off I feel we are. Not the *amount* of publicity but the lessening amount of it—that's the measure right now.

The hearing today on the Norway shipment had two things of particular interest.* (1) It got L.L.S. out in the open with his opposition. Before, he had managed to get it in executive sessions (two of them) from which I had been *excluded*. He had predicted such terrible things that would follow from his "disclosures" that it's good to have it out in the open. My guess is that his position will be a dud.

(2) Senator Vandenberg took out after me for saying on the record, more than once, that there were reflections on Norway in what had been said about our sending isotopes to the Norwegian Military Institute. "Let there be no more talk about reflections on Norway," sezze he, in his best statesman's voice. Joe Volpe, at my side, said, "Drop it," but I thought to myself: if he doesn't want anything said about it, it must be a pretty good argument, and one that hurts. So I said, with a grin, that though it might mean being taken to the woodshed, nevertheless it was relevant whether a nation receiving isotopes was friendly or unfriendly, and stuck to my guns.

Helen and I went to a garden party "in honor of His Majesty the King's" birthday, at the British Embassy. Very pleasant; got a salute of respect from quite a few people whose good opinion counts for a

---

* Hickenlooper charged that an AEC shipment of radioactive isotopes sent to Norway in April was in violation of the Atomic Energy Act. Strauss, who had voted against the shipment at the time, later stated the reasons for his opposition in a letter to McMahon which was read into the hearing record.

lot with me—people like John Lord O'Brian, the Eugene Meyers, and some people I haven't seen for a long time such as George Morris, Commissioner Mahaffie of the ICC, Joe Davies, etc.

JUNE 11, 1949
AT HOME

About a month of great strain. Part of it's just plain nightmare— nothing else can describe it—just nightmare. Some of it the exultation and excitement of winning. Most of it in the glare of the publicity and the apparatus that goes with it these days: batteries of newsreels; huge searchlights and such that accompany the modern horror, the television camera; radio microphones taking every syllable; and the floor at one's feet as you testify filled with men with cameras, waiting to pounce at you, bulbs banging, when you make the least spontaneous movement. Time was when having a transcript taken and six men asking questions at one time was about all I could take; now I've gotten so none of this bothers me—I mean this whole array that was loosed on this investigation.

As things stand today, Hickenlooper has not convinced many people who didn't believe all along I was no damn good: the Hearst people and their readers (or many of them), the reactionary groups generally. My friends (who I am sure were upset and puzzled and perhaps a bit scared I'd gone off the deep end somehow) are all reassured, I know; and the in-betweeners, so important, have dismissed the whole thing as another piece of political skulduggery, I would guess, and have gone on to something else.

It has been tough, and I look it, frankly. But only once did I flare up—just for a minute Friday morning. I'd had too much sleeping pills and strain, and for a moment or two snapped at my colleagues. Mostly I've been collected enough, esp. on the stand, and no sense of panic. Disgusted at times, of course.

Worked a bit on the book (*This I Do Believe*) today. So anxious to get it off and on its way.

JUNE 16, 1949
IN THE SENATE CAUCUS ROOM (NOON)

Zinn, head of our huge Argonne Laboratory, has been testifying all morning mostly about whether "the" bottle that was "lost" was brown or clear glass, etc. I have been more depressed about this job this morning than I have been for a long, long time. Chiefly, I suppose, because all this seems such a frittering of time and emotion and energy, such triviality in a world that is really faced with great and grave troubles. Such a waste of good men's minds. I am tired, rather badly tired, I suppose, and it is difficult to summon the sense of humor and perspective I need to manage to get through this dull, miserable, and humiliating experience.

JUNE 29, 1949
AT HOME (EARLY)

Ups and downs. Yesterday a bad down: continued evidence of political mauling of the atom: O'Mahoney's Approp. Committee proviso that would require advance Budget Bureau approval of any construction cost beyond initial estimates, and so do everything to divide responsibility and delay making headway. You'd think there never had been an exceeded estimate in the Govt. before. Will cause padded estimates, as customary in old line depts.—this is a kind of fraud I want none of.

Hearing gets duller by the day. Down to garbage cans yesterday—even lower, the slab beneath them!†

Baruch here; saw him for an hour Monday, 27th. If Cong. persists in mixing in politics, he thinks I ought to tell Pres., "Look around for another Chairman." Thinks Eng. going to hell in a hand basket and this country in danger going along. Very handsome and charming, but his vanity is hurt by fact Pres. will have none of him.

David's commencement was a great joy to us.

Worked Sat., Sun., and Monday on the new book. Should rest, but want so much to have it out. Trying a lot of rewriting or additions.

JULY 14, 1949
MEETING AT BLAIR HOUSE,‡ 8–10:45 P.M.
(NOTES WRITTEN AT HOME, 11:15 P.M.)

Present:

The President (looking wrinkled around his eyes as I don't remember ever having seen him before; and as the evening wore on—he said almost nothing after the opening and by way of closing—looking quite tired and old, not the jaunty man at all).

† Hickenlooper spent much time on various administrative problems and housekeeping shortcomings at AEC installations, including garbage cans.
‡ At this meeting, the Administration explained to a few top Senators and Congressmen its proposal for a broader program of atomic cooperation with Britain and Canada. The "Modus Vivendi" of 1948 was to expire at the end of 1949 and the British were pressing for the kind of partnership they felt entitled to because of their wartime contributions. The U.S., on its side, needed the cooperation of Britain for an assured supply of uranium ore.

The Secretary of State, looking very cool and serene, doing a beautiful job of exposition; somehow professorial, I thought, compared to the others, rather than the distinguished lawyer he usually is.

The Secretary of Defense (Johnson).

The Vice President (Barkley).

The Speaker of the House (Rayburn).

General Eisenhower (who told me, "I sure *was* sick"; and "After being a chain smoker for 35 years I had to quit and it has been tough—four months and it is still tough!").§

Senators Connally, Vandenberg, McMahon, Hickenlooper, Tydings (who left early with a bad cold); Congressmen Durham and Cole.

Bill Webster of MLC, Joe Volpe, Gordon Arneson of State.

Dean, after the President, read some notes about how important this is; stated that the Modus came to an end before long; described the status of our former partnership, asked me to describe the raw materials picture (which I did in three sentences that hit most everybody with a dull thud) and then the proposal. Then Johnson and Ike told about how interrelated we are with our ally.

Vandenberg was "shocked." Two "prejudices." One, he recalled meeting in Forrestal's office, and then went on to bring up (as I had predicted he would) the Cyril Smith incident; and he quoted Van Bush as saying, "Of course, we shouldn't be giving away that 'know-how.' "❡ Prejudice 2: doesn't want to keep on giving things to the British.

Eisenhower spoke on how important the British are to us; how important good faith and mutual trust is in an ally. Eisenhower told off Hickenlooper and his talk about how we must stand alone and protect the world; telling him that if he thinks this country can fight a war without Britain, he is crazy; or that if we think we can depend on the atomic bomb to win a war, we are crazy; or the idea that we don't need the rest of the world "in order to live."

Connally, at the end, surprised me by a very fine statement, simple and humble, about how the people of this country feel about working with the British (this to answer Vandenberg and Hicken-

§ Eisenhower was at this time president of Columbia University, but served Truman as a consultant. (He had been ill that spring.)

❡ The meeting in Forrestal's office was in 1947, when Vandenberg had insisted on the rescinding of a wartime executive agreement requiring British approval of any American use of atomic weapons. (The agreement was ended shortly afterward.) The Smith incident was in the summer of 1948. Dr. Smith believed he had authority to exchange certain technical metallurgical information with British scientists; before he conferred with them, his instructions were explicitly amended to exclude such information.

looper, who said the people wouldn't stand for our giving our "know-how" to the British, etc.).

This last was a particularly silly business: I kept saying, "That 'know-how' . . . the British helped make that 'know-how'; you are only kidding yourself." And still they kept on making the same statement. Vandenberg and Hickenlooper talking like small-bore politicians.

After Vandenberg had talked so much about how much we were giving, Acheson and Rayburn and Barkley said something very good: Our foreign policy is *not* founded on helping someone else so much as it is that by helping them we are taking the best way to help our own country. Vandenberg said, "Yes, I know that and have said it," but you could see that he never had understood what he had said and didn't understand it now.

The newspapers had had stories this afternoon about a meeting, and the President was asked about it at his press conference this afternoon. It was supposed to be secret. It was agreed that on leaving tonight we would all say, "If there is any comment, it must come from the President." There must have been 50 newspapermen on the sidewalk outside when we left—after 10:30—quite a lot of excitement.

Bill Webster said, "Well, this was history." I replied, "This will probably be just a lot of talk."

There will be more talk before Congressional committees. To suppose that this can be kept from leaking seems pretty hopeless.

JULY 18, 1949
IN THE BASEMENT STUDY OF OUR NEW HOME: 5126 ALBEMARLE

So many many things happening, and I haven't had that extra spark of energy to pay any attention to the journal.

Besides, most of them would have been recorded at a time of considerable discouragement—I even used the word "despair" one day, and this is an emotion that under no circumstances should a human being permit himself. Fatigue, cumulative, had a lot to do with it. Have had to contend, too, with quite a lot of a gnawing kind of physical pain and discomfort, that grates on the nerves, and hence erodes the patience and spirit, more than one is willing to admit.

The futility of so much of what the Joint Committee has been dishing out, the interminable hearings (mostly wind), the fine testimony of those who say we have done a remarkably good job, with almost no attendance and little news coverage (good words rarely being news comparable to charges), McMahon's efforts to get legislation to increase the prestige and power of his committee and of himself, the Appropriations Committee's whacks at us—well, it hasn't been too good at best, and quite bad when a fellow is rather worn down.

But there have been some very wonderful things, too, and this morning, refreshed physically from a good weekend, and that "new start" that has always been my salvation, these good things loom large again.

David, for instance. He is a capital young man. His criticism of a difficult chapter of the book was excellent, and led to a whole new slant on what the chapter should be about. He is thoughtful, full of steam, and fine to look upon. His letters this morning tell of his first two days as a "newspaperman" on the *Post-Dispatch*—full of detail of people whom he meets, doing much better—much—than I did at his or subsequent ages. And his first story hit page one—an amusing one with photo, of two housewives who got tired waiting for the city to repair a hole in the street and did it themselves. He and his friend John Simon have an article on academic freedom pending with *Harper's Mag.*, with a division of opinion about it among the eds., but this gives one a feeling he has what it takes, too.

Nancy, too, has been part of the brighter news; for though Sylvain hasn't yet an assistantship for sure, she turned down our suggestion that they postpone the wedding till they do know how they'll manage, in a firm, sweet, but quite adult letter, the letter of a girl very much in love and not afraid of anything; but with no adolescent cracks about Mother and Dad not "understanding"—just that this is what they're going to do, and they'd rather figure out things together than separated.

The House has been a Godsend; it is almost the ideal answer—for Helen's ideas, translated into the remodeling, are incredibly wonderful, giving a look out into the garden and woods, and yet the net effect is not of a plush and swank house, above our means, but quite otherwise. The garden *has* me, and we again have something we do together.

The Book has been another good spot in the tough weeks, for though I wish I had more time to work on it, it is not going to be bad at all; and the challenge has been met, to spend weekends writing and polishing it, and get it out in spite of the pressure of the investign.

The office has been a lifesaver in every way. I don't think I would have survived but for Martha Jane and Joe Volpe, each of whom in their way have that kind of thoughtfulness and friendliness that gets one over the hill that seems too steep even to try. So there has been a lot of good with the sour.

JULY 19, 1949
IN A CLOSED SESSION OF THE JOINT COMMITTEE (3:30 P.M.)

It is absolutely quiet in here now; seven Senators (including chairman and ranking member of the Committee on Foreign Relations) and eight Congressmen are reading the security file on Miss B., an employee at Los Alamos, her drinking habits and where she slept, according to some.

Fine subject for Congressional attention, I must say. And the great issue about our relations with U.K. has to wait; and a dozen Commission people sit here.

What a way to run a railroad!


(AT HOME)

There were many little touches at the Blair House meeting of last Thurs. night. Some serious, some just plain horseplay of the American politico at his warm, human best.

The meeting was in a rather small room. Huge picture, painting, of F.D.R. dominated the room, hanging over a very yellow sofa on which Arthur Vandenberg not so much sat as sprawled.

F.D.R. kept his composure throughout, despite the following: Hickenlooper talking, running on: "One of these wartime agreements is so extra-or-rdinary that the U.S. hasn't even a copy; I had to see it in photostat." Truman, looking like a tired owl, sitting bolt upright in a chair in the corner of the room, suddenly woke up (he was surveying H. with a dry passivity). He stuck his finger, arm outstretched, at H. and said, "I've got that document; got it locked up in my safe in the White House and that's where it stays." H. said, nonplused, "I don't refer to the Quebec agreement; I have another one in mind." The Pres. didn't bat an eye: "I know the one you mean, and don't you worry about that; I've got it." The "artists" present appreciated that exchange.

As the evening wore on, Vandenberg turned to the Pres., who sat with Acheson between them. "Do you work here?" he said. "If you do, maybe you know how to get a drink of water."

"You'll have better than a drink of water." (Which he did, later.)

Most everyone had said something. Not Hickenlooper. Vandenberg gave him a build-up: "And now we ought to hear from one of the best-informed men . . ." So H. began in that flowing-stream manner, in which one phrase runs into another, and when it is over you wonder what went on. Opposed the President's plan, of course. "Amurikun peepl be opposed to giving away . . . We must protect our own security first and foremost; everything depends on our keeping this vi-tal seekrut to ourselves; we stand alone, etc. Joining with others upon whom after all we can't be sure . . . etc."

Eisenhower, who sat on H.'s right, looked at him, first quizzically, then in consternation; then he finally had his fill: this was all contrary to Ike's thesis of our dependence, in a military sense, on the two countries being together, a sense of oneness he had described vividly out of his experience in landing an invasion army, etc. He scowled like hell, broke in: "Do I have to begin by making a speech defending my Americanism?" And then he went to town on Hick. "When it comes to the absolute necessity of this ally, I speak with some experience," he said, "but even leaving aside the matter of military necessity, we can't live alone in this world: tin, manganese," etc. It was a massacre.

My own contributions were few: comments on raw materials; later, answering H.'s remarks that it would be better to get along with what we have in raw materials than give away our know-how, and besides we had all this stuff in tanks in the ground that was in effect a huge mine:* on the first part, I said we were kidding ourselves if we thought the former partners didn't know how to make bombs, reciting their wartime Los Alamos participation; on the second, the fallacy of this would be apparent, to everyone, in a few months after we dropped back to a lesser apportionment of raw material.

It was asked: What about asking Britain to stop [their plan to make their own weapons] and we give them no information or partnership, but hold some of our weapons and earmark them for them? I said (as did Acheson) this would be so humiliating a proposal, considering their place in the world and their contribution to this enterprise, that it would do more harm to make the offer than just to ride along; and I added, if the alternative were full partnership *or* continuing the limited area-by-area arrangement under the Modus Vivendi, my personal view would be to drop the whole thing and each go it alone, because the present arrangement leads to friction because it is almost impossible to administer, since the facts don't come in these neat little compartments of the agreement, so we have increased ill will against us, and the creation of good will and mutual confidence and trust (emphasized by Ike in his statement) is defeated rather than furthered; that whether the British were justified or not in their view, they did feel they'd been badly dealt with from the end of the war.

JULY 22, 1949
AT HOME
(MEETING WITH THE JOINT COMMITTEE, JULY 20)†

A full attendance, almost, except Tydings and Kilday. In the jammed little room in the Capitol, 48G.

---

* The "stuff in tanks" was radioactive waste from the Hanford plutonium plant, stored in huge underground tanks; this contained some fissionable material, potentially recoverable by chemical processes.

† This meeting was to present to the Joint Committee the proposed broader program of atomic cooperation with Britain and Canada which had been discussed earlier at the Blair House meeting of July 14.

I sat at a table facing the committee, between Dean Acheson on my left and Gen. Eisenhower on my right, with Secy. Johnson on his right. Behind the committee is a huge old-fashioned mirror. I noticed the Secy. of State in it, and the world-famous Ike grin, but who is that long-faced, solemn, tired-looking guy between them—face vaguely familiar? Oh, for crying out loud, that's me.

Dean began, as at Blair House, soon passing the ball to me on raw materials. I was questioned by Hickenlooper and Millikin, who tried to make our operating reserve seem more imposing than we had. Knowland, pouting like a big, bad-tempered adolescent, his eyes red and smaller than ever, obviously holding his temper not too well: did we assert we had authority to do this without Congress? Then Dean called on Johnson, who passed it at once to Eisenhower, but without having stated what the program of the Pres. was, or what Ike was supposed to cover in the presentation (that is, Dean didn't state it, and this led to considerable deterioration; why he didn't, I don't know, but it worked out badly, I thought, and so did Joe Volpe).

Eisenhower didn't supply the broad foundation of our existing relations with U.K. and our mutual need; he seemed a bit set back by Vandenberg's needling at Blair House: that the British need us, that we are always shelling out to them, etc. But he endorsed the program, which unfortunately Dean had not yet explained. So when Ike was questioned, which he was extensively, the large strategic advantages somehow he made fuzzy, and kept saying: just speaking as a soldier and for the Joint Chiefs, we want the raw material, here, all of it if we can get it, and how this is done we don't care. Had he considered the serious public relations effect of "giving away the secret"? No; he could see what Hickenlooper meant, implied it had a lot to it, backed away from it; though later he said he understood from Dr. Rabi that the U.K. knew everything anyway, that our information wasn't necessary for them, might save them a month only. "I'm just a soldier; don't know about all these political currents." He said it was clear that all atomic weapons except for a very few ought to be stored this side of Atlantic.

He deprecated and deplored idea that atomic weapons could win a war in a sudden attack on us, or against an enemy holding the huge Eurasian land mass. (Wonder who he meant? These euphemisms of soldiers are as bad as those of diplomats.) If we are subject to sudden attack, he said, we mustn't let our people feel there is nothing we can do. (This for the theory that an atomic war would be over in a brief time, something I recall he helped promote with his articles in *Look*, I believe it was—72-hr. war.) We must protect ourselves against that kind of feeling among our people—panic, he called it, and complacency.

People "need just enough information to protect ourselves against that kind of panic" is what some of my shorthand scribbles say. "This is not just another weapon. You can say it is just another and different weapon—a soldier can say this—but it would not be true because of the fearful effect of it upon the mind, and in war that is what you are dealing with, the minds of men."

Could this agreement as proposed be made without Congressional approval? Does the President have legal authority to go ahead and negotiate? Of course, said Dean, the Constitution authorizes and makes that his responsibility, to negotiate; but we intend to consult with this committee as things go along; can't say now whether have legal authority, finally, without first having the results of talks with the U.K.

Dean stated the legal position, that the McMahon Act authorizes "technical cooperation," including weapon information, where common defense and security are thereby strengthened, as here.

Knowland blew his top—the redness in his face changed to pale white; he intended to take the floor and try to get Congressional action to prevent an agreement without Cong. approval—yelling and pretty out of control. Millikin more quietly said he was considering the same; that the President couldn't even initiate talks with the British on information! Dean said he could do that, but it would be against the public interest. Connally said he was "regusted" with such talk—politics, partisan politics, he grunted, and left the room. Dean said there was no intention to conclude an agreement without continuous consultation, but this didn't seem to placate Knowland at all.

Hickenlooper asked me if the Commission's position was unanimous. I said: after the President had taken a position, it followed that the Comm. was bound by and adopted that view, since we were responsible to him. (Would that this were true in fact.) But as of Feb. 9, when the Commission considered what it would recommend to the President, there was "partial disagreement." Four of us (Bacher and Waymack then on Comm.) had believed that how negotiations carried on was not for us but for Secy. of State; Strauss had disagreed, felt whole arrangement depended upon insisting on certain conditions precedent, such as that all weapons and weapons material production be solely in the U.S., etc. Four of us thought information exchange should continue; Strauss thought it should be suspended, except as to health, physics, and the like. On objectives we seemed to be in full agreement.

I could see Strauss very unhappy, back of me (by mirror). He stood up; later was recognized, said he wanted to amplify: Reason he was opposed to continued information exchange was because we had learned through our scientists that the U.K. was engaging in a weapons program, whereas we thought it was to be non-weapon; thought this was illegal. (No question of legality had he raised during all the Commission discussions, but in last two weeks it is "illegal.")

His statement fell with the explosive roar of a pillow being dropped on a featherbed. Then he went on: "It is correct, as the Chairman has said, that I was in a minority of one at that time; but I am glad to say that my two new colleagues, Mr. Dean and Dr. Smyth, have had a chance to review the matter and I have hopes that I will not continue in the minority."

On the legal question, Acheson said: If exchange of information "for industrial purposes" is illegal, then the Jan. 7 Modus Vivendi is illegal. "That was an agreement which this committee approved." (Not a peep from the committee on this. Millikin said later, lamely, that the exchange of *weapon* information was illegal, implying that he distinguished this from the earlier industrial information under the Modus and implying, of course, that that had been legal.)

Vandenberg made him quite a speech at the end. Acheson had said: In this world one has to face not black and white, but alternatives. This is one of those cases. Don't back away from it because it has things about it you don't like.

So V. started to boom: "I don't back away from it; but it must be an utter last resort." "I think the distinguished Sec. of State will lose whatever influence at every internatl. conference that exists, if he has a partner there in this secret." "It is a psychological fact that a major source of our influence in these councils is due to the fact that we are in temporary possession of this awful thing." It may be that the U.K. does have almost all the knowledge; but the people of the country don't know that, they think we are the sole possessors of the secret. They will react violently if they hear that we gave that to the British.

McMahon took him on: should we be driven by public opinion, as responsible leaders, when we know that opinion is ignorant of the facts, or should we inform the public? V. didn't like this; but it was a fair though rough way of putting it; later McM. apologized for what he said; but he should have been sorry only for how he said it. V. kept saying: it may well be an illusion, but it is believed and we would risk our necks to violate that illusion.

It had been my hunch that the case turns on getting the facts about the extent of British knowledge to the committee, and to the country; so they had before them three or four memos from Robert Oppenheimer, Norris Bradbury, Hans Bethe, etc., making mincemeat of the notion that the British didn't know much (an idea fostered assiduously by Groves). But they are naturally loath to give up so comforting a thought, and with it the prospect of a nice, juicy, resounding political issue against Truman: he gave away the Secret. So Millikin and Knowland and Hickenlooper kept sounding off in the same vein— let us keep the secret from the British. H. even suggested (as Strauss has from the start) that we abrogate our raw materials arrangements and deal separately with Belgium: a kind of blackjacking of a partner that would sadly impair our moral position, not only with the British but all over.

Johnson did a neat rug-pulling job on Dean (who may have asked for it by his failure to keep the ball a bit more firmly, as the President's spokesman on this) by saying: Don't shoot off on the Senate floor, and we promise in the military to study the things you've said and maybe we will come back with something different. He is supposed to be the great political peacemaker; but if we don't come back with something different, then the committee *will* be mad; and if we do, it will show they can keep on whittling on the President's position; and they will.

As I left, in the tiny elevator with Johnson and Eisenhower, the latter seemed quite upset: "I never realized," Ike muttered, "what a lot of cross-currents there are; I just don't know what all that sort of thing is about." He may have something there.

JULY 23, 1949
AT HOME

Have had a good deal to do—might be fair to say it much stronger than that—with what could become the most important single change in the relation of the President to the military establishment in peacetime, except that this isn't peacetime.

The evidence of such a change will be a letter from the Pres. It will direct that a requisition of the military relating to the Commission's function [of providing atomic weapons expressed in quantities and rates of production] be the subject of consideration and report by the Natl. Security Council. Basic factors of our whole policy for the protection of the country are involved.

What makes it most important—I don't want to refer to details here, which I can easily remember—is that instead of having a conclusion of the military staffs handed to the Pres. (always urgent, of course—just in time for him to sign his name and no questions asked) as essentially an accomplished fact, it would now be regarded as a proper subject for staff work before he decides; and that staff work is not just from the interested military, but includes the Secy. of State (foreign policy staffing) and the AEC and the Bureau of the Budget.

The insistence that the Pres. must no longer be handed a kind of ultimatum, requiring him to differ with a unanimous conclusion of the Joint Chiefs, a terrible spot to be in, goes back quite a way with me.

I found the Pres. with no staff support of his own whatever on such an issue and a Defense Secy. who had lost his backbone—Forrestal—just handing things to the Pres. to o.k. Jim Webb fought valiantly to get some sense, some review and appraisal, into this. It is an old story, so old that in my first visit with Louis Johnson he said, "The President—*no* President—can disagree with a unanimous conclusion of the Joint Chiefs."

When another recommendation from the military for expansion of weapon facilities came along, a whopper, we were expected to develop a physical program to make it effective, and throw it at the Pres.; if we had not been a civilian agency—mark this well—there would have been no one who would have raised the questions I insisted be raised and answered, not by saying, "The Joint Chiefs say so," but asking: why and wherefore, and what about basic policy, what kind of war is this to be, what are we to do afterward, is this to be piled on top of all the other defense expenditures, etc.???

If we were part of the military, or subordinate to them, or if I didn't find that they are just like any other group of experts and specialists, even more so, there would have been no opportunity to develop a governmental mechanism to give the Pres. a chance to decide such a question on the basis of a rounded staff picture and with real freedom to use his high discretion. (The "custody" issue of last summer at this time was another illustration of how a *real* measure of civilian participation saves the Pres. from simply o.k.ing military conclusions.)

How many atomic bombs, set off within a short space of time, will so contaminate the atmosphere as to kill off a substantial part of the world's population? Stafford Warren and others have emoted about this, placing it very low; E. O. Lawrence and his people think this is rot, and place the figure very high. Now we get a report, from one individual only but pursuant to a request I made, that puts it very low. We must try to get a reasonable answer.

What a business!

(LATER: my mother's birthday—and I'll phone her tonight)

Yesterday Nancy bought her wedding dress! *Not* a frilly pink bonnet, her first baby bonnet, which I shall always remember; not her first barrette to hold back her hair after the first "bob" haircut, nor the first pair of square-toed brown shoes with stiff soles. Nope, a wedding dress, and material for a veil, and lace gloves, and such.

This particular "father of the bride," being notorious for weeping on all sentimental occasions (including high school commencements and movies), at the moment doesn't feel weepy at all, and I hope this continues through the ceremony. Nancy has her problems, but somehow she'll meet them. But they are *her* problems, not mine: that I think sums up my feeling about the children, as things now stand.

The wedding is in two weeks—August 7. "Weather permitting" (i.e., rain, for it will be hot and sticky as everyone knows, barring a Washington miracle), it will be in our "back yard," as we'd say in Indiana ("garden" to Washington), under a crab-apple tree, beside our little water-lily pool, with the guests on the lower-level lawn.

Nancy had quite a "crisis" about who would marry her: result, a Jewish rabbi, David Seligman by name, of the Central Synagogue in N.Y. Sylvain felt deeply that they should be married in the Jewish faith, because this would mean everything to his parents, who have had to suffer much, and lost all their worldly goods, because of their Jewishness; he wrote us a beautiful if quite mystical letter about it. But it seems, in the Jewish religious law, one's faith is determined by the faith of the mother. Nancy couldn't be married by a rabbi (even a most liberal "reform" kind, which Seligman is, apparently) unless she concluded to join or identify herself "with the Jewish community." So she spent two weeks finding out what this was all about, studying with the rabbi, etc., and concluded that this is what she wanted to do; how many parts love and how many parts conviction this is, no one knows. It didn't seem to faze Helen a bit, even less than that. I feel that preoccupation with religious forms is a major distraction from religious feeling. My father was actually a rebel on the whole "setup," as he called it. The children got some religious education, but it wasn't Jewish except, of course, as the once-over-lightly sort of Protestant Sunday school, etc., going is founded on Jewish bases.

They still don't know where they will be this fall.

David's first week as a reporter sounded wonderful in his letters. He is ambitious to become a Good (not merely a Competent) Reporter. His enthusiasm and good spirits are refreshing. He'll make it.

We're enjoying the house enormously. The place is full of birds, and a refuge in the quite monumental heat and humidity of Wash. in summer.

Mark Childs did a column yesterday headed "Lilienthal's Successor," stating I had plans to get out, and would when the infighting on me made it possible, perhaps by the first of the year. I'm saying nothing further on the subject, and doubt if I can really retire before the end of my term in June next—i.e., 1950. But unless there is somehow an early recognition that I'm not staying in public service, or in this job, indefinitely, I am put in a hole where it may be much more difficult to get out, if come next spring I still feel (as I certainly do—poignantly) that I want a crack at private life for ten years. So I think, at the moment, the Childs piece not bad timing, provided there isn't much more said from here on out. I can't pull out suddenly; a good successor must be named, and a decent transition effected. But I want to serve notice far enough in advance, and in a public way, so that I can minimize the effect of the inevitable tales that I am being forced out, or won't be reappointed, etc.


JULY 25, 1949
AT HOME (7 P.M.)


Have just come from an hour with the Secy. of State: subject—where do we go from here? Wed. P.M. we meet with the Joint Committee again. The Pres. wants to make clear he doesn't want to go ahead with broader cooperation with the U.K. until there has been adequate discussion and a fair degree of assent in Congress: this amounts to saying that legislation will ultimately be needed, if we get anywhere with the U.K., which, as the Secy. says, in a matter of such large international importance is the way we do things in this country.

A specific proposal for Wed.: want to go ahead having the Secy. explore the matter with the British, by first proposing a 6- or 12-month extension of the Modus; in the meantime there'll be time for the hotheads to cool off, and for the country to get the feel of this thing.

If Dean can persuade the Joint Committee on this (which may not be easy, as having tasted blood they may want to move in and have the kill), this seems wise, but only provided some things are understood about the interim period while these things are being explored and the extension worked out: that a public statement be made by the Pres. or Secy. State after the meeting that will say (a) the earlier agreement will, we hope, be extended (or words that convey that the interim period takes care of an operating crisis) while we work out something to bring back to Congress; (b) a statement is made making clear this is in a broad context of British-American relations, which to me has always been central, and not just a haggling match about swapping uranium for "secrets" and that sort of stuff, with bludgeons exhibited on both sides; (c) that if we continue a limited item-by-item kind of technical cooperation, we realize it can be the source of irritation and charges of bad faith, hence we try to ascertain what the U.K. wants before we agree to the extension. After 30 minutes I was glad to note that Dean agreed.

JULY 28, 1949
AT HOME

The first galleys of *This I Do Believe* arrived at seven this morning; they look beautiful, in large and beautifully designed type. The pile of scattered MS is actually going to be a book.

Wrestling with another ugly and tough one. Mr. Z is the holder of an AEC fellowship, granted him by the National Research Council. He chose to study at the U. of X, and requested that Dr. B. serve as his supervisor. Mr. Z is close to the end of his work for a doctorate in theoretical physics, in non-secret work. He is without anything in his record at all; he worked at Oak Ridge, on classified work, and therefore knows a certain amount of "secret" matter on the K-25 plant. He was cleared by the Manhattan project, and so was Dr. B., who likewise was privy to secret information.

Two months ago we learned that the mysterious Scientist X about which the Un-American Activities Committee had been issuing statements is Dr. B.; and requested the National Research Foundation to have Z's supervisor changed to someone else. They did nothing effective about it, U. of X saying they knew no reason for such a course.

Now we learn that the Justice Dept is considering asking that Dr. B. be indicted for perjury, in swearing he was not a Communist Party member when in fact he had been; also that there was some testimony to the effect that he had passed classified information on to a Soviet agent.

If we order the U. of X to provide the student with a different supervisor, we are directing a university in its internal affairs; if we approach the student, and ask him if B. has tried to pump him, this somehow is shocking. We spent hours on this. U. of X now says they will try to make a shift voluntarily, and Mr. Z will be interviewed by the FBI and our people and asked about Dr. B.'s conduct, as part of the inquiry into Dr. B. But here we see how widespread are the ill consequences of secrecy.


(10:30 P.M.)

Submitted to Clark Clifford the suggested text of statement we would issue today announcing the [next weapons test]; then on Sat. Pres. would comment on this as progress, and also comment on our sixth report to Congress. Best way to answer the dragging investigation is by affirmative statements of results.

Clark called me shortly before the President's press conference of today: Pres. read our statement re T; said it should not be made; seem too warlike at this time, as if we had belligerent intentions. But he is commenting on the report, and did issue a statement on the U.K.-Canada matter which we helped work up yesterday after the hearings, in a late afternoon session with Dean Acheson and his boys; helpful in that it again emphasized how much Britain had helped and knew, and hence how punk a political hooraw it is shouting about "giving away the secret."

The meeting with the Joint Committee yesterday was not well attended, judged by the earlier one: no Connally or Russell or Vandenberg. Dean read them a statement the Pres. had authorized, and that we had spent an hour on Monday late P.M. Comprised an assurance by the Pres. that though conversations with the British would go forward, looking toward a broader arrangement, plus an extension of the Modus Vivendi of January, 1948, no commitment would be made without consultation with the committee, at which time it would be determined whether legislation was necessary.

It was a very, very conciliatory position; and judging from a telephone conversation Dean had with the Pres. while I sat with him yesterday P.M., Dean had to persuade the Pres. to take it easy and calm them down; Dean doubtless had in mind that he has about all he can handle up there now, with the Aid to Arming Europe and the ECA programs both in difficulties.

What I feared was that someone—presumably Hickenlooper— would challenge the whole program, and insist on terminating any technical cooperation at all during the discussion period. Hickenlooper did just this, but in such a namby-pamby way (since he got no real support anywhere) that it petered out into one of his vaguest and most hopelessly weak performances.

Millikin used an argument, which he "suggested" (meaning he could pull away from it if it didn't go), that was about as oily and super-subtle and devious as anything I'd heard for some time: that even to discuss continuing the status quo was in itself a recognition that Britain had a claim and standing of partnership with us, and instead of maintaining the status quo, the extension conversations weakened our own position. I have rarely seen Acheson with more repugnance, intellectual, on his face.

Knowland was far more reasonable and civil; but he wanted the Pres. to state that he had no powers to proceed without Cong. approval, as bald a proposition concerning the Presidential power as I've heard. Dean handled this admirably.

When we saw Dean at 5:15, he seemed quite harried and drawn; but he showed me a group of magnificent gladioli in his office—very proud; raised and sweat over every one. An extraordinarily fine man, and just what the country needs right now.

AUGUST 4, 1949
AT HOME

When we moved to the new house (I was in bed with grippe at the time), we left Penny at the vet's in Bethesda. She had become more and more a very old dog; but she would have her moments, when that grace and charm she had would win your heart completely. She had had nephritis for more than a year, taken penicillin, etc. and as a result her odor, nine days out of ten, was really sickening, so we had to keep her outside all the time, which broke her heart.

Helen and I talked it over; shouldn't we have her life ended, mercifully, and not have it drag on? It was a burden on Helen, and I found myself preferring to have her have this added trouble, and messy trouble at times, to the pain I'd get having Penny destroyed. Helen talked to the vet, a very kindly and understanding man. He had handled Penny for two years, she would never know what happened; he couldn't do anything to make her better, she was almost 16 years old.

So one day after we moved here—just when Helen didn't tell me— she phoned the vet and Penny went out, and was buried in an orchard back of his house in Bethesda.

We all miss her; read a poem last night about a loyal dog, and felt quite blue for a while. We never have a fine bone, at table, or hear a dog yelping in a high excited tone through the woods next door that we don't think about her.

Mac given away. Penny dead. Doesn't seem too important: just a horse, just an old cocker spaniel. But those things are important, somehow.

AUGUST 5, 1949
AT HOME

Senate passed our approp. bill, with almost no debate, and no broadside attacks such as might have occurred if the Hoopinvestigation had yielded some harvest. But it contained a rider requiring full FBI investigation and Comm. clearance for scholarship-holders in non-secret fields—an extreme that confirmed everything I said during those first days in May when I tried to stem a tide that went over me like the sea over a kid's sand-castle. The way I feel now, I think we ought to drop the fellowship program entirely rather than inject this business onto scores of college campuses. They also adopted a rider limiting our flexibility on new construction projects; not as bad as the one originally proposed, but in principle quite wrong.

Yesterday noon I finished correcting the last galleys of the book and sent them back. I haven't the foggiest notion how well this book will hit people; I guessed wrong and so did Harper's on *Democracy on the March;* I hope it will have a good audience, for it is timely. But it may seem like a collection or compilation of twice-told things, which will pretty well kill its chances.

The expansion-of-production discussion is apparently going to get me into a look at military ways of laying plans, on a large scale. I find already how impatient they are at the idea that their conclusions (as professionals and experts, and those responsible for the country's safety) should be examined and critically questioned by those who are not ultimately responsible, or equally expert. The idea is always repugnant to an expert. And in the case of the military they can point to the failure to fortify Guam, the unwillingness to rearm in 1938 and 1939, etc.

Sat. night last we went to dinner at Mike Monroney's; present: Speaker Rayburn (a delightful man, the more I see of him); Senator Kerr of Okla., a huge fellow with an "act" of the country boy from the wide-open spaces, a fine though deliberate story-teller; and Mrs. Fred Vinson, Roberta to everybody.

She is a remarkable gal. As small-town and middle-class as humanly possible—but this is true of half of Wash. officialdom or more—but she makes no pretense or effort to palm herself off as anything else, and this is really quite engaging, though at times startling. For example, she told in detail how she heard about Vinson's appointment as Chief Justice, and how mad she was, and how she cried. Since he had come to Congress they had been bedeviled by lack of money, the boys to educate, a dream of a cattle farm to go back to, etc. Now the time had come; and then he up and took an appointment at a salary for Wash. quite limited (as I know, for my own income is in about that range, and he can't supplement it at all) and for life—no way to resign, actually. The hope of having some money and going back to Kentucky gone.

Well, to cry because your husband has one of the great posts of the world for life seems like an act, but not with her; oh, perhaps a tiny bit. "I can't be a Mrs. Stone or Mrs. Hughes," she says, which is true. After dinner we talked about their trials and tribulations through a long public service; he came to Wash. in 1933, with his backlog about gone.

Wed. night went to a big shindig a flamboyant old character from Mobile, Cong. Frank Boykin, gave in honor of Sam Rayburn; it was one for Sam and ten for Frank. But I got a strong impression of the fraternal feeling among professional politicians, and how much alike they are, in temperament, manners. A likable lot, relaxed that way.

Sat between Scoop Jackson, who is a prize in any contest, that boy, and Admiral Jerry Land, who (at 70, I suppose) looks still like a mischievous boy.

AUGUST 8, 1949
AT HOME

The wedding is over. Another "deadline" met, behind us. A happy, gay event, with Nancy beautiful, composed; the weather (a major figure for a garden wedding) just perfect summer. The only excitement—and temporary exasperation: the groom was late, 45 minutes or so, while the bride had been put into her rig, calmed and ready for her entrance, the "congregation" out on the lawn, standing and waiting.

The reception was friendly and informal, no swank nor rum and riot. A minimum of newspaper photographers, by our request and their cooperation. Ted took a color film on our movie camera, the same camera I bought at Palos when David was a few months old, and on which a long succession of baby and childhood "sequences" were so successfully recorded.

Sylvain was so nervous he couldn't hold the cup of wine—his hands shook, not trembled, and without the Rabbi's help he'd never got the ring on our composed daughter's hand. A lovely ring, two thin platinum bands interwoven, and set with diamonds all around, quite lovely. They took off with no rice, no tin cans on their car, but quite decorously and sweetly—"My friends," said the groom, gravely, "won't make our exit that kind." He seems very fine and thoughtful, and they have a good chance; a better than good chance, I'd think.

David, back after 2½ weeks of reportership, looks wonderful, likes learning, is proud that he is under a "tough" city ed., is self-possessed, handsome, and so considerate and interested in everybody—a vast improvement over his father, meaning he looks like me and has some of my intensity but a large admixture of his mother's fine balance and outgiving sweetness.

Helen was the star all over again. The Rabbi made it much too difficult for her; more than necessary, a kind of pep talk to Nancy, a recent "convert," and he was keyed up by having in his close audience a Jew "of whom we are proud," etc. (but can't count on). But Helen took it with no shadow; we kept our eyes glued on each other, across the space between, where our daughter was being prayed over and made one with a "stranger." Today she is still going strong, laughing upstairs as I write, exchanging talk with brother Ted and the Elder Statesmen—

her sobriquet for her Uncle Gayl and Dad, both of whom enjoyed themselves—though, of course, Dad enjoys himself anywhere any time these years.

## AUGUST 9, 1949

Miss Kirschman of my office put in a call to Admiral Sidney Souers, Executive Director of the National Security Council at the White House; I wanted to speak to him. She was told: "Admiral Souers is busy now. He's in a war council meeting." This, I think, tops the stories of secretarial helpfulness; I wonder what a newspaper reporter would think if he was given that kind of response!

## AUGUST 10, 1949

The Hickenlooper "investigation" is certainly a burning issue of great and intense interest: just had word that for the *fourth* time in ten days scheduled meetings of the Joint Committee have been canceled! I suggested last week to McMahon that perhaps the best and most eloquent "report" that could be written would be no report at all. The country has already written its own report: dud.

The evils of the Federal Government getting its nose into education are illustrated in still another way (and the soundness of my testimony last early May, in the first days of the fellowship row) by a letter I have just received from Rep. Kilday, endorsing someone who has applied for a fellowship. A whole new area in education—influence on a political basis.

## AUGUST 13, 1949
### AT HOME

Everything looks set for a departure next Thursday morning for the Vineyard, and six weeks of rest and vacation. I'm pretty tired, though far better than I'd have hoped for.

Had half-hour visit with Sen. Vandenberg yesterday noon; his office. He was genial and friendly, and extraordinarily candid.

After greetings, he said he'd just been talking to the Secy. of State, telling him to get in out of the rain on the Military Aid to Europe bill. I commented that sense enough to come in out of the rain was mighty handy in a Secy. of State; that I thought the experience we had on the

U.K. atom matter showed he did; as a matter of fact, the way it was handled showed the consultation process at its best, almost a classic example of the give and take inherent in the democratic process.

Yes, he agreed. Some of his critics, he said (he doesn't like criticism worth a damn, despite the fact he gets almost nothing but praise, a trait he does not have all to himself—I note that the more praise I get, the less I can easily toss off criticism of a sort—it isn't logical, but it happens) . . . some of his critics say that a bipartisan foreign policy is a me-too policy. "I say," he said, "that may be the way it looks from the outside; but it overlooks the things that go on before agreement is reached and announced"—meaning, of course, that he is able to get a different policy by the opposition, etc., that precedes a public bipartisan policy agreement.

That is why, I suppose, Dean Acheson predicted, before the first Blair House meeting, "I know what Van will say; he will open by saying this is outrageous, and he can't be counted on to support it. That's the way he always begins any discussion of a new policy."

Vandenberg made no reference to the U.K.-Canada matter.

Well, he said, the investigation is over, for all practical purposes. (I had said I had called to say good-bye before going on a rest-holiday, which he seemed to approve.) "But now *we* have something to do that is harder than anything the Comm. faced during the investigation," he said, "how to write a report."‡

"Millikin and Knowland and I," he said, looking out of the window, and then contemplatively pulling at his cigar, "have a very tough position. We know that there was nothing disclosed—I patiently sat through almost every session—that even distantly or remotely resembles 'incredible mismanagement.' If we say that, it will just kill Hickenlooper. He's a nice fellow, very nice fellow. He thinks he and he alone stands between the security of the nation and disaster. But we can't say that, of course. But some of the avid Democrats will want a report that will take advantage of the failure of the charges to be sustained; they'll want to say Hick. is a louse and you are wonderful. They'll use that to plow Hickenlooper under.

"So for just sheer political reasons we'll have to write a report—of course, there'll be two of them, as I've already told McMahon—that will say that Hickenlooper has rendered a great public service by his actions, that it has uncovered some things in the way of laxity that have since been corrected due to his charges, etc. Then, in a very small P.S. down at the bottom"—he grinned over the top of his glasses as he demon-

‡ The Joint Committee on October 12 decided that the Hickenlooper charges were without foundation, voting 9 to 6 along party lines.

strated—"we'll have to say there has been no 'incredible mismanagement.'"

I made no comment at all, and kept a poker face through this.

He brought up the question of personnel clearances. I said there'd been a meeting Thurs., sorry he couldn't be there, as it was interesting. Hick.'s position, he said, seems to be that if there is anything in the FBI file at all that casts any suspicion whatever, the person should be fired or not employed.

I commented that this was indeed his theory, but when he was pressed with questions, the unfairness of this was too much for him, and he'd say: find out *who* it was who made the derogatory statement, etc.; in other words, evaluate. I said Hickenlooper had even said there was no sense sending these reports to a board like the Roberts Board.

Yes, Vandenberg responded, Hickenlooper believes that if there is anything in that file, that's the end of it. V. didn't say so explicitly, but I gather he wouldn't go for that, but he made it clear that he doesn't think I'm tough enough, saying, "There is the difference between us: I would be more suspicious than you would be, generally speaking."

In 3 years, X months, and 14 days, he said, "I'm going to have the pleasure of being philosophical about this Government"—referring to his plans to retire at the end of his term. "I'm going to say that we have managed to make this Government work so far because it has been flexible; but it may be near the end because we've set up too many bottlenecks. Too great inflexibility. Look at this appropriation situation right now." (He referred, I took it, to the way the European Cooperation Administration thing had been handled—six months of hearings, riders, item-by-item appropriation involving policy not money, really, with chaos and indecision and general breakdown. I recalled what I had said in my book on this score, and felt less concerned that I had written it, for it is critical. But right.)

"Another thing that is endangering the future are the commentators and columnists: fantastic effect—not long-range, perhaps, but at the moment. That Fulton Lewis goes on the air and I am flooded—flooded —" (He looked at his desk angrily as if the flood of mail was there right then.) "Walter Lippmann sits back and writes a column and I'm flooded with mail."

I said, standing to leave: once during the early days of the investigation I began to feel a bit sorry for myself; then I remembered how pale and polite what I was getting was compared with, say, Jefferson when Governor of Va. He looked rather sad: "God, how did we ever get through the Civil War; how did we ever do it? What it must have been like to be in the Senate at that time—nothing but blackness, nothing to hope for."

AUGUST 17, 1949
AT HOME
(MEETING WITH THE PRESIDENT IN HIS OFFICE, MONDAY, AUGUST 15,
11:35–11:50 A.M.)

After greetings—the President seemed quite relaxed and happy,
though worn—told him I had been in to see him the morning the roof
fell in—the Monday when Hickenlooper's blast appeared—and he had
sent me out of his office rarin' to go.

"Well, you've survived, I see," he said, grinning from ear to ear.
"I told you what you were up against: a couple fellows" (he held up two
fingers) "up for re-election" (meaning McMahon and H.) "and that it
wouldn't turn up a thing—and it didn't. You came out of it better than
ever."

Then he started to talk about Cong. investigations and charges,
comparing his own conduct of the Truman Committee with Senator
"Hooey" (he said that's the way it ought to be pronounced) and his
piddling around with trifles . . . the Vaughan attacks, trying to hit the
President through Vaughan and others around him, instead of looking
into things that would help the country.§

I told him the three months' Hickenlooper investig. had cost the
Commission heavily in lost momentum, distraction of key personnel,
but that we just had to go to work and build it back.

He said something about the way the mossbacks always predict
the end of the world and charge him with putting over a "welfare
state"—whatever that is—this was Byrnes and Herb. Hoover. Which
started him on Hoover. "He's a nice enough old man," he said. "Of
course," and here he had a big laugh, "he's to the right of Louis the Four-
teenth. But he deserves to be treated with respect as an ex-President.
Roosevelt couldn't stand him and he hated Roosevelt. But he straightened
out the food problem in S. America back there in 1945, and he can
do some things. No reason to treat him other than with respect. But he
doesn't understand what's happened in the world since McKinley."

Told him I was going on a vacation; he said that's a sensible idea,
and after what I've gone through, sure had it coming. . . . "Have a
good time."

Only matter of business mentioned was the anti-trust suit against
AT&T: imitated Tom Clark saying out side of his mouth, "Hayll . . .
we ainta gonta stop usin' telephones because we trying to separate AT&T

§ Maj. Gen. Harry H. Vaughan, the President's military aide, was a figure in
the "five-percenter" investigation of influence-peddling in Government contracts.
Senator Clyde Hoey was chairman of the investigating subcommittee.

and Western Electrik." He laughed; said the suit was a good idea, was all for it. "If we don't keep after these fellows, we'll get some cartelizing here, too, bad thing."

Pleasant visit. I made no reference to Commission internal troubles.

AUGUST 18, 1949
AT HOME

Hour with Jim Webb Aug. 16, P.M. He is to handle the negotiations with U.K. & Canada, at least initially. Fine, solid, intense man; devoted to him.

Said he and Admiral Souers had lunch with Secy. Johnson few days ago; this matter came up. Johnson amazed and confused them, saying: (1) Secy. of State's legal position all wet—no legal authority for the Modus Vivendi, repeating the now Strauss position phrase for phrase; (2) Lilienthal now in the minority at the Comm., 3 to 2, with Strauss in charge; (3) Commission no damned good, inefficient, wasteful, eager to "give away the secret," etc. Whole proposition re U.K. no good. Making allowances for his reputation for wild statements, and his technique of raising hell and attacking everyone (Dean A. gets it all the time: "Reds in the State Department," etc.), they wondered: What the hell. Are you for the President's program as announced or against it? (This he told me in confidence, i.e., Webb, so I can't tell my colleagues explicitly.)

Also said he was on the yacht, *Williamsburg,* with Truman last Sunday. Pres. took him aside, said, "Acheson is a gentleman. He won't descend to a row. Johnson is a rough customer, gets his way by rowing. When he takes out after you, you give it right back to him." Mystified Webb; doesn't me.

Told Jim the setting of whole matter wrong: the idea we and U.K. are just trading a hunk of uranium for a hunk of "secrets"—all wet. This is a broad-gauge effort to fill, temporarily, the gap left by the failure of acceptance of the American proposal for internatl. control—etc., etc. Gave same picture to Souers yesterday, and to Clifford.

Talked to Clifford and Admiral Souers yesterday, met Lt. Gen. Quesada, great airman and head of Task Force for our next [test]— handsome guy, lots personality, as they say. Cleaned up my desk; heard that *This I Do Believe* will be a book in fact by Sept. 15 or sooner—gosh, and more dead than alive but happy, set off for home, where soon our new son-in-law and our "married daughter" appeared. I accept new facts with amazing ease: seems so natural that they are man and wife. Seem very happy. I like Sylvain more each time I see him and they seem to enjoy each other—their jokes, experiences. Our roof is no darned good so I have the troubles of a householder; and it will set me back a thousand bucks.

But the important news is: in a couple hours we set off for the Vineyard and no work for weeks and weeks—I hope (except Monday, when we have an all-day conference there with Pike, Wilson, Volpe).

SEPTEMBER 19, 1949
AT THE ALLEN HOUSE ON MARTHA'S VINEYARD

We have been here a month, today.

The days have gone by, and then the weeks. There have been days so beautiful in the brilliance of the light, the deep blue of the Sound, the quiet softness of the meadow and trees outside (as today, with the half-rain, or a few days ago when a deep fog took over) that the rest of the world seems far, far away. It is on such days more difficult to believe in that hurly-burly of Washington than it is to believe in the midst of the pull and haul of my normal living that the Vineyard is actually out there, so lovely and serene.

This morning I padded out to the kitchen to put on the coffee water, and for fifteen minutes or so was so absorbed in the ancient apple tree outside that everything else stopped, ceased to exist. Out of a deep hole in the old tree, and from the crevasse of a great crack in one of the old boy's major limbs (the sleet storm of last winter did that to him), blue birds poured in and out. I've never seen them at such close range, in repose. Then a huge flicker; beside him, almost comic, a busy independent downy woodpecker, whacking away with none of the cautionary looks to right and left of the big flicker. Then the soft gray of kingbirds. Then two crested sleek gray birds, ones I'd never seen before, possibly Bohemian waxwings. The sound of birds out there now, and the distant soft sound of the water of the Sound, rolling over the stones of the shore—that's what I have to live with.

It's been an almost perfect holiday, for us at this time. We were both very weary, very. I've never seen Helen look as she did. I was a touch apprehensive of what a sudden let-up might do; sometimes it doesn't work so well. Actually, we tapered off, you might say. The Monday after we got here on Saturday, Sumner Pike, Carroll Wilson and Joe Volpe came for the day, to go over the problems Sumner would inherit as Acting Chairman, he having been on his vacation for the preceding month. Then on Tuesday our friends from Knoxville, the Tours, Harry and Jean, arrived to be with us for a week. We did quite a bit of sight-seeing, visiting, etc., and though it wasn't resting (and at the time I wanted to rest and nothing else), it was fun, pleasant, absorbing when we talked about plans for the house we wanted to build on our new "Topside" nine acres. When they left, we really were ready for the sleep kind of holiday. For three weeks we have been going to bed about 9 (at times even earlier) and up 11 or 12 hours later, oftener than not, with a nap for me in the afternoon.

In the past week in particular I've been thinking a good deal about the future; during the month I've written quite a few letters, including some fairly serious ones: e.g., to Clark Clifford about the President's Phila. speech on foreign relations, and in general on his state papers; one to the President on the matter of appointing a Negro as a Federal Judge in the East. Penna. district; one to Anne O'Hare McCormick on her wonderful column "The First Decade Is Not the Hardest"; I've also typed out notes for possible use in the speech I'm to make on receiving the Freedom House Award Oct. 13; I've thought about *This I Do Believe*, from the promotion aspect; we've seen a few people, chiefly the Houghs, Pat, Henry, Betty; the Nortons, Charley and Bea, our neighbors; Tom and Rita Benton one evening, Robert and Leah Louise Duffus, the Roger Baldwins.

Helen and I have talked a good deal about the future: an issue that the calendar and the end of my term of office next June 30 (1950) make inescapable. The talks about the future—"What do we do next?"—are sharpened by the desire and need for more income. We want to build a summer house, but to do so along the line of the plans Helen has drawn (a very simple place) or remodeling Joan Mitchell's old house (the Edward Luce place) involves not less than $10,000, probably more, to start, which is more than my present liquid assets (savings bonds). We've had to increase our help to Dad and Mother. Nancy and Sylvain will need more help right along, perhaps for several years. David may well want to return to graduate work, or want help to buy a paper, etc. We've been spared costly illness, but that could come. If I set up my own law office, or join with others in it, or some other kind of independent business venture, I need cash to live on while the new venture gets going. And so on.

I vowed I'd not make a decision, or say I had, about being available for another nomination, after June 30, until I'd had a rest, and the sour memory of the Hickenlooper episode, and the appropriations nightmare, were well past. They are past now, and hardly in mind at all. I'm not a "new man" and never will be; but I'm no longer acutely weary, and certainly this is a place to develop some perspective.

Right now, it seems clear: get out of Government service not later than the end of this term.

A good many reasons stand back of this conclusion. They range around the 360 degrees. Some relate to my feeling that I have to get out sometime, and this is the best timing, when there is still time, presumably, to develop an alternative way of earning a living for the present and the years of semi-retirement. Some are reasons of caution, self-protection, selfish reasons: if I am reappointed, there would no doubt be a confirmation fight, probably another cooked-up "scare" or "scandal" like the U-235 Argonne bottle scare; it could be bitter and a strain, and a damned nuisance. Helen said wearily yesterday, as we had our breakfast coffee on the front stoop, "If we have another one," (referring to the Hickenlooper business) "I'll resign."

Some of the reasons are cautionary in another, and equally selfish sense: things are in quite good condition now, the responsibility has been met, the country has the weapons it needed, in the stockpile, I'm vindicated—get out when the market is high; the sort of thing Willkie always used to preach (but, in the end, failed to follow, in the real test) or that Baruch does so often. I've made the reason somewhat less honorable than it is: there is no way of seeing this job through to the end—it is a job for 50 years—and the first segment is in good shape, so it is honorable to ask for one's discharge in favor of another set of hands.

Then there are other selfish reasons: Lewis has made it almost impossible to enjoy the Commission as a family, as we did when we started out, something I worked hard to develop. I would continue to serve if it were necessary; but it doesn't seem so. Well, the other reasons are many—money, a desire for a new and less arduous (or emotionally wearing) life than cohabiting with destructive forces provides, etc.

I confess freely to a funk, a blue, blue one, about making the change to "private" life. After spending what will be in June, 1950, about 19 years (Feb., 1931, to June, 1950—yep, 19 years, whaddya-know!) on a salary so low that one never thought about it, just had the check deposited and drew till it was gone, the transition from that to setting up an office, signing a lease, hiring people, waiting for clients, etc.—on a very slim cash margin, this gives me a considerable pause. Every now and then I say to myself: Who in the hell will want to bring a legal problem to you? I'm hedging on that by planning a lecture tour, some articles, perhaps even engaging a literary agent; but this would only carry me a year or so, for two reasons: (a) my market value as a free-lancing writer and speaker would decline by that time, a year after I no longer speak with the authority of my position; and (b) I would not like the life for much longer than that, though I hope I'll always write and speak, as a "side-line."

Today we expect to get a look at *This I Do Believe*, in advance copies. Secretly I keep hoping that it will take on, sell perhaps 20,000 copies in the year (which is a best-seller, in the current book market). Actually, I know this is a fond dream, that 9,000 would be very good; that a series of "faint-praise" reviews, or "this is a collection of Mr. L's speeches, warmed over" reviews, could actually make it a dim bulb, just another book. But it is rather exciting, having this kind of gamble ahead. And it was a grand experience, doing—grand for Helen and me to have this to do together, and good to find I could push through even the vast glacier of troubles of this spring and get it done right on the nose of a schedule made up when all looked rosy, serene, and full of time.

SEPTEMBER 21, 1949
IN THE ALLEN HOUSE ON THE VINEYARD

These are notes of a remarkable twenty-four hours in the life of a vacationer.

11 P.M. Monday night, Sept. 19. Driving up to "Norton Circle," returning with Pat Hough and Helen, from dinner with the Henry Houghs and Bob Duffuses in Edgartown. A heavy ground-fog. Just at the Circle (the Wuthering Heights background of the goat field and its boulders faintly visible), the headlights pick out the figure of a man, hatless, squinting into the lights, looking bemused, hooking his thumb in the hitchhiker's gesture (though, of course, there's nothing beyond to hitch to but the gate). I said quietly, "It's Jim McCormack" (being Brigadier General James McCormack, AUS, Director of the Division of Military Applications of the U.S. Atomic Energy Commission). As if I frequently found him on a windswept moor, in the dead of night, on an island, outside a goat field. "It was he." No questions; said he had lighted a candle in our house. Had he parachuted; what was this?

11:30 P.M. Helen downstairs; General Jim and I lighted a kerosene lamp in this room, with its Charles Addams cartoon flavor, esp. at night. He said things, jestingly (in part), about the traditionally rude fate of messengers with bad news. Then he gave me the news, rather dead-pan, its unambiguous nature rather fuzzy; some reference to the shock and impact, the recriminations, the whole box of trouble it portended.◖ The coal-oil lamp between us, the shadows all around; outside, through these windows, the Great Dipper and the North Star off toward the lights of New Bedford and Falmouth. I took it with no outward evidence of anything more than a budget problem, etc. The President might say something tomorrow at 4 P.M. to the world. I got two bottles of beer out of the "real ice" box; we drank them. I told Helen I'd be leaving at seven, be back tomorrow (saying nothing else to her, of course). We turned in. I slept less than perfectly. "Are you troubled, disturbed?" she asked as we said good night. "Oh, some; one of those things. Probably be back by night"; I didn't believe it.

◖ The news was that our detection system had evidence of an atomic explosion, by the Russians.

6 A.M. Awake; better make an earlier departure, better chance to get back same day. Put on lovely faded overalls, blue sweater, down the hill to the engine to pump her up tight, keep Helen in water two days; stopped at barn for filling of water jug. Poplar tree filled with the slender, tufted birds I'd seen morning before, so beautiful; then they left, in a cloud, flew into the sunrise, swinging as a cloud from side to side, spreading out, closing in, disappearing. Told Helen and Jim about them, over bacon and eggs.

8:20 A.M. Flying in a big Army C-47, plush, over Noman's Land. Got my electric razor, shaving myself. A bit shocked by the ultimate in quick change—shaving by electric razor flying over the ocean, so soon after the rather crudities—and simple wonders—of Vineyard life. Long talk with General Jim about atomic weapons, what is ahead, about his war experience, about the life of a military careerist. And thinking hard and in some considerable anguish.

11:30 A.M. In my office, the old familiar things seeming not familiar; what am I doing here? The possibilities that this is something else disposed of flatly—Robert Oppenheimer positive, unequivocal; even Bob Bacher almost without a "qualification." The feeling in the abdomen— here it is. [What we'd feared ever] since January, 1946, [in our first Board of Consultants meeting in] the American Trucking Building. Vermont affair, we are here.* Calls to Webb: [He said:] positively nothing [should be announced] today, [would bring] things too near panic abroad, in N.Y. [at the UN General Assembly meeting]. Great admiration for Webb's way of protecting the decision of his Chief. But all of us, seen separately, then together—Gordon Dean, H. Smyth, Lewis (first visit with him alone for months), and wonderful Sumner, Joe Volpe, Carroll—all same, with J.R.O. (who is frantic, drawn). Bob B. (deeply worried), felt it should be announced and right away: let's not muff the duty to initiate the facts, rather than shore up a "leak" (inevitable with 300 people knowing it) or have the other fellow say it. Call to Admiral Souers: [told him] that's how we feel.

12:30 P.M. Admiral Souers called: "The President said he wanted to talk to you about it, 3:45 today, back entrance."

3:45 P.M. The President was reading a copy of the *Congressional Record,* as quiet and composed a scene as imaginable; bright sunlight in the garden outside, the most unbusy of airs. Started talking about it: debate on reciprocal trade agreements (won by a close margin); tells me of the humorous incident—teller made mistake, Barkley's retort. Jolly, amused. Points to stack of newspapers, *Star* of that afternoon on top; reads them, lots of them, not for news, but to get the propaganda

---

* Vermont was a code for what was later called Joe I, the first Russian atomic device.

angle. Important to do that. People want the facts, he gives that to them. But see the "crises" all over the front; esp. the effect through world of British devaluation, crazy threats of strikes.

He said: want to talk about this detection report—knew about it— knew it would probably come—German scientists in Russia did it, prob- ably something like that. Be glad to call in Joint Committee chairman, ranking minority member, tell them just what I'm telling you now; don't want you to be in trouble with them. Not going to say anything myself now; later, when this (pointing to news reports re sterling deval- uation troubles) quiets down, maybe in a week; realize may leak, lots people know—still take that chance, meet it when it comes.

I said: may I have permission to state views, despite fact you have reached conclusion? He took off glasses, first time I saw him without them, large, fine eyes. Considerate, fine air of patience and interest. I tried to set out affirmative virtue of making it [announcement] now and initiating matter rather than plugging leaks. Advantages would be three in number. First, would show Pres. knows what is going on in Vermont [Russia]; that would reassure auto mechanic in Vineyard Haven, etc. Second, Pres. knowing and saying so would show him not scared, hence others needn't be; third, would show Pres. will tell people when things come along they need to know that won't hurt being told.

[He agreed that] maintaining confidence of people in him, taking cue from his own calm, was good point, but not afraid of that. Can't be sure, anyway [that the Russians actually have a bomb]. I stepped into that: is sure, substantial—and great surprise even to most pessimistic. Really?—sharp look, question: how compare with tri?†

But [announcement] by him [might] cause great fears, troubles. They [Russians] changed; sending Big Shot [Vishinsky, to UN Assembly in N.Y.]; talking very reasonably again, things look better; this may have something do with it. Not worried; took this into account; going to work things out. Most of [my] points borne down on most of yesterday P.M.: Johnson, Early, Bradley, then Joint Chiefs. [He said he had] thought about it last night; not going to add it to situation in N.Y. [at the UN]. [I said:] you have whole picture, and responsibility; that's the answer. [He said:] as to [informing Joint Atomic Committee] chairman & ranking member; risk in that; hold it in abeyance till see how things develop.

4:15 P.M. Walks with me to door; I open it and he steps through; outside, the personal staff, Genl. Vaughan, etc. Vaughan says [referring to the "five-percenter" investigation], "Oh, they didn't get after me hard,

† "Tri" (for "triangle") was not the President's word but was my notation. My recollection is that "tri" referred to a method of confirmation of the air filter detection evidence. (In the entry, I did not record my response.)

they really went after you." President's hands in coat pockets, looking fresh, amused—considerably heavier.

4:16 P.M. With Admiral Souers, long talk. [He said that] Bradley, Johnson, Steve Early, and three Joint Chiefs made terrific case [to the President that an announcement be made at once]: integrity of the government [at stake], etc. Told him how things stood re [Joint] Committee; that all of us felt should be done [i.e., inform the committee], but [the President's] conclusion [was to defer this] and we'd be for it; what about Lewis, he asked, will he feel bound to report this to Republican members? No, I felt sure he would feel that it [the President's position] was a mistake, but wouldn't do that.

5 to 6 P.M. With Comm., Gen. Mgr., Gen. Counsel. [President's deferral of an announcement a] mistake, but he has had the [contrary] views presented [to him], directly. J.R.O. feeling badly: "Are you going to tackle Acheson? If he changes, Pres. will." "Of course not." J.R.O. badly upset: "We mustn't muff this; chance to end the miasma of secrecy— holding a secret when there is no secret." [I asked:] "Weren't you surprised?" "Yes, yes." "A good deal?" "Yes, a good deal. Always hoped, half-thought our troubles would have . . ."

6:10 P.M. "No," says Martha Jane, "we're not going to have you phoning in; if you'll go back tonight, less danger having the rest of your holiday spoiled." Same with Wilson, Pike—fine, friendly consideration. To Pike's for tall drink of good whiskey, talk, borrowing some books.

6:55 P.M. Off the ground, in a B-25; reading corresp., magazines, stuff from the office.

8:40 P.M. Back on the Vineyard.

10:30 P.M. Long visit with Helen before the fireplace, from the light of limbs from the old dead apple trees, the wind blowing like mad, the Wuthering Heights touch again as it goes through the loose house; to bed.


SEPTEMBER 21, 1949

We walked up the hill together, to the mailbox at the Circle. This time it was there—a package from Harper's. Inside, two books, THE book. We sat down on the bank in the sunshine and looked at our child —a handsome one, too, we feel.


SEPTEMBER 23, 1949
THE VINEYARD

Last night the heavens opened, after a long, long dry spell, and we had rain, and the most melodramatic thunderings and lightning. The rain continued this morning; a fine, husky rain. I went down to the pump house, to do my stuff. As I finished, I heard Mrs. Norton calling from her house. I knew, somehow, it was Pike calling from Washington. Which it was.

He told me that the President was issuing a statement on the "atomic explosion"; that is, had just done so (it was about 12:20 when we talked) at 11. He read me the statement. I was pleased and relieved; it did help to talk to the President after all; some of the points were reflected in the statement, not in the terse, cryptic one he was considering when I was in Wash. Tuesday. Thus, the reference back to his statement four years ago that of course other nations would in time have atomic weapons. I especially liked the opening statement—not carried on the radio reports today, though—that the public is entitled to know. Pike and Frances Henderson both thought no need for my return; at least until we assess things Monday.

We're still debating: should we build on the Vineyard; can we afford to sink $5,000 in it now, another 5 in the next couple years?

SEPTEMBER 26, 1949
ON THE VINEYARD

The vacation is about over. In my mind—which is where vacations are spent, pretty much—it's been over since a week ago tonight. But the days since then have had some wonderful hours in them, up here. Yesterday I walked down at noon for a swim. The sunlight through the trees on the trail was pure magic, and the clump of young beech trees, their feet in the warm green moss, were so beautiful I stood and watched them, simply transfixed. The air is so clear and sparkling, the water of the Sound a blue so deep that you can hardly believe it is water.

Yesterday we settled the matter of the house, walking over the site with Hariph Hancock, the builder, pointing out the stakes where we wanted it, getting his restrained but clear approval that there really was a spot to build a little house—for the view was one to take one's breath. It should be all ready for next summer. A big step for us.

Which led Helen and me to visit over our lunch about the many changes that have taken place since the end of our Vineyard holiday last summer at about this time—a bit earlier—and today; and to speculate that other things will probably happen during the time that lies between the end of next summer's holiday and this.

What were the things—none of them foreseeable a year ago—that took place in the year? (1) That the Russians have developed an atomic bomb, and that we were able to detect it at once. (2) That Nancy would become engaged and married—last year she was with us, and had barely met Sylvain, at this time. (3) That we would write a book and have it published. (4) That we would buy a house in Washington. (5) That we would buy a piece of land on the Vineyard, and contract to build a house on it. (6) That David would have picked a journalistic career, definitely, and have a job on the *Post-Dispatch*. (7) That I would be "investigated" again. (8) That I would get the Freedom Award.‡ (9) That I would so firmly resolve to leave public service by this time next year or sooner. Well—that's quite a list.

Can next year hold a candle to this, for changes?

SEPTEMBER 29, 1949
FLYING TO THE VINEYARD IN A C-47, ABOVE THE OVERCAST
(3:45 P.M.)

Yesterday asked Jim Webb (now Acting Secretary of State) to have lunch with me today. Spent from 1:00 until 2:30 with him, and during the last 45 minutes, with George Kennan (Acheson's chief adviser).

I could not have called to see him at a more timely moment.

This morning (or was it yesterday?) at National Security Council or Cabinet meeting he reported to the President that the U.K.-Canadian talks had failed; that what U.K. proposed was something the Joint Committee, or members of it, would not "take." The Vice President counseled against trying to get anything on this subject through the present session of Congress that involved a fight, which the proposal made by the British certainly would, in his opinion.

The President stated to the Cabinet (or the Council, wherever Webb made his report) that he believed he had legal authority to proceed to make an agreement that he believed furthered the common defense and security, and that nothing in the Atomic Energy Act impinged on that; if it was construed to do so, the Act was unconstitutional as an invasion of his Presidential powers. The President said (with Johnson of Defense there) that Acheson and Lilienthal agreed, Johnson disagreed. But he was advised not to go ahead (at this time at least) and test that power he felt sure he had, but to try to work out something the committee would go for. He directed Jim to "sound out" the committee on the proposition as it now stands.

That proposition by the British is clearly *not* what they would have been willing to propose, *themselves,* as a fair allocation of joint effort between friends and former partners. It has been my view since the very beginning that the *spirit* in which these discussions are carried on is the important thing, that from that spirit a theme or compass-heading will appear, and it is that, rather than the detailed dickering,

‡ The Freedom House Award for 1949 was a double award, to General Lucius D. Clay and to me.

that will bring an answer. If we take the course of the hard-boiled banker, or try to blackjack the British, or deprecate them, they will respond as almost any human beings would respond, by also being difficult, by insisting on doing things atomically that would not be the most economical division of labors and of materials between real partners, but just to assert their pride and place in the world. This is what Hickenlooper, and Strauss, and others have accomplished with their pecking away at technical cooperation, and the kind of things that were said at the time of the last Blair House meeting. It is a shameful record of the tyranny of a tiny minority.

The U.K. has been quite willing to see that we get raw materials completely adequate for our immediate needs. They are quite unwilling to transfer their (bomb) production activities to this hemisphere, as we proposed, but insist that they will go ahead with this on their own; they ask for complete interchange of all technical information.

Kennan had a meeting with them for two o'clock. He was for telling the U.K-Canadian group that they must go back to England; that what they proposed would not be accepted by the Joint Committee, and that therefore however we might feel about our ability (as between the President, the Secretary of State, etc.) to work something out, the way the Joint Committee has acted and would act means that there is nothing we can do further that holds promise.

I urged strongly against this course. I said it was by no means sure just what the Joint Committee would accept. Some of them would agree to nothing. Others would like to escape responsibility entirely. But the entire issue depended upon public *knowledge* and public *discussion* by the President and many, many others, of what was involved in this issue. I thought they should be told that the British were most cooperative about raw material, which was the point about which the committee members, particularly Vandenberg, were most vocal and "hard-boiled." This would take the edge off things. The business of supplying the British with information had taken a different slant, I thought, since the announcement that the crude and "backward" Russians had "The Secret"—I meant this half-facetiously, but it does have a point in it.

Kennan seemed impressed, and left for the meeting, saying he would accept the point about not telling the British that the reason no agreement was reached was because the Joint Committee would not accept it—I hope to hell he sticks to that point.

Jim asked, "What do I do about 'sounding out' the committee on the U.K. proposition, as directed by the President?" I said I thought this was ill-advised, if by that he means to tell the committee what the U.K. proposition was, and to ask their approval of it. The President could only accomplish such a negotiation as this if he were authorized to do so, and the consequences of his not being so authorized were grave, graver now than ever before. Somehow *that* was the issue that must be clarified and put before the country.

Jim said: suppose the President sends a message to the committee saying he cannot dispatch his responsibility properly by the kind of discussions now going on; send along a proposed joint resolution asserting the approval of Congress to his going ahead to make an agreement, and then if they reject it, as they will, make a public issue of it between now and Jan. 1, and if the stalemate continues, trying to go ahead without Congressional approval or concurrence. (This last portion is quite another matter, and has a fatal bug in it: the British would not be interested in an agreement that had such uncertain standing.)

So I am to assemble the reasons why the "sounding out" idea isn't good; why the resolution is; and perhaps what kind of language could accompany the resolution when the President sends it to the committee, if he decides to do so.

Talked to Jim about his statement on international control—that we were willing to consider any proposition that was better than ours. I thought it was just right—of course, we should be. Suggested that perhaps there should be another group brought together, like our Board of Consultants, to "take another look."

He certainly talks plainly about Louis Johnson. He says "the President is certainly fed up with him." Johnson "makes the most irresponsible statements; for example, he said that if AEC were efficiently operated, we could carry out the expanded program with the savings we would make"—and since that runs into 350 millions it is evident what dopey talk this is. Jim recalled the President's statement to him aboard the *Williamsburg;* my recollection of that Jim corrected: the President said he was not to take anything off Johnson, meaning that Johnson was full of hot air and that he should bring their differences to him for settlement. Jim states flatly that "The President has lost confidence in Johnson." On four recent issues the President has decided every one against Johnson and for State. When Acheson isn't present (as now) for Security Council meetings, when the President leaves the meeting, he asks Jim Webb (age 42 or so, and Under Secretary) to preside rather than Johnson; this "burns Louis up."

I talked to Jim frankly about my present plans, as I now see them. He asked me if the President knew my "cut-off" date. I said he knew I did not intend to stay beyond my present term because I had asked to get out as of a year ago, but that he had urged that I stay on until "things quieted down," i.e., after the elections. Jim asked me what I wanted to do; I tried to describe my need for income, by deciding for a time to write and speak and in this way serve the public. He asked about my becoming the head of a foundation, like Brookings, or would I be interested in association with a law firm like Acheson's, with a drawing account, and a share on new business I brought in? He said he would like to talk to Dean about this later, if I were willing, when he returns, Oct. 12.

## POSTSCRIPT: WRITTEN OCTOBER 10, 1949

The sequel to this is:

1. The British did return to England.

2. The public was told that things were progressing "fine"—!

3. It was decided to spend the next two weeks trying to draw up a paper that would represent the American position as of now.

4. A report was made to the Joint Committee, but not very definite.

I was on the Vineyard at the time this occurred.

## OCTOBER 10, 1949

Waiting to hear the President's decision about our proposed expansion program: a whopping big one. More and better bombs. Where this will lead—that is, whether it will lead to something good—is difficult to see. We keep saying, "We have no other course"; what we should say is "We are not bright enough to see any other course."

The day has been filled, too, with talk about supers, single weapons capable of desolating a vast area. Ernest Lawrence and Luis Alvarez in here drooling over the same. Is this all we have to offer?

Later: the President greeted Frank Pace and Lawton of the Budget Bureau with the statement: "I have decided not to send up a request for an AEC supplemental appropriation at this time." No further information. Admiral Souers opines that it was based on timing —which is certainly bad.

This despite unanimous recommendation of Joint Chiefs of Staff, etc., etc. He makes his *own* decisions.

## OCTOBER 16, 1949
### AT HOME

Had a solid hour and a half with Nehru, the Prime Minister and leader of India, last evening, from 9:30 until after 11; in his living room in the Tower of the Waldorf, in N.Y. The meeting was definitely of his doing, and he was set to keep up the visit for I don't know how long, when I broke it up, as both of us had had a long day. Twice Helen spoke to his sister, the Ambassador to the U.S., Madame Pandit, suggesting that the Prime Minister must want to rest, etc.; she said, "My brother is having a wonderful time, this is what he enjoys, thoughtful talk."

A remarkable and I should judge a wonderful man, with real elements of greatness. Since he had asked to see me (and had everyone in a tizzy Thursday and Friday trying to locate me, and insisting I come back to Wash. to see him, which I declined to do) I let him do the talking, except when he asked questions; but after 45 minutes he was so full of excitement with my responses and his own sequence of thought that it became a conversation of some animation. His face glowed as he warmed to the themes he talked about. He speaks with a grace of expression one rarely hears.

Our raw materials people (Gustafson) said, of course, what Nehru must have on his mind in urgently asking to see me was the discussions concerning beryl ore deposits in India and technical help to them, a very limited matter. I doubted this, somehow, and I was right: Nehru never came even close to it. It was river development, industrialization, how does one develop among the intense Indian nationalistic young people a knowledge of how to make things happen. He ask for names of men who could be chief engineer, etc., of the Damodar River development, which he wanted patterned on the TVA.

He and his sister and daughter had come to tea at John Gunther's, where Helen and I were guests. He answered questions about Kashmir and Pakistan, and what not, for 90 minutes, I guess. He was quite insistent that he must see me soon; what about Monday? I said I couldn't come back to New York (which set him back somewhat); what about later that day, i.e., yesterday? No, they were full up; but when I said I didn't see how I could make it any other time, they said 9:30. While he was talking, he said Mr. Lilienthal should pay a visit to India; I said that considering the unattractive competing things that held me in Wash., this was a good offer; I was halfway there already. Which seemed to amuse him.

The party at Gunther's included his new wife, a quite beautiful tall girl, about 30. At first she had a kind of spoiled beauty look about her, but part of it was just nerves—the idea of having a flock of people and the great Nehru descend on her home, complete with police escort, and her cook just given notice. But as the evening wore on, I thought she was not only exceptionally pretty, but intelligent, independent of view, and generally quite a gal.

Those others present: The Kaltenborns (he said every time he vouched for me, as he has quite often, it would produce "more mail and more deep feeling than about any other person of a public character in the news—some of the mail quite passionate"—anti, this part). The Shirers—a very relaxed-appearing man he is. Raymond Swing, who has now apparently decided that the world is going to hell in a hand basket so fast that there's nothing to be done about it—this is exactly what he told Helen. A man from *McCall's*, who snagged Mrs. Roosevelt from the *Ladies' Home Journal*—gent in the widest chalk-stripe suit ever saw, and face to match. Jay Allen. Gardner and Fleur Cowles. The Thomas Finletters (she's very attractive; when she was introduced to me in Phila. three years ago, just after our State Dept. report, it went like this: "And this is Mr. Lilienthal." She: "Oh, yes, Mr. Acheson Lilienthal").

OCTOBER 25, 1949
ON THE TRAIN, BEFORE LEAVING NEW YORK FOR WASHINGTON

Spent 45 minutes with a real "character" this afternoon: W. Colston Leigh, a tough baby, who told me the facts of life—or a few selected bits thereof—of the business of exploiting human reputations known as "the lecture platform." It was fascinating: this is the way, says he, with Vincent Sheean, Mrs. Roosevelt, Archie MacLeish, etc.

"As for Lilienthal, I make no bones about it, I want a five-year contract with you and I want it bad. You are today the most controversial character in the country; more people hate you and more people think you are beyond praise than anybody, not excluding Truman. The ones who hate you want to see you—they are interested—and the ones who want to applaud you—well, that's easy. If you want to squeeze out every dollar, I can make you quite a lot of money. If you want to handle it on the basis of getting the kind of hearing you want for your ideas, I can do that, too, but you won't make so much. You can average $500 to $750 gross a lecture for as many as you care to handle for three to four months." He wants a contract right now, subject to my later decision about when it can be effective. I told him I was just looking over the field, would let him know when I knew more.

Another visit with Baruch. He thought the minority report on the Hickenlooper investigation was pretty thin; they backtracked. Had a very interesting hour with him.

Squeezed 30 minutes in at the Metropolitan, seeing the Van Gogh exhibition, which is wonderful; with my Cousin Beatrice and Sylvain's mother, Mrs. Bromberger. Was recognized; in some cases people spoke to me, one a very handsome young lady who said, "Aren't you Lilienthal?" (without the "Mr."). Beatrice was amused and a little taken aback, too.

The speech to the Herald Tribune Book and Author Luncheon was rather fun—a huge audience, mostly women, filling the place to the top gallery. I told Irita Van Doren, who was a great friend of Willkie, that the last time I was there I had debated Wendell—this was in 1935. But the circumstances—how different.

Had dinner and spent the evening with Sengier and Robiliart, of Union Minière, our Belgian partners. A perfectly wonderful meal it was, too, in their apartment. Sengier was in fine fettle, full of amusing and interesting stories of Africa, China, what lies ahead for the English, etc. He said the fear of Russia in Western Europe was so great that people were rather giving in to it—spending their money and saying what the hell.

OCTOBER 29, 1949
AT HOME (AFTER AN ALL-SATURDAY SESSION)

[*Early in October, Strauss expressed the opinion that "We should now make an intensive effort to get ahead with the Super"—that is, a thermonuclear or fusion weapon, later called the hydrogen or H-bomb— and recommended that we consult the General Advisory Committee. I then requested the GAC to meet with us and provide an analysis of our whole position in the light of the Soviet atomic explosion, including a review of the technical and other considerations involved in expediting existing research at Los Alamos on the possible development of a "Super" bomb. The following entry contains my own notes of one of the meetings with the GAC. (Here, and in later entries, I used the term "Campbell's"—standing for "soup," that is, "super"—in referring to the H-bomb.)*]

With the General Advisory Committee (minus only Seaborg) all day. Subject: what now, centering around "Campbell's." Genl. Bradley; Norstad, chief of Air Force planning and operations; Admiral Parsons, Genl. Hull.

It's quite evident that the full import of the Russians' success, and their prospect of a substantial stockpile in the next —— years, hasn't yet sunk in, so far as the Natl. Military Establishment is concerned; too busy with the inter-service row, or just not too able to grasp it.

The conclusion or adding-up I got out of the day with such fine minds and spirits as were there was that the Russian bomb has changed the situation drastically, and that the talk about our having anticipated everything and following the same program we had before is the bunk.

It will take Europe years to get rearmed and strong enough to withstand the great manpower of a Russian attack. Would we launch an atomic attack on R. if she moved into Europe, if we knew this meant Russian bombs on London, say? A close question, they said—meaning, I guessed, that we wouldn't. (Harry Luce saw this point when I saw him some time back.) Defensive countermeasures could be rather effective, better for a single point, London, N.Y., than a big country where they come from all sides, and here Russia is harder to defend than England.

"Campbell's" made the eyes light up; but chief value of such a weapon "psychological"—Bradley's only comment. What about having AEC step up our present level of production? No answer; Norstad came to me later to say, "We've got no answer; we are studying it once each six months."

A dramatic setting: Oppenheimer at the end of the table. Conant looking almost translucent, so gray. Bradley very G.A.R.-ish, country-man's accents.

In the P.M. session, just the Commission and the General Advisory Committee: Conant flatly against it [the H-bomb]. Hartley Rowe, with him: "We built one Frankenstein." Obviously Oppenheimer inclined that way. Buckley sees no diff. in moral question $x$ and $y$ times $x$, but Conant disagreed—there are grades of morality. Rabi completely on other side. Fermi, his careful enunciation, dark eyes, thinks one must explore it and do it and that doesn't foreclose the question: should it be made use of? Rabi says decision to go ahead will be made; only question is who will be willing to join in it. I deny there is anything inevitable in political decisions. Lewis says the decision won't be made by a popular vote, but in Wash. Conant replies: but whether it will stick depends on how the country views the moral issue.

Conant makes firm point at outset: Can this be declassified—i.e., the fact that there is such a thing being considered, what its effect would be, if it could be made successfully, etc.? I said President certainly could announce it if he wished to. (Privately, doubt if he would—then the arms race fat would be in the fire. He'd more likely say: well, move along but don't say anything about it.) Cyril Smith strong for the Conant point, as was I. Lewis quite dubious, evidently.

Conant says, "This whole discussion makes me feel I was seeing the same film, and a punk one, for the second time."

I commented that if the strongest ground (Bradley's) was "psychological"—a big question. That's what was said about the "little brother": did it provide a sense of security to us, or much elbow room? What happened to the "deterrent"—hadn't we seen how thin these arguments had proved in the past; why would it be different in the future?

Meet again Sunday at ten.

OCTOBER 30, 1949
AT HOME (SUNDAY)

Spent from 10 until 11:30 with the GAC; then we sat together, the five of us, with Carroll Wilson and Joe Volpe, until 1:30 or so. At 1:45 canceled part of my Midwest trip. Some terrible and deeply important things to work out in my mind.

This isn't one of those things where my long experience and habit of trying to find a ground where a group can agree is useful; on the contrary, it is a function that tends to confuse what needs to be a pretty clear line. I'm urging all of us to reach his individual answer, rather than try to bring himself to agree with his associates.

Yesterday it appeared that less than half of the eight [GAC members], never more than five, would be for going ahead all-out; today they were in full agreement: that they would not be for it; two, however, conditional on a rather thin proposal that if the other fellow refused to agree not to go ahead, we would.

Reports from Los A. and Berkeley are rather awful: the visiting firemen saw a group of scientists who can only be described as drooling with the prospect and "bloodthirsty." E.O. [Lawrence] quite bad: there's nothing to think over; this calls for "the spirit of Groves," and the ground is laid for the Joint Committee members to come back and demand that we plunge ahead and think about it, if at all, on vacation or something.

At present the issue seems to me fairly simple, and fairly conclusive: this would *not* further the common defense, and it might harm us, by making the prospects of the other course—toward peace—even less good than they now are. The difference between what we have or are working on and this is one of kind. There is no scientific or non-military by-product—it is straight gadget-making.

I've a date to see the Pres. Monday the 7th, on my personal situation. Things are certainly coming to the showdown stage and fast.


OCTOBER 31, 1949

Further recollections of Saturday and Sunday.

1. Military clearly no longer favor "outlawing" the bomb (though, of course, they consider themselves bound by the official policy) because without it (coupled with the "political fact," as they assert, that this country will not raise a mass army in peacetime) there is nothing we can do to prevent or deter Russia taking over Europe; with Europe overrun there is nothing we can do (without the bomb), as Europe "does not want to be liberated again."

2. The view of some of the military is that war is inevitable. The top, however, do not go so far; they believe it's "likely" in a relatively short time, four to five years. After it comes we must use the atomic bomb, as we can't hold Europe without it.

3. The opinion among the top military seems clear: "Further negotiation with the Russians is useless."

4. "If we knew the Russians were in a position to drop A-bombs on London, would we use A-bombs to prevent Russia overrunning Europe?" "It is a close question; it would be a difficult and a close decision."

5. "We regard the next four to five years the most critical in the entire history of the country."

6. "If substantial numbers of atomic bombs are on both sides, then we know we can't win the next war, certainly if it comes before the rearming and re-establishment of Western Europe, say six to ten years."

7. "It would have psychological value." Referring to "Campbell." No other comment.


NOVEMBER 1, 1949
FLYING TO SOUTH BEND FROM WASHINGTON

Spent 45 minutes with Dean Acheson this morning. I told him the essence of the "Campbell" business; said my present point I could confine to this: that I regard the matter not as one for the Commission merely, or chiefly, but essentially a question of foreign policy for him and the President. He was somber enough when I began; after a few questions he was graver still. I did a better than usual job of statement, and I think he got the point, therefore, at once, judging by his questions.

He recalled this possibility, from 1946, but understood that it was then considered only a remote chance. I explained that some more work had been given to it, and that now it was considered a 50-50 chance, somewhat better than the initial prospects. As to the capability of others, he assumed that this was not out of the question; I told him it certainly could not be so considered. I suggested that in my opinion he ought to mention it to the President soon; I planned to present it to him in some detail later, when the Commission had done more thinking about it, but the time factor was related to the Joint Committee being steamed up on the subject. He asked: We may then be forced to follow this course whether we think we should or not— was that what I feared? It certainly was.

As to the point made by the GAC (I left their document with him to read) that a statement should be made forswearing development along this line, I said this did not seem very attractive or useful, to me, unless it could be coupled with some proposal, which might perhaps best be a rather broad one, and not simply related to the atom. (The more I think of this, the better it makes a certain amount of sense; the mere declaration of intention not to make use of something one doesn't have to use, in itself, puzzles me as an approach. Later, in talking this over with my colleagues, it was one thing they rather liked. I insisted, however, that it should not be made a *condition* of our not going down this road, but simply coupled with the broad proposal.)

What a depressing world it is, said Dean, looking quite gray.

I rose to go after ten minutes or so; he waved me down. So we talked somewhat more about this. Again I started to leave. I had said that some other time I would like to discuss a matter of my personal plans, but not now. He asked me to tell him about this. He said he didn't see how I had stood it as long as I have, "living with this grim thing all the time." He referred to the performance of the Congressional committee—months of attacks of every detail of our work, and the agony of having always to chew things over with four others, however good that might be. "But nevertheless it is sad that after you have acquired as great a knowledge of the workings of Government as you have, that this should be lost."

What did I plan: return to the practice of law? I said that I hadn't been able to make any plans, and couldn't until it was known publicly that I was going, but that law practice would seem the best answer I could think of at the moment. "What about being the President of a university?" I hadn't thought of that; my financial needs wouldn't permit of teaching; I might do a certain amount of speaking and writing, but actually law practice, of the right kind, seemed to be the most flexible thing. He said he didn't know that he would go back to the law when he got out; he had found it very disappointing, how difficult it was to get clients to follow any kind of broad course that he recommended, and told me about a large anti-trust case; how he had tried to get his client and the Justice Department to go at it in a sensible way, but that both got mad and now his partners are going to spend years "of the dreary business" of a long anti-trust case.

Yesterday I told Jim Webb the essentials of the situation. He is a fine, earnest, devoted man, and I always feel better after I have talked to him. He seems somewhat young and untried for his great responsibility, but that probably only shows that I am getting seedy myself.

Last evening the five of us spent a couple hours, in my office, with Senator McMahon. Pretty discouraging. What he is talking is the inevitability of war with the Russians, and what he says adds up to one thing: blow them off the face of the earth, quick, before they do the same to us—and we haven't much time.

He uses all sorts of words to justify this, and part of the time he is practicing speeches on the floor of the Senate at us. The whole world revolves about the exploding atom, as he sees it—that's the whole of it, and there is no hope. I said, " I don't believe that." Apparently one isn't supposed to say that, for he didn't like it. I was asked for "evidence" to support my belief that things aren't as cut and dried and desperate as he painted them.


NOVEMBER 3, 1949
FLYING BACK FROM CHICAGO (10 A.M.)

Some ten years ago, General "Ironpants" Johnson, answering a question at the Press Club in Washington, said he thought the best timber available for the Presidency was Wendell Willkie, president of Commonwealth & Southern. Willkie was almost unknown at the time, except as the fellow who had finally been compelled to sell out to TVA, that transaction having just been completed. A newspaperman called Willkie at Birmingham, for comment. He said, "Well, at the rate the Government is taking over my business I'll soon be out of a job—and this is the best offer I've had so far."

This came to my mind yesterday when I had a visit with Chancellor Hutchins of the University of Chicago. He wanted to see me, presumably about getting money—which is a university president's chief aim in life. And, of course, this is what we did get to before I left. But he began by saying, "How would you like to be dean of the Chicago Law School? You can have it if you want it, and we'll pay more than the Government does." I felt like Willkie: well, at least this is the best offer I've had so far.

I rather thought he was kidding, at first—he has quite a sense of— well, not humor exactly, but of satire. But he wasn't. So I said that it was true that my term expires soon, and I have been giving some thought to what I do with myself; that I had thought I would try to practice law. But I certainly didn't think I was enough of a lawyer any more to head one of the best law schools in the country, that the bar wouldn't consider me qualified. Well, he thought otherwise, etc. I was polite enough to ask some questions: how big a school is it; what did he expect of the school? As to salary, he said it was now $15,000, but that they would pay me $20,000 or $25,000. This is actually for three-quarters of the year.

Would I be interested, he asked, in being a university president?

That is really what I ought to do; that what I am now doing is like that, except that what I am doing is like running ten Universities of California at the same time, and with the left hand, he said. No, I said, I didn't think much of that, but actually I didn't know quite what a president did, and how he got things done; I understood that faculty members were completely secure, and that the schools within the university were almost autonomous. Yes, he said, a president is a dictator without any power (whatever that means), but he knew that President Sproul was looking for someone to head UCLA, to succeed Dykstra, and that the University of North Carolina was "in the market."

We talked about law practice: he said there had been times when he got so fed up he was thinking of that himself, but concluded that clients never took a lawyer's advice anyway, so it was a rather futile way to live.

I thought about the Law School with some degree of seriousness for about five minutes, partly because it would be so easy a life, and I could do so many other things—travel, lecture, write, and look wise without much effort. But this is not for me. I don't want to live in Chicago; I don't want to be so far removed from reality. While the world is proceeding to go to hell in a hand basket, I'd hate to be doing crocheting.

Had a long visit with Zinn. Seemed much more relaxed than usual. Urey, Szilard, etc., are cooking up some kind of an attack on us, but except for that the rest seemed the usual round of "this is where I came in" problems.

Spoke at the North Shore Forum, an activity of the Temple Israel in Glencoe. Very large audience, filling every nook and cranny, people standing, on the platform so I could hardly move, etc. I enjoyed myself, as I usually do before an audience—as I certainly did before a wonderful packed chapel full of students, priests and nuns, at Notre Dame the evening before. I answered questions both evenings. At the North Shore I asked that they be written. To my surprise they came in by the dozens—all kinds of questions. I had a lot of fun with them, and they did, too.

I was given an "honorarium" (fee to you) of a thousand dollars. Since I didn't write a special speech for the occasion and had a very enjoyable release from the anxieties of "Campbell's," this seems very nice indeed. I could do more of this sort of thing without taxing my energies at all, indeed refreshing them, if it didn't come too much at a time. Not that a net thousand dollars for an evening is in the cards many times, but for some time this would not be so bad as a way of paying the rent—now I shall have to change the metaphor—paying the bank, it should be.

I was asked: "Do you agree with President Truman's position on international control as recently stated?" After stating what it was, I said that I did—had had a part in formulating the American position. Then I paused, grinned, and said, "If I didn't agree with President Truman's position, however, considering that I was directly responsible to him, well . . . I guess one of us would have to resign." This amused the audience considerably—one of those laughs that goes off bang, then starts to die away, and then breaks out again—which is fun to observe.

[*What follows are some notes I made on November 3, 1949, during an airplane flight from Chicago to Washington. Writing such notes was (and still is) a familiar and useful way for me to "think out loud" about the issues and problems confronting me in the course of my work. These notes, as in the case of many others made over a period of years, I decided at the time to include as a part of the regular Journal entry, and consequently they are included in this volume.*

[*The reason that I now, in 1964, single out these particular Journal notes of 1949 for comment is that they deal with what was then a most secret and complex issue and one still controversial, that of the thermonuclear or hydrogen bomb. These notes were an early attempt to think out, for myself, the major pros and cons of an issue that was a part of my responsibility: whether the security of the United States would be served by a program of attempting to make this super-weapon.*

[*What I wrote informally on this airplane ride in November should not be taken as my "position" on an issue which was yet to be argued out and decided within the high councils of government. Such a formal and considered opinion was presented by me on January 31, 1950—some three months later—at the final meeting of a special committee of the National Security Council. This committee had been appointed by President Truman to advise him on the H-bomb issue. Its members were Secretary of State Acheson, Defense Secretary Johnson, and myself. At noon on that same day, January 31, we reported to the President, who then authorized the H-bomb program and directed it to proceed. That afternoon I dictated a memorandum in which I repeated the views I had earlier in the day presented to Secretaries Acheson and Johnson. This memorandum, once secret but now declassified, is reproduced in this volume at page 623.*

[*These informal November notes may be of use to those who will one day write a definitive history of the H-bomb issue. To my mind, however, they are primarily of value as an example of the process of thought and analysis and feeling that men of affairs must go through, each in his own way, to reach conclusions on problems that are not abstract or academic, but real human issues, often (as in this case) of great urgency.—D.E.L.*]

Spent the last hour or so trying to write down my own conclusions about Campbell; these notes are attached, in handwritten form, as part of this journal.

I. Commission state that it is the Commission's (or Commissioners') judgment that the President decide against Commission proceeding with program.* "Proceeding" means:
>a. Directing Los Alamos to assign high or highest priority to accomplishment of test of X [H-bomb] in shortest possible time. "Proceeding at highest priority" involves:
>>(1) Bringing in new talent for X theoretical and experimental work.
>>(2) Emphasizing reaching stage of testing X at a cost (indeterminate but considerable) to [the progress on] current and expanded [A-bomb] program of Los Alamos; probably Sandia, etc. [as well].
>[b.] Assumption: "proceeding" cannot be in secret, i.e., essentials [will become] public [knowledge].

2. [*A proposed course as an alternative to "proceeding" with H-bomb.*]
>1. "Expansion" [of A-bomb program], to go ahead with highest priority.
>2. Emphasis on [weapon] engineering to make for *greater tactical value*, i.e., less mass or saturation or indiscriminate bombing use. (Involves, in general, emphasis on numbers and manageability, against emphasis on increasing by large factors size of individual explosion, or an increase in poisoning effects.)
>3. A statement by the President that X [H-bomb] is something we have considered and decided against, what it is, how feasible, what results, if made, if used: using President's *same statement* to press for active reconsideration throughout the world of a Plan, Pact for World Survival, of which control of weapons of mass annihilation (negative aspect) one part, but *affirmative* proposals to assure World Survival are even greater part. Renunciation of X [by U.S.] must be followed by Russian Opening of Borders. Opening

---

* The Commission decided not to take a position on the H-bomb issue; instead, the Commissioners' individual views were submitted to the President.

of Borders is beginning. Without that, nothing else can
follow but suspicion, fears . . . and piling up of X and $X^2$.

*Or*

3. Statement [by President, as above] plus Council of Citizen Advisers to the President (or Secretary of State or National Security
Council) to advise President on his effort to accomplish World Survival
by a step-by-step program.

[*Analysis of arguments presented* favoring *H-bomb*]:

1. Purpose of "proceeding" [with H-bomb]:
   Deterrent against the Russians' [war-like course]
*But:* [That would be] no additional deterrent to the present and
   currently projected [expanded A-bomb] program [without the
   H-bomb].

2. Purpose: To use in a war, assuming war "inevitable in 3 to 6
   years"
*But:* On this assumption, [we ought to] strike now (on some kind
   of rationale) while [we are still] able to inflict damage [on
   Russia] at low cost to us or our European allies.

3. Purpose: (i.e., of "proceeding") To hasten international agreement [on nuclear control].
*But:* Isn't it more of an ultimatum, or declaration of intention [to
   go to war], if not [actually] of war?

4. Purpose [of proceeding with H-bomb]: To reassure our friends
   in Europe.
*But:* Does it reassure anyone, anywhere, that the humanitarian
   and peace-loving U.S.A. takes the initiative (again) in
   weapons of mass annihilation involving risks to large areas
   of the Caucasian world? Is it reassuring to those under the
   shadow of Russia's armies and present air force (and later its
   A-bombs) that we take a step that may be construed by the
   U.S.S.R. as an ultimatum, or declaration that war is inevitable,
   i.e., only a matter of when—or who takes the first conven-
   tionally overt step?

5. Purpose [of H-bomb program]: To reassure American people.
*But:* After telling them that we had a "secret" [—the A-bomb]
   probably for a generation, and having this press-relations tale
   fold so miserably, will [H-bomb] mean reassurance, except to
   those few who now today believe the only question is our
   physical survival, and this group would not be reassured by
   bigger bombs in 1955 (or 1958) but [only by actually] using
   what we have in 1950.

[*An alternative to H-bomb program*]:

   To maintain the opportunity to take advantage of every

[chance] to develop a situation in which U.S.S.R.–U.S. relations will simmer down to less than boiling, and then gradually be accepted as rivalry and opposition, but not enmity that verges daily on war; in short, to persist in efforts to win the Cold War by a stalemate at about the present stage (add and subtract a bit from year to year) or to win it, by Russian inability to make further net inroads, or win it by the Russian Politburo's unwilling but pragmatic acceptance of her own internal strengthening as her measure of her own political success. This projected on a 20- to 25-year time segment. "But what happens then?" Well, let some other, perhaps wiser men try to solve that one then.

NOVEMBER 4, 1949

Conversation with Jim Webb this morning. I told Jim I had not seen Secretary Acheson since our conversation about the "Campbell" matter. He said:

1. The Secretary had "touched base with the President" as I had suggested; that he had made the point to the President that this was a matter that was important and complex; that the President should not be rushed into anything without great thought. It was identified as a major problem with the broadest domestic and international ramifications. I told Webb I thought this was very reassuring; that I would mention to the President when I saw him on Monday that we are in the process of preparing some kind of a paper, presumably of recommendations on the subject.

2. I asked him if the Commission should try to elicit the views on "Campbell" of State and Defense and present these all together in a package to the President; that I thought not; that we should submit only our views. He said offhand he agreed with that; that we might recommend to the President how we thought the matter should be coordinated within the Government but that we should not try to do it ourselves.

3. He said that Kennan and his staff had been in for a couple of hours. They had been instructed to spend the next two or three weeks laying out the whole picture as it confronts the Secretary; that this kind of staff work was absolutely essential.

Oppenheimer is seeing Secretary Acheson this afternoon on this subject.

The Commissioners do not seem willing to take a position. I have stated my own view as being flatly against this project, partly to get the thing off dead center and partly because I feel better when I take a position and don't fiddle with it; but my example has not proven contagious.

## NOVEMBER 6, 1949
### AT HOME

Gardened yesterday and this morning: dug up the rock garden, redid the soil, mixing in the luscious leaf mold we brought from Rockville, lime and bone meal; then planted Siberian iris, primula, candytuft, some bulbs, dianthus, sedum—had wonderful time.

Tomorrow noon the calendar moves along: I see the President at twelve, and expect to tell him that I've done my stint, that he should have in mind getting a successor. My fear is he will agree "in principle" but be unwilling to do something in public about it before Congress returns, when I can very easily get into some row that will make withdrawal mean and bad-tasting all around. I hope he doesn't feel I'm "running out on him"—don't see why he should.

If there ever was any uncertainty about the necessity of my getting out, the past days helped clear it out—boy. The interminable talk-talk-talk, the incredible amateur touch about how a large organization runs, yet with no humility at all about their inexperience, on the contrary. I'm really fed up to the ears.

More seriously, the "Campbell" discussion in the emotional atmosphere following on the President's announcement of the Russian bomb on Sept. 23rd confirms my feeling that we are all giving far too high a value to atomic weapons, little, big, or biggest; that just as the A-bomb obscured our view and gave a false sense of security, we are in danger of falling into the same error again in discussion of "Campbell"—some cheap, easy way out. And what I have said in public about the Myth I ought to say more clearly by disassociating myself from a means of deception [continuing reliance on big bombs].

## NOVEMBER 7, 1949
### AT HOME

Another step taken, and more successful and more definite than I had hoped for. In other words, I told the President I must move on, fairly soon; we've discussed it, and he has—as you might say—accepted it in principle, and certainly with no ill feeling or sense that I am running out, etc.

As I entered his office—I was ahead of schedule about seven minutes (due at 12, in at 11:53), I felt a sinking feeling in my midriff. Crossing the threshold, it came over me, with a rush, the many

times I'd gone through that door, in so many different states of mind
(the A. E. Morgan "trial"; the last time I saw F.D.R. when he was pressuring me to take the Surplus Property job to avoid the row with
McK.; the day I first met Truman as President and so on) and a feeling:
how will it be like to be out—no more of this kind of thing, entering
that door with responsibility????

The President was quietly reading, and after greeting me with a
huge grin (that showed how relaxed he is, despite the tired eyes, but
also how much plumper he has become), he said, "For amusement I've
been reading old man Ickes' speech about Dulles Saturday night—
listen to this." Then he quoted some barb, and leaned back and laughed;
we both laughed. Then he said, "Listen to this: 'Willkie was the bare-
foot boy of Wall Street; Dulles is Wall Street itself, on stilts. . . .
Dewey has been bitten by the Presidential hornet, and nothing will cure
him of it but embalming fluid.' "

I never saw the President so full of hard laughter, and couldn't
help thinking: this is certainly a break for me, and how smart to come
in when he is sure the election tomorrow will go his way, whereas
Wed. I take a risk that it might not.

"The old man is funny; but it isn't half so funny when he isn't
on your side," he said. I said I knew about that, and he nodded; yes,
he did, too.

"Well," he asked me, "what are you thinking about these days,
how are things going, now you've once more disposed of those fellows
on the Hill?"

So I went into my story, with no frills. I had been in public service
for 19 consecutive years, come next Feb., always in a controversial
field. I have to move on, and I've come in to talk it over with him, not
only as the President, but also on a personal basis, as my friend.

"Well, I'm certainly sorry to hear you feel that way, and I'll try
to persuade you to change your mind, if I can. But I can certainly see
why you feel as you do. We just must make sure" (here he glared,
through his thickish glasses) "that those bastards on the Hill don't
get a chance to say they forced you to quit. What would you plan to
do after you left? I don't suppose you quite know."

I explained that I didn't; that part of the trouble is that until it is
announced, I can't talk to anyone, or make any plans, for it won't be
known, nor can it be, that I am free to make plans. I'm not like a
fellow who is on leave of absence from another job, or with a lot of
money, or a law firm or something to rejoin. Yes, he could see that.
And having been in public service all those years, though we always
lived within our income, I don't have reserves enough to go very long.
So I need to plan as far ahead as I can, though it has its difficulties.

My term expires June 30 in any case, and he'd probably be naming new men, or renaming men, by April, say.

"What about your saying on Dec. 30, that you won't be serving beyond June 30?" he said. No, I said that wouldn't help too much; I ought to leave before then, but an announcement by that time would be almost necessary, then I could stay on a month or two to help my successor.

"Successor," he said. "That's not going to be easy. I can't just open the front door and pick up a man who can stand up to those fellows on the Hill, who think they are the board of directors of this thing, or who'd be willing to take it on, or capable of it—that's going to be tough, to find such a man. Remember the position that U.S. Steel fellow took—he'd be willing to come only if he continued to get his steel salary—that's the kind of thing some fellows put up to you" (he shook his head as with a foolish child). (This was Ilgenfritz, who was turned down for the Munitions Board by the Senate.)

I said one of the most difficult things about the job, and that would have to be considered in a successor, is the way this is set up —an outfit with five heads. The wear and tear of that is terrific, and many men wouldn't put up with it. I've tried to make it work, but it really should be re-examined. Yes, he said—ought to be a Chairman, but with executive powers, or something like that. But we'll talk of that later.

"You've got to be thinking of who I could get," he said. I said I would; but I didn't volunteer any thoughts at this point.

"Practicing law would be interesting," he said (but he didn't look as if he thought so), "and I'm sure you'd make some fine connections, but I should think with your wide experience in running things you'd find it more interesting to become head of some big commercial organization, where your unique experience would be so valuable—like a large chain store outfit or something." I said that I hadn't thought much of that, but I did know that what I needed was to get away from the atom for a while before beginning anything else, and I planned a trip more or less around the world. "Point Four," he broke in, just like that . . . yes, to see some of these great opportunities for development, such as India, Africa.

Then he was off. For ten minutes he waxed enthusiastic about what I should see on such a trip, what a great thing it would be. He got up abruptly, shoulders squared, and marched across the room to his big globe, and said, "Now here is the finest opportunity for development in the world" (pointing to the valleys of the Tigris and Euphrates). "They have the money, money's no problem, they have it by the barrels—oil under every foot. They have to know how to do things. We can show them that. Then here" (northern India) "and here" (the Paraná, in S. America, and the great plateaus of Brazil) "and here" (the Belgian Congo). And so on and on—and Alaska. His eyes snapped, he was happy. "We might even use an atomic bomb to change the course of some river."

He certainly endorsed that world-tour proposal, and (as in the case of Clark Clifford) it certainly helped sell the idea of my leaving.

"Well, I'd like you to stay on," he said. "We have to find a good successor if you don't. I hate like the dickens to see you go. Don't say anything about it to anyone" (I said if I do, Hickenlooper and McMahon will know it ten minutes later) "until I talk to some of the boys here —Charley Ross and John Steelman, and before I go to Key West we'll try to find some way to handle it to meet your personal situation. I'll have to think about the rest of the Commission, too—there's one fellow there I don't plan to reappoint, there may be others. I'll see you —I'll send for you pretty soon. You think about who I could get, who could handle it—that's going to be hard. We don't want someone who will let that Joint Committee run things; we don't want a military-minded civilian, he must be someone who sees the necessary military setting, how it fits in, but he must be someone who doesn't regard that as our objective—and we're going to use this for peace and never use it for war—I've always said this, and you'll see. It'll be like poison gas (never used again)."

He added: "I've got a serious—a very serious—problem about this to decide before long" (referring to "Campbell"). He looked solemn but not gray and worried as he said this.

"We are worrying it around," I said, "and hope to get a memo to you that may help, have our Gen. Advisory Comm. in to advise the AEC." "Yes," he said, "I want the facts; of course, it's a policy question." I told him our concern was that this would get up a head of steam from some of the scientists and from McMahon and his Committee to try to put on a blitz to get a quick decision.

"I don't blitz easily." He grinned hard.

NOVEMBER 9, 1949
AT HOME

Have just come from handing our memo on "Campbell" to the President § (at about 5:10 P.M.) I feel wonderful. [Orally] I said only that I am against it, for the reason that it may ruin his program for peace—just that. He certainly gave me the distinct impression that in

§ This memorandum contained a summary of the individual view of each Commissioner; there was no recommendation from the AEC as a whole.

emphasizing that point, in my "Views of DEL" memo that accompanied the report, I had guessed right on the kind of argument that would appeal to him in his present frame of mind, and his sanguine temperament. I said McMahon and others who thought the world was going to hell in a hand basket wanted this because apparently they thought the only thing to do was to blow up the world, but I didn't feel that way. He grinned like the dickens and said, "Oh, just wait till Brien is re-elected and he won't think we're going to hell in a hand basket."

I went over to the WH with the package, to hand it to Matt Connelly. Instead, he opened the door to the President's office and waved me in. I was startled, and said, "Matt, it was you I wanted to see." But he pushed me in anyway, saying it'd be better that way and then I could tell the President anything I wanted about it. So there I was.

The President asked me to have a chair, and settled back for a chat. I said something about: Was he happier as I had seen him Monday, anticipating a victory, or after it had happened? "Well," he said, "I am happy, and I'll tell you why. This election in N.Y. State carried out the very thing I pounded away in that long, hard campaign last summer—I guess it was the hardest campaign there's ever been in this country. They've dragged out statism and all that stuff and they've got their answer. I had a long talk with Foster Dulles—he was sitting right there where you are—and I advised him not to get off the high international plane or he'd get licked; that he'd been making millions for the big fellows so long he didn't know what people really thought and were like. Well, he didn't take my advice, and look at this." He held out a telegram: "YOU WIN. JOHN FOSTER DULLES." (I got a big laugh out of the drama with which he told this tale.)◖

When I first handed him the report, he said, grinning like anything, "I've already read it." I said, "You are a miracle man, but this has just come from the typewriter—I don't see how . . ." He was amused, and said, "You do look mystified. I read Johnson's copy before he saw it himself." This got me even more mystified, until I finally understood that he meant the Defense memo had come in and it was the subject he was referring to, not our own report. At least that's the best I could make out of it.

He said, "Have you thought anything further about someone to take your place?" Well, I hadn't, but I described Chester Barnard. Yes, he knew him. Wasn't he pretty much to the right? Yes, I said, in a way he is, as a telephone executive, but he has independent views, approved my book on TVA, etc. "Give me his full background," he said,

◖ Dulles was defeated by Herbert Lehman in the New York election for U.S. Senator. It was an off-year and most of the contests in the nation were for city and state offices; the Democrats were generally successful.

"also anyone else you can think of." I mentioned one name. "He's a fine man," he said, "lots of courage, but he goes off half-cocked, without all the facts. He did that once and I had to cut the ground out from under him. That's something that won't do on your job, as you know—that's the reason you've done so well, you didn't go off half-cocked."

I suggested Lee DuBridge; the President was interested but not responsive. He asked, "What do you think about Paul Porter? He has done a fine job, and he can stand up to the Hill the way you did and he's in our corner." (I'd never thought of him, but I certainly will now, for I am sure'n hell anxious not to get caught here for a long time for lack of a successor.)

NOVEMBER 11, 1949
AT HOME

Gardening again—after doing business by phone. Very warm and wonderful day.

Spent some time with Clark Clifford late P.M. yesterday. As I was sitting waiting for him to finish with a visitor, Charley Ross came plowing past me in the anteroom, agitated as a hound dog on the scent, and then out he came with Clark in tow. I later learned that Cap Krug had resigned from Interior, to the papers, before the Pres. had recd. his resignation! Not a sensible way to leave, I must say.

Told Clark about "Campbell." To my joy, relief, and delight, he pulled a copy of our memo out of his desk drawer; said the Pres. had handed it to him, said he wanted to talk to him about it in a few days. I summarized the facts, said we differed about the course the Pres. should take, but that this was helpful as it tended to bring out all sides.

(In P.M. saw Robert LeBaron of the Military Liaison Committee, who was mystified about the Pres.'s remark about having already seen it, i.e., Johnson's report, "before he saw it"; said Defense had not even gotten under way with much of a staff study in the Joint Chiefs; didn't consider it [the H-bomb] fit in as an "offensive" gadget; only value was "retaliation" if the visiting team had it; Bradley away on "a week's leave"; no one steamed up over there. Hardest problem he has ever faced—which last amused me.)

So I'll have a chance to keep in touch with developments at the WH—very reassuring.

Talked personal things with Clark, too; finally said before he decides what he is going to do I'd like to discuss with him whether we might not work together, as I would enjoy this, and thought he "has the best judgment of any man I'd ever known." He seemed pleased (not surprised since our long evening together recently and a prior meeting with him foreshadowed such an interest).

I'm thinking hard about how to take off on the issue of a complete revamping of the whole Comm. setup, limitation upon the Joint Comm., description of what the investigation has done to the Comm., and an insistence that the Commissioners confine themselves to policy matters. Nat Finney is doing a story, Morse Salisbury told me, predicting my retirement Jan. 1 because of the snarl with the Joint Comm. and no man of stature would take it as things stood.

Ed Murrow talked five minutes last evening on his program about *This I Do Believe*—and did he go all out—nothing brief or subtle— "I want to persuade you to read a book." It was something.

NOVEMBER 14, 1949
IN THE COMMISSION CONFERENCE ROOM

When I have a day—or a week—of boredom in the "new life," this note is to be read to remind myself of the boring boredom in this job. We are now in the second hour of droning on about details of operation which are supposed to have some relation to the functions of this Commission—and perhaps they do. But it is dull, unproductive, tiresome, frustrating, and, generally, a waste of an irreplaceable part of my life. So when I have to do dull, unproductive, etc., things in the future, don't let me get away with "regrets"—no feeling that if I were still in public life I wouldn't have such dullness and boredom and irrelevance.

NOVEMBER 18, 1949
AT THE OFFICE

Clifford said, "I'd lay it right on the line; say you want to send in a resignation right away; that otherwise Hickenlooper and his crowd will start something—they've already undertaken something—and then you'd have to leave under fire."

This was at 11:15, after he had looked over a top secret two-page report to the Pres. on where things now stand, and a memo suggesting names (of successors).

So that is what I did; it worked. I came out of the President's with a load off my chest. He said, "I hate this like the dickens," etc., etc., again and again; but the prospect of my being under fire and then leaving, giving these devils the satisfaction and political advantage— that argument took. So now I am readying myself to write that letter, and hope to have it accepted by this time next week, to take effect Dec. 31. At long last, the door of the pen looks ajar.

The thing that did the business, I think, was his reading a two-page report on where we now stand—"That's a fine report," he said, reading it through. I said the Hickenlooper investig. had caused us to lose a good deal of drive; he said that would be cured by the three-man committee of the National Security Council (Acheson, Johnson, and myself) he was having set up to study "Campbell" and argue the points out. (A non sequitur, as far as I can see.)

Then I showed him a sheaf of editorials on the outcome of the investig.—he read the titles and chuckled. Then I said: This is where we stand, and it is good. If I leave now, it will be one thing. But if I wait around until Congress is back, this crowd will start a row. . . . "We don't want you leaving under fire," he said. "I hate it like the dickens, but you can send it in. No, I don't need to see it in advance, but it is all right to check it with Clark."

Then I showed him a long memo on a successor, including some names. It began: the Commission should be abolished and an Administrator substituted with an Advisory Board. He said, "That makes sense. I know Wilson, and Porter, of course; don't know DuBridge." I volunteered that there is no one over here now who could do it among the Commissioners; no, there certainly isn't, he said.

I somehow didn't quite give the impression of sadness at leaving that I suppose I should have, or make any speeches about it—thinking perhaps that I'd save those till it was a reality. It was a bit awkward at the end. But I guess I was so glad to get the hell out.

NOVEMBER 20, 1949
AT HOME

I had just finished reading aloud the latest—and last, I hope— draft of my letter of resignation. And then suddenly, with no warning, I started to cry—a curious sort of sobbing business. People are funny. I have been so darned relieved—and then reading my words, and their finality, as if an epitaph soon to be made use of, I bust out weeping.

It ought to be out and public by Wed. or Friday at the latest, if I'm lucky.

No regrets; just the usual one that after so long a time, such a change stirs something in me.

NOVEMBER 22, 1949

Visited with David K. Niles, administrative assistant to the President, at his request. He gave me a five-sheet statement criticizing the

Commission's performance from the standpoint of "the scientific community." When I finished reading it, I said, "What else did Leo Szilard say?"

Szilard took the position with Niles that he, Szilard, was trying to prevent this paper being released to the press signed by "130 scientists." Niles, of course, was the doctor who was going to save us all from this disaster. I said I didn't think it would be a disaster at all; that a good many of the things in the paper are true as a matter of judgment; that some of them are cockeyed. Szilard was using this with Niles to get him an appointment with the President, etc., etc. The old gag!

NOVEMBER 26, 1949
AT HOME

This has been quite a week.

Last Sunday night I finished the letter to the President, and some notes Clark asked for of points that might be made in the reply.

Monday at 11:30 I handed the letter to Clark, who read it and thought it "splendid." But he told me some disturbing news. At the Saturday staff meeting the Pres. said he had been asked by me to accept my resig., and "I as much as told him he could." But he'd been thinking and didn't know whether he could permit it; that there was the "Campbell" thing outstanding, a report would have to be made in which I took a part, so he couldn't see how he could let me go Jan. 1.

My innards sank 40 feet. But I said: tell him that report will certainly be ready by Dec. 31 if it is any good at all; if it isn't, you can assure him I'll stay till it is, perhaps two weeks later. The important thing is: get the announcement out pronto, before things get gummed up by his enemies and mine so he can't let me go except under fire. I was not too serene after that. Clark said he'd say just that. That evening he said, "The Pres. talked it over with me, said he wanted to take the letter to Blair House and think the whole thing over and see how it looked by morning."

Tuesday noon Clark said the Pres. had it up at staff meeting that morning, at some length. Charley Ross helped in supporting my position, with Clark, so the Pres. asked that Bill Hassett, his secretary, get a draft of a letter up accepting the resignation, and then he'd think about it further. Boy, this was close sailing. That P.M. I visited with Charley, asked him to get word to me so I'd have time to tell my associates, etc. He was very considerate.

Wednesday noon the Comm. was in a session on what is the role of the Comm.—important discussion. It went on late. About noon Martha Jane came in with note: "Charley Ross wants to speak to you at once."

I raced down the hall to my office. He said, "The letter of acceptance has been signed, both it and yours to be released today if that's o.k." I said we'd better not risk leak; let her go, as of 4 p.m. Then returned to meeting, which went on till 1:10, when I asked the C-ers to remain. Told them. Said I hadn't been authorized to discuss it before. Smyth was obviously hit between the eyes—he knew, for I had told him in answer to a direct question that I'd hoped for this, but to have it over . . . Dean and Sumner were very nice indeed. Lewis seemed quite upset, colored, nervous. Said, "You beat me by a couple months; planned to leave Feb. 1." Said privately, "Want to talk to you Friday." (But he didn't.)

Telephoned to the AEC regional managers, and answered the phone to newsmen: Friendly, Carl Levin, Leviero, Sevareid, etc. Talked to Ed Murrow, to put into effect our plan for an interview in his show tonight. He phoned the questions, I talked with him about them a bit, wrote some lines, Frances and Helen criticized them, then Helen and I went to CBS studio, me with a cold. Never had done a two-way thing like that (Ed was in N.Y.); but it went rather well, I was told, sounding relaxed and what I said improved the news stories.

Thursday morning papers (and Wed. broadcasts) very friendly, nice touch, no talk of my "running out." Hickenlooper said, "I did it." Banner eight-column heads in Chicago *Trib*, Balt. *Sun*, Wash. *Star*. Helen's crack to me Tuesday, which I used when asked what am I going to do went over big: "Don't know, but my wife has given me a resignation gift: a tin cup." Thurs. noon, long visit with Jim Carey, terribly interesting guy. Reminded him that when I took on the Commie United Electrical crowd, CIO issued a reprimand to me; now they threw them out. Would have helped if they'd been in there pitching earlier. He took it well.

Good many wires on hand Friday morning. Lecture bureaus; law practice (Arthur Garfield Hays). Genl. feeling of relief. Invited to dine with Phil Murray and Arthur Goldberg, CIO's general counsel. Morning spent hour or so with newsreel and still cameramen. Lunch and a long visit with Gordon Dean; we made headway on the kind of understanding that we would have accomplished months ago but for the damned investigation, which upset everything. He is a very decent fellow, with good instincts, and most diligent.

Much worried over trend of Comm. to be negative, critical, to want to re-examine decisions of management that might "cause trouble on the Hill," which of course creates utter confusion and centralization, caution, lack of drive. About decided that in this spot an advisory part-time commission better than full-time one.

Phil Murray is a delightful man when he is in a relaxed mood, and that he was last evening; dinner in his rooms at the Carleton. I congratulated him enthusiastically over the steel pension strike* and throwing the bad unions out of CIO; reminded him I knew about steel strikes, from my youth in Gary, said what a great advance had been made since then. Goldberg, a keen and very decent fellow, said, "We read about your wife's gift to you and Phil has designs on you." So Phil told about their contract with U.S. Steel, which provides for a board of arbitration and conciliation to administer the contract. Ralph Seward was chairman; the company wanted him out; the post was open. It paid $25,000 and expenses, with a staff. He would like to suggest my name to the company, if they agreed, which he thought they would, etc. Very much a full-time job. Said I didn't think it was the dish for me; but would think it over as he urged.

NOVEMBER 27, 1949
AT HOME

I didn't miss my "timing" on the resignation by much; pin-pointing is what one might call it.

Big Ed Johnson, Sen. from Colorado, made a big mess of things in a television show last Nov. 1; arguing against relaxation of secrecy in a debate, he said things that he had no business to†—the *Post* here did a job on it, ten days or so later, then editorialized. The last time I saw the President—was it the 16th?—the *Post*'s piece had appeared that morning. The President was mad as hops, started off by cussing Johnson and the Joint Committee out; said he was writing Johnson a hot letter. Then last Friday Atty. Gen. McGrath and McMahon saw the Pres., came out to admit he had raised cain about security lapses, which was taken to be a blow at Johnson, so he was in some hot water.

Johnson's idea of how to get out of it was to let fly at me, which he did in a nasty statement in this morning's papers—I headed a dastardly plot to give the secrets of a super bomb to Britain and Canada. Made me rather sick at the stomach for a while: if taken seriously—and the wire services carry it over the country, and it was page one in two out of three papers I saw this morning—it amounts to a charge of treason or in any event of illegal action. But at tomorrow's press conference—which will probably be well attended with all this—I know what I *should do*: no comment to anything along this line, for the

* The nationwide steel strike had ended earlier in the month; the companies agreed to provide pension benefits.

† Johnson said progress was being made on a bomb "1,000 times deadlier" than the Nagasaki bomb. He was the first person with access to secret information to speak publicly about a super bomb.

worst thing is not having a nasty attack made, but answering and joining in on it when there is no way of getting at the facts.

NOVEMBER 30, 1949

Dinner at the French Embassy Wednesday night. Sir Oliver Franks and I had a little visit at his suggestion. He expressed concern about the way the [U.S.-U.K. atomic cooperation] talks have been going—the amount of fencing; the fact that both parties' representatives were there with fixed instructions and that this was hardly the way for two great nations to work out a program in their common interest. This was just what has been troubling me about it, and I said so frankly. He said he thought he ought to talk with the Secretary of State about it. I told him I thought he should, too.

It was a very pleasant evening, as a matter of fact. Francis Biddle; Ambassador Bonnet, who is very interesting about French youth and education and how badly Europe needed "a long period of peace"; Joe Davies and Mrs. Davies in their incredible state of wealth; Justice and Mrs. Frankfurter.

DECEMBER 3, 1949
AT HOME

Another week: quite a week indeed.

Last Sunday I was pretty mad at the sock Sen. Ed Johnson had taken at me: head of a "nefarious plot" to betray the country by giving secret, etc., to Britain. I fumed a bit, called Morse Salisbury—then realized that it was another case where humor was in order. Can't be too literal in public affairs: what he accused me of amounted to his effort to get off the hook of his own indiscretions in his famous television debate in favor of secrecy!

Monday was a looloo. Began with a briefing on the U.K.-Canada talks. Then at ten a big press conference—more than 100 of the top correspondents. It went much better than I had feared. On the "nefarious plot in which Sen. Johnson says you're engaged" (question by Elmer Davis), I laughed, said I was trying hard to be disengaged, and let it go at that—a moral victory, for Sun. I was really outraged and sore. Nat Finney saved the conference by reminding them that our reactor announcement was important news, and from there on we left the questions about Russia, the bomb, Sen. Johnson, etc.

Monday at four met with David Lawrence and his *U.S. News* staff, for an "interview"—I was wound up, and when I saw they didn't have much idea of what an isotope is, I talked too much and too hard. It is to appear tomorrow, and after editing, not too bad.

Tuesday I blew open my feeling that the "role of the Commission" had proved so difficult to define because a full-time Comm. was a mistake, under present circumstances, that it ought to be abolished and an Administrator plus part-time Comm. substituted. I probably erred in making it so emphatic and so sudden, for Dean was "shocked" and the others felt, I think, that I was unrealistic and rather implied the Comm. hadn't done much—not what I said but the implications were the sour things. The staff was there to say to us what they had been saying to Carroll and themselves: unless the Comm. defined its area and encouraged execution rather than just worried about mistakes, nothing but trouble was ahead. They came up with illustrations that chiefly related to internal machinery troubles; though they stem from the Comm. role, most of them didn't sound like anything but defects of management. Quite a back-set, temporarily, to my effort to clarify the limited role of the Comm., which I think should be major policy only, plus a buffer with the public and Congress and interpretation—speeches, seeing people, fixing of goals, holding management to them.

Talked lecture management with Bill Leigh, a rough, tough, but interesting cuss; thinks I can earn a fair amount that way. I hate to tie myself up on it. Will see another manager later in the week.

This is a period of soul-searching, and a tough one. For to change your way of living and earning a living, for a conscientious guy with a reputation and standing he wants much to maintain, means you must ask and find answers to tough questions: Just what is it you want out of life; how much importance does money have to you; can you stand a quiet, reflective life, such as writing or teaching, or must you keep on eating the racy, fiery fruit of management and turmoil?

Spent almost two hrs. with Jim Webb and Fred Morrison, head of Max Gardner's old firm of lawyers: purpose, to look me over and vice versa, re practicing Washington, D.C., law. Result: skepticism on my side, and, I would guess, on his. Lunched with my dear friend John Lord O'Brian: his advice—don't try law practice. It is tedious and boring after what you've lived through; you've been out of it too long to pick up law practice and handle it without strain and uncertainty; most Wash. practice is the kind of thing you would find against your principles. Why not business management or running a foundation? Chief advice: take your time about deciding, don't be in a hurry, give yourself time to think it over, give the country time to realize you are available.

Lunch with Justice Frankfurter. Advice: you will find law practice here not to your standards, not that it is "corrupt" in the crude sense, but

. . . Told him Barton Leach, and later John Gaus, said there was interest in my teaching at Harvard. That F.F. thought a sound idea. It gives the most needed of all things for you: freedom. Freedom to say and think; great freedom of time. I was much moved by what he said.

About the best advice I've had, because it was basic, came from Martha Jane Brown: You have to live with yourself, and don't forget that. Only talk, now, to those people, few in number, in whom you have implicit confidence; start with that. It is not a problem of how you earn money, but how you are going to live and spend your energies. Said with such directness and sweetness that I realized again I have not only a secretary second to none, but someone of a rare comprehension and character.

Bob Hutchins had a suggestion or two: head a U. of Chicago study of social, etc., implications of the atom; head an organization to be created and financed—future—to spread the Point Four idea—TVA for the world.

DECEMBER 11, 1949
AT HOME

Much of this week has been spent thinking about "What next"— what do I do with my life from here out, and how do I earn a living while doing it—or should or must the question be the other way around —how earn money, the answer to that question in effect answering what I do with the unknown but finite number of hours of energy I have left in the X number of years ahead.

Only one specific thing resulted: I now have a contract for lecture management with Bill Leigh, the gravel-voiced, energetic tough guy who is W. Colston Leigh, Inc. Two-year period; only commitment is for four weeks in March and April, as a try-out. A good contract, thanks to Ed Murrow's advice; he had me insist on a 60 percent of the gross (except that I pay my personal expenses en route), and I have reserved the right to reject any date. This will provide a source of income for the first months on my own.

Most of the week spent considering the same subject, but with very different people.

Monday: at 11:30 I visited with Stringfellow Barr and Scott Buchanan, trustees of the World Government Foundation (with Bob Hutchins), who offered to pay me to think, and to pay for a trip to far places to see what there is to the Point Four development scheme as basis for a bigger Foundation grant from old (84) Mrs. Emmons Mc-Cormick (Reaper) Blaine. About one thing they're clear: they want to grab holt of me, and seem willing to make it wholly without strings. But the strings are there, I fear. And the notion of making a career of foreign development, something that will take not ten but a hundred years to show much results, is one to be cautious about, at age 50.

Well, my next appointment was at lunch with former Ambassador Joe Davies, at the baronial place they have here; we lunched in his version of a Russian country place—dacha—with liveried servants all over the place. After dismissing the servants he said (and very well he said it, too) that America must now carry "the white man's burden" (he used that expression, too) as did Britain in the days of Elizabeth. Foreign economic development as an outlet for American risk capital, encouraged by tax incentives here, and protected by UN assurances against confiscation, etc.

What a curious converging; as different motives between the Barr-Buchanan team and sharp-eyed money-maker Davies it would be hard to imagine: one of the dramatic-scene things that are too dramatic for the stage! His line was this: I shall doubtless practice law. Best area, become counselor to and help organize investment group re foreign development, taking an equity, the only way now one can acquire a fortune. But it was vague and tentative. One advice I thought sound: don't jump fast, don't take first thing that comes along.

Saw people from *Life* mag. (Emmett Hughes, text editor) and from *Reader's Digest*. They want articles, willing to pay well; when I frowned at "regular rate" of $1,500 or $2,000, they doubled it at once, and such payments would interest me.

Tuesday P.M. went to New York, stayed at the Murrows. Ed was steamed up over the current sensation: Fulton Lewis, Jr.'s "exposé" that Hopkins and Wallace, etc., were pressuring through uranium shipments, etc., to the Soviet: "Hopkins handed the atom bomb to Russia on a platter." As of today it appears Lewis has had another one blow up in his face—and is being criticized in the respectable press for it, but this doesn't seem to faze him (though he acts outraged at the "unfairness") as his listeners are the kind who believe everything he says, especially if it is stabbing F.D.R. or anyone connected with him.

Breakfasted leisurely with Ed on Wed. Paley of CBS says "No" on the weekly broadcast idea for me; two reasons: would be too serious to have much justification, and second, he'd be stuck with me—"You can't just drop a man like Lilienthal after you've started with him." I thought Ed was over-sanguine on this anyway, so I'm not disappointed—query whether I could have done it. Ed says he'll speak to Sarnoff of NBC, but the whole idea seems to me something that might come later, several years later, not now. NBC has asked me, as have two other stations, about doing a series, but I've put it over for the time being. One guy suggests 15 or 20 debates with Fulton Lewis!

At eleven spent an hour and half with Leroy Wilson, pres. of AT&T. Very appealing fellow, "Terry Hut," Indiana, is what he still is, in speech and easy manner—more authentic than Willkie was on this. Talked intensely for an hour, to me, about how he tries to keep close to people— story of a young woman, small stockholder, wife of an employee, let out —never quite knew what the story's point was, but he felt it deeply. A man on the defensive, like so many of the top of industry, but a good man, sincere, thoughtful, groping. He proposed pensions be raised by AT&T from $50 to $100 a month; was attacked by CIO union—"busting the union." This hurt and baffled him. My purpose was two: tell him what a fine job they're doing (under Bracken of Western Electric, etc.) at Sandia; second, to get better acquainted with him. Bishop Oxnam's name was brought in by him: he seems to want guidance for his problems, such as the pension matter. I told him how Oxnam had helped to get better public understanding of our Board of Consultants' report.

Lunched Wed. with Gerard Swope; talked to him about the foreign develort. thing; he thot private capital unlikely, referred to Stettinius' failure in Liberia; this I didn't know; apparently Ed did more than fail, he depleted his fortune. The Rockefellers had done better, he said. Offered to make me chairman of Institute of Pacific Relations (he now is), and in this role Helen and I would start off Jan. 20 on a four- or five-month world trip, all expenses paid. I declined; want to find out how I earn a living first—not the time to be gone that long. But it made me pleased just to think of it.

Afternoon Wed. with Bill Leigh; then Jim Szold, who also thought the foreign investment thing a poor prospect. I said I wanted to earn some money; what for? he said. Those who have no financial problems can be very detached about that area. He's a fine man, and a very successful one as a businessman; as a young man was considered the radical black sheep of the Szold family.

Thurs. 11 to 12:30 with Rafferty of Union Carbide, later with Haggerson, the president. They are spent men, discouraged, puzzled, fearful, unhappy; yet since 1920 they built an empire and changed the course of American life. Why do they seem so isolated, so disillusioned, so *poorly paid?* is another way to put it. I'd like to think about that a lot.

Lunched Thurs. with Phil Reed, chairman of GE, Anne Ferris' brother. Charming, handsome fellow, young-appearing, intelligent. He asked: What has gone wrong that we are so close to war, in spirit, with Russia? Will our preparedness bankrupt us? He wanted to know what I planned to do. He seemed sincerely desirous of helping suggest things. Grand fellow. As to atomic energy incentives to private concerns (following on my *U.S. News* thing), which had brought some enthusiasm from the Carbide people (as much as they are capable of in their burned-out condition), Reed would have none of it; they [GE] "don't want to get tarred with the Du Pont (i.e., 'merchants of death') brush," don't want to make profit out of it.

3 P.M. till the Congressional left, with Jim Warburg; he's an intense and intelligent and wonderfully articulate man. All on fire with a Point Four campaign to make it Point One, he says; wanted me to become chairman of a Citizens Committee to push for legislation, etc. I'm chary of that. Read his pamphlet; he has made it seem a short-range as well as long-range (100-year) thing, to make up for the deficiencies of our Marshall Aid and Atlantic Pact strategy; I doubt this like hell. But it fits in, again, with the world trip idea. He must have heard that Baruch is interesting himself in me; regards him, Luce, etc., as imperialists, and their course fatal.

Friday, lunch with Bob La Follette. How does one "adjust" to non-public life? Make the most of its advantages, for one thing, he says. Don't saddle yourself with a big law office. Told me about his consulting work, for United Fruit and Sears R. Bitter against those in labor and Govt. who are out to wreck the private business system, while they talk the other way; I have much sympathy for this, I must say, though, it came strange from a La Follette. How they are hated now in Wisconsin by their former supporters; had dinner with one of them (casual business of being recognized on train), and he regarded them as turncoats of the worst kind, the way the rich did F.D.R.

Gridiron dinner last night, rather late, guest of Lowell Mellett. Sat next to Merle Thorpe, *Nation's Business,* whose outlook put me in mind of a speech I'd like to make: "Let's Bury Our Dead." Long talk with C. R. Smith of American Air Lines, big tough guy, "goddammit" every other word, but attractive in a hard kind of way; told of seeing rivers from the air in northern India, that fall a thousand feet at one fall. Foreign development 200-year job, he says. No soil most places.

Terribly pleased to have Paul Hoffman come way around to speak to me at table; he said, "Before, we divided McKellar's venom, now I have to take it alone." Gov. Lausche of Ohio also came over; curious-looking man, hair like a Zulu, shrewd face. Met Henry Ford II, who spoke—no sensation, superficial, pleasant. Secy. Louis Johnson spoke to me at length—read in some column—was it Tris Coffin?—I had left because of a fight with him, said he knew "nothing to it." The military folks are nervous about reports I'm going to take out after them, which I've no cause or intention of doing. Frank Kent, the columnist, who recited how he'd supported me in confirmation, asking who, but who, can we get now for AEC? Skits very so-so, I thought, rather dull, slow, middle-aged, like too many of the guests and members. Not all the skits, but not a super-show at all. A mean anti-British one, bad and not funny at all.

Beginning to clean out my papers—old Wis. files mostly, headed for junking.

Leave soon for Chicago, last important conferences.

DECEMBER 17, 1949
AT HOME

Xmas eve a week from tonight. And our children—all *three* of them this time—will be home. Happy day.

Troubled this morning by a Mark Childs piece about the U.K. business, which includes a stiff dig at Lewis about his bitter animus toward the British, etc. L. and I have recognized that we are on difficult terms, but since my return from holiday we've been trying to get over that. This Childs piece and the Joe Alsop piece last Sunday have re-opened the sores. It is easy to say that "This is Washington" and that it goes on all the time, but that doesn't help much. I've been consulting L. again on personal matters, and in other ways trying to show that I wish things could be, if not friendly, certainly not inflamed. Gordon [Dean] was sore, naturally, by Joe Alsop's remarks about his appointment being a political one, i.e., at McMahon's insistence or sponsorship.

(At this point I was interrupted by two interesting developments. It is now Sunday, 11 A.M., December 18.)

Item 1: A call (I mean a visit) from Larry Martin, asst. editor, Denver *Post,* and Barnet Nover, *Post's* Wash. bureau head. Purpose: to ask me on behalf of Ep Hoyt of the *Post* whether I'd consider a contract to write for a group of newspapers, under *Post* sponsorship, on an open-end basis, that is, write when I felt I had something I wanted to say, rather than on a deadline or so many times a week basis, as in the case of a syndicate contract. I was enough interested, need I say, to talk to them over an hour about it, they getting more steamed up by the minute as I told of my idea of a trip to far parts, etc. Hoyt may make me a definite proposal, money included, sometime next week.

Item 2: Jim Webb phoned about 3:45 P.M. Fred Morrison, of Gardner, Morrison & Rogers, had visited with Jim, at M.'s initiative, to say he thought it over and was definitely interested in making me a proposal to join that office; could I come down to talk to Jim about it? I did. Jim not "authorized to make a proposal," etc., etc., but Morrison asked him to describe it to me, and get my reaction. Firm would guarantee me a minimum of $40,000 a year; i.e., if I got in no business of my own, but only worked on their business, I'd be able to count on that much; with a share in added business, future growth of the firm, etc. I'd have independence to work or not on a particular client's work, freedom to come and go, to lecture and write (with income therefrom to be deducted from the $40,000, I gather). Would wish I'd not "carry a torch" too much the first year or so. They'd have troubles with some of their clients, e.g., Carolina Power & Light, but, etc.

So this has added to the things to think about, hard. Item 2 worries me, in that the firm is a question mark to me—big textile people, Coca-Cola, Penna RR. But you can't have your cake and eat it: if I want to be relieved of the worry of having no reserve for our "declining years" and the worries of setting up an office of my own—which this course would eliminate—I've got to expect some other concerns to pay for that.

Most of the week spent at Argonne Lab. Left Sunday P.M., returned late Wed. night.

Meeting of managers and lab directors. Quite encouraging. Spirit good, just the right amount of "griping." No sign of cliques, or of deep disaffection. I urged them to try to understand the virtues of keeping cost records, and making use of cost accounting and budgeting, rather than regard it as unnecessary red tape, esp. in a Govt.-financed undertaking where there are no standards, much, except the willingness of Congress to put up more money. Said, don't get mature, organizationally, too soon—too smooth an operation is not too good a sign.

Monday evening had an hour or so with Bob Hutchins, at the pres.'s home. Met his new and young wife, formerly his secretary. A very pretty and impressive young woman, dark, gentle, and looking in that huge house and beside the very tall and sophisticated Hutchins like a kindergarten teacher called in to look out for his children, perhaps. He is very proud of her, even to the point of bragging about her in a restrained and nice way—she redecorated and remade the huge library in which we visited. I'm terribly glad for him: he has had a very rough time.

We talked further about Mrs. Emmons Blaine and her dough. Bob says they, i.e., the World Govt. Foundation trustees, are willing and desirous of making a good deal of money available for me to "think" about economic development abroad, or for a long trip to take a look-see, or both. The sticking point with me is the adverse comment there would be, or might be, because this old gal was a principal supporter of Henry Wallace's last candidacy; Scott Buchanan, one of the trustees, likewise. She is old (84) and very rich (perhaps $100,000,000) and from a distinguished business family. But a misstep by me at this juncture might easily cost me the confidence, across most of the board, I now have, and money can't pay for that, whatever the money's source.

Friday spent 1½ hours with George Kennan. Remarkable man. Peeled off his coat, exhibiting farm-type galluses over his thin and bent shoulders. Then he nervously started rolling back his sleeves, folding them back by stages till they were way above his elbows.

Told him State's representatives (Paul Nitze, who succeeds George Jan. 1, while G. is on a year's leave) hadn't contributed much so far in the "Campbell" discussion. He showed me a lengthy memo and had me read it—showing they had been doing a lot of thinking and working but weren't ready to disclose it till Acheson had seen this; even then they'd be well advised to hold it pretty closely; but it could be a basis for discussions among the three members of the Special Committee, which I hope may begin next week.

Webb told me, Sat. P.M., that relations with U.K. were frayed; Franks called last Wed. (this he said he intended doing when we saw each other briefly in a crowd at the Gridiron) to tell Acheson just that.‡ This is not good news, though not necessarily final, and in my view it is not surprising. The way we have dealt with U.K. makes U.K. countermoves, if only for bargaining, inevitable—so I've thought for two or more years.

Sorting through old Wisconsin brown envelopes—and burning up or throwing away eight-ninths, I'd say. What an active buzzard I was indeed! But one can't keep all the accretions of his life.

I am struck by the soundness of the prose in my writing, including letter-writing, of that period. Also, by my cockiness in taking the lead in the country in utility regulation—correspondence from all over the 48 states about.

Long time ago.


DECEMBER 22, 1949

President:
Back a man up? That's the way to get loyalty.

Phone call last night from Ted: Dad is in a pretty bad way. Sinking attacks, increased weakness. Took him to the hospital. Ted is going down. I spent a rather worried night. Talked to Dad's doctor this morning. Very high blood presure—200—and chronic nephritis, albumen

‡ In the atomic information exchange talks, the British were pressing demands to which the Defense Department in particular was opposed. It seemed clear that no real agreement could be reached.

pumping through, very tired-out heart. But, he said, no emergency, nothing critical. Just wearing out. Dad is at the hospital, where they are
running tests, etc. Mother, too, is not in good health; complaining of
chest pains, taking an examination this morning.

So it goes. But they are a wonderful pair!

DECEMBER 24, 1949
AT HOME

Another heavy and eventful week: Visit with the President; good
confab at lunch with George Kennan, about "Point Four" sort of thing;
with NSC committee headed by Z.§

(VISIT WITH THE PRESIDENT ON WEDNESDAY, DECEMBER 21, 12–12:15
P.M.)

The President looked fine, brown, clear-eyed, even plumper than
before, and very friendly. His first full day in the office since he got
back from Key West. We chatted about this and that for nearly five
minutes—something he doesn't go in for when he is in a feeling of
tension. Then I said it was evident that the report [on the H-bomb]
couldn't be finished by the 31st, and since I promised I would stay on if
that were the case I was prepared to do so, but wanted the date a final
one and made known publicly. His face became very serious, suddenly,
said he would certainly appreciate this a lot, that he had been thinking
it might be necessary for me to stay even as long as February 1. I said,
"In view of how very much you have done for me, Mr. President, the
least I can do is to accede to your request. So we won't have to consider
another extension, which would be bad and make it hard for me to
make plans, let's make it February 15."

He seemed very appreciative. It has been tough lately: Sidney
Souers preceded me in his office and I later learned had fixed on an
immediate resignation;◖ Clark Clifford had an agreement to leave on
Feb. 1 (we had talked about my visit before I went in, and it was Clark
who suggested I offer Feb. 15 rather than Feb. 1, so we wouldn't both
leave on the same day—that the Pres. felt "the bottom had fallen out of
things with so many leaving him").

I went on to say I didn't think it was good for me to be too active
in regular AEC matters, hence that Pike should carry on as Acting

§ The special committee of the National Security Council (Acheson as chair-
man, Louis Johnson and myself as members) named to report to Truman on the
H-bomb issue.
◖ As Executive Secretary of the National Security Council.

Chairman except on the reports I want to make, etc. We agreed I'd write him, he'd respond, this would take care of the record, he'd announce it over there.

I told him Lewis Strauss had told us he planned to resign soon, and that I didn't see any occasion for that; he, L., didn't have the kind of problems I had, no reason why he should not stay on. The President said he would talk to him. Thought it was good thing to have a fellow in a group like that who was always disagreeing, good for everybody, had them in his Cabinet. I agreed, said we had always given L. more than ample time to voice his objections in those few areas where we could not work out agreement. My quarrel and basis of objection—and Waymack, Pike, and Bacher felt the same way—was not his difference with our views, but his unwillingness to accept the decision of the rest and regard that as the team decision. Yes, the Pres. agreed, couldn't have that.

He got to talking about how things ought to be run, following on my warm expression about the way he made me always feel he was behind me. That's the only way, he said. "I can't even kid a fellow," he said; used to do it, and if others were present it was like a whip-lash, so regarded, and if alone, fellow felt it keenly; realized you can do that if you are a Senator—can't if you are (here he glanced at his desk in a characteristic way) the President. Too bad, too; then he said this fine thing: "You know, kidding is part of our American way of doing business."

DECEMBER 24, 1949
AT HOME

Yesterday noon Gordon Dean (Smyth was with us, in my office, Strauss had just left us, for his holiday, Pike was away) said, "I'm troubled by the growing number of attacks on Lewis"—meaning in newspapers. There was the Joe Alsop column, then Mark Childs' crack about anti-British animus on L.'s part, then the *Post-Dispatch* editorial. If there were an issue, that would be one thing. Lewis wouldn't accept another five-year term for worlds, he intends to resign in the spring. If he were trying to be Chairman, as the dope stories have it, then there'd be some point in their trying to chop off his head. But this is a synthetic issue. It hurts him; he has many British friends. Because of his racial background he can't fight back on the issue, etc., etc., etc.

I agreed there was no good could come of such a row in the papers, at this time. I've resigned. It would be bad all around and no point in it. Then I asked to see the *Post-Dispatch* editorial. One statement made as fact did seem most unfair: that he was part of a clique to overthrow civilian control in favor of military. This is far from the fact, as far as possible. So I thought about it a good deal, and with some agitation of mind, for it does not usually make any sense to write letters to the editor —Ickes made a fool of himself along this line. But as much as my confidence in Lewis has been shaken—almost 100 percent—and much harm as he has done with his methods of seeking to undo Comm. decisions not to his liking, *this* wasn't true and was unfair.

I like to think I don't bear grudges and am forgiving. So I wrote a telegram to Dilliard of the *P–D*. I did it because the habit of feuding and ungenerosity and ruthless fighting is a toxic thing for anyone who has any part of it, and the only way to flush it out of the system is to be fair to the point of naïveté.

Yesterday morning talked by phone with Dad's doctor at Daytona Beach, Morris Seltzer. No emergency; giving him X-ray exam., blood transfusion to correct low count. Had me speak to him on phone, which was wonderful. Dad didn't know Ted was coming down from Indiana. Ted called last night; Dad not too bad, Mother very peppy. So no crisis, and the chances are I'll see them fairly well on Jan. 8th.

Nancy and Sylvain arrived as we were having late breakfast. Seem happy though tired from sitting up all night on the train, and a pretty confining life at Cambridge.* Wonderful to have them. Nancy and I have again cut a Xmas tree from our own place, as we did last year and years ago, when she was five, at Palos. The day is beautiful. David arrives this evening.

CHRISTMAS DAY, 1949
AT HOME
(MEETING OF SPECIAL COMMITTEE ON THE H-BOMB, DECEMBER 22, 10:30–12:15)

1. Opened by Z [Acheson]: a fine bit of exposition by a master of the craft. He at one end of the table, I at the other. He said: not here to reach decision, but to think together.

2. Passed then to the man on his right [Johnson]. He very relaxed. Like to hear from me—issue to them [Defense], a very limited one.

3. I referred to telephone call of almost exactly four years ago, to me at Knoxville [from Acheson, when he asked me to head the Board of Consultants]; I'd been in it ever since.

Conditions since then have changed. Hence need to take another

* Both were working toward advanced degrees.

look. Consider [go-ahead] decision not limited; may close the door to any other course.

The Strong Man [Johnson] says he doesn't see what any of that has to do with the matter before us. I insist they are related.

He doesn't agree; says the light at the end of the tunnel is the "minimum," the very minimum, can't be made less, all agreed in his place on that.†

Man on Z's [Acheson's] left, more schoolmasterish-looking even than usual in civilian dress [General Bradley], wants to correct [my point that an H-bomb go-ahead might be closing the door on a great step toward peace]. [He says:] may be very opposite, great deterrent. Psychological value. I say: I don't know what that means.

4. Man of Heroic Mould [Johnson] states their position, with which all civilians in his shop fully agree. Other matters unrelated. Liaison Lad [LeBaron of the Military Liaison Committee] chimes in; finding many military uses for this longer look at it (I guess he means it'll be a handy thing around the house, as it were). No relation to anything else.

5. I break in—couldn't disagree more; purpose and course of mankind wrapped up in this; that's the trouble and has been, treating this as if gadgets can be dealt with without relation to men's objectives and philosophy (he [Johnson] had said some slighting things about not getting philosophy mixed in here).

Man on my left [Smyth], who came with me, adds his bit at this point, with feeling, and in support.

Head of table [Acheson] takes no position. He said he spent two hrs. with schoolmasterish guy [Bradley] asking questions, day before, on what you do with such things, etc. Wants some more of that; I ask to be invited; Big Boy [Johnson] says he'd like to "argue with me" about it sometime.

6. We reached no conclusion, which is good. But going is tough. Karl Compton has written a strong letter, Big Boy says, as if to settle all question about where "the scientists" stand, as if only question is squeamishness of some. I say it isn't only scientists who have doubts (and of course many scientists don't).

7. It's now clear that sponsors [of the H-bomb] are scientists and military establishment, active and ardent.

8. We'll meet again, sometime.

9. Z [Acheson] listed changes [since 1945]: (a) monopoly no longer fact; (b) early and great peacetime use now regarded "inconsequential," with which I disagree but didn't butt in to say so.

---

†That is, the only reason the Defense Department would accept for not proceeding with the H-bomb would be Soviet agreement to the U.S. international atomic control plan.

DECEMBER 27, 1949

Walter Williams, tough, forthright fellow, asked could he see me for five minutes. Was obviously embarrassed, fidgety. "I saw you go through that confirmation hearing and got some idea of the kind of man was at the head of this thing. Then I saw you go through that investigation, and take the blame for things without any passing of the buck to anyone. I just want to say that here I have been working for a man. That's all I wanted to say."

DECEMBER 30, 1949
AT HOME (8:30 A.M.)

Spent an hour yest. late P.M. with ABZ [Acheson]. Told me at length of his talks with chairman [Bradley of the Joint Chiefs].

[Acheson] said he [Bradley] had a 67-page memo "beautifully rendered" on the whole problem, but when got through didn't clear things up at all. So he [Acheson] sat down and wrote out a whole lot of questions; they reminded me of Jacobowsky and the Colonel: if this happens, then still there are two alternatives, etc., etc. Then he read these analytical questions to the chairman [Bradley]. Net result: now they are thinking about military policy. Said to Johnson, "Now don't come into this meeting and say the Joint Chiefs say so and so, and that's our position. Then all the President has is what staff says; he wants us to think this through ourselves. If he wanted staff's view he would have asked for it."

I felt much encouraged. ABZ [Acheson] has analyzed the policies we now follow, and also the current problem. And his questioning leads to real doubt about how solid our present accepted formula is, if continued. And the contradiction between our [international atomic] control policy and our military policy—"If we keep saying we want the control policy when we don't, we are perhaps fooling others, but we shouldn't commit a fraud upon ourselves." Where will this leave a future Government? In the soup. Exactly.

Can't write much more right now. See the chairman [Bradley] this morning.

As [for atomic information exchange with the] U.K., [Acheson said] Johnson pitched it all out the other day (as I predicted). Now it needs direct communication between the men who can say what our purpose is: is it to tie U.K. up as much as we can, or is it something else? I said I had always thought the real issue wasn't technical but the relations between the countries.

DECEMBER 31, 1949
AT HOME

Ruppel, editor of *Collier's,* just phoned: would I be interested in this proposition: two-yr. contract, six articles a year at $5,000 each, a total minimum for the two yrs. of $60,000, to be paid if I submitted the articles, whether they accepted them or not, no censorship, use of an office and secretary in Washington; if I went on trips connected with articles, they'd pay expenses, even carry part of cost of trip to India, Brazil, etc. This wouldn't exclude my lecturing; in fact, they'd fit together, feed each other; nor apparently exclude radio work, certainly not business or legal consulting work, could live in Washington. What about it?

I didn't commit myself, said I thought I could do six pieces a year (which is six in ten months, counting out vacations) readily enough; if I did more, they'd pay for them at same $5,000 rate.

This was outgrowth of word getting around that Satevepost was after me, also *Reader's Digest,* and *Collier's* effort to become more lively. Would exclude newspaper syndicate deal, which "Ep" Hoyt said yesterday from Denver was cooking along, sending McKinney and a Des Moines *Register* syndicate expert to talk to me about it Wed.

Must say, this begins to look like something. If lecturing isn't too strenuous and a bore (and I've had enough experience with it not to be too concerned), then between them (without radio or business consultation fees) this should produce not less than $60,000 a year, which is a lot of money for this guy, working at the very things he wants most to do. This would leave, I calculate, at least a six weeks' stretch each year for public service of some kind, uncompensated. If this isn't the answer, then I'd like to see the color of something better, f'r-heaven's sakes.

Not a very pretty picture, sezz I as Harry [Smyth] and I left the mild warrior's [Bradley's] office.

[Bradley said:] All we have right now, but all, is [our A-bomb stockpile]. Without that we are helpless to aid our friends and must, if they are overrun, try to hold our foes off from home base; never again able to normandize [invade Europe]. [If the Russians overran Western Europe and then were forced back, it would] take our friends 10 to 15 years to get rebuilt; even then, [Europe might not survive]. If they [Russians] were on yon side of the Pripet [marshes in western Russia], as historically, then long lines of supply, etc., bad for them; but they and their dumps are on this side.

He [Bradley] says "caint" and when he uses a profane adjective, it is as mild as if your aged grandmother used it.

Yes, replying to my question about inconsistency in saying get rid of [bombs] and we can't manage without, yes. And our get-rid-of plan is the "minimum."‡ But if it [control plan] was adopted would mean no troubles being planned [by Russians]—we think. Maybe their huge land forces, etc., only a dictator's way of hanging onto power—inventing foreign devils, etc. Sweet smile of self-amusement at this, to himself, halfway. If trouble long time off, he said, best to keep forces down to nucleus; but they *know* what is going to happen, we can only guess, so we compromise between being ready to meet an early and a more remote crisis. If we do more, can be exhausted and resources worn away.

I asked: what would be effect of withdrawing our get-rid plan, [face up to the fact we are in an arms race] in view of events? First reaction—never thought of that one, he said—bad on our friends. But come to think of it, might have something be said for it: would bear thinking about. Sezz I: might make plainer that we don't live in a world at peace—look at our expenditures for non-essentials.

I asked: Is [A-bomb stockpile] with or without "Campbells" really a deterrent—will it be five or ten years hence? He admitted [bombs] of declining value, but still war would leave both sides beat up so bad little value in using them.

‡ Our policy was to get rid of atomic weapons through international control on one hand, and yet our military was relying on these weapons as virtually our only means of defense.

# VI

# THE ATOMIC ENERGY YEARS

# 1950

A warm, warm day. Writing this in trunks, having been in for long swims twice today. Plenty of snoozes. Storing up for the coming sprints, the three-week lecture session in March, and what have you.

(Ding Darling just dropped by; full of affection for Bill Waymack we were.§ Then he talked about fish and shrimp and why the fish population is so hard hit around here.)

Friday the 6th gardened at home; weather warm beyond belief (71 deg.), dug wood soil and pumped it into our garden, transplanted narcissus bulbs that hadn't been moved for years and years. That night, we went to Ambass. Davies' for dinner. About the most elegant dinner and surroundings I've ever seen, though the guest list was not. The house is a museum of beautiful and invaluable things—vases, Russian ikons, cameos, God knows what. The decoration of the dining table, for 30, was as rich and beautiful as one can imagine—huge silver vases, four feet high from the table, filled with bushels of red roses. Candelabra on the buffet with 12 or 16 candles, delicate gold filigree work. Butlers in livery . . .

I thought: take a quick look at this splendor, my lad, for it is about gone, forever. Between a change of taste in such things and the tax bills, it is gone except in a few places, such as this. The Davies' are most

§ Ding Darling was the cartoonist for Waymack's Des Moines *Register and Tribune*.

accomplished and friendly hosts—know how to do it and work at it. Ambassador Pandit, the honor guest; also Secretaries Gray (Army) and Matthews (Navy); Mrs. Daisy Harriman; Earl of Jellicoe; and some Washington fixtures, such as the Pratts, ex-Sen. Bingham, etc.

Spent a good deal of the week before we left, i.e., the week after New Year's, on things connected with what next. Agreed with Bill Leigh that I'd do a speech to the Scrap Iron Institute in Wash. Jan. 23, after much argument by him. Reason: fee of $1,500, which he hopes may set a precedent for future convention speeches. Talked to Denver *Post* people (McKinney and Nover), and it was clear that they couldn't run a syndicate, and that periodicals rather than papers was the thing for me. Talked with Lowell Mellett at lunch: he thought the *Collier's* idea a sound one. Didn't think I needed an agent; I'm not so sure. Agreed with Leigh that I'd lecture this fall, two weeks in Oct., three in November; he thinks he can net $4,000 a week for me; if he can, this is just too much to pass by.

Left Sat., Jan. 7, for Daytona. Dad at station, to my surprise and concern. Seemed old but not gone by any means. Mother perky. Their new home very nice. Helen and the folks walked out onto the stage of the Civic Auditorium, and it must have been a picture, Dad and Mom, just as relaxed as anything, with 2,800 people out there applauding them. My talk went quite well. Meant a lot to the folks. Talked to Dad's doctor, Morris Seltzer, young, nice-looking man. Dad's just running down, arteries in heart region hardening, cells not functioning too well; can't expect him to last much longer, but no crisis imminent; responded to blood transfusions.

Tues., the 9th, to Winter Park, spoke to Town Hall Forum, old but cultivated audience, packed; tried an informal talk, which went rather well. Answered some written questions; then said I'd take some from floor. Man got up, started to ramble; Miss Lockhart said what is your question; he pulled out something from pocket. "Suppose you wonder where I got this?" Then he purported to read from *TVA Handbook* (which is a public document) about labor policy, words indicating TVA favored labor unions—after more needling and restlessness from audience, who were getting fed up with him, finally asked question: "How do you square your definition of democracy, etc., with fact that there's a closed shop in TVA and AEC?" By this time people were rustling and Miss Lockhart was in somewhat of a tizzy. I said there was no closed shop, so basis of question was missing. He rose again, and Miss L. adjourned the meeting. He pursued me to the stage, started to argue, then got out a camera and began pointing at me, with a strange thing attached to it; I got mad and told him no one had right to take one's picture without permission— I was frankly a bit upset that he was a nut and this gadget he had would go off—a kind of silly idea, no doubt, but I kept thinking: if anything happens, "they" will never let me go out without security protection again.

### JANUARY 23, 1950

"Any publicity concerning intelligence is potentially detrimental to the effectiveness of intelligence and of national security."
What do you think about that!

### JANUARY 26, 1950
AT HOME

You are participating in a great and tragic issue, I reminded myself. So stop being so sorry for yourself; it's grim, but you are alive.

[Acheson] very composed; like a spring day, the window open, we seated as if we had all time in world.◖
1. Told him, "I am looking at a *man*." Replied: After a while you get tired of the curs yiping, and have to have your say. Understand some criticism in this bldg.; don't give a damn.
2. Conclusion stated. Reasons: if take time to get re-examination, meantime not giving green light, such a row that atmosphere not conducive either to negotiation, new look, etc. But firm: high-level look.*
3. I indicated my reservations (to this conclusion): a go-ahead would tend to confirm [present] wrong policy; [that big bombs] offer assurance [of military security] when none exists.
4. If answer first [last November] had been Yes, no broad inquiry would have taken place.
5. [Acheson said:] If not for [Russian] investiture of [East] Germany, [present] policy might work.
6. [Acheson said:] This kind of war—strategic bombing—not a useful means of effecting national policy, in a democracy. Doesn't break the

◖ Acheson and I were meeting in his office, the day after he had made his famous comment: "I do not intend to turn my back on Alger Hiss." (Hiss had just been sentenced that day.) The paragraph numbered 1 refers to that episode. The remainder is concerned with the H-bomb issue, about to be decided by the President.
* The gist of our conversation here was this: Acheson indicated his belief that the President should direct the AEC to go ahead ("green light"). He seemed to feel that this could be combined with what I believed was needed before a commitment to the H-bomb was made by the President, namely a serious re-examination ("high-level look") of the prevailing policy of almost exclusive military reliance on big bombs. I gathered that it was his view that without such an immediate go-ahead from the President the excited atmosphere ("row") in Congress and in the Government would make most unlikely any useful "new look" at our military and political posture and policies.

will of population, destroys them. So can only be considered to effect sheer survival, not winning, i.e., achieving national purpose.

7. [He] frowns on preventive war—because in 1970 something may happen, don't make sure of it in 1950. Too many things may happen in your favor.

8. Two years ago we were winning. Now China, things going other way. China may—possibly—be partial undoing.

9. Atom can't be dealt with separately any more; part of over-all settlement.

JANUARY 28, 1950
(VISIT WITH THE PRESIDENT, 12:05–12:20 P.M.)

Pres. was a bit behind schedule. Looked worn, color florid, eyes puffed.

Wanted talk about Comm. Only 2½ weeks till leave. Did he have successor, if he wanted to say? No, haven't; "haven't given it much thought, to tell you the truth." (No reference to staying on, so I'm in the clear, surely, God be praised.) "May I make suggestion?" Sure, want them. Need someone to take over soon as I leave. New man may take time. Strongly urge man whose loyalty runs to him, the Pres.,—not to McMahon or Hickenlooper, but to the President. Also good, solid judgment and knowledge of program. Pike that man. I said couldn't think of better man than Pike.

Pres. said he'd think about it, had always liked him, knew him long time. I said whole program turned on people, on staff, assembled fine lot, few in Govt. service before; credit should go to Wilson, general manager, though he was seldom heard of. He asked, "How would it be to put him on the Comm?" I said he would make an excellent Chairman, but in any event thought a pat on the shoulder would help, a note perhaps. "What is his name?" he said, getting pad and pen. "Oh, yes, I know him," wrote his name.

About "Super." I said disappointed been such a long delay in report [Special Committee report (Acheson, Johnson, myself)]; meeting for today, Fri., canceled. He said, "Very much hope can get agreement." I told him much accomplished already because for first time Acheson took time to apply that wonderful mind of his to the problem, to ask the military the right questions. He said some fine things about Acheson; loyal, sensible, not like some men who are brilliant. President said ought to reach him with some report promptly. Baruch has just announced his conclusion, publicly, I said, and they'll all be sounding off now the Joint Committee is having hearings.

At the word "Baruch," he grinned in a most mischievous and boyish way, and for some minutes he went over B.M.B. with a light and devastating touch. "I've known him a long, long time—he's the same old Bernie. Gave $5,000 to Dewey; then day after election and I won, tried to give Bill Boyle money for us Democrats. Nothing doing. He's behind Byrnes"† (all this said grinning, not bitter, just final) "financing him. He's just a disappointed man; he had F.D.R. down at his place in South Carolina; had news photographers take pictures of bathroom where F.D.R. would go, bed he'd sleep in, etc., and with Bernie's picture big over it all. Next day, after this appeared, F.D.R. went straight home."

I said there'd be a lot of stories about my position, that I would lead a "crusade" against my Pres., etc. I told him I had called Charley Ross to say hooey; Charley said forget it. President said, "Now don't let those things affect you—if they bother me, *I'll* tell you; don't give it a thought. Now take Clark—why there's not an unethical bone in that boy's body. But because he's in a financial hole and has to dig his way out by practicing law, they're saying he'll have a pipe line to the White House and all that. Nonsense."

I rose to leave; showed him some maps I had along of South America, India, etc., and reminded him of my projected trip. Looked pleased. "When you come back, be sure to come in; tell me all about it." Walked to door with me: "Come in any time. And about that trip—maybe when you come back we can set up some kind of world-wide TVA."

Yest., Fri., a big day.

1. The Pres. confirmed, and therefore "declassified," the existence of a problem or matter to be decided, i.e., H or super bomb. This was in his afternoon press conf., on being asked for comment on Baruch's position urging that we go ahead. This is a major event, and a large step in the effort we've made to keep the Steamroller from rushing this through without adequate thot.

2. Urey got off a speech that is the E. O. Lawrence–Strauss line: if we don't get this super first, we are sunk, the U.S. would surrender without a struggle—in other words, overemphasis on a gadget-concept of life. Will stir up the animals. This means that a public discussion is inevitable.

3. On the personal front:

Gene Black, pres. of the World Bank, asked me if I'd be at all interested in working for the Chase Bank, of which he used to be senior V.P.—as an officer concerned with atomic energy—as other former AEC people are being hired by utilities, etc. I said I might do some

† The former Secretary of State had been making public attacks on the President's programs.

consultation on that, but no full-time job. But what about going to S. America for them and others? Went into this.

JANUARY 29, 1950
AT HOME

Closing his broadcast Fri. night, Ed Murrow spoke of the H-bomb issue and then said, in effect: Thank goodness this is something you and I don't have to spend our weekend wrestling with.

Well, I am wrestling, and have been. It is tough and wearing. Have a feeling it is coming to a showdown, at long last. The air is full of statements—Connally, Urey, Baruch, Bridges, etc.

No sense brooding about it, and I really don't. What I'd like to do is be effective, in getting as much by way of a commitment that will enable us to see that gadgets won't give us security alone; and if I don't exploit this point now [before the decision to go ahead is made], there may not be another chance as good, from here on.

*On the morning of January 31, 1950, was held the final meeting of the special National Security Council Committee appointed by President Truman to advise him on the H-bomb issue. That afternoon I dictated a memorandum of that meeting, which at that time was classified as secret. The memorandum is reproduced here, after having been formally declassified by the AEC on February 17, 1964, at my request.*

*The noon meeting between President Truman and the NSC committee is recorded in the regular Journal entry which follows the memorandum.*

JANUARY 31, 1950

*Meeting of the members of the Special Committee of the National Security Council on the Super Bomb, 10:15 A.M., Room 216, Old State Building.*
*Present: Secretary Acheson, Secretary Johnson, Undersecretary Early, Mr. Lilienthal, Dr. Smyth, Gen. Burns, Mr. LeBaron, Mr. Fisher, Mr. Arneson, Adm. Souers and Mr. Lay.*

Secretary Acheson opened the meeting. He stated that the Committee had had one meeting, that there had been a certain amount of staff work, papers prepared and discussions by the members of the Committee; that it appeared to him that the proper procedure was for the members of the Committee to agree upon a recommendation, to be followed by a paper written by staff, after staff knew what members of the Committee were prepared to recommend. Secretary Acheson then said he had before him a paper which he said summarized the background. He said that it was not necessary to read the paper if the members of the Committee did not particularly desire this, that it would suffice to read the conclusions reached in the paper. He thereupon read the following:

In the light of the foregoing considerations, the following recommendations are made:

(a) That the President direct the Atomic Energy Commission to proceed to determine the technical feasibility of a thermonuclear weapon, the scale and rate of effort to be determined jointly by the Atomic Energy Commission and the Department of Defense; and that the necessary ordnance developments and carrier program be undertaken concurrently;

(b) That the President defer decision pending the reexamination referred to in (c) as to whether thermonuclear weapons should be produced beyond the number required for a test of feasibility;

(c) That the President direct the Secretary of State and the Secretary of Defense to undertake a reexamination of our objectives in peace and war and of the effect of these objectives on our strategic plans, in the light of the probable fission bomb capability and possible thermonuclear bomb capability of the Soviet Union.

(d) That the President indicate publicly the intention of this Government to continue work to determine the feasibility of a thermonuclear weapon, and that no further official information on it be made public without the approval of the President.

Secretary Acheson then handed out a proposed statement which the President might make in conformity with Paragraph (d) of the recommendations. The proposed statement is as follows:

There has been much public discussion about a project for testing the possibility of a so-called hydrogen or super bomb. The democratic process requires that the people of this country be informed in an orderly manner of decisions which are being made which affect their security.

It is part of my responsibility as Commander-in-Chief of the armed forces to see to it that our country is able to defend itself against any possible aggressor. Accordingly, the Atomic Energy Commission has been directed to continue with the development of all forms of atomic weapons. This work includes a project looking toward a test of the feasibility of the hydrogen bomb. Like all other work in the field of atomic weapons it is being and will be carried forward on a basis consistent with the over-all objectives of our preparedness program.

It is important that this project be viewed in its proper perspective. No preparedness program can rely on any single weapon. This is all the more true of a weapon which, given the agreement of others to effective international control, we propose be banished from national armaments. Furthermore, no preparedness program, no matter how effective, can do more than provide the shield behind which we persevere in our struggle to foster the idea and the reality of individual freedom and human dignity. Our sense of dedication must be directed to the pursuit of an honorable course and to the strengthening of the free world, for there is no short cut or easy way to security or to international peace and justice.

Secretary Johnson then commented on Secretary Acheson's proposal. He said that the Defense Establishment was in agreement with the recommendations; they had two suggestions to offer. One was that Recommendation (b) be eliminated. Recommendation (b) reads:

That the President defer decision pending the reexamination referred to in (c) as to whether thermonuclear weapons should be produced beyond the number required for a test of feasibility.

Secretary Johnson also submitted an alternative draft of statement for the President to make. It is much briefer than the one proposed by Secretary Acheson; a copy was not supplied to me but it was read aloud.

Secretary Acheson said we appeared to be in agreement; should we not see if we could compose the differences between the two proposed public statements.

Mr. Early said he recommended that the statement be made by the President in the form of a hand-out by Charles Ross rather than at a press conference. Secretary Johnson agreed, saying that the thing to do was to play it down, make it just one of those things. Mr. Early further said that the last paragraph of the State Department version seemed better left off. Secretary Johnson thought the first paragraph better be omitted and that we should add something from the statement he recommended about continuing this development until international agreement was reached.

I urged that a sentence be added strengthening the idea that it was not only international agreement that was involved, but a reexamination of our whole position, so I wrote out the following: "We shall also continue to examine all those factors that affect our program for peace and this country's security." The words I prepared were accepted.

I also suggested that the statement say that the President's direction related to *continuing* work, rather than give the impression of suddenly beginning something wholly new. I proposed amending the sentence as it originally read in the State Department draft from: "Accordingly, the Atomic Energy Commission has been directed to continue with the development of all forms of atomic weapons. This work includes a project looking toward a test of the feasibility of the hydrogen bomb." to "Accordingly, I have directed the Atomic Energy Commission to continue its work on all forms of atomic weapons, including the hydrogen bomb." This was accepted.

In its approved form the recommended statement by the President read as follows:

> It is part of my responsibility as Commander-in-Chief of the armed forces to see to it that our country is able to defend itself against any possible aggressor. Accordingly, I have directed the Atomic Energy Commission to continue its work on all forms of atomic weapons, including the so-called hydrogen or super-bomb. Like all other work in the field of atomic weapons, it is being and will be carried forward on a basis consistent with the over-all objectives of our program for peace and security.
>
> This we shall continue to do until a satisfactory plan for international control of atomic energy is achieved. We shall also continue to examine all those factors that affect our program for peace and this country's security.*

At this point I asked an opportunity to express my views, which was afforded me.

I began by stating that I was under no illusions about the limited value or effect of advice to the President from me, when it conflicted with a recommendation agreed to by both the Secretaries of State and Defense. Nevertheless, my reservations about the course recommended, in some important respects, were so great that I felt it necessary to refer to them very briefly. Following is my recollection of my remarks.

For three years, since the beginning of the Commission, I had made efforts to have the Commission function in the spirit and the letter of a law providing for civilian control of atomic weapon development. The statute provides that the President annually should determine the rate and number and kind of weapons produced. Annually the Commission and the Secretary of Defense transmitted jointly to the President a memorandum on this subject which the President approved, and which thereupon became the Commission's directive. At no time was the Commission supplied with any of the information or views of the Military Establishment upon which the Military recommendations had been based. Therefore the Commission at no time examined into the underlying assumptions and the policies and plans of the Military Estab-

* The President did issue this statement publicly.

lishment in respect to the necessity for or the adequacy of the number of weapons provided for and the rate of their production. I did not think this represented a serious issue, except in the abstract, up to the time of the expansion program proposal of last spring. The reasons this is so is that saying that we needed everything that could come out of the spigot was so obviously right that no examination of assumptions was required.

When the expansion program came along last spring and summer a different situation appeared. The President himself directed that the assumptions underlying this proposal be examined into by a special committee of the National Security Council, consisting of the same members as of this committee.

But this move to examine into the military assumptions and policies did not succeed. I said the reasons why it didn't succeed were not particularly relevant at this juncture.

The proposal for accelerated research and development toward a thermonuclear weapon, however, presented a clear case where the underlying assumptions, policies and plans of the Military Establishment to provide for our defense needed to be examined independently if there was to be substance to the principle of civilian control of atomic weapons by the Commission. If a military conclusion could not be examined into and was not examined into independently by the Secretary of State, the Atomic Energy Commission, and of course by the President, but was regarded as the whole answer to the ultimate question, then this definitely removes any notion of civilian participation in a fundamental policy question.

A beginning of an examination of military assumptions, policies and plans for the security of the country by members of this Committee, and by staff has been made in the past weeks. I stated as my opinion that this represented substantial progress. I stated that the recognition that the Secretary of State as well as the Secretary of Defense had a right and a duty to examine into these assumptions and see if they furthered our over-all national purposes was an important outcome of this whole consideration of the super bomb.

Accordingly, I thought Recommendation (c) was an important element in this whole matter; namely, a real inquiry into the basic question: what is the best way to further the common defense and security, to which questions as to our atomic bomb programs and the plans for their use, and the thermonuclear development are subsequent.

I said moral questions, questions of the utter frightfulness of this weapon, questions of again seeking international control—all are relevant but none seem to me the central questions.

A principal misgiving and grave reservation about the wisdom of the recommendation to proceed forthwith with the thermonuclear research at an accelerated pace, and proceed prior to this all-important reexamination of our present course was as follows: that I felt that such a direction by the President, prior to that reexamination and perhaps re-setting of the course would be highly prejudicial to the examination itself.

I recognized that the atmosphere of excitement resulting from a further delay of a decision of the President would not be the best atmosphere in which to function. I was, however, impressed, in my own mind, with the counter consideration: that the atmosphere resulting from the decision to go ahead would produce at least equally unfavorable conditions under which to conduct the examination and would probably make a new approach to the atomic weapons race impossible. The injury to vital concerns affecting our security and our position in the world and to the likelihood of a searching objective reexamination, outweighed in my mind the troubles inherent in the course of taking a new look first.

The central question seems to me not whether we should build the super bomb or not build it. Rather we should first face up to weaknesses in our present national position and not threaten by a decision now what might be the last chance to adopt a less certain course of danger. The decision to proceed before exploring those weaknesses and see what we could do about them might well mean we would not later be able to face up to them, or we just would not face up to them, or facing up to them would come too late. I admitted that the weaknesses I saw in our present course might not be confirmed by such a hard new look, or might be even worse than I feared. But unless we faced up to them as a principal problem, they would plague our future Secretaries of State and Secretaries of Defense, Chiefs of Staff, and Presidents and bear them down with perhaps overwhelming problems; whereas if perhaps faced up to now they were not unmanageable.

The decision recommended here is to proceed now to "augment to the greatest extent possible the effort devoted to (super-bomb) research" and to proceed with a test in 1952 as a target, that is a test "at the fastest practicable rate." The disadvantages of this course that I see are of several characters. First the *act* of directing that this proceed can not be minimized by mere statements such as we recommended to the President. It is too great an act for that. It is more eloquent and meaningful than any words that accompany it, or any speech saying it means this or that.

The act, I feared, would be widely regarded as a confirmation in the clearest possible terms of our present chief and almost sole reliance upon this kind of armament against the Russians.

It seemed to me that the present course of having, as General Bradley indicated, virtually nothing else but the atomic bomb that we could use for the defense of Europe today, or in the near future, is clearly a weakness; we would hide from ourselves the existence of that weakness by magnifying and redoubling and multiplying our efforts along the same course, a course that seems to me highly doubtful of value today.

I stated that in my opinion we are today relying on an asset that is readily depreciating for us, i.e., weapons of mass destruction. The President's decision would tend to confuse and, unwittingly, hide that fact and make it more difficult to find some other course.

The act of going ahead would tend to provide a false and dangerous assurance to the American people that when we get this new gadget "the balance will be ours" as against the Russians.

I referred also to comments of leading members of the Congress during the past week or so. These comments include those of the Chairman of the Committee on Foreign Relations of the Senate and of the Minority Leader Senator Wherry. They show that assumptions will be drawn from proceeding with this development which I do not believe are justified, and I fear will make more difficult a facing up to the wasting and dwindling value to this country of weapons of mass destruction as the principal basis of the defense of this country and of Europe.

I said I was concerned that the act of going ahead, far from strengthening our defense or atomic program, would magnify its weaker aspects. These aspects include such matters as (1) the value of A-bombs since [the Soviet atomic test of] September 23 to deter or to prevent Russia over-running our European allies; (2) the impact of the decision to proceed on the feeling of the inevitability of war, and therefore weakening the basis of our present course, which is there will be no war soon.

At this point I interpolated that the present assumption of this Government is clearly that there will be no war with the Russians in the immediate future, that is to say in the matter of two or three years. If this is not a sound assumption, if the assumption is that war is likely in the next two or three years then the question of proceeding with the H-bomb is an easy one; but more important than that we should be getting ready for war, whereas at the present time we are *not* getting ready for war. I said we ought on that assumption to send my son back into the service; we should be really taxing ourselves; we should stop the making of pleasure automobiles, etc. etc.

But this is not the assumption. The assumption is that we are not going to have a war with the Russians in the next few years. Therefore why can we not spend a few months for an intensive and realistic re-examination of the worsening of our position as the result of our preoccupation with atomic weapons. It seemed to me that this was a far wiser course than to make a decision, prejudicing the reexamination and, I feared, making it increasingly difficult if not impossible to face the realities, or to take another course that might save the world from the fury of the atomic arms race and the tension between the USA and USSR.

It seems to me that unless the assumption is an early war we have the time to realign our policies and ought to do nothing to make that realignment more difficult or perhaps (as I believe) well-nigh impossible.

I said there were other weaknesses in our present course which I feared the decision at this time might make harder to correct. Thus, we take a position as a nation that atomic weapons should and must be eliminated. But our military leaders are depending almost entirely upon atomic weapons in the event of war. This kind of contradictory position is not merely a defect of reasoning, a faulty argument. It is a positive danger to continue both those courses at the same time. To go ahead on a new cycle of atomic weapons, the super, might well make it more difficult for that defect to be faced and something done about it.

The net of my reservation about this recommendation therefore was this: the decision to proceed forthwith, with nothing more, may be, and I fear will be to miss an opportunity to reexamine and realign our policy, a better opportunity than may ever appear again to better our security and promote something better than a headlong rush to a war of mass destruction weapons.

Following my statement, Secretary Acheson said that he found little in what I said with which he would disagree. He said further, however, that it still did not offer an alternative course that appealed to him, that he felt that the pressure for a decision was so great, that the discussion and feeling in the Congress had reached such a point that to defer the decision to this purpose was an alternative that he could not recommend. Secretary Johnson apparently agreed. We must protect the President, he said.

We then proceeded to a discussion of the recommendations themselves. Dr. Smyth suggested to me that Paragraph (b) which the Secretary of Defense urged be left out, should be retained. His point was that (b) left in tended to justify and strengthen the idea of a reexamination. Secretary Johnson said that he felt (b) was not needed and that he had other objections (which he did not explain) to it. It was stricken out.

Paragraph (c) directing the reexamination of objectives was then discussed. It was pointed out that in the paper presented by Secretary Acheson the Chairman of the Atomic Energy Commission was omitted from the group [to reexamine U.S. policy]. The reasons for this, the Secretary of State stated, were several. He said there was first of all the obvious difficulty of working with a five-man Commission in a matter of this kind. The second point was that to have the Commission on the same level as the head of a Department might seem inappropriate. Third, that the Commission's function was actually related to the technical aspects rather than the issues that were the subject matter of this direction. Admiral Souers pointed out that this reexamination would involve discussion of strategic war plans, and the whole field of our world relations. Secretary Acheson added that our relations with the Russians were now in a worsening condition.

The inference I drew from this discussion was that this participation in basic policy examination was regarded as rather remote from the functions of the Commission as conceived by the other members of the Committee. Secretary Acheson asked my opinion about the omission of the Commission. I said that I would defer to Dr. Smyth's opinion on this since I was practically out of office, and it was a matter of direct concern for my colleagues and my successor. With this qualification I stated that I was in agreement that the five-man Commission point was a good one; that the problems of the Chairman of the Commission or the representative of the Commission serving as a co-equal with individuals who are the heads of their departments and could speak for them was a real and substantial difficulty.

Secretary Acheson said there was the further difficulty that under the law and the Commission's practice the Joint Committee on Atomic Energy was kept informed by the Commission on almost a day-to-day basis; that the inclusion of the Commission in this study would doubtless require that the current investigation into this matter be supplied to the Joint Committee while the discussions were tentative and even though they included matters of the utmost secrecy; this was a major objection.

I said that I could not say this was not a valid point. Dr. Smyth said he was inclined to agree that this was a real point; that he thought the five-man Commission point could be worked out but that the Joint Committee problem was a real one in this kind of a situation. Admiral Souers concurred about this Joint Committee phase of the matter. Secretary Acheson said further, however, that it would be his purpose and intention to consult on technical matters with a technically qualified member of the Commission, presumably Dr. Smyth. Furthermore, he said that specifically the General Advisory Committee to the Commission or members of that Committee would certainly be consulted, particularly since they had taken a strong and critical view about our present policies in this whole matter.

Secretary Johnson then recommended that we go to the White

House at once and get a decision. He said he already had an appointment at 12:30 and we could use that. He said the heat was on in the Congress and every hour counted in getting this matter disposed of.

\* \* \*

(MEMORANDUM OF MEETING WITH THE PRESIDENT, OF THE SPECIAL COMMITTEE OF NATIONAL SECURITY COUNCIL ON THE SUPER BOMB. PRESENT WERE SECRETARIES ACHESON AND JOHNSON; MR. LILIENTHAL; ADM. SOUERS; AND MR. LAY, ASSISTANT EXECUTIVE SECRETARY.)

The three members of the committee, with Admiral Souers and Mr. Lay, entered the President's office at about 12:35. We left about seven minutes later. Secretary Acheson stated that an agreement had been reached on a recommendation to him on the super bomb matter and handed him a sheet of paper containing these recommendations. Sec. Acheson stated that Chairman Lilienthal also had some comments he wished to make.

The President, turning to me, said that he had always believed that we should never use these weapons and that our whole purpose was peace; that he didn't believe we would ever use them but we had to go on and make them because of the way the Russians were behaving; we had no other course.

I said that I appreciated the opportunity to state briefly the grave reservations I had to the course recommended. I said that I didn't overrate at all the value of my judgment in the face of agreement by the Sec. of State and the Sec. of Defense, but try as I could I could not honestly avoid stating that I thought this course not the wisest one and that another course was open. I thought the decision the President would make, however carefully worded, however casually issued, would be construed throughout the country as confirming our present course in respect to how the country could best be defended; that it magnified some of the weaknesses that were growing greater every month, namely, our chief reliance upon atomic weapons in the defense of this country and Europe. The President interrupted to say we could have had all this re-examination quietly if Senator Ed Johnson hadn't made that unfortunate remark about the super bomb; since that time there has been so much talk in the Congress and everywhere and people are so excited he really hasn't any alternative but to go ahead and that was what he was going to do.

I said there were one or two additional points concerning my grave reservations about this course, but since I was an adviser only, to insist upon making the points would be a discourtesy.

While putting his signature on the statement for the press and on the recommendations, the President said that he recalled another meeting that he had had with the National Security Council concerning Greece a long time ago; that at that time everybody predicted the end of the world if we went ahead, but we did go ahead and the world didn't come to an end. He felt this would be the same case here.

Except for some cordial words of a personal nature to me about my departure on February 15, this was the substance, as I recall it, of this meeting.

(AT HOME)

No denying, this is a night of heartache. But there is some personal satisfaction, where there is nothing but pain for the decision made today. For I found my manhood sufficient for one of the hardest tests I've ever had: to "stand up in meeting" and say "No" to a steamroller, knowing it would be so easy to equivocate, or to acquiesce silently, be a good sport, etc. Whether time proves me right and the Pres.'s two Secretaries, and the Hill boys, and the E. O. Lawrences wrong, I suppose no one will ever know; mostly things become too blurred with the passing of events to say, with a surety. But I played the part better than I feared I might, for it was a hard one.

If I had anything but the most unbounded admiration for Dean Acheson, and compassion for his terrible load, or less than the deepest loyalty and fealty for the President, it wouldn't have been so hard. But Dean was so distressed that I would raise such doubts (we both share them, he, I think, at least as greatly as I) that might confuse the Pres. without holding out a clear or workable alternative (as he thought), and the Pres. was so clearly set on what he was going to do before we set foot inside the door, that I had a terrible temptation, of course. But when the two Secs. had agreed, and they were about to pass on to when do we see the Pres., what should he say in public, it was as plain as anything has ever been that if I went out of that room without making my point and making it strong, I'd been crumpled inside the rest of my life. So at the point it was easy. What I said was as well said as anything I've done in a long time, based on a few notes of analysis made this morning in the few minutes before the meeting.

Now to be a good sport about it all—this won't be easy.

I carried the news in to the GAC. It was like a funeral party— especially when I said we were all gagged. Should they resign? I said definitely not, on the contrary. This would be very bad. Though before long a number of them may, just because they feel their standing is impaired.

It was a hard experience, and my views didn't prevail. I hope I was wrong, and that somehow I'll be proved wrong. We have to leave many things to God; this one He will have to get us out of, if we are to get out. As I said in comment on Dr. Urey's silly speech about surrendering if an ultimatum backed by super bombs is given us: it isn't so important how long one lives; what is important is that while he lives he lives as a man.

FEBRUARY 2, 1950
AT HOME

The roof fell in today, you might say. After the gay and happy time, the going-away party given me by the employees last night, this was quite a contrast. The news, I learned at about seven when I left the office, will be out when the man§ is arraigned in London tomorrow at about twelve our time. Then, as the President is reported to have said to Admiral Souers, tie on your hat.

It took place during the war project; but he had been here since, which drags us in. It is a world catastrophe, and a sad day for the human race.

It seems to me I have drawn about my fair share of these crises and alarms.

Saw the President (on a last-minute request) at about 3 P.M. Asked him to name an Acting Chairman soon, so I can be freer to finish up. Said he would in few days, but didn't say whether it'd be Pike. May well be Dean. (Strauss insists he's sending in his letter of resignation tomorrow.)

Talked at length before I could get to this, about how hopeful he and Acheson were they'd find something to work out a way with the Russians—but he didn't sound convincing. He had some ideas, the Pres. said; might work. Then he explained how hard they were to deal with, with long recital about how wives (Russian women) of our Embassy employees disappeared when we insisted they be allowed to come out.

Pres. referred to my trip—said, "Before you go I want to talk to you, have some ideas."

Tomorrow will be a hard one, as has today.

FEBRUARY 3, 1950
AT HOME

Last night, when I left the office about seven, this was clear: the British were going to arraign Fuchs at Bow Street at what would be twelve o'clock noon our time, today. We checked this with State (Arneson) and later with Souers. When I said that would be six o'clock, a

§ Klaus Fuchs.

funny time, nevertheless that was it. So the boys set out to write a statement to be used at noon today, and I went on home. Sleep wasn't too easy: the vision of "the top blowing off things," antagonism increased between U.S. and Britain, witch-hunts, anti-scientist orgies, etc.

I got to the office at about 9, having set a Comm. meeting for 9:15, walked in my office to find an agitated bunch; the word was on the radio, the British had announced it at twelve o'clock *their* time . . . six o'clock ours. I was as calm as I can remember being; insisted we put into the statement the strongest language about what Fuchs knew and was part of: "a wide area of the most vital weapons information," including Fuchs' attendance at a 1947 declassification conference with the British.

The Joint Committee had set a meeting for 10:30, with a good attendance, much picture-taking. When called on, I told the story in terms of what he [Fuchs] knew, emphasized this was no periphery guy, or a courier, or a dumb spy, but a scientist who knew most of the weapons stuff because he had helped work out many of the most difficult of the problems. I poured it on: there wasn't a bright light in the whole picture. This had a good, sobering effect. They were most courteous (my resignation perhaps), asked what advice I had. I said, "This is bad; but let's not panic the country; keep your shirt on, don't wallow in it. And let's hope this won't so disturb the Los Alamos outfit, or investigations so harass everyone that the new super program is held up."

FEBRUARY 14, 1950

Farewell day: with the President, with the press corps at the White House, and then (shades of solemnity) threw a big and successful party to the press, radio, and newsreel people in my office. Tomorrow is the last.

Meeting with the President was highlighted by his warmth and evidence of friendliness, and by his telling me he had named Pike Acting Chairman. This relieved me a lot, for otherwise it would have been a blow to Pike, and to me, and it makes the transition much easier and happier.

I went to see the President to make sure he didn't take any stock in stories that I was going out to "blast" him, his atomic policies, lead a crusade against the H-bomb, etc., etc. I think he was fully persuaded that I do want to help, not pick at him, and that my theme of Atoms for Peace is just what the country needs. I didn't mention *Collier's*— just that I would lecture and write.

It was one of the happiest sessions I've ever had with him, and my admiration and wonder at his relaxed way of looking at things, and his obvious good health (he looked tip-top today, his eye clear, lost a bit of weight he didn't need) reached a new high.

We talked about everything: about my forthcoming trip to Brazil, for example. I said I would go to see the Par-an'-a River. He said, "I've been callin' it Par'ana—that's probably wrong, but anyway." Now can you imagine a ruler any place else in the world talking like that? Of course, my pronunciation is purely extempore—but such a sweet kind of humility just bowls me over.

He said he had seen me on television—Mrs. Roosevelt's show yesterday◖—"You were good, too," he said, "just as natural as could be." Thought the show was interesting; good thing, too. "Good thing to have these things talked about." (This relieved me a lot.) I said Mrs. R. asked me and I am a pushover for her; when she asks me to do anything, I do it, no matter what it is. "I feel the same way about her," he said. "When I was in real trouble, before the election, she said she wanted me to know she would do anything she could to help; said she couldn't do anything with her three boys (they were sitting there at the phone while she talked). She made a recording in Paris and had it played here and it helped. I never forget when someone helps out when you need it badly. She told me about the television show, and I said, fine, go ahead.

"About these scientists," he said, "such as those on the show, we need men with great intellects, need their ideas. But we need to balance them with other kinds of people, too." No anti-intellectualism at all.

Said he now had two vacancies, with Strauss resigning. He said, sorry he wanted to leave now, hoped he'd stay till spring, need fellows who have different kinds of views, need them so you get all kinds of angles. "In my Cabinet, have Brannan, New Dealer, and Snyder, have Sawyer and Acheson. But when the decision is made, then I don't want anyone cutting my throat."

As I left the President's office, I made a strong statement to newsmen: not going out blasting the Pres., but try be helpful, thought his policy showed great leadership.

◖A premiere of her weekly TV program. Atomic energy—and the H-bomb—were discussed.

# APPENDIX A

*The Conference on Atomic Energy Control
at the University of Chicago
September 20–21, 1945*

This conference was held just a few weeks after the first atomic bombs were dropped at Hiroshima and Nagasaki. Its sponsor, the University of Chicago, had a historic role in the development of atomic energy: it was at Chicago in 1942 that the first atomic chain reaction was achieved, and University scientists had taken an important part in the wartime bomb project.

With the war's end, Chicago became the rallying point for the atomic scientists, who began campaigning for effective international atomic energy control and for a broad public understanding and discussion of the issues involved. In this, they were at odds with the Army, which continued to maintain severe wartime security restrictions.

Most of the fifty or so participants in this September conference were university professors. Many were scientists, including some—like James Franck and Leo Szilard—who had worked on various aspects of the bomb project.

These notes on the discussions, transcribed from my shorthand made at the time (or, in the case of my comments, that same day), are terse summaries of major points; therefore they do not do full justice to the speakers. It is remarkable, however, to see the extent to which the issues raised then—in 1945—have remained lively, unresolved, and basic to American policy throughout some two decades of our history.

## THE ATOMIC BOMB

THURSDAY A.M. (SEPTEMBER 20)

JACOB VINER (*economist, University of Chicago*): Atomic bomb cheapest way of killing human beings.

With two giants (Russia and United States) world government impossible.

Degree of peace we have had in the past two or three centuries has been due to uncertainty as to who was your natural enemy against which to fight a preventive war. Now no ambiguity as to target, where there are only two giants. Already having psychological effects in this country.

Atomic bomb warfare more largely a war of nerves; "only safe place to be will be in Army." Psychological warfare begins when two countries have atomic bombs.

Denies that surprise is important, assuming aggressor and victim both have atomic bomb.

Deterrent effect of atomic bomb brings back the importance of the small country, brings it back, though by a different course, to the position it occupied in eighteenth century. They can make their conquest cost too much.

Atomic bomb not a threat to *biological* survival. Important factor in political survival, etc.

Believes atomic bomb will be peacemaking in effect; deterrent effect—the cost when it is used against you.

EDWARD M. EARLE (*School of Economics and Politics, Institute for Advanced Studies, Princeton*): Must remember atomic bomb is *addition to* other weapons.

VINER: Notion that wars are never fought unless nation feels it can win is contrary to history. Sometimes psychological factors require you to take the step though you know it is fatal. Yugoslavia against Germany in this war; Finland against Russia.

Small countries now have improved their position, relatively, to do damage—not to win wars.

Atomic bomb reduces the possibility of two giants, and in that sense is a contribution to peace, because a number of countries become factors, and not Russia and United States alone.

Will the very fact that some small country begins to produce atomic bombs be enough to cause one of the large countries to act to prevent them from proceeding? Taking Belgium—who will annihilate Belgium if she should start producing atomic bombs? Viner says, of this time, we would not act on the basis of that alone.

*Disposition of uranium:* Only large rich deposits now known are in northern Canada and Belgian Congo, though of course present in sea water, etc. Others may be discovered and probably will be.

EARLE: Germany is only great power that is now invulnerable to atomic bomb because all her major cities are flattened. She will rebuild her cities with that in mind. She will sell her services to some new coalition—with Russia, for example. Not just two great powers: can't exclude idea of development of new coalitions.

THEODORE SCHULTZ (*agricultural economist, University of Chicago*): We are much more insecure than ever before; we are beginning to take on the characteristics of a nation that feels insecure. Russians' behavior will be more that of a secure people (presumably because of great land mass and the fact that they will have such bombs in a few years).

WILLIAM FOX (*research associate, Institute of International Study, Yale*): How long will *peacetime* uses now known shorten the time it would take to go into *bomb* production? Shorten time by six months to one year.

JAMES FRANCK (*physical chemist, University of Chicago*): It would be possible to agree on an international limitation on weapons, but that would still make feasible to produce radioactive material for non-military uses now known, such as "tracers" in industry.

ROBERT HUTCHINS (*Chancellor, University of Chicago*): Asks if analogy of easy conversion of German peacetime industry to war not applicable. Answer not clear except that training of personnel and knowledge in the field important factors, which might shorten time schedule to get into bomb production in the order of a year.

(While Fox speaks of United Nations organization—"an organization upon which the hopes of the world have been pinned"—[Col. Charles A.] Lindbergh intensely examines his pencil and half-smiles; Hutchins looks sardonically amused. These two very friendly, in recesses. Don't know what the background is. Hutchins is an extraordinarily handsome man in his early middle age; heavier, less sharp, more repose. That constant look of sardonic amusement puzzles me.)

KURT RIEZLER (*philosopher, New School*): Re *mutual inspection* as proposed by Edward Shils (sociologist, University of Chicago). A really efficient system of inspection would be so contrary to the traditions of the Russians and their philosophy of government that they would consider such a proposal as an attack on their whole system of government and way of life. (A sophisticated, shrewd, and rather disillusioned European face.) He urges, in alternative, an ultimate proposal to be made by us that United Nations Charter be amended to provide that no nation may use atomic bombs without the unanimous approval of the United Nations—i.e., a veto by any *one* great nation would make it illegal.

HUTCHINS (to Shils): If inspection scheme would require change in system of government of Russia, and if they can produce the atomic bomb in three years anyway, Riezler's point seems well taken.

Russians' objection would be based on fundamental considerations: their ideology (referring to fact that Government does not permit disclosure —i.e., secrecy is a *state* policy). A dictatorship is inconsistent with free talk.

FRANCK: Would not this inspection scheme encounter difficulties in this country—how does General Electric know, when government inspectors for Russia, etc., poke and nose around, they are not looking for other things? Thinks it impossible anyway—number of people required, etc. True that you cannot have mutual trust without mutual inspection; but there should be a kind of mutual inspection that is feasible.

IRVING LANGMUIR (*chemist, inventor, General Electric*): We only have two or three years of being ahead. The inspection proposition might be developed in, say, 15 years. But we cannot persuade the other countries to this idea in the time we have. We must press for a lesser step.

Inspection of specified uranium mines ignores possibility of other fields not yet known—low-grade ores may be very plentiful.

First step is improving relations with Russians by every means and all means. Try to reach situation where, *if* Russia has the atomic bomb, that neither nation will use them—at least for 15 or 20 years while we are developing a world government.

We must not strive now for ultimate security. During the next two years allay suspicion on the part of Russia. When those two years are up, we will have one important demonstration: we *did not use* our atomic bombs when we knew we had them and she did not.

HUTCHINS: If we could get this inspection agreement, we wouldn't need it.

RIEZLER: One of the worst parts of such a scheme is that the very process of negotiation of such an agreement itself breeds suspicions, as it goes along; and that is very dangerous. Stalin won't say "No"; he will propose a defective system of inspection which we will reject because we don't trust him. That is very dangerous.

(Curious to note as we go along how much prestige I have acquired among these scientists because I have been through a successful fight with political forces, which seems a miracle of accomplishment because it is so far out of the experience of these men. Seems far more important than it is, for that reason.)

OSWALD VEBLEN (*mathematician, Institute for Advanced Studies, Princeton*): The United States has not made as great a contribution to the atomic bomb as Denmark nor probably as Great Britain, depending upon how much importance you place on the theoretic side.

Bear in mind that fission is only one of the ways to convert matter into energy. (This seemed very important to me; wish he had said more.)

The realistic approach is the quixotic one.

LILIENTHAL: I note that all these proposals address themselves to the particular kind of hell that the scientists have brewed in the atomic bomb, by fission of the atom. Would it not be important to make plain to the American people—if such is the fact—that you fellows have other things cooking, not related to atomic explosions, that may be just as bad or worse? Why work ourselves blue in the face to develop a method of, say, inspecting uranium mines by an international commission when science has other, equally destructive things on foot that do not involve either uranium or even the atom?

We are, I rather assume, going to have a whole series of crises as a result of increasing scientific knowledge that is adaptable to blowing the hell out of the world. If we had a series of Smyth reports on these, possibly people would see that this is an issue that can't be easily sidestepped by such simple schemes as "mutual inspection" and limited agreements not to develop a *particular* kind of destructive force.

DAVID HILL (*physicist, University of Chicago*): I agree with that position. The fact is that there are several such in the course of exploration, some at advanced stages.

The fact is that mankind now knows enough to control the universe and nature. In a very few years we will have enough concentrated energy so that we can destroy all vestige of life in an area 1,000 miles by 3,000, by a series of bombs.

FRANCK: *What is the secret?*

1. Design of the bomb itself. Two designs were developed in two years; hence other countries could find a solution for that. Scientists think it is not a secret.

(Even if kept secret, progress of science *not* impeded.)

2. Exact details of manufacturing processes and the nature of barriers for diffusion processes—this took some time. This is a secret that will take time for others to discover. Secret not of process but of technical materials to use.

(This has scientific interest, but if secrecy necessary can still go ahead in the development of science, especially in case of armament race.)

3. Direct chemical process used to separate plutonium from other materials. Regarded as a secret but he thinks it is not super-secret. Four or five different possible methods were developed.

(No great advantage to keep this secret.)

4. Development by industry of remote control devices for handling radioactive materials. This is technical process of great skill. If you have the blueprints, you can do it more quickly.

5. Production rates of critical materials. Regarded as super-secret. Based on assumption that danger of retaliation would be less if others do not know this fact. We (the project scientists) are not supposed even to guess. Host of other details that could be revealed, that are regarded as secrets.

(Probably should be kept secret if fear of an armament race.)

(LILIENTHAL: My point that "military security" as enforced in terms of Army standards may actually *imperil* the security of the nation, in the short *and* the long run.)

FRANCK (continued): There is good reason, if one really wants to keep a secret, to keep even the basic scientific aspects secret.

Our guess is that for another nation to make such weapons two years is the minimum if it is not revealed; six to eight years as a maximum. Say five years. In effect, these are only trade secrets.

EARLE (*civilian adviser to Air Forces*): Need a peace conference between U.S.A. and Russia; we're on our way to talk ourselves into a war with Russia. We need psychological disarmament.

Jellied gasoline just as destructive to Tokyo as atomic bomb. A-bomb just one more weapon.

LANGMUIR: Total bombardment of all B-29s over Japan less than the two atomic bombs. Atomic bomb is absolutely unique—not just like another weapon. So has different order of magnitude.

FRANCK: Reason gas was not used in this war is that it *would not have produced a decision* under the conditions of war of movement. Atomic bomb could produce a decision.

Shelters protect against ordinary bomb. Probably not useful in case of atomic bomb—probably have to be half-mile deep.

(Haven't spoken with Lindbergh; can't understand quite why he is here. His hatred of the Russians is apparently fantastic. Yesterday he said that the Russians were the modern barbarians who are "taking over our homeland.")

FRIDAY A.M.(SEPTEMBER 21)

REDFIELD (*anthropologist, and Dean of Social Sciences, University of Chicago*): Responsibility of the University did not end with the discovery of this instrument of destruction.

FRANCK (on secrecy): What is the effect of secrecy on *progress of science?*

Not in the interest of science to have one or two men, administrators with many other functions, to decide *what* should be secret.

Conclusions: There should be as little regulation as possible. If regulation necessary to a part, regulation should not be exercised from the top without consultation with the scientific people in the field. Same as to publications. Now whoever finds something new, if it falls within field of nuclear physics he cannot publish, whether necessary in interests of secrecy or not. This rule must be stopped if United States is to keep up. This would be a kind of Maginot Line of science.

Under existing Army censorship, information from one center of scientific inquiry would not be available to others. People at Chicago didn't know what scientists at other places were doing. When questions were put as between centers (Oak Ridge, Chicago, etc.), the questions were not intelligible.

Cannot teach science if you must always worry about whether what you are teaching will put you in jail. Not a single scientist feels he can work under these circumstances. Not a single scientist does not realize that in the event of armament race (which seems probable) some things must be secret.

LILIENTHAL: Toward the close of yesterday's session I said I had the impression that intelligent discussion of these grave policy issues was inhibited by the Army's general restrictions, exemplified by the Army's effort to obstruct the holding of this very meeting; and that I thought most of the efforts toward censorship of the scientists is nonsense. What has been said here since more than confirms that impression.

You must realize that we are caught in a circle.

This is the circle:

First: Unless the people are properly informed of the facts, the resulting public policy regarding the atomic bomb will be neither sound nor enduring.

Second: The people cannot be informed so long as the scientists are prevented from speaking out.

Third: *Whether* the scientists may speak out is a matter of public policy.

And so we are in a circle—chasing our tail.

The most illuminating statements that can be made concerning these grave issues will come from the men who have been immersed in it for two or three years, the scientists themselves. That has been here demonstrated.

We've heard about "secrecy." But that relates to rate of production of weapons and weapons material. That's *not* the issue, as I see it. These scientists are under a rule—whether legally enforceable or not is immaterial—that they will submit everything they say, before a Congressional committee, say, or elsewhere, to the "review" and "approval" of the Army. That's not "secrecy." Nothing of the kind has ever been proposed, so far as I know: that a citizen's *opinions* shall be subject to a pre-audit by the military in peacetime. What happens to the "right to talk," the denial of which in Russia was said yesterday to be a chief characteristic of a dictator nation? What happens to the spirit of the scientist?

This pre-audit over the opinions of men of high professional standing will create a paralysis, a *creeping* paralysis. First, it will be mental. Then it will be ethical, moral. And though this whole discussion here, somewhat to my amazement, has been wholly in terms of power politics, surely it is assumed that there are other forces at work in the world than the pressures and fears of nations and of force, that there are within the individual controls and disciplines and urges, those things we call moral compulsions.

I want to warn the scientists that they are, by a curious circumstance, the trustees of a great moral responsibility in this issue of whether they shall insist on the duty to speak out so the public may know.

(These extemporaneous remarks I delivered with some little feeling, created a stir, and after the meeting I got fervent approval and handshakes from a curious assortment of men, notably Barnard, president of New Jersey Bell Telephone Company; Hecht, a scientist from Columbia; and from most of the atomic project scientists.)

REDFIELD: The Army has just announced that it will seek legislation placing atomic bomb research under their control!

LEO SZILARD (*physicist, University of Chicago*): Basic belief:

1. That danger atomic bomb presents increases rapidly. Quotes Oliphant (British physicist) as saying that atomic bombs corresponding to one million and to ten million tons of TNT, and area of ten square miles destroyed, are entirely possible.

(Hiroshima's bomb 20,000 tons of TNT.)

Earth consists of crust and water and air. Can we blow this up? Two questions: (a) Is the earth, water, or air combustible? It is. If we applied an appropriate match to it, will it explode? Don't yet know the answer. (b) Can we construct a match suitable to set it off? My guess is that the answer to (b) would *take longer* than (a).

If either combustible, sooner or later we will find a match. The situation in 10, 15, 20 years will be somewhere between the ultimate solution and Hiroshima.

2. We did not stop manufacturing after Hiroshima. We don't make them to drop on Russia, but we reserve that right.

We are in an armament race.

If Russia starts making atomic bombs in two or three years—perhaps five or six years—then we have an armed peace, and it will be a durable peace.

But we will not have permanent peace at lesser cost than world government. But this cannot come without changed loyalty of people. If we can't have that, all we can have is a durable peace. Only purpose of a durable peace would be to create conditions 20–30 years from now can bring about world government. That requires shift of loyalties.

If we are *sure* to get a Third World War, the later it comes the worse for us.

Victor of next war will *make* a world government, even if that victor should be United States, having lost 25 million people dead.

Believes chance of avoiding Third World War is only 10 percent.

A 10 percent chance of adoption of any proposal to preserve peace and the world would therefore *not* be too slender. A chance to proceed upon.

LANGMUIR: Premises:

1. Within five years, more likely three, Russia can build atomic bombs and within few years after that build bombs as great as to be comparable with ours.

2. In that interval of time we will not nor should we attack Russia to *prevent* her having atomic bombs.

3. Within 2–5–7 years we will have Russia and United States substantially equal in regard to power, with the possibility that Russia may increase her power at faster rate than we can.

What can we do about it?

Both United States and Russia looking toward peace, both place culture on high plane of desirability.

We should go just as far as we can in working with Russia toward world government.

In the meantime, we must find some solution short of world government, which will take longer than the period of grace we have.

REINHOLD NIEBUHR (*Union Theological Seminary, New York*): Techniques not known—that's all the secret there is.

There is a secret that there is *no* secret.

Assume that there will be a conscious or unconscious use of advantage in dealings with Russia. This represents great danger.

Secrecy presents grave issue. This is more the Army tendency to maintain censorship; part of power politics.

Secrecy or no secrecy important question of public policy.

Control is not the primary problem. Record of history is that all efforts to outlaw weapons never successful. Possibility of evasion of inspection great; very process of inspection creates suspicion. Must subordinate control to the larger issue; to wit, world government.

But world government is not part of this period of history. See no communal basis for world government at this time.

Alternative:

1. Control of bomb.
2. Creation of world government.
3. Use of bomb; policy concerning *use* of bomb should be part of major policy in respect to dealings with Russia.

Always the question: Can we *psychologically disarm* ourselves? Tremendously difficult.

How can we relate atomic bomb policies to general policies of psychological disarmament?

VINER: Area of agreement:

1. All agreed on *urgency* of the problem. All that the atomic bomb adds to other horrible weapons in existence is urgency.

2. Secrecy:

There is a secret—perhaps a six-months' secret, but still a secret.

Will six-months' secret generate another six-months' secret—can we remain six months ahead indefinitely? This would be of great importance in dealing with Army.

Procedures:

1. World government not in the picture at present, for dealing with this problem.

World government as a concept not inherently impossible.

2. Atomic bomb may have such tremendous power for damage may lessen importance of giants' size (i.e., U.S. and U.S.S.R.).

CHARLES MERRIAM (*Political science, University of Chicago*): Haven't submitted enough with reference to *peacetime* uses.

After my denunciation of pre-censorship a number of men who worked on the bomb project came to me with stories of how insidious were the restrictions put on them. Stearns (former director of the Chicago Metallurgical Laboratory) told me a number: (a) One young fellow "had the finger put on him" because he went to a Russian ballet one evening. (b) An investigator asked one leading scientist, in investigating a particular man as to his loyalty, "Did he vote for Roosevelt?" This went too far and the man was "disciplined," so the FBI said. (c) On the stupidity as well as the arbitrariness: A number of the scientists on the project asked permission to attend the Jubilee held last June in Moscow by Russian scientists. Permission was denied to all of them who had been invited. The ground was that the Russians might "ply" them with liquor and find out something. But the Russians could see that of all the American scientists invited none in the field of *nuclear physics* attended, so they would know what was up. On the other hand, the British physicists were permitted to and did attend, including several who were working on the project and had complete knowledge of all the super-secrets! Langmuir attended only after his company (GE) put up a big fight; he reported that there was little drinking and that he was permitted to see anything he wanted through all the laboratories, and was asked no questions.

# APPENDIX B

*Excerpt from Testimony of David E. Lilienthal, February 4, 1947, at Hearing on Confirmation of the Atomic Energy Commission before the Senate Section of the Joint Committee on Atomic Energy.*

Senator McKELLAR. Mr. Lilienthal, did you, acting for the TVA, complain of the OPA price of around $37 per ton on ammonium nitrate fertilizer?

Mr. LILIENTHAL. Senator, I don't remember. I can get the file in, and we can see.

Senator McKELLAR. I think you had better see. You do not know what price, then, you got the OPA to set? I wish you would get that too, as you do not seem to carry figures in your head.

Mr. LILIENTHAL. This sort of thing was carried on by the managers of the TVA.

Senator McKELLAR. You do not carry that in your head, although you were the head of it, and you really were the TVA after Dr. A. E. Morgan left.

Mr. LILIENTHAL. Judging from my memory on these details, apparently not. But I am sure that the men who did these things were responsible men, and whatever they did I was responsible for.

. . . .

Senator McKELLAR. . . . I think it is very important what your views are on communistic doctrine, and I have no doubt the committee feels that way about your views on communistic doctrine.

What about them?

Mr. LILIENTHAL. This I do carry in my head, Senator.

Senator McKELLAR. You do not?

Mr. LILIENTHAL. This I do carry in my head. And I will do my best to make it clear.

Senator McKELLAR. Yes, sir?

Mr. LILIENTHAL. My convictions are not so much concerned with what I am against as what I am for—and that excludes a lot of things automatically.

Traditionally, democracy has been an affirmative doctrine rather than merely a negative one.

I believe in—and I conceive the Constitution of the United States to rest, as does religion, upon—the fundamental proposition of the integrity of the individual; and that all Government and all private institutions must be designed to promote and protect and defend the integrity and the dignity of the individual; that that is the essential meaning of the Constitution and the Bill of Rights, as it is essentially the meaning of religion.

Any forms of government, therefore, and any other institutions, which make men means rather than ends in themselves, which exalt the state or any other institutions above the importance of men, which place arbitrary power over men as a fundamental tenet of government, are contrary to this conception; and therefore I am deeply opposed to them.

The communistic philosophy, as well as the communistic form of government, falls within this category, for its fundamental tenet is quite to the contrary. The fundamental tenet of communism is that the state is an end in itself, and that therefore the powers which the state exercises over the individual are without any ethical standards to limit them. That I deeply disbelieve.

It is very easy simply to say one is not a Communist. And, of course, if despite my record it is necessary for me to state this very affirmatively, then this is a great disappointment to me. It is very easy to talk about being against communism. It is equally important to believe those things which provide a satisfactory and effective alternative. Democracy is that satisfying affirmative alternative.

And its hope in the world is that it is an affirmative belief, rather than simply a belief against something else, and nothing more.

One of the tenets of democracy that grow out of this central core of a belief that the individual comes first, that all men are the children of God and their personalities are therefore sacred, is a deep belief in civil liberties and their protection; and a repugnance to anyone who would steal from a human being that which is most precious to him, his good name, by imputing things to him, by innuendo, or by insinuation.

And it is especially an unhappy circumstance that occasionally that is done in the name of democracy.

This I think is something that can tear our country apart and destroy it—if we carry it further.

I deeply believe in the capacity of democracy to surmount any trials that may lie ahead provided only we practice it in our daily lives.

And among the things that we must practice is this: that while we seek fervently to ferret out the subversive and anti-democratic forces in the country, we do not at the same time, by hysteria, by resort to innuendo and sneers and other unfortunate tactics, besmirch the very cause that we believe in, and cause a separation among our people, cause one group and one individual to hate another, based upon mere attacks, mere unsubstantiated attacks upon their loyalty.

I want also to add that part of my conviction is based upon my training as an Anglo-American common lawyer. It is the very basis and the great heritage of the English people to this country, which we have maintained, that the strictest rules of credibility of witnesses and of the avoidance of hearsay and gossip shall be excluded in courts of justice.

And that, too, is an essential of our democracy.

And whether by administrative agencies acting arbitrarily against business organizations, or whether by investigating activities of the legislative branches, whenever those principles fail, those principles of the protection of an individual and his good name against besmirchment by gossip, hearsay, and the statements of witnesses who are not subject to cross-examination: then, too, we have failed in carrying forward our ideals in respect to democracy.

This I deeply believe.

# INDEX

L. means David E. Lilienthal

Acheson, David, 449, 469

Acheson, Dean G., 10, 14, 25, 30, 31, 33, 39, 41, 58, 68, 74, 84, 97, 101, 115, 116, 120, 123, 127, 129, 132, 143, 145, 153, 158-59, 161, 167, 182, 209, 210, 214-16, 257, 329, 417, 469-70, 489, 521, 528, 561, 562, 636, 638; Atlantic Pact, 520; atomic energy control issue, 10-11, 12-13, 27, 43-44, 49-53, 73, 213-16; Baruch plan, 55, 58, 59, 131; H-bomb issue, 583-84, 590, 598, 610, 611n, 613, 614, 615, 620-21, 620n, 623-25, 630-31, 633; -L. Report, 27, 33, 44-45, 47; Secretary of State, 448, 448n, 449; Under Secretary of State, 10n, resignation (1947), 200, 200n, 213; U.S.-U.K. atomic energy cooperation, 24-26, 455, 462, 465, 467, 544, 545, 548-51, 555, 557, 574, 602

Acheson, Mrs. Dean G. (Alice), 417, 449, 469

Acheson Committee. See State Department

Acheson-Lilienthal Report, 25, 26, 27-28, 27n, 29-30, 31, 33, 35-36, 38, 41ff., 47, 49-53, 58-59, 60-61, 60n, 64, 66, 67, 69, 70ff., 83, 91, 127, 130, 149, 161, 215-16, 244, 258, 461, 579, 606. See also State Department, Board of Consultants on International Control

Adams, Franklin P., 193

Adams, J. Donald, 404

Administration, 7, 15, 113, 115-16, 214, 343, 467, 489, 529-30, 597, 609. See also Civilian atomic control issue

Adrian, William L., 86

Advisory Panel on Atomic Energy. See State Department, Board of Consultants on International Control

Agar, Herbert S., 129-30, 130n

Agar, Mrs. Herbert S., 129, 130

*Age of Innocence, The,* 398

Ager, Paul W., 111

Agriculture Department, U.S., 42, 42n, 46, 55, 174

Agronsky, Martin, 104, 143, 491

Aiken, George D., 184

Air Force, U.S., 185, 214, 220, 230, 464, 484

Allardice, Corbin, 399

Allen, Jay, 579

Allen, Raymond B., 517

Alsop, Joseph, 44, 104, 129, 425, 608, 612

Alvarez, Luis, 577

American Association for the Advancement of Science, 406, 407, 410

American Federation of Labor, 55, 352, 354, 411

*American Magazine,* 268, 268n

*American Mercury,* 111

American plan. See Baruch plan